Lecture Notes in Artificial Intelligence   1418

Subseries of Lecture Notes in Computer Science
Edited by J. G. Carbonell and J. Siekmann

Lecture Notes in Computer Science

Edited by G. Goos, J. Hartmanis and J. van Leeuwen

Springer
Berlin
Heidelberg
New York
Barcelona
Budapest
Hong Kong
London
Milan
Paris
Singapore
Tokyo

Robert E. Mercer   Eric Neufeld   (Eds.)

Advances in Artificial Intelligence

12th Biennial Conference of the Canadian Society
for Computational Studies of Intelligence, AI'98
Vancouver, BC, Canada, June 18-20, 1998
Proceedings

Springer

Series Editors
Jaime G. Carbonell, Carnegie Mellon University, Pittsburgh, PA, USA
Jörg Siekmann, University of Saarland, Saarbrücken, Germany

Volume Editors

Robert E. Mercer
Department of Computer Science, University of Western Ontario
London, ON, N6A 5B7, Canada
E-mail: mercer@csd.uwo.ca

Eric Neufeld
Department of Computer Science, University of Saskatchewan
57 Campus Drive, Saskatoon, SK, S7N 5A9, Canada
E-mail: eric@cs.usask.ca

Cataloging-in-Publication Data applied for

Die Deutsche Bibliothek - CIP-Einheitsaufnahme

Advances in artificial intelligence : proceedings / AI '98,
Vancouver, BC, Canada, June 18 - 20, 1998. Robert Mercer ; Eric
Neufeldt (ed.). - Berlin ; Heidelberg ; New York ; Barcelona ;
Budapest ; Hong Kong ; London ; Milan ; Paris ; Santa Clara ;
Singapore ; Tokyo : Springer, 1998
    (... biennial conference of the Canadian Society for Computational
    Studies of Intelligence ; 12) (Lecture notes in computer science ; Vol.
    1418 : Lecture notes in artificial intelligence)
    ISBN 3-540-64575-6

CR Subject Classification (1991): I.2

ISBN 3-540-64575-6 Springer-Verlag Berlin Heidelberg New York

© Springer-Verlag Berlin Heidelberg 1998
Printed in Germany

Typesetting: Camera ready by author
SPIN 10637401   06/3142 – 5 4 3 2 1 0   Printed on acid-free paper

Preface

AI'98 is the 12th in the series of biennial Artificial Intelligence conferences sponsored by the Canadian Society for Computational Studies of Intelligence/Société canadienne pour l'étude de l'intelligence par ordinateur. As in recent years the conference is being held in conjunction with the annual conferences of two other Canadian societies and is collectively known as AI/GI/VI'98.

The Canadian AI conference has a long tradition of attracting international papers of high quality from a variety of AI research areas. All papers submitted to the conference received three independent reviews. Fewer than half of the submitted papers were accepted to appear in the proceedings. A journal version of the best paper of the conference will be invited to appear in Computational Intelligence. The conference has always explicitly cultivated international participation. Papers were received from six continents, and this diversity is represented in these proceedings. Once again we have maintained a single track format but for the first time have provided the authors with two different presentation venues: a number of topic focussed plenary sessions and a general poster session. A highlight of the conference continues to be the invited speakers. This year, four speakers, Oren Etzioni, Ken Ford, Stuart Russell, and Jonathan Schaeffer, are our guests.

Conference success depends upon the hard work of a large number of individuals. We gratefully acknowledge the members of the program committee who helped coordinate the refereeing of all of the submitted papers. They also made a number of important recommendations regarding various aspects of the program. Thanks also to the many referees who reviewed the papers. Their efforts were obvious in the detailed and constructive reviews, all done within a very tight schedule. Our gratitude goes to those who organized various conference events and helped with other conference matters: Franz Oppacher, Una-May O'Reilly, Wayne Davis, Rob Walker, Sandra McKay, Marjorie Francis, Luiz Merkle, and Jim Morey. We also appreciate the cooperation we have received from Springer-Verlag, especially Alfred Hoffmann.

Finally, we would like to acknowledge the participants. Enjoy yourselves.

April 1998

Bob Mercer
Eric Neufeld
Program Co-chairs, AI'98
The University of Western Ontario
and
The University of Saskatchewan

Organization

AI'98 is organized by the Canadian Society for Computational Studies of Intelligence/Société canadienne pour l'étude de l'intelligence par ordinateur.

Program Committee

Conference Chair:	Wayne Davis, The University of Alberta (emeritus)
Program Co-chairs:	Robert E. Mercer, The University of Western Ontario
	Eric Neufeld, The University of Saskatchewan
Organizing Chairs:	Dan Fass, Simon Fraser University
	Fred Popowich, Simon Fraser University
Workshops:	Franz Oppacher, Carleton University
	Una-May O'Reilly, Massachusetts Institute of Technology
Committee Members:	Peter van Beek, University of Alberta
	Craig Boutilier, University of British Columbia
	Chrysanne DiMarco, University of Waterloo
	Jim Greer, University of Saskatchewan
	Howard Hamilton, University of Regina
	Graeme Hirst, University of Toronto
	Dekang Lin, University of Manitoba
	Charles Ling, University of Western Ontario
	Joel Martin, National Research Council
	Paul McFetridge, Simon Fraser University
	Peter Patel-Schneider, AT&T Research
	Jonathan Schaeffer, University of Alberta
	Fei Song, University of Guelph
	Bruce Spencer, University of New Brunswick
	Ahmed Tawfik, Wilfred Laurier University
	Andre Trudel, Acadia University
	Yang Xiang, University of Regina
	Qiang Yang, Simon Fraser University

Referees

Aijun An	Jim Greer	Brad Nickerson
John Barron	Russell Greiner	Charlie Obimbo
Peter van Beek	Howard Hamilton	Franz Oppacher
Yngvi Bjornsson	T. Heift	Wanlin Pang
Craig Boutilier	Graeme Hirst	Denis Papp
Christina Carrick	Morten Irgens	Peter F. Patel-Schneider
Brahim Chaib-draa	W. Ken Jackson	Sharad Sachdev
Jianhua Chen	Andreas Junghanns	Jonathan Schaeffer
Howard Cheng	Edward Kim	Danny Silver
Paulina Chin	George K. Knopf	Fei Song
Veronica Dahl	Catherine Leung	Bruce Spencer
Nicolas Demers	Dekang Lin	Ahmed Tawfik
Chrysanne DiMarco	Charles Ling	Janine Toole
Roy Eagleson	Hanan Lutfiyya	Davide Turcato
Eugene Eberbach	Brien Maguire	Andre Trudel
Wael Farag	Joel Martin	George Tsiknis
Denis Gagne	Stan Matwin	Kay Wiese
Daya Gaur	Paul McFetridge	Y. Xiang
Lev Goldfarb	Guy Mineau	Qiang Yang

Sponsoring Institutions

BC Advanced Systems Institute
Simon Fraser University

Table of Contents

Planning, Constraints, Search and Databases

Applications

Genetic Algorithms

Learning and Natural Language

Posters

Reasoning

Uncertainty

Learning

Sokoban: Evaluating Standard Single-Agent Search Techniques in the Presence of Deadlock*

Andreas Junghanns, Jonathan Schaeffer
Email: {andreas, jonathan}@cs.ualberta.ca

University of Alberta
Dept. of Computing Science
Edmonton, Alberta
CANADA T6G 2H1

Abstract. Single-agent search is a powerful tool for solving a variety of applications. Most of the academic application domains used to explore single-agent search techniques have the property that if you start with a solvable state, at no time in the search can you reach a state that is unsolvable (it may, however, not be minimal). In this paper we address the implications that arise when states in the search are unsolvable. These so-called deadlock states are largely responsible for the failure of our attempts to solve positions in the game of Sokoban.

Keywords: single agent search, heuristic search, Sokoban, deadlocks, IDA*

1 Introduction

Single-agent search (A*) has been extensively studied in the literature. There are a plethora of enhancements to the basic algorithm – a programmer's tool box – that allows one to tailor the solution to the problem domain to maximize program performance (such as iterative deepening [7], transposition tables [12] and pattern databases [2]). The result has been some impressive reductions in the search effort required to solve challenging applications (see [10] for a recent example).

Many of the academic applications used to illustrate single-agent search (such as sliding-tile puzzles and Rubik's Cube) are "easy" in the sense that they have some (or all) of the following properties: simple and effective lower-bound estimators, small branching factors and moderate solution depths. These domains also have the nice property that given a solvable starting state, every move preserves the solvability. This means that one can construct a real-time search (anytime algorithm) that can be guaranteed to find a (non-optimal) solution [9].

In the real world, one often has to make irrevocable decisions. Similarly, search applications (particularly if they are real-time) have to deal with this

---

* This is a revised and updated version of a paper presented at the IJCAI workshop on Using Games as an Experimental Testbed for Artificial Intelligence Research, Nagoya, August, 1997.

complexity. In competitive games programs (such as for chess), the irreversible moves mean that one may play a move that loses. In the context of single-agent search, an irreversible move means that one may move from a solvable state to an unsolvable one. A short-term decision (within the constraints of real time) may lead to a long-term disaster (problem cannot be solved). How to deal with this is a difficult problem.

Sokoban is a popular one-player game. Given a topology of rooms and passageways, the object is to push a number of stones from their current locations to goal locations. Of interest is that since you can only push, never pull, a single move can transform the problem from being solvable to being unsolvable. Many of these so-called deadlock states are trivial to identify (and avoid in the search), but some require extensive analysis to prove their existence. For example, one can easily construct an unsolvable Sokoban position that will require a massive search tree that is hundreds of moves deep to verify the deadlock.

Sokoban is a difficult search application for many reasons:

1. it has a complex lower-bound estimator,
2. the branching factor is large and variable (potentially over 100),
3. the solution may be very deep in the search tree (some problems require over 500 moves to solve optimally), and
4. some states are provably unsolvable (deadlock).

For sliding tile puzzles, for example, there are easy algorithms for generating a non-optimal solution. In Sokoban, because of the presence of deadlock, often it is very difficult to find *any* solution. Finding an optimal solution is much more difficult.

In this paper, we evaluate the standard single-agent search techniques while trying to optimally solve Sokoban problems. We identify the existence of deadlock as a new property of the search space that has not been addressed in previous research. We argue that even though standard search techniques have a dramatic impact on the size of the search, they are insufficient to solve most of the standard Sokoban problems.

We have constructed an IDA*-based program to solve Sokoban problems (*Rolling Stone*). In addition to using the standard single-agent search enhancements (such as transposition tables and move ordering) we introduce a good lower-bound estimator, deadlock tables, the inertia heuristic and macro moves that preserve the optimality of the solution. Despite these enhancements chopping orders of magnitude from the search tree size, we can solve only 16 of the 90 benchmark problems. Although this sounds rather poor, it is the best reported result to date. We believe our techniques can be extended and more problems will be solved. However, we also conclude that some of the Sokoban problems are so difficult as to be effectively unsolvable using standard single-agent search techniques.

2 Sokoban

Sokoban is a popular one-player game. The game apparently originated in Japan, although the original author is unknown. The game's appeal comes from the simplicity of the rules and the intellectual challenge offered by deceptively difficult problems.

The rules of the game are quite simple. Figure 1 shows a sample Sokoban problem (problem 1 of the standard 90-problem suite available at http://xsoko-ban.lcs.mit.edu/xsokoban.html). The playing area consists of rooms and passageways, laid out on a rectangular grid of size 20x20 or less. Littered throughout the playing area are *stones* (shown as circular discs) and *goals* (shaded squares). There is a *man* whose job it is to move each stone to a goal square. The man can only push one stone at a time and must push from behind the stone. A square can only be occupied by one of a wall, stone or man at any time. Getting all the stones to the goal nodes can be quite challenging; doing this in the minimum number of moves is much more difficult.

To refer to squares in a Sokoban problem, we use a coordinate notation. The horizontal axis is labeled from "A" to "T", and the vertical axis from "a" to "t" (assuming the maximum sized 20x20 problem), starting in the upper left corner. A move consists of pushing a stone from one square to another. For example, in Figure 1 the move *Fh-Eh* moves the stone on *Fh* left one square. We use *Fh-Eh-Dh* to indicate a sequence of pushes of the same stone. A move, of course, is only legal if there is a valid path by which the man can move behind the stone and push it. Thus, although we only indicate stone moves (such as *Fh-Eh*), implicit in this is the man's moves from its current position to the appropriate square to do the push (for *Fh-Eh* the man would have to move from *Li* to *Gh* via the squares *Lh, Kh, Jh, Ih* and *Hh*).

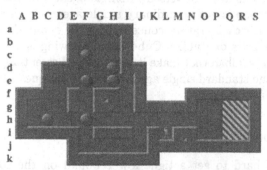

He-Ge Hd-Hc-Hd Fe-Ff-Fg Fh-Gh-Hh-Ih-Jh-Kh-Lh-Mh-Nh-Oh-Ph-Qh-Rh-Rg Fg-Fh-Gh-Hh-Ih-Jh-Kh-Lh-Mh-Nh-Oh-Ph-Qh-Qi-Ri *Fc-Fd-Fe-Ff-Fg-Fh-Gh-Hh-Ih-Jh-Kh-Lh-Mh-Nh-Oh-Ph-Qh-Qg* *Ge-Fe-Ff-Fg-Fh-Gh-Hh-Ih-Jh-Kh-Lh-Mh-Nh-Oh-Ph-Qh-Rh Hd-He-Ge-Fe-Ff-Fg-Fh-Gh- Hh-Ih-Jh-Kh-Lh-Mh-Nh-Oh-Ph-Pi-Qi Ch-Dh-Eh-Fh-Gh-Hh-Ih- Jh-Kh-Lh-Mh-Nh-Oh-Ph-Qh*

Fig. 1. Sokoban problem 1 and a solution

The standard 90 problems range from easy (such as problem 1 above) to difficult (requiring hundreds of stone pushes). A global score file is maintained that gives the best solution achieved to date (at the above www address). Thus solving a problem is only part of the satisfaction; improving on one's solution is equally important.

Note that there are two definitions of an optimal solution to a Sokoban problem: the number of stone pushes and the number of man movements. For a few problems there is one solution that optimizes both; in general they conflict. In this paper, we have chosen to optimize the number of stone pushes. Both optimization problems are computationally equivalent. Using a single-agent search algorithm, such as IDA* [7], one stone push decreases the solution length by at most one, but may increase it by an arbitrary amount. Optimizing the man movements involves using non-unitary changes to the lower bound (the number of man movements it takes to position the man behind a stone to do the push).

Sokoban has been shown to be NP-hard [1, 3]. [3] show that the game is an instance of a motion planning problem, and compare the game to other motion planning problems in the literature. For example, Sokoban is similar to Wilfong's work with movable obstacles, where the man is allowed to hold on to the obstacle and move with it, as if they were one object [14]. Sokoban can be compared to the problem of having a robot in a warehouse move a number of specified goods from their current location to their final destination, subject to the topology of the warehouse and any obstacles in the way. When viewed in this context, Sokoban is an excellent example of using a game as an experimental test-bed for mainstream research in artificial intelligence.

3 Why is Sokoban so Interesting?

Although the authors are well-versed in single-agent search, it quickly became obvious that Sokoban is not an ordinary single-agent search problem. Much of the single-agent search literature concentrates on "simple" problems, such as the sliding tile puzzles or Rubik's Cube. The following is a listing of problems encountered with Sokoban that make it difficult and essentially cause a program based solely on the standard single agent-search techniques to fail to solve more than a handful of problems.

3.1 Lower Bound

In general, it is hard to get a tight lower bound on the solution length for Sokoban problems. The tighter the bound, the more efficient a single-agent search algorithm can be. The stones can have complex interactions, with long elaborate maneuvers often being required to reposition stones. For example, in problem 50 (see Figure 2), the solution requires moving stones *through* and *away* from the goal squares to make room for other stones. Our best lower bound is 100 stone pushes (see section 4.1), whereas the best human solution required 370 moves – clearly a large gap, and an imposing obstacle to an efficient IDA* search. For some problems, without a deep understanding of the problem and its solution, it is difficult to get a reasonable bound.

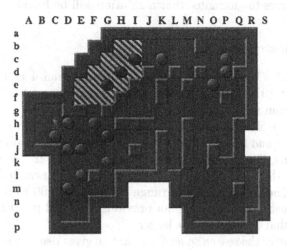

Fig. 2. Sokoban problem 50

3.2 Deadlock

In most of the single-agent search problems studied in the literature, all state transitions preserve the solvability of the problem (but not necessarily the optimality of the solution). This is a consequence of all state transitions (moves) being reversible (there exists a move sequence which can undo a move). Sokoban has irreversible moves (e.g. pushing a stone into a corner), and these moves can lead to states that provably cannot lead to solutions. In effect, a single move can change the lower bound on the solution length to infinity. If the lower bound function does not reflect this, then the search will spend unnecessary effort exploring a sub-tree that has no solution. We call these states *deadlocks* because one or more stones will never be able to reach a goal.

Deadlocks can be as trivial as, for example, moving a stone into a corner (in Figure 1, moving Ch-Bh[1] creates a deadlock state; the man can never get behind the stone to push it out). Some deadlocks can be wide ranging and quite subtle, involving complex interactions of stones over a large portion of the maze (in Figure 1, moving Fh-Fg creates a deadlock). Any programming solution to Sokoban must be able to detect deadlock states so that unnecessary search can be curtailed.

The presence of deadlock states in a search space creates a serious dilemma for a real-time search applications (anytime applications). If we have to commit to a move (because of resource constraints) we may move to a deadlock state,

---

[1] This is in fact an illegal move in that position, since the man can't reach the stone. We assume here, that the stone on Fh was not in the maze.

guaranteeing insolvability. Since many of these deadlock scenarios cannot be determined without search, the real-time algorithm will have a difficult time allocating resources to guarantee that a solution will be found.

3.3 Size of Search Space

Sliding tile puzzles have a branching factor of less than 4 and the maximum solution length for the 15-puzzle is 80. Rubik's Cube has a branching factor of 18 and a maximum solution length of 20 [10].

The large size of the search space for Sokoban is due to potentially large branching factors and long solution lengths, compared to the previously studied problem domains. The number of stones ranges from 6 to 34 in the standard problem set. With 4 potential moves per stone, the branching factor could be well over 100! The solution lengths range from nearly 100 to over 650 pushes. The trees are bushier and deeper than previously studied problems, resulting in a search space that is considerably larger.

The large size of the search space for Sokoban gives rise to a surprising result. Consider problem 48 (Figure 3). Our program computes the lower bound as 200 moves. Since human players have solved it in 200 moves, we can conclude that the optimal solution requires exactly 200 moves. Knowing the solution length is only part of the answer – one has to find the sequence of moves to solve the problem. In fact, problem 48 is difficult to solve because of the large branching factor. Although IDA* will never make a non-optimal move according to its heuristic estimate of the distance to the goal, it has no idea what order to consider the moves in. An incorrect sequence of moves can lead eventually to deadlock. For this problem, to IDA* one optimal move is as good as another. The program builds a huge tree, trying all the optimal moves in all possible orders. Hence, even though we have the right lower bound, our program builds an exponentially large tree and fails to solve problem 48.

4 Towards Solving Sokoban

Although we believe that standard search algorithms, such as IDA*, will be inadequate for solving all 90 Sokoban problems, as a first step we decided to invest our efforts in pushing the IDA* technology as far as possible. Our goal is to eventually demonstrate the inadequacy of single-agent search techniques for this puzzle. This section discusses our work with IDA* and the problems we are encountering.

4.1 Lower Bound

A naive but computationally inexpensive lower bound is the sum over the distances of all the stones to their respective closest goal. It is clear however that only one stone can go to any one goal in any solution. Since there are as many

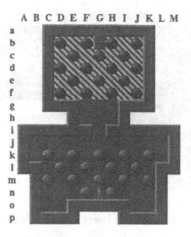

Fig. 3. Sokoban problem 48

stones as there are goals and every stone has to be assigned to a goal, we are trying to find a *minimum cost* (distance) *perfect matching* on a complete bipartite graph. Edges between stones and goals are weighted by the distance between them, and assigned infinity if the stone cannot reach a goal.

Essentially the problem can be summarized as follows. There are n stones and n goals. For each stone, there is a minimum number of moves that is required to maneuver that stone to each goal. For each stone and for each goal, there is a distance (cost) of achieving that goal. The problem then is to find the assignment of goals to stones that minimizes the sum of the costs.

Minimum cost perfect matching for a bipartite graph can be solved using minimum cost augmentation [11]. Given a graph with n nodes and m edges, the cost of computing the minimal cost matching is $O(n * m * log_{(2+m/n)}n)$. Since we have a complete bipartite graph, $m = n^2/4$ and the complexity is $O(n^3 * log_{(2+n/4)}n)$. Clearly this is an expensive computation, especially if it has to be computed for every node in the search. However, there are several optimizations that can reduce the overall cost. First, during the search we only need to update the matching, since each move results in a single stone changing its distance to the goals. This requires finding a negative cost cycle [6] involving the stone moved. Second, we are looking for a perfect matching, which considerably reduces the number of possible cycles to check. Even with these optimizations, the cost of maintaining the lower bound dominates the execution time of our program. Most of the lower bounds used in single-agent search in the literature, such as the Manhattan distance used for sliding tile puzzles, are trivial in comparison.

One advantage of the minimum matching lower bound is that it correctly returns the parity of the solution length (Manhattan distance in sliding tile puzzles also has this property). Thus, if the lower bound is an odd number, the solution length must also be odd. Using IDA*, this property allows us to iterate by two at a time.

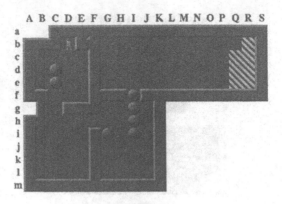

Fig. 4. Illustrating lower bound calculations

There are a number of ways to improve the minimum matching lower bound. Here we introduce two useful enhancements. First, if two adjacent stones are in each other's way towards reaching their goal, then we can penalize this position by increasing the lower bound appropriately. We call this enhancement *linear conflicts* because of its similarity to the linear conflicts enhancement in sliding-tile puzzles [5]. Figure 4 shows an obvious example. The four stones on *If*, *Ig*, *Ih* and *Ii* are obstructing each others' optimal path to the goals[2]. We have to move two stones off their optimal paths to be able to solve this problem (for example, *Ig-Hg* to allow the man to push *If*, and *Ii-Hi* to move the stone on *Ih*). In each case, two additional moves are required. In addition, the stones on *Cd* and *Ce* have a linear conflict. Hence, in this example, the lower bound will be increased by six.

The second enhancement notes that sometimes stones on walls have to be *backed out* of a room, and then pushed back in just to re-orient the position of the man. In Figure 4, the stone on *Gi* has a *backout conflict*. Consider this stone while pretending there are no other stones on the board. The man must move the stone to a room entrance (*Gi-Gh*), push it out of the room (*Gh-Fh-Eh-Dh*), and then push it back into the room it came from (*Dh-Eh-Gh-Hh*). This elaborate maneuver is required because the man has to be on the left side of the stone to be able to push it off the wall. In this problem, there is only one way to get to the left of the stone – by backing it out and then back into the room. This conflict increases the lower bound by six[3].

Table 1 shows the effectiveness of our lower bound estimate. The table shows the lower bound achieved by minimum matching (MM), inclusion of the linear conflicts enhancement (+LC), inclusion of the backout enhancement (+BO), and

---

[2] The optimal path is defined as the route a stone would take if no other stone was in the maze obstructing its movements.

[3] Another increase by 4 is achieved by observing that stones moving into the goal room and targeted at the two lower goals need two extra pushes each to allow the man into the room, before pushing it to the right.

the combination of all three features (ALL). The upper bound (UB) is obtained from the global Sokoban score file. Since this file represents the best that human players have been able to achieve, it is an upper bound on the solution length. The table is sorted according to the last column (Diff), which shows the difference between the lower and upper bound. Clearly for some problems (notably problem 50) there is a huge gap. Note that the real gap might be smaller, as it is likely that some of the hard problems have been non-optimally solved by the human players.

#	MM	+LC	+BO	ALL	UB	Diff	#	MM	+LC	+BO	ALL	UB	Diff	#	MM	+LC	+BO	ALL	UB	Diff
51	118	118	118	118	118	0	62	235	235	237	237	245	8	25	326	330	364	368	386	18
55	118	118	120	120	120	0	72	284	288	284	288	296	8	90	436	436	442	442	460	18
78	134	134	136	136	136	0	77	360	360	360	360	368	8	49	96	96	104	104	124	20
53	186	186	186	186	186	0	54	177	177	177	177	187	10	42	208	208	208	208	228	20
83	190	194	190	194	194	0	56	191	191	193	193	203	10	61	241	243	241	243	263	20
48	200	200	200	200	200	0	76	192	194	192	194	204	10	28	284	286	284	286	308	22
80	219	225	225	231	231	0	47	197	199	197	199	209	10	68	317	319	319	321	343	22
4	331	331	355	355	355	0	8	220	220	220	220	230	10	39	650	652	650	652	674	22
1	95	95	95	95	97	2	27	351	353	351	353	363	10	46	219	219	223	223	247	24
2	119	119	129	129	131	2	86	122	122	122	122	134	12	67	367	369	375	377	401	24
3	128	132	128	132	134	2	44	167	167	167	167	179	12	23	286	286	424	424	448	24
58	189	189	197	197	199	2	17	121	121	201	201	213	12	32	111	113	111	113	139	26
6	104	106	104	106	110	4	59	218	218	218	218	230	12	16	160	162	160	162	188	26
5	135	137	137	139	143	4	87	221	221	221	221	233	12	85	303	303	303	303	329	26
60	148	148	148	148	152	4	43	132	132	132	132	146	14	89	345	349	349	353	379	26
70	329	329	329	329	333	4	34	152	154	152	154	168	14	24	442	442	516	518	544	26
63	425	427	425	427	431	4	71	290	294	290	294	308	14	15	94	96	94	96	124	28
73	433	433	437	437	441	4	40	310	310	310	310	324	14	33	140	140	150	150	180	30
84	147	147	149	149	155	6	35	362	364	362	364	378	14	26	149	149	163	163	195	32
81	167	167	167	167	173	6	36	501	507	501	507	521	14	11	197	201	201	207	241	34
10	494	496	506	506	512	6	41	201	203	219	221	237	16	75	261	263	261	263	297	34
38	73	73	73	73	81	8	45	274	276	282	284	300	16	29	124	124	122	122	164	42
7	80	80	80	80	88	8	19	278	280	282	286	302	16	74	158	158	172	172	214	42
82	131	135	131	135	143	8	22	306	308	306	308	324	16	37	220	220	242	242	290	48
79	164	166	164	166	174	8	20	302	304	444	446	462	16	88	306	308	334	336	390	54
65	181	185	199	203	211	8	18	90	90	106	106	124	18	52	365	367	365	367	423	56
12	206	206	206	206	214	8	21	123	127	127	131	149	18	30	357	359	357	359	465	106
57	215	217	215	217	225	8	13	220	220	220	220	238	18	66	185	187	185	187	325	138
9	215	217	227	229	237	8	31	228	232	228	232	250	18	69	207	209	217	219	443	224
14	231	231	231	231	239	8	64	331	331	367	367	385	18	50	96	96	96	100	370	270

Table 1. Lower bounds

4.2 Transposition Table

The search tree is really a graph. Two different sequences of moves can reach the same position. The search effort can be considerably reduced by eliminating duplicate nodes from the search. A common technique is to use a large hash table, called the transposition table, to maintain a history of nodes visited [13]. Each entry in the table includes a position and information on the parameters that the position was searched with. Transposition tables have been used for a variety of single-agent search problems [12].

One subtlety of Sokoban is that saving exact positions in the transposition table misses many transpositions. While the exact positions of the stones is critical, the exact position of the man is not. Two positions, A and B, are identical if both positions have stones on the same squares and if the man in

A can move to the location of the man in *B*. Thus, when finding a match in the transposition table, a computation must be performed to determine the reachability of the man. In this way, the table can be made more useful, by allowing a table entry to match a class of positions.

4.3   Deadlock Tables

Our initial attempt at avoiding deadlock was to hand-code a set of tests for simple deadlock patterns into *Rolling Stone*. This quickly proved to be of limited value, since it missed many frequently occurring patterns, and the cost of computing the deadlock test grew as each test was added. Instead, we opted for a more "brute-force" approach.

Rolling Stone includes a pattern database [2] that we call *deadlock tables*. An off-line search is used to enumerate all possible combinations of walls, stones and empty squares for a fixed-size region. For each combination of squares and square contents, a small search is performed to determine if deadlock is present or not. This information is stored in a tree data structure. There are many optimizations that make the computation of the tree efficient. For our experiments, we built two differently shaped deadlock tables for regions of roughly 5x4 squares (containing approximately 22 million entries).

When a move *Xx-Yy* is made, the destination square *Yy* is used as a base square in the deadlock table and the direction of the stone move is used to rotate the region, such that it is oriented correctly. In Figure 4 if the move *Gi-Gh* is made, then a deadlock table could cover the 5x4 region bounded by the squares *Eh*, *Ee*, *Ie* and *Ih*. Note that the table can be used to cover other regions as well. To maximize the usage of the tables, reflections of asymmetric patterns along the direction the stone was moved in are considered.

Although a 5x4 region may sound like a significant portion of the 20x20 playing area, in fact many deadlocks encountered in the test suite extend well beyond the area covered by our deadlock tables. Unfortunately, it is not practical to build larger tables.

Note that if a deadlock table pattern covers a portion of the board containing a goal node, most of the effectiveness of the deadlock table is lost. Once a stone is on a goal square, it need never move again. Hence, the normal conditions for deadlock do not apply. Usually moving a stone into a corner creates a deadlock, but if the square is a goal node, then the position is not necessarily a deadlock.

4.4   Macro Moves

Macro moves have been described in the literature [8]. Although they are typically associated with non-optimal problem solving, we have chosen to investigate a series of macro moves that preserve the solution's optimality. We implemented the following two macros in *Rolling Stone*.

Tunnel Macros In Figure 1, consider the man pushing a stone from *Jh* to *Kh*. The man can never get to the other side of the stone, meaning the stone can only be pushed to the right. Eventually, the stone on *Kh must* be moved further: *Jh-Kh-Lh-Mh-Nh-Oh-Ph*. Once the commitment is made (*Jh-Kh*), there is no point in delaying a sequence of moves that must eventually be made. Hence, we generate a macro move that moves the stone from *Jh* to *Ph* in a single move.

The above example is an instance of our *tunnel macro*. If a stone is pushed into a one-way tunnel (a tunnel consisting of articulation points[4] of the underlying graph of the maze), then the man has to push it all the way through to the other end. Hence this sequence of moves is collapsed into a single macro move. Note that this implies that macro moves have a non-unitary impact on the lower bound estimate.

Goal Macros As soon as a stone is pushed into a room that contains goals, then the single-square move is substituted with a macro move to move the stone directly to a goal node. Unlike with the tunnel macro, if a goal macro is present, *it is the only move generated*. This is illustrated using Figure 1. If a stone is pushed onto the room containing the goal squares (such as square *Oh*), then this move is substituted with the goal macro move. This pushes the stone all the way to the next highest priority empty goal square (*Rg* or *Ri* if it is the first stone into the goal area). The goals are prioritized in a pre-search phase. This is necessary to guarantee that stones are moved to goals in an order that precludes deadlock and preserves optimality of the solution.

In Figure 1 a special case can be observed: the end of the tunnel macro overlaps with the beginning of the goal macro. The macro substitution routine will discover the overlap and chain both macros together. The effect is that one longer macro move is executed. In the solution given in Figure 1, the macro moves are underlined (an underlined move should be treated as a single move).

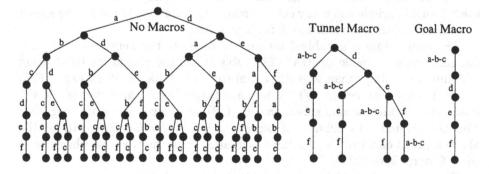

Fig. 5. The impact of macro moves

Figure 5 shows the dramatic impact this has on the search. At each node in the figure, the individual moves of the stone are considered. There are two

---

[4] Squares that divide the graph into two disjoint pieces.

stones that can each make a sequence of 3 moves, *a-b-c* for the first stone, and *d-e-f* for the second stone. The top tree in Figure 5 shows the search tree with no macro moves; essentially all moves are tried, whenever possible, in all possible variations. The left lower tree shows the search tree, if *a-b-c* is a tunnel macro and the lower right tree if *a-b-c* is goal macro.

4.5 Move Ordering

We have experimented with ordering the moves at interior nodes of the search. For IDA*, move ordering makes no difference to the search, except for the last iteration. Since the last iteration is aborted once the solution is found, it can make a big difference in performance if the solution is found earlier rather than later ([12] comment on the effectiveness of move ordering in single-agent search). One could argue that our inability to solve problem 48 (Figure 3) is solely a problem of move ordering. For this problem, we have the correct lower bound – it is just a matter of finding the right sequence of moves.

We are currently using a move ordering schema that we call *inertia*. Looking at the solution for problem 1 (Figure 1), one observes that there are long runs where the same stone is repeatedly pushed. Hence, moves are ordered to preserve the *inertia* of the previous move – move the same stone in the same direction if possible.

5 Experimental Results

Given 20 million nodes of search effort, our program can currently solve 16 problems. Table 2 shows these problems and contains in the second column the number nodes needed to find a solution (all search enhancements enabled).

These results illustrate just how difficult Sokoban really is. Even with a good lower bound heuristic and many enhancements to dramatically reduce the search cost, most problems are still too difficult to solve.

The later columns in table 2 attempt to quantify the benefits of the various enhancements made to IDA*. The table shows the results for IDA* using minimum matching enhanced with: a transposition table (128k entries – TT), deadlock table (5x4 region – DT), macro moves (goal and tunnel macros – MM), linear conflicts and backout enhancements (CB), and inertia move ordering (IN). The ALL column is the number of nodes searched by *Rolling Stone* with all the above features enabled. The columns thereafter show the tree size when one of these features is disabled.

These experiments highlight several interesting points:

1. Because of macro moves, the size of the search tree for problem 1 is *smaller* than the solution path length!
2. The program can find deep solutions with nominal depth. For example, the solution to problem 78 is 136 moves, and yet it is found by building a tree that is only 64 levels deep!

Problem	ALL	ALL-TT	ALL-DT	ALL-MM	ALL-CB	ALL-IN
1	61	61	70	116	61	160
2	1,646	1,036,503	6,855	370,213	>20,000,000	1,798
3	876	42,732	15,225	16,289	26,940	1,470
4	213,670	>20,000,000	>20,000,000	>20,000,000	>20,000,000	743,639
6	10,004	>20,000,000	10,846	>20,000,000	11,393	10,003
7	88,890	>20,000,000	6,166,124	744,912	253,404	77,539
17	126,121	>20,000,000	155,506	>20,000,000	>20,000,000	133,439
38	1,063,178	>20,000,000	2,958,995	8,999,852	1,267,181	450,017
51	125,413	>20,000,000	182,125	19,817,875	>20,000,000	103,021
63	256,835	>20,000,000	415,011	>20,000,000	>20,000,000	6,233,537
65	4,203,390	>20,000,000	6,438,584	13,561,416	>20,000,000	>20,000,000
78	76	76	76	154	1,195	1,902
80	237	237	237	627	>20,000,000	2,524
81	11,887,844	>20,000,000	>20,000,000	>20,000,000	>20,000,000	7,864,587
82	1,167,457	>20,000,000	1,989,577	>20,000,000	1,359,703	1,101,122
83	200	232	200	764	13,003	318

Table 2. Experimental Data

3. Problem 63 has a solution length of 431 moves and yet it is found with a search of only 257,000 nodes.
4. Transpositions tables are much more effective than seen in other single-agent and two-player games. For example, removing transposition tables for problem 6 increases the search by more than a factor of 2000!
5. Without the improvements of the lower-bound estimator (linear and backout conflict), the search tree for problem 80 increases by over a factor of 84,000! All the other improvements on the other hand have no or only minor effect on the search tree size.
6. Each of the enhancements can have a dramatic impact on the search tree size (depending on the problem).

Rolling Stone spends 90% of its execution time updating the lower bound. Clearly this is an area requiring further attention.

6   Enhancing the Current Program

Our program is still in its infancy and our list of things to experiment with is long. The following details some of the ways we intend to extend our implementation.

- To help detect larger deadlocks, we propose using localized searches that prove that for a certain stone combination no solution exists to push them to goals. It remains to be investigated if the search effort spent in testing for deadlocks will be offset by the savings gained from avoiding sub-trees with no solution.
- Our version of IDA* considers all legal moves in a position (modulo goal macros). For many problems, *local* searches make more sense. Typically, a

man rearranges some stones in a region. Once done, it then moves on to another region. It makes sense to do local searches rather than global searches. A challenge here will be to preserve the optimality of solutions.

- The idea of *partition search* may be useful for Sokoban [4]. For example, partition search could be used to discover previously seen deadlock states, where irrelevant stones are in different positions.
- A pre-search analysis of a problem can reveal constraints that can be used throughout the search. For example, in Figure 1 the stone on *Ch* cannot move to a goal until the stone on *Fh* is out of the way. Knowing that this is a prerequisite for *Ch* to move, there is no point in even considering legal moves for that stone until the right opportunity.
- So far, we have constrained our work by requiring an optimal solution. Introducing non-optimality allows us to be more aggressive in the types of macros we might use and in estimating lower bounds.
- Looking at the solution for Figure 1, one quickly discovers that having placed one stone into a goal, other stones follow similar paths. This is a recurring theme in many of the test problems. We are investigating dynamically learning repeated sequences of moves and modifying the search to treat them as macros.
- Sokoban can also be solved using a backward search. The search can start with all the stones on goal nodes. Now the man *pulls* stones instead of pushing them. The backward search may be useful for discovering some properties of the correct order that stones must be placed in the goal area(s) (the inverse of how a backward search can pull them out). This is an interesting approach that needs further consideration.

7 Conclusions and Future Work

Sokoban is a challenging puzzle – for both man and machine. The traditional enhanced single-agent search algorithms seem inadequate to solve the entire 90-problem test suite, even with their dramatic impact on the search tree size.

The property of deadlocks contained in a search space adds considerable complexity to the search. Since deadlock situations are an important consideration in real world applications, the notion of deadlock needs further attention. Deadlock tables are beneficial but inadequate to handle these situations. Further work is needed to identify when deadlocks are likely to occur and either avoid them (if possible) or invest the resources (search) to verify their existence. The problem of deadlocks is critical for any real-time application.

8 Acknowledgments

The authors would like to thank the German Academic Exchange Service, the Killam Foundation and the Natural Sciences and Engineering Research Council of Canada for their support. This paper benefited from interactions with Yngvi Bjornsson, John Buchanan, Joe Culberson, Roel van der Goot, Ian Parsons and Aske Plaat.

References

1. J. Culberson. Sokoban is PSPACE-complete. Technical Report TR 97-02, Dept. of Computing Science, University of Alberta, 1997. Also: http://web.cs.ualberta.ca/~joe/Preprints/Sokoban.
2. J. Culberson and J. Schaeffer. Searching with pattern databases. In G. McCalla, editor, *Advances in Artificial Intelligence*, pages 402–416. Springer-Verlag, 1996. Proceedings of CSCSI'95.
3. D. Dor and U. Zwick. SOKOBAN and other motion planing problems, 1995. At: http://www.math.tau.ac.il/~ddorit.
4. M. Ginsberg. Partition search. In *Proceedings of the National Conference on Artificial Intelligence (AAAI-96)*, pages 228–233, 1996.
5. O. Hansson, A. Mayer, and M. Yung. Criticizing solutions to relaxed models yields powerful admissible heuristics. *Information Sciences*, 63(3):207–227, 1992.
6. M Klein. A primal method for minimal cost flows. *Management Science*, 14:205–220, 1967.
7. R.E. Korf. Depth-first iterative-deepening: An optimal admissible tree search. *Artificial Intelligence*, 27(1):97–109, 1985.
8. R.E. Korf. Macro-operators: A weak method for learning. *Artificial Intelligence*, 26(1):35–77, 1985.
9. R.E. Korf. Real-time heuristic search. *Artificial Intelligence*, 42(2–3):189–211, 1990.
10. R.E. Korf. Finding optimal solutions to Rubik's Cube using pattern databases. In *AAAI National Conference*, pages 700–705, 1997.
11. H.W. Kuhn. The Hungarian method for the assignment problem. *Naval Res. Logist. Quart.*, pages 83–98, 1955.
12. A. Reinefeld and T.A. Marsland. Enhanced iterative-deepening search. *IEEE Transactions on Pattern Analysis and Machine Intelligence*, 16(7):701–710, July 1994.
13. D. Slate and L. Atkin. Chess 4.5 — The Northwestern University chess program. In P.W. Frey, editor, *Chess Skill in Man and Machine*, pages 82–118, New York, 1977. Springer-Verlag.
14. G. Wilfong. Motion planning in the presence of movable obstacles. In *4th ACM Symposium on Computational Geometry*, pages 279–288, 1988.

A Heuristic Incremental Modeling Approach to Course Timetabling

Don Banks[1], Peter van Beek[1], and Amnon Meisels[2]

[1] Department of Computing Science
University of Alberta
Edmonton, Alberta, Canada T6G 2H1
{banks,vanbeek}@cs.ualberta.ca
[2] Department of Mathematics and Computer Science
Ben-Gurion University of the Negev
Beer-Sheva, Israel 84105
am@cs.bgu.ac.il

Abstract. The general timetabling problem is an assignment of activities to fixed time intervals, adhering to a predefined set of resource availabilities. Timetabling problems are difficult to solve and can be extremely time-consuming without some computer assistance. In this paper the application of constraint-based reasoning to timetable generation is examined. Specifically, we consider how a timetabling problem can be represented as a Constraint Satisfaction Problem (CSP), and propose an algorithm for its solution which improves upon the basic idea of backtracking. Normally, when a backtracking routine fails to find a solution, there is nothing of value returned to the user; however, our algorithm extends this process by iteratively adding constraints to the CSP representation. A generalized random model of timetabling problems is proposed. This model creates a diverse range of problem instances, which are used to verify our search algorithm and identify the characteristics of difficult timetabling problems.

1   Introduction

Timetabling problems arise in many real world situations. Although many computerized techniques exist for timetable construction, obtaining acceptable results is often difficult. In this paper we address the problem of constructing a master timetable of multiple-section courses, along with scheduling students into sections of their requested courses. Thus the global problem consists of two subproblems—often called in the literature the master timetabling subproblem and the student sectioning (or grouping) subproblem. The two subproblems have been addressed separately in the past (see, for example, [1, 9, 10] and references therein). More recently, methods have been proposed which solve the two subproblems in tandem. Aubin and Ferland [1] propose an iterative method to solving the global problem which alternately solves the two subproblems until no further improvement to the solution can be found. The method is heuristic and is not guaranteed to find a global optimum. Hertz [6] adopts the solution method of Aubin and Ferland and shows how tabu search techniques can be used to potentially find an improved optimum.

In recent years, constraint-based reasoning has gained much attention in the Artificial Intelligence community. Previous constraint-based approaches to timetabling only address one of the two subproblems. For example, Meisels et al. [8] and Yoshikawa et al. [13] consider a high school timetabling problem where each class of students remains together for the entire term and Lajos [7] and Henz and Wurtz [5] address the master timetabling subproblem in a university setting. Feldman and Golumbic [3] address the use of priority constraints in their CSP solution to the student sectioning or grouping subproblem. Chan, Lau, and Sheung [2] present a constraint-based approach to time-tabling that iteratively relaxes some constraints and then "repairs."

In this paper, we propose a novel constraint-based model and solution technique to the global problem for modeling general timetabling problems found in high schools in Edmonton, Alberta, Canada. The problem involves creating a master timetable of multiple-section courses and creating individual student schedules. The schools being studied have eight periods per week, and the weekly schedule remains constant throughout the term. Courses are divided into sections of students, and each section is scheduled into its own period. The input to the problem consists of a list of students' course selections. The objective is to satisfy as many of the student course selections as possible by scheduling the sections of the courses into the eight weekly periods subject to a limit on the size of the classes, limits on the number of teachers of each subject, and a limit on the total number of rooms in the school.

In our CSP model of the problem, we define binary constraints to occur between pairs of courses chosen by the same students, and non-binary constraints to occur over groups of courses to enforce constraints on available teachers and rooms. A novel feature of our CSP model is that our model is heuristic. Satisfying all of the constraints does not guarantee 100% students satisfaction. While the non-binary teacher and room constraints are exact in the model, the domains of the variables are drastically pruned before solving and the binary constraints are heuristic estimations of complex non-binary constraints. However, we find that adding all of the possible binary estimation constraints between pairs of chosen courses often results in no solution existing. The proposed solution method heuristically and incrementally models and solves a timetabling problem. By prioritizing the various binary estimation constraints, our algorithm will iteratively add the constraints to the problem, building upon the solution until no further improvements can be made.

Our algorithm, which iteratively adds constraints before proceeding with a backtracking search, should be contrasted with (i) Aubin and Ferland [1] who iterate between the two subproblems of assigning students to the generated master schedule and *regenerating* a master schedule (that solves also the conflicts that result from the assignment of students to the last master schedule), and (ii) Chan, Lau, and Sheung [2] who iteratively *relax* constraints rather than strengthen constraints. Our approach can also be contrasted with a widely used optimization technique for CSPs which incrementally adds a constraint which enforces a new cost bound and resolves the model [12, p.94]. In our method all potential constraints are generated by the students' selection of courses. The iterations are generated by incrementally adding more constraints (from a *fixed set*) to the problem. A constraint weighting function is required to decide which constraints will satisfy the most students. A threshold value is used to determine the minimum weighting to include the binary constraints, and a forward checking routine is used to solve the specified CSP—which implies assigning periods to sections—and a master timetable is specified. Then, the procedure iterates and raises the threshold to include more binary constraints, which should increase the number of students successfully scheduled. The iterations continue until too many binary constraints have been added and no solution can be found. In further contrast to Aubin and Ferland, in their method the problem is *modeled* exactly using an integer linear programming formulation and then is *solved* heuristically. In our method, the problem is modeled heuristically—in that we add constraints that prune away large parts of the search space (and may prune away an optimal solution)—and then is solved exactly. Similar to Aubin and Ferland, we do not both model and solve our model exactly because it is computationally infeasible to do so [1].

We demonstrate the robustness of our algorithm by defining a random timetabling problem generator, based on actual high school data, and then solving a diverse range of timetabling problems. We show that in the majority of test cases, our algorithm can satisfactorily schedule 98% of the students on the randomly generated data and the amount of computational time required by the algorithm is reasonable. Furthermore, the generator helps us to identify difficult to solve timetabling problems. These problems can then be recreated for testing on future timetabling algorithms.

The software we have developed is a batch scheduling system. We envision the current scheduler as being part of an interactive decision support system where it would provide the initial schedule which the user could then analyze and modify (see, for example, [4]).

2   The Timetabling Problem

The high school timetabling problems that are the center of the present investigation arise from schools in Edmonton, Alberta, Canada. They are large problems ranging in size from 250 to 2200 students and having between 45 and 400 courses to timetable. A *course* is defined as a group of students who meet three times per week for instruction. There is one and only one teacher assigned to instruct each of these three lessons. The students have much freedom in the courses they will take. Each student provides the school with a list of desired courses four months in advance of the school year. Students have individualized schedules based on the courses that they select.

	Mon.	Tue.	Wed.	Thr.	Fri.
9:00	1	2	1	2	1
10:00	3	4	3	3	2
11:00	5	5	4	5	4
13:00	6	7	6	6	7
14:00	8	8	7	8	–

Fig. 1. Sample blank timetable

There are 8 periods in each week, with each period divided into 3 non-overlapping time slots of one hour in duration. Each day has 5 time slots. A sample blank timetable is shown in Fig. 1. If a student is scheduled to have Chemistry 30 in period 1, she would attend this class every Monday, Wednesday and Friday at 9:00 am. A student may register in at most 8 different courses in a term, but may register in fewer.

Some courses may be in high demand and hence be divided into multiple sections, where each section refers to a specific group of students who will always meet at the same period for the lesson. Most courses have between 1 and 4 sections, but some, such as English 10, have as many as 13. Each section will then be assigned a period number of 1 through 8. Therefore, part of the goal of this timetabling problem is, given all of the student's requests, assign a period number from 1 to 8 to each section of each course, and assign the students to a section for each course chosen, such that no student is assigned to more than one section in the same period. An important constraint is that no more than 30 students may be scheduled into one particular section. Another constraint is that we may not have more courses scheduled in any one period than there are rooms in the school.

The other piece of the puzzle is scheduling the teachers. However, the actual process of determining the teachers' schedules is not a part of the problem at hand, since the administration of the high school prefers to do this themselves. Nonetheless, one of our goals is to have a final solution which *guarantees* that valid teachers' schedules can be generated from the resulting master timetable. Two constraints are that no teacher may teach two lessons at the same time and there is one and only one teacher for every section. Another constraint is that teachers are only available to teach certain subjects. For example, suppose there are exactly 3 Physics teachers. A constraint would therefore assert that no more than 3 Physics courses can be scheduled in the same period, otherwise there would not be enough teachers for all of them.

The overall terminology and definition of the problem is as follows:

- A school has n students, r rooms, and offers c courses from s subjects.
- Every course C_i, $1 \leq i \leq c$, has an associated subject. For example, Math 10 through Math 33, all belong to the subject, Math.
- Every course C_i, $1 \leq i \leq c$ is subdivided into sections. The local policy is that a section of a course can have at most 30 students in it. Thus, the number of sections needed for a course is determined by dividing the number of students enrolled in the course by 30 and rounding up to the nearest integer.
- Each subject S_i, $1 \leq i \leq s$, has a number of available teachers T_i.
- Each student submits a list of desired courses L_i, $1 \leq i \leq n$, where each $L_i \subset \{C_1, \ldots, C_c\}$.

The problem is to generate a master schedule which assigns each section of each course to a period from $1 \ldots 8$. Additionally, we desire the n individual student timetables to be generated from the resulting assignment of periods to sections, such that each list of course selections L_i is satisfied. This goal is also subject to the constraint that no more than 30 students can be scheduled into one section. The main constraint, that the students must have the courses they have chosen available to them, is of the not-equals variety (e.g. there must be sections of all these courses that are *not assigned equal* periods). However, there are also two distinct capacity constraints in this problem: (i) the total number of sections of each subject S_i must not exceed T_i during any period, and (ii) the total number of sections must not exceed r during any period. The quality of a master schedule is measured by how many students have conflict free schedules. Any solution is guaranteed to have conflict free schedules for the teachers.

3 A Constraint Satisfaction Model

The constraint satisfaction model is a simple means of representing a wide variety of problems. The CSP has three components: *variables*, *domains*, and *constraints*. Each CSP consists of a set of variables $\{x_1 \ldots x_n\}$, each with an associated domain of values $D_1 \ldots D_n$. A solution to a constraint satisfaction problem is an instantiation of each variable to one particular value from its domain, such that none of the constraints are violated. Constraints, therefore, are relations between variables which describe their legal values. For example, suppose variable x has the domain $\{1, 2, 5\}$ and variable y has the domain $\{2, 3, 4\}$. A *binary* constraint—one that proposes the valid instantiations between *two* variables—may exist which says that $x \neq y$. Not all constraints are binary. A *unary* constraint is one that applies to a single variable. A non-binary constraint which includes all n variables of the CSP is known as a *global* constraint.

In order to formulate the timetabling problem as a CSP, we must define what are to be the variables, domains, and constraints.

3.1 Variables

Each variable represents a course C_i, such as Math 10, and all sections of that course. Associated with each variable or course is a number of attributes including the number of students enrolled in that course and the subject S_i of that course. Assigning a value to a variable represents assigning a time period to each section of that course.

3.2 Domains

The domains of the variables each consist of an m-tuple of periods, where m is the number of sections of each course. Each tuple consists of m periods in the range $\{1 \ldots 8\}$. Therefore, in the general case a 3-sections course would have the domain values $(1, 1, 1), (1, 1, 2), (1, 1, 3), \ldots$ and so on. The result of this choice is that domain sizes becomes an unmanageable 8^m, where m is the number of sections of the course. We can remove equivalent solutions by enforcing that the periods occur in ascending order since master timetables that differ only in that they swap two sections of the same course are equivalent. Further, a natural heuristic for the domains we have discovered is to exclude the possibility of duplicate periods appearing in the corresponding tuple of values. If we enforce that no period's value appears more than once in each permutation, then the domain values for the 3-section course become $(1, 2, 3), (1, 2, 4), (1, 2, 5), \ldots (6, 7, 8)$. The domain size in this case would be 56, instead of 512. The natural heuristic of disallowing multiple sections in the same period reduces the size of the domains from 8^m to at most 70, and therefore the total search space is reduced exponentially, albeit at the expense of potentially ruling out valid solutions. The maximum domain size of 70 occurs when the number of sections is four. This heuristic directly corresponds to what the actual high school schedulers do; only rarely will a course be "doubled up" in the same period.

A variable representing a course with 8 sections would have a domain size of 1, simply containing $(1, 2, 3, 4, 5, 6, 7, 8)$. In the event that the course has more than 8 sections, some overlap is impossible to avoid. So, in this case we assume that the first 8 sections of the course have the implicit $(1, \ldots, 8)$ distribution, while the remaining sections obey the non-overlap rule.

3.3 Constraints

Student Course Selection Constraints. The given input to the problem consists of the student course selections. The resulting final timetable must be one that somehow has the necessary available sections open for all of the student requests.

We propose a binary constraint which will *estimate* the section assignment needs, the *subset* constraint. Subset constraints occur between courses in the same term. This constraint between two courses says that one course's permutation of period values cannot be a subset of the other. The idea of this constraint is to avoid a student being left with the same period as the only open time for two courses that he/she is registered for. For example, suppose a student chooses three courses, A, B and C, the first two having two sections, and the latter with one section. If both A and B are given the permutation (4,7), one might conclude that this was fine, the student could take A in period 4, and B in period 7. However, if C were now given the value (4), this is not acceptable. Thus, between *one* pair of these courses there is a subset constraint necessary, which would deem that the two courses' permutation may not be equal to or a subset of the other. With just one subset constraint, together with the natural heuristic of avoiding duplicate courses, we have now guaranteed that the assignment of periods to sections for these three courses will satisfy the student. The general rule for applying estimator constraints is given below, together with examples.

Estimator Rule: If a student selects a course of n sections, and also selects d courses (in the same term) with n or fewer sections, $d \geq n$, the n-section course is subset-constrained by $d - n + 1$ of the other courses.

Example 1. A student picks 3 courses, A, B, and C. A has 1 section, B has 2, C has 3. No binary constraints are needed. Any combination of values for A,B and C will allow the student to attend all three courses. Applying the rule specifically to course C, n is equal 3 sections, but d is equal to 2 sections with 3 or fewer courses. Since d is less than n, the estimator rule does not apply.

Example 2. A student picks 5 courses, A through E. A, B, and C each have 3 sections, D has 2, E has 1. Subset constraints are needed between A-B, A-C and B-C. These will guarantee that 5 different periods will appear in the permutations of A, B and C. D and E could then be anything, and are not constrained.

Example 3. A student picks 8 courses, A through H. Course A has 7 sections, while the rest have only 1. Course A must be constrained with one of the other courses, while each pair of courses B through H must be constrained, for a total of twenty-two binary constraints.

In the third example, the algorithm was left with a seemingly arbitrary choice of which single section course to constrain with course A. However, this selection need not be done randomly. Our algorithm would first check if there are any existing constraints, from previously examined student selections, between course A and courses B through H. If there are any, no new constraint would be needed involving course A. Otherwise, the selection may be made by choosing the course B through H which has the *most* students also registered in course A.

Non-binary Constraints. The non-binary constraints are not meant to be estimations, instead they are exact. All of the non-binary constraints are included in any solution attempt. There exists a non-binary teacher's constraint, which is designed to ensure the final solution will allow for successful scheduling of the teachers. There is one such constraint for each of the sixteen subjects, and the constraint covers all of the courses in each subject. If there are T_i full-time teachers for a given subject, this constraint says that there may not be more than T_i courses of the subject scheduled at one particular period. The other non-binary constraint is the global room constraint. This constraint is meant to enforce that the school cannot exceed its' capacity. If there are r rooms, then there may not be more than r courses scheduled during one particular period.

4 Solving the High School Timetabling Problem

A CSP with no solution is highly undesirable, since there is nothing of value returned to the scheduler. We need some additional rules which dictate the number of constraints to be used by the CSP solver routine. The algorithm we have developed operates iteratively. The CSP begins with no binary constraints at all, and some instantiation of the variables is found which satisfies the non-binary and unary constraints. The process continues by adding binary constraints that pertain to courses of one section and later to courses with more sections. In other words, the CSP is "repaired" by adding more binary constraints. This value, one section, may be thought of as a threshold. The threshold will be incremented as necessary until there is either 100 percent student satisfaction or no solution is found—and the algorithm halts. The general pseudocode of the algorithm is summarized below.

TIMETABLING ALGORITHM
0. Determine enrollment matrix
1. Initialize thresholds
2. **Repeat**
3.   GenerateCSP(threshold)
4.   **For** i=1 to $n_{attempts}$ **Do**
5.   Randomly order domains
6.   Heuristically order variables
7.   Solve CSP
8.   Schedule students
9.   Add constraints by increasing thresholds
10. **Until** no solution exists, or $n_{sat}\%$ of the students are scheduled

Step 0. Determine Enrollment matrix. The enrollment matrix is used to determine which pairs of courses are taken together by students, and the frequency of these combinations.

Step 3. GenerateCSP(threshold). This step determines which binary constraints are included in the problem, based on the current thresholds. The algorithm considers adding a binary constraint between two courses only if one or more students has requested that pair of courses. The decision of whether or not to include a binary constraint is based on how many sections each of the courses has and on how many students have requested that pair of courses. Initially, binary constraints are only added between courses that have a single section and which have high demand. On the next iteration, binary constraints are added between single section courses that have moderate demand. On the iteration after that, those with low demand. On the iteration after that, binary constraints are added between courses that have one or two sections and high demand, and so on.

Step 4. For i = 1 to $n_{attempts}$. Within this algorithm lies a loop that randomizes the domains and solves the CSP, $n_{attempts}$ number of times. For our experiments, $n_{attempts}$ was set at two.

Step 6. Order Variables. The order of the variables refers to the order in which the backtracking routine will assign values to the variables. A good heuristic ordering of the variables can greatly reduce the cost of finding a solution [11]. In our work, the best ordering strategy that has been found is by domain size, smallest to largest.

Step 7. Solve CSP. This step involves most of the computational time and could be any existing CSP algorithm. For our experiments we use a backtracking algorithm known as *forward-checking*. If no solution is found (either because it is proven that no solution exists or because some predefined time limit has been exceeded), for *all* of the $n_{attempts}$ CSPs at the current threshold settings, the program terminates, since too many constraints have been added. (Proceeding to add more binary constraints to an over-constrained problem could not possibly help). The solution found which satisfies the most students course selections is then returned.

Step 8. Schedule the students. After the CSP has been solved, and we are left with a master timetable, the individual students must be scheduled so that their course requests are met. We have determined that the ordering of the students to be scheduled can make a difference. We choose to order the *most* difficult to schedule students first; a "difficult" student to schedule is one who chooses many courses with few sections in them, thereby causing less flexibility in the student's timetable. The number of successfully scheduled students is recorded. If this value exceeds the previous best, the solution is saved, and will be available once the program terminates.

Step 9. Adding constraints by increasing the thresholds. The thresholds are manipulated in order to increase the number of constraints that are in the CSP, and hopefully yield a better solution.

Step 10. Program halting criteria. The algorithm halts once no further improvements can be made. The user can also specify a pre-desired student satisfaction rate, which also results in program termination, once attained. For our experiments, n_{sat} was 99%. In reality, high school timetablers in large schools are pleased to reach 95% student satisfaction.

5 Experimental Results

We gathered data from three local high schools, but we did not proceed to solve the actual high school timetabling problems as some of the data was incomplete and unexplained. As well, each school had their own "exceptions" to the scheduling process. For example, some schools have half credit and double credit courses that last a single term rather than the full year; some courses are taken by correspondence and not actually attended at the school, and one school has an International Baccalaureate Program whose students are treated differently in the scheduling process. The local high school timetablers solve the problem by hand on a school by school basis, a project with requires many hours of effort beginning months in advance of the new school year.

The approach we took was to create an abstract random model of the high school timetabling problem based on courses that are all full year and one credit. Our goal was to create a wide range of realistic data in order to examine what effect varying the parameters of our problem has on the time required to solve the problem and the overall quality (number of students scheduled) of the solution. A further motivation in creating a random problem generator is in identifying "hard" timetabling problem instances. Our random problem generator is able to create a broad range of timetabling problems, including some that are particularly difficult to solve.

We first identified three critical parameters of the high school timetabling problem at hand: n, the numbers of students in the school; c, the number of courses offered by the school; and r, the number of rooms in the school. We varied the number of students from 750 to 2000 by increments of 250, and the number of courses from 100 to 200 by 50. The number of rooms is a function of the capacity of the school. Given the n students, who choose from the c courses, the minimum value of r is the smallest number of rooms which can accommodate all of the resulting classes. The actual value of r will include "spare" rooms, varied at 0.0%, 2.5%, 5.0% and 7.5% of the minimum in our experiments.

To generate a random timetabling problem, one needs a random set of student course selections. From these selections, the constraints can be formulated, as described in Section 3. The student course selections are modeled by four discrete random variables. There is one random variable to model the grade that the student is in (grade 10, 11, or 12) and one to model the number of courses selected (between 1 and 16). Students from a particular grade are not limited to choosing courses of their grade level. The frequency of the random course selections, as well as frequency of students choosing particular courses at a higher or lower grade level, were estimated from data supplied by local high schools.

Some of our experimental results on our random timetabling model are shown in Table 1. The values shown in the table are the averages of 100 experiments at each of the different values of n, the number of students, c, the number of courses, and r, the number of rooms. For all experiments, the timetabling algorithm was run with $n_{attempts}$ equal to 10 (see Step 4, Section 4), and the algorithm halted if a predefined limit of 100 backtracks was reached (see Step 7) or the number of satisfied students, n_{sat}, was greater than or equal to 99% (see Step 10).

The results are encouraging. In the case where the percentage of spare rooms was 2.5% or greater, which are the realistic cases, we found a master timetable that satisfied 98% of the students in approximately two-thirds of the experiments. The most difficult to solve problems occurred when the number of courses offered was high in comparison to the number of students, such as when 750 stu-

Table 1. Effect of varying number of students, number of courses, and percentage of spare rooms, on percentage of students satisfied. Each data point is the average of 100 trials on random problems. In all trials, the algorithm was terminated when 99% student satisfaction was attained.

(a) Percentage of spare rooms is 0%

Courses	Students					
	750	1000	1250	1500	1750	2000
100	88.6	84.5	94.3	84.7	53.0	62.0
150	72.7	78.9	70.9	81.2	45.7	38.9
200	67.5	67.8	72.9	75.7	47.4	39.6

(b) Percentage of spare rooms is 2.5%

Courses	Students					
	750	1000	1250	1500	1750	2000
100	91.4	98.9	99.2	99.6	99.9	99.9
150	82.1	95.2	99.1	99.1	99.3	99.7
200	75.8	85.7	94.5	98.9	99.1	97.2

dents could select from 200 different courses. In this case, the number of courses with just one section of students (less than thirty enrolled) is high. These courses are the most difficult to schedule, since there is the least flexibility for the students, as they are only offered at one time. Because of the Estimation Rule, these single section courses participate in the most binary subset constraints. In general, as the number of courses (variables in the CSP) increased, the quality of the solutions decreased.

Further results can be seen in viewing the data as the number of students in the random model is varied. In general, as the number of students increase, the overall quality of the solutions also increased. This trend is also a consequence of having fewer single section courses. Having more students in each course results in more sections being allotted, which gives greater flexibility as the students are scheduled into courses.

Varying the number of courses and students has a direct implication on the number of binary constraints in the problem. In order to manipulate the *non-binary* constraints, we have also varied the number of rooms in the school. The global capacity constraint says that no more than r courses can be scheduled at one period, given that there are r rooms in the school. As the number of rooms decreases, the quality of the solutions decrease, because in some cases no solution exists at all. For example, when the percentage of spare rooms is 0.0%, the average success rate of the algorithm on a school with 2000 students and 200 courses is 39.6%. However, of the 100 experiments on random problems at these settings, 60 of the experiments terminated with no initial solution found, and in that case the recorded result was 0% student satisfaction. No statistically significant difference was found between the results for 2.5% spare rooms and the results for 5.0% and 7.5%. This is somewhat surprising since for the smaller problems where the minimum number of rooms is around 25, 2.5% spare rooms only adds one room slack, and for the larger problems where the minimum number of rooms is around 60, 2.5% spare rooms only adds two rooms slack. Nevertheless, it was found that having this few of a number of "spare" rooms was sufficient and greatly improved the quality of the master schedule found by the algorithm as measured by the number of satisfied students.

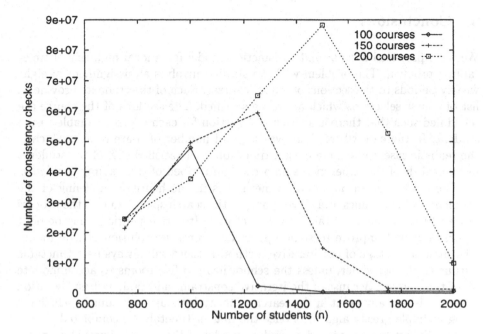

Fig. 2. Effect of number of students on number of consistency checks. For these experiments, the parameters are $c = 100$, 150 and 200 courses, and $r = R_{min} + 2.5\%$ rooms. Each data point represents the average of 100 trials.

The experimental results are also encouraging for their low required run-time. Each solution attempt, whether terminating with no solution, or completing with a master timetable and individual timetables, required less than one hour on a Sun SS4/70-32. The most difficult problems, found when the number of courses was 200 and the number of students was 1500, required approximately 90 million consistency checks on average to reach 99% student satisfaction. On these problems the average run-time was 2107 seconds and the hardest problem took 3404 seconds. The experiments with poor results (less than 80% satisfaction) actually terminated quite quickly, requiring between one and two million consistency checks. The easiest problems occurred when the number of courses was low, and the number of students was high. These problems achieved 99% student satisfaction in roughly two hundred thousand consistency checks—less than five minutes of run-time. Therefore, we conclude that some problems are naturally easy, while in some cases good solutions can be found with more iterations of adding binary constraints. The average number of consistency checks is displayed in Fig. 2. We found that in our experiments the number of consistency checks was an extremely good predictor of run-time and that a plot of average run-time gives the same qualitative shape as in Fig. 2. Thus, for each value c, number of courses, there is an associated number of students n where a peak in problem difficulty is observed.

6 Conclusions

We have proposed a constraint satisfaction model for a local high school time-tabling problem. The problem we have studied involves an assignment of eight weekly periods to the sections of school courses. Each of the students provides a list of course selections which are to be satisfied. The sections of the course are scheduled such that there is at least one section for each course available to the student. In the case where there was a small number of spare rooms, which is the realistic case, we found a master timetable that satisfied 98% of the students in two-thirds of the experiments on a random testbed of timetabling problems.

The innovation in our solution method is in the heuristic modeling of the problem—which prunes away large parts of the search space—and in the process of *iteratively* adding constraints to the network. Iterative solutions may be poor at first but will improve to some upper limit, until no solution can be found. The main advantage of our iterative method is there will always be a timetable output to the scheduler, unless the school has too few rooms to accommodate all of the courses. Because of the iterative constraint addition, a "best" solution always exists at any point in the search. The students are individually scheduled using a simple greedy algorithm once the master timetable is completed.

Finally, we have proposed a random model of the school timetabling problem. By identifying the three critical parameters of number students, number of classrooms and number of courses, we have created a diverse testbed of realistic timetabling problems. Furthermore, we have identified some particularly difficult to solve timetabling instances. These particular instances can be *recreated*, by giving the generator the same parameters and same random seed, so that comparisons can be made with other, improved timetabling algorithms.

References

1. J. Aubin and J.A. Ferland. A large scale timetabling problem. *Computers & Operations Research*, 16:67–77, 1989.
2. H. W. Chan, C. K. Lau, and J. Sheung. Practical school timetabling: A hybrid approach using solution synthesis and iterative repair. In *Proceedings of the Second International Conference on the Practice and Theory of Automated Timetabling*, pages 123–131, Toronto, Canada, 1997.
3. R. Feldman and M. C. Golumbic. Constraint satisfiability algorithms for interactive student scheduling. In *Proceedings of the Eleventh International Joint Conference on Artificial Intelligence*, pages 1010–1016, Detroit, Mich., 1989.
4. J. A. Ferland and C. Fleurent. SAPHIR: A decision support system for course scheduling. *INTERFACES*, 24:105–115, 1994.
5. M. Henz and J. Wurtz. Using Oz for college time tabling. In *Proceedings of the First International Conference on the Practice and Theory of Automated Timetabling*, pages 162–180, 1995. Available as: Springer Lecture Notes in Computer Science 1153.
6. A. Hertz. Tabu search for large scale timetabling problems. *European Journal of Operational Research*, 54:39–47, 1991.

7. G. Lajos. Complete university modular timetabling using constraint logic programming. In *Proceedings of the First International Conference on the Practice and Theory of Automated Timetabling*, pages 146–161, 1995. Available as: Springer Lecture Notes in Computer Science 1153.

8. A. Meisels, J. El-Saana, and E. Gudes. Comments on CSP algorithms applied to timetabling. Technical report, Department of Mathematics and Computer Science, Ben-Gurion University, 1993.

9. A. Schaerf. A survey of automated timetabling. Technical Report Report CS-R9567, Centrum voor Wiskund en Infirmatica (CWI), Amsterdam, The Netherlands, 1996. To appear in *Artificial Intelligence Review*.

10. G. Schmidt and T. Strohlein. Timetable construction — an annotated bibliography. *The Computer Journal*, 23:307–316, 1979.

11. E. Tsang. *Foundations of Constraint Satisfaction*. Academic Press, 1993.

12. P. van Hentenryck. *Constraint Satisfaction in Logic Programming*. MIT Press, Cambridge, Massachusetts, 1989.

13. M. Yoshikawa, K. Kaneko, Y. Nomura, and M. Watanabe. A constraint-based approach to high-school timetabling problems: A case study. In *Proceedings of the Twelfth National Conference on AI*, pages 1111–1116, Seattle, Wash., 1994.

Planning Strategy Representation in DoLittle

Jacky Baltes

Department of Computer Science
Tamaki Campus
University of Auckland
Private Bag 92019
Auckland, New Zealand

h.baltes@auckland.ac.nz

Abstract. This paper introduces multi-strategy planning and describes its implementation in the DOLITTLE system, which can combine many different planning strategies, including means-ends analysis, macro-based planning, abstraction-based planning (reduced and relaxed), and case-based planning on a single problem. *Planning strategies* are defined as methods to reduce the search space by exploiting some assumptions (so-called *planning biases*) about the problem domain. *General operators* are generalizations of standard STRIPS operators that conveniently represent many different planning strategies. The focus of this work is to develop a representation weak enough to represent a wide variety of different strategies, but still strong enough to emulate them. The search control method applies different general operators based on a strongest first principle; planning biases that are expected to lead to small search spaces are tried first. An empirical evaluation in three domains showed that multi-strategy planning performed significantly better than the best single strategy planners in these domains.

1 Introduction

Strategical planning, in particular the classical planning paradigm has long been an active research area in artificial intelligence. One reason for this popularity is that many practical problems can be interpreted as strategical planning problems, e.g., scheduling of machines in a factory, file system maintenance in an operating system, or cargo delivery.

Unfortunately, theoretical results show that planning is intractable even in simple domains [3, 5]. To be practical, a planner must therefore reduce the size of the search space. Based on the notion of an inductive bias in machine learning [12], I introduce *planning bias* to describe these assumptions. Examples of planning biases include assumptions about the structure of the search space, the domain description, the plan structure, the problem set, and the order of the problems.

A *planning strategy* is any method that exploits some planning bias by removing, re-ordering, or restructuring part of the search space. The distinction between planning bias and planning strategy is important since (a) there may be different strategies for exploiting a bias, and (b) since different planning biases may lead to the same planning strategy. For example, if the designer of a domain assumes that earlier plans are subtasks of later ones (a problem order bias), she may either create macros to encapsulate earlier solutions or use a case-based system with a specific similarity metric. On the other hand, Iba's and Korf's macro-planners use the same planning strategy (macros), but are based on very different planning biases (peak-to-peak heuristic ([9]) vs. serial operator decomposability ([10])).

2 Motivation

Planning systems based on particular planning strategies work well if the underlying assumptions (biases) are met, but fail (often spectacularly) if they are not. Many different planning strategies have been developed, but no single bias has been found to be superior or even sufficient in all domains. Recent research shows that planners must use different planning biases in different domains [14].

The motivation for multi-strategy planning is that instead of developing a new planning strategy, the planner is based on partially successful, well known planning strategies. So far, the work focused on macro-based, case-based, and abstraction-based planning. The problem is to determine when a given planning strategy is appropriate for a domain and solve the problem with it. Unfortunately, there are many examples in which a single planning strategy is not sufficient for a domain or even a single problem. Instead, some parts of the problem can be solved efficiently by a particular planning strategy, but another planning strategy is needed for the remainder. Therefore, a multi-strategy planning system must (a) break the problem up into subproblems, (b) select planning strategies and solve the subproblems, and (c) combine the solutions to the subproblems.

The remainder of this section is a brief example, to give the reader a feeling for the essence of multi-strategy planning. Therefore, the comparison is based solely on the necessary search depth and ignores other factors such as the branching factor. A completely worked example can be found in [1].

This work aims at developing a strategical planning system for a kitchen robot. To simulate this environment, I developed a kitchen domain; it consists of an one-armed, mobile robot whose task it is to prepare different beverages. The kitchen domain is a complex domain. It contains 51 operators and 45 objects and has an average branching factor of 3.5. Plans contain many primitive operators, e.g., making a cup of tea, which is one of the simplest tasks, takes 30 steps and is shown in Tab. 1.

Assume that in the kitchen domain, the goal is to prepare a cup of instant coffee with sugar. The solution to this problem contains 42 primitive operators and is shown in Tab 2.

Case-based planning retrieves a plan (in this example, the plan for making tea) and adapts it. This requires replacing the tea box with the instant coffee jar (steps 23,25), replacing the tea bag with instant coffee (steps 29), adding steps

Table 1. Making tea in the kitchen domain

1 OPEN-DOOR CUPBOARD	; get a cup and fill it
2 PICK-UP-FROM-CUPBOARD CUP1	; with water
3 MOVE-ROBOT AT-TABLE AT-SINK	
4 PUT-IN-SINK CUP1	
5 FILL-WITH-WATER CUP1	
6 TURN-WATER-OFF	
7 PICK-UP-FROM-SINK CUP1	; heat the cup with water in
8 MOVE-ROBOT AT-SINK AT-TABLE	; the microwave and put it
9 PUT-ON-TABLE CUP1	; on the table
10 MOVE-ROBOT AT-TABLE AT-STOVE	
11 OPEN-DOOR MICROWAVE	
12 MOVE-ROBOT AT-STOVE AT-TABLE	
13 PICK-UP-FROM-TABLE CUP1	
14 MOVE-ROBOT AT-TABLE AT-STOVE	
15 PUT-IN-MICROWAVE CUP1	
16 CLOSE-DOOR MICROWAVE	
17 HEAT-WATER-IN-MICROWAVE CUP1	
18 OPEN-DOOR MICROWAVE	
19 PICK-UP-FROM-MICROWAVE CUP1	
20 MOVE-ROBOT AT-STOVE AT-TABLE	
21 PUT-ON-TABLE CUP1	
22 MOVE-ROBOT AT-TABLE AT-SINK	
23 PICK-UP-FROM-SHELF TEA-BOX	; get a tea-bag and put it in
24 MOVE-ROBOT AT-SINK AT-TABLE	
25 PUT-ON-TABLE TEA-BOX	; the cup, dispose of it
26 OPEN-CONTAINER TEA-BOX	; afterwards
27 GET-TEA-BAG	
28 MAKE-TEA CUP1	
29 MOVE-ROBOT AT-TABLE AT-SINK	
30 PUT-IN-GARBAGE-CAN OLD-TEA-BAG	

to get a spoon (steps 27-28), and removing operators to throw out the used tea bag. A case-based planner can perform these adaptations relatively quickly by comparing the old and new goal predicates. However, the case-based planner has to create a suffix plan to get the sugar jar and open it, and then scoop the sugar into the coffee. This takes an additional 19 steps in the kitchen domain and the previous plan does not contain any information that can help a case-based planner to speed up this process.

Table 2. Making instant coffee with sugar in the kitchen domain

```
   . . .
22 MOVE-ROBOT AT-TABLE AT-SINK               ; identical to the
                                             ; plan for making tea
23 PICK-UP-FROM-SHELF INSTANT-COFFEE-JAR     ; replace tea-box
                                             ; with
24 MOVE-ROBOT AT-SINK AT-TABLE               ; instant-coffee-jar
25 PUT-ON-TABLE INSTANT-COFFEE-JAR
26 OPEN-CONTAINER INSTANT-COFFEE-JAR
27 OPEN-DOOR DRAWER                           ; add steps and use
28 PICK-UP-FROM-DRAWER SPOON                  ; a spoon
29 SCOOP-INSTANT-COFFEE
30 POUR-INSTANT-COFFEE CUP1
31 STIR CUP1                                  ; stir instant coffee
32 PUT-DOWN-ON-TABLE SPOON
33 MOVE-ROBOT AT-TABLE AT-SINK
34 PICK-UP-FROM-SHELF SUGAR-BOX
35 MOVE-ROBOT AT-SINK AT-TABLE
36 PUT-ON-TABLE SUGAR-BOX
37 OPEN-CONTAINER SUGAR-BOX
38 PICK-UP-FROM-TABLE SPOON
39 SCOOP-SUGAR
40 ADD-SUGAR CUP1
41 STIR CUP1
42 PUT-ON-TABLE SPOON                         ; done
```

Macro-based planning exploits often used operator sequences in the domain. Because of the large variety of possible location for the utensils in the kitchen domain, there are few long recurring operator sequences. The average length of the useful macros in the kitchen domain is about four operators. For example, the following macro fills a cup with water (put $Cup in sink, fill $Cup with water, turn water off, pick up $Cup). Given that macros only contain small number of operators, they can not reduce the search space sufficiently. For example, in this case, the search depth is still at least ten steps.

Abstraction-based planning creates an abstract plan to make instant coffee with sugar: (get a cup, fill cup with water, heat the water by either using the microwave or the stove, add instant coffee, get the sugar jar, add sugar). However, the refinement of each of those abstract operators is non-trivial in itself, and abstraction-based planning does not provide any guidance when searching for the refinement. For example, the refinement of the "heat-the-water" operator consists of ten primitive operators.

Multi-strategy planning uses all planning strategies to make instant coffee with sugar. It uses case-based planning to find an initial plan. However, it is able to employ other planning strategies when searching for the suffix plan to add sugar. An abstract plan to add the sugar is easily found: get the sugar jar and add the sugar. The refinement of these abstract operators is sped up by providing macros for often recurring subsequences, e.g., fetching a jar or opening a jar. In this case, the search depth is two steps only.

As can be seen in the previous example, no single problem solving strategy (macros, cases, abstractions) was able to solve the problem efficiently, but a combination had to be used.

3 Planning Paradigm

Korf has previously analyzed the planning problem as a state space search problem [10]. In this framework, planning is interpreted as a graph search problem. The nodes of the graph represent world states and edges correspond to application of an operator. Although intuitive, this framework is not powerful enough to represent other planning strategies, such as abstraction-based planning since it reasons about sets of world states.

This section develops a practical definition of planning strategy as a language for evolving plans and a set of plan transformations. This work uses the plan-space search paradigm, which was first introduced to analyze partial order planning [4] but can be extended to include recent new planning paradigms [2, 6]. Planning is interpreted as search through evolving plans. In this framework, a planner is defined as follows:

Definition 1 (Planner). *A planner* $\mathcal{P}$ *is a tuple* $(\mathcal{L}_S, \mathcal{L}_G, \mathcal{L}_O, \mathcal{L}_P, \mathcal{T}, \mathcal{M})$.

- $\mathcal{L}_S$ *is the state language, describing possible world states.*
- $\mathcal{L}_G$ *is a goal description language.*
- $\mathcal{L}_O$ *is a description language for operators,*
- $\mathcal{L}_P$ *is the plan language, the language describing evolving plans. The plan language must be able to express plans, that is a set of operators, an ordering on the operators in the set, and a set of constraints on variable instantiations. Early planning systems supported only totally ordered, fully instantiated plans. More recently, partial-order planners support partially ordered plans with co- and non-codesignation constraints of variables.*
- $\mathcal{T}$ *is a set of plan transformations. A plan transformation t is a function that takes a plan expression from* $\mathcal{L}_P$, *and returns a new candidate plan c expressed in* $\mathcal{L}_P$.

- *M is the plan selection method. Given a set of possible plans P expressed in $\mathcal{L}_\mathcal{P}$, M selects the plan p to be tested next.*

The state $\mathcal{L}_\mathcal{S}$, goal $\mathcal{L}_\mathcal{G}$, and operator $\mathcal{L}_\mathcal{O}$ languages determine the description of a domain, since they define the input to the planning system. As many other planning systems, this work uses a variant of the STRIPS representation. Therefore, the representational classification is ignored in the remainder of this paper.

The operational classification is determined by three components: the plan description language $\mathcal{L}_\mathcal{P}$, the set of plan transformations T, and the plan selection method M. Plan selection methods are usually derived from well-known search methods such as depth-first, breadth-first, or best-first.

The following subsections discuss some popular planning systems in the plan space search paradigm. Although there are many possible variations of the different strategies, the following discussion focuses on the most common implementations.

3.1 Forward chaining planning

Forward chaining planning is a simple planning system that applies operators until a goal state is found. The plan language represents a totally ordered and fully instantiated operator sequence. There is only a single plan transformation: append an operator to the operator sequence.

3.2 Means-ends analysis

Means-ends analysis contains two totally ordered and fully instantiated sets of operators, the plan head and the plan tail. The plan head contains operators that are already applied and the plan tail contains operators that still need to be applied. There are three plan transformations: (a) append an operator to the plan head, (b) prepend an operator to the plan tail, and (c) apply the first operator of the plan tail.

3.3 Macro-based planning

Macro-based planning is similar to means-ends analysis planning, but the plan language and the plan transformations are extended to include sequences of operators instead of single operators only.

3.4 Abstraction-based planning

Abstraction-based planning extends the plan language to allow for different levels of abstraction. The set of plan transformations from means-ends analysis are extended to include a transformation that adds the generation of a new subproblem space at the next lower abstraction level.

3.5 Case-based planning

Case-based planning uses a similar plan language to means-ends analysis, but a much larger set of plan transformations (insert, remove, reorder, replace, and instantiate an operator). The operator selection method is based on a similarity metric instead of relevance.

Table 3, which is described in [1], summarizes the results presented above and includes the plan language and set of plan transformations for other planning strategies.

Table 3. Operational classification of different planning systems

Planner	Plan lang. $\mathcal{L}_\mathcal{P}$	Transform. set T
Forward Chaining	Total order Instantiated variables Plan head	Append to plan head Advance current op.
Means-ends	Total order Instantiated variables Plan head and plan tail	Append to plan head Prepend to plan tail Advance current op.
Case-based CHEF	Total order Instantiated variables Plan skeleton Concurrent plans	Insert operator Remove operator Reorder operator Replace operator Change var. bindings Move current op.
Auto. subgoals STEPPING STONE Relaxed Abstraction	Total order Instantiated variables Uniform trees Plan head and plan tail	Append to plan head Prepend to plan tail Advance current op. Create probl. space
Abstraction ALPINE	Total order Instantiated variables Uniform trees Plan head and plan tail	Append op. at level i Prepend op. at level i Advance curr. op. (i) Create probl. space $(i+1)$
Macros MACLEARN	Total order Instantiated variables Plan head	Append op. sequence Advance current op.
Multi-strat. DOLITTLE	Total order Instantiated variables Plan skeleton Non-uniform trees	Move current op. Insert op. sequence Remove, -order, -place ops. Change var. binding Create problem space
Partial-order TWEAK	Partial order Constrained variables	Add operator Add variable constraint Add operator ordering

Note that this representation is not the only one possible. There are many other weak representations, for example, Gould's APS system uses a pattern weight representation [7]. The main focus of this work is a representation that is weak enough to cover a wide variety of strategies, yet strong enough to emulate them. For example, it may seem that the reorder and replace plan transformations in case-based planning are superfluous, since they can be achieved by sequences of insertion and removal of operators. From a representational point of view, operator insertion and removal are the only ones necessary, since any plan can be created with these two transformations alone. However, this neglects the fact that these transformations have specific conditions under which they are applied. For example, in Hammond's Chef planner [8], an operator can only be replaced if it solves a missing precondition or unwanted side effect conflict. As Hammond showed, the power of Chef stems from the fact there is a small set of these transformations and applicability conditions that can solve most problems in the cooking domain.

4 Multi-strategy Planning in DoLittle

This section discusses the design of DoLITTLE, a multi-strategy planner that can combine forward chaining, means-ends analysis, case-based, automatic subgoaling [13], abstraction-based, and macro-based planning.

Extending the analysis of different planning strategies in the plan space paradigm described in section 3, the plan language and the set of plan transformations necessary for a multi-strategy planning system can be determined. In particular, the plan language must be able to represent: (a) totally ordered operator sequences, (b) instantiated variables, (c) a plan skeleton, and (d) trees of problem spaces. The set of plan transformations must include (a) operator transformations (application, insertion, removal, reordering, replacement of an operator sequence), (b) changing a variable binding, and (c) the creation of different subproblem spaces for subproblems, serial subgoals, and abstract spaces.

The design of a multi-strategy planner requires three key components: (a) applicability conditions for planning strategies, (b) a representation for different planning strategies, and (c) a search strategy that emulates different planning strategies.

4.1 Applicability conditions

Previous work has shown that simply extending the set of plan transformations is not sufficient. Minton showed that the creation of macro-operators alone must be carefully controlled to avoid a decrease in performance due to the increase in branching factor [11]. The situation is even worse for a multi-strategy system that adds many more plan transformations. Therefore, a multi-strategy planning system must also provide powerful methods for specifying when a given plan transformation should be applied. There are many possible features of a planning process that may be useful in determining whether to apply a planning strategy, e.g., the current state, the goals the planner is trying to achieve, the problem space, the current subgoal hierarchy, the current operator and its binding, the results of the indexer, the set of rejected plans, and additional domain knowledge. Many of these features are planning strategy dependent. For example, there is no concept of a subgoal hierarchy (means-ends analysis) in case-based planning and vice versa for the results of the indexer. Therefore, DoLITTLE's applicability conditions are based on a common subset of these features: the current state and the set of goals the planner is trying to achieve (so-called open goals).

The language for DoLITTLE's applicability conditions supports conjunction, disjunction, and negation of preconditions and open goals. For example, DoLIT-TLE can specify that a given planning strategy should only be used when the current state contains either (ON CUP1 TABLE) or (IN CUP1 MICROWAVE) and the planner is trying to achieve (IN CUP1 SINK) but not when it is trying to achieve (ON CUP1 SHELF). For more detail, the reader is encouraged to refer to [1].

4.2 Representation of planning strategies

DoLITTLE uses general operators, a generalization of STRIPS operators, to represent applicability conditions and planning strategies. Associated with a general operator is a set of refinements. A refinement is a sequence of general or primitive operators that guarantees that the effects of the parent operator are achieved, but it may have additional pre-conditions and effects.

The following general operator is an example from the kitchen domain and illustrates the key features:

General operator example

```
GEN-PICK-UP-FROM-CUPBOARD
      Variables $OBJECT
      Preconds (ARM-EMPTY)
              (IS-AT ROBBY AT-TABLE)
              (IS-IN $OBJECT CUPBOARD)
      Open goals (HOLDING $OBJECT)
      Effects (HOLDING $OBJECT)
              (NOT (IS-IN $OBJECT CUPBOARD))
              (NOT (ARM-EMPTY))
      Refine. 1 PICK-UP-FROM-CUPBOARD($OBJECT)
      Refine. 2 ABSTRACT-SUBGOAL
```

The general operator GEN-PICK-UP-FROM-CUPBOARD can be used to pick up an object from the cupboard independent of whether the cupboard is open or not. The preconditions and open goals refer to the planner state, not the world state. The preconditions of the operator establish that the planning strategies described in the refinements are applicable, if the current world state matches them, i.e., the arm is empty, the robot is at the table, and $OBJECT is in the cupboard. Note that DoLITTLE will not subgoal on the preconditions in the planner state, only on those of the refinements. Furthermore, one goal that the planner is trying to achieve is (HOLDING $OBJECT). Adding another literal to the set of open goals results in a conjunction. To represent a disjunction, a new general operator must be created:

General operator example

GEN-PICK-UP-FROM-CUPBOARD-2
    Variables $OBJECT
    Context
    Preconds (ARM-EMPTY)
         (IS-AT ROBBY AT-TABLE)
         (IS-IN $OBJECT Cupboard)
    Open goals (NOT (IS-IN $OBJECT Cupboard))
    Effects (HOLDING $OBJECT)
        (NOT (IS-IN $OBJECT Cupboard))
        (NOT (ARM-EMPTY))
    Refine. 1 PICK-UP-FROM-CUPBOARD($OBJECT)
    Refine. 2 ABSTRACT-SUBGOAL

Given the two general operators, the strategies described in their common set of refinements are applicable if the planner is trying *either* to achieve (HOLDING $OBJECT) *or* to negate (IS-IN $OBJECT Cupboard).

General operator example (continued)

REFINE. 1: MACRO
    Variables $OBJECT
    Preconds same as parent plus
        (IS-OPEN CUPBOARD)
    Effects (HOLDING $OBJECT)
        (IS-IN $OBJECT Cupboard)
        (ARM-EMPTY)
    Sequence PICK-UP-FROM-CUPBOARD($OBJECT)

The first refinement is of type MACRO and consists of the single primitive operator PICK-UP-FROM-CUPBOARD. This refinement has the additional precondition that the cupboard must be open when picking up the object. If DoLITTLE selects this refinement, but the cupboard is closed, it will subgoal and generate a plan to open the cupboard. Note that in practice DoLITTLE selects the refinement that best matches the situation and would return the second refinement, discussed below, if the cupboard is closed. The deletions of (IS-IN $OBJECT Cupboard) and (ARM-EMPTY) are side-effects of PICK-UP-FROM-CUPBOARD. The difference between a MACRO and CASE refinement is that only CASE refinements can be adapted by for example replacing operators. MACRO refinements can only be added to the plan.

General operator example (continued)

REFINE. 2: ABSTRACT SUBGOAL
        Variables $OBJECT
        Preconds same as parent plus
                (NOT (IS-OPEN CUPBOARD))
      Effects (IS-OPEN CUPBOARD)
             (HOLDING $OBJECT)
             (NOT (IS-IN $OBJECT CUPBOARD))
             (NOT (ARM-EMPTY))
        Sequence empty

The second refinement is a reduced abstraction refinement, which does not contain an operator sequence. It contains one additional precondition (NOT (IS-OPEN CUPBOARD)) and one additional effect (NOT (IS-OPEN CUPBOARD)). DoLITTLE recursively searches for a plan that achieves all effects of the refinement. However, since the search space is classified as an abstract search space, the planner is constrained to plans that do *not* change the values of the literals in the general operator. For example, while searching for the plan to pick up the cup, DoLITTLE will reject any plan that changes the position of the robot ((IS-AT ROBBY TABLE)) or picks up an object ((ARM-EMPTY)).

4.3 DoLittle's search control

The representation of different planning strategies is alone not sufficient for a multi-strategy planning system. The representation of cases and macros are very similar, both are sequences of operators. However, their effect on the search space is very different. Macros are simply selected and concatenated, whereas cases are selected based on a similarity metric and are adapted. The situation is similar to that of asking for the inherent meaning of a bit-pattern (e.g., 11101010), which of course depends on whether it is interpreted as a binary number (signed or unsigned?), a machine code instruction (for which processor?), a character string, or a floating point number. Therefore, a multi-strategy planning system must also provide a search control method that emulates the effect of a given planning strategy on the search space.

DoLITTLE's search control method is based on a strongest-first heuristic: planning strategies that result in the smallest search space are tried first. Checking a small search space first has two benefits: (a) if a solution exists in this space, it can be found quickly, and (b) if no solution exists, the failure can quickly be recognized. Note that since planning strategies are not complete, they may remove the part of the search space with the solution.

DOLITTLE uses a domain independent similarity measure to retrieve the most similar general operator to the current problem and to select the refinements. If the operator or refinement represents a macro that exactly matches a problem, a solution is found (macro-based planning). Otherwise, the operator sequence is adapted to the current situation (case-based). If there is no case or macro available, a subproblem search space is created. At present, there are three different types of search spaces in DOLITTLE: an abstract subgoal space, a serial subgoal space, and a general subgoal. The different search spaces represent different constraints on the search.

5 Evaluation

This section discusses briefly the results of an evaluation of DOLITTLE's performance on a set of problem domains. For a detailed description of the methodology and the statistical analysis, please refer to [1]. The evaluation included three domains: (a) the blocks-world, (b) the towers of Hanoi, and (c) the kitchen domain.

The goal of this evaluation was to evaluate empirically the performance of multi-strategy planning (DOLITTLE) against that of four single strategy planners: a means-ends analysis planner, a case-based planner, a macro-based planner, and an abstraction-based planner. The performance of DOLITTLE was also compared against that of a problem coordinated multi-strategy planner with an oracle (PC-MSP-O), that is a planner that selects from a set of possible planners the best one for a given problem. Although in practice, selecting the best strategy is impossible a priori, the entries for the hypothetical PC-MSP-O planner were generated by selecting the minimum of the single strategy planners. However, in contrast to DOLITTLE, the planning strategy is fixed for a problem, that is, PC-MSP-O is not able to switch between planning strategies when solving a single problem.

For the evaluation, a set of 150 training problems were randomly generated and the different planners were trained on these problems. Then a new set of 250 test problems were generated and the performance of the different planners was tested. Solving problems in the kitchen domain is difficult. Therefore, the solution length of the problems in the test and training set was slowly increased by increasing the number of drinks and ingredients in a plan. For example, a simple problem maybe to prepare a glass of milk, whereas preparing a glass of milk with honey or two cups of tea are more difficult (as measured by the minimum solution length) problems. The idea is that by solving small problems first, the planners are able to learn enough information to solve more complex problems later.

The comparison included the cumulative number of nodes generated and the cumulative running times for the different planners as well as the relationship between the time limit and the total running time of the system. Figure 1 shows the cumulative running time in the kitchen domain. The X-axis is a set of 250 test problems that are increasingly more difficult.

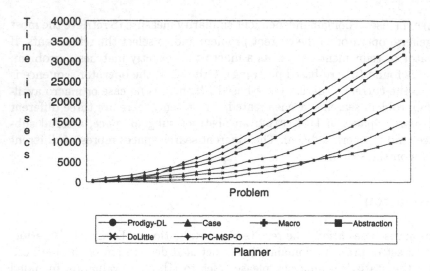

Fig. 1. Cumulative running times in the kitchen domain

The single strategy planners did improve performance with case-based planning being the best single strategy planner in this domain. In the kitchen domain, variations of earlier problems are often subtasks in later ones, which favors a case-based approach. Multi-strategy planning provided a significant higher speed up than single strategy planning. DoLittle performed better on the more difficult problems than PC-MSP-O. This difference statistically significant, which shows that especially in complex domains, a multi-strategy planner should be able to switch planning strategies while solving a problem.

In the kitchen domain, DoLittle gained much of its power by combining case-based planning with either macro operators or abstract operators. Initially, it would select a case and adapt it to the new situation. It would use macros, abstractions, and sometimes even other cases for difficult adaptations.

The empirical evaluation also showed that no single strategy planner was superior. For example, although case-based planning lead to the biggest improvement in the kitchen domain, it performed worse than abstraction-based planning in the towers of Hanoi domain.

6 Conclusions

So far, the main focus of the research has been on methods for combining different planning strategies on a single problem. Current work investigates the interaction of different planning strategies.

The uniform representation in DoLITTLE also makes it an ideal test-bed for the comparison of different planning strategies. This work may result in a better understanding of the applicability conditions of different planning strategies. This will lead to better methods of determining when a given planning strategy is appropriate for a domain.

Development on DoLITTLE is continuing at the University of Auckland. Currently, we are working on a project that uses DoLITTLE as the strategic planning component of an autonomous, mobile robot. The intended applications for the robot are mail delivery in an office environment, and other household and security tasks.

This new application will require the addition of new planning strategies and new learning methods. So far, DoLITTLE's learning methods are limited since they only learn from successful solutions. There are many more problem solving events that may prove helpful in learning to improve the performance of the planner, such as failure, subgoal interaction, or expensive refinements.

References

1. Jacky Baltes. *DoLittle: a learning multi-strategy planning system*. PhD thesis, University of Calgary, June 1996.
2. A. Blum and M. Furst. Fast planning through plan-graph analysis. In *Proceedings IJCAI-95*, 1995.
3. Tom Bylander. Complexity results for planning. In *Proceedings of the Twelfth International Joint Conference on Artificial Intelligence*, pages 274–279, Sydney, 1991.
4. David Chapman. Planning for conjunctive goals. *Artificial Intelligence*, 32:333–378, 1987.
5. Stephen V. Chenoweth. On the np-hardness of blocks world. In *Proceedings Ninth National Conference on Artificial Intelligence*, volume 2, pages 623–628, Stenlo Park, July 1991. AAAI Press/The MIT Press.
6. Matt Ginsberg. A new algorithm for generative planning. In *Proceedings KR-96*, 1996.
7. Jeffrey Gould and Robert Levinson. Experience-based adaptive search. In Ryszard Michalski and Gheorghe Tecuci, editors, *Machine Learning: A multi-strategy approach*, volume 4, pages 579–603, San Francisco, Ca, 1994. Morgan Kaufmann Publishers.
8. Kristian J. Hammond. *Case Based Planning*. Academic Press Inc., 1989.
9. Glenn A. Iba. A heuristic approach to the discovery of macro-operators. *Machine Learning*, 3:285–318, 1989.
10. R. E. Korf. Planning as search: A quantitative approach. *Artificial Intelligence*, 33(1):65–88, 1987.
11. Steven Minton. *Learning Search Control Knowledge: An Explanation-based Approach*. Kluwer Academic Publishers, Boston, 1988.
12. Tom Mitchell. The need for biases in learning generalizations. In J. Shavlik and T. Dietterich, editors, *Readings in Machine Learning*, pages 184–191. Morgan Kaufmann, 1990.
13. David Ruby and Dennis Kibler. Steppingstone: An empirical and analytical evaluation. In *Proceedings of the Ninth National Conference on Artificial Intelligence*, pages 527–532, Menlo Park, July 1991. AAAI, AAAI Press/The MIT Press.

14. Peter Stone, Manuela Veloso, and Jim Blythe. The need for different domain-independent heuristics. In Kristian Hammond, editor, *Proceedings of the second international conference on artificial intelligence planning systems*, pages 164–169, Menlo Park, 1994. AAAI Press.

Establishing Logical Connectivity between Query Keywords and Database Contents

Dong-Guk Shin and Lung-Yung Chu

Computer Science & Engineering, University of Connecticut,
191 Auditorium Road, U-155, Storrs, CT 06269, USA
{shin, chu}@cse.uconn.edu

Abstract. Recent advances in Internet and client-server technology provide unprecedented opportunities for users to directly access multiple databases. One major problem in this environment is that users suffer difficulties in formulation query expressions due to their unfamiliarity with the target database schemas and contents. It seems imperative that the query interface should exhibit some intelligent behavior in assisting user's query formulation process. In this work, we present a query formulation assistance system, called *Qassist*, which was designed to map input query keywords or phrases into various components of the database constituents. Once the mapping is performed, *Qassist* generates skeletons of query expressions that can be considered as plausible interpretations of the input phrases. At the core of the mapping process is the use of database schema modeling knowledge. We present an example illustrating how use of such a modeling knowledge enables us to generate the interpretations of query phrases.

1 Introduction

For the past few years, thanks to the proliferation of various specialty databases and advances in the Internet, we have witnessed a tremendous growth in the end-user population who wishes to access databases by themselves. One of the challenging problems in this scenario is to build a query interface that allows them to express queries quicker and easier. One criticism of the SQL query interface that its syntax can be very complicated [2], [3]. Another serious problem, which has often been overlooked in the literature, is that formulating SQL queries requires user to understand the database schema. For those who are not familiar with someone else's database schema, formulating query expressions is not a trivial task. Initially, users may develop questions in their mind, but without knowing how data has been organized into the database, they will have a difficulty in determining how to initiate formulating the query, for example, which specific table names, or attribute names they should use in formulating the query.

As an example, consider a biologist wishes to perform the following query "Show me the known sequences of cystic fibrosis transmembrane conductance regulator." Formulating a proper SQL expression for this question can be a real challenge for her even if she is a SQL expert [7]. This is because the answers to this query are stored in two different databases and she must form a distributed query which requires her to understand the schemas of both databases. When each database contains more than 100 tables, getting familiarized with both of the schemas can be quite demanding.

With this particular problem in mind, we developed a query assistance system capable of recognizing limited set of noun phrases or keywords, mapping them to corresponding components of the schemas, and finally producing the skeletons of the corresponding SQL expressions. The philosophy behind the architecture of this system is different from that of the previously attempted natural language interface for databases (e.g., [4], [6]). One major difference is that this system does not aim at translating the entire query given in a natural language. Instead, it attempts to find out whether a given set of input keyword terms can be mapped to any meaningful combination of database schema elements and the data values stored in the database. Once any meaningful mapping is discovered, the discovery is presented to the user who will then use it to complete the rest of the SQL query formulation. By doing so, the user speeds up the query formulation. This system may aim at a smaller, modest goal, but it would not cause the well-known problem of the full-blown natural language interfaces for databases – that is, the users would not suffer from the lack of knowledge of the conceptual boundary between what the system can do and can not do.

The rest of this paper is organized as follows. Section 2 includes the overview of the system architecture. In Section 3, we briefly describes the knowledge representation language $\mathcal{L}_k$. In Section 4, we show how the database schema modeling knowledge can be represented in $\mathcal{L}_k$. In Section 5, we describe the mapping methodology. Section 6 includes an example illustrating the overall process. Finally, Section 7 is the conclusion.

2 System Architecture

2.1 Two features

We developed a prototype query interface, called *Qassist*, that aims at assisting users to express SQL queries quicker and easier in a multiple database environment. *Qassist* provides various features that enable user to express queries graphically. It also provides a way of accessing remote database schemas conveniently. Most importantly, however, *Qassist* provides a feature that is unique and bears some characteristics of an intelligent system. That is, *Qassist* attempts to "recognizes" query keywords or phrases. If a user enters a keyword, the system will find in which database(s) the keyword appears and in what form - i.e., whether a keyword appears as a relation name, an attribute name, or an attribute value. When the user enters a phrase, the system interprets it into potential partial SQL expressions.

2.2 System components

Figure 1 shows the overview of the system architecture and various components the system contains. We briefly explain some key components.

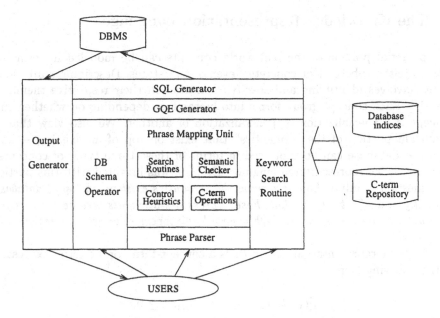

Fig. 1. Overview of the system architecture

Database Indices: A set of inverted files are created for each database available. These inverted files contain indices for certain table columns whose values might be input by the user as query keywords. Inverted files are also created for the database schema so that input keywords can match table names as well as attribute names.

Concept-term Repository: A collection of what we call concept-terms (or c-terms) is built and stored in a repository. Each of these concept-terms represents a certain real world concept modeled into relational schema. These concept-terms are expressed in the knowledge representation language $\mathcal{L}_k$. These concept-terms are used as the resources for producing the mapping between query phrases and the database schemas.

Phrase Mapping Unit: This module contains four subcomponents, Search Routines, Control Heuristics, Semantic Checker, and C-term Operations. This module constitutes the computation engine responsible for generating the mapping between query phrases and the database schemas.

Phrase Parser: This module is responsible for parsing the query phrase into keywords and passing the result to the Phrase Mapping Unit.

Graphical Query Expression (GQE) Generator: Once mapping is established by Phrase mapping unit, this module is responsible for generating and graphically displaying the skeleton SQL expressions from the mapping data. It needs to interact with Keyword Search Routine, Phrase Mapping Unit, and DB Schema Operator which is responsible for providing information about other related database schemas.

3   The Knowledge Representation Language

A substantial portion of the real world concepts can be modeled in terms of entities (either abstract or concrete), events, and states. Describing states and events involves identifying and specifying entities in their respective thematic roles [1]. Each concept group forms into hierarchies depending on whether one concept is a specialization or generalization of another. We also view that a significant portion of the "semantics" that exist on top of an existing − i.e., legacy − database can be expressed in terms of these three types of concepts. The knowledge representation language $\mathcal{L}_k$ [8, 9] was invented with this particular question in mind: *How to express the semantics existing on top of database explicitly and effectively so that those expressed statements become sources for manipulating data semantics which generally disappear once schema designs are completed?*

The basic representation unit in $\mathcal{L}_k$ is a concept-term, or a c-term, expressed in the following form:

$$l[c_1 : t_1, c_2 : t_2, .., c_n : t_n], n \geq 0,$$

where l is called the *head concept label*, and $c_i : t_i$, $0 \leq i \leq n$, is called a *restrictor*, c_i, a *concept-connector* of the restrictor, and t_i, the *target* of the concept-connector c_i. Here t_i itself can be a c-term. Depending on whether the head concept label l denotes an entity, a state, or an event in the real world, the c-term beginning with l is then categorized into an entity, a state, or an event c-term. Once c-terms are expressed, a pair of c-terms can be conjoined by two special symbols, $\dot{\in}$ and $\dot{\subseteq}$, to represent the "is-an-instance-of" relationship and the "is-a-specialization-of" relationship, respectively. These pairs of c-terms expressed with $\dot{\in}$ and $\dot{\subseteq}$ collectively form into hierarchies.

Some examples of c-terms are:

(1) CAR   (3) CAR[color:RED, style:CONVERTIBLE]
(2) CAR[color:RED]   (4) OWN[agent:SUE, object:CAR[color:RED]]

The expression (1) is a simple c-term without any restrictor. This expression is meant to denote a "car." The rest of the expressions show the case where one or more restrictors can be included. In particular, the expression (4) show the nesting of c-terms. (2) is meant a "red car," and (3) a "red convertible car." (4) refers to a state "Sue owns a red car."

One unique feature of $\mathcal{L}_k$ is that the language includes a set of c-term manipulation operations that are designed to perform common reasoning steps and various forms of associations. There are

O1. Upward label substitution   O2. Restrictor Release
O3. Downward label substitution   O4. Restrictor introduction
O5. Restrictor inheritance   O6. Membership identification
O7. Concept-connector identification   O8. Label-target rotation

The details of the operations can be found in [8,9]. One example is given below. Assume that CAR in (3) and CAR in (4) mean the same object. Then by using O4 (Restrictor introduction) the two c-terms (3) and (4) can be merged to produce another c-term,

"OWN[agent:SUE, object:CAR[color:RED, style:CONVERTIBLE]]"

which is meant "Sue owns a red convertible car."

4   Using Concept-Terms to Describe a Database Schema

We use c-terms to express how concepts and facts have been modeled into a database schema. The general expression is the following format of c-terms:

$$object\ [\ attribute_1{:}DB\_col\_1,\ \cdots,\ attribute_n{:}DB\_col\_n\ ]$$

In the above, *object* is the name of the entity being described, $attribute_i$ is a property or characteristics of the entity *object*, and DB_col_i is the particular table column in which the target values of the corresponding property of the object are stored. Since we are dealing with a multi-database environment, DB_col_i is expressed in terms of a dot-interconnected expression, such as databasename.tablename.columnname, which uniquely points out a table column in certain database. We indicate that specifying the table column information in the concept-connector's target position is a reasonable solution, because the target is supposed to contain the information about the potential values for the concept-connector, and because, in each database, those values appear in columns of a table.

Example: Let the table called LOCUS be in the gene mapping database GDB. Let another table called SEQUENCE be in the nucleotide sequence database GSDB. Suppose each table contains attributes as illustrated below.

```
LOCUS ( locus_id, locus_name, sequence, locus_symbol )
SEQUENCE ( id, sequence, length )
```

By examining the above relation schemas, we initially generate c-term expressions, each describing how concepts has been modeled into a relation schema. The results are given below.

locus [identifier:gdb.locus.locus_id, name:gdb.locus.locus_name,   (4.1)
            symbol:gdb.locus.locus_symbol, sequence:sequence]

sequence [identifier:gsdb.Sequence.id, sequence:gsdb.Sequence.sequence, (4.2)
             length:gsdb.Sequence.length]

Figure 2 shows how the two c-terms (4.1) and (4.2) are expressed in tree structures.

The above method of using c-term expressions to describe how concepts are expressed by a database schema is not yet sufficient for our intended goal. We augment the c-term structure to include additional information. The general format for the augmented c-term expressions in *Qassist* is the following.

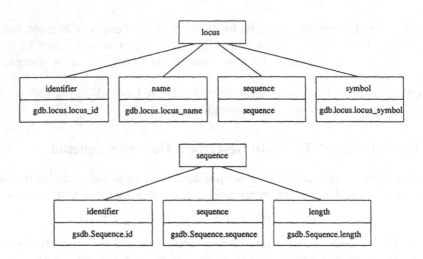

Fig. 2. Two c-terms recording database schema modeling

(head_label_0, DB_location_0) [
    (connector_1, DB_location_1, att_type_1):(head_label_1, DB_location_12),
    (connector_2, DB_location_2, att_type_2):(head_label_1, DB_location_22),
    ···]

Here att_type can have either I, C, or N as its value. The meanings of these values are explained shortly. The two example c-terms (4.1) and (4.2) are then augmented into the following expressions (4.3) and (4.4), respectively.

(locus, gdb.locus) [(4.3)
    (symbol, gdb.locus.locus_symbol, I):(STRING, dom_locus_symbol),
    (sequence, gsdb.Sequence, C):(sequence, gsdb.Sequence),
    (name, gdb.locus.locus_name, I):(STRING, dom_locus_name)]

(sequence, gsdb.Sequence) [(4.4)
    (sequence, gsdb.Sequence.sequence, I):(TEXT, dom_sequence),
    (length, gsdb.Sequence.length, N):(INT, dom_sq_length),
    (identifier, gsdb.Sequence.id, I):(STRING, dom_sq_id)]

Figure 3 shows the two augmented c-term expressions (4.3) and (4.4) in tree structures. In the tree structure representation, there are two types of nodes, namely node_A type nodes and node_B type nodes. Here node_A nodes can have zero or more children of node_B type nodes. The node_B type nodes contain connector, class_type information, and DB_location indicating the database location of connector. Each of node_B type nodes can have only one child node of node_A type. Note that, in the figure, "I" means that the target values for the corresponding connector can uniquely identify the objects being described; "C" means that the target values for the corresponding connector is a compound object which itself can have children; and "N" means that the target values for

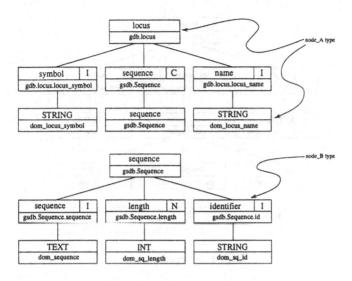

Fig. 3. Augmented representation of data modeling

the corresponding connector is terminal. In fact, all I type connectors are also terminal.

5 Mapping Between Input Keywords and Database Content

5.1 Keywords vs. noun phrases

Users can input fragmented query in two ways. One method is to have the system allow users to enter keywords. In this case, the system treats each keyword separately and return as the results the database constituents mapped to the individual keyword. For example, three example keyword sets are given below, each including the gene name CFTR.

(a) {sequence, CFTR}; (b) {CFTR, sequence}; (c) {length, CFTR, sequence}

In this case, both (a) and (b) inputs are treated same. Discovering database content mapping to each keyword is straightforward. The second method is to have the system allow users to enter noun phrases. Three examples are given:

(d) sequence of CFTR; (e) CFTR sequence; (f) length of CFTR sequence

Our goal is to design a system that is capable of interpreting both (d) and (e) in the same way and also produces a mapping that forms the basis of expressing the query whose execution returns CFTR sequences.

Currently, *Qassist* handles a limited subset of noun phrases which are of the following forms where each A_i is a noun:

1. A_1 of A_2 of $\cdots$ of A_n
2. A_1's A_2's $\cdots A_n$
3. $A_1 A_2 \cdots A_n$

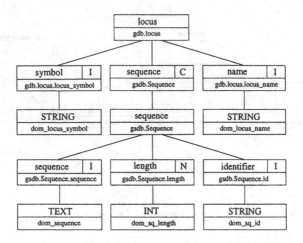

Fig. 4. Merged c-term

5.2 C-term Manipulation

Once a noun phrase, say *np* is input, *Qassist* parses it and isolates nouns. Each isolated noun is then mapped against the concept-term library to discover how it is mapped to database constituents. The discovered outputs are c-terms. The next step is to manipulate these discovered c-terms to produce a derivative which can be considered as an interpretation of the noun phrase *np*. For the c-term manipulation, *Qassist* currently uses two operations among the eight c-term manipulation operations list in Section 3.

Concept-connector identification: This operation is alternatively called *Merge* and is somewhat similar to the join operation of Sowa's Conceptual Graph [10]. This operation takes place when two c-terms share one same label, specifically when a target embedded in one c-term match the head-concept label of the other c-term. As an example, consider the two c-terms shown in Figure 3. The label "sequence" appear in both c-terms. These two c-terms are merged to produce a new one and the result is shown in Figure 4.

Upward Label Substitution: This operation occurs when a type value replaces the type label. As an example, consider the c-term examples in Figure 3. The operation occurs when the target value for the concept-connector 'symbol' replaces the head-concept label 'locus.' Likewise, the target value for 'name' can also replace 'locus.' This operation is plausible because instances generally inherit properties of their type. This operation is prohibited for the concept-connector which are not I type. For example, a target value for 'length' cannot replace "sequence."

5.3 Semantic Check

Once multiple c-terms are combined and modified by using "Merge" and "Upward Label Substitution," the system produces a data structure that we call the final c-term tree (FCT). The system checks whether or not the meaning associated with the FCT is plausible.

First, we define the *level* of a node in FCT. Given an FCT t, let A be a node in t. The level of A, denoted by $L(A)$, is the number of the edges of the path between A and the root node of t. Suppose $L = A_1$ of A_2 of $\cdots A_i$ of $\cdots$ of A_n is the user's input, and the FCT contains all A_i nodes, where $1 \leq i \leq n$. When $L(A_i) = L(A_{i+1})$ and the class_type of A_{i+1} is "I", A_{i+1} is said *promotable* to its immediate parent node using Upward Label Substitution. The input keyword set I is *soundly interpretable* if and only if after all the promotable nodes are promoted and the following conditions is satisfied:

$$\text{For each } i,\ 1 \leq i \leq n - 1,\ L(A_i) \geq L(A_{i+1}).$$

The relationship between a parent node p and each of its children nodes, q, in a c-term tree is that "q is an attribute (property) of p." In general, if a noun phrase is of the form "A of B," then the relationship between A and B is generally, "A is an attribute (property) of B." We determine the plausibility of an FCT by using such a structural similarity between a c-term tree structure and this particular class of noun phrases. The following algorithm is designed to check the plausibility of an FCT.

Algorithm: Semantic Check
1. Move up all the promotable nodes among A_1 to A_n using Upward Label Substitution
2. Find the maximally indexed node A_n from the FCT and set $i = n - 1$.
3. Find A_i from A_{i+1}'s children.
4. If not found, then declare failure and exit.
5. If found, then set $i = i - 1$, and goto Step 3 until $i = 1$.
6. Declare success and exit.

Declaring "success" means that *Qassist* produced a plausible interpretation for the input I. It also means that *Qassist* can translate the interpretation, i.e., the corresponding FCT, into an SQL expression. Declaring "failure" means that either no FCT can be generated or the FCT generated may not be a plausible interpretation with respect to the given database schema.

For example, if one entered the phrase "car's employee," its FCT will be determined not plausible. Also if one entered the phrase "employee's car," where no vehicle information is available in the database, no corresponding FCT will be generated, indicating that there is no way to interpret that phrase. Of course, if the database contain information about vehicle, "employee's car" will be mapped to an FCT to indicate the plausible interpretation.

Figure 5.(a) illustrates the case where the semantic check produces "success" for an input FCT. Figure 5.(b) illustrates the case where the semantic check produces "failure." The basic idea of the algorithm is that a path can be found that interconnects all the recognized nodes in sequence in the given FCT.

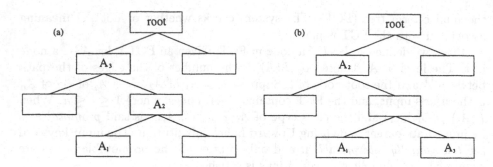

Fig. 5. (a) Plausible FCT; and (b) Implausible FCT

5.4 Generate Graphic Query Form from c-term Tree

Once the FTC is determined plausibly interpretable with respect to the database schema, the next step is to transform the FTC into a graphical SQL expression (GQE) , an approach similar to the one presented in [11]. The transformation rule is given below.

Procedure: C-term To GQE Transformation

1. For each node_A type node, if there are no children, then ignore it. If it contains children, then create a table widget according to the DB_location field.
2. For each node_B type node, if its database name and relation name are the same as that of its parent, then create a column widget and attach it to the table widget created from its parent.
3. For each node_B type node, if its database name or relation name differs from that of its parent, then create a table widget according to its relation name, and a column widget according to the attribute name. Then find a joinable path between this new table and the table created by its parent. Insert all tables and columns in this joinable path if they are not yet inserted in GQE.

Figure 6 shows the GQE generated from the FCT given in Figure 4.

6 Illustration by Example

We illustrate step by step how *Qassist* works by using an example. Suppose that a user is interested in finding "all the reported sequences for the CFTR gene," where CFTR is a gene name for cystic fibrosis. The user enters the phrase "sequence of CFTR" to see how such a phrase fragment is mapped against multiple databases available. We assume that *Qassist* maintains a c-term repository like the one given in Figure 7.

Step 1: Parse the input phrase. Qassist parses the input phrase "sequence of CFTR." It treats "sequence" and "CFTR" as two keywords, and recognizes "of" as the preposition that connects the two keywords.

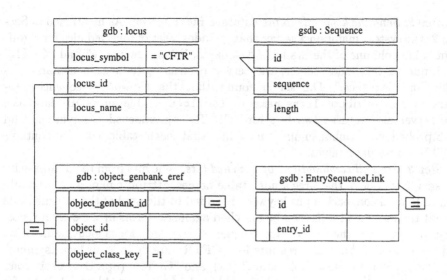

Fig. 6. The GQE generated from a final c-term tree

```
(locus, gdb.locus) [
    (symbol, gdb.locus.locus_symbol, I):(STRING, dom_locus_symbol),
    (sequence, gsdb.Sequence, C):(sequence, gsdb.Sequence),
    (name, gdb.locus.locus_name, I):(STRING, dom_locus_name),
    (modifier, gdb.persons, C):(modifier, gdb.persons),
    (type, gdb.locus_type_dict, C):(type, gdb.locus_type_dict) ]

(probe, gdb.probe) [
    (symbol_summ, gdb.probe.locus_symbol_summ, I):(STRING, dom_probe_symbol),
    (sequence, gsdb.Sequence, C):(sequence, gsdb.Sequence),
    (id, gdb.probe.probe_id, I):(INT, dom_probe_id) ]

(type, gdb.locus_type_dict) [
    (locus_type_desc, gdb.locus_type_dict.locus_type_desc, I):
        (STRING, dom_locus_type),
    (locus_type_key, gdb.locus_type_dict.locus_type_key, N):
        (INT, dom_locus_type_key) ]

(sequence, gsdb.Sequence) [
    (sequence, gsdb.Sequence.sequence, I):(TEXT, dom_sequence),
    (length, gsdb.Sequence.length, N):(INT, dom_sq_length),
    (identifier, gsdb.Sequence.id, I):(STRING, dom_sq_id) ]

(persons, gdb.persons) [
    (first_name, gdb.persons.pers_first_name, N):(STRING, dom_first_name),
    (last_name, gdb.persons.pers_last_name, N):(STRING, dom_last_name) ]
```

Fig. 7. A c-term repository

Step 2: Send the keywords to the database index server. As mentioned in Section 2, the system maintain a server that includes a set of inverted files for significant table columns of the available databases. When "sequence" and "CFTR" are input to this index server, the server returns "gdb.locus.locus_name" as a hit for "sequence." The server found that the keyword "sequence" appears in the attribute locus_name of the locus table in GDB database. The server also returns two hits for "CFTR," "gdb.locus.locus_symbol" and "gdb.probe.locus_symbol_summ," meaning that each table column contains "CFTR" in its data values.

Step 3: Find all combinations of returned hits. The hits from the database index server are one of the three kinds - table names, attribute names, or attribute values. In addition, each input keyword is added to the pool of the returned hits so that the modified hit list can be matched against c-terms in the c-term repository. In summary, the two hits for "sequence" are "gdb.locus.locus_name" (h_1^1) and "sequence" (h_2^1). The three hits for "CFTR" are "gdb.locus.locus_symbol" (h_1^2), "gdb.probe.locus_symbol_summ," (h_2^2), and "CFTR" (h_3^2). Overall six combinations $C_1 - C_6$ are possible: C_1 for (h_1^1 and h_1^2); C_2 for (h_1^1 and h_2^2); C_3 for (h_1^1 and h_3^2); C_4 for (h_2^1 and h_1^2); C_5 for (h_2^1 and h_2^2); and C_6 for (h_2^1 and h_3^2).

Step 4: Find all the matched c-term groups. For each of the possible combinations $C_1 - C_6$, find all possible matched c-term groups from the c-term repository. So, for each of the above combinations, the following c-term groups result.

(a) Case C_1 - The matched c-term tree is:

```
(locus, gdb.locus) [
    (symbol, gdb.locus.locus_symbol, I):(STRING, dom_locus_symbol),
    (sequence, gsdb.Sequence, C):(sequence, gsdb.Sequence),
    (name, gdb.locus.locus_name, I):(STRING, dom_locus_name),
    (modifier, gdb.persons, C):(modifier, gdb.persons),
    (type, gdb.locus_type_dict, C):(type, gdb.locus_type_dict) ]
```

Note that in this case, both of the keywords "sequence" and "CFTR" are found in the same c-term tree.

(b) Case C_2 - The matched c-term trees are:

```
(locus, gdb.locus) [
    (symbol, gdb.locus.locus_symbol, I):(STRING, dom_locus_symbol),
    (sequence, gsdb.Sequence, C):(sequence, gsdb.Sequence),
    (name, gdb.locus.locus_name, I):(STRING, dom_locus_name),
    (modifier, gdb.persons, C):(modifier, gdb.persons),
    (type, gdb.locus_type_dict, C):(type, gdb.locus_type_dict) ]

(probe, gdb.probe) [
    (symbol_summ, gdb.probe.locus_symbol_summ, I):
        (STRING, dom_probe_symbol),
    (sequence, gsdb.Sequence, C):(sequence, gsdb.Sequence),
    (id, gdb.probe.probe_id, I):(INT, dom_probe_id) ]
```

(c) Case C_3 - The matched c-term tree is:

```
(locus, gdb.locus) [
    (symbol, gdb.locus.locus_symbol, I):(STRING, dom_locus_symbol),
    (sequence, gsdb.Sequence, C):(sequence, gsdb.Sequence),
    (name, gdb.locus.locus_name, I):(STRING, dom_locus_name),
    (modifier, gdb.persons, C):(modifier, gdb.persons),
    (type, gdb.locus_type_dict, C):(type, gdb.locus_type_dict) ]
```

Note that since there is no matched c-term tree for "CFTR," this case is ignored.

(d) Case C_4 - The matched c-term trees are:

```
(sequence, gsdb.Sequence) [
    (sequence, gsdb.Sequence.sequence, I):(TEXT, dom_sequence),
    (length, gsdb.Sequence.length, N):(INT, dom_sq_length),
    (identifier, gsdb.Sequence.id, I):(STRING, dom_sq_id) ]
```

```
(locus, gdb.locus) [
    (symbol, gdb.locus.locus_symbol, I):(STRING, dom_locus_symbol),
    (sequence, gsdb.Sequence, C):(sequence, gsdb.Sequence),
    (name, gdb.locus.locus_name, I):(STRING, dom_locus_name),
    (modifier, gdb.persons, C):(modifier, gdb.persons),
    (type, gdb.locus_type_dict, C):(type, gdb.locus_type_dict) ]
```

(e) Case C_5 - The matched c-term trees are:

```
(sequence, gsdb.Sequence) [
    (sequence, gsdb.Sequence.sequence, I):(TEXT, dom_sequence),
    (length, gsdb.Sequence.length, N):(INT, dom_sq_length),
    (identifier, gsdb.Sequence.id, I):(STRING, dom_sq_id) ]
```

```
(probe, gdb.probe) [
    (symbol_summ, gdb.probe.locus_symbol_summ, I):
        (STRING, dom_probe_symbol),
    (sequence, gsdb.Sequence, C):(sequence, gsdb.Sequence),
    (id, gdb.probe.probe_id, I):(INT, dom_probe_id) ]
```

(f) Case C_6 - The matched c-term tree is:

```
(sequence, gsdb.Sequence) [
    (sequence, gsdb.Sequence.sequence, I):(TEXT, dom_sequence),
    (length, gsdb.Sequence.length, N):(INT, dom_sq_length),
    (identifier, gsdb.Sequence.id, I):(STRING, dom_sq_id) ]
```

Note that, since there is no matched c-term tree for "CFTR," this case is ignored.

Step 5: Merge all the c-terms in the matched c-term groups into one c-term. Only four matched c-term groups were found: (a), (b), (d), and (e). For each of them, the c-term trees were examined for possible merging into a single c-term tree. The results are listed below: (a) There is only one c-term tree in this matched c-term group, so, no merge is necessary. (b) The c-term trees in this group cannot be merged, so this case is subsequently ignored. (d) The c-term trees in this group can be merged. (e) The c-term trees in this group can be merged.

Step 6: Check the semantic meaning of all merged c-term trees. From the previous step, only (a), (d), and (e) remain. For each of them, the semantics check algorithm is applied to verify the semantic meaning. The case (a) is ruled out because it results in an "instance" of an "instance" type, which is not possible.

Step 7: Show all the possible solutions to users. It is concluded that two possible interpretations are (d) and (e). Since more than two interpretations are produced, the input "sequence of CFTR" is considered ambiguous. For ambiguous inputs, the system presents all the possible interpretations, and the user makes the final decision.

The meaning associated with (d) is "sequence of CFTR which is an instance of attribute locus_symbol of relation locus in GDB database." The meaning associated with (e) is "sequence of CFTR, which is an instance of attribute locus_symbol_summ of relation probe in GDB database." The user has an option to choose one or all the the possible interpretations. The system automatically generates the skeleton SQL expressions graphically.

Step 8: Complete the query and examine. The system presents graphical SQL expressions in order to identify semantically correct ways of joining multiple tables. The user then may specify other restrictions and/or projection conditions as he wish. Once the query formulation is completed, the system executes the query and presents the query results. By looking at the results from the query, the user may finalize which of the two interpretation is what he originally intended.

7   Conclusion

We have presented a framework for a system designed to assist users to form SQL queries in a multiple database environment. Our approach focuses on how to help users get started in formulating queries when they initially have little knowledge of the contents or the schemas of the databases they are using. Our proposed framework maps the input query keywords into database constituents that include table names, attribute names, and data values. We showed that the mapping can be computed if correspondences between conceptual terms and database constituents are properly established a priori using c-terms of $\mathcal{L}_k$.

The fundamental premises of the proposed approach are different from those of the previously reported natural language (NL) interfaces for databases (e.g., [4], [5]). Unlike in NL interfaces, the target users of our system are not novice, casual users who would like to avoid using SQL. Our system targets SQL experts who like to use SQL, but who would still need assistance from the system in understanding third party databases that they have little knowledge about. Unlike in NL interfaces which aim at translating a complete NL query statement into a database native query language, our system aims at determining only how fragmented noun phrases or input keywords are mapped to database constituents. The system's outcome provides initial cues to the SQL experts about how to proceed and complete the rest of the query. From our experiences in using the prototype system, we conclude that the combination of the query phrase mapping and the graphical way of presenting queries can significantly help SQL experts deal with little known or very complex databases.

Currently we are investigating ways of enhancing our noun phrase handling component. Producing a more sophisticated noun phrase handling component alone constitutes a significant research problem. We expect that the rest of the proposed framework would be reusable even if we replace the noun phrase handling module with a better one.

References

1. J. F. Allen. *Natural Language Understanding*. The Benjamin/Cummings Publishing Co., Inc., Menlo Park, CA, 2nd edition, 1995. Chapter 8.
2. J. E. Bell and L. A. Rowe. An Exploratory Study of Ad Hoc Query Languages to Databases. In *Proc. of the 8th IEEE Int'l Conf. on Data Engin.*, pages 606–613. 1992.
3. G. J. Clark and C. T. Wu. DFQL: Dataflow query language for relational databases. *Information & Management*, 27:1–15, 1994.
4. B. J. Grosz, D. E. Appelt, P. A. Martin, and Pereira F. TEAM: An experiment in the design of transportable natural-language interfaces. *Artificial Intelligence*, 32:173–243, 1987.
5. G. Jakobson et al. An intelligent database assistant. *IEEE Expert*, pages 65–79, Summer 1986.
6. C. Kellogg. From data management to knowledge management. *Computer*, 19(1):75–84, 1986.
7. V. Markowitz and A. Shoshani. Object queries over relational databases: Language, implementation, and applications. In *Proc. of the 9th IEEE Int'l Conf. on Data Engin.*, Vienna, Austria, April. 1993.
8. D. G. Shin. $\mathcal{L}_k$: A language for capturing real world meangings of the stored data. In *Proc. of the 7th IEEE Int'l Conf. on Data Engin.*, pages 738–745, Kobe, Japan, April 1991.
9. D. G. Shin. An expectation-driven response understanding paradigm. *IEEE Trans. on Knowledge and Data Engineering*, 6(3):430–443, 1994.
10. J. F. Sowa. *Conceptual Structures: Information Processing in Mind and Machine*. Addison Wesley, Reading, MA, 1984.
11. K.-Y. Whang, A. Malhotra, G. H. Sockut, L. Burns, and K.-S. Choi. Two-Dimensional Specification of Universal Quantification in a Graphical Database Query Language. *IEEE Trans. on Knowledge and Data Engineering*, 18(3):216–224, 1994.

Test-Driving TANKA: Evaluating a Semi-Automatic System of Text Analysis for Knowledge Acquisition

Ken Barker[1], Sylvain Delisle[2] and Stan Szpakowicz[1]

[1]School of Information Technology and Engineering
University of Ottawa
Ottawa, Canada   K1N 6N5
{kbarker, szpak}@site.uottawa.ca
[2]Département de mathématiques et d'informatique
Université du Québec à Trois-Rivières
Trois-Rivières, Canada   G9A 5H7
Sylvain_Delisle@uqtr.uquebec.ca

Abstract. The evaluation of a large implemented natural language processing system involves more than its application to a common performance task. Such tasks have been used in the message understanding conferences (MUCs), text retrieval conferences (TRECs) as well as in speech technology and machine translation workshops. It is useful to compare the performance of different systems in a predefined application, but a detailed evaluation must take into account the specificity of the system.

We have carried out a systematic performance evaluation of our text analysis system TANKA. Since it is a semi-automatic, trainable system, we had to measure the user's participation (with a view to decreasing it gradually) and the rate at which the system learns from preceding analyses. This paper discusses the premises, the design and the execution of an evaluation of TANKA. The results confirm the basic assumptions of our supervised text analysis procedures, namely, that the system learns to make better analyses, that knowledge acquisition is possible even from erroneous or fragmentary parses and that the process is not too onerous for the user.

1   Introduction

This paper describes the evaluation of the trainable semi-automatic text analysis system TANKA (Text ANalysis for Knowledge Acquisition). TANKA aims to build interactively a semantic representation of a technical text. Throughout the development of TANKA we have performed diagnostic evaluations of the system's components. Now that these components are complete, the whole system must be tested on new texts in different domains.

There has been increased interest in the evaluation of natural language processing tools over the last few years. The message understanding conferences (MUCs) are a direct reaction to a lack of standardization in the evaluation of such tools. The MUC competitions compare the performance of different systems on some uniform, predetermined text processing task. The motivation for and background of the MUC competitions are described by Grishman & Sundheim [13].

Although these competitions have successfully emphasized the importance of evaluation for the NLP community, they have also revealed certain limitations. In particular, researchers have noted that the predefined tasks in evaluation competitions result in applications that are designed to score well, but are not portable [16]. Furthermore, little attention has been paid to the evaluation of interactive systems and the role of users [14].

To address these issues, Sparck Jones and Galliers ([18], [19]) offer more general strategies for evaluating generic NLP systems. They note that "there is far too much variety in the situations and subjects of evaluation to come up with a definite [evaluation] scenario" [19: 193].

Hirschman & Thompson [14] note that different kinds of evaluation make different assumptions about the distribution of test data. While it is important to test a system on all types of input it is designed to handle, such a *diagnostic evaluation* does not reflect the performance of the system on actual texts. The distribution of linguistic phenomena in the test suite of a diagnostic evaluation is almost certainly not the same as the distribution of phenomena in complete real texts, which form the test suite for a *performance evaluation*. For performance evaluations, it is important to identify *criteria* (what is being evaluated), *measures* (what properties of performance reflect the criteria) and *methods* (how the measures are analyzed to arrive at an evaluation of the criteria).

The evaluation methodology described in this paper is necessarily specific to TANKA. Nonetheless, we have attempted to adhere to the precepts of a more rigorous approach to NLP system evaluation.

2 The TANKA System

Analysis in TANKA consists of recognizing semantic relationships signalled by surface linguistic phenomena. The system uses as little *a priori* semantic knowledge as possible. Instead, it performs detailed syntactic analysis using publicly available part-of-speech lists and lexicons and produces a tentative semantic analysis. This analysis is proposed to a participating user who usually approves the system's proposal. In the case of an incorrect or incomplete analysis, the user may also be required to supply elements of the semantic interpretation. Delisle *et al.* [12] offer a detailed description of TANKA.

2.1 The DIPETT Parser

Syntactic analysis in TANKA is performed by DIPETT (Domain Independent Parser of English Technical Texts), a broad coverage Definite Clause Grammar parser whose rules are based primarily on Quirk *et al.* [17].

DIPETT takes an unedited, untagged text and automatically produces a single initial parse of each sentence. This first good parse tree is a detailed representation of the constituent structure of a sentence. If DIPETT is unable to produce a single complete parse of a sentence within a time limit imposed by the user, it will attempt to produce parses for fragments within the sentence (such as if possible, clauses and phrases). Delisle [10] and Delisle & Szpakowicz [11] present a complete discussion of DIPETT and related parsing issues. A WWW version of the parser with a simplified interface will be released soon.

2.2 The HAIKU Semantic Analyzer

Semantic Relationships. Given the parse trees produced by DIPETT, the HAIKU semantic analyzer [12] identifies the semantic relationships expressed by related syntactic constituents. The semantic relationships are expressed at three levels: between connected clauses, within clauses (between a verb and each of its arguments) and within noun phrases (between a head and each of its modifiers). The semantic relationships that HAIKU assigns to syntactic structures at each of these levels appear in Table 1. The *clause level relationships* (*CLRs*) are assigned to connected clauses, the *cases* are assigned to verb-argument pairs and the *noun modifier relationships* (*NMRs*) are assigned to modifier-noun pairs.

There are several observations to make about these semantic relationships. The lists are amalgams of similar lists used by researchers in discourse analysis, case and valency theory and noun phrase analysis. For each of our three lists, we identified an initial set of relationships and then did an extensive survey of the lexical items that mark them. This survey identified several omissions and redundancies in the lists. We further validated the relationships by checking their coverage on real English texts. Details of the construction process and validation appear in our publications [7, 2], as well as comparisons of our relationships to other lists [6, 3].

The next observation is that HAIKU does not depend on these particular lists of relationships. The techniques it uses at each level of analysis would work with any other closed list of semantic relationships.

Finally, several relationships appear in more than one list, reflecting the fact that the same semantic relationship may be realized at different levels of syntax. Merging the relationships into a single unified list for all three levels is a consideration for future work.

Semantic Analysis. HAIKU tries to assign semantic relationships with a minimum of *a priori* hand coded semantic knowledge. In the absence of such precoded semantics HAIKU enlists the help of a cooperating user who oversees decisions during semantic

CLRs	*Cases*		*NMRs*	
Causation	Accompaniment	Location_to	Agent	Object
Conjunction	Agent	Manner	Beneficiary	Possessor
Cooccurrence	Beneficiary	Material	Cause	Product
Detraction	Cause	Measure	Container	Property
Disjunction	Content	Object	Content	Purpose
Enablement	Direction	Opposition	Destination	Result
Entailment	Effect	Order	Equative	Source
Precedence	Exclusion	Orientation	Instrument	State
Prevention	Experiencer	Purpose	Located	Time
	Frequency	Recipient	Location	Topic
	Instrument	Time_at	Material	
	Location_at	Time_from		
	Location_from	Time_through		
	Location_through	Time_to		

Table 1. Semantic relationships in HAIKU

analysis. To lessen the burden on the user, the system first attempts automatic analysis. It compares input structures to similar structures in the text for which semantic analyses have been stored. Since it does not have access to a large body of pre-analyzed text, HAIKU starts processing from scratch for a text (or a collection of texts) and acquires the needed data incrementally.[1]

Clause level relationships are assigned whenever there are two or more connected finite clauses in a sentence. For each clause, DIPETT provides a complete syntactic analysis including tense, modality and polarity (positive/negative). It gives us the connective (usually a conjunction) and the type of syntactic relationship between the clauses: coordinate, subordinate or correlative.

The CLR analyzer looks up the connective in a dictionary that maps each connective to the CLRs that it might mark. Since the connectives are a small closed class, the construction of such a marker dictionary is not a large knowledge engineering task. Once constructed, it can be used for any text. Using the subset of CLRs, HAIKU holds competitions between each pair of relationships based on the syntactic features of the clauses. The CLR with the most points after all competitions is the one suggested to the user for approval. The CLRs and the CLR analyzer are described by Barker & Szpakowicz [6].

Within a clause, the parser identifies the main verb and its arguments: subject, direct and indirect objects, adverbials and prepositional phrases. From this information, the case analyzer builds a *case marker pattern* (CMP) made of the symbols psubj, pobj, piobj, adv and any prepositions attached to the verb. To assign cases to the arguments of a given verb, the system compares the given verb+CMP to other verb+CMP instances already analyzed. It chooses the most similar previous verb+CMP instances and suggests previously assigned cases for this verb+CMP. Delisle *et al.* [12] and Barker *et al.* [7] describe case analysis and the cases in detail.

Within noun phrases, the parser identifies a flat list of premodifiers and any postmodifying prepositional phrases and appositives. The NMR analyzer first brackets the flat list of premodifiers into modifier-modificand pairs [4], and then assigns NMRs to each pair. NMRs are also assigned to the relationships between the head noun of the noun phrase and each postmodifying phrase. To pick the best NMR, the system first finds the most similar modifier-modificand instances previously analyzed. Next, it finds the NMRs previously assigned to the most similar instances and selects one of these relationships to present to the user for approval.

3 The Evaluation Exercise

TANKA is intended to analyze an unedited English technical text. Technical texts usually lack humour, intentional ambiguity, and other devices that would make

---

[1] An alternative to starting analysis from scratch would be to accumulate the semantic analyses from session to session. The extent to which the acquired knowledge from one text (or domain) would be useful in the analysis of a different text is a consideration for future work.

analysis more difficult. Copeck *et al.* [9] describe a study to investigate the character of texts typically considered technical. So in order to evaluate TANKA we ran it on a real, unedited technical text.

Individual components of DIPETT and HAIKU have been tested on a variety of technical texts including an income tax guide, a fourth generation programming language manual, a building code regulatory text and a computer installation guide.

The most thorough previous test of the system was reported by Barker & Delisle [5]. For that experiment, we chose a text [15] with fairly simple syntax to ensure a high number of successful parses. That text describes a technical domain (weather phenomena) using simple language. We refer to this book as the *clouds* text and the experiment as the *clouds* experiment. We chose a simpler text in the belief that the higher parse success rate would allow the system to acquire more knowledge (since semantic analysis is based on the results of syntactic analysis). What we found instead was that the simpler text used very general terminology and carried less content. We also noted that even if a sentence was parsed incorrectly or in fragments, much of the knowledge in the sentence could still be acquired, either from the incorrect or incomplete parse tree, or from other sentences containing the same or similar concepts (we refer to this as *conceptual redundancy*).

For the evaluation described in this paper, we chose a more syntactically complex text [1]. The text has more complex constructions, but it also uses more specific terminology and contains more information and less "fluff". We refer to this book as the *small engines* text and the experiment as the *small engines* experiment.

3.1 The Evaluation Methodology

The *small engines* experiment was held at l'Université du Québec à Trois-Rivières over five days. Just over 15 hours were spent during timed semantic analysis interaction. One of the authors drove the system while another timed the interaction on each sentence and recorded details of the interaction. All interaction decisions were made collectively, adding time to the interactions for discussions, but hopefully also eliminating personal biases. The system was run in Quintus Prolog 3.2 on a Sparc-20 with a 120 second CPU time limit for parsing per sentence.

The first step in running DIPETT and HAIKU on a text is to build a lexicon for the text. DIPETT has a built-in part of speech labeller. The labeller uses the Collins wordlist to create a lexicon containing all parts of speech of all the words in the text. The resulting lexicon contains extraneous entries, since not every part of speech of every word appears in the text. We used a concordance tool to check the lexicon for extraneous entries. We should note that the lexicon construction stage is not as much work as tagging the text with part of speech information; nor does it give parsing as big a headstart. Many words appear more than once as different parts of speech in the text. The lexicon may contain several entries for each word, even after deleting the extraneous entries. The construction of the lexicon required a short day's work for 1200 words.

For the analysis of each sentence, we started a stopwatch as soon as parsing was complete. We then examined the parse and recorded details of parse completeness and correctness. Interaction then proceeded through clause level relationship analysis, case analysis and noun modifier relationship analysis. For each of these levels of analysis, we recorded the degree of difficulty of the interaction. After all interactions in semantic analysis were complete, we stopped the stopwatch and recorded the total interaction time for the sentence.

The degree of difficulty of interaction (what we refer to as *onus*) was recorded as an integer from *0* to *3*. *0* means that the interaction is trivial. *1* is assigned to an interaction that requires a few moments of reflection. *2* rates an interaction as requiring serious thought, but eventually a semantic relationship is assigned. *3* means that even after much contemplation no relationship is deemed appropriate for the given input.

3.2 Examples of Interaction

To understand the criteria of our evaluation better, it is useful to show the reproductions of the different kinds of interactions with HAIKU. The user's input is shown bold and underlined

Figure 1 shows the interaction for the CLR assignment for sentence 119 from the *small engines* text. The sentence has two finite clauses connected by the subordinator *as*. From the parse tree, the system identifies the connective, the main clause and the subordinate clause. It looks up *as* in the marker dictionary and finds that it may mark Cooccurrence (ctmp), Causation (caus), Enablement (enab), Entailment (entl) or Prevention (prev). The system holds competitions between each pair of relationships (ten competitions for this example) based on the syntactic features of the clauses. The CLR analyzer chooses Causation as the most appropriate for the sentence, since it finishes with the most points.

Figure 2 shows the case interaction for sentence 164 from the *small engines* text.

String #119:   *As the crankshaft rotates, its gear turns the gear on the camshaft and causes it to rotate, too.*

```
There is a Clause-Level Relationship marked by 'as':

    its gear turns the gear on the camshaft and causes it to
    rotate, too
       as
    the crankshaft rotates

CLR competitions among [ctmp,caus,enab,entl,prev]
Results (maximum is 8):
    ctmp    caus    enab    entl    prev
  +------+------+------+------+------+
     2       8       1       6       3
The CLR Analyzer's best suggestion(s) for this input:
    (1)    Causation (caus)
> Please enter a number between 1 and 1: 1

Your CLR assignment will be stored as:
    the crankshaft rotates
       <causes>
    its gear turns the gear on the camshaft and causes it to
    rotate , too
```

Figure 1. Clause level relationship analysis interaction for sentence #119

String #164:   *Electric starter motors **crank** an engine by spinning the flywheel.*

```
CURRENT SUBJ    : electric starter motors
CURRENT VERB    : crank
CURRENT COMPL   : an engine by spinning the flywheel

CMP found by HAIKU: psubj-pobj-by
> Do you wish to overrule this CMP? N

S4: new verb with known CMP; new CP (relative to this verb).
Candidate CPs with example sentences:
 (1) agt-obj-inst  the carburetor controls the crankshaft speed
                   by the amount of fuel/air mixture it allows
                   into the cylinder.
 (2) agt-obj-manr  they do this by seeing that the oil is
                   changed at the proper time and that greasing
                   and tune-ups are carried out regularly.

if appropriate, enter a number between 1 and 2: 1
CMP & CP will be paired as: psubj/agt pobj/obj by/inst
```

Figure 2. Case analysis interaction for sentence #164

This sentence has one clause with the main verb *crank*. The case analyzer constructs the case marker pattern psubj-pobj-by based on information in the parse tree. In the previous sentences, the verb *crank* has never occurred. However, the system has seen the CMP twice: once with the verb *control* and once with the verb *do*. In those two instances the corresponding case patterns were Agent-Object-Instrument and Agent-Object-Manner. The system suggests these two case patterns to the user, who chooses the first, since "spinning the flywheel" is the Instrument (or *method* used) to "crank an engine".

For the noun phrase *the threaded part of the plug* in sentence 142, the NMR analyzer will assign two NMRs: one between *threaded* and *part* and one between *part* and *plug*. The interaction in Figure 3 shows the interaction for *threaded part* only. The system has never seen *threaded* as a modifier of *part*, but it has seen *threaded* as a modifier of other modificands and *part* as a modificand with other modifiers. NMRA calculates a score for each of the NMRs that have been previously assigned when *threaded* was a modifier and when *part* was a modificand. Property receives the highest score for this pair.

String #142:   *The lower electrode is fastened to the **threaded part** of the plug.*

```
HAIKU: Noun-Modifier Relationship Analysis of current input ...

Match type 3: (threaded, _, nil) or (_, part, nil)
[prop]: 4.66667

For the phrase 'threaded part'
> Do you accept the assignment:
  Property (prop): threaded_part is threaded

  [n/a/<nmr>/Y] Y
```

Figure 3. Noun modifier relationship analysis interaction for sentence #142

4 The Evaluation

Three main criteria guided the evaluation of our system. First, we wanted to evaluate the ability of HAIKU to learn to make better suggestions to the user. Since the system starts with no prior analyses on which to base its suggestions, the user is responsible for supplying the semantic relationships at the beginning of a session. To measure HAIKU's learning, we compared the cumulative number of assignments required from the user to the cumulative number of correct assignments suggested to the user by the system over the course of analyzing the *small engines* text.

Second, we wanted to compare the number of relationships that HAIKU analyzed with the total number of such relationships in a text (*i.e.*, the number it *should have* analyzed). Since it would not be feasible to count by hand the total number of relationships even in a text of several hundred sentences, we sampled relationships at random from the text to find the proportion that HAIKU analyzed. This proportion can be thought of as a measure of *Recall*[2] of the kind of knowledge HAIKU has been designed to acquire.

Third, we wanted to evaluate the burden that semi-automatic analysis places on the user. Since burden is a fairly subjective criterion, we looked at the amount of time spent by the user on each sentence as well as the onus rating described in section 3.1.

4.1 Evaluating the Parser

In order to evaluate the performance of HAIKU, it is important to look at the results of parsing, the input to HAIKU.

Of the 557 sentences that we analyzed, 55% received a complete parse. That does not necessarily mean that the parses were correct. In fact, only 31% of the 557 parses were perfect. Another 9% were good enough not to affect semantic analysis. That means that for 60% of the sentences, parse errors were serious enough to affect semantic analysis. Most often, these errors meant that HAIKU was unable to make a semantic relationship assignment for a given input. Fortunately, due to the *conceptual redundancy* mentioned in section 3, much of the knowledge in these difficult sentences was acquired by the system anyway.

4.2 Evaluating CLR Analysis

The HAIKU module most affected by parse errors is the clause level relationship analyzer. In order to make an assignment, CLRA needs a complete and correct parse at the top-most level. A second problem with CLR analysis is that CLR data is the sparse: every sentence usually has several noun phrases and at least one finite clause, but relatively few have multiple connected finite clauses. Note however that because

---

[2] All semantic relationship assignments are either accepted by the user if correct or supplied by the user if the system's assignments are incorrect. Therefore, *Recall*'s partner *Precision* is a meaningless measure in HAIKU (*i.e.*, it is always 100%).

the CLR data is so sparse, the proportion of relationships analyzed by HAIKU can be measured directly without sampling.

In the *clouds* experiment, the system correctly determined 73% of the CLRs assigned, while the user assigned the other 27%. In the *small engines* experiment, the system determined 76% of CLRs automatically. For the *clouds* text, there were 76 connected clauses requiring CLR assignments, 67% of which received analysis. For the *small engines* text, however, only 28% of the clause pairs received analysis. The small number of clause level relationships actually captured by HAIKU for the *small engines* text is a direct result of the error rate in complete parses of structurally complex sentences.

4.3 Evaluating Case Analysis

For case analysis we first compare the number of case patterns that the system determined correctly with the number the user had to supply directly. 584 clauses in the *small engines* text received a case analysis. The system is considered to have determined the case pattern correctly if the correct case pattern was among those suggested to the user. The system made an average 4.4 suggestions for clauses for which it could make any suggestions at all.

Figure 4 plots the cumulative number of assignments made by the user against the cumulative number of correct assignments among the system's suggestions. After fewer than a hundred clauses, the number of correct system assignments overtook the user assignments for good. By the end of the experiment, the system had suggested a correct case pattern for 66% of the assignments.

In order to evaluate the proportion of clauses in the text that received a case analysis, we took 100 verbs at random from the text, determined their case marker pattern manually and found that for 97 of them there was a corresponding case pattern in HAIKU's output. Therefore, with 95% confidence we claim that HAIKU extracted between 91.5% and 98.9% of the case patterns in the text. This high coverage is due

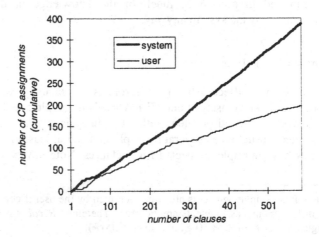

Figure 4. Case pattern assignments

to the fact that the user is given the opportunity to correct case marker patterns that are incorrect because of misparses.

4.4 Evaluating NMR Analysis

In the *small engines* experiment, 886 modifier-noun pairs were assigned an NMR. As with case analysis, we consider the system's assignment correct when the correct label is among its suggestions to the user. The system made an average 1.1 suggestions (when it could make any suggestions at all).

Figure 5 shows the cumulative number of NMR assignments supplied by the user versus those determined correctly by the system. Again, after about 100 assignments, the system was able to make the majority of assignments automatically. By the end of the experiment, the system had correctly assigned 69% of the NMRs.

To evaluate the number of modifier-noun relationships that HAIKU captured, we took 100 modifier-noun pairs at random from the text and found that 87 of them appeared in HAIKU's output. At the 95% confidence level, we can say that HAIKU extracted between 79.0% and 92.2% of the modifier-noun relationships in the *small engines* text.

4.5 User Burden

We said in section 3 that the *clouds* text was chosen for its relatively simple syntax to ensure a large number of successful parses. Correct parses guarantee the maximum amount of semantic analysis (and therefore user interaction). Making the user as active as possible would allow us to observe trends in user time and burden over the course of a session with TANKA. The main trends observed were that user time was directly related to sentence length and complexity, and that the average user time (adjusted for sentence length) decreased over the course of analyzing the text. As it turns out, we observed the same trends in the *small engines* experiment.

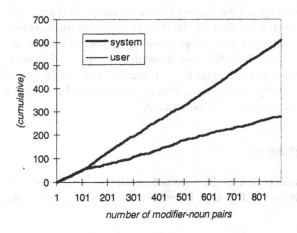

Figure 5. Noun modifier relationship assignments

The average number of tokens (words or punctuation) in the *small engines* sentences was 15.4. The average number of CLRs per sentence was 0.05, while the average number of case patterns was 1.2 and the average number of NMRs was 1.7. On average, we spent 1 minute, 49 seconds on each sentence. By coincidence, the average user time for the *clouds* experiment was also 1 minute, 49 seconds for an average of 0.1 CLRs and 0.9 case patterns per sentence (NMRs were not evaluated in the *clouds* experiment).

The *onus* numbers for each level of semantic analysis in the *small engines* experiment appear in Table 2.

onus	0	1	2	3	average
CLRA	18	4	0	0	0.19
CA	480	89	15	0	0.20
NMRA	808	71	7	0	0.10

Table 2. Onus ratings for semantic analysis

5 Conclusions

Three main conclusions can be drawn from the evaluation, corresponding to the three criteria presented in section 4. The first is that the system learns. By using partial matching on a growing set of semantic patterns, the system can come up with analyses of inputs that it has never seen before.

The second conclusion is that the system can acquire knowledge from the text even with fragmentary parses and misparses, although case analysis and NMR analysis are less sensitive to parse errors than CLR analysis. As mentioned earlier, this result is due to two things. First, many of the key concepts in a text are repeated frequently. Second, the fragments in fragmentary parses are often large enough to cover one or more phrases or even whole clauses. This conclusion is significant, since one of the main problems of systems that rely on detailed parsing is the parse error rate, due to the brittleness of grammars. Our evaluation shows that the amount of knowledge acquired is not necessarily limited by the proportion of perfect parses.

Finally, the evaluation showed that our system is not too onerous for the user. We extracted fairly complete knowledge from more than 500 sentences in a technical domain in just a few days. We also showed in section 4 that after a brief training period the system made the majority of semantic relationship assignments, with the user merely accepting the analyses. Finally, we observed that the average user time decreased over the course of the experiment.

Acknowledgments

This research is supported by the Natural Sciences and Engineering Research Council of Canada and by le Fonds pour la Formation de Chercheurs et l'Aide à la Recherche.

References

1. Atkinson, Henry F. (1990). *Mechanics of Small Engines.* New York: Gregg Division, McGraw-Hill.
2. Barker, Ken (1996). "The Assessment of Semantic Cases Using English Positional, Prepositional and Adverbial Case Markers." TR-96-08, Department of Computer Science, University of Ottawa.
3. Barker, Ken (1997). "Noun Modifier Relationship Analysis in the TANKA System." TR-97-02, Department of Computer Science, University of Ottawa.
4. Barker, Ken (1998). "A Trainable Bracketer for Noun Modifiers." *Proceedings of the Twelfth Canadian Conference on Artificial Intelligence,* Vancouver.
5. Barker, Ken & Sylvain Delisle (1996). "Experimental Validation of a Semi-Automatic Text Analyzer." TR-96-01, Department of Computer Science, University of Ottawa.
6. Barker, Ken & Stan Szpakowicz (1995). "Interactive Semantic analysis of Clause-Level Relationships." *Proceedings of the Second Conference of the Pacific Association for Computational Linguistics,* Brisbane, 22-30.
7. Barker, Ken, Terry Copeck, Sylvain Delisle & Stan Szpakowicz (1997). "Systematic Construction of a Versatile Case System." *Journal of Natural Language Engineering* (in print).
8. Cole, Ronald A., Joseph Mariani, Hans Uszkoreit, Annie Zaenen & Victor Zue (1996). *Survey of the State of the Art in Human Language Technology.* http://www.cse.ogi.edu/CSLU/HLTSurvey/
9. Copeck, Terry, Ken Barker, Sylvain Delisle, Stan Szpakowicz & Jean-François Delannoy (1997). "What is Technical Text?" *Language Sciences* 19(4), 391-424.
10. Delisle, Sylvain (1994). "Text processing without A-Priori Domain Knowledge: Semi-Automatic Linguistic analysis for Incremental Knowledge Acquisition." Ph.D. thesis, TR-94-02, Department of Computer Science, University of Ottawa.
11. Delisle, Sylvain & Stan Szpakowicz (1995). "Realistic Parsing: Practical Solutions of Difficult Problems." *Proceedings of the Second Conference of the Pacific Association for Computational Linguistics,* Brisbane, 59-68.
12. Delisle, Sylvain, Ken Barker, Terry Copeck & Stan Szpakowicz (1996). "Interactive Semantic analysis of Technical Texts." *Computational Intelligence* 12(2), May, 1996, 273-306.
13. Grishman R & B. Sundheim (1996). "Message Understanding Conference - 6: A Brief History." *Proceedings of COLING-96,* 466-471.
14. Hirschman, Lynette & Henry S. Thompson (1996). "Overview of Evaluation in Speech and Natural Language Processing." in [8].
15. Larrick, Nancy. (1961). *Junior Science Book of Rain, Hail, Sleet & Snow.* Champaign: Garrard Publishing Company.
16. MUC-6 (1996). *Proceedings of the Sixth Message Understanding Conference.* Morgan Kaufmann.
17. Quirk, Randolph, Sidney Greenbaum, Geoffrey Leech & Jan Svartvik (1985). *A Comprehensive Grammar of the English Language.* London: Longman.
18. Sparck Jones, Karen (1994). "Towards Better NLP System Evaluation." *Proceedings of the Human Language Technology Workshop, 1994,* San Francisco: Morgan Kaufmann, 102-107.
19. Sparck Jones, Karen & Julia R. Galliers (1996). "Evaluating Natural Language Processing Systems: An Analysis and Review." *Lecture Notes in Artificial Intelligence* 1083, New York: Springer-Verlag.

An Object Indexing Methodology as Support to Object Recognition

Guy W. Mineau, Mounsif Lahboub, Jean-Marie Beaulieu

Dept. of Computer Science, Université Laval
Quebec City, Quebec, Canada
{mineau, lahboub, beaulieu}@ift.ulaval.ca

Abstract. This paper presents an object recognition methodology which uses a step-by-step discrimination process. This process is made possible by the use of a classification structure built over examples of the objects to recognize. Thus, our approach combines numerical vision (object recognition) with conceptual clustering, showing how the latter helps the former, giving another example of useful synergy among different AI techniques. It presents our application domain: the recognition of road signs, which must support semi-autonomous vehicles in their navigational task. The discrimination process allows appropriate actions to be taken by the recognizer with regard to the actual data it has to recognize the object from: light, angle, shading, etc., and with regard to its recognition capabilities and their associated cost. Therefore, this paper puts the emphasis on this multiple criteria adaptation capability, which is the novelty of our approach.

1 Introduction

Artificial vision for semi-autonomous vehicles was one of the main research issues of the IIT Project, the Interactive Image Technologies Project, sponsored by both M3i and ATS, two Canadian companies, and managed by CRIM, le Centre de Recherche Informatique de Montréal [1]. In this project, we were asked to come up with an organization for an image database, that would provide support for different recognition tasks associated with object recognition. The main idea was to propose an organization which would facilitate the selection of appropriate recognition modules in light of the actual data available. Such modules take care of different aspects of object recognition such as the recognition of lines, segments, text, color, shapes, etc. By helping the selection of the appropriate recognition modules, we make the recognition process adapt to the actual data it is faced with, hoping to facilitate its task and improve its efficiency.

Our application domain was the recognition of road signs, as it is relevant to the navigational task of semi-autonomous vehicles. This domain was ideal for testing our proposed organization, since road signs are composed of simple shapes, made of specific contrasting colors, and occasionally bearing some simple textual headings. They are well described: road laws, which use them, describe both their function and design. So there is background knowledge about road signs. However, as with any visual recognition task in natural environments, lighting, shading, backdrops and angle parameters affect perception. Consequently, using the background knowledge we have, we can determine to what degree these parameters hinder the perception of the object, and we can propose to select recognition modules accordingly. We can also take into consideration the actual cost of using certain modules: recognizing color may be more expensive in terms of the required equipment than recognizing shape for instance, though it could be faster. In brief, a cost function could intervene in this selection mechanism as well.

Basically, in a discrimination process, potentially interesting objects are identified. Then, the assessment of some condition on these objects eliminate some of them, producing a *remainder set*, i.e., the set of objects which fulfilled the condition. Discrimination is done iteratively until only one object remains, until all objects within the remainder set are indistinguishable i.e., no condition could reduce it further, or until the set is empty. The selection of the conditions to assess must be done wisely in order to optimize some criteria. This criteria could be: 1) convergence, minimizing the time it takes to isolate a single object, 2) cost, i.e., the actual cost associated with the application of some recognition module, 3) availability, set up by the actual hardware architecture of the vision system, and 4) precision, which depends on the application domain, i.e., on the complexity of the objects to be recognized, the background, the admissible error rate, the sensitivity of the application to errors, and so on. These criteria can be pondered in a cost function used by the recognition process to favor certain recognition activities over others.

In an object recognition system, discrimination will be based on what the vision system can perceive: basic visual attributes such as shape, lines, color, headings, etc., which are low-level information (attributes) describing the way objects will appear in the environment. However, having background knowledge on these objects (as with road signs), we know how these attributes fit in, i.e., how they are related to one another, what part of the sign they describe. So, the discrimination process can use this background knowledge to identify what attribute should be checked next in order to exclude objects from the remainder set. By identifying particular attributes, it proposes to use certain recognition modules to carry out this verification. At this point, a cost function could be used by the recognition system to ponder the selection of the appropriate recognition module. Since a dialog between the discrimination and the recognition processes takes place so that module selection is achieved, discrimination can be used to guide the recognition process, adapting it to the actual situation according to the cost function (a complete example will be given in Section 2 below).

Since discrimination is done on how the object should look according to how and where it is used, and according to what we know about the object so far, full description of road signs, incorporating low-level information, should be acquired as input data to the discrimination process. Of course, to facilitate discrimination, we need to structure this data. We could precompute clusters of similar objects (according to their description), and relate them in a partial order of inclusion. This relation would identify quickly what remainder set would result from the assessment of particular conditions, identifying those which are applicable to the situation on hand. This structuring is precisely what conceptual clustering techniques produce. Consequently, the proposed methodology below presents such a technique applied on object descriptions as acquired from both background knowledge and the vision system.

2 Proposed Methodology

This section first describes the proposed methodology which seeks to organize the input data (object descriptions) into some classification structure (Section 2.1). This structure will help the discrimination process, as exemplified in Section 2.2.

2.1 The Object Indexing Methodology

As said before, we will apply a conceptual clustering technique on object descriptions that primarily come from the knowledge base we have on road signs. However, since the classification structure produced will be used by the recognition process that can perceive only low-level attributes describing the object, we need to incorporate this type of information into the descriptions that the background knowledge provides us with. This must be done manually before the full object descriptions are given to the clustering algorithm. In brief, we will build exemplars of the objects under different perception parameters (where light, shading and angle will vary); and we will hand these descriptions, these multiple examples of the same road signs, to the clustering process. More formally, here is our proposed methodology; it is made of two distinct and consecutive phases: 1) the acquisition of the exemplars, and 2) their clustering.

The Acquisition Phase:

Step 1:   Select the objects to be recognized, called the *sample set* $S = \{O_i\}$ $\forall i \in [1,n]$, where n is the cardinality of S. It may be the case that a vehicle will not encounter all road signs,[1] so selecting only the relevant ones reduces the complexity associated with their recognition. In this step, we identify the types of road signs that the vision system will eventually have to recognize on the road.

Step 2:   From the knowledge base we have on road signs, extract the high-level descriptions of these objects. The set of these descriptions, $\{H_i\}$ $\forall i \in [1,n]$, provide prototype descriptions of each object, i.e., each H_i is a description of the type of object O_i is. For instance, Figure 1 below shows the description of a typical pedestrian crossing sign. These high-level descriptions have been encoded using conceptual graphs [2]. They must include a concept for each low-level attribute that a vision system may

---

[1]   For instance, some vehicles will never go on highways. Thankfully, this limits the size of S, the sample set. For our application, as testbed, we selected only 22 signs normally encountered in residential areas.

perceive: color, shape, headings, etc. These attributes, appearing as *concepts* in a conceptual graph, are not instantiated with particular values since {H_i} contains only generic descriptions.

Step 3: According to the particular settings in which the object will be recognized, determine all parameter values[2] under which the object should be recognized, such as: different angles, different lighting conditions, and so on. This will provide the number of different shots k, one should take of the same object, each shot representing an image of the object under a different combination of these parameter values.

Step 4: For each object O_i, take k shots of it under the various conditions identified in step 3, producing {D_{ij}} $\forall i \in [1,n]$ $\forall j \in [1,k]$, the set of all k shots of the n objects of S. This set, called I, represents the $N=n*k$ exemplars that are passed on to the clustering algorithm as input data.[3] Each D_{ij} is the original description of the generic object O_i as described by H_i, where the appropriate low-level attributes, represented by concepts in H_i, were instantiated to particular values (as perceived by the vision system). Of course, this step, as the first three, requires manual intervention.

The Clustering Phase:

Step 1: Pass the N object descriptions of I to the conceptual clustering technique we use, called MSG. The MSG, Method of Structuring by Generalization [3,4], produces a classification structure where clusters represent groups of objects described by conceptual subgraphs shared by these objects. It also relates all clusters in a partial order of inclusion defined over these subsets of objects.[4] From I, its input data, the MSG produces such a classification structure called *Knowledge Space*, KS[5], which can be seen as the organization we wish to produce in order to support the discrimination process (see Section 2.2 below).

---

[2] As mentioned earlier, these parameters are related to the different perspectives from which the object will need to be perceived later on by the recognition system.

[3] The clustering algorithm will treat these N objects as different objects, ignoring that there are k versions of each object.

[4] The MSG will not be presented here since it is not the focus of this article which presents the discrimination process based on such a classification structure, where low and high level information intervene, along with a cost function.

[5] A KS is not a tree but rather a hierarchy where there is a partial order of generality induced upon the different nodes.

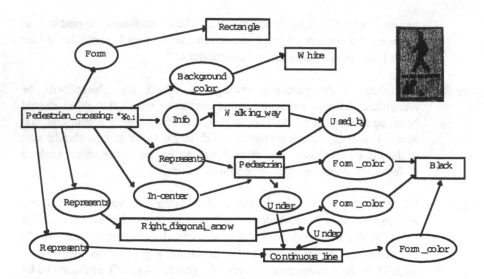

Fig.1. A description of a pedestrian crossing sign using a simple conceptual graph.

We used the MSG because it is applicable on structured objects since it was designed to handle conceptual graphs. Another important advantage with regard to our current application, is that it is incremental. So, upon feedback from the vision system, it could incorporate other exemplars of recognized objects into the KS in order to refine its discrimination capability and improve its performance the next time around. In brief, its expertise base can grow within reasonable complexity bounds (unlike non-incremental methods which must start from scratch each time a new object is considered). Derived from lattice theory [5], a KS has sound mathematical foundations. The MSG is related to formal concept analysis [6], except that it is based on simplifying assumptions that make it possible to address very large sets of objects. For our current application, the loss of information that these assumptions entail are insignificant with regard to our objective of linking conceptual subgraphs to the clusters of objects that they describe.

Figure 2 below shows a simple KS built with three road signs. It shows that three clusters were formed: 1) a cluster for red signs, labeled (1,3), 2) a cluster for rectangular signs, labeled (2,3), and 3) a cluster for all signs, where the discrimination process normally starts from, represented by the root node, labeled (1,2,3). There exists a complexity analysis that shows that with prototype descriptions (as in this application), the size of the KS is O(N), that is, both the number of nodes and links are O(N), where N is the total number of objects passed as input data to the MSG [4]. This complexity analysis also shows that the worst-case time requirement of the MSG is $O(N^2)$, though it is subquadratic in average. So, with our conceptual clustering method, building a classification structure over object descriptions acquired as described above is feasible.

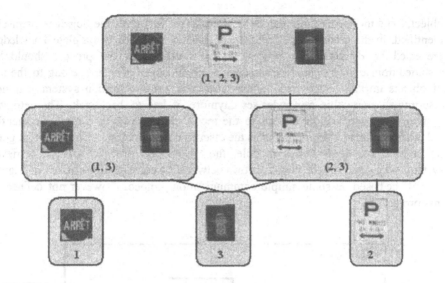

Fig.2. An example of a simple classification structure built with three signs.

2.2 The Discrimination Process

Now, we must show how the object recognition process may use this classification structure to adapt and improve its performance. So, this section describes a typical vision system that would implement such a discrimination process. The architecture of the vision system is given in Figure 3. It is composed of a perception module, a segmentation module, a recognition process, a retrieval system, some recognition modules, a knowledge base describing these modules, the road signs and a cost function, and a classification structure as produced in section 2.1 above.

Examining Figure 3, we see that the perception module acquires the image in which the object to be recognized appears. The segmentation module identifies potential objects in this image. Then the recognition process sends a query to the retrieval system of the classification structure in order to inquire about what steps to take next. By answering this query, the retrieval system tells the recognition process what attributes to verify, and in what part of the object this verification should take place.[6] The recognition process, in light of the cost function and the recognition modules it has access to, sends a request to the segmentation module so that the appropriate recognition module is used to verify the selected condition. The result of this verification is sent back to the retrieval system in order to update the remainder set accordingly. This discrimination process continues with the retrieval system proposing other conditions to verify, until one of these three terminating conditions are met: 1) the remainder set contains one object, 2) the remainder set contains no

---

[6] It could even tell the recognition process to verify that some other object is present, leading to a recursive cooperation between these processes.

object, 3) no more conditions can be verified. In the first case, the object is precisely identified. In the second case, some inconsistency or some incomplete knowledge prevented the discrimination process to work efficiently: the process should be restarted from an intermediary remainder set,[7] or the object does not belong to the set of objects initially considered. In the third case, the recognition system can not discriminate upon this remainder set anymore; it has to backtrack. The retrieval system, by its verification requests to the recognition process in order to constantly reduce the remainder set, implements the discrimination process. The dialog that goes on between the segmentation module, the recognition process, and the retrieval system, symbolized by the double arrows between the corresponding boxes in Figure 3, could be based on some simple communication protocol (however not defined in this project).

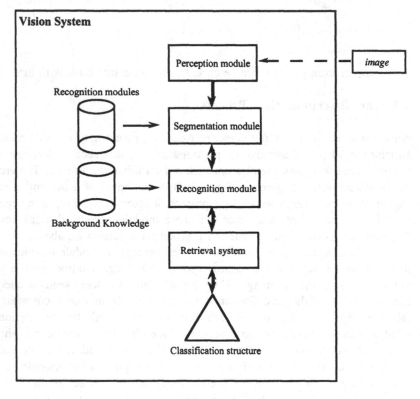

Fig.3. Overview of the proposed architecture.

---

[7] We should mention that the retrieval system, upon failure of previous verification requests, can backtrack and request some new verification from some previous remainder set.

Here is an example of using a classification structure to request particular attribute verifications. Figure 4 represents the road signs used in this example.[8] Our example aims at identifying object #20 correctly. Figure 5 shows the classification structure that we will use for this example.[9] Here, we will only show the interaction between the recognition process and the retrieval system, using natural language. The conditions to verify, which are requests made to the recognition process, would normally appear as conceptual subgraphs describing the nodes of the classification structure. For simplicity reasons, we did not include them in Figure 5. Also for simplicity reasons, we suppose that each condition can be evaluated successfully on the objects of the remainder set (otherwise, backtracking would be needed).

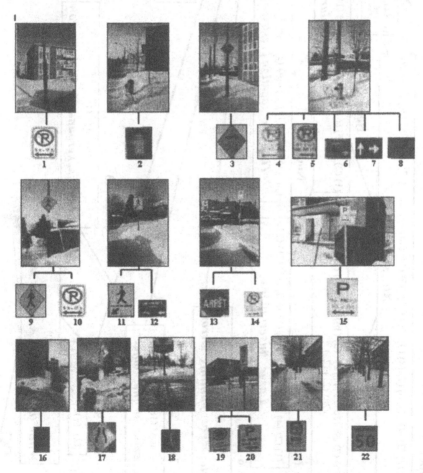

Fig.4. The 22 road signs used in our test application.

---

[8] Since we could not benefit from the segmentation algorithm being developed by some other team of the IIT Project, we had to isolate these signs by hand.

[9] For this application, we only took one shot of the 22 road signs of Figure 4, some of which are similar.

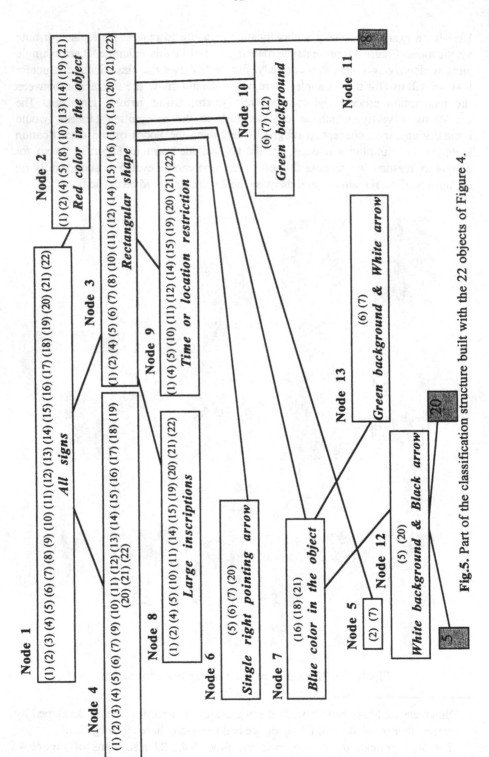

Fig.5. Part of the classification structure built with the 22 objects of Figure 4.

First, an object (a potential road sign) is identified in the image, by the segmentation module.[10] We now have to precisely recognize it. Starting from the root node of the structure (node #1), we have three initial choices to test this object: 1) find if something is red in the object (and go to node #2), 2) find if the object is of rectangular shape (and go to node #3), or 3) simply eliminate object #8 (and go to node #4). This third alternative is not considered because it does not improve our search sufficiently.[11] Since the recognition process knows that all signs are either of rectangular, polygonal, or diamond shaped, it decides to go for the second alternative (which is simple to verify).

Then, starting from node #3, for the same reasons as above, nodes #5 and #10 can be discarded. This leaves 5 alternatives; we can look for: 1) some blue color in the object (and go to node #6), 2) a single right-pointing arrow (and go to node #7), 3) large inscriptions (text or symbols) (and go to node #8), 4) a time or location restriction inscription (text or symbol) (and go to node #9), or 5) a green background (and go to node #10). Because of its associated cost, the recognition process chooses to postpone as much as possible the recognition of colors, which discards alternatives 1 and 5. As for inscriptions, since the recognition of arrows is certainly the easiest of the remaining alternatives, the recognition process chooses this option.[12]

Then, from node #7, only two alternatives are possible: 1) test for the background color (which, if green, would take us to node #13, otherwise, to node #12), or 2) test for the color of the arrow (which, if white, would take us to node #13, otherwise, to node #12). Of the two conditions, it is easier to test for the background color, which offers a higher degree of confidence. The recognition process decides to go with the first alternative, which results in the negation of the condition, i.e., the background color is not green.

Finally, from node #12, different conditions can be evaluated. For instance, the retrieval system could propose: 1) to check to see if there is a big red circle in the top part of the sign (if so, then it represents object #5, otherwise, it represents object #20), or 2) to test the color of the textual inscriptions (again, if red, it would be object #5, otherwise, it would be object #20). Again, the first condition is perceived as easier by our recognition module which chooses to evaluate it. Having no red circle in the top part of the sign, the retrieval system informs the recognition process

---

[10] This was the assumption that we could make in the IIT Project, as other researchers were dealing with this issue.

[11] Noisy or exceptional objects create clusters which are not discriminative enough (as node #4). They also create clusters which are abnormally small in terms of their parent nodes. In either case, the recognition process chooses to disregard them; otherwise, it could imply a lot of backtracking later on. This decision is based on some discrimination metric devised to assess inter-class dissimilarity, and will not be presented in this article because of space limitation.

[12] Frequencies of occurrence for certain text headings or symbols may be contained by the knowledge base which is consulted by the recognition process in order to select the next condition to verify.

that the remainder set contains only object #20. Its prototype definition being available in the knowledge base of the system, additional verifications could take place. For instance, the exact textual inscriptions may be read once more in order to be precisely decrypted, a capital letter P may be looked for at the top of the sign, etc.

It should be obvious by now that object recognition was guided by this discrimination process in a way that allowed its adaptation to the perceptual constraints of the environment, the architectural constraints of the vision system, and the cost constraints of the application. Also, we wish to add that the methodology proposed here also allows probabilistic matching between objects under recognition and class descriptions, even though our research did not take us that far yet. Probabilistic matching could be useful for ranking different matches, providing some confidence level associated with each action, and providing alternatives when backtracking is needed.

3 Literature Survey

In artificial vision, it is widely acknowledged that the availability of background knowledge helps the recognition process [7]. With our application domain, background knowledge was available. It has also been shown that machine learning techniques could help the vision process, particularly in robotics environments [8]. Learning techniques can help the recognition process by extracting generalizations from the data, in such a way that noise or environmental parameters affecting perception statistically vanish. They help the extraction of salient features of objects [9]. One project particularly successful in extracting salient features of perceived objects used a connectionnist approach [10]. However, contrarily to that approach, we aimed at learning *symbolic* descriptions of objects so that we could implement a discrimination process based on a dialogue between a vision module and some task-support module. Nevertheless, the discovery of salient features of perceived objects through a learning method is totally relevant to our goal. As proposed in [11], the variations affecting the recognition of objects should be taken into account by the learning method. That prompted us to sample the objects according to the possible variations of the perception parameters (light, angle, etc.), resulting in multiple exemplars of the same objects taken under various environmental conditions.

As for the particular learning technique that we used, since we aimed at implementing a discrimination process from the start, it seemed that a classification structure would provide an organization that would facilitate this discrimination. Classifier systems were used in [8, 9, 12] successfully. We anticipated even greater results with our application domain since our data is highly structured and is already classifiable (road signs have predefined shapes and colors, for instance), contrarily to the data of [12] where the SKICAT system seeks to cluster constellations and galaxies. So, in summary, according to the ideas presented in [13], we proposed an architecture for a vision system where adaptive control of the recognition process is possible through the use of a classification structure inferred from different exemplars of the same objects (see Figure 3).

Under the methodology that we propose, each sample of an object mixes high-level and low-level information describing the object. The high-level information comes from the background knowledge that we have; while the low-level information comes from the perception module, influenced by particular perception conditions. Applying the learning technique on data being described by both types of knowledge allows a dialogue between the segmentation module (where low-level information is the only data available) and the recognition module (where high-level information must be used to exploit the background knowledge we have on the application domain) to take place.

[14] describes such a system where high and low-level information are mixed in order to describe perceived objects, but where these two types of information are linked by relations that are inferred both from the background knowledge and the actual data which visually describe the object. In contrast to this work, our methodology does not specify how these two types of information could be mixed. We believe that rules could be used to define which attribute is represented by which concept in the conceptual graph describing the object. However, it is obvious that extensive knowledge about the visual attributes (and their domains) must be acquired and exploited in a way that will facilitate the matching of two exemplars of the same object (by the learning algorithm). We believe that this is highly dependant upon the application domain. In contrast to the work of [14], we propose to use the two types of information (low and high-level) in a learning process that will form clusters of objects described by symbolic descriptions useful for the dialogue required by the discrimination process. The ultimate goal of our approach is to provide support for this discrimination process, and not so much as to discover relations between high and low-level descriptions of the same objects.

4 Conclusion

In this paper, we presented a methodology that aims at improving object recognition through a discrimination process made possible by the use of a classification structure built over exemplars of the objects to recognize. We described how object descriptions could be acquired under this methodology, mixing both high and low-level information. High-level information comes from background knowledge we have on the application domain; low-level information comes directly from the vision system. Mixing these two types of information in the object descriptions is what makes the discrimination process possible, connecting high and low-level object recognition activities. Through the use of a simple example, we showed how discrimination was possible.

The methodology that we propose here is certainly useful and easy to achieve. However it is based on the major assumption that the segmentation module can identify potential objects from the original image, which is our starting point. With the road sign application, this is certainly the case, as road signs are designed to contrast from the background visual information. However, this may not be the case with other applications, restraining the applicability of our method. For our methodology to work well, we must have an application domain for which: 1) background knowledge about the objects to recognize is available, 2) the objects are easily identifiable from the background information of the image, 3) the vision system's capabilities are sufficient to discriminate between the objects, that is, the requests made by the retrieval system can be carried out, and 4) the objects are visually different enough from one another so that their differences can be detected (and could support the discrimination process).

Unfortunately, the IIT Project did not get to the point of integration yet; so we do not know at the moment how useful our methodology really is when faced with real size applications. Other than our own example of 22 objects, no other on-the-field testing was carried out. However, a subsequent phase of the IIT Project is planned. We simply hope that our methodology, being simple, will be adopted by vision system developers, so that testing in real-life environments becomes possible, providing additional insights about its shortcomings. Nevertheless, we think that we have demonstrated its potential usefulness and its simplicity.

By using a conceptual clustering method to build the classification structure used by the discrimination process, this article also shows how different AI techniques can come together to support the implementation of some high-level cognitive task. Once more, this makes a case for multi-strategic approaches in AI-related applications. For this reason and all of the above, we hope to have created an interest for this methodology.

References

1. Li, Y., Saldanha, C. & Lalonde, M., (1996). Geomodeling: Georeferencing Real World Objects. In: Proceedings of Vision Interface 1996. May. Toronto. 71-76.
2. Sowa, J. F. *Conceptual Structures: Information Processing in Mind and Machine*. Addison-Wesley, 1984. 481 pages.
3. Mineau, G., (1991). *Méthode de structuration par généralisation*. Thèse de doctorat. Département d'informatique et de recherche opérationnelle. Université de Montréal.
4. Mineau, G.W. & Godin, R., (1995). Automatic Structuring of Knowledge Bases by Conceptual Clustering. In: IEEE Transactions on Knowledge and Data Engineering, volume 7, no 5. 824-829.
5. Godin, R., Mineau, G.W., Missaoui, R. & Mili, H., (1995). Méthodes de classification conceptuelle basées sur les treillis de Galois et applications. In: Revue d'Intelligence Artificielle, volume 9, no 2. 105-137.
6. Wille, R., (1982). Restructuring Lattice Theory: an Approach Based on Hierarchies of Concepts. In: I. Rival (Ed.), *Ordered Sets*. Dordrecht-Boston: Reidel. 445-470.
7. Dean, T., Angluin, D., Basye, K., Engelson, S., Kaelbling, L., Kokkekis, E., Maron, O., (1995). Inferring Finite Automata with Stochastic Output Functions and an Application to Map Learning. In: Machine Learning Journal, vol. 18. Kluwer Academic Publishers. 81-108.

8. Dorigo, M., (1995). ALECSYS and the AutonoMouse: Learning to control a real robot by distributed classifier systems. In: Machine Learning Journal, vol. 19. Kluwer Academic Publishers. 209-240.
9. Watanabe, L. & Yerramareddy, S., (1991). Decision Tree Induction of 3-D Manufacturing Features. In: Proceedings of the 8th International Workshop on Machine Learning. Morgan Kaufmann. 650-654.
10. Thint, M., Wang, P., (1990). Feature Extraction and Clustering of Tactile Impressions with Connectionnist Models. In: Proceedings of the 7th International Workshop on Machine Learning. Morgan Kaufmann. 253-258.
11. Segen, J., (1988). Learning Graph Models of Shape. In: Proceedings of the 5th International Workshop on Machine Learning. Morgan Kaufmann. 29-35.
12. Fayad, U. M., Weir, N. & Djorgovski, S., (1993). SKICAT: A Machine Learning System for Automated Cataloging of Large Scale Sky Surveys. In: Proceedings of the 10th International Workshop on Machine Learning. Morgan Kaufmann. 112-120.
13. Whitehead, S. D. & Ballard, D. H., (1991). Learning to Perceive and Act by Trial and Error. In: Machine Learning Journal, vol. 7, no 1. Kluwer Academic Publishers. 45-83.
14. Klingspor, V., Morick, K.J. & Rieger, A.D., (1996). Learning Concepts from Sensor Data of a Mobile Robot. In: Machine Learning Journal, vol. 23. Kluwer Academic Publishers. 305-332

Oracles and Assistants: Machine Learning Applied to Network Supervision

Richard Nock[1] and Babak Esfandiari[2]

[1] Laboratoire d'Informatique, de Robotique et de Microélectronique de Montpellier,
161, rue Ada,
34392 Montpellier, France
nock@lirmm.fr
[2] Mitel Corporation,
350 Legget Drive,
P.O. Box 13089,
K2K 1X3, Kanata, ON, Canada
babak_esfandiari@mitel.com

Abstract. This paper presents an application of machine learning in network management and supervision, in order to help the processing of the large volume of event notifications received by network operators. In this paper, we provide theoretical and experimental results on learning patterns called chronicles, in order to design a machine assistant to network supervision operators. We first define a learning model that suits our framework, and study from a theoretical point of view the ability to learn chronicles. We quantify the effects of the network behaviour on learning and prove to what extent help can be brought by oracles, possibly the operator, or another learning assistant, to increase the assistant accuracy. We also have implemented and tested our machine assistant and we give experimental results obtained in two distinct realworld situations. They show experimentally the circumstances for which chronicle learning is possible without the help of the operator or another assistant.

1 Introduction

The aim of this paper is to show how Artificial Intelligence techniques (such as machine learning and multi-agent systems) can be applied to network management and supervision in order to help the processing of the large volume of alarms and various event notifications received by network management platforms. Actually, many of these alarms prove to have a user-depending utility and have to be filtered. Other events become meaningful when associated to their context, which partly consists in the previous and following events, which dates of detection may vary depending on the traffic. Therefore time has to be explicitly taken into account. We have chosen the Chronicle model [7] in order to incorporate temporal reasoning in our experimental platform. Thus some of the tasks (alarm filtering, log recording, fault detection...) can be automated via a chronicle recognition system [2], letting the supervision operator focus on more important tasks. Although it is possible to have a model-based approach, we will assume that we do not have a complete knowledge of the network, and that the model can evolve quickly.

Therefore "on-line" knowledge acquisition seems to be a good solution. We have been mainly inspired by Pattie Maes's Interface Agents [13], where an agent learns by "looking over the shoulder" of the human operator. The association of the chronicle recognition system and the chronicle acquisition system can eventually provide us a true intelligent assistant to network management and supervision. But chronicle learning can raise theoretical problems, and we have to know which assumptions are reasonable to build such a system. For example, [2] advocates for the dialog between the learner and the experts. This paper brings some theoretical results showing how much such a dialog can be useful, and provide some algorithms which have been tested so far. We have implemented a simplified simulation of a network management platform which respects network management standards (GDMO and CMIS) and encloses our assistant. The algorithms present in some cases the desirable properties [2] to provide neither too specific, nor too general chronicles.

The theoretical learning model we present and its extensions are a generalization of a previous model [14]. Section §2 presents some definitions refering to chronicles; section §3 presents the assistant's structure. Positive and negative results for chronicle learning are investigated in section §4, followed in section §5 by the algorithms and the practical results that were obtained.

2   Definitions

Temporal knowledge is required for reasoning on events, actions and change [7], in order to model facts such as : precedence, overlapping, simultaneity between events. While "numerical" approaches based on Operations Research are not adequate for symbolic reasoning, classical and modal logic approaches have problems in finding a good balance between semantic expressivity and algorithmic complexity. The *chronicle model* proposed by Ghallab is based on two elementary types of formulaes taken from the reified temporal logic : *events* and *holds*.

- a "hold" expresses that some ground domain attribute holds over some interval, for instance : *Hold (position (robot1, docking-site), (t5, t6))*. In this examples, the hold means that between *t5* and *t6*, *robot1* stays at its *docking-site*.
- an "event" specifies a discrete change of the value of an attribute, for instance :
  Event (state (switch): (off, on), t8). In this example, the event means that at time *t8*, the *switch* changes of state, passing from *off* to *on*.

A chronicle model is a set of *event patterns* and temporal constraints between them and with respect to a context specified by *hold* assertions. If some observed events match the event patterns, and if their occurence dates meet the specified constraints within its context, then an instance of this chronicle occurs. Here is an example of a chronicle taken from [7] :

```
Chronicle RobotLoadMachine {
event (Robot: (outRoom, inRoom), e1);
event (Robot: (inRoom, outRoom), e4);
event (MachineInput: (UnLoaded, Loaded), e2);
event (Machine: (Stopped, Running), e3);
e1 < e2;
1' ≤ e3 - e2 ≤ 6';
3' ≤ e4 - e2 ≤ 5';
hold (Machine: Running, (e2, e2));
hold (SafetyConditions: True, (e1, e4));
when recognized {report ''Successful load''; }}
```

Realtime (and therefore with low complexity) chronicle recognition [2] is processed in several steps :

- Transform "holds" into "forbidden events", *i.e.* an event should not change the value of the "held" attribute within the duration of the "hold".
- Possibly create a new instance of a possible chronicle and update (in fact this is always a restriction as time goes by) the *window of relevance* (acceptable time intervals for the expected events to complete a chronicle pattern) of all possible chronicles when a new event has been observed.
- Detect "deadlines" and occurences of "forbidden events". In these cases, the corresponding chronicle will be removed from the list of the possible chronicles.
- Trigger off the action corresponding to the completed chronicle.

3   The assistant's structure

Our machine assistant is mainly inspired by Pattie Maes's Interface Agents [13]. An Interface Agent is "a computer program that employs Artificial Intelligence techniques in order to provide assistance to a user dealing with a particular computer application. Such agents learn by 'watching over the shoulder' of the user and detecting patterns and regularities in the user's behaviour". Since we had to deal with realtime aspects and time was a very important parameter, we chose to manipulate chronicles. As shown in figure 1, our assistant has two main components :

- The Chronicle Recognition System (RS), which goal is to receive time-stamped event notifications (such as alarms) and try to match them with chronicles stored in the so-called Confirmed Chronicle Base. Whenever a chronicle has been recognized, the RS processes the corresponding action (such as filtering, fault diagnosis...). If the received events do not match any chronicle, it is up to the supervision operator to take a decision. For more details about the Recognition System, see [2].

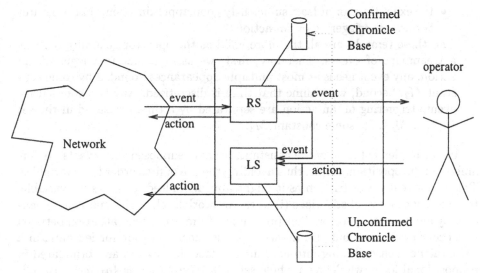

RS : Recognition System

LS: Learning System

Fig. 1. The assistant's structure

- The Learning System (LS), which goal is to watch "over the shoulder" of the supervision operator when he takes a decision, in order to feed the Recognition System with new chronicles. New chronicles are stored in a so-called Unconfirmed Chronicle Base before being "mature" enough in order to be confirmed (*i.e.* transferred to the Confirmed Chronicle Base). In this paper, we describe more precisely this component.

4   Learnability and chronicles

First, in order not to laden our notations, we shall make our learning study on chronicles whose "holds" have been removed. Indeed, in all our positive learning results, provided we can manage "events", we can also manage "holds" quite similarly, since they can be treated as forbidden events [2]. The main difficulty of the learning task stems from the management of all the "events". Our model for learning chronicles is adapted to our framework. It uses properties on the operator and event appearances. These can be presented as follows:

- The operator is human. Our task is to provide an assistant to model his behaviour. Therefore, we can suppose that the set of different actions being learnt is a constant, albeit very big. Call $\alpha = \{\alpha_1, ..., \alpha_{M_1}\}$ this set of actions, where M_1 is a constant.
- Any human operator, be him as efficient as possible, cannot recall
  - events that are too spaced out,
  - how many times some event has appeared, beyond some threshold,

- the exact time, or at least sufficiently good approximation, that separates two events triggering off an action.

And these remarks are all the more valid as the operator generally receives a treamount of events. Therefore, first, we assume that to trigger off an action, any event needs at most multiple appearances bounded by some constant M_2. Second, we assume that time is discretized. Any two consecutive events triggering off an action are separated by a time measured in the set $\{0, 1, ..., M_3\}$, for some constant M_3.

In our implementation of the assistant, we have supposed that events are formulated in propositional logic, thus avoiding the use of first-order logic variables. This is not really a restriction as it might appear. Indeed, to any such variable, there are not many substitutions (i) at the network level, or (ii) that can be handled by any human operator. This prevents us from using generalization between first-order predicates, but still allows us to use generalization for learning, in a "Montaigne" sense. Taking into account the fact that events are formulated in propositional logic, we define a whole set of nM_2 events $a = \{a_1, a_2, ..., a_{nM_2}\}$. This set contains, for any first-order defined event, the corresponding whole set of propositional events where each event is obtained by substituting each variable of the original event by possible constants for this variable.

There are 2^{nM_2} subsets of the whole set of events. Given a subset of k events, there are $\binom{nM_2}{k} = (nM_2)!/((nM_2 - k)!k!)$ couples of events, and for each couple, if there exists a time constraint between the events of the couple, it is measured in the set $\{-M_3, -M_3+1, ..., M_3\}$. Given some action, we obtain an upperbound for the number of chronicles that can be described over the nM_2 events that is (largely) upperbounded by $(4M_3 + 4)^{n^2 M_2^2}$. Although this bound is larger than the real one, it illustrates that the limitations we have applied so far do not affect the number of chronicles that can be built. As another consequence of our formalization, we can view a chronicle as a *monotonous formula* described over a set of Boolean variables whose size is no more than $nM_2 + M_3\binom{nM_2}{2}$. Recall that a variable is Boolean iff it can take two values : "0" or "1" (respectively negative and positive literals). A monotonous formula contains only positive literals. It therefore becomes possible to look for the translation of any positive result concerning Boolean formulae into positive results for learning chronicles.

4.1 Modelling the probability of appearance of events

Our model allows variations of probabilities according to laws that can be unknown, but whose variations take place in a convenient range. We allow the appearance probability of any event a_i at time t, $w_t(a_i)$, to behave as $w_t(a_i) \leq \frac{1}{\beta} w_{t'}(a_i), \forall t' \leq t$. β is a constant. The more β tends to 0, the more our model fits to reality, but the bigger the learning time, the bigger the number of examples needed to learn.

This model is very convenient for our framework. Indeed, the strongest constraint it puts on the weights is that for any event a_i, if $\exists t : w_t(a_i) = 0$, then

$\forall t' > t, w_{t'}(a_i) = 0$. This does not represent a constraint in our model : indeed, recall that the assistant learns chronicles that it puts in the Confirmed Chronicle Base, where they are no longer modified. The authorization of appearance of events at some points could artificially increase the error probability of a chronicle, independantly of the real performances of the assistant. We call $D_\beta(t)$ the probability distribution of events at time t.

4.2 Learning chronicles

We suppose that the assistant has access to *oracles*, that supply events, actions and/or messages ("Yes", "No") according to some fixed protocol. We present them from the most passive of them, to the most active ones, for which there can be interactions between the assistant and the oracles. We have on purpose tried to make the oracles behave as simply as possible. In particular, we did not try to adapt the complex behaviour of experts recommended by [2], because we wanted to define the canonical possible behaviours for experts.

• The most simple of these oracles is entirely passive, and simply supplies on-line streams of events from a and actions from α, according to their appearance on the network. We refer to him as PASSIVE(α). Typically, this one represents the network itself.

• The second oracle behaves as PASSIVE(α), except that its output does not present *overlapping*. PASSIVE$^S(\alpha)$ supplies "examples", that is, couples (stream of events, action) that can be viewed as chronicles subsumed by the chronicles to model. The learner knows that the events provided are exactly those that have triggered off α; PASSIVE$^S(\alpha)$ therefore can be viewed as providing a "one-way help", from the operator to the assistant (the assistant knowing that there is no overlapping). From this point of view, PASSIVE$^S(\alpha)$ is an interesting intermediate between PASSIVE(α), where no explicit help exists between the assistant and the operator, and the following oracles, that represent "two-way helps".

• ACTIVE$_{MQ}(\alpha)$ takes for parameter some subset of events from a (without time stamps) and some action from α, and is answered "Yes" or "No", depending on the action can be triggered off by this set of events.

• ACTIVE$_{EQ}(\alpha)$ takes for parameter a chronicle (or a set of chronicles) involving an action from α, and is answered (by the operator) either "Yes" if it is judged correct (and the chronicle is added to the Confirmed Base), or "No", and in that latter case, a stream of events with dates is provided by the operator, for which the chronicle fails.

At the network level, these two latter oracles can represent either an assistant, or a human operator. The aim of the assistant is to guarantee, with a certain confidence, that, from a fixed and reasonable time, he shall trigger off the actions from α approximatively "at the same time" they are triggered off in the stream he receives from the passive oracle(s). This means that, if the operator is removed (when we can consider that the learning task for α has ended, see figure 1), and if, say, the assistant receives a stream $s_{i_t}, s_{i_{t+1}}, \ldots$ where s_{i_t} (resp. $s_{i_{t+1}}$) is the stream of events triggering off α_{i_t} (resp. $\alpha_{i_{t+1}}$), then its "failure" probability will be no more than, say $0 < \epsilon < 1$. Which means that, with probability $1 - \epsilon$, α_{i_t} will be triggered off after the appearance of the last event of s_{i_t}, but not after the appearance of the first event of $s_{i_{t+1}}$.

Our learning model is related to the PAC-learning model [16]. We note $c(\alpha)$ the set of chronicles to learn, that trigger off the actions from α, $|c(\alpha)|$ the size of the writing of $c(\alpha)$, and Ω some oracle(s) belonging to the previously enumerated set. PAC-learning aims at proving that the *class* of chronicles $\mathcal{C}_\alpha$, containing $c(\alpha)$, is learnable. That means that for any element of $\mathcal{C}_\alpha$, the learning task is possible. Note that $\mathcal{C}_\alpha$ is just a product set, between any of the classes $\mathcal{C}_{\alpha_i}, i \in \{1, ..., M_1\}$. $\forall i \in \{1, ..., M_1\}$, the class $\mathcal{C}_{\alpha_i}$ can be understood as the class from which any set of chronicles triggering off α_i is always taken. It can be *e.g.* the class of single chronicles, having no more than 10 events. We use the shorthand "α is PAC-learnable" for "$\mathcal{C}_\alpha$ is PAC-learnable". Recall that we have access to a set $a = \{a_1, ..., a_{nM_2}\}$ of events, and $\alpha = \{\alpha_1, ..., \alpha_{M_1}\}$.

Definition 1 *We shall say that α is PAC-learnable using Ω if there exists a learning algorithm L using Ω and a polynomial $p(.,.,.,.,.)$ such that, for any $0 < \epsilon, \delta < 1$ (resp. accuracy and confidence parameters), for any $\beta > 0$ and initial distribution $D_\beta(0)$, for any $c(\alpha) \in \mathcal{C}_\alpha$, after a time t bounded by $p(n, \frac{1}{\beta}, \frac{1}{\epsilon}, \frac{1}{\delta}, |c(\alpha)|)$, L puts a set of chronicles $\{c'(\alpha_1), ..., c'(\alpha_{M_1})\}$ in the confirmed chronicle base such that*

$$\forall i \in \{1, ..., M_1\}, \forall t' \geq t, P(P_{D_\beta(t')}(\alpha_i \text{ fails}) > \epsilon) < \delta$$

As the reader shall remark, the algorithm proposed for the assistant in section §5 of this paper uses a threshold to put the learnt chronicles in the confirmed base, corresponding to a number of times the actions of the corresponding chronicle were triggered off. The agorithm is inspired by the algorithm of [10, 12], that learns monotonous monomials from positive examples only. We have extended it to handle streams of events, overlapping between chronicles, and multiple chronicle learning.

The threshold t_{α_i} for putting an action α_i in the confirmed base can be calculated in the same way as [15], theorem 4. We obtain a sufficient number of activations of α_i whose expression is

$$t_\alpha = \frac{1}{\beta\epsilon} \left(\log |\mathcal{C}_{\alpha_i}| + \log \left(\frac{1}{\delta} \right) \right) \tag{1}$$

If α_i is triggered by k (constant) chronicles, depending on the fact that the size of a chronicle can be considered as unfixed or constant, the dependance on n in t_{α_i} is reduced from $\mathcal{O}(n)$ to $\mathcal{O}(\log(n))$. The logarithmic dependance in n is important, as n can be very large, and therefore the human factor limitations can be of great help for the threshold calculation.

4.3 Theoretical results for learning chronicles

Proposition 1 *If any action from the set α can be supposed to appear in a single chronicle, then*

1. α *is PAC-learnable using $PASSIVE^S(\alpha)$.*
2. α *is PAC-learnable using $ACTIVE_{MQ}(\alpha)$ and $PASSIVE(\alpha)$, and the chronicles built are at least as accurate as those of 1.*

This proposition raises the problem of learning using only PASSIVE(α), when there exists overlapping between chronicles. It is not straightforward to prove that PAC-learning is preserved. In that case, we can consider that efficiency is measured with respect to the ideal chronicle at the network level, and not the ideal "theoretical" chronicle. This can be a much more complex chronicle, involving overlapping with the definition of other chronicles involving other actions, but in that case, we preserve the PAC-learning property. Concerning the cases where an action can be triggered off by multiple chronicles, the learning problem is at least as difficult as for k-term-DNF, which was shown to be intractable [11]. This explains why as we shall see, learning a particular type of chronicles called filters is difficult in practice.

To prove negative results even when the assistant has access to different oracles, we make the following assumptions on the learning framework: calls to PASSIVE(α), PASSIVE$^S(\alpha)$, and ACTIVE$_{EQ}(\alpha)$ are authorized. We fix as $k-$complex-Chronicles the set of chronicles involving no more than k events, where $k \leq n$ can be a function of the whole number of events. RP denotes the class of polynomial-time randomized algorithms as defined by [1].

Proposition 2 *Unless $RP = NP$,*

- $k-$ *complex-Chronicles are not PAC-learnable.*
- *Even if the events appear at different times each, with constant time between events and actions, if α is triggered off by only three chronicles, α is not PAC-learnable.*

(Proof made by reduction from the Set-Cover problem for 1, and from Graph-3-Colorability for 2 [6]). The human operator can be of great help in the form of an oracle ACTIVE$_{MQ}(\alpha)$. Indeed, with access to ACTIVE$_{MQ}(\alpha)$, the first previous negative result in proposition 2 becomes positive. It is worthwhile remarking that the human operator is of greater help when behaving like ACTIVE$_{MQ}(\alpha)$ than like ACTIVE$_{EQ}(\alpha)$.

5 The learning assistant

Before beginning the description of our system, let us assume that the set of events and actions is finite and "relatively small", in order to generate a reasonable amount of chronicles with enough genericity. We will furthermore consider a particular action called "silence", which does not correspond to any actions of the supervision operator, but which is useful to generate particular chronicles : filters.

Definition 2 *A filter is a chronicle*

{ SetOfEvents, SetOfTimeConstraints, SetOfHolds } ⇒ *silence*

Filters are used to decrease the sum of the events displayed to the operator: when the corresponding events are received, the system simply ignores them. Given that many different sequences of events can lead to the action "silence", it is hard to learn them without using the operator or the assistants' help (see section §4). Learnt chronicles will consist in a set of events terminated by an action. We will see later how we deal with temporal constraints and "holds". As the supervision operator has to interact with the Learning System (for instance to confirm chronicles), it is important for him to understand how our system learns. We believe that incremental learning is easier to follow by a human operator. Furthermore, if the learning algorithm is fast enough, it can be used in realtime, just like the Recognition System, thus enabling better cooperation. The chronicle learning is processed in three steps : the chronicle creation, the chronicle evaluation and the chronicle confirmation.

5.1 The chronicle creation

A chronicle is created in two cases:

- When the supervision operator triggers an action: the created chronicle is the set of the received events before the action, plus the action itself.
- When nothing happens during a given time interval (neither received events nor actions) : the created chronicle, which will be used as a filter, is the set of received events since the previous action, followed by the action "silence".

In some cases, the operator triggers several actions in a row, without waiting for the reception of new events. This can have several meanings:

1. these actions all correspond to the whole sequence of the received events;
2. each action corresponds to a subsequence of the received events;
3. a combination of the two previous possibilities.

In the actual system, we have assumed that we only have to face the first possibility. The sequence of actions is therefore considered as one single action which is the concatenation of the sequence. The second possibility corresponds in fact to the more general problem of overlapping chronicles, which is hard to manage. This issue has been discussed in section §4.3. A possible fast heuristic is to bufferize the k last received events independently of the triggered actions. When the sum of the received events reaches a certain threshold T which models the memory capacity of the operator, only the T last events are buffered (this also helps to satisfy learnability constraints expressed in section §4). Obviously, when the action is triggered off by the Recognition System, the corresponding events are deleted, since the corresponding chronicle has already been learnt.

5.2   The chronicle evaluation

Operations : now we have to know whether the created chronicle is worth being added to the Unconfirmed Chronicle Base. First we need to define two operators: the inclusion ($\subset$) and the subtraction ($\backslash$) between two chronicles. A chronicle A is included in chronicle B iff their actions are equal and A's sequence of events is a "subword" of B's sequence of events. Dates of occurence of the events are not compared. If A $\subset$ B, then we can subtract A from B by removing A's events from B's sequence of events and replacing B's action with the action "silence", to create a "filter". Of course the result of a subtraction can depend on how to select the subword in B. An easy way is to select the first occurence of each event. For more "realism", it can be interesting to minimize the date differences, but this can be too costly, except if we do not want to obtain necessarily the "best" subword.

The evaluation algorithm : here is the evaluation of a new chronicle C, created following the chronicle creation step, given his action a :

Algorithm 1: EVALUATE(C)

% C is a chronicle with an action a
begin
  $Trust(C) := 1$
  for *each* $C' \in$ *the CB so that* $C'(action) = a$ **do**
    switch C **do**
      case $C \subseteq C'$: exit
      case $C \supset C'$: create-and-evaluate-filter $C'' := C \backslash C'$; exit
      case $C \neq C'$: continue

  for *each* $C' \in$ *the UCB so that* $C'(action) = a$ **do**
    switch C **do**
      case $C \subset C'$
        add C to the UCB; $Trust(C) := Trust(C') + 1$
        remove C' from the UCB; create-and-evaluate-filter $C'' := C' \backslash C$
      case $C \supseteq C'$
        create-and-evaluate-filter $C'' := C \backslash C'$; widen C' time interval;
        $Trust(C')$++
      case $C \neq C'$: continue

  add (C) to the UCB
end

Basically, when inclusion is found between two chronicles, the shorter one (*i.e.* the most general one) is kept, and the other one is discarded. The trust value of the chronicle is incremented, and the remainder of the substraction between the chronicles is used to create a filter.

Temporal constraints : another operation is the creation of temporal constraints. By increasing time intervals, we can somehow "generalize" chronicles by accepting chronicles with the same sequence of events and with different time stamps. Obviously, we only create temporal constraints between two consecutive events, since otherwise trying to create some kind of adequate "constraint-tree" (the root being the first event) would be too costly and not necessarily useful. Remember that we try to preserve a realtime learning algorithm !

Filters : filters, like C'', created during the evaluation algorithm must also be evaluated. However, their evaluation is easier, since we do not need to create other chronicles during the evaluation. However, as we know (section §4) that learning filters is difficult and risky (we would not want to filter important events!), it is better to keep the most specific ones, contrarily to the other chronicles.

Overlapping : it must be noted that the above algorithm is a valid learning algorithm when no overlapping of events occurs. However, when it is not the case, it becomes a heuristic, unless we deal with theoretical chronicles at the network level (section §4.3). We have already proposed and tested a heuristic that deals explicitly with overlapping, that could not be included in this paper because of the lack of space, but that can be found in [4]. Here is, however, the general idea : given that we abandon in this case the idea of learning different chronicles that lead to the same action, we can use a "longest common subsequence" operation on two chronicles that lead to the same action, and replace them both by the newly calculated sequence.

5.3 The Chronicle Confirmation

Now that we have put chronicles in the Unconfirmed Chronicle Base, the question is : when can we put those in the Confirmed Chronicle Base ? We have basically two ways of doing this :

- When the "trust" in a chronicle reaches a certain threshold, it can be automatically confirmed.
- The operator can confirm manually a chronicle by simply "clicking" on it. Here, the operator plays approximatively the role of the $ACTIVE_{EQ}$ oracle. To play it completely, it would be necessary for him to bring the assistant a case where the chronicle fails.

Note that there is a need for a coherence maintenance system in the Confirmed Chronicle Base. Indeed, if the system encounters cases where the same sequence of events leads to different actions (ambiguity), it has to detect them.

This is done by comparing each new chronicle to those stored in the Chronicle Base and trying to find inclusions (this time with different actions). Coherence maintenance is not important concerning the Unconfirmed Chronicle Base, since those chronicles are not used yet in the recognition system. But this could also help creating "holds": the events obtained by the subtraction of two chronicles with different actions would correspond to "holds".

5.4 Experimentation and first results

The learning system has been integrated in our experimental and simple network management platform, MAGENTA [5], which is roughly compatible with ISO and CCITT specifications, namely the Manager-Agent model, GDMO [9] and CMIS [8]. See [14] for a complete description of MAGENTA's interface.

The assistant has been tested with data taken from a simulation of a french packet-switched data network. The actions to be triggered off are part of these data (they have been generated by a specific expert system). Results show that with a very small sample of events corresponding to thirty hours of simulation, the assistant behaves quite well, learning five acceptable chronicles out of ten that reached the confirmation threshold. These results are all the more valid as these data contain lots of overlaps, and the actions are not necessarily triggered off by a single sequence of events: these two cases could make the algorithm behave quite badly (recall the remark of section §4.3).

We have also tested the assistant on a problem where we could reasonably suppose that there were no overlaps: the data were generated by the behaviour of a user of a programming environment. Some of the generated chronicles were very pertinent and really corresponded to the desire of the user.

6 Conclusion and perspectives

In this article, we present a chronicle learning system that has been implemented and tested in a realworld domain: network management. We have also studied a learnability model relevant to our framework and raised theoretical results that distinguished two main problems when dealing with learning sequences of events in a real-time world:

- different sequences of events leading to the same action,
- overlapping of sequences.

In the paper we proposed an algorithm that deals with the first problem, and sketched another one (the complete description can be found in [4]) that deals with the second one. We empirically discovered that it is difficult to deal with the two problems at the same time. A formal theoretical proof would be highly interesting.

The other aspect studied in this paper is the quantification of the help provided by an oracle to the assistant, and what is the exact kind of minimum help that can make a learning task possible. But since in certain cases the needed help would be too much to require from a human operator, it is possible, as in [13], to think of linking the assistants together so they can also play the oracle role to each other. We have started experimenting this ([3]), and the first results are promising.

References

1. J. L. Balcazar, J. Diaz, and J. Gabarro. *Structural Complexity I*. Springer Verlag, 1988.
2. Christophe Dousson. *Suivi d'évolutions et reconnaissance de chroniques*. Thèse d'université, Université Paul Sabatier, Toulouse, LAAS, Septembre 1994.
3. B. Esfandiari. *Techniques d'Intelligence Artificielle Distribuée pour la Supervision-Maintenance des Réseaux*. PhD thesis, Université Montpellier II, 1996.
4. B. Esfandiari, G. Deflandre, J. Quinqueton, and C. Dony. Agent-oriented techniques for network supervision. *Annals of Telecommunications*, 51(9–10):521–529, 1996.
5. Babak Esfandiari, Michel Plu, Joël Quinqueton, and Gilles Deflandre. A multiagent perspective for assistance to a network supervision operator. In *MAAMAW poster session*, 1996.
6. M.R. Garey and D.S. Johnson. *Computers and Intractability, a guide to the theory of NP-Completeness*. Bell Telephone Laboratories, 1979.
7. Malik Ghallab. Past and future chronicles for supervision and planning. In Jean Paul Haton, editor, *Proceedings of the 14th Int. Avignon Conference*, pages 23–34. EC2 and AFIA, EC2, Paris, Juin 1994.
8. ISO/DIS 9595. *Information Technology - Open Systems Interconnection - Common Management Information Service Definition*, Janvier 1990. 2nd DP N3070.
9. ISO/DP 10165-4. *Information Technology - Structure of Management Information - Part 4. Guidelines for the Definition of Managed Objects*, Juin 1990.
10. M. J. Kearns. *The Computational Complexity of Machine Learning*. M.I.T. Press, 1989.
11. M. J. Kearns, M. Li, L. Pitt, and L. Valiant. On the learnability of boolean formulae. *Proceedings of the Nineteenth Annual A.C.M. Symposium on Theory of Computing*, pages 285–295, 1987.
12. M. J. Kearns and U. V. Vazirani. *An Introduction to Computational Learning Theory*. M.I.T. Press, 1994.
13. Pattie Maes and Robyn Kozierok. Learning interface agents. In *Proceedings of the 11th Nat Conf on Artificial Intelligence*. AAAI, MIT-Press/AAAI-Press, 1993.
14. J. Quinqueton, B. Esfandiari, and R. Nock. Chronicle Learning and Agent oriented techniques for network management and supervision. In Chapman & Hall, editor, *International Conference on Intelligent Networks and Intelligence in Networks (Invited paper)*, pages 131–146, 1997.
15. R.L. Rivest. Learning decision lists. *Machine Learning*, pages 229–246, 1987.
16. L. G. Valiant. A theory of the learnable. *Communications of the ACM*, pages 1134–1142, 1984.

A Common Multi-Agent Testbed for Diverse Seamless Personal Information Networking Applications

Suhayya Abu-Hakima, Ramiro Liscano, Roger Impey

Seamless Personal Information Networking (SPIN) Group,
Institute for Information Technology,
National Research Council of Canada,
Building M-50, Montreal Rd.,
Ottawa, Ontario, Canada, K1A 0R6
web: www.nrc.ca/iit/SPIN_public
{abu-hakima, impey, liscano}@iit.nrc.ca

Abstract

The paper describes the design and implementation of a unique cooperative agents testbed intended for diverse applications in seamless personal information networking. The real-world SPIN^{TM1} testbed is aimed at two applications, namely seamless messaging and intelligent network management. Both are agent-driven and share agent behaviours. The messaging agents rely on the network management device diagnostic agents for input. The first generation of Seamless Messaging^{TM} is described in detail. It is user-centric and assumes heterogeneous communication environments intended to support today's nomadic users. A prototype is introduced for the management of messages across distributed information networks. Its aim is to intercept, filter, interpret, and deliver multi-modal messages be they voice, fax, video and/or e-mail messages. A user's Personal Communication Agent^{TM} (PCA) is charged with delivering messages to the recipient regardless of their target messaging device be it a telephone, a pager, a desktop, a wireless laptop or a wireless phone. PCAs classify and act on incoming messages based on their content. A Secretary Agent^{TM} routes and tailors urgent messages appropriately to the Device Manager Agent^{TM} which delivers the message to a device that the user may be roaming or active on. What makes Seamless Messaging unique is its approach to treating a message in a universal manner, its ability to mediate between different messaging environments and devices, and its capability of tracking and finding users.

1 Introduction

The intensely distributed workspaces of today require users to communicate and compute across heterogeneous networks and applications. The paper describes the design and implementation of a cooperative agents testbed for seamless personal information networking (SPIN). The SPIN testbed is aimed at two difficult applications, Seamless Messaging and Intelligent Network Management. In the remainder of the paper we describe: in section 2 what SPIN is about and why Seamless Networking requires

---

1. SPIN^{TM}, Personal Communication Agents^{TM}, Diagnostic Agents^{TM}, Message Watcher Agents^{TM}, Device Manager Agents^{TM}, Service Provider Agents^{TM}, Secretary Agents^{TM}, Universal Message Box ^{TM} and Seamless Messaging^{TM} are all trademarks of the National Research Council of Canada.

agents; in section 3 relevant work; in section 4 network management concepts; in section 5 seamless messaging concepts; in section 6 the first generation seamless messaging testbed prototype; and in section 7 future work and conclusions.

2 What is Seamless Personal Information Networking (SPIN)?

SPIN is the vision of personal information networking technologies that allow users to seamlessly interchange information in today's distributed workspaces how, when, where, and if they want to. The assumption is that every user has a unique and distributed workspace. In it, a user can have heterogeneous devices (telephones, computers), running on heterogeneous networks (wired, wireless, voice, data, multimedia) and all integrating a variety of heteregeneous applications (voice mail, email, fax, word processors, web browsers, electronic calendars, etc.).

Why do you need Agents in Seamless Networking?

Many reasons come to mind why agents are an ideal evolution of the traditional distributed computing paradigm for seamless networking. Agents are accepted as software entities that can act autonomously or with some guidance on the user or software system's behalf. Agents are active computational entities that are persistent, can perceive, reason and act in their environments and can communicate with other agents [Huhns and Singh 95]. Agents are ideal for applications that require some form of distributed intelligent cooperation.

Networks are inherently distributed hence making any centralized intelligent software function to support users unreliable. A centralized system will surely fail in a world with 2 billion telephones and over 125 million Internet users. Networks are managed through their partitioning into subnetworks. Thus, seamless networks designed to support user needs require distributed intelligent processes to manage them. In SPIN, we are addressing this need by developing Diagnostic Agents that live in network nodes.

Users require both heavyweight or complex reasoning processes in the form of personal assistants that can manage their computing and communication needs as well as lightweight or simple processes that can act as proxies on their behalf in the network. As a user roams from place to place, they require distributed support to access their information as the need arises. Active information processes embodied as agents can provide such support. Intelligent personal assistants that can act autonomously on a user's behalf are essential in dealing with the overflow of information arriving in a user's workspace. If the information is urgent, a user's personal communication assistant has to track the roaming user and deliver the key information content. This is only possible through customisation of personal agents. A personal agent must be created and empowered to find the user as the need arises.

IIT's Living Lab: SPIN's Real-World Multi-Agent System Testbed

For the SPIN vision to be achieved, a real-world networking environment must be used as the underlying environment for the agent testbed. At the Institute for Information Technology (IIT) we have set up the heterogeneous environment known as the IIT Living Lab. The idea behind the Living Lab is to allow agents to be created, to monitor themselves, to co-exist, to spin-off proxies and to be killed or expire when they have fulfilled their duties. Both the Seamless Messaging and the Intelligent Network Management application agents share the testbed. The intent is for the PCAs of the seamless messaging application to make use of the Diagnostic Agents (DAs) of the network management application. For example, if a PCA needs to forward information to a user device that is not responding it could ask the device DA or its parent DA 'why is the active user device not responding?'

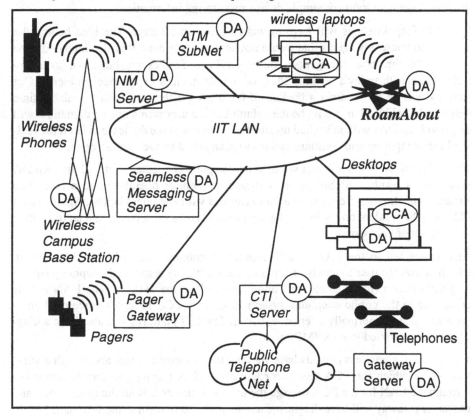

Fig. 1. The IIT Living Lab

Figure 1 illustrates the IIT Living Lab. It is centered around a typical enterprise LAN. The Institute LAN has daily operational and experimental traffic for an organization of over 100 users with hundreds of interconnected devices over seven subnetworks. Initially, we are launching the agents into the SPIN subnetwork which has over 30 desktop devices which are also accessible from home by dialing in. The SPIN subnetwork includes connected network devices such as printers, and routers. PCAs will typically reside on the user desktops.

In the case of a user with a number of desktops (the average at SPIN is three: two at the office and one at home), the user PCA can reside on a single device but monitor activity on the other devices. This will be possible through the DAs which will reside on every networked device and work as proxy agents of SNMP agents (SNMP is the Simple Network Management Protocol from the Internet Engineering Task Force). SNMP agents are fast becoming an Industry standard with any new network device [IETF references on SNMP are all on-line at www.ietf.org]. SNMP agents are very simple and function to place respective device information in a Management Information Base (MIB). The MIB is very much like a database that can be browsed by network management tools for simple device monitoring information.

Both SPIN applications will have agents resident on a server. The idea behind the server is to house any agents that would not be device resident. It is also intended to be the place for the persistent agents to be stored if user devices are shut down (as is typically done with today's desktop PCs) or if user devices experience problems. Our strategy will be to maintain a backup of the PCA for the user with a scalable time delay (a day-old backup would be the default but if a user wants one on demand it will be provided). DAs will be backed up similarly. Here we take the lessons from the real-world in computing and communications to plan ahead to avert catastrophe.

The IIT LAN has a RoamAbout wireless access point connected to it with its own DA proxy to its resident SNMP agent designed to monitor operation and access. The RoamAbout allows a user to walk around campus with a wireless laptop. Again, a user PCA may be resident on a wireless laptop or may send a PCA proxy to a laptop with a reduced set of behaviours.

Also connected to the LAN is a Computer Telephony Integration (CTI) platform which allows the user to receive telephone calls with any associated telephony signalling information (for example, incoming caller id) to the desktop. The LAN is thus connected to the public telephone system so that the PCA accesses voice mail environments that are normally telephone-driven. The CTI platform will also have a diagnostic agent proxied to its SNMP agent.

Furthermore, a wireless campus base station allows a user to roam about with a wireless phone which the PCA can also route calls to. A paging gateway is accessible through the LAN for the PCA to page the user as instructed. Both the base station and the pager gateway will have diagnostic agents attached to them to monitor their health. Proxy PCAs with simplified behaviours may be dispatched to a cellular phone or pager as long as the device can host it. For the devices to host a PCA proxy, we assume some processing capabilities on board. This will soon be facilitated to some extent as pager and wireless phone manufacturers deliver JAVA-enabled devices with JAVA virtual machines on board. In this manner, the PCA proxy implemented in JAVA can be hosted. At the moment JAVA-enabled pagers and wireless phones are not part of our testbed and we simply rely on device-compatible gateways to deliver text or voice information to the pager or cellular phone.

Finally, an Asynchronous Transfer Mode (ATM) switch allows the user access to high speed multimedia applications such as video on demand. Most ATM switches are now SNMP-enabled and thus our DA can work as a proxy to the switch's SNMP agent.

The IIT Living Lab makes an ideal testbed into which we have launched our seamless networking applications. The Living Lab's heterogeneous networks are essentially transparent to the user and are simply used by the personal communication agent to route user information as needed. The networks are also being managed by a set of diagnostic agents which share some behaviours with the personal communication agents. Furthermore, the PCAs rely on some of the monitoring information from the DAs to fulfil their obligations. Thus, in a *single* testbed, SPIN is ensuring the reusability of agent behaviours and the interoperability of two agent-based applications. This is a key aspect to our work which we believe is a goal for many researchers but is fairly rare if non existent in other multi agent system testbeds.

3 Relevant Work

Networks can be seen as a natural domain for the application of distributed artificial intelligence, and more particularly, agent-based computing technology [Reinhardt 94]. In particular, Weihmayer and Velthuijsen suggest a number of reasons for this, including their inherent distribution (e.g. along spatial, functional, and temporal lines), the proliferation of heterogeneous devices and services associated with them (this is particularly true of multi-vendor mixed computing-communications networks), the growing need for privacy, the sustained demands for high performance, and the increasing desire for "intelligence" in the network [Weihmayer and Velthuijsen 94].

Modelling messaging in organization services as a collection of coordinated agents results in a number of benefits. For example, a degree of virtual homogeneity is brought to otherwise heterogeneous networks of computer-telephony messaging services and devices (such as voice mail, e-mail or fax mail); relatedly, a more open network architecture facilitating more rapid and effective deployment of "plug and play" messaging services is made possible. All the same, the agent metaphor does not, in and of itself, directly resolve any of the technical issues related to system interoperability such as sharing remote resources, guaranteeing a particular quality of service or resolving the network feature interaction problem. Rather, as Laufmann points out in [Laufmann 94] "the metaphor provides a model of coordination that addresses real-world issues of the computing and communications marketplaces, and in so doing leverages the deployment of new technical solutions as they become available". In this respect, the *Seamless Messaging Personal Communication Agents and the Secretary agent* are analogous in scope and purpose to Laufmann's coarse-grained agents or CGAs [Laufmann 94]. The Diagnostic Agents can also be assumed to be CGAs.

These agents, like those supported by the Carnot project's Distributed Communicating Agents (DCA) tool [Huhns et al. 93], are essentially high-performance problem solvers which can be located anywhere within and among networked enterprise resources. These agents are intended to communicate and cooperate with each other, and with human agents. Through the use of models of other agents and resources within the enterprise, SPIN's agents, like DCA agents, will cooperate to provide integrated and coherent management of information in heterogeneous computing-communications environments [Huhns and Singh 95].

The convergence of networks and the need for personal digital assistants with embedded agents that interface to all the information accessible through a web of networks (Internet, World Wide Web, etc.) has also been cited as a key reason to develop cooperative multi-agent systems [Rosenschein and Zlotkin 94]. SM agents are being developed to enable users to share valuable messaging services such as voice and e-mail as if in a single seamless network across a variety of devices that include cellular phones, PDAs, wired telephones and wireless laptop computers.

The Multi-Agent Network Architecture (MANA) described in [Gray et al. 94; Abu-Hakima et al. 95] is designed to provide services across communication networks. In some ways, its objectives are similar to those of the concepts in Seamless Messaging. However, its agents are coarse-grained agents which are compiled at run-time and hence lack the flexibility to adapt as would be necessary in a seamless messaging environment. Personal Communication Agents will also be able to launch proxy PCAs as mobile agents which are fine-grained agents that are light weight specifically designed for reactive situated behaviour. THe MANA agents did not incorporate fine-grained agents mobile or static.

Bradshaw and his colleagues in describing KAoS (Knowledgeable Agent-oriented System) describe an open agent architecture that mirrors in its goals what SPIN is aiming for in its testbed [Bradshaw et al. 97]. The goal of the SPIN agent framework is not to take on monolithic reasoning capabilities but rather to tailor their behaviours to the context of their world. Thus, the personal communication agent of a user will aim to provide situated personalized functionality to the user while relying on other agents such as the Secretary agent and the Device Manager agent to provide more generic functionality. The PCA will also rely on the diagnostic agents of the network management application to provide monitoring information if the PCA fails to deliver required personal messaging information to the user. Furthermore, the PCA will rely on software modules that are mediated by an agent wrapper or that are accessible through open APIs (Application Programming Interfaces) to fulfil its responsibilities. For example, a PCA will not take on any computer-telephony functionality but will access the CTI server through a common application interface to gain knowledge about messaging information as it needs it. Thus, in one world, the agents are designed to rely on an open, mediated approach to gaining more functionality without taking it on. In some sense, this is what is known as *good old software engineering* where a system is partitioned carefully to maximize the use of generic blocks of code with well-defined interfaces rather than repeating the blocks for each instantiation.

Jim White of General Magic Inc. introduced TeleScript and its Magic Links with mobile agents in the mid 1980s [White 97]. SPIN in many ways is aiming for some of the functionality that White described in allowing users to be mobile and have information that can roam on their behalf in the form of mobile agents. TeleScript and the Magic Links did not succeed as they assumed a closed world that did not interoperate with much of the user's workspace (the telephone being the most obvious example). SPIN is quite focused on user-centric computing and communications. The vision starts from the user workspace and works outwards. We do not assume that we can force the user to buy special purpose PDAs to acquire seamless messaging. We insist on making use of Industry and commonly accepted standards and good user practices. We recognize that for the vision to succeed, we must adopt the user's constraints and recognize that each user has a unique and individual workspace. This is why the PCAs are highly personalized to the user's workspace and habits. The PCAs also assume a very open world with no borders and take it on as a challenge to address user-centric requirements rationally. This is by no means an easy problem. We also believe that General Magic continues their valuable vision with more open languages and platforms.

4. SPIN's Network Management Application

What is NM?

Network Management (NM) is typically achieved in today's complex environments through a Network Control Centre NCC). The NCC has five primary functions: administration, planning, operations, security, and application development.

- The Administration-related functions concentrate on the policy and procedures of the organization and their reflection in the implemented network. A key administrative function is **accounting** for both the network resources and its use.
- The Planning-related functions include the design and the evolution of the network. Initially, the network is designed with a certain margin (sometimes 50%) for growth. The network is continuously evaluated and its capacity monitored for expansion.
- The Operations-related functions are the primary concern of a network manager, mainly to "keep the network running" for the users. Operations include **monitoring** events, **trending** the performance of the network, **fault recovery**, taking configuration actions when needed, issuing trouble tickets, the provision of a help desk and providing technical support when needed.
- The *Security-related* functions include maintaining the integrity of the data on the network and putting in place procedures to prevent a breach of the network by unwanted intruders (or hackers).
- NCC functions often include some specialized activities that are Application Development-related. These may include setting up electronic mail, specialized databases or workflow management software such as Lotus Notes.

The five activities that are included in the five layers of the network management standard are accounting, monitoring, performance trending, fault recovery and security.

(These are shown in boldface in the text above.) Many vendors developing network management tools strive to include these five key functions in their products.

Where SPIN agents fit into NM?

SPIN's strategy is to make use of the adopted Industry standard known as SNMP. Through the SNMP agents, we are developing proxy diagnostic Agents (DAs) that can monitor a device and provide some self-healing functionality. The DAs have both a peer-to-peer and an adopted parent DA relationship. In a future paper we will provide greater detail on the NM agents in the SPIN MAS testbed.

5 SPIN's Seamless Messaging Application

What is SM?

Seamless Messaging provides users with the capability to work freely in distributed personal workspaces. It allows the creation, encoding, filtering and delivery of messages across heterogeneous networks. Thus, users can seamlessly deliver voice or electronic mail to wireless or wired mail environments. For example, a user can send a multimedia e-mail from a laptop computer and have it received by a voice-only cellular phone which is the recipient's currently active device. The SM paradigm requires that the recipient of the message be located through an electronic secretary and the message be tailored to the recipient's active device user interface. As such, SM is not an easy endeavour.

Where agents fit into SM?

Each user can customize a Personal Communication Agent (PCA) through a PCA launch tool. This tool allows the user to tailor PCA behaviours in terms of classifying and acting on incoming messages from email, voice mail, fax, and video mail environments. In addition, an event-driven Message Watcher agent is triggered on the arrival of any messages. It routes the messages to the respective PCA which may call on the services of a Secretary agent to find the user. Furthermore, a Device Manager agent can tailor a message to the target user device be it a cell phone, pager, desktop, etc.

6 First Generation Seamless Messaging Prototype in Agent Testbed

6.1 Seamless Messaging Application Requirements

Seamless Messaging must: manage both asynchronous and isochronous (where immediate access to the user must be established) messaging, be easily customized by the end user, and be modular enough allowing features to be easily added or removed. For asynchronous messaging, a universal message box that can handle multi-modal messages is maintained. Thus, in a single unified view, the user can examine a list of any incoming voice mail, email, fax or video messages. Voice mail and fax messages in the list show the number of the caller, their organization (if caller id can pick it up) and an icon which can be selected to hear the voice mail or view the fax. Isochronous messaging requires immediate delivery of the message to the roaming user and the possibility of establishing a connection in the case of voice calls. Figure 2 provides a high level view and the flow of information between the seamless messaging agents. Note that there are 2 paths for a message to take, either into the universal message box if it is asynchronous (connectionless) or directly connected through the Device Manager Agent to the output device for isochronous communications. The event loop is used to control the flow of communication between the agents.

The Seamless Messaging application is based on five sets of generic agent behaviours: the *Message Watcher*, the *Personal Communication Agent*, the *Secretary*, the *Service Provider* and the *Device Manager*. The *Message Watcher Agent* is designed as an event monitor as in a typical blackboard approach that waits for incoming messages and formulates these messages into a unified representation for the system to process. The *Personal Communication Agents* are designed to act based on a set of user speci- fied constraints that the PCA interprets as rules at runtime. Note that the constraints are customizable at any point while the seamless messaging application is running. The user can even telephone the system and get into a dialogue with an automated speech interface to the PCA to modify their messaging requirements. The *Secretary* agent cooperates with the PCA to find the user to act on a message where the user has instructed the PCA action behaviour to 'contact or find me'. The *Service Provider Agents* fulfil specialized behaviours in transforming messages from one form to another (for example, text-to-speech). Finally, the *Device Manager* Agent delivers the message by invoking its appropriate device driver behaviour and passing it the tai- lored information for delivery to the user's active device.

6.2 Workflow

The *Event Loop* is used to illustrate that the agents communicate by placing inter- agent message blocks into a common area that other agents have access to. Message blocks contain an identification tag which triggers the appropriate recipient agent to take the message out of the common area and interpret it. The system is easily extended by defining a new agent and the type of messages the agent should respond to. Although conceptually any agent can communicate with another on the *Event Loop*, in reality the workflow is constrained.

The system is triggered by an event in the form of a message arrival (a message can be email, fax, voice mail, etc.). The workflow is initiated by the *Message Watcher Agent* which places a control block on the *Event Loop* together with the identification tag that will indicate the next operation to be performed on the message. Normally, the identification tag will trigger the PCA *Classifier* behaviour to read the control block and retrieve the required information about the message.

The *Classifier* formats a new control block which it places on the *Event Loop* indicat- ing the message has been successfully classified. The next step by the PCA is taken by the *Action Definer* which defines the action to be performed based on the class of the message. Again, a new control block is created by the *Action Definer* and placed on the *Event Loop*. This time the *Secretary* agent is triggered whose role is to interpret any of the actions associated with the message. There will be some situations where the *Secretary* may not have sufficient information to process the message, for example when the message is of an *urgent* type and the user must be located. In this case additional resources are required to help find the user[1].

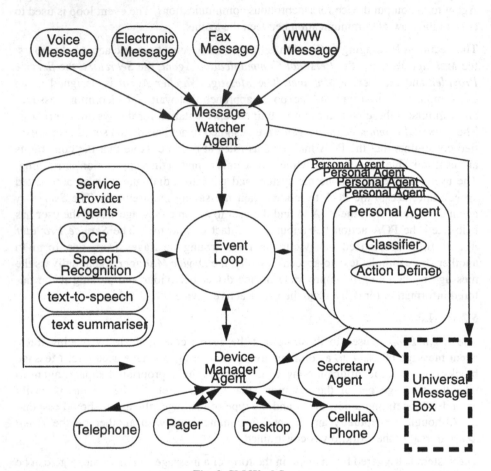

Fig. 2. SM Workflow

Once the *Secretary Agent* determines what device the message should be targeted to, a control block is created and placed on the *Event Loop* to trigger the *Device Manager Agent* to determine what device to use to contact the user. The device driver may need

---

1. A PeopleFinder agent has been implemented that can help find the user but it is out of the scope of this paper. It extends the work by [Ferguson and Davlouros 95].

to tailor the body of the message into an appropriate format for the physical device. For example, if the message is text only and the target device is only able to handle voice, (i.e. a telephony device), some text to speech conversion must be carried out. In this case it may be necessary to invoke one of the *Service Provider agents* to perform a mapping of the message into another format.

6.3 Personalizing the System

This particular system contains three personalization functions: *Classifier and Action Definer behaviours* associated with the PCA, and a *Secretary* agent. The end user personalizes the system by specifying his/her desires to constrain the PCA and the Secretary agents.

6.3.1 PCA Classifier Behaviour

The *Classifier's* role is to look through an incoming message and classify the message as instructed by the user. The user can define any number and any type of classes for a message along with a set of rules that helps determine if the message fits the defined class type.

The general structure of the rules is as follows:
DEFINE class_name AS
    ((attribute [operator] value)
    OR (attribute [operator] value).....
    AND ((attribute [operator] value)
    OR (attribute [operator] value)...)
    ...

In this example, the class_name will be associated with the messages that evaluate the expression after the keyword AS to TRUE. This expression is composed of a number of (attribute [operator] value) sets connected by Boolean operators. The currently available attributes are sender, recipients, number of recipients, date received, number of lines, subject, message body, and other defined classes. The operators available are =, !=,), >=, <, >. Obviously, not all are applicable to all fields, and the operator meaning can differ. For example, "number of recipients = 2" means an equality, whereas "body = 'this is an example'" means "body contains 'this is an example'".

6.3.2 PCA Action Definer Behaviour

The *Action Definer's* role is to take a classified message and attach to that message an action to be performed on the message. Specification of the type of action to be performed to the message is similar to that done for the classifier agent, i.e. as a set of rules that map classes of messages to actions.

A typical example of a rule has the following form,

IF class_name

ACTION (action_1, action_2, ..., action_n).

Which specifies that if a message has been classified as class_name perform actions (action_1, action_2, ..., action_n).

Actions are divided into 2 types: direct and subjective actions. Direct actions are actions that can be resolved directly by the *Device Manager Agent* and require little or no interpretation. These actions can be serviced directly by the *Device Manager Agent*. Subjective actions require more interpretation and therefore are processed by the *Secretary Agent* before being serviced by the *Device Manager*. Examples of these two types of actions are the following, "phone_me '276-2389'" is a typical direct action, while "contact_me" is a subjective action requiring further interpretation. These more abstract subjective actions are open to interpretation and are contextually interpreted based on the situated belief of the user's availability.

6.3.3 Electronic Secretary Agent

The *Secretary* agent's role is to act upon any of the actions attached to a message. The *Secretary* must first decide the type of action the message has, is it a direct or a subjective action. If it is a direct action then it can be passed directly to the *Device Manager Agent* so it can process the message. If the message has the subjective action then the *Secretary* has to interpret the action. An example of this is the *contact_me* action.

The *contact_me* action requires the Secretary to use whatever resources are at its disposal to determine where the user may be. At the moment it uses a unique hierarchical scheduling structure to determine the availability of the user. The scheduling concept uses a three tier hierarchy representing three abstractions of time management. Commencing from a default description of a user's typical day (e.g. 9-5 Workday), to a more refined blocked-off scheduled events (e.g. 10-12 talk, 2-4 meeting), to finally a set of temporary changes which reflect the instant picture of where the user is located (e.g. 11-12:30 John's Office). The more detailed temporary changes take precedence over the user's scheduled events which in turn take precedence over the default day. Note that temporary events can be called and recorded by the PCA to dynamically alter the user's availability.

6.4 Mediating the Devices: the Device Manager Agent

Devices are mediated using the *Device Manager* whose primary role is to determine the appropriate manner to deliver a message to a particular user device. This agent can use any of the available services from the *Service Provider Agents* to map a message to a particular format suitable for the device. Currently the system can call on two *Service Providers* for two types of mapping, a text-to-speech conversion (which is performed directly by the Computer Telephony server) and a text filter or summarizer trained on particular feature sets of a message. The later is used to interpret text messages and deliver them to a pager which is constrained by the number of text characters it can accept.

6.5 The Message Filter Agent: Text Summarizer

Electronic mail messages commonly have a subject line. However, sometimes the subject line is not descriptive enough for summarizing the objective of the full message. Keyphrases extracted directly from the message provide a useful starting point for releasing the objective of the message. Thus, an individual who receives many e-mail messages daily and does not have the time to look at them all immediately selects those of relative importance to read first. Keyphrases from the message are helpful in guiding the user in ranking their email. Furthermore, forwarding an e-mail message to a device with low bandwidth such as a pager requires a set of keyphrases since a pager can only display a limited number of characters (maximum is ~160 characters!). The goal of the *Text Summariser Agent* is to be a text e-mail filter to filter out keyphrases that can reflect the content of the message.

Let us examine the system level design of the e-mail filter [Sin 96]. First, *human judgement* in the form of user input is used to pick up keyphrases manually from the e-mail message. The same e-mail message is then passed to the e-mail filter, which extracts keyphrases automatically. These *automatic keyphrases* are then compared to the *manually selected keyphrases*. The ultimate goal is to make the automatic keyphrases more or less equivalent to the manually selected keyphrases, so that human judgement can be replaced by the e-mail filter [to try out the keyphrase extractor go to: http://www.nrc.ca/iit/II_public/demos].

6.6 Implementation of Seamless Messaging

The system has been implemented using Lotus Notes as the underlying development environment [Gordon 96; Yu 96; Sin 96]. The system, as currently implemented, can manage both voice and e-mail messages. Electronic mail messaging is a typical example of asynchronous communications and e-mails are therefore immediately stored into the Universal Message Box and processed. If a message is categorized to be immediately delivered to the end-user, the system takes the action to actively deliver the message through a pager, a telephone (using text to speech), fax, or by forwarding it to another e-mail address. Any message that is not categorized to be delivered to the user is kept in the Universal Message Box and can be retrieved, via the telephone or using an email client on a workstation. Voice calls are an example of isochronous communication and are not immediately forwarded to the Universal Message Box. Instead the incoming call is classified and delivered immediately to a device that can manage isochronous voice communications by connecting the calling party to the user in real-time. If this is not possible a voice message is taken and stored in the Universal Message Box. The voice message appears in the list of user messages and is manipulated in a manner similar to e-mail. The first generation has been actively in use as of 1996.

7 Future Work and Conclusions

Our future work will include the full implementation of the Network Management agents and the second generation seamless messaging prototype. The second prototype will introduce more complex behaviours to the PCA that would include reasoning based on more complex structures. This would allow the end user to state in simple terms more complex directives about managing their messages. We also recognize the need for a PCA firewall to protect it from being snooped on by other PCAs or by external Service Providers who may wish to target market messaging services based on user preferences. We are also working on a PCA launch tool that would incorporate more GUI support for the user's definition of classification and action rules.

We believe Seamless Personal Information Networking presents a complex real-world problem to the agents community. We are developing a single unified testbed that incorporates diverse agent applications with shared behaviours and cooperative reasoning. Our emphasis is on the use of off the shelf computing and communications components in unison with the agent paradigm which provides an additional challenge to our work.

Acknowledgments

We would like to acknowledge the full SPIN team at NRC. We would also like to acknowledge our collaborators in the Mobile Agents Alliance at the University of Ottawa and Mitel Corporation. Finally, we would like to acknowledge Nortel Ltd. for their support with the wireless PCS 1900 BTS and their ATM Passport switch.

References

Abu-Hakima S., Liscano R., and Impey R., [1996] "Cooperative agents that adapt for seamless messaging in heteregeneous communication networks," IJCAI-96 Workshop on Intelligent Adaptive Agents, August 4, 1996, Portland, Oregon, Technical Report WS-96-04, AAAI Press, Menlo Park, California, pp.94-103.

S. Abu-Hakima, I. Ferguson, N. Stonelake, E. Bijman, and R. Deadman. [1995], A Help Desk Application for Sharing Resources Across High Speed Networks Using a Multi-Agent architecture. Proceedings of the workshop on AI in Distributed Information Networks, IJCAI-95, Montreal, Quebec, August 19, 1995. pp. 1-9.

J.M. Bradshaw, S. Dutfield, P. Benoit, and J. D. Woolley, [1997] "KAoS: Toward an Industrial-Strength Open Agent Architecture", Chapter 17, Software Agents, AAAI / MIT Press.

I. Ferguson and J. Davlouros, [1995] On Establishing Multi-Sensory Multi-Channel Communications Among Networked Users. Proceedings of the workshop on AI in Distributed Information Networks, IJCAI-95, Montreal, Quebec.

Gordon, P. [1996] "Message Handling Application", NRC Work Term Report.

T. Gray, E. Peres, D. Pinard, S. Abu-Hakima, A. Diaz, and I. Ferguson. [1994] A Multi-Agent Architecture for Enterprise Applications. In *Working Notes AAAI-94 Workshop on Artificial Intelligence in Business Process Re-engineering*, Seattle WA, July 1994, pp. 65-72. NRC 37140.

M.N. Huhns, and M.P. Singh, [1995] Cooperative Information Systems, IJCAI-95 tutorial Notes, August 21, 1995, Montreal, Quebec, Canada, 68 pages.

M.N. Huhns, N. Jacobs, T. Ksiezyk, W. Shen, M. Singh, and P.E. Cannata. [1993] Integrating Enterprise Information Models in Carnot. In *Proceedings of the First International Conference on Intelligent and Cooperative Information Systems*.

Laufmann, S. [1994] The Information Marketplace: The Challenge of Information Commerce. In *Proc. of the Second International Conference on Cooperative Information Systems*, May, 1994, pp. 147-157.

A. Reinhardt. [1994] The Network with Smarts. *Byte*, October, 1994 pp. 51-64.

J.S. Rosenschein and G. Zlotkin. [1994] Designing Conventions for Automated Negotiation. *AI Magazine* 15(3), 1994, pp. 29-46.

Sin, E., [1996] "Filtering eMail Using Keyphrase Extraction", NRC Student Report.

R. Weihmayer and H. Velthuijsen. [1994] Application of Distributed AI and Cooperative Problem Solving to Telecommunications. In *Proc. of the International Workshop on Distributed Artificial Intelligence*, Lake Quinault WA, July 1994.

J. White, [1997] "Mobile Agents", Ch. 19, Software Agents, AAAI / MIT Press.

Yu Q., [1996] "Seamless Message Handling Application", NRC Student Report.

A Hybrid Genetic Algorithm for the Vehicle Routing Problem with Time Windows

Jean Berger, Martin Salois and Regent Begin

Defence Research Establishment Valcartier, Decision Support Technology Section
2459 Pie-XI Blvd. North, Val-Bélair, PQ, Canada, G3J 1X5
email: jean.berger@drev.dnd.ca

Abstract. A variety of hybrid genetic algorithms has been recently proposed to address the vehicle routing problem with time windows (VRPTW), a problem known to be NP-hard. However, very few genetic-based approaches exploit implicit knowledge provided by the structure of the intermediate solutions computed during the evolutionary process to explore the solution space. This paper presents a new hybrid genetic algorithm for VRPTW. It investigates the impact of using explicitly domain knowledge and a priori knowledge/characteristics about expected solutions during the recombination and mutation phases of the algorithm. Basic principles borrow from recent hybrid and standard genetic algorithms, and features of well-known heuristics to drive the search process. Designed to support time-constrained reasoning tasks, the procedure is intended to be conceptually simple, easy to implement and allow fast computation of near-optimal solution. A computational experiment has been conducted to compare the performance of the proposed algorithm with similar and standard techniques.

1   Introduction

In the vehicle routing problem with time windows [1,2], a set of customers with specific demands is serviced by a homogeneous fleet of vehicles of limited capacity, initially located at a central depot. Routes are assumed to start and end at the central depot. Each customer provides a time period in which they require service, consisting in a particular task to be completed such as repair work or loading/unloading the vehicle. Hard time window constraints impose customer service to be initiated within a predetermined specific time interval. It is worth noticing that the time window requirement does not prevent any vehicle from waiting at a customer location before servicing, even though opportunistic waiting implicitly incurs a penalty in route cost. The primary objective is to minimize the number of tours or routes, then the total route (travel and waiting) time such that each customer is serviced in its time window and, the total load on any vehicle associated with a given route does not exceed vehicle capacity.

A variety of algorithms including exact methods and efficient heuristics have already been proposed for VRPTW [1,2]. However, recent performance shown by some metaheuristics and evolutionary approaches, such as genetic algorithms [3,4] and tabu search [5,6] relying on stochastic-based search techniques to explore the solution space, make these techniques extremely promising [7-11]. The problem-solving methodology of genetic-based algorithms has definitely been one of the most suitable approaches to tackle the VRPTW [7-10] so far. The algorithm proposed by Blanton and Wainwright [10] consists in encoding individuals by representing a chromosome as a sequence of customers. Search is driven toward suitable orderings of customers based upon precedence relationship (temporal, spatial, mixed) as well as a fixed a priori global precedence order defined over customer time window lower bounds. Genetic operators are proposed to generate new customer sequences or orderings from previous ones. The decoding procedure relies on a greedy heuristics reminiscent of the bin-packing algorithm, in which ordered customers from the chromosome are successively inserted in the solution. On the other hand, the approach proposed by Thangiah [8,9] relies on an alternate two-phase process, namely customer clustering and cluster-based customer routing. Customer clustering uses a genetic-based method in which individuals encoding (chromosome) are represented by a sequence of neighboring sectors originating from the central depot and describing respectively clusters of customers. Local cluster-based customer routing is then achieved using a particular heuristic. As for the algorithm proposed by Potvin [7], it mainly relies on the basic principles of genetic algorithms disregarding explicit solution encoding issues for problem representation. Genetic operators are simply applied to a population of solutions as opposed to a population of encoded solutions (chromosomes). The search is mainly driven by heuristic information about the problem domain. The evolution of the population is achieved considering the best features shown by parent solutions.

The classical genetic algorithm paradigm primarily operates at the encoding level (chromosomes) and therefore do not exploit explicitly any useful information about a particular problem domain. In counterpart, hybrid genetic algorithms [4] attempt to make use of particular knowledge of the problem domain to drive the search process, as illustrated by some of the recent methods described earlier for VRPTW. However, we conjecture that most of the genetic-based algorithms proposed for this problem do not capture enough explicit domain knowledge and a priori knowledge/characteristics about expected solutions that tend to possibly improve the search process. The contribution of such knowledge to the selection of favorable domain-dependent strategies might contribute to explore more efficiently the solution space, while speeding-up the generation of near-optimal solutions, a desirable property to achieve time-constrained reasoning.

In this paper a new hybrid genetic algorithm for VRPTW is proposed. It investigates the impact of using explicitly domain knowledge and a priori knowledge/characteristics about expected solutions, during the recombination and mutation phases of the algorithm. Basic principles borrow from recent hybrid and standard genetic algorithms and features of well-known heuristics to drive the search process. Designed to support time-constrained reasoning tasks, the procedure is intended to be conceptually simple, easy to implement and allow fast computation of near-optimal solution. Despite the fact that the algorithms are neither admissible nor complete, we contend that the proposed technique is well suited to support time-constrained reasoning tasks, involving limited computational resources.

The paper is outlined as follows. Section 2 introduces the basic concepts of genetic algorithms. It describes the general principles of the technique and then presents preliminary observations about an early investigation of the method for VRPTW. An overview of the proposed hybrid genetic algorithm is then given. The main features of the procedure are briefly presented with a special emphasis on the recombination and mutation operators. Then, in Section 3, we present the results of a computational experiment to assess the value of the proposed approach. The performance of the method is compared with similar and standard techniques, and the strengths and weaknesses of the algorithm are briefly discussed. Finally, we conclude with a short summary in Section 4.

2   Genetic Algorithm Approach

2.1   General Principles

A genetic algorithm [3,4] is an evolutionary computation technique inspired from the principles of natural selection to search a solution space. It evolves a population of individuals encoded as chromosomes by creating new generations of offsprings through an iterative process until some convergence criteria or conditions are met. Such criteria might, for instance, refer to a maximum number of generations or the convergence to a homogeneous population composed of similar individuals. The best chromosome generated is then decoded, providing the corresponding solution. The underlying reproduction process is mainly aimed at improving the fitness of individuals; a measure of profit, utility or goodness to be maximized while exploring the solution space.

The creation of a new generation of individuals involve primarily four major steps or phases: representation, selection, recombination (crossover) and mutation. The representation of the solution space consists in encoding salient features of a solution as a chromosome (chromosome encoding), defining an individual member of a population. Typically pictured by a bit string, a chromosome is made up of a sequence of genes which capture the basic characteristics of a solution. The evolution of the encoded solutions or population members is driven by the selection, recombination and mutation phases, respectively. The selection phase consists in choosing randomly two parent individuals from the population for mating purposes. The probability of selecting a population member (parent) is generally proportional to its fitness in order to emphasize genetic quality while maintaining genetic diversity. Biased toward the best chromosomes, selection is aimed at propagating good solution features from one generation to the next. The recombination or reproduction process propagates genes of selected parents to produce offsprings that will form the next generation. It combines characteristics of chromosomes (parent solutions) to potentially create offsprings with a better fitness. As for mutation, it consists in randomly modifying gene(s) of a single individual at a time to further explore the solution space and ensure, or preserve, genetic diversity. The occurrence of mutation is generally associated with a low probability. A new generation is created by repeating the selection, reproduction and mutation processes until all chromosomes in the new population replace those from the old one. A proper balance between genetic quality and diversity is therefore required within the population in order to support efficient search.

2.2 Preliminary Observations

A preliminary investigation of some variants of the known genetic-based techniques has been conducted for VRPTW in order to identify their strengths and weaknesses. An extension of the algorithm proposed in [10] to further exploit data distribution of the problem instance was first explored. It consisted in generating various customer orderings, considering several a priori precedence relationships based upon time window lower and upper bounds, as well as statistical distribution over the distance separating two customers for a problem instance. The generalized precedence ordering scheme was randomly used in concert with specialized recombination operators. A particular ordering selection was based on a probability distribution reflecting the data distribution of the problem instance. As a result, the extended procedure outperformed the original algorithm, the introduction of additional domain and problem structure knowledge consistently improving the quality of the computed solution. The next observation relates to the importance of encoding schemes, as illustrated by the quality of results obtained using different approaches [7-10]. Comparative results show that encoding strategies can play a key role in the quality of the computed solution, and/or its convergence rate. However, given that suitable and proper encoding for VRPTW may be extremely complex to achieve, it appears that traditional explicit encoding might not necessarily represent an absolute requirement to design very efficient genetic-based techniques as shown in [7]. Similarly to the work reported in [7], the approach proposed in this paper overlooks explicit encoding issues.

The last observation refers to Potvin's work [7] in which some genetic operators can be very costly, and therefore can significantly impair the performance of the algorithm. In effect, the attempt to build a feasible route by connecting two route segments from two parent solutions while successfully inserting unrouted customers during the recombination phase can be very time-consuming. The failure to insert unrouted customers being very likely, alternate parent solutions need to be repeatedly examined until a feasible child solution can be generated. Local search performed in the mutation phase may be quite prohibitive as well. In the latter case, an iterative procedure repetitively attempts to move around several sequences of customers with various cardinality, and resorts to a potentially expensive repair procedure to perform local optimization. Consequently, special attention must be paid to the cost of search and methods used, such as repair procedures and, in a lesser extent, local optimization techniques to find feasible solutions if a tradeoff between solution quality and run-time computation is a primary concern for a targeted application.

2.3 Hybrid Genetic Algorithm

Designed to support time-constrained reasoning tasks related to VRPTW, the procedure is intended to be conceptually simple, easy to implement and allow fast computation of a near-optimal solution. The proposed algorithm uses explicitly domain knowledge and a priori knowledge/characteristics about expected solutions during the recombination and mutation phases. It borrows from recent hybrid and standard genetic algorithms, and also includes features of well-known heuristics to drive the search process. Typical a priori knowledge about an expected solution involving route-based and customer-based characteristics, include:

- waiting time and total route distance are minimum
- average travel time and variance amongst route customers tend to be minimum
- nearest customers (aggregate) tend to be part of the same route
- customers with a large number of close neighbors can be inserted in multiple routes
- customers with large/narrow service time window are easier/harder to schedule
- early/late route customers are scheduled earlier/later over their service time window
- a lower bound on the number of routes necessary (based on vehicle capacity and customer demand) can be computed
- small routes (small number of customers) tend to be merged within larger routes
- remote route customers tend to be inserted in nearest routes (route centroids)
- average and variance (distribution) of: service time, time window parameters (lower, upper bounds and length), travel time (customer distance)
- average travel time (between two customers) over average time window ratio

This knowledge is used to derive/design new strategy knowledge, in order to select routes or customers of parent solutions to be recombined or modified, namely:

- select routes of parent solution with the largest waiting time
- select a route neighborhood from the second parent for mating considerations
- select route customers (to be moved) of parent solution with:
    the largest waiting time
    large time window
    large slack time (deadline - effective service time)
    the largest travel time to its immediate (route customer) neighbors

The proposed approach consists in defining a suite/family/sequence of route-based genetic operators based on this knowledge, as well as features of well-known heuristics to drive the search process. Restricted to customer nodes specified through the routes of the mating parent solutions, a heuristic is locally applied during the recombination and mutation phases, to incrementally build feasible routes at low cost. The use of a heuristic is coupled to a random customer removal procedure, reminiscent of the principles of the simulated annealing technique, to further explore the search space and escape local minima. Some of the heuristics being investigated include features of insertion-based techniques [12] and the nearest-neighbor procedure. The proposed hybrid genetic algorithm has been built on top of the GAlib [13] genetic algorithm library and implemented in C++.

Representation. A solution is represented by a set of feasible routes, an individual being implicitly encoded as a chromosome formed of multiple segments. A chromosome segment (sequence of genes) represents a feasible route, referring to a sequence of customers to be visited by a vehicle. A segment is delimited by two separators to specify the related route. Admissible genes are therefore defined by indexed customers and separator symbols.

$$/C_3C_4C_2C_{11}C_5/ \ C_1C_9C_8C_{10}/ \ C_{12}C_6C_7/...////$$
$$/---- \text{Route 1} ----/--- \text{Route 2} ---/- \text{Route 3} -/...////$$

Fig. 1. Chromosome encoding

A chromosome encoding is shown in Figure 1. It illustrates a string of symbols involving indexed customers (C_i) as well as separator (/) occurrences. A maximum number of separator occurrences can easily be determined (upper bound on the maximum number of routes, e.g. the number of vehicles available) to ensure a fixed chromosome length for each individual (solution).

Selection. The selection process consists in choosing two individuals (parent solutions) within the population for mating purposes. The selection procedure is stochastic and biased toward the best solutions using a roulette-wheel scheme [3]. In this scheme, the probability to select an individual is proportional to its fitness. Delayed to the completion of a new generation, an individual fitness is computed as follows:

$$\text{fitness}_i = R_i - R_{min} + \min \ \{D_i, 2D_{min}\}/D_{min} . \qquad (1)$$

where

R_i: number of routes in solution i

R_{min}: number of routes of the best solution in the current population

D_i: total traveled distance associated with solution i

D_{min}: total traveled distance associated with the best solution in the current population

The proposed fitness expression indicates that better solutions include fewer routes, and then involve smaller total traveled distance.

Recombination. The insertion-based (IB_X) crossover operator creates an offspring by combining iteratively various routes r_1 of a parent solution P_1 with a subset of customers, formed by r_1 nearest-neighbor routes from parent solution P_2. Using criteria based on a priori domain and expected solution characteristics knowledge, a removal procedure is first carried out to remove from r_1 some key customer nodes believed (mostly subject to a priori knowledge) to be suitably relocated within some alternate routes. These customer nodes will further be visited for insertion in future route constructions of the child solution. Then an insertion-based routing heuristic inspired from [12] is locally applied to incrementally build a feasible route at low cost, considering the modified partial route r_1 as the initial solution. A standard heuristic [12] is coupled to a random customer acceptance procedure, in order to insert one of the best candidate customers on the route. For each new customer insertion to the partial route, the random acceptance method successively examines the sequence of best candidate nodes determined during the current iteration of the standard heuristic, until one is inserted. The method includes principles somewhat reminiscent of the simulated annealing technique to further explore search space, and escape local minima. Once a route construction is completed, the overall process is repeated for a random number of different routes r_1 of P_1. The child then inherits the remaining altered routes of P_1, if necessary, and any unrouted customers simply form additional one-customer routes. The process can be reiterated to generate a second child by interchanging P_1 and P_2.

The proposed insertion-based (IB_X) crossover operator includes the following steps:

Step 1   Select a random number of routes of P_1 to be visited.

   Step 2

        Repeat

    2.1   Select randomly a new route r_1 (chromosome segment) from P_1 (chromosome) according to a certain criterion. Probability for route selection is proportional to its relative total waiting time.

    2.2   Select a subset RS2 of routes from P_2 located in the neighborhood of r_1. Neighboring routes of r_1 are determined by routes of P_2 whose centroids are located within a certain range of r_1 (centroid). This range primarily determines the number of routes of P_2 to be considered.

    2.3   Remove some customers from r_1 using a specific customer removal procedure.

    2.4   Build a route child solution: apply an insertion-based routing heuristic considering the modified route r_1 as the initial partial solution and the pool of customers formed by the routes of RS2 and possibly already visited (but unrouted) customers.

             Insertion of unrouted but already visited customers will be examined again when building the next route.

    2.5   Inserted nodes are then removed from the remaining subset of routes of P_1 to be visited.

        Until (the selected random number of routes of P_1 has been visited).

Step 3   Inherits the remaining unvisited routes of P_1 (if any) while eliminating customers already routed.

Step 4   For each remaining unrouted customer (if any), build a new one-customer route.

As mentioned in step 2.2, the neighboring routes of r_1 are determined by routes of P_2 whose centroids are located within a certain range of r_1 (centroid). This range is primarily determined by the average distance separating r_1 from its neighbor P_2 routes. A distance measure between two routes is defined by the Euclidean distance or the travel time separating their respective centroid. A route centroid corresponds to a virtual site or customer whose coordinates refer to the average position of its specific routed customers.

The stochastic customer removal procedure indicated in step 2.3 involves three kinds of knowledge from which strategies are defined. The related approaches consist in removing either randomly specific customers, rather distant customers from their successors (or alternately from route centroid) based on average route successors distance, or customers with waiting times (or alternately large time windows) above route customer average. Strategies are chosen randomly by the removal procedure based on a user-defined a priori probability distribution. This step is first aimed at moving candidate customer nodes subject to be relocated, and therefore create better opportunities for alternate key node insertions.

The insertion-based routing heuristic used in step 2.4 mainly exploits some features of the method proposed in [12]. Limited to the construction of a single route for the child solution, the procedure considers the modified route r_1 (step 2.3) as the initial partial solution and restricts the set of customers to be explored to RS2 (step 2.2) as well as already visited (but unrouted) customers. The procedure inserts one customer at a time. Accordingly, it determines for each candidate customer left, the best possible location to be inserted, and then the best one to be added next to the partial route. The best possible location for a candidate customer is evaluated using domain knowledge criteria characterized by various adjustable parameters [12]. Parameters of the routing heuristic are selected randomly for each crossover execution. As for the insertion of the best candidate customer per se, an embedded random acceptance procedure is used. The probabilistic method successively examines the sequence of best candidate nodes determined during the current iteration until one is inserted. The probability for node insertion follows a periodic pattern, in which a schedule governing a linearly non-decreasing function determines a probability value over a given number of generations (period). If the best customer node to be inserted is rejected, the second best is then considered and, then the third, and so forth. A successful customer is eventually inserted. The procedure tends to create room for alternate customers, by rejecting best customer nodes to be inserted, and therefore escape local minima. The whole process (next customer insertion) is then repeated until no more customer can be inserted.

Mutation. The mutation operator is aimed at reducing the number of routes of solutions having only a few customers, and/or, evolving routes or escaping local minima by locally reordering customers. Three mutation operators are proposed namely, IB_M, NNR_M and DCR_M.

The insertion-based (IB_M) mutation operator attempts to move customers from the smaller route(s) (small number of customers) of a solution, to alternate existing routes, using the insertion-based routing technique described earlier. Alternate routes for customer insertion are randomly visited. The operator can be summarized as follows:

Step 1   Select the smallest route(s) of a solution.
Step 2   For each customer of the selected route do
2.1   Repeat
2.1.1   An alternate route is randomly examined for customer insertion.
2.1.2   Try to relocate/insert the related customer using the insertion-based routing technique described above.
           Until (customer insertion OR all available routes have been unsuccessfully examined).

The nearest neighbor-based reordering (NNR_M) mutation operator attempts to reorder customers by applying locally the nearest-neighbor procedure [14] to each route of the targeted solution. The scheme is aimed at evolving the solution on a local basis, using an alternate routing heuristic biased toward a specific domain attribute; namely distance.

Step 1   For each route of a solution do
    1.1   Reorder locally customers based on the nearest-neighbor procedure. If reordering is not possible the route remains unchanged.

The distant customer reordering (DCR_M) mutation operator consists, for a specific route of the targeted solution, in trying to move remote customers regarded as significantly distant from their route successor (immediate neighbor), to an alternate route whose centroid is located within its immediate vicinity. A customer is assumed distant from its route successor, if the travel distance to each other is larger than the average travel distance separating route successors over the route. The operator can be summarized as follows:

Step 1   For each route of a solution do
    1.1   Compute average travel distance separating customers over the route.
    1.2   Remove customers regarded as significantly distant from their route successor, that is customers whose travel distance to their successor (immediate neighbor) is larger than the average distance computed in step 1.1.
Step 2   For each removed customer in step 1.2 do
    2.1   Examine insertion in neighboring routes whose centroid is located within its immediate vicinity. The nearest routes (centroid) are visited first. Attempts for customer re-insertion to a different route make use of the insertion-based routing technique introduced earlier for the recombination phase.
Step 3   Build new routes from remaining unrouted customers (if any) emerging from step 1.2, by aggregating as much customers as possible on the same route using a nearest-neighbor routing heuristic.

3   Computational Experiment

A computational experiment has been conducted to compare the performance of the proposed algorithm, with similar and standard techniques, and therefore assess the value of the proposed approach. The algorithm has been applied to a standard set of VRPTW instances [12]. Each instance involves 100 customers randomly distributed over a geographical area. The travel time separating two customers corresponds to their relative Euclidean distance. Customer locations for a problem instance are either generated randomly using a uniform distribution (problem sets R1 and R2), clustered (problem sets C1 and C2) or mixed, combining randomly distributed and clustered customers (problem sets RC1 and RC2). The standard set defines two classes of problem instances, namely, (R1, C1, RC1) and (R2, C2, RC2). The former includes problem instances characterized by a narrow scheduling horizon and small vehicle capacity. The latter involves problem instances characterized by a large scheduling horizon and large vehicle capacity. A narrow scheduling horizon generally requires a large number of routes (vehicles) to timely satisfy customer demands, whereas a large horizon involves fewer routes as a larger number of customers can be serviced by the same vehicle. More details about these problems and related data set may be found in [12].

The experiment has been conducted under specific conditions. Typical parameters and settings for the investigated algorithm include:

- Population size: 50 (2 populations)
- Maximum number of generations: 100
- Migration: 5
- Population replacement scheme: elitism
- Recombination rate: 60%
    IB_X:
    customer removal procedure (from route r_1 of parent solution P_1):
        random: 25%
        distance-based: 25%
        largest waiting time: 50%
    customer insertion acceptance procedure:
        scheduling period T: 20 generations
        insertion probability (over T generations): min $\{1/2 + i/T, 1\}$, $i=1..T$
- Mutation rate: 60%
    if best fitness improves from one generation to the next then
        IB_M
    else apply with a 50% probability an alternate mutation operator:
        NNR_M: 70%
        DCR_M: 30%

In order to emphasize genetic diversity, the simultaneous evolution of two populations has been considered. The migration parameter, a feature provided by GAlib, refers to the number of (best) chromosomes exchanged between populations after each generation. Population replacement is based upon an elitic scheme, meaning that the best solution ever computed from a previous generation is automatically replicated and inserted as a member of the next generation, before the reproduction (selection) process even starts. Each initial population has been generated randomly using a nearest-neighbor procedure to construct feasible solutions.

The results for the 56 Solomon's problems are summarized in tables 1-6. For each problem set, the performance of the proposed algorithm is compared with the best computed results reported in [11] and obtained from various similar (tabu search and genetic-based) and standard (operations research-based [15]) techniques. The second column presents the number of routes and total traveled distance, respectively, for the best computed solution, whereas the third column refers to the corresponding results for our algorithm. An entry with a star symbol indicates a problem instance in which the number of routes for a computed solution matches the best known solution.

Results show that computed solutions easily compete with most of the best known solutions. The method proves to be quite satisfactory for clustered problems (C1, C2), as computed solution quality (distance and number of routes) nearly match best published results. But the procedure slightly degrades in quality, as total distance may differ up to 8% for R1 and RC1. This observation becomes more apparent for R2 and RC2 showing some algorithm weaknesses in efficiently combining routes (or vehicles) having a large number of customers. The particular subset of knowledge used and/or genetic operators currently designed are believed to insufficiently reduce and confine the search space to good solution neighborhoods for these problem instances

(R2, RC2). Nevertheless, it is worth noticing that for all standard test problems the computed number of routes mostly corresponds or slightly differs from the best repor-

Table 1. Performance comparison for R1 problem set

Problem Set R1	Routes/Total Distance (best)	Routes/Total Distance (Hybrid GA)
R101	18/ 1607.7	19/ 1688.4
R102*	17/ 1434.0	17/ 1567.1
R103	13/ 1207.0	14/ 1310.2
R104*	10/ 982.0	10/ 1081.1
R105*	14/ 1377.1	14/ 1406.7
R106*	12/ 1252.0	12/ 1367.6
R107	10/ 1159.9	11/ 1145.8
R108	9/ 980.9	10/ 1002.6
R109	11/ 1235.7	12/ 1230.5
R110	10/ 1080.4	11/ 1133.5
R111	10/ 1129.9	11/ 1174.3
R112*	10/ 953.6	10/ 1031.1

Table 2. Performance comparison for C1 problem set

Problem Set C1	Routes/Total Distance (best)	Routes/Total Distance (Hybrid GA)
C101*	10/ 827.3	10/ 828.9
C102*	10/ 827.3	10/ 837.3
C103*	10/ 828.1	10/ 848.4
C104*	10/ 824.8	10/ 852.4
C105*	10/ 828.9	10/ 828.9
C106*	10/ 827.3	10/ 828.9
C107*	10/ 827.3	10/ 828.9
C108*	10/ 827.3	10/ 828.9
C109*	10/ 828.9	10/ 828.9

Table 3. Performance comparison for RC1 problem set

Problem Set RC1	Routes/Total Distance (best)	Routes/Total Distance (Hybrid GA)
RC101	14/ 1669.0	15/ 1696.7
RC102*	13/ 1477.5	13/ 1638.7
RC103*	11/ 1110.0	11/ 1392.1
RC104*	10/ 1135.8	10/ 1238.7
RC105	13/ 1733.6	14/ 1652.9
RC106*	12/ 1384.9	12/ 1416.8
RC107*	11/ 1230.9	11/ 1303.0
RC108	10/ 1170.7	11/ 1191.9

Table 4. Performance comparison for R2 problem set

Problem Set R2	Routes/Total Distance (best)	Routes/Total Distance (Hybrid GA)
R201*	4/ 1281.6	4/ 1448.5
R202	3/ 1530.5	4/ 1248.3
R203*	3/ 948.7	3/ 1075.6
R204	2/ 869.3	3/ 821.2
R205*	3/ 1063.2	3/ 1162.6
R206*	3/ 833.0	3/ 1056.4
R207*	3/ 814.8	3/ 891.9
R208*	2/ 738.6	2/ 761.9
R209	2/ 855.0	3/ 996.0
R210*	3/ 967.5	3/ 1047.5
R211	2/ 949.5	3/ 820.2

Table 5. Performance comparison for C2 problem set

Problem Set C2	Routes/Total Distance (best)	Routes/Total Distance (Hybrid GA)
C201*	3/ 591.6	3/ 591.6
C202*	3/ 591.6	3/ 591.6
C203*	3/ 591.2	3/ 600.2
C204*	3/ 590.6	3/ 616.6
C205*	3/ 588.9	3/ 588.9
C206*	3/ 588.5	3/ 588.5
C207*	3/ 588.3	3/ 588.3
C208*	3/ 588.3	3/ 588.3

Table 6. Performance comparison for RC2 problem set

Problem Set RC2	Routes/Total Distance (best)	Routes/Total Distance (Hybrid GA)
RC201*	4/ 1249.0	4/ 1616.1
RC202*	4/ 1165.6	4/ 1380.7
RC203*	3/ 1079.6	3/ 1222.3
RC204*	3/ 806.8	3/ 903.3
RC205*	4/ 1333.7	4/ 1465.2
RC206	3/ 1212.6	4/ 1215.3
RC207*	3/ 1085.6	3/ 1510.4
RC208*	3/ 834.97	3/ 960.7

ted solutions. On the other hand, the computation of a near-optimal solution is reasonably fast (1-10 minutes on a Sun SPARC 10) due to low cost operator execution. In that respect, additional speed-up could easily be achieved by optimizing the current algorithm implementation.

Even though recent tabu search [16,17] techniques developed for this problem slightly outperform the proposed algorithm, the latter has shown similar or better performance than any previously reported (published) genetic-based methods. The stochastic procedure is conceptually simple, easy to implement and allows for the fast computation of a near-optimal solution; a desirable real-time feature when dealing with time-constrained reasoning constraints.

4 Conclusion

This effort toward solving VRPTW aims at investigating the impact of explicitly using domain knowledge and a priori knowledge/characteristics about expected solutions during the recombination and mutation phases of a genetic algorithm. The approach is based upon some principles of recent hybrid and standard genetic algorithms and features of well-known heuristics to drive the search process. Simple and easy to implement, the stochastic procedure allows for the fast computation of a near-optimal solution, a suitable property to address time-constrained reasoning constraints. A computational experiment shows that even though the proposed hybrid genetic algorithm does not outperform some recent tabu search techniques yet, computed solutions remain very competitive and nearly match some of the best known solutions. Future work will explore the introduction of new features to the proposed hybrid genetic algorithm. Accordingly, a combination of various routing heuristics aimed at diversifying problem-solving strategies to search the solution space will be investigated. The contribution of alternate knowledge will also be examined to enrich the recombination phase of the algorithm. Additional research directions include the impact of partial constraint relaxation during problem-solving as well as knowledge associated with statistical distribution of key domain attributes over problem instances.

References

1. Desrosiers, J. and al.: Time Constrained Routing and Scheduling. In: Handbooks in Operations Research and Management Science, Vol. 8. Network Routing, M.O. Ball, T.L. Magnanti, C.L. Monma, G.L. Nemhauser Eds, North-Holland, Amsterdam, (1995) 35-139
2. Solomon, M.M. and Desrochers, J.: Time Window Constrained Routing and Scheduling Problems. Transportation Science 22 (1988) 1-13
3. Goldberg, D.E.: Genetic Algorithms in Search, Optimization, and Machine Learning. Addison-Wesley, New York, (1989)
4. Reeves, C.R.: Modern Heuristics Techniques for Combinatorial Problems. Halsted Press, New York, (1993)
5. Glover, F.: Tabu Search - Part I. ORSA Journal on Computing 1 (1989) 190-206
6. Glover, F.: Tabu Search - Part II. ORSA Journal on Computing 2 (1990) 4-32
7. Potvin, J-Y. and Bengio, S.: The Vehicle Routing Problem with Time Windows Part II: Genetic Search. INFORMS Journal on Computing 8(2) Spring (1996)
8. Thangiah, S.R. and al.: Vehicle Routing with Time Deadlines using Genetic and Local Algorithms. Proceedings of the 5th International Conference on Genetic Algorithms, University of Illinois at Urbana-Champaign, (1993) 506-513

9. Thangiah, S.R.: An Adaptive Clustering Method using a Geometric Shape for Vehicle Routing Problems with Time Windows. Proceedings of the 6th International Conference on Genetic Algorithms, University of Pittsburg, (1995) 536-543

10. Blanton, J.L. and Wainwright, R.L.: Multiple Vehicle Routing with Time and Capacity Constraints using Genetic Algorithms. Proceedings of the 5th International Conference on Genetic Algorithms, Champaign, IL, (1993) 452-459

11. Rochat, Y. and Taillard, E.D.: Probabilistic diversification and intensification in local search for vehicle routing. Journal of Heuristics 1(1) (1995) 147-167

12. Solomon, M.M.: Algorithms for the Vehicle Routing and Scheduling Problems with Time Window Constraints. Operations Research 35(2) (1987) 254-265

13. Wall, M.: GAlib - A C++ Genetic Algorithms Library, version 2.4. (http://lancet.mit.edu/galib-2.4/), MIT, Mass., (1995)

14. Bodin, L. and al.: The State of the Art in the Routing and Scheduling of Vehicles and Crews. Computers and Operations Research 10(2) (1983)

15. Desrochers M., and al.: A New Optimization Algorithm for the Vehicle Routing Problem with Time Window. Operations Research 40 (1992) 342-354

16. Taillard, E.D. and al.: A Tabu Search Heuristic for the Vehicle Routing Problem with Soft Time Windows. Transportation Science 31 (1997) 170-186

17. Badeau, P. and al.: A Parallel Tabu Search Heuristic for the Vehicle Routing Problem with Time Windows. Transportation Research-C 5 (1997) 109-122

Maintaining Genetic Diversity in Genetic Algorithms through Co-evolution

Jason Morrison and Franz Oppacher

{morrison,oppacher}@scs.carleton.ca
Intelligent Systems Lab
School of Computer Science
Carleton University
Ottawa, ON K1S 5B6

Abstract. This paper presents a systematic approach to co-evolution that allows concise and unified expression of all types of symbiotic relationships studied in ecology. The resulting Linear Model of Symbiosis can be easily added to any regular Genetic Algorithm. Our model helps prevent premature convergence to a local optimum by maintaining the genetic diversity in a population. Our experiments show that co-evolutionary Genetic Algorithms outperform regular Genetic Algorithms on some difficult problems including one (Holland's Royal Road function) which was specifically designed to highlight the strengths of a regular Genetic Algorithm.

1 Introduction

Genetic Algorithms (GAs), by simulating evolution have proven to be powerful optimization techniques that can be applied to a wide variety of problems. However, most applications of GAs suffer from the following drawback: as a GAs population evolves, its individuals approach a local optimum of the optimization problem. This convergence to a local optimum creates lower genetic diversity among individuals surviving into successive generations. This loss of genetic diversity is not observed in natural systems. In natural systems the observed tendency is that genetic diversity is sustained within a sufficiently large population.

This particular difference between GAs and natural systems is of concern because the loss of genetic diversity in a GA often eliminates the possibility of the GA obtaining the global optimum. Since a GA relies on the loss of genetic diversity to raise the probability of reproducing fit individuals, it would not be desirable to completely prevent the loss of genetic diversity.

The solution that we propose, to increase the accuracy of the GA model and the performance of GAs, is to add a "plug-in", tunable co-evolution module to the canonical GA. We begin with a brief description of related work, then we give the definitions necessary for our model and subsequently describe the model. Then we present some results showing the feasibility of our method to sustain genetic diversity and increase performance. We conclude with a discussion of the model's capabilities and future work.

2 Background and Previous Work

GAs use an individual's fitness to determine the probabilities that the individual will survive and/or reproduce. Each individual in a population is a potential solution to the problem that the GA is attempting to solve and the fitness function is usually a measure of how well an individual solves that problem. Since higher probabilities of survival and/or reproduction are allocated to individuals with higher fitness values, it is expected that individuals with higher fitness will be present in the next generation.

In co-evolutionary systems the fitnesses of individuals depend not solely on their ability to solve a problem but also on other individuals. By adding this dependency we hope to model the interactions, relationships and dependencies seen in nature.

A variety of approaches have been taken in modelling co-evolution in GAs. One of the most popular [4, 8, 10, 13] involves a tournament approach to fitness functions called the "Competitive Fitness Functions" (CFFs) by Angeline and Pollack [1], is defined by its calculation of the fitness function. To calculate a CFF requires two (or more) individuals to compete in a game and their fitness values are then based on relative performance in the game. The key idea is that given different pairs (or groups) of individuals the fitness value of a specific individual varies. Hence an individual's fitness is affected by other individuals in its population and therefore GAs that use CFFs are co-evolutionary.

A second approach to co-evolution in GAs is to use multiple populations [6, 9]. Typically a problem is broken into components and each component is assigned a different GA. The fitness value of an individual is calculated by randomly choosing the necessary individual(s) from the other population(s) and then evaluating how well this group of individuals solves the problem. The individual being evaluated is then assigned its fitness according to how well it assisted in the solution or according to how well the entire group solved the problem. Since the fitness of an individual depends on the other individuals chosen, this system is also co-evolutionary.

Hillis [4], Sims [10] and Paredis [8] find solutions which were either not possible without co-evolution or achieve a more accurate or efficient solution using co-evolution. Unfortunately, most previous work in co-evolution and GAs is limited because few solutions are reusable (i.e., the co-evolutionary models are designed specifically for the problems originally considered). We attempt to remedy this drawback by proposing a model of co-evolution that is applicable to all GAs.

Of all the approaches that qualify as co-evolutionary only one group provides a generalizable technique. In the Niche and Species approach[1] selection is performed on separate sub-groups of the population. This allows diversity to drop within a specific selection group while the overall diversity remains high. These techniques are co-evolutionary because within a given population an individual's fitness is determined by which selection group it belongs to. Although these methods were created solely to increase genetic diversity without attention to how accurately nature is modelled, they only delay loss of genetic diversity and do not prevent it indefinitely.

3 Definitions

We provide a consistent set of definitions and a clear notation to eliminate the confusing and contradictory interpretations in previous work[2]. Since we are modelling the interaction between individuals a formal definition of this interaction is required. Drawing on terminology used to describe ecosystems [7, 11] we define the term "symbiosis".

Definition 1. Symbiosis *is a relationship between two individuals such that the fitness of one individual directly affects the fitness of the other individual.*

This is somewhat controversial because symbiosis is commonly used to refer to co-dependent mutualism. Even within the ecological community there is debate as to what the term "symbiosis" should mean. However this choice is made to be consistent with [11] where many ecological terms are defined. However saying that A is in symbiosis with B does not fully describe the relationship between A and B. Thus we define the term "connection" (see Definition 2) to more accurately convey the relationship.

Definition 2. *Given that there is a symbiosis between two individuals A and B, a connection (denoted: $A \rightarrow B$, read: A affects B) exists if and only if the fitness of A has a direct effect on the fitness of B.*

While this notion of "connection" is very general there are two common types (protagonist and antagonist connections) which are used to define most forms of symbiosis.

Definition 3. $A \overset{\pm}{\to} B$ *(read: A protagonizes B) if and only if there exists a connection $A \rightarrow B$ such that as the fitness of A increases, the fitness of B increases and as the fitness of A decreases the fitness of B decreases.*

---

[1] Deb and Goldberg give a survey of this material in [3]

[2] A well known example is Hillis' use of "Parasite" in a model that involves competitors.

Definition 4. $A \stackrel{-}{\rightharpoonup} B$ *(read: A antagonizes B) if and only if there exists a connection $A \rightarrow B$ such that as the fitness of A decreases, the fitness of B increases and as the fitness of A increases the fitness of B decreases.*

As previously stated, fitness in a GA is usually taken to measure how well an individual solves the problem which the GA is working on. We divide fitness into two categories: absolute and expressed fitness.

Definition 5. *The absolute fitness of individual x_i at time t, $f_i^a(t)$, is the individual's fitness without any effects by other individuals. Thus absolute fitness $f_i^a(t)$ is dependent on the genotype and phenotype of x_i and time t.*

Definition 6. *The expressed fitness of individual x_i at time t, $f_i^e(t)$, is the individual's fitness including the effects of all individuals. The expressed fitness is therefore dependent on the genotype and phenotype of x_i, time t and all individuals x_j such that $x_j \rightarrow x_i$.*

With these definitions in place it is possible to describe the various forms of symbiosis that exist in nature. Using [11] as a base classification scheme and expanding it to include all cases of pairwise relationships generates the classification scheme given in Table 1. Within our model of co-evolution, individuals in symbiosis are in one of these basic forms of co-evolution.

4 Model

We begin the description of our model with Equation 1 which calculates expressed fitness at time t (i.e. generation t). In words, the expressed fitness of individual x_i at time t, $f_i^e(t)$, equals the expressed fitness of individual x_i at time $t-1$, $f_i^e(t-1)$, plus the total change, $C_i(t)$, in the fitness of x_i at time t.

Type of Symbiosis	Connection
Adaptism	$Individual_A \rightarrow Individual_A$
Amensalism	$Host \stackrel{-}{\rightharpoonup} Amensal$
Commensalism	$Host \stackrel{+}{\rightharpoonup} Commensal$
Mutualism	$Symbiont_A \stackrel{+}{\rightharpoonup} Symbiont_B$
	$Symbiont_B \stackrel{+}{\rightharpoonup} Symbiont_A$
Predation	$Predator \stackrel{-}{\rightharpoonup} Prey$
	$Prey \stackrel{+}{\rightharpoonup} Predator$
Competition	$Competitor_A \stackrel{-}{\rightharpoonup} Competitor_B$
	$Competitor_B \stackrel{-}{\rightharpoonup} Competitor_A$

Table 1. Pairwise forms of symbiosis.

$$f_i^e(t) = f_i^e(t-1) + C_i(t) \tag{1}$$

This enigmatic "total change", $C_i(t)$, can be broken down into two components: i) changes due to connections to individuals and ii) a change in absolute fitness of the individual.

Connections, are assumed to be independent of one another so that the first component of change, i.e., the total effect of all connections, is the sum of all effects due to individual connections. We represent the effect of connection $x_j \rightarrow x_i$ at time t by $c_{ij}(t)$.

The second component of total change can effectively be ignored for most GAs because absolute fitness (i.e. how well an individual solves the problem) is static.

To determine initial conditions, assume that a new individual x_i is born at time t. since x_i has not been affected by other individuals, its initial expressed fitness is its absolute fitness, $f_i^e(t) = f_i^a(t)$. Similarly, since there was no previous fitness the total change is equal to the initial fitness $C_i(t) = f_i^a(t)$. Using this idea of birth, and assuming that all individuals are born at time t=0, the initial conditions of expressed fitness can be stated in Equation 2.

$$f_i^e(0) = f_i^a(0)$$
$$C_i(0) = f_i^a(0) \tag{2}$$

Equation 3 represents the full formulation for $C_i(t)$ (Note: it is assumed that there are S individuals in the set of all individuals).

$$C_i(t) = \sum_{j=1}^{S} c_{ij}(t) + (f_i^a(t) - f_i^a(t-1)) \tag{3}$$

This leads to Equation 4 which is the defining equation for our model of symbiosis.

$$f_i^e(t) = f_i^e(t-1) + \sum_{j=1}^{S} c_{ij}(t) + (f_i^a(t) - f_i^a(t-1)) \tag{4}$$

Using the simplest function for a connection leads to the linear connection. As given in Equation 5, the linear connection c_{ij} is a protagonist connection when $\alpha_{ij} > 0$ and an antagonist connection when $\alpha_{ij} < 0$. Throughout the remainder of this paper the values α_{ij} will be referred to as connection strengths or weights.

$$c_{ij}(t) = \alpha_{ij}C_j(t-1) \tag{5}$$

The Linear Symbiosis Model of Co-evolution is a model of co-evolution that uses only linear connections. Given the form of the linear connections it is possible to restate the basic equation of the symbiosis model (Equation 4). Thus let $F^a(t)$ be the vector of absolute fitnesses for all S individuals in all populations $[f_1^a(t), \ldots, f_i^a(t), \ldots, f_S^a(t)]$. Similarly let $F^e(t)$ be the vector $[f_1^e(t), \ldots, f_S^e(t)]$ and $C(t)$ be the vector $[C_1(t), \ldots, C_S(t)]$. Finally let $\mathcal{A}$ be the matrix with components α_{ij}. Using these definitions with Equations 5 and 4 produces the defining equation of the linear model given in Equation 6.

$$\begin{pmatrix} f_1^e(t) \\ \vdots \\ f_S^e(t) \end{pmatrix} = \begin{pmatrix} f_1^e(t-1) \\ \vdots \\ f_S^e(t-1) \end{pmatrix} + \begin{pmatrix} \alpha_{11} \ldots \alpha_{1S} \\ \vdots \ddots \vdots \\ \alpha_{S1} \ldots \alpha_{SS} \end{pmatrix} \begin{pmatrix} C_1(t-1) \\ \vdots \\ C_S(t-1) \end{pmatrix}$$
$$+ \begin{pmatrix} f_1^a(t) \\ \vdots \\ f_S^a(t) \end{pmatrix} - \begin{pmatrix} f_1^a(t-1) \\ \vdots \\ f_S^a(t-1) \end{pmatrix}$$
$$F^e(t) = F^e(t-1) + AC(t-1) + F^a(t) - F^a(t-1) \tag{6}$$
$$\text{where} \quad C(t) = F^e(t) - F^e(t-1)$$

Thus a GA with our linear model of co-evolution uses the vector $F^e(t)$ as the fitnesses of all individuals instead of $F^a(t)$.

5 Implementation and Experiments

In order to implement the expressed fitness of an individual, several questions concerning births and deaths must be answered. These questions are: How does the death of an individual in symbiosis affect its partners? How does a newborn affect expressed fitnesses? How does the system change as a whole because of births and deaths?

Suppose a child x_j is born at time $t+1$. At the time of birth the expressed fitness of x_j should be equal to the absolute fitness of x_j plus any effects felt at time t. However, since the child was not alive in the previous time then $C_j(t) = 0$. The remainder of the equations apply. In the model explored here each child is assigned its connections at birth and they remain constant throughout its life. Should any individual die then the new child that is created to replace it will inherit the dead individual's connections. This is only possible because, in the implemented GA, the population size is constant.

Death and its effects are also critical to the implementation of the model. Consider again Equation 4. Suppose at time t an individual x_j is alive and affects individual x_i, and at time $t+1$ x_j is dead. This means that the change $C_j(t)$ in x_j between times $t-1$ and t will not affect individual x_i at time $t+1$ (i.e., $C_j(t) = 0$, regardless of $f_j^e(t)$ and $f_j^e(t-1)$).

Suppose that an individual x_i is in symbiosis with x_j and that x_j lives at time t and is dead at time $t+1$. Further suppose that at time $t+1$ a new individual is born and takes x_j's place. Since the death and birth both indicate that $C_j(t) = 0$ there is nothing further to model. If x_i and x_j are connected as shown in Figure 1, then in our model, their fitnesses would be calculated as shown in Table 2.

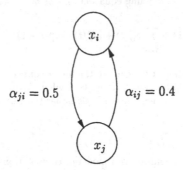

$$\alpha_{ji} = 0.5 \qquad \alpha_{ij} = 0.4$$

Fig. 1. Graph for Birth/Death Example. Connections are displayed as directed edges and individuals are nodes.

Quantity	$t-1$	t	$t+1$	$t+2$	$t+3$
$f_i^a(t)$	10	10	10	10	10
$f_i^e(t) = f_i^e(t-1) + c_{ij}(t) + f_i^a(t) - f_i^a(t-1)$	19.6	20.2	20.2	21.4	21.4
$c_{ij}(t) = \alpha_{ij}C_j(t-1)$	1.6	0.6	0	1.2	0
$C_i(t) = f_i^e(t) - f_i^e(t-1)$	1.6	0.6	0	1.2	0
$f_j^a(t)$	5	5	11	11	11
$f_j^e(t) = f_j^e(t-1) + c_{ji}(t) + f_j^a(t) - f_j^a(t-1)$	13.5	14.3	11.3	11.3	11.9
$c_{ji}(t) = \alpha_{ji}C_i(t-1)$	2.5	0.8	0.3	0	0.6
$C_j(t) = f_j^e(t) - f_j^e(t-1)$	2.5	(0.8) 0	3	0	0.6
Event		Death of x_j	Birth of new x_j		

Table 2. The values in the column time $t-1$ are assumed to have been taken from midpoint in the individuals' lives. It is important to note the change in $C_j(t)$ to 0 once the death has occurred. The bracketed value is the value that would have been appropriate had the death not occurred.

In this paper we present tests of only a select group of symbiosis patterns. These patterns are the basic types that include feedback between individuals (i.e. Mutualism, Predation, Competition and Adaptism – See Table 1). In the case of Adaptism each individual is simply given a connection to itself and no other connections are made. The other cases involve pairing individuals x_i and x_{i+1} were $i = 0 \pmod 2$. Each pair is then given connections appropriate to the type of symbiosis being tested. Thus in a population of S individuals there are $\frac{S}{2}$ symbioses of the same type. Furthermore all connection weights are assigned a single magnitude (i.e. $|\alpha_{ij}| = \alpha$). This allows a direct comparison of the effect of connection strength between otherwise equivalent experiments.

Our GA implementation uses standard parameter settings to avoid unfairly favouring the co-evolutionary GA. The selection technique is the Ranked Based Selection by Baker [2] which gives the regular GA the most genetic diversity without implementing a specialized crowding or niche scheme. To ensure the best performance on the problems the GA is elitist with a 90% replacement rate in a population of 100 individuals. The mutation and uniform crossover rates used are 0.001 and 0.60 respectively.

Three different problems are tackled in the experiments. The first two are modified versions[3] of classical Operations Research functions i.e., Rosenbrock's and Griewangk's Functions (Equations 7 and 8 respectively). Their parameters are given in Tables 3 and 4. For both of these problems an individual x_i is represented by a binary string which is mapped to two numbers y_{i1} and y_{i2}. The third problem is Holland's Royal Road function [5]. This problem takes a single binary string and assigns a value based on the bits that are 1's. The idea is that sections of consecutive bits are rewarded in increasing amounts for having a specific number of bits (m^*) equal to 1. However, if those bits contain all 1's then the most reward is offered. Bonus awards are given for having consecutive sections with all 1's. Thus the maximum occurs when all of the bits are 1's. The problem is difficult to solve because there are many local optimum where there are m^* 1's in a particular section. The parameter settings for the Royal Road function are displayed in Table 5.

$$f_i^a(t) = -100(y_{i1}^2 - y_{i2})^2 - (1 - y_{i1})^2 \qquad (7)$$

Because Rosenbrock's function is non-linear and non-separable normal line search techniques are largely ineffective. However, this function can be solved using a special adaptation of linear search [12, p. 5].

Parameter	Value
Max (y_1, y_2)	$(2.048, 2.048)$
Min (y_1, y_2)	$(-2.048, -2.048)$
Total Bits	32

Table 3. Rosenbrock's Function: The maximum fitness attainable is at (1,1) and is equal to 0.

$$f_i^a(t) = -1 - \sum_{j=1}^{2} \frac{y_{ij}^2}{4000} + \Pi_{j=1}^2 \left(\cos(\frac{y_{ij}}{\sqrt{i}}) \right) \qquad (8)$$

Griewangk's function is also a very difficult function to solve with normal line search. The two dimensional case is used because it has been shown [12] that higher dimensional cases of the problem are easy to solve.

Parameter	Value
Dimensions	2
Max(y_1, y_2)	$(511, 511)$
Min (y_1, y_2)	$(-512, -512)$
Total Bits	32

Table 4. Griewangk's Function: The maximum fitness attainable is at (0,0) and is equal to 0.

Holland's Royal Road function was created as an example of a function which is relatively easy for GAs while being relatively difficult for other search techniques. It is included to show that our co-evolutionary technique can improve GAs even on problems that are specifically designed for the GA.

Parameter	Value
k	4
b	8
g	7
m^*	4
v	0.02
u^*	1.0
u	0.3
$f_i^a(t)$	see [5]

Table 5. Holland's Royal Road Function: Using these defaults the max fitness is 12.8 and the min is -0.9.

---

[3] The modification was a multiplication by -1 to transform them into maximization problems.

6 Results

Several measures of performance are given in this section. The best fitness[4] of every individual (best ever fitness) and the best fitness of current individuals (current best fitness) are given to indicate the optimization capability of the system. To measure the genetic diversity the average Hamming distance[5] of the survivors to the best current survivor is cited. This gives a direct measure of the amount of genetic diversity that survives in the system.

Before describing the specific results for the different problems a description of behaviour common to all problems is warranted. Since the effects on expressed fitness are cumulative, an individual's expressed fitness may become higher than the global optimum of the absolute fitness. This leads to two possible stages in a co-evolutionary GA.

In the first stage, during the early generations, the co-evolutionary GA behaves similarly to a regular GA. The exact behaviour seems dependent on the form of symbiosis used as well as the problem itself. However, the interesting stage occurs in the later generations.

After the co-evolutionary GA has converged for a while, the amount of change introduced by the new individuals is lower, i.e., the average $C_i(t) = f_i^e(t) - f_i^e(t-1)$ is smaller. This implies that new individuals survive less frequently into the next generation. At some point the value of $C_i(t)$ is too small to allow new individuals to survive. It is at this point that the co-evolutionary GA changes to its second stage of behaviour. From this point onward the surviving population freezes, i.e., changes become more and more infrequent and eventually stop. This means that after this point the genetic diversity remains constant. Improvement in the best ever fitness, as compared to a standard GA, is achieved because of the constant random recombination of the existing genetic diversity into new individuals. Thus the second stage of behaviour is equivalent to a random search.

The beginning of the change between the two stages and the length of time during which the change occurs depend on the form of co-evolution, the strength of the connections and the problem structure. The results show that co-evolutionary GAs can outperform the regular GA. That is, the best individual found (in absolute fitness) by the co-evolutionary GA is on average better than that found by the regular GA.

Adaptism, Mutualism and Predation show very similar behaviour to one another. Each of these symbiosis patterns preserves genetic diversity and can outperform the regular GA. Since in Competition the effects of connections balance one another, Competition is not significantly different from the regular GA. The results given here have been selected because they display typical behaviour. A much more detailed presentation of results and analysis will be available in a forthcoming paper. For each combination of connection strength (α), symbiosis type and problem, the results show the average of 200 experiments.

Figure 2 shows the best absolute fitness ever achieved by Adaptism while optimizing Rosenbrock's Function. Clearly both extremes of α perform better than the regular GA. It is important to note that the co-evolutionary GAs continue to improve while the regular GA converges to a local optimum.

Figure 3 shows the average Hamming distance from the survivors to the current best survivor achieved by Adaptism while optimizing Rosenbrock's Function. For this problem even the weakest connection weight causes a dramatic increase in genetic diversity. Also important is the fact that genetic diversity plateaus very early (7th to 20th generation) and never decreases further.

Figure 4 shows the best absolute fitness achieved by Predation while optimizing Griewangk's Function. The curve for $\alpha = 0.8000$ shows that the survivors freeze too early. Despite a lot of diversity the co-evolutionary GA is unable to outperform the regular GA. The curve for $\alpha = 0.0125$ shows that the population freezes too late. Despite converging to a high fitness level the lack of genetic diversity once the survivors do freeze restricts the overall performance of the co-evolutionary GA. Finally $\alpha = 0.0750$ is the compromise that outperforms all others tested.

---

[4] The fitnesses referred to in this section unless otherwise noted are the absolute fitnesses.
[5] The Hamming distance between two binary strings is the number of bits that are different between the two strings.

Figure 5 shows the average Hamming distance from survivors to the current best survivor achieved by Predation while optimizing Griewangk's Function. For this problem there is a wide range of increase in genetic diversity with varying α. Also important is the fact that once genetic diversity plateaus in the co-evolutionary GA it never decreases further.

Figure 6 shows the best absolute fitness achieved by Adaptism while optimizing Holland's Royal Road Function. The curve for $\alpha = 0.80$ shows that the survivors freeze too early. Despite a lot of diversity the co-evolutionary GA is unable to outperform the regular GA. The curve for $\alpha = 0.05$ shows that the population freezes too late. Despite converging to a high fitness level the lack of genetic diversity once the survivors do freeze restricts the overall performance of the co-evolutionary GA. Finally $\alpha = 0.40$ is the compromise that outperforms all others shown.

Figure 7 shows the average Hamming distance from survivors to the current best survivor achieved by Adaptism while optimizing Holland's Royal Road Function (binary string length is 240 bits). For this problem there is a wide range of increase in genetic diversity with varying α. Also important is the fact that once genetic diversity plateaus in the co-evolutionary GA it never decreases further. The $\alpha = 0.40$ curve does not plateau because by the 100th generation it does not have a frozen set of survivors.

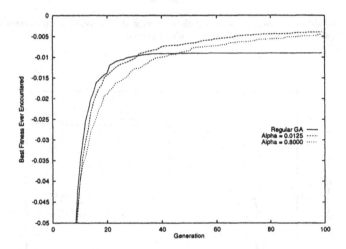

Fig. 2. This graph shows the best absolute fitness ever achieved by Adaptism while optimizing Rosenbrock's Function.

7 Conclusions and Future Work

We have described a co-evolutionary model that maintains genetic diversity in a population. While this is not the first attempt to maintain diversity through co-evolution (see Section 2) our model seems to be the first systematic approach to co-evolution. Using the Linear Model of Symbiosis, it is possible to add co-evolution to any GA.

More importantly, this co-evolutionary "add-on" is a tunable system, where an increase in the strengths of connections results in an increase in the sustained genetic diversity. This relationship holds across a wide variety of possible absolute fitness functions.

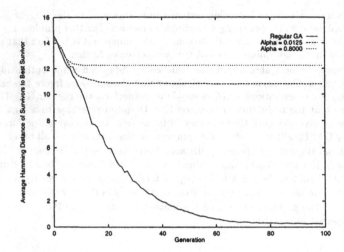

Fig. 3. This graph shows the average Hamming distance from the survivors to the current best survivor achieved by Adaptism while optimizing Rosenbrock's Function.

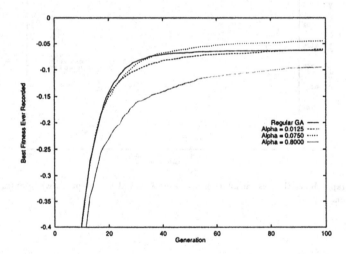

Fig. 4. This graph shows the best absolute fitness achieved by Predation while optimizing Griewangk's Function.

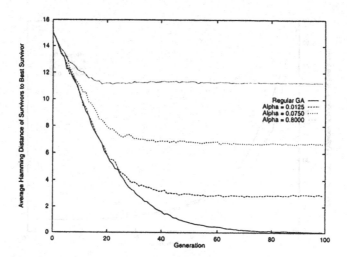

Fig. 5. This graph shows the average Hamming distance from survivors to the current best survivor achieved by Predation while optimizing Griewangk's Function.

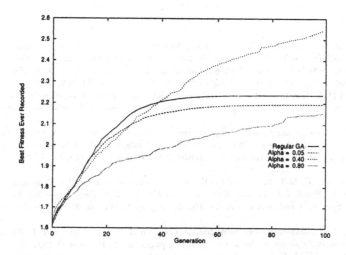

Fig. 6. This graph shows the best absolute fitness achieved by Adaptism while optimizing Holland's Royal Road Function.

As a tool, our co-evolution model works without explicitly measuring genetic diversity. In previous systems, genetic diversity was maintained by monitoring the diversity and not allowing similar, or alike individuals to survive. This unnatural control of survival demands that the selection operator be tailored for each type of system and eliminates it as a general purpose system.

A dynamic fitness function represents a difficult challenge for regular GAs when the fitness function changes too slowly the GA will converge to a local optimum and lack sufficient genetic diversity to re-converge once the fitness function changes. This limitation is removed with the addition of co-evolution.

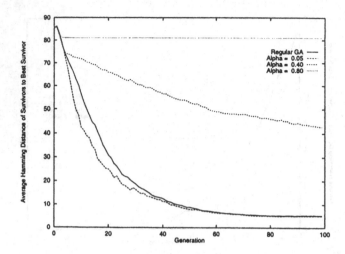

Fig. 7. This graph shows the average Hamming distance from survivors to the current best survivor achieved by Adaptism while optimizing Holland's Royal Road Function (binary string length is 240 bits)

References

1. P. J. Angeline and J. B. Pollack. Competitive Environments Evolve Better Solutions for Complex Tasks. In *Fifth International Conference on Genetic Algorithms*, pages 264–270, 1993.
2. J. E. Baker. Adative Selection Methods for Genetic Algorithms. In J. J. Grefenstette, editor, *International Conference on Genetic Algorithms: ICGA '85*, pages 101–106, 1985.
3. K. Deb and D. E. Goldberg. An Investigation of Niche and Species Formation in Genetic Function Optimization. In J. D. Schaffer, editor, *International Conference on Genetic Algorithms: ICGA '89*, pages 42–43, 1989.
4. W. D. Hillis. Co-evolving parasites improve simulated evolution as an optimization procedure. In *Artificial Life II, SFI Studies in the Sciences of Complexity*, volume 10, pages 313–323.
5. J. H. Holland. Royal roads functions. *Internet Genetic Algorithms Digest*, 7:issue 22, August 12 1993.
6. P. Husbands and F. Mill. Simulated Co-Evolution as The Mechanism for Emergent Planning and Scheduling. In *Fourth International Conference on Genetic Algorithms*, pages 264–270, 1991.
7. D. Lewis. Symbiosis and mutualism. In *The Biology of Mutualism: Ecology and Evolution*, pages 29–39.
8. J. Paredis. Co-evolutionary Constraint Satisfaction. In H. S. Y. Davidor and R. Männer, editors, *Parallel Problem Solving from Nature - PPSN III*, pages 46–55, Berlin, Oct 1994. Springer-Verlag.
9. M. A. Potter and K. A. DeJong. A Cooperative Coevolutionary Approach to Function Optimization. In H. S. Y. Davidor and R. Männer, editors, *Parallel Problem Solving from Nature - PPSN III*, pages 249–257, Berlin, Oct 1994. Springer-Verlag.
10. K. Sims. Evolving 3D Morphology and Behavior by Competition. In R. Brooks and P. Maes, editors, *Artificial Life IV*, pages 28–39, 1994.
11. M. Starr. A generalized scheme for classifying organismic associations. *Symposia of the Society for Experimental Biology*, 29:1–20, 1975.
12. D. Whitley, K. Mathias, S. Rana, and J. Dzubera. Evaluating evolutionary algorithms. *Artificial Intelligence*, 85:1–32, 1996.
13. X. Yao and P. J. Darwen. Evolving Robust Strategies for Iterated Prisoner's Dilemma. In X. Yao, editor, *Progress in Evolutionary Computation*, pages 276–292, 1994.

The Effect of Genetic Operator Probabilities and Selection Strategies on the Performance of a Genetic Algorithm

Kay Wiese and Scott D. Goodwin

Department of Computer Science, University of Regina
Regina, Saskatchewan, S4S 0A2, Canada
Phone: (306)-585-5210, Fax: (306)-585-4745
email: wiese@cs.uregina.ca, goodwin@cs.uregina.ca

Abstract. This paper presents a comparison of two genetic algorithms (GAs) that use different selection strategies. The first GA uses the standard selection strategy of roulette wheel selection and generational replacement (STDS), while the second GA uses an intermediate selection strategy in addition to STDS. Our previous research has shown that this intermediate selection strategy, which we call "Keep-Best Reproduction (KBR)", found solutions of lower cost for a variety of travelling salesman problems. In this paper, we study the effects of crossover and mutation probabilities on STDS as well as on KBR. We study the effect of recombination alone, mutation alone and both together. We compare the performance of the different selection strategies and discuss the environment that each selection strategy needs to flourish in. Overall, KBR is found to be the selection strategy of choice. We also present empirical evidence that suggests that KBR is more robust than STDS with regard to operator probabilities.

Topic Area: Evolutionary Computing, Genetic Algorithms, Search

1 Introduction

Genetic algorithms were originally designed to work on bitstrings. These bitstrings encoded a domain value of a real valued function that was supposed to be optimized. They were originally proposed by Holland [Hol75]. More recently, researchers have focused on applying GAs to combinatorial optimization problems, including constraint optimization problems such as the travelling salesman problem (TSP) and the job shop scheduling problem (JSSP). Most research on applying GAs to the TSP has been focused on designing new representations and new operators. Other work has compared the performance of different operators. Most of this research has focused on the effect of recombination (crossover) alone. Mutation was not used at all in most works including [Gol85] and [Gre85]. The selection process was done via roulette wheel selection, and the new offspring were inserted into the new generation.

We have designed a new selection strategy which keeps good previous genetic material in the population as well as facilitating the insertion of highly fit new chromosomes into the new generation. We will refer to this selection strategy as *keep-best reproduction* (KBR). One of the reasons why mutation is not studied in many papers is because of its disruptive effect on good chromosomes and because often researchers want to test their new recombination operators in isolation. This paper presents the results of three studies that are aimed at answering the following questions. What is the effect of recombination alone? What is the effect of mutation alone? What are good operator probabilities if both recombination and mutation are used? The study investigates both standard selection with generational replacement (STDS) as well as KBR. The outcome of the study is significantly different for the two selection strategies. Overall, KBR proves to be the selection strategy of choice. Previously we have published initial results on KBR in the TSP domain that showed that KBR can outperform STDS [Wie98a]. The study presented here puts KBR in a perspective with other selection strategies; it emphasises the role and properties of selection mechanisms and provides an in depth study of the effect of operator probabilities. This study demonstrates when and where KBR is better than STDS.

Section 2 gives a brief overview of the role that selection plays in evolutionary algorithms. In Sect. 3, we review the traditional selection step and its shortcomings, and discuss how KBR can achieve the objectives outlined in Sect. 2. Section 4 presents the results of a study that compares STDS and KBR on different sized travelling salesman problems. The study clearly shows the superiority of KBR if both recombination and mutation are being used. After our conclusion in Sect. 5, we discuss some ideas and thoughts for further research in Sect. 6.

2 Selection in Evolutionary Algorithms

Selection plays a vital role in every evolutionary algorithm. Without selection the search process becomes random and promising regions of the search space would not be favoured over non-promising regions. In order to have an efficient and effective search there must be a search criteria (the fitness function) and a selection process that gives individuals with higher fitness a higher chance of being selected for reproduction, mutation and survival.

Depending on the selection strategy that is used, there will always be a tradeoff between *exploration* and *exploitation* of the search space. Informally, exploration is the part of the search that "discovers" new and hopefully promising regions in the search space, while exploitation is the part of the search that stays in one region of the search space and tries to improve individuals in that locality. Both exploration and exploitation are important for a successful search and do usually compete with each other in the sense that too much exploration means too little exploitation and vice versa.

The selection strategy that is employed determines how much exploration and how much exploitation is done. One measure to quantify selection strategies is the *selection pressure*. Informally, a high selection pressure means that highly fit individuals are selected in disproportionate numbers of samples, while individuals of lower fitness are often not selected at all and are lost during the search process.

A higher selection pressure leads to less exploration of the search space, and more exploitation of so-called "super-individuals", which often leads to a loss of diversity in the population and ultimately to premature convergence. On the other hand, a selection strategy with low selection pressure does not differentiate as much (or at all) between good and bad individuals. This ultimately leads to less exploitation of highly fit individuals and can slow down the convergence speed of the search. Too low a selection pressure could prevent the search from converging at all if the selection strategy forces the search to "jump" from one part of the search space to another all the time. There is a variety of different selection schemes for GAs, genetic programming and evolution strategies. To discuss them and their properties is beyond the scope of this paper and we refer the reader to [Thi97] and [Bae96] for an overview.

What properties do we want a selection strategy to have? First, we want to preserve previous good genetic material, so it can be exploited further. Second, we want the search to make progress in the form of highly fit individuals, so that new promising regions of the search space can be explored. Third, we want to have fast convergence (by increasing the selection pressure) but avoid premature convergence (by maintaining diversity).

3 Keep-Best Reproduction: How to Get Better Results Through an Intermediate Selection Strategy

Most of the research since 1985 on applying GAs to the travelling salesman problem has focused on designing new representations and genetic operators and comparing their performance [Gol85,Gre85,Oli87,Whi89,Sta91].

Surprisingly, not much research has been published on the effect of different selection strategies in this problem domain. Most researchers have used roulette wheel selection, a global selection strategy, and either generational replacement or steady-state reproduction. Roulette wheel selection is global selection, since an individual's fitness is compared to the sum of the fitnesses of all individuals. Each time the GA enters the selection phase, two individuals are chosen randomly by "spinning" the roulette wheel. This random global selection is biased towards the individuals that are highly fit. While roulette wheel selection is fitness proportionate selection, people have also used ranking methods such as tournament selection [Thi97] for the parent selection. The study presented here uses only roulette wheel selection to select the parents.

In order to achieve objective one and two of Sect. 2, which were to preserve good genetic information as well as to introduce new, good genetic information into the population, we propose the following intermediate selection strategy: Keep only the best of the 2 offspring chromosomes and replace the other by the best parent. Since this ensures that both the best offspring and parent chromosome are kept, we call this technique *keep-best reproduction* or short KBR. Also KBR has a higher selection intensity than STDS. They both use the same parent selection strategy but KBR employs an additional selection step on the parents and children in order to decide who will survive into the next generation. By keeping the best child we seek to achieve fast convergence. By keeping one (the best) parent we seek to prevent premature convergence.

Alternatively, we could have chosen to keep the 2 best out of the set consisting of the two parents and the two offspring. Yet, there is a potential danger in this approach. In case that the parents frequently have better evaluations than the offspring, the GA would not make significant progress, using the same strings over and over again. The other case where both offspring would have better evaluations than the parents is not likely to happen too often. STDS, which always keeps both offspring, is shown to have inferior performance on our test problems, so the likelihood of consistently generating offspring that are both superior is highly unlikely. This exact idea of keeping the two best of the family of two parents and two children was employed in a study by Thierens and Goldberg in [Thi94]. However they used random parent selection (we use roulette wheel parent selection) with crossover probability 1 and developed a simplistic model for the case of optimizing the bit counting function (onemax). They showed that their selection strategy, called "elitist recombination" has the same convergence characteristics as standard tournament selection of size two in this simplistic model.

KBR is a novel approach and should not be confused with tournament selection. Tournament selection is a parent selection method that randomly chooses s individuals from the population and the best of those s individuals becomes a parent. Here s is the size of the tournament. Increasing s increases the selection pressure. KBR works locally only on the set of the parents and the set of the children. It does not have the same random component as tournament selection has. Also tournament selection only decides who is chosen for reproduction, KBR decides who will live into the next generation.

Figure 1 shows a modification of a standard genetic algorithm that incorporates KBR. In the following section we discuss the results of an empirical study of KBR versus STDS.

4 Comparison of Traditional Selection and Keep-Best Reproduction

We have conducted a large number of tests on asymmetric travelling salesman problems using 33, 50 and 100 cities. The cost between two cities was a random integer number between 0 and *maxcost*, where *maxcost* was set to 100 times the number of cities. Our implementation is based on the algorithm displayed in Fig. 1. The parent selection was done via roulette wheel selection. The mutation operator was a simple swap operation that picks two random locations in the tour, and exchanges the two cities in those locations. The crossover operator

```
┌─────────────────────────────────────────────────┐
│                                                 │
│          Genetic Algorithm with Keep-Best        │
│                 Reproduction                     │
│          ==============================          │
│                                                 │
│   Initialize a population of chromosomes;        │
│   Evaluate the chromosomes in the population;    │
│                                                 │
│   while (stopping criteria not reached) do       │
│       for i=1 to sizeof(population)/2 do         │
│           select 2 parent chromosomes;           │
│           apply crossover operator to them;      │
│           apply mutation operator to them;       │
│           evaluate the new chromosomes;          │
│           compare the parents' fitnesses and     │
│           remember the best parent;              │
│           replace the offspring chromosome with  │
│           lower fitness by the best parent chromosome; │
│           i = i + 1;                             │
│       endfor                                     │
│       update stopping criteria;                  │
│   endwhile                                       │
│                                                 │
└─────────────────────────────────────────────────┘
```

Fig. 1. Keep-Best Reproduction

we used was the partially mapped crossover (PMX). A detailed description of PMX can be found in [Gol85]. To be able to study the effects of KBR with fewer variables, we decided to not include elitism in our study. The fitness function we used was $f_i = c_{max} - c_i$, where c_i is the actual tour cost of individual i and c_{max} is the maximum cost in the population.

We have run tests for population sizes of 200, 400, 600, 800, 1000, and 1500. Three independent studies were done. The first study looks at the effect of recombination alone. Many researchers have tested their genetic algorithms without mutation. This study allows us to compare the performance of KBR with the technique other researchers have used. The second study only investigates the effect of mutation. We would expect STDS not to converge significantly with mutation alone. The third study investigates the effects of having both recombination and mutation. Again we need to show that KBR benefits from a combination of recombination and mutation, and thus is a true enhancement of the underlying genetic algorithm. 4320 different runs were logged for the varying problem sizes, population sizes, selection techniques, and operator probabilities.

4.1 Recombination Alone

Table 1 displays the results of a GA run on a 100 city problem. For STDS the best tours are found with a crossover probability between 0.5 and 0.7. Higher crossover probabilities cause a sharp increase in the cost of the best tour found. With STDS and higher crossover probabilities the population starts to diverge, which can be seen by comparing the worst and best tour in the population after 300 generations. KBR however converges rather rapidly over the full range of crossover probability settings. With a population size of 600, no more than 69 generations were needed to reach a state of equilibrium, where all individuals are the same, see Table 1. Here higher crossover probabilities find better solutions.

Table 1. Results for the 100 city problem with a population size of 600. The columns labeled P_c and P_m contain the crossover probability and the mutation probability, respectively. The individual entries in the table contain the cost of the best tour after i generations. In the cases where $i = 300$ the population has not converged yet

	Recombination			Mutation	
P_c	STDS	KBR	P_m	STDS	KBR
	best tour i	best tour i		best tour i	best tour i
0.0	425,016 16	425,016 7	0.0	425,016 16	425,016 7
0.1	273,964 115	341,099 25	0.1	190,428 300	136,385 300
0.2	237,869 163	274,485 49	0.2	180,631 300	106,458 300
0.3	259,308 82	290,090 29	0.3	199,513 300	108,782 300
0.4	233,675 143	296.718 35	0.4	199,369 300	117,792 300
0.5	203,258 221	277,104 42	0.5	204,071 300	108,964 300
0.6	169.938 300	249,705 48	0.6	228.071 300	103,631 300
0.7	270,750 300	248,030 46	0.7	238,164 300	114,537 300
0.8	386,417 300	227,186 60	0.8	272,712 300	108,035 300
0.9	380,276 300	230,589 62	0.9	283,378 300	101,534 300
1.0	400,208 300	187,644 69	1.0	303,777 300	117,909 300

The overall result is that STDS finds better tours up to a crossover probability of 0.6. If the probability is higher than that, KBR finds better tours, see Fig. 2. Although the solutions found by KBR using crossover probabilities of more than 0.6 are better than with STDS, they are not better than the best tours that STDS can find with lower crossover probability settings. In general, KBR does not find better solutions than STDS if only recombination is used and crossover probabilities are fine-tuned to yield optimal performance.

The higher the crossover probability, the better the quality of the tours found by KBR. This is not surprising since with low crossover probability KBR converges very rapidly in between 25 and 49 generations according to Table 1. These solutions are produced in the following way: The best individuals in the population get an increased amount of samples in the parent population due to the fitness proportional roulette wheel selection. Then crossover is applied. If the probability test is not passed then the parents are simply duplicated. When the KBR selection is applied, the best parent and its child copy are kept and put into the new generation. In the next generation, these individuals will have duplicates and increase their chance of being chosen as parents again. Thus low crossover probabilities lead to a rapid loss of diversity in the population and to premature convergence. See Fig. 3 for a run on a 100 city TSP that shows the premature convergence of KBR after 48 generations.

At first this seems to be a rather discouraging result. The reason for this "under-performance" lies in the nature of KBR. By only inserting one offspring into the next generation after recombination and keeping the best parent, there is going to be less diversity in the population, thus leading to a faster convergence. Fast conversion itself is not what is undesired, it is the convergence to tours of higher cost. There is a simple way to introduce diversity into the population, the use of mutation.

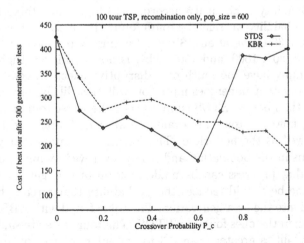

Fig. 2. The x-axis shows the crossover probability P_c, while the y-axis shows the cost of the best tour after 300 generations or less (in thousands) for a 100 city random TSP. No mutation was used. The population size was 600

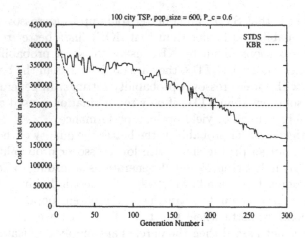

Fig. 3. The x-axis shows the generation number i, while the y-axis shows the cost of the best tour after i generations for a 100 city random TSP. No mutation was used. The crossover probability was set to $P_c = 0.6$. The population size was 600

4.2 Mutation Alone

Studies of mutation alone are usually not done within the genetic algorithm community since without any form of recombination the algorithm cannot be considered a true GA. We include this study to show that KBR is not just a local hill-climber in disguise. Subsection 4.3 shows that the best results can be obtained by a combination of recombination and mutation.

Using STDS, the cost of the tours is found to be within a similar range up to a mutation probability of about 0.5 according to Fig. 4 and Table 1. Increasing the mutation probability worsens the tours found. In no case is there any sign of convergence after 300 generations. Similar findings were made with population sizes of 200, 400, 800, 1000, and 1500. This is not surprising. Higher mutation probabilities simply have too much of a disruptive effect on good tours. With STDS a good tour that undergoes mutation will most likely have a higher cost after mutation than before. STDS simply keeps the worse tours and moves on.

With KBR, however, tours are evaluated after mutation, and the best parent is kept as well as the best child. The former guarantees that good genetic material remains in the population and is not destroyed by mutation, while the latter ensures that progress can be made in form of new genetic information. Keeping only the best child reduces the probability that a really bad mutated child is inserted into the next generation. The tours found with KBR are of much better quality than the ones found by STDS. The tour costs are similar for most mutation probabilities greater than 0.3 for population sizes of up to 400 and greater than 0.1 for population sizes 600, 800, 1000 and 1500. Figure 5 shows a single run for STDS and KBR with mutation only.

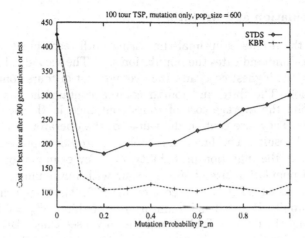

Fig. 4. The x-axis shows the mutation probability P_m, while the y-axis shows the cost of the tour after 300 generations or less for a 100 city random TSP. No recombination was used. The population size was 600

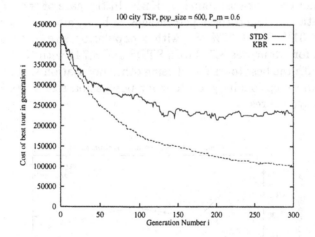

Fig. 5. The x-axis shows the generation number i, while the y-axis shows the cost of the best tour after i generations for a 100 city random TSP. No recombination was used. The mutation probability was set to $P_m = 0.6$. The population size was 600

As discussed in Subsect. 4.1, if the probability test for the mutation operator is not passed for either child, then the best parent and its child clone make it into the next population, thereby introducing a loss of diversity. Why does our data show such good results for small mutation probabilities? Since the mutation operator is applied individually and not on the set of children, the chance that at least one child will be mutated increases. This decreases the probability that KBR only keeps the best parent and its child clone.

4.3 Recombination and Mutation

Table 2 shows the results of optimal runs using both recombination and mutation. The first column indicates the population size. The second column contains the lowest cost, the highest cost, and the average cost of tours contained in the initial population. The third and fourth column contain the lowest cost, the highest cost, and the average cost of tours contained in the population after 300 generations. They also contain the values of the operator probabilities that yielded optimal results. The first number is the crossover probability P_c, the second number is the mutation probability P_m. For example for the 100 city problem and a population size of 800 the tour with minimum cost found after 300 generations using STDS had a cost of 131,597. This was achieved with a crossover probability $P_c = 0.3$ and a mutation probability $P_m = 0.1$.

By examining the data in Table 2 and Fig. 6 we see that KBR significantly improves the results obtained with the genetic algorithm. For the 100 city problem the cost of the cheapest tour found by STDS is between 55% and 68% higher than the tour-cost found by KBR. In our initial study [Wie98a] we also investigated 33 and 50 city problems with encouraging results. We found that for the 50 city problem the cost of the cheapest tour found by STDS is between 25% and 59% higher than the tour-cost found by KBR. In the case of the smallest problem with 33 cities we found these percentages to be significantly lower, ranging from 0.33% to 31%. The 0.33% was with a population size of 1000, where the minimum cost for a tour was 8,770 with STDS and 8,741 with KBR. Comparing these results with the best tours found using other population sizes, it seems that STDS found an exceptionally good tour for population size 1000. We consider this to be an atypical result.

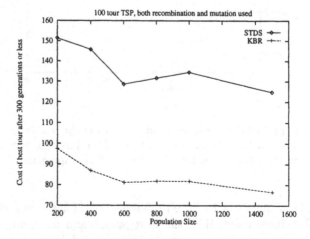

Fig. 6. The x-axis shows the population size, while the y-axis shows the cost of the best tour after 300 generations or less for a 100 city random TSP. For each population size the operator probabilities P_c and P_m were fine-tuned to yield optimal performance

Table 2. Best results after 300 generations for the 100 city problem. Both recombination and mutation were used. The crossover probability P_c and the mutation probability P_m were finetuned in each case to yield optimal algorithm performance

pop-size	Initial	STDS	KBR
	best tour worst tour average tour	best tour worst tour average tour P_c, P_m	best tour worst tour average tour P_c, P_m
200	430,672 581,774 499,398	151,374 192,703 162,810 0.5, 0.09	97,449 120,032 102,125 0.6, 0.6
400	430,672 581,774 500,781	145,714 185,052 154,692 0.6, 0.02	86,891 111,588 88,335 1.0, 0.5
600	425,016 600,179 500,520	128,600 182,331 136,592 0.5, 0.08	81,115 116,207 90,410 0.8, 0.9
800	413,272 600,420 500,571	131,597 178,439 137,883 0.3, 0.1	81,775 108,604 84,236 0.9, 0.4
1000	413,272 600,420 500,416	134,433 181,588 143,040 0.4, 0.05	81,767 113,471 85,686 1.0, 0.7
1500	413,272 600,420 500,528	124,668 176,807 135,370 0.5, 0.04	76,451 118,576 84,666 0.7, 0.8

We have found mutation rates of up to 10% useful for STDS. With KBR we were able to speed up the convergence of the GA by using higher mutation rates, as one can see from the mutation rates in Table 2. This should not come as a surprise. While with STDS, mutation is performed and the mutated chromosomes are inserted into the next generation, KBR only keeps the best child. In case mutation lowers the fitness of the offspring, there is always the good genetic material of the best parent that is kept. So higher mutation rates are not as disruptive as with STDS. On the other hand, without mutation, KBR very rapidly converges to local optima of low quality (see Subsect. 4.1). The higher mutation rates reintroduce diversity and help steer the GA away from these inferior local optima. One should note, however, that KBR is not the equivalent of an iterative improvement or random search. Mutation rates of 100% are not beneficial, optimal results were typically obtained with 40% to 90% for 100 city problems.

We also find that higher recombination rates are beneficial when KBR is used. In Table 2 the recombination rates that yielded optimal results were between 60% and 100%. With STDS, this rate was significantly lower, between 30% and 60% for the 100 city problem. Figure 6 shows the costs of the best tours found by STDS and KBR for different population sizes. A single run is shown in Fig. 7. Note that after 118 generations KBR found a tour of similar cost to the cost of the best tour found by STDS after 600 generations.

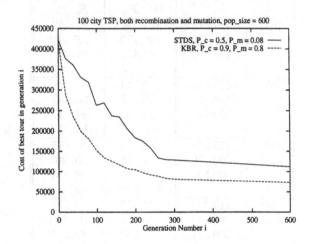

Fig. 7. The x-axis shows the generation number i, while the y-axis shows the cost of the best tour after i generations for a 100 city random TSP. The population size was 600

We would like to clarify the meaning of crossover probability as used in this paper. Crossover with KBR produces one child and clones one parent. A crossover probability of for example 60% is thus equivalent to a crossover probability of 30% with STDS, since only 30% of the chromosomes in the new population were created by crossover. However, intermediately two children are created by KBR in every crossover step. Thus, a crossover rate of 60% for KBR means that $0.6 \times sizeof(population)$ new chromosomes are created through crossover in each generation, but only $0.3 \times sizeof(poulation)$ are inserted into the new generation.

4.4 Varying Operator Probabilities

KBR also makes the underlying GA more robust in the sense that small changes in genetic operator probabilities do not lead to a large change in algorithm performance. For example, for the 100 city problem with a population size of 600, crossover probabilities varying from 0.1 to 1.0 and mutation probabilities varying from 0.01 to 0.10 for STDS and mutation probabilities varying from 0.1 to 1.0

for KBR the best tour that was found with STDS had cost 128,600, the worst tour had a cost of 402,533. The best tour found by KBR had cost 81,115 and the worst tour 127,938. This means that the worst tour found by STDS was 213% more expensive than the cheapest tour whereas the worst tour found by KBR was only 58% more expensive than the cheapest tour (percentages rounded to the next integer). This shows that KBR consistently finds better solutions than STDS. KBR is not affected as much by small changes to operator probabilities as is STDS. Table 3 shows the effect of a small change in the crossover probability from 0.6 to 0.7. While the tour found by KBR is about 7.25% cheaper after the change in crossover probability, the tour-cost increases by 100.1% if STDS is used.

Table 3. Performance difference after small change of operator probabilities. While the mutation probability P_m was not changed, the crossover probability P_c was changed from 0.6 to 0.7

STDS	KBR
best tour P_c, P_m	best tour P_c, P_m
168.018	100.513
0.6, 0.05	0.6, 0.5
337.193	93.230
0.7, 0.05	0.7, 0.5

5 Conclusion

We have proposed a new intermediate selection strategy, that compares parent encodings and child encodings and keeps the best parent as well as the best child. We call this selection strategy *Keep-Best Reproduction*. We have three conclusions to make. First, if recombination is used only, then KBR fails to find better tours than STDS. The optimal crossover probability for STDS lies between 0.5 and 0.7 for our test problems. Higher probabilities lead to a sharp increase in tour costs. Using KBR, the highest crossover probabilities yield the tours with lowest cost. The cost of these tours however is still higher than the ones found with STDS and lower crossover probabilities. Second, if only mutation is used, then KBR finds better tours than STDS over the full range of mutation probabilities. KBR finds similarly good tours for almost all mutation probability settings, while the tours found with STDS tend to have higher costs with higher mutation probabilities. Third, if we combine recombination and mutation, KBR outperforms STDS significantly on our test problems, especially as the problem size increases. Our study also shows that GAs are complex and brittle systems. Had we only implemented and tested KBR within the context of recombination we would have to report that KBR is not competitive with STDS. Introducing mutation and fine-tuning operator probabilities, however, showed that KBR can lead to impressive improvements. Even with significantly smaller population sizes, KBR finds better solutions than STDS with much larger populations. This means that a better solution can be found with less function evaluations and thus with less total computing time. KBR also converges faster, yielding better results faster, and in this way further contributes to a reduction in total computing time. The optimal results found with KBR have significantly different operator settings than STDS. Another observation we made is that KBR is less susceptible to a change in crossover probability and mutation probability. This makes GAs that use KBR more robust, i.e., the performance does not so heavily depend on parameter settings such as population size, crossover probability and mutation probability.

6 Further Research and Discussion

We are primarily interested in genetic operators such as selection, crossover, mutation and how they interact. Other non-GA approaches such as taboo search often outperform pure GAs in many problem domains. On the other hand, any GA can find solutions of at least the quality of any other local search algorithm if the GA is hybridized with this particular local search algorithm. However, the computing time might increase by doing so. This paper was intended to investigate KBR and the effect of genetic operator probabilities in the TSP domain for a pure (non-hybrid) GA. Undoubtedly there are many other very efficient GAs to solve the TSP, however, most of these could be combined with KBR and we believe that doing so would improve the quality of solutions found and/or improve the efficiency of the algorithm.

Since KBR as a selection strategy works on fitness values only, it should work well in other problem domains. This however remains to be shown empirically in every individual case. KBR can easily be added to any existing generational GA, which makes it easy for others to try KBR with their particular application.

We need to test KBR on some benchmark problems as well as on larger travelling salesman problems. We are confident however, that on these problems we will still be able to get better results with KBR than with STDS. Since KBR enforces some sort of local elitism we should compare KBR with a GA that uses STDS and elitism. It would be interesting to see how other GA techniques such as other parent selection strategies (tournament, random, ...) and other genetic operators (OX, PBX, CX, ...) affect the performance of KBR versus STDS.

Our intention is to build a distributed genetic system for constraint optimization. We will implement a distributed GA with KBR on a MIMD system with 64 transputer nodes. We will compare STDS and KBR for this parallel implementation and are confident that we will accomplish similar good results as in the sequential case.

In order to put KBR in context with other advanced selection strategies we will do a theoretical analysis of KBR in order to determine its selection intensity, and convergence characteristics and compare KBR with its most similar family competition scheme elitist recombination [Thi94]. We will also test KBR in other application areas, such as finding good linear error correction codes [McG98] and dynamic channel assignment for cellular radio [San98].

7 Acknowledgements

The authors would like to thank the Institute of Robotics and Intelligent Systems (IRIS/PRECARN) for funding this research. This research is part of the Intelligent Scheduling Project IC-6.

References

[Bae96] Baeck, T., "Evolutionary Algorithms in Theory and Practice: Evolution Strategies, Evolutionary Programming, Genetic Algorithms", Oxford University Press, 1996.

[Gol85] Goldberg, D.E. and Lingle, R., Jr., "Alleles, Loci, and the Traveling Salesman Problem", *Proceedings of the 1st ICGA*, pp. 154–159, 1985.

[Gre85] Grefenstette, J.J., Gopal, R., Rosmaita, R., and van Gucht, D., "Genetic Algorithms for the Traveling Salesman Problem", *Proceedings of the 1st ICGA*, pp. 160–168, 1985.

[Hol75] Holland, J.H., *Adaptation in Natural and Artificial Systems*, Ann Arbor, MI, University of Michigan Press, 1975.

[McG98] McGuire, K.M. and Sabin R.E., "Using a Genetic Algorithm to Find Good Linear Error-Correcting Codes", *Proceedings of the 1998 ACM Symposium on Applied Computing SAC'98*", pp. 332–337, 1998.

[Oli87] Oliver, I.M., Smith, D.J., and Holland, J.R.C.,, "A Study of Permutation Crossover Operators on the Traveling Salesman Problem", *Proceedings of the 2nd ICGA*, pp. 224-230, 1987.

[San98] Sandalidis H.G., Stavroulakis P.P., Rodriguez-Tellez J., "A Combinatorial Evolution Strategy for Dynamic Channel Assignment in Cellular Radio", *Proceedings of the 1998 ACM Symposium on Applied Computing SAC'98*", pp. 303–307, 1998.

[Sta91] Starkweather, T., McDaniel, S., et. al, "A Comparison of Genetic Sequencing Operators", *Proceedings of the 4th ICGA*, pp. 69–76, 1991.

[Thi94] Thierens, D. and Goldberg, D.E., "Elitist Recombination: An Integrated Selection Recombination GA", *Proceedings of the 1st IEEE World Congress on Computational Intelligence*, pp. 508–512, 1994.

[Thi97] Thierens, D., "Selection Schemes, Elitist Recombination and Selection Intensity", *Proceedings of the 7th International Conference on Genetic Algorithms ICGA-97*, pp. 152–159, 1997.

[Wie98a] Wiese, K. and Goodwin, S.D., "Keep-Best Reproduction: A Selection Strategy for Genetic Algorithms", *Proceedings of the 1998 ACM Symposium on Applied Computing SAC'98*, pp. 343–348, 1998.

[Wie98b] Wiese K. and Goodwin, S.D., "Parallel Genetic Algorithms for Constrained Ordering Problems", *Proceedings of the 11th International Florida Artificial Intelligence Research Symposium, FLAIRS'98*, to appear, 1998.

[Whi89] Whitley, D., Starkweather, T., and D'Ann Fuquay, "Scheduling Problems and Traveling Salesman: The Genetic Edge Recombination Operator", *Proceedings of the 3rd ICGA*, pp. 133–140, 1989.

The Impact of External Dependency in Genetic Programming Primitives

Una-May O'Reilly

The Artificial Intelligence Lab,
Massachusetts Institute of Technology,
545 Technology Sq, Cambridge, MA, 02139, USA
WWW home page: http://www.ai.mit.edu/people/unamay
Email: unamay@ai.mit.edu

Abstract. The power of genetic programming arises from its ability to identify and promote appropriate subprograms of the "true" solution via its fitness based selection and inheritance mechanism ("survival of the fittest") and then combine them via blind variation in terms of subtree crossover. Both control and data dependencies among primitives impact the behavioural consistency of subprograms in genetic programming solutions which in turn taxes the efficiency of selection. We present the results of modelling dependency through a parameterized problem in which a subprogram exhibits internal and external dependency levels that change as the subprogram is successively incorporated into larger subsolutions. We find that the key difference between non-existent and "full" external dependency when a solution is composed of subsolutions with exponentially scaled fitness contributions is a longer time to solution identification and a lower likelihood of success as shown by increased difficulty in identifying and promoting correct subprograms.

1 Motivation

One reason our understanding of genetic programming [Koza, 1992] is imprecise is the lack of an adequate account of how program dependencies impact the effectiveness of selection and crossover. Program dependencies can be decomposed into two classes: control and data. A control dependency between two program statements means that they must be executed in specific order so that the program proceeds correctly. A data dependency between two statements means that one statement sets up a data state (e.g. variable) which the other one subsequently needs to reference.

We contend [O'Reilly and Oppacher, 1995] that program dependency is a key issue in GP. In our view a subprogram has both *internal* dependencies and *external* dependencies. Internal dependencies are data and control relationships that stay within the subprogram. External dependencies denote a data or control relationship between the subprogram and code that either precedes it in execution or follows it in execution.

Regardless of how code surrounding a subprogram changes, the part of its behaviour that depends on internal dependencies never changes. In the case of external dependencies, quite the opposite is true. The code which surrounds a subprogram influences the effectiveness of its externally dependent behaviour. This has the following consequences:

Based on the concept of a schema [Goldberg, 1989], a genetic algorithm acquires estimates of the value of a component of a solution ("schema") via sampling potential solutions which embed it and assessing their fitness. Selection promotes components which demonstrate above average fitness in this manner each generation. Dependency implies that the subprogram fitnesses the GP algorithm estimates and then uses to guide promotion of subprograms are inaccurate. When a subprogram has external dependencies the average of any population sample is probably a poor estimate of the true average. If the value of a subprogram is over-estimated, it will be promoted through selection even if it is not truly worthy. Or, if the value of a subprogram is under-estimated, it will be incorrectly ignored. Concisely, external dependencies imply that the fitness distribution of a subprogram's instances (embedded in programs) has high variance. This leads to inaccurate estimates of a subprogram's fitness. This could result in inappropriate subprograms being identified as solution components by GP.

Second, a critical number of external dependencies will make it hard to use a subprogram in multiple parts of a program because it does not exhibit modular behavior.

Third, to some extent external dependencies mimic epistasis or feature interdependence as the term is used in GAs. The critical difference is that external dependencies resolve as subprograms combine but epistasis is stationary. Considering dependency without resolution: If each subprogram has many external dependencies the situation is similar to high epistasis in GAs. In the case of GP (compared to linear bit string GAs) understanding how the algorithm handles them is even more complicated. GP's non-binary alphabet and representation which varies in length and structure enlarge the size of the search space and increase the range of behavioural combinations.

Finally, consider the case where a subprogram has an internal dependency but there is a large amount of code between the statements which are dependent upon one another. Crossover has a high probability of disconnecting the dependent statements because they span a large amount of code. Broadly, useful subprograms with long range dependencies are nonetheless vulnerable to being lost because of crossover.

How the paper proceeds

Given these complicated issues surrounding program dependencies, we have designed a simple model of program dependency in terms of external and internal dependency and in terms of a dependency resolution scheme which assumes that external dependence decreases as a subprogram is subsumed into progressively larger subsolutions. This model consists of a parameterized problem which GP is asked to solve. The problem is constructed deliberately to isolate and control the dependency issues and to permit monitoring of microscopic GP phenomena such as time of subsolution identification, critical levels of subsolution quantities, and their correlation with the rate of fitness improvement. Section 2 describes the problem and indicates how it can be used to model dependency and monitor GP. In this paper we vary the problem parameter controlling external dependency from one extreme to the other. Section 3 first sets out experimental hypotheses and questions. It then provides the run parameters of the investigation. Finally, it presents experimental results and analysis which from which conclusions are drawn. The paper ends with a necessarily short list of future work in Section 4.

2 A Function Modelling Dependency

Reminiscent of a Royal Road function [Mitchell et al., 1992] our constructed problem uses a primitive set composed of dummy functions and terminals. Instead of executing a program and examining its final state or output to determine its fitness, a program is directly inspected to see what combinations of primitives it contains that are subprograms of an optimal solution. For any subprogram of the optimal solution, the program receives a variable contribution (up to a pre-designated maximum) to its overall fitness. The variable contribution reflects dependency and associated behaviour.

The central merit of constructing a problem is that knowledge of the structure of a problem can be used to "watch" the algorithm execute on the level of subsolution identification and combination. It is computationally too expensive to monitor all possible subprograms in a standard GP problem because the subprograms of the optimal solutions are not competely specified in advance.

Our choice of a primitive set was fairly arbitrary. Each primitive of the set {A,B,C,D,E,F,G,H,I} has corresponding arity {3,3,2,2,1,1,0,0,0}. We designated a set of solutions in which each solution embeds each primitive twice. The expressed portion of each solution is the same but non-expressed portions may differ. A solution must be rooted at the root of the program it is found in. The solution set is shown as a program parse tree (with wildcard subtrees denoted by "*") in Figure 1. It can be described with s-expression notation that also uses wildcards:

$$(D(A*(B*(DIG)*)(C(EH)(F*)))(B(CIH)*(A*(E(FG)))*))$$

We chose to assign fitness contributions to a designated set of subprograms that progressively overlap and increase in size (see Table 1). In terms of combination this hierarchy is intended to make the problem straightforward for GP to solve. At the bottom (i.e. level 1) there are 17 subprograms of length 1. They comprise every correct pairing of primitives found in the solution. The subprograms at level 2 are 8 overlapping pairwise combinations of level 1 subprograms. They are all of length 2. Level 3 is 4 overlapping pairwise combinations of level 3 subprograms, level 4 is the 2 overlapping pairs of level 3 subprograms and, finally, level 5 is the combination of both level 4 subprograms. Subprograms of levels 1 through 4 do not have to be embedded in a program tree at the root or any other special location.

Level	Ref. No.	Subprogram
1	1	$(*(A*(B***)*))$
	2	$(*(A**(C**)))$
	3	$(*(CE*))$
	4	$(*(C*F))$
	5	$(*(B*(D**)*))$
	6	$(*(DI*))$
	7	$(*(D*G))$
	8	$(*(EH))$
	9	$(*(DA*))$
	10	$(*(D*B))$
	11	$(*(BC**))$
	12	$(*(B**A))$
	13	$(*(CI*))$
	14	$(*(C*H))$
	15	$(*(AE**))$
	16	$(*(EF))$
	17	$(*(FG))$
2	18	$(*(A*(B*(D**)*)*))$
	19	$(*(DIG))$
	20	$(*(A**(C*(F*))))$
	21	$(*(C(EH)*))$
	22	$(*(CIH))$
	23	$(*(D*(B(C**)**)))$
	24	$(*(B**(AE**)))$
	25	$(*(E(FG)))$
3	26	$(*(A*(B*(DIG)*)*))$
	27	$(*(A**(C(EH)(F*))))$
	28	$(*(D*(B(CIH)**)))$
	29	$(*(B**(A(E(FG))**)))$
4	30	$(*(A*(B*(DIG)*)(C(EH)(F*))))$
	31	$(*(D*(B(CIH)*(A(E(FG))**))))$
5	32	$(D(A*(B*(DIG)*)(C(EH)(F*)))$ $*(B(CIH)*(A(E(FG))**)))$

Table 1. Subprograms of the solution set. An asterisk denotes any syntactically legal s-expression.

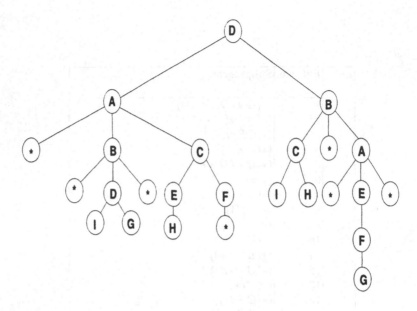

Fig. 1. The solution set of the dependency problem. An asterisk denotes any subtree as acceptable.

The fitness contribution of a subprogram is the sum of *content* and *placement* components:

The placement component provides fitness pressure to manoever a complete solution towards the root of a program tree. Designate d as the the distance in tree edges between the root of the solution and the root of its embedding program tree. Designate h as the maximum tree height parameter of the GP run. The placement component of a level 1 to 4 subprogram is zero. The placement of a level 5 subprogram, is $h - d$.

The *maximum* content fitness that a subprogram at level k can contribute to its embedding program increases non-linearly to model our assumption that some non-linear aspect of program behaviour makes a subprogram at level $k+1$ worth more than the sum of its two parts at level k. The progression of maximum fitness contributions for a block of each level is presented in Table 2.

Level	1	2	2	4	5
Max content Fitness	1	2	8	32	64
Max placement Fitness	0	0	0	0	h

Table 2. Fitness Components of subprograms. Values given are maximum.

To model dependency the problem is specifically designed with two parameters:

1. D: the fraction of external dependency exhibited by a subprogram
2. R: the rate at which external dependency is resolved by subprogram combination.

Together the parameters control the *actual* content fitness contribution of a subprogram. Internal dependency $(1 - D)$ is multiplied by maximum content fitness to obtain a static component of content fitness contribution. External dependency (D) is multiplied by a random value RN from $(0 \ldots 1)$, maximum content fitness and the (as yet to be explained) resolution factor R_l to obtain a variable component of fitness contribution. The subscript l refers to the level of the largest subprogram which subsumes the subprogram in question.

These fitness contribution products equate to the following two conditions: First, if a subprogram has no external dependencies once it is subsumed by a larger subprogram, it contributes its maximum content fitness to the program that contains it. Second, when a subprogram has external dependencies, the fixed and variable components are added together to compose its actual content fitness.

The justification is that the part of a subprogram's behaviour that depends on internal dependencies never changes. Thus its value to a program that embeds it is constant. In the case of external dependencies, because the code which surrounds a subprogram influences the effectiveness of its externally dependent behaviour, this part of a subprogram's fitness contribution varies. We simulate this variance by drawing a random coefficient which is used to make the fitness contribution based on external dependency variable.

We presume that when two subprograms of one level combine to form one of the next level some of their external dependencies are with each other. These become internal dependencies of the combined subprogram. However, some external dependencies remain because they are not resolved by the combination. As subprograms get larger we presume that the number of external dependencies decreases because more and more external dependencies among constituent blocks are resolved as the block gets longer. We control this resolution with parameter R, the resolution schedule.

Table 3 presents the dependency resolution schedule used. It basically states a quantified relation such that when a block of level k is embedded in a block of level $k + 1$ or higher, only a fraction R_l of the level k's block's variable fitness contribution is subject to external dependency factors. As a block is subsumed by blocks of higher and higher levels its variable fitness contribution decreases and its fixed contribution increases.

3 The Dependency Variation Experiment

3.1 Hypothesis

We shall observe GP solving the function when D is set to its minimum $(D = 0)$ and when D is set to its maximum $(D = 1)$. A sensible initial hypothesis is

Level of Subsuming Subprogram	2	3	4	5
Resolution Factor		0.80	0.60	0.40	0.20

Table 3. Dependency Resolution Schedule. The variable fitness contribution of the given subprogram is reduced by a factor of R_l corresponding to the subsuming block's level

that when subprograms are highly dependent on external code (e.g. $D = 1$), the fitness variance of the initial sample of subprograms conducted early in GP will be great. This will more frequently lead GP to select and promote copies of inappropriate subprograms and result in lower probability of success and longer expected number of evaluations to find an optimal program. When subprograms are relatively insensitive to external code (e.g. $D = 0$), GP will have a more accurate estimate of a subprogram's fitness and, because the fitter subprograms combine into the optimal solution, use this to efficiently discover the optimal solution.

3.2 Run Parameters

We ran the GP algorithm with standard parameter settings listed in Table 4.

Parm	Setting
pop size	300
max gen	300
Selection	Fitness Proportional, 1 elite individual
init tree height	random to height 5
max tree height	12
crossover	unbiased point selection
$D = 0$, experiment size	103 runs
$D = 1$, experiment size	60 runs

Table 4. GP Run Parameters

3.3 Experimental Results

One question is whether the macroscopic phenomena of best individual and population fitness time series indicates a difference between the extremes of D. Figure 2 is the mean values of 103 and 60 runs respectively. Error bars are not plotted because they are very short and do not intersect. The plots show that when there is no external dependency, GP progresses towards a solution at a faster rate and attains higher best individual and population fitness. Thus, dependency, even when it resolves itself as subsolutions combine, makes a problem harder for GP to solve.

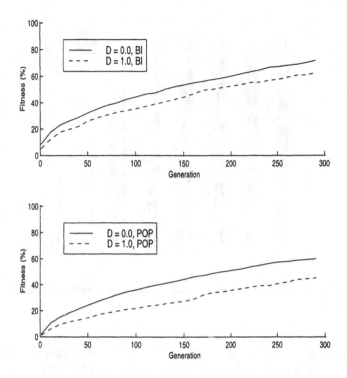

Fig. 2. Fitness Time Series (experiment average). Best Individual is upper plot, population is lower plot.

Figure 3 indicates the magnitude of difficulty in terms of the fraction of runs that were able to attain a given number of distinct subprograms. Its information can be correlated with the information in Figure 4 which indicates at what generation a given number of subprograms was first found.

With or without external dependency, all runs of an experiment were able to evolve at least one program with 26 of the 33 different required subprograms. While this "pace" was kept up by the $D = 0$ case up to approximately 30 subprograms, the $D = 1$ case immediately started to fall off. Only 85% of $D = 1$ runs attained 29 subprograms and, while approximately one third did find a program having all of the 32 subprograms properly combined, none of these runs were able to move the combined subtree up to the root of the program where it would perfectly express the correct solution. The $D = 0$ runs dropped off from 100% success later, that is, when 31 subprograms were inspected. Only three quarters of the runs found a program with at least 31 subprograms and only one third found all the subprograms (i.e. 32). However, almost all of these latter runs successfully moved the solution combination to the root position.

The tendency to experience a lower likelihood of subprogram combination and discovery is not perfectly correlated with the time required to find a specific quantity of subprograms (see Figure 4) or to find one more subprogram (see Figure 5). This reveals a complication in the algorithm (and model and statis-

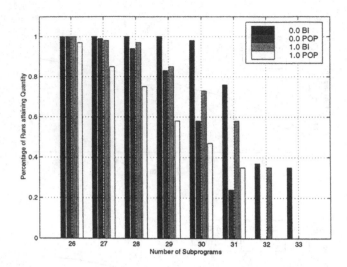

Fig. 3. Fraction of runs in experiment discovering a program with specified quantity of subprograms.

tics compilation) deserving of future attention. On average, the $D = 0$ runs found a program with 26 subprograms after 25.48 (10.81)[1] generations and the $D = 1$ runs reached them after 42.33 (23.87) generations. Note the considerably higher standard error in the latter case. It stems from higher variance in $D = 1$ subprogram fitness estimates.

It appears somewhat puzzling that the generation of acquisition was later for $D = 1$ for 27 to 31 subprograms yet both $D = 0$ and $D = 1$ runs, on average, found their first program with 32 subprograms around generation 205 (with approximately the same standard error). As well, after 28 subprograms, $D = 1$ actually acquires correct new subprograms at a faster rate.

One partial explanation for this could be that this a statistical artifact. Recall that Figures 4 and Figures 5 only compiled data from runs where the quantity of hits was *actually* found (i.e. truncated data): Fewer $D = 1$ runs attained between 29 and 31 subprograms. Presuming we could correctly estimate the out of range data values which were truncated, we would expect higher variance, and perhaps more correlation between likelihood of acquisition and time of acquisition or time to acquire. We are considering non-parametric statistical tests as a means of overcoming the censored data problem.

Another possible explanation is that by the time a $D = 1$ run manages to find a program with 28 correct subprograms, it has so many copies of the compositional subprograms that it is more likely that crossover can chance upon a combination yielding a 29th subprogram.

Level statistics are shown in Figures 6 and 7 and Table 5. As per subprogram acquisition, smaller fractions of runs of $D = 1$ are able to complete levels 2, 3

---

[1] Std-error

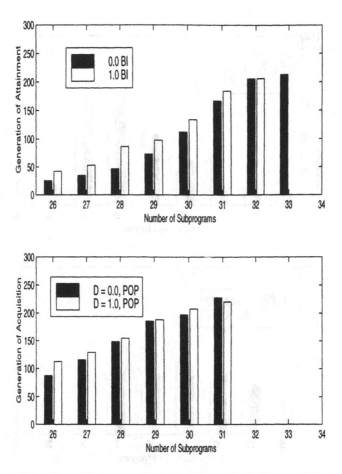

Fig. 4. Generation when subprogram quantity is acquired. Upper plot applies to best individual (BI) of run acquiring the quantity and lower plot to the population (POP) acquiring the quantity on average. Data is truncated.

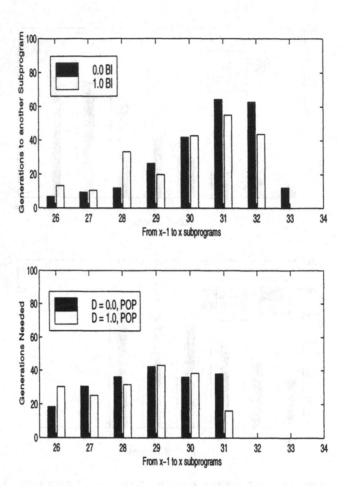

Fig. 5. How many generations it takes for a one subprogram improvement. Upper plot applies to best individual (BI) of run acquiring one more subprogram. Lower plot shows the generations required by the population (POP) to, on average, attain another subprogram. Data is truncated.

and 4. Each successive fraction is also smaller than the previous. However, once again, for both $D = 0$ and $D = 1$ 35% of the runs successfully acquire level 5 (which is consists solely of subprogram 32). Less runs of $D = 1$ find all the subprograms of level 4 than $D = 0$ but, when the $D = 1$ runs do so, they find the level more quickly. They require on average 5 fewer generations, *in the case where a run acquires the level.* Figure 7 indicates that acquisition of level 3 and level 4 subprograms overlaps. This is not the case with levels 4 and 5 because overlap is impossible.

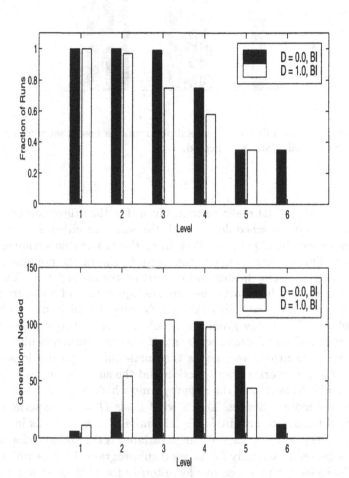

Fig. 6. Upper plot shows fraction of runs where best program (BI) discovered all subprograms of a level. Lower plot indicates the generations required for the best program to find all the subprograms of a level. Data is truncated.

Why do a higher percentage of runs which attain 31 subprograms reach 32 subprograms in the $D = 1$ case than in the $D = 0$ case? And, why, though less runs of $D = 1$ acquire level 4, do they do so more quickly than those of $D = 0$?

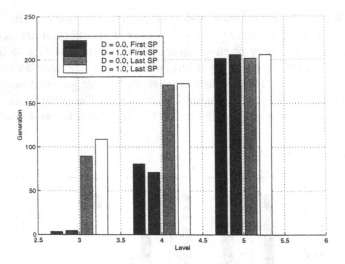

Fig. 7. Generation when first and final subprogram of a level's set were all co-located in the Best Individual. Data is truncated.

The answer lies in first realizing that, given that the fitness contribution components and resolution schedule are both the same for either $D = 0$ or $D = 1$, the differences can be explained solely in of the observable variance in fitness when $D = 1$. This variance impacts the mean fitness of the population and the fitness difference between the best individual and the mean fitness. This, in turn, impacts selection which dictates the expected quantities of a subprogram from one generation to the next. There are no "wrong" or misleading subprograms in this problem. GP is only given the problem of allocating optimal quantities and proportions of subprograms such that a correct solution is discovered. The negative impact of fitness variance is that non-uniform proportions of subprograms of a levels may arise from selection and the subprograms of a level which are present will "crowd out" the subprograms which need to be discovered by being allocated more instances. This is what leads $D = 1$ to experience a higher percentage of failures to acquire levels 2,3 and 4 or subprograms in quantity 27 through 31. The positive impact of fitness variance is the ability to for selection to "quickly" seize on a randomly found good subprogram (i.e. one which has large external dependency but which has fortuitously found itself in a good context) when it is discovered. This will happen when the subprogram and its embedding program have higher fitness than average. This situation is enabled by the fact that the expected fitness of externally dependent subprograms is lower and this lowers the mean fitness and makes the difference between the best individual and the mean fitness relatively large. This positive situation is what we conjecture happens when subprogram 31 or level 4 is acquired: while a smaller fraction of $D = 1$ runs find the subprograms of level 4 (or attain 31 subprograms), when these successful runs "stumble on the happy event" they immediately exploit their discovery, reproduces copies of subprograms quickly and provide crossover with the opportunity to find another fortuitous combination.

Table 5 reveals that among the pool of best programs there was, on average, more than one copy of a subprogram in each program at the time every level was acquired by the best program (see BI Density where BI stands for Best Individual and density is the number of instances of the subprogram as a fraction of the BI pool).

However, BI Coverage indicates that not every one of these programs had at least one copy during the acquisition of levels 1 through 3. Coverage is the fraction of programs in a pool that embed at least one copy of the subprogram.

The density of a level's subprograms in the population is drastically different between $D = 0$ and $D = 1$ for levels 1,2, and 3. While $D = 0$ populations have a density less than one, $D = 1$ populations have a density very close to 1 or higher. The differences between $D = 0$ values and $D = 1$ values can be explained by the variance in actual fitness of $D = 1$'s subprograms. More copies are required to ensure a high likelihood that at least one expresses higher than average fitness.

	BI Coverage		BI Density		Pop Coverage		Pop Density	
L	0.0	1.0	0.0	1.0	0.0	1.0	0.0	1.0
1	0.83	0.86	1.64	1.86	0.51	0.58	0.86	1.16
2	0.82	0.90	1.35	1.87	0.49	0.64	0.85	1.44
3	0.93	0.98	1.28	1.29	0.57	0.60	0.84	0.93
4	1.00	0.99	1.04	1.10	0.42	0.41	0.51	0.47
5	1.00	1.00	1.00	1.00	0.00	0.00	0.00	0.00

Table 5. BI and Population Level Coverage and Level Density at Generation of Level Completion in BI. Data is truncated and applies only to runs where BI did achieve the level.

In general, the differences in coverage and density suggest implications in real GP problems. Problems with a large measure of external dependency in their primitives will have to acquire more instances of correct subprograms before these can be exploited by selection because, despite being appropriate for the correct solution, the correct subprograms' behaviour is variable and provides only noisy indication of the ultimate value. If external dependencies do not span long sections of code, crossover has the same disruptive and combinative effects on problems with different external dependencies. However, if a problem with external dependencies also has a solution that has long spanning dependencies, crossover will be less likely to provide combinative effects and thus there will be a requirement for even more copies of the subprogram to improve the odds of a combinative event. Alternatively, unexpressed "junk code" may be beneficial in reducing the likelihood that a long spanning pair of dependent subprograms are disrupted by crossover.

3.4 Conclusions

Without restating the detailed findings, a quick summary is: Problems which employ primitives that have external dependency properties similar to those of our model with $D = 1$ (i.e. external dependency causes fitness variance yet decreases with subprogram combination) are more difficult for GP to solve than those employing primitives with less dependency on surrounding primitives such as the model with $D = 0$. Difficult can be taken to mean less likelihood of a run succeeding and longer time periods to formulate improved solutions. However, there is some evidence that problems with external dependence can exploit lucky events which on less frequent occasions allow them to find solution faster. This depends on the relative value of subprograms and how selection affects the fitness distribution of the population.

4 Future Work

There is obviously more data analysis to be done with these parameters of the dependency model. We still have data from intermediate settings of D that space does not permit us to discuss. In addition both the dependency resolution schedule and fitness contributions which were fixed in the present experiments could be varied in isolation for controlled comparison. A uniform fitness contribution rather than the non-linear scheme of Table 2 might clarify some of the more complicated phenomena we have reported. Beyond exploring the model, we plan to figure out how to calibrate it to dependency in real GP problems. For this we are considering dependency flow analysis and Monte Carlo sampling approaches.

Acknowledgments

The author is grateful for support from ONR under contract number N00014-95-1-0600 and from a Natural Sciences and Engineering Research Council (Canada) Post Doctoral Fellow award.

References

[Goldberg, 1989] Goldberg, D. E. (1989). *Genetic Algorithms in Search, Optimization, and Machine Learning*. Addison-Wesley, Reading, MA.

[Koza, 1992] Koza, J. R. (1992). *Genetic Programming: On the Programming of Computers by Means of Natural Selection*. MIT Press, Cambridge, MA.

[Mitchell et al., 1992] Mitchell, M., Forrest, S., and Holland, J. H. (1992). The royal road for genetic algorithms: Fitness landscapes and GA performance. In Varela, F. J. and Bourgine, P., editors, *Proceedings of the First European Conference on Artificial Life. Toward a Practice of Autonomous Systems*, pages 245–254, Cambridge, MA. MIT Press.

[O'Reilly and Oppacher, 1995] O'Reilly, U.-M. and Oppacher, F. (1995). The troubling aspects of a building block hypothesis for genetic programming. In Whitley, L. D. and Vose, M. D., editors, *Foundations of Genetic Algorithms*, volume 3, San Mateo, CA. Morgan Kaufmann.

Quality Control in the Concept Learning Process

Udo Hahn & Klemens Schnattinger

(ⓒF) Text Knowledge Engineering Lab, Freiburg University
Werthmannplatz 1, D-79085 Freiburg, Germany
http://www.coling.uni-freiburg.de

Abstract. A natural language text understanding system with advanced learning capabilities is presented. New concepts are acquired on the fly by incorporating two kinds of evidence – knowledge about linguistic constructions in which unknown lexical items occur and knowledge about structural patterns in ontologies such that new concept descriptions can be compared with prior knowledge. On the basis of the quality of evidence gathered this way concept hypotheses are generated, ranked according to plausibility, and the most credible ones are selected for assimilation into the domain knowledge base.

1 Introduction

We propose a text understanding approach in which continuous enhancements of domain knowledge bases are performed given a core ontology (such as WordNet [3]). New concepts are acquired taking two sources of evidence into account: the prior knowledge of the domain the texts are about, and linguistic constructions in which unknown lexical items occur. Domain knowledge serves as a comparison scale for judging the plausibility of newly derived concept descriptions in the light of prior knowledge. Linguistic knowledge helps to assess the strength of the interpretative force that can be attributed to the grammatical construction in which a new lexical item occurs. Our model makes explicit the kind of quality-based reasoning that lies behind such a process.

We advocate a *knowledge-intensive* model of concept learning from sparse data that is tightly integrated with the non-learning mode of text understanding. Both learning and understanding build on a given core ontology in the format of terminological assertions, and hence make abundant use of terminological reasoning facilities. The "plain" text understanding mode can be considered as the instantiation and continuous filling of roles with respect to *single concepts* already available in the knowledge base. Under learning conditions, a *set of alternative concept hypotheses* are managed for each unknown item, with each hypothesis denoting a newly created conceptual interpretation tentatively associated with the unknown item.

In order to illustrate some important aspects of the learning process, let us suppose, your background knowledge of the information technology domain tells you that *Aquarius* is a producer in the IT world. By convention, you know absolutely nothing about *Megaline*. Imagine, one day your favorite computer

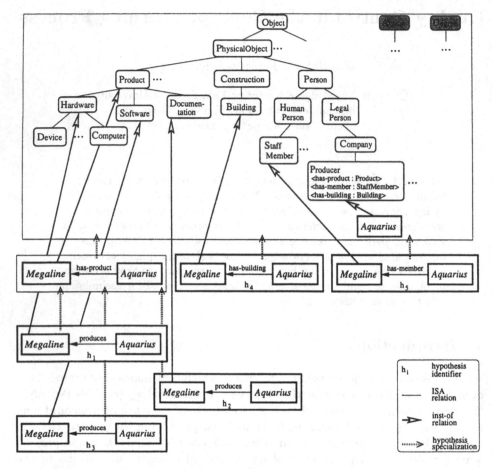

Fig. 1. A Sample Learning Scenario: Setting for *"Megaline of Aquarius ..."*

magazine features an article starting with *"Megaline of Aquarius .."*. Has your knowledge increased? And if so, to what extent, i.e., what did you learn already from just this short phrase?

Fig. 1 attempts to outline an answer to these questions by considering the initial setting of a sample learning scenario. The incremental concept formation process starts upon the reading of the unknown lexical item *"Megaline"*. In this initial step, the corresponding hypothesis space incorporates all the top level concepts available in the ontology for the new lexical item *"Megaline"*. So, the concept MEGALINE may be a kind of an OBJECT, ACTION, etc.

Continuing with the processing of the phrase *"Megaline of Aquarius ..."* brings in *a priori* knowledge associated with *Aquarius*. The *linguistic* structure of the phrasal pattern *Noun-"of"-Noun (1.)* licenses some conceptual relation between the concepts MEGALINE and AQUARIUS to be established but *(2.)* places no additional constraints on the kinds of conceptual relations that may be selected for consideration (besides the fact that numerical expressions are excluded by the nonnumerical nature of the unknown concept MEGALINE). Considering, however, the *conceptual* attributes (roles) it is related to (some of which are inherited from more general concepts, some of which are unique for a producer), we may then select all nonnumerical conceptual relations associated with AQUARIUS, and relate AQUARIUS via each of these relations to MEGALINE.

As an immediate consequence, the processing of this phrase lets us exclude several top-level hypotheses such as ACTION or DEGREE, since they cannot be related to AQUARIUS in any way (cf. the darkly shadowed boxes). But we may still derive more specific hypotheses about the very nature of MEGALINE. This is due to the fact that the range of each of these relations emanating from AQUARIUS has attached to it a conceptual range restriction constraining the type of possible role fillers. When filling the conceptual roles HAS-PRODUCT, HAS-MEMBER, HAS-BUILDING, etc. with MEGALINE, as a consequence, MEGALINE is tentatively assumed to be a kind of PRODUCT, STAFFMEMBER, BUILDING, etc. of AQUARIUS (we here restrict ourselves, of course, to a subset of conceptual relations associated with AQUARIUS). Any of these hypotheses are kept in a special hypothesis space, and additional evidence from later text passages will be taken into account for each of them – either to further refine a hypothesis or to invalidate it in the light of incoming information.

The knowledge intensity of our approach is even more visible when one has a closer look at one of the above hypotheses, *viz.* the one indicating that AQUARIUS HAS-PRODUCT MEGALINE. In this case, further conceptual constraints help to immediately refine that hypothesis (we here refer to definitions of conceptual relations such as the one given by (P3) in Section 2.1). This is due to the fact that a PRODUCER in our application always produces either HARDWARE, SOFTWARE or DOCUMENTATION material, and nothing else. Hence, we may be more specific already in that we specialize the original hypothesis, MEGALINE INST-OF PRODUCT, to three more informative hypotheses, namely MEGALINE INST-OF HARDWARE, MEGALINE INST-OF SOFTWARE, and MEGALINE INST-OF DOCUMENTATION. This is exactly the result of the first concept formation round that is mirrored by five different hypothesis spaces — h_1, h_2, and h_3 cover the refined PRODUCT reading in three different subspaces, h_4 relates to the BUILDING and h_5 to the STAFFMEMBER hypothesis, respectively. Any of these five hypotheses will be subject to further updates by information that flows into the system as more data about MEGALINE is made available in the text (cf. Table 1)

2   A Model of Quality-Based Learning

Fig. 2 depicts how linguistic and conceptual evidence are generated and combined for continuously discriminating and refining the set of concept hypotheses (the unknown item yet to be learned is characterized by the black square). The *language processor* (for an overview, cf. [6]) yields structural dependency information from the grammatical constructions in which an unknown lexical item occurs in terms of the corresponding *parse tree*. The kinds of syntactic constructions (e.g., genitive, coordination, comparative), in which unknown lexical items

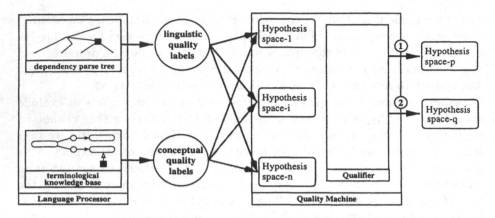

Fig. 2. Architecture for Quality-Based Learning

appear, are recorded and later on assessed relative to the credit they lend to a particular hypothesis. The conceptual interpretation of parse trees involving unknown lexical items in the *terminological knowledge base* is used to derive *concept hypotheses*, which are further enriched by conceptual annotations reflecting structural patterns of consistency, mutual justification, analogy, etc. These kinds of initial evidence, in particular their predictive "goodness" for the learning task, are represented by corresponding sets of *linguistic* and *conceptual quality labels*. Multiple concept hypotheses for each unknown lexical item are organized in terms of a corresponding *hypothesis space*, each subspace holding different or further specialized concept hypotheses.

The *quality machine* estimates the overall credibility of single concept hypotheses by taking the available set of quality labels for each hypothesis into account. The final computation of a preference order for the entire set of competing hypotheses takes place in the *qualifier*, a terminological classifier extended by an evaluation metric for quality-based selection criteria. The output of the quality machine is a ranked list of concept hypotheses. The ranking yields, in decreasing order of significance, either the most plausible concept classes which classify the considered instance or more general concept classes subsuming the considered concept class (cf. [13] for details of this metareasoning process).

2.1 Linguistic Quality Labels

Linguistic quality labels reflect structural properties of phrasal patterns or discourse contexts in which unknown lexical items occur – we assume here that the type of grammatical construction exercises a particular interpretative force on the unknown item and, at the same time, yields a particular level of credibility for the hypotheses being derived thereof. As an example of a high-quality label, consider the case of COMPOUND. This label is generated for constructions such as *"...the @A@ unit ..."*, with "@..@" denoting the unknown item. The compound almost unequivocally determines "@A@" (considered as a potential noun)[1] to denote an instance of the concept class UNIT. This assumption is justified independent of further conceptual conditions, simply due to the nature of the linguistic construction being used. Still of good quality, but less constraining, are occurrences of the unknown item in a CASEFRAME construction as illustrated by *"... @B@ is equipped with memory ..."*. Here, case frame specifications of the verb *"equip"* that relate to its PATIENT role carry over to *"@B@"*. Given its final semantic interpretation, *"@B@"* may be anything that is equipped with memory. Hence, considering an utterance like *"The Megaline is equipped with memory ..."*, we may hypothesize that, in an information technology domain, at least, MEGALINE can tentatively be considered, e.g., a COMPUTER.

Let us now return to the discussion of the phrase *"Megaline of Aquarius ..."* in more technical terms. We use a concept description language (for a survey, cf. [14]) for representing both the content of texts and the emerging concept hypotheses. One possible translation of this phrase into corresponding concept descriptions yields:

(P1) *Aquarius* : PRODUCER
(P2) *Aquarius* HAS-PRODUCT *Megaline*
(P3) PRODUCES $\doteq$
PRODUCER|HAS-PRODUCT|(HARDWARE $\sqcup$ DOCUMENTATION $\sqcup$ SOFTWARE)

Assertion P1 indicates that the instance *Aquarius* belongs to the concept class PRODUCER, P2 relates *Aquarius* and *Megaline* via the binary relation HAS-PRODUCT. The relation PRODUCES is defined as the set of all HAS-PRODUCT relations which have their domain restricted to PRODUCER and their range restricted to the disjunction of the concepts HARDWARE, DOCUMENTATION or SOFTWARE. Similar representation structures could be developed for (P4) *Aquarius* HAS-BUILDING *Megaline*, as well as (P5) *Aquarius* HAS-MEMBER *Megaline*.

Depending on the type of the syntactic construction in which the unknown lexical item occurs, different hypothesis generation rules may fire. In our example, *"Megaline of Aquarius ..."*, the *Noun–"of"–Noun* pattern places only few constraints on the item to be acquired. In the following, let *target* be the unknown item *("Megaline")* and *base* be the known item *("Aquarius")*, whose conceptual relation to the target is constrained by the syntactic relation in which their lexical counterparts co-occur. The main constraint for the above syntactic pattern says that the target concept fills (exactly) one of the n roles of the base concept (for more details on hypothesis generation rules, cf. [5]). Since the correct role cannot be yet decided upon, n alternative hypotheses have to be posited (unless additional constraints apply), and the target concept has to be assigned as a filler of the i-th role of base in the corresponding i-th hypothesis space. As a consequence, the classifier is able to derive a suitable concept hypothesis by specializing the target concept (initially TOP, by default) according to the value restriction of the base concept's i-th role. Additionally, this rule assigns a

---

[1] Such a part-of-speech hypothesis can directly be derived from the inventory of valence and word order specifications underlying the dependency grammar model we use [6].

syntactic quality label to each *i-th* hypothesis indicating the type of syntactic construction in which target and base co-occur.

Continuing with our example, the target concept MEGALINE is already predicted as a PRODUCT in one interpretation of the phrase *"Megaline of Aquarius ..."*. This is the immediate result of the instantiation of the HAS-PRODUCT relation by AQUARIUS HAS-PRODUCT MEGALINE. (The other two alternative interpretations, MEGALINE as a kind of BUILDING or STAFFMEMBER, respectively, still persist, but will not be considered here.) The conceptual representation of PRODUCT is given by:

$$\text{PRODUCT} \doteq \forall\text{PRODUCT-OF.COMPANY} \ \sqcap \ \forall\text{HAS-SIZE.SIZE} \ \sqcap$$
$$\forall\text{HAS-PRICE.PRICE} \ \sqcap \ \forall\text{HAS-WEIGHT.WEIGHT}$$

This expression reads as "all fillers of PRODUCT-OF, HAS-SIZE, HAS-PRICE, HAS-WEIGHT roles must be concepts subsumed by COMPANY, SIZE, PRICE, WEIGHT, respectively". Because of these type restrictions, only the role PRODUCT-OF as the inverse relation of HAS-PRODUCT must be considered. So, the target MEGALINE, as a tentative PRODUCT, is now related to its base concept AQUARIUS, an instance of PRODUCER that is subsumed by COMPANY, via the PRODUCT-OF relation, i.e., MEGALINE PRODUCT-OF AQUARIUS.

The classifier, in turn, immediately specializes HAS-PRODUCT to PRODUCES, since the domain of the HAS-PRODUCT relation has already been restricted to PRODUCER. Hence, three distinct hypotheses can be immediately derived due to the range restrictions of the role PRODUCES, *viz.* HARDWARE, DOCUMENTATION, and SOFTWARE. These are managed in three alternative hypothesis spaces, namely h_1, h_2, and h_3, respectively. Similarly, the readings (P4) and (P5) yield two additional hypotheses for MEGALINE, as a kind of BUILDING and as a kind of STAFFMEMBER, respectively. We roughly sketch these preliminary results by the following concept descriptions (note that for *Megaline* we also include parts of the implicit *is-a* hierarchy):

$(Megaline : \text{HARDWARE})_{h_1}, (Megaline : \text{PRODUCT})_{h_1}, ..,$
$(Aquarius \ \text{PRODUCES} \ Megaline)_{h_1}$
$(Megaline : \text{DOCUMENTATION})_{h_2}, (Megaline : \text{PRODUCT})_{h_2}, ..,$
$(Aquarius \ \text{PRODUCES} \ Megaline)_{h_2}$
$(Megaline : \text{SOFTWARE})_{h_3}, (Megaline : \text{PRODUCT})_{h_3}, ..,$
$(Aquarius \ \text{PRODUCES} \ Megaline)_{h_3}$
$(Megaline : \text{BUILDING})_{h_4}, (Megaline : \text{CONSTRUCTION})_{h_4}, ..,$
$(Aquarius \ \text{HAS-BUILDING} \ Megaline)_{h_4}$
$(Megaline : \text{STAFFMEMBER})_{h_5}, (Megaline : \text{HUMANPERSON})_{h_5}, ..,$
$(Aquarius \ \text{HAS-MEMBER} \ Megaline)_{h_5}$

2.2 Conceptual Quality Labels

Conceptual quality labels result from comparing the representation structures of a concept hypothesis with other hypotheses and with already existing representation structures in the underlying domain knowledge base from the viewpoint of structural similarity, incompatibility, etc. The closer the match, the more credit is lent to a hypothesis. A very positive conceptual quality label such as M-DEDUCED is assigned, e.g., to multiple derivations of the same concept hypothesis in different hypothesis (sub)spaces. Positive labels are also assigned to terminological expressions which share structural similarities, though they are not identical. The label C-SUPPORTED, e.g., is assigned to any hypothesized relation $R1$ between two instances when another relation, $R2$, already exists in the knowledge base involving the same two instances, but where the role fillers occur in "inverted" order ($R1$ and $R2$ need not necessarily be semantically inverse relations such as with *"buy"* and *"sell"*). This rule of cross support captures the inherent symmetry between concepts related via quasi-inverse relations.

Considering our example, for MEGALINE the concept hypotheses HARDWARE, DOCUMENTATION and SOFTWARE were derived independently of each other in different hypothesis spaces. Hence, PRODUCT as their common superconcept has been multiply derived by the classifier in each of these spaces, too. Accordingly, this hypothesis is assigned a high degree of confidence by the classifier which derives the conceptual quality label M-DEDUCED for the three hypothesis spaces involved, *viz.* h_1, h_2, and h_3:

$$(Megaline : \text{PRODUCT})_{h_1} \quad \sqcap \quad (Megaline : \text{PRODUCT})_{h_2} \quad \Longrightarrow$$
$$(Megaline : \text{PRODUCT})_{h_1} \quad : \quad \text{M-DEDUCED} \quad \dots \dots$$

2.3 Quality-Based Classification

Whenever new evidence for or against a concept hypothesis is brought forth in a single learning step all concept hypotheses are reevaluated. First, weak or even untenable hypotheses are eliminated from further consideration. The quality-based selection among hypothesis spaces is grounded in *threshold levels* (later on referred to as **TH**). Their definition takes linguistic evidence into account. At the first threshold level, all hypothesis spaces with the maximum of COMPOUND labels are selected. If more than one hypothesis is left to be considered, only concept hypotheses with the maximum number of CASEFRAME assignments are approved at the second threshold level. Those hypothesis spaces that have fulfilled these threshold criteria will then be classified relative to two different *credibility levels* (later on referred to as **CB**). The first level of credibility contains all hypothesis spaces which have the maximum of M-DEDUCED labels, while at the second level (again, with more than one hypothesis left to be considered) those are chosen which are assigned the maximum of C-SUPPORTED labels. A comprehensive specification of the entire qualification calculus is given by [13].

Once again, consider the phrase *"Megaline of Aquarius ... "*. Five hypothesis spaces have been generated, three of which stipulate a PRODUCT hypothesis. Since the conceptual quality label M-DEDUCED has been derived by the classifier, this result yields a ranking with these three PRODUCT hypotheses preferred over those associated with BUILDING and STAFFMEMBER (cf. Table 3, learning step 1). As far as the sample phrase *"Megaline ... in a mini tower case"* is

	Phrase	Semantic Interpretation
1.	*Megaline of Aquarius* ...	(PP-Attach,Aquarius,has-product,Megaline)
2.	... in a *mini tower case*	(PP-Attach,Megaline,has-case,MiniTowerCase.1)
3.	*Megaline's CPU* ...	(GenitiveNP,Megaline,has-cpu,CPU.1)
4.	*Megaline* is *equipped with* ...	(CaseFrame,equip.1,patient,Megaline)
5.	... *2 MB working memory*	(CaseFrame,equip.1,co-patient,Memory.1)
		↦ (Megaline,has-memory,Memory.1)
6.	... and two	(CaseFrame,equip.1,co-patient,FloppyDiskDrive.1)
	floppy disk drives	↦ (Megaline,has-drive,FloppyDiskDrive.1))
7.	... the *Megaline unit* ...	(Compound,Megaline,instance-of,Unit.1)

Table 1. Learning Steps for a Text Fragment Featuring *"Megaline"*

concerned (cf. Table 1, second learning step, and also Table 3) only the hypotheses STAFFMEMBER (the owner of the MINITOWERCASE) and specializations of HARDWARE (viz. PC, WORKSTATION, DESKTOP, NOTEBOOK, and PORTABLE) have a reasonable interpretation for that phrase. All other hypotheses are no longer tenable. Due to additional quality constraints, not discussed here, only PC, WORKSTATION and STAFFMEMBER pass the threshold level **TH**. Again, the qualification label M-DEDUCED leads us to prefer PC and WORKSTATION (with the common superconcept COMPUTER) over the hypothesis STAFFMEMBER.

3 Evaluation

In this section, we present some data from an empirical evaluation of the text learner. We start with a consideration of canonical machine learning performance measures (such as recall, precision, etc.) and then focus on the more pertinent issues of learning accuracy and the learning rate. Due to the given learning environment, the measures we apply deviate from those commonly used in the machine learning community. In concept learning algorithms like IBL [1] there is no hierarchy of concepts. Hence, any prediction of the class membership of a new instance is either true or false. However, as such hierarchies naturally emerge in terminological frameworks, a prediction can be more or less precise, i.e., it may approximate the goal concept at different levels of specificity. This is captured by our measure of *learning accuracy* which takes into account the conceptual distance of a hypothesis to the goal concept of an instance, rather than simply relating the number of correct and false predictions, as in IBL.

In our approach, learning is achieved by the refinement of *multiple* hypotheses about the class membership of an instance. Thus, the measure of *learning rate* we propose is concerned with the reduction of hypotheses as more and more *information* becomes available about one particular new instance. In contrast, IBL-style algorithms consider only one concept hypothesis per learning cycle and their notion of *learning rate* relates to the increase of correct predictions as more and more *instances* are being processed.

We considered a total of 101 texts (= **SizeofTestSet** above) taken from a corpus of information technology magazines. For each of them 5 to 15 learning

	Camille	–	TH	CB
Correct	*	100	100	99
OneCorrect	*	21	26	31
ConceptSum	*	446	360	255
RECALL := $\frac{\text{Correct}}{\text{SizeofTestSet}}$	44%	99%	99%	98%
PRECISION := $\frac{\text{Correct}}{\text{ConceptSum}}$	22%	22%	28%	39%
PARSIMONY := $\frac{\text{OneCorrect}}{\text{SizeofTestSet}}$	14%	21%	26%	31%

Table 2. MUC Performance Measures

steps were considered. A *learning step* consists of the inferences being made at the level of hypothesis spaces after new textual input has been processed in which the target occurs. In order to clarify the input data we supply, consider Table 1. It consists of seven single learning steps for the unknown item *"Megaline"* that occurred while processing a complete text. Each learning step is associated with a particular natural language phrase in which the unknown lexical item occurs and the corresponding semantic interpretation data (linguistic quality labels are supplied as the first argument). The knowledge base on which we performed our experiments currently comprises 325 concept definitions and 447 conceptual relations.

3.1 Canonical Performance Measures

In a first series of experiments, we evaluated our system in terms of its *bare off-line* performance. By this we mean its potential to determine the correct concept description at the end of each text analysis considering the outcome of the final learning step only. Following previous work on evaluation measures for learning systems [8] and proposals by [2] that have shaped as evaluation standards for the MUC community, we here distinguish the following parameters:

- **Hypothesis** denotes the set of concept hypotheses derived by the system as the final result of the text understanding process for each target item;
- **Correct** denotes the number of cases in the common test set in which **Hypothesis** contains the correct concept description for the target item;
- **OneCorrect** denotes the number of cases in the test set in which **Hypothesis** is a singleton set which contains the correct description only;
- **ConceptSum** denotes the sum of the concepts generated for all of the target items.

Measures were taken under three experimental conditions (cf. Table 2) — in the second column (indicated by –) we considered the contribution of only the terminological reasoning component to the concept acquisition task, the third column contains the results of incorporating the (linguistic) threshold criteria (denoted by **TH**), while the fourth one incorporates (linguistic as well as conceptual) credibility criteria (designated by **CB**). The data indicate a surprisingly high recall rate. The slight drop for **CB** (98% relative to 99%) relates to a single selection fault during processing. The values for precision as those for parsimony are consistently in favor of the full qualification calculus (**CB**).

In an attempt to relate these results to a system close in spirit to our approach, we chose CAMILLE [8], considering versions 1.0, 1.2, 2.0, and 2.1, and the results reported for recall, precision, and parsimony in the assembly line and the terrorism domain (cf. Table 2, column one). Not surprisingly, the precision of our terminological reasoning component (LOOM [9]) is equal to CAMILLE's,[2] but our system outperforms CAMILLE significantly on the evaluation dimensions **TH** and **CB** both with respect to recall and parsimony. Unlike CAMILLE is our learner consistently improving as more and more information becomes available for an unknown target item (cf. also the following section).

3.2 Learning Accuracy

In a second series of experiments, we investigated the *learning accuracy* of the system, i.e., the degree to which the system correctly predicts the concept class which subsumes the target concept under consideration. Learning accuracy (LA) is defined here as (n being the number of concept hypotheses for a single target):

$$
LA := \sum_{i \in \{1 \dots n\}} \frac{LA_i}{n} \quad \text{with} \quad LA_i := \begin{cases} \dfrac{CP_i}{SP_i} & \text{if } FP_i = 0 \\ \dfrac{CP_i}{FP_i + DP_i} & \text{else} \end{cases}
$$

SP_i specifies the length of the *shortest path* (in terms of the number of nodes being traversed) from the TOP node of the concept hierarchy to the maximally specific concept subsuming the instance to be learned in hypothesis i; CP_i specifies the length of the path from the TOP node to that concept node in hypothesis i which is *common* both for the shortest path (as defined above) and the actual path to the predicted concept (whether correct or not); FP_i specifies the length of the path from the TOP node to the predicted (in this case *false*) concept and DP_i denotes the node *distance* between the predicted (false) node and the most specific common concept (on the path from the TOP node to the predicted false node) still correctly subsuming the target in hypothesis i. Figures 3 and 4 depict sample configurations for concrete LA values involving these parameters. Fig. 3 illustrates a correct, yet too general prediction with $LA_i = .75$, while Fig. 4 contains an incorrect concept hypothesis with $LA_i = .6$. Though

---

[2] Hastings mentions ([8], page 71) that "... classifier systems [like LOOM] provide a very similar inference mechanism to CAMILLE's." This statement is backed up by our precision data which exhibit equal values for our system and CAMILLE. Hastings (ibid.) also rightly observes that "... they [the classifier systems] stop short of inferring the best hypotheses." The specialization procedure he has developed for CAMILLE resembles the one we use in our approach. Contrary to Hasting's approach, however, we evaluate the different, more specific hypotheses with respect to linguistic and conceptual evidence and arrive at a ranked list of hypotheses based on **TH** and **CB** criteria. This way, more specific hypotheses simultaneously pass an evidential filtering mechanism that significantly increases the system's learning performance.

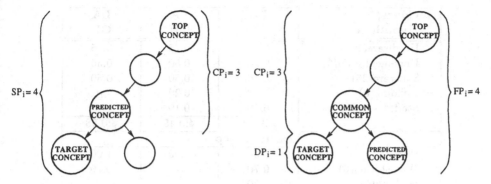

Fig. 3. LA for an Underspecified Concept Hypothesis

Fig. 4. LA for a Slightly Incorrect Concept Hypothesis

the measure is sensitive to the depth of the concept graphs in a knowledge base, it produced adequate results in the information technology domain we considered. As the graphs in knowledge bases for "natural" domains typically have an almost canonical depth that ranges between seven to ten nodes from the most general to the most specific concept, our experience seems to generalize to other domains as well.[3]

Given this measure, Table 3 illustrates how the various concepts hypotheses for MEGALINE develop in accuracy from one step to the other, relative to the data from Table 1. The numbers in brackets in the column **Concept Hypotheses** indicate for each hypothesized concept the number of concepts subsumed by it in the underlying knowledge base; **LA CB** gives the accuracy rate for the full qualification calculus including threshold and credibility criteria, **LA TH** for threshold criteria only, while **LA –** depicts the accuracy values produced by the terminological reasoning component without incorporating any quality criteria. As can be seen from Table 3, the full qualification calculus produces either the same or even more accurate results, and the same or fewer hypothesis spaces (indicated by the number of rows). Usually, though not in this example (cf. step 6), the full qualification calculus derives the correct prediction more rapidly than the less knowledgeable variants.

Fig. 5 depicts the learning accuracy curve for the entire data set (101 texts). We also have included the graph depicting the average growth behavior of hypothesis spaces (Fig. 6). For both figures, we distinguish again between the measurements for **LA –**, **LA TH** and **LA CB**. In Fig. 5 the evaluation starts from LA values in the interval between 48% to 54% for **LA –/LA TH** and **LA CB**, respectively, in the first learning step, whereas the number of hypothesis spaces (**NH**) range between 6.2 and 4.5 (Fig. 6). In the final step, LA rises up

---

[3] We tested the *WordNet* lexical database [3], a commonsense ontology, to determine concept paths of maximal length. In the computer subnet the maximum path length amounts to eight nodes. The maximum path length ever (of eleven nodes) was found in the biology domain for which fairly detailed classification systems already exist. These experiments were conducted by one of our colleagues, Katja Markert.

Concept Hypotheses	LA -	LA TH	LA CB
Hardware(101)	0.75	0.75	0.75
Documentation(5)	0.50	0.50	0.50
Software(26)	0.50	0.50	0.50
Building(0)	0.29	0.29	
StaffMember(0)	0.19	0.19	
	ϕ:0.45	ϕ:0.45	ϕ:0.58
Learning step 1			
PC(0)	1.00	1.00	1.00
Workstation(0)	0.70	0.70	0.70
Desktop(0)	0.70		
Notebook(0)	0.70		
Portable(0)	0.70		
StaffMember(0)	0.19	0.19	
	ϕ:0.66	ϕ:0.63	ϕ:0.85
Learning steps 2, 3, 4, 5, and 6			
PC(0)	1.00	1.00	1.00
Workstation(0)	0.70	0.70	0.70
Desktop(0)	0.70		
Notebook(0)	0.70		
Portable(0)	0.70		
	ϕ:0.76	ϕ:0.85	ϕ:0.85
Learning step 7			

Table 3. Some Concept Learning Results for a Text Featuring *"Megaline"*

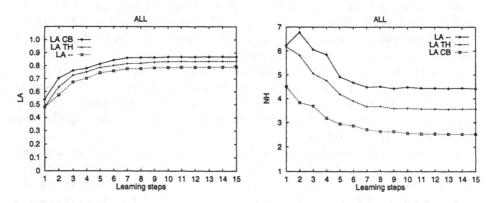

Fig. 5. Learning Accuracy (LA)   **Fig. 6.** Number of Hypotheses (NH)

to 79%, 83% to 87% for **LA −**, **LA TH** and **LA CB**, respectively, and the **NH** values reduce to 4.4, 3.6 and 2.5 for each of the three criteria, respectively.

The pure terminological reasoning machinery always achieves an inferior level of learning accuracy and generates more hypothesis spaces than the learner equipped with the qualification calculus. Also, the inclusion of conceptual criteria (**CB**) supplementing the linguistic criteria (**TH**) helps a lot to focus on

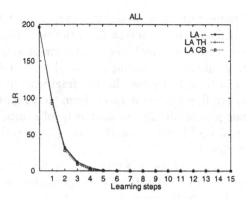

Fig. 7. Learning Rate (LR)

the relevant hypothesis spaces and to further discriminate the valid hypotheses (on the range of 4% of precision). Note that an already significant plateau of accuracy is usually reached after the third step (*viz.* 67%, 73%, and 76% for **LA -**, **LA TH**, and **LA CB**, respectively, in Fig. 5; the corresponding numbers of hypothesis spaces being 6.1, 5.1, and 3.7 for **NH -**, **NH TH**, and **NH CB**, respectively, in Fig. 6). Obviously, our approach finds the most relevant distinctions in a very early phase of the learning process, i.e., it requires only *few* examples.

3.3 Learning Rate

The learning accuracy focuses on the predictive power of the learning procedure. By considering the *learning rate*, we supply data from the step-wise reduction of alternatives of the learning process. Fig. 7 depicts the mean number of transitively included concepts for all considered hypothesis spaces per learning step (each concept hypothesis denotes a concept which transitively subsumes various subconcepts).

Note that the most general concept hypothesis, in our example, denotes OB-JECT which currently includes 196 concepts. In general, we observed a strong negative slope of the curve for the learning rate. After the first step, slightly less than 50% of the included concepts are pruned (with 93, 94 and 97 remaining concepts for **LR CB**, **LR TH** and **LR -**, respectively). Again, learning step 3 is a crucial point for the reduction of the number of included concepts (ranging from 16 to 21 concepts). Summarizing this evaluation experiment, the quality-based learning system exhibits significant and valid reductions of the predicted concepts (up to two on the average after all learning steps).

4 Related Work

Our approach bears a close relationship to the work of Mooney [10], Gomez & Segami [4], Rau *et al.* [12] Hastings [8], and Moorman & Ram [11], who all aim at the automated learning of word meanings from context using a knowledge-intensive approach. But our work differs from theirs in that the need to cope with *several competing* concept hypotheses and to aim at a *reason-based selection* is not an issue in these studies. Learning from real-world textual input usually provides the learner with only sparse, highly fragmentary evidence such that multiple hypotheses are likely to be derived from that input. So, we stress the need for a hypothesis generation and quality control component as an integral part of large-scale real-world text understanders [7] operating in tandem with concept learning devices.

The work closest to ours has been carried out by Rau *et al.* [12] and Hastings [8]. They also generate concept hypotheses from linguistic and conceptual data. Unlike our approach, the selection of hypotheses depends only on an ongoing discrimination process based on the availability of these data but does not incorporate an inferencing scheme for reasoned hypothesis selection. In the light of our evaluation study in Section 3, the difference in learning performance (compared, e.g., with Rau *et al.*'s approach [12]) amounts to 8%, considering the difference between **LA** - (plain terminological reasoning) and **LA CB** values (terminological metareasoning incorporating the qualification calculus). Similarly strong arguments hold for a comparison of our results with Hasting's approach [8] at the precision dimension, with an even greater advantage for the full qualification calculus (39%) over pure terminological reasoning in the CAMILLE System (22%). Hence, our claim that we produce competitive results.

5 Conclusion

We have proposed a knowledge-based methodology for updating and enhancing a given domain ontology on the fly. The approach is based on the incremental assignment and evaluation of the quality of linguistic and conceptual evidence for emerging concept hypotheses in terms of a strict notion of *"quality control"*. No specialized learning algorithm is needed, since learning is a (meta)reasoning task carried out by the classifier of a terminological reasoning system. However, heuristic guidance for selecting between plausible hypotheses comes from the different quality criteria. Our experimental data indicate that given these heuristics we achieve a high degree of pruning of the search space for hypotheses in very early phases of the learning cycle.

In our experiments learning was still restricted to the case of a single unknown concept in the entire text. Generalizing to n unknown concepts can be considered from two perspectives. When hypotheses of another target item are generated and incrementally assessed relative to an already given base item, no effect occurs. When, however, two targets (i.e., two unknown items) have to be related, then the number of hypotheses that have to be taken into account is equal to the product of the number of hypothesis spaces associated with each of them. In the future, we intend to study such test cases. Fortunately, the number of hypothesis spaces decreases rapidly (cf. Fig. 6) as does the learning rate (cf. Fig. 7) so that the learning system should remain within feasibility regions.

Acknowledgements. We would like to thank our colleagues in the CLIF group for fruitful discussions and instant support, in particular Joe Bush who polished the text as a native speaker. K. Schnattinger is supported by a grant from DFG (Ha 2097/3-1).

References

1. D. Aha, D. Kibler, and M. Albert. Instance-based learning algorithms. *Machine Learning*, 6:37–66, 1991.
2. N. Chinchor. MUC-4 evaluation metrics. In *Proceedings of the 4th Message Understanding Conference – MUC-4*. San Mateo, CA: Morgan Kaufmann, 1992.
3. C. Fellbaum, editor. *WordNet: An Electronic Lexical Database*. Cambridge, MA: MIT Press, 1998.
4. F. Gomez and C. Segami. The recognition and classification of concepts in understanding scientific texts. *Journal of Experimental and Theoretical Artificial Intelligence*, 1:51–77, 1989.
5. U. Hahn, M. Klenner, and K. Schnattinger. A quality-based terminological reasoning model for text knowledge acquisition. In N. Shadbolt, K. O'Hara, and G. Schreiber, editors, *Advances in Knowledge Acquisition. Proc. of the 9th European Knowledge Acquisition Workshop (EKAW'96)*, pages 131–146. Berlin: Springer, 1996.
6. U. Hahn, S. Schacht, and N. Bröker. Concurrent, object-oriented natural language parsing: the PARSETALK model. *International Journal of Human-Computer Studies*, 41(1/2):179–222, 1994.
7. U. Hahn, K. Schnattinger, and M. Romacker. Automatic knowledge acquisition from medical texts. In J. Cimino, editor, *Proc. of the 1996 AMIA Annual Fall Symposium (formerly SCAMC). Beyond the Superhighway: Exploiting the Internet with Medical Informatics*, pages 383–387. Philadelphia, PA: Hanley & Belfus, 1996.
8. P. Hastings. *Automatic Acquisition of Word Meaning from Context*. PhD thesis, Department of Computer Science and Engineering at the University of Michigan, 1994.
9. R. MacGregor. A description classifier for the predicate calculus. In *AAAI'94 – Proc. of the 12th National Conference on Artificial Intelligence. Vol. 1*, pages 213–220. Menlo Park, CA: AAAI Press & MIT Press, 1994.
10. R. Mooney. Integrated learning of words and their underlying concepts. In *CogSci'87 – Proc. of the 9th Annual Conference of the Cognitive Science Society*, pages 974–978, 1987.
11. K. Moorman and A. Ram. The role of ontology in creative understanding. In *CogSci'96 - Proc. of the 18th Annual Conf. of the Cognitive Science Society*, pages 98–103. Mahwah, NJ: L. Erlbaum, 1996.
12. L. Rau, P. Jacobs, and U. Zernik. Information extraction and text summarization using linguistic knowledge acquisition. *Information Processing & Management*, 25(4):419–428, 1989.
13. K. Schnattinger and U. Hahn. A sketch of a qualification calculus. In *FLAIRS'96 – Proc. of the 9th Florida Artificial Intelligence Research Symposium*, pages 198–203, 1996.
14. W. Woods and J. Schmolze. The KL-ONE family. *Computers & Mathematics with Applications*, 23(2/5):133–177, 1992.

Grapheme Generation in Learning to Read English Words

Charles X. Ling[1] and Bei Zhang[2]

[1] Department of Computer Science
The University of Western Ontario
London, Ontario, Canada N6A 5B7
E-mail: ling@csd.uwo.ca
URL: http://www.csd.uwo.ca/faculty/ling
[2] Foreign Language Teaching and Research Section
Shanghai University of Engineering Science
Shanghai 200336, P.R. China

Abstract. A learning system for a more complete process of learning to read aloud English words should consist of three major steps: alignment, mapping learning, and grapheme generation. In a previous paper, we discussed a basic alignment algorithm and several improvements that effectively accomplish the alignment and mapping learning simultaneously. In this paper, we focus mainly on grapheme generation. We present several criteria for constructing graphemes, and demonstrate that graphemes generated improve the predictive accuracy in learning to read aloud.

1 Introduction

Reading English text aloud has been studied successfully for many years with numerous laboratory systems and some commercial systems (see, e.g., Allen, 1976; Allen, Hunnicutt, & Klatt, 1987; Kurzweil, 1976; Klatt, 1982, 1987). In this paper, we focus on only one aspect of reading aloud: isolated word text-to-phoneme conversion (ignoring visual recognition, text analysis, intonation and stress analysis, speech synthesis, and so on). Our focus is on automated learning of text-to-speech conversion, rather than, for example, conversions specified by manually designed rules. Our learning system can be used to construct automatically in a very short time prototypes of reading machines for English or other languages.

Given a set of words, each with an orthographic representation (spelling or alphabet letters) and a phonological representation (pronunciation or phonemes), the basic learning task is to learn a mapping from spelling to pronunciation, and to predict the pronunciation of unseen words with a high accuracy. A natural approach to model the *complete* learning process of single-word spelling-to-phoneme conversion requires three major steps (see (Ling & Wang, 1998) for the justification, and other approaches and their weaknesses). The first step is to align spelling letters with phoneme letters. The second step is to learn the mapping from spelling to phonemes, and the last step is to generate graphemes (see later). These three processes are intimately tied together, and are very complicated to model. Most previous work models only one of the three processes. For example, NETtalk by Sejnowski and Rosenberg (1987), and models by Seidenberg and McClelland (1989) and Plaut, McClelland, Seidenberg, and Patterson (1996) only dealt with the mapping learning task; the alignment was done manually, and no graphemes were generated.

The goal of this study is to show that all of the three processes of learning to read aloud can be modeled effectively by our learning system. Our learning system solves a larger task but it requires much less work by the user. The system is much more autonomous and the performance is superior: the predictive accuracy of our system is very high, comparing to previous learning systems with a much limited scope.

1.1 Alignment

We assume that the starting point of spelling is 26 letters (plus two marks for the beginning and ending of the word). The phoneme representation, on the other hand, is a small set of about 40 standard phonemes as the sound building blocks for EnglishBelow are examples of letter-to-phoneme mappings of some single words: **speech** → spEtS, **thought** → T*t, and **thrill** → Tril.

The first task of aligning spelling and phoneme letters is necessary because often n spelling letters of a word maps to m phonemes in pronunciation with $m < n$.[3] For example, the word **thought**, which has 7 letters in spelling, has only 3 phonemes, T*t, in the phoneme representation that we use.[4] Therefore, the mapping from spelling to phoneme is not one-to-one. To make the second (learning mapping) and third tasks (grapheme generation) possible, we have to properly align letters with phonemes so that the learning programs know which letter (or letter combination) maps to which phoneme. For **thought**, the first alignment below is correct,[5] while the second and third are not.

thought	thought	thought
T_*___t	T*t____	T*___t_

Clearly, there is a total of $\binom{7}{4} = 35$ different ways of inserting 4 spaces in T*t, or 35 ways of aligning **thought** with T*t.

In Sejnowski and Rosenberg's NETtalk, a silent phoneme is inserted manually so the alignment is done before learning. That is, the mapping **thought** → T_*___t would be given to NETtalk so the mapping is always one-to-one.

---

[3] There are four cases where a single letter maps to more than one phoneme. They are x as in box (maps to ks in bo<u>ks</u>), j as in just (maps to dz in <u>dz</u>∧st), o as in one (maps to w∧ in <u>w</u>∧n), and u as in fuel (maps to yU in fy<u>U</u>l). To simplify learning, these "macro" phonemes are replaced by single letters not used in the original phonological representation.

[4] In the phoneme string T*t, T represents the sound th in <u>th</u>ought, * represents the sound ough in th<u>ough</u>t, and t represents the sound t in though<u>t</u>.

[5] There are other correct alignments of thought with T*t, such as _T*___t or _T_*_t. In general, as long as T is aligned with one letter in th, and * with one letter in ough, the alignment is regarded as correct.

1.2 Mapping Learning

The second task is to learn a complicated mapping from letters to phonemes from pairs of letter strings to phoneme strings which *have been aligned*. Such a mapping is only *quasi-regular* (many disjunctive rules with many exceptions), and is more complicated than some other language-learning tasks, such as the mapping from verb stems of English verbs to their past tenses (Ling & Marinov, 1993; Ling, 1994).

It is important to realize that the result of alignment directly affects mapping learning: *Each possible alignment combination represents one possible mapping to be learned.* As mentioned, the mapping is only quasi-regular, with many exceptions. It could be that, if thought is aligned with T*t___, t maps to T, h maps to *, o maps to t, and the rest of the letters ught map to a blank phoneme — *this might be a legitimate mapping* to be learned. That is, a bad alignment also constitutes a mapping. Since many words in the training set have more than one alignment (e.g., thought has 35), the combination of possible alignments of all the words in the training set is huge, but each represents one possible mapping to be learned. As an example, the data set we use in our study originated from Seidenberg and McClelland (1989); the dataset contains a total of 2,998 words. The combination of all of these alignments of the corpus is estimated to be over 12,000.

The question is, with so many possibilities, how can a learning program learn the correct alignment of all words *and* mapping based on the newly-learned alignment effectively?

1.3 Grapheme Generation

The third difficult task is the grapheme generation. A grapheme is a sequence of two or more consecutive letters (such as th, ea, ch, tch, oar, ough, eigh) that map to a single phoneme (Wijk, 1969; Venezky, 1970). Since the spelling-sound regularities of English are primarily grapheme-phoneme correspondence (GPC) rules, the regularities are most elegantly captured if appropriate graphemes are used in the orthographic representation (Plaut et al., 1996). Taking the example of thought again (the correct alignment is T_*___t), th functions as a *single* component, and pronounces (or maps to) a single phoneme T. So does ough. A complete learning system of reading English words should be able to *learn* proper graphemes, a higher-level orthographic representation, rather than remaining at the level of 26 alphabet letters.

However, grapheme generation, a seemingly simple task, is not that simple. Even with the correct alignment, it is hard to ensure that only "useful" graphemes are produced. For example, given the correct alignment, T_*___t, of thought, t could map to T, houg as a grapheme could map to *, and ht as a grapheme could map to t. Why are these (houg and ht) not graphemes? If letters and phonemes are not aligned correctly, more such useless "graphemes" would be generated, and further, it may not be possible to find the desired graphemes. For example, if thought is aligned incorrectly with T*___t_, it is not possible to have th as a grapheme mapping to T, since th maps to more than one phoneme (i.e., T*).

The role of graphemes in reading is often overlooked. Since graphemes are only a re-representation of the training data, they do not affect much the training procedure and training errors. Therefore, one tends to think that they are only a convenience. After a more careful study, we show in this paper that graphemes also improve the predictive accuracy of unseen words. In thought → T_*__t, if we have found the proper graphemes, th and ough, we can use two high-level symbols (say A and B respectively) to replace them. Therefore, thought becomes ABt, which maps to T*t. Clearly, this not only compresses orthographic representation, it also makes *the mapping learning much easier* — the mapping becomes one-to-one.

In a previous paper (Ling & Wang, 1997), we presented several alignment algorithms which utilize a decision tree algorithm C4.5 (Quinlan, 1993) for the mapping learning. This paper focusses on methods of generating useful graphemes. Later, we test our learning algorithm thoroughly with real English words unused in the training set, and show that graphemes generated improve generalization ability of the learning system.

2 Learning Mappings with Automatic Alignment

In a previous paper (Ling & Wang, 1997), we presented several alignment algorithms that utilize C4.5 as the mapping learning algorithm. We will only provide a very brief summary here.

The key idea in solving the alignment problem is that most of the 12,000 possible alignment combinations discussed in Section 1 do not contain much regularity in mapping. That is, if many words are aligned incorrectly or inconsistently, there is little regularity to be learned, and it becomes almost impossible to predict the phonemes of a new word. Therefore, the basic alignment algorithm is based on the fact that the proper alignment should be consistent among words, and the prediction based on aligned words should be consistent with the correct alignment of the new word.

The basic alignment algorithm is a hill-climbing algorithm that gradually builds up the set of aligned words. From a set of words (we call it a *converged set*) that have already been aligned (not necessarily all correctly), a decision tree is built using C4.5, and it is used to choose the best alignment of an unaligned word. The best alignment is then added into the converged set. More specifically, an unaligned word from the *unconverged set* (containing all unaligned words) is aligned in the following way: whenever the new word has more than one possible alignment (that is, the word is an $n \rightarrow m$ mapping with $n > m$), a prediction of the word using the decision tree built on the current converged set (of aligned words) is produced first. As we discussed earlier, the prediction based on aligned words should be consistent with the correct alignment of the new word. The prediction is thus compared with all possible alignments of the word, and the alignment most consistent[6] with the prediction is chosen as the correct one. The chosen alignment, which hopefully is correct, is then added into the converged set, the decision tree is updated with the inclusion of the newly aligned word, and the process is repeated. As the set of the aligned words increases, the decision tree algorithm learns more varieties of mappings from letters to phonemes, the alignment of the new words becomes more and more accurate.

We found that the basic alignment algorithm makes an excessive number of misalignments: the error rate[7] is over 10%. Thus, we studied several extensions and improvements of it. These improvements include incorporating a tie breaking policy, ordering the words from easy to complex, employing a conservative criterion for accepting aligned words, and correcting previously misaligned words. More details can be found in (Ling & Wang, 1997).

3 Automatic Grapheme Generation

Recall that a grapheme is a sequence of two or more consecutive letters that map to a single phoneme in some consistent manner, and therefore should be treated as a single "macro" letter. Examples of commonly used graphemes are th, ough, ee, and tch. Graphemes are very important in English reading, since the spelling-sound regularities of English are primarily grapheme-phoneme correspondence (GPC) rules, so they are most elegantly captured with appropriate graphemes in the orthographic representation (Plaut et al., 1996).

This seemingly easy task is not so easy. Look at the example of thought again. The correct alignment of thought is T_*__t. However, there are many possible letter sequences that map to single phonemes, and all of them can *potentially* be graphemes. For thought → T_*__t, there are 12 possible letter sequences that map to single phonemes:

th → T,
ho → *,
hou → *,
houg → *,
hough → *,
ou → *,
oug → *,
ough → *,
ht → t,
ght → t,
ught → t, and
ought → t.

---

[6] The consistency between two words (i.e., prediction and alignment) is determined simply by the number of different phonemes in the two words at the corresponding positions.

[7] Since no "teacher" provides correct alignment to the learning program, this is essentially an unsupervised learning task. The error rate here is thus the testing error rate instead of the training error rate in supervised learning.

Why, among these 12 possibilities, are the only useful graphemes th (mapping to T), and ough (mapping to *)?

To generate useful graphemes from the data set alone, we use three important properties of useful graphemes:

1. Graphemes compress orthographic representation
2. Graphemes appear frequently in the spelling of the words
3. Graphemes map to single phonemes with few exceptions

A letter sequence is an *exception* as a grapheme if it maps to two or more phoneme letters. For example, th appears frequently in words, and *all* appearances of th in the dataset map to either T (as in thought and bath) or D (as in smooth, that and the). That is, there is no exception for th in the dataset we use[8] if the th part of all words are aligned correctly. For example, if thought is aligned incorrectly with T*＿＿t, th is an exception for grapheme since it maps to two phonemes (T and *). This illustrates again the importance of correct alignment for grapheme generation. By the same reason, among possible letter sequences for thought, ho is not a valid grapheme because it maps to more than one phoneme (i.e., two phonemes) in many other words (such as hot → hot, hold → hOld). If a letter sequence has too many exceptions, it should not be regarded as a useful grapheme, because when predicting a new word in which a letter sequence maps to more than one phoneme, the prediction is always incorrect, since that letter sequence is always treated as a grapheme and mapped to one phoneme.

Note that, as th can map to T or D, a grapheme can map to more than one single phoneme in different words. Which phoneme a grapheme maps to depends on the neighbouring letters and previously-learned graphemes, and that mapping can also be learned using the decision-tree algorithm. That is, after graphemes are generated, they are replaced in all words by single "macro" letters not used in current orthographic representation, and the mapping from the new orthographic representation with graphemes is *re-learned* using the same decision-tree learning algorithm. When a new word to be predicted contains graphemes, they will be replaced by the "macro" letters first, and the decision tree (built with graphemes) is then used to predict the phonemes (therefore, if the letter sequence is an exception, i.e., not a grapheme, the prediction of the word is always incorrect).

As we noted earlier, a grapheme is useful if it compresses the orthographic representation, it appears in words frequently, and it maps to single phonemes with few or no exceptions. Based on these properties, we devise the following heuristic steps for finding useful graphemes.

In the first step, a table storing all potential letter sequences, their frequencies, and the number of exceptions is constructed. For each word in the training set, all possible letter sequences that map to single phonemes (e.g., thought has 12 as indicated above) are recorded in the table. This results in a large table

---

[8] There are some compound words in which th is an exception (but no such words appear in the data corpus). For example, in hothouse and lighthouse, th is not a grapheme since it maps to two phonemes, t and h.

of 444 letter sequences with their statistics. Note, however, that most of these letter sequences are not graphemes. The next step *ranks* the letter sequences and finds out useful graphemes.

In the second step, several empirical evaluation criteria are used to rank the letter sequences in the table. The better a letter sequence is regarded as grapheme, the earlier it is listed in the ranked list. Assuming C and D are any two letter sequences in the table, the following three criteria rank C and D. The first criterion states that

if $f_1(C) > f_1(D)$ then rank C before D (i.e., C is a better grapheme)

where

$$f_1(X) = (\text{X-total-occurrences} - \text{X-exceptions}) \times (|X| - 1).$$

Since $(|X| - 1)$ indicates the number of letters that are eliminated if X is used as a grapheme, f_1 calculates the total saving in the orthographic representation that the grapheme achieves for the whole training sample. Clearly, this criterion prefers the grapheme to achieve more savings in the orthographic representation. As an example, ough is prefered over gh, if everything else is equal, since it saves 3 letters per occurrence while gh saves only 1.

The second and third criteria deal with the exceptions of the letter sequences as graphemes. In case the first criterion produces a tie between C and D, the second criterion is applied:

if $f_2(C) < f_2(D)$ then rank C before D

where

$$f_2(X) = (\text{X-exceptions})/(\text{X-total-occurrences}).$$

Clearly, this criterion prefers a grapheme with a small percent of exceptions. The third criterion is actually a filter that removes letter sequences from the table if they have too many exceptions (or ranks the letter sequences to the very end of the long list):

if $f_2(C) > 0.1$ then delete C from the table.

As we discussed earlier, good graphemes should have no or few exceptions, since the prediction is always incorrect if the testing word has a letter sequence that maps to more than one phoneme. Restricting the ratio of exceptions and total occurrences of a letter sequence to 0.1 or lower implies that, overall, the predictive error caused by such errors would not be higher than 10% (assuming that exceptions of letter sequences as graphemes are distributed evenly in the training and testing sets).

Note that these three criteria represent roughly a minimum length principle: you want to compress the encoding (using graphemes) while reducing exceptions and errors.

After ranking and filtering the list of letter sequences using the three criteria above, only 45 letter sequences are left. The third step orders these letter sequences such that a super-string is moved before a sub-string. For example, **ough** is a super-string of **ou** and **gh**, and it is moved before **ou** and **gh**. For the same reason, **tch** should always be placed before **ch**. This step is necessary because during grapheme replacement in training and testing examples, super-string graphemes should always be replaced first. Otherwise, they will never be replaced or used if their sub-string graphemes are ranked and replaced before them.

These three steps produce a ranked list of 45 letter sequences, and they are taken as useful graphemes. These 45 ranked graphemes are (most useful first): **tch, ear, ch, ea, th, sh, our, eer, ee, are, oor, oo, ough, ck, ar, lle, ai, ore, ll, dge, ow, or, oar, oa, ire, ss, ier, ur, aw, wh, ie, ir, ere, eigh, augh, ew, er, au, oi, igh, wr, kn, oe, mb**, and **ugh**. As we can see, most of these 45 letter sequences, especially the ones appearing early in the list (such as **tch, ch, ea, th, ee, oo** etc.), are very common graphemes, frequently appearing in English words.[9]

4 The Generalization Ability

In this section, we test our learning algorithm's predictive performance on real English words. Testing on real words is much more rigorous, since each word has only one correct answer (the one given in the dataset we have), and both regular and exception words (such as **have**) may appear in the testing set. It is an ultimate test for a learning system to be useful in real-world applications.

Ten runs of experiments are performed for a reliable assessment of our learning algorithm. In each run, the whole set of data, 2998 words, is randomly split into an 80% part for training and a 20% part for testing without overlap. To evaluate the role of graphemes in the model's performance, we *gradually* inject (instead of using none or using all) the 45 graphemes generated in Section 3 into the orthographic representation. That is, for each 80/20 split of the training and testing sample, 9 learning sessions are run, each with 5 additional graphemes from the ranked list injected into the orthographic representation. Then C4.5 is applied to the training sample with the new orthographic representation. The predictive accuracies on testing words with gradual grapheme usages are reported in Table 1, and average predictive accuracies are plotted in Figure 1.

We can observe several exciting results from the table. First, the average predictive accuracy on 20% of English words unseen in the training set is increasing gradually with more and more graphemes injected — from the average accuracy of 72.6% without using any graphemes, to 80.3% with 45 graphemes. This meets our expectation that graphemes make the learning easier, which, in turn, makes the prediction of new words better.

Second, the predictive accuracy of our learning algorithm on unseen words is very high. It achieves over 95% correct at the phoneme level, and 80% correct at the word level, on words not supplied in the training set. This accuracy is

---

[9] Some long graphemes are listed early in the list because they are super-strings of other useful graphemes.

Table 1. Predictive accuracies with standard errors (s.e.) on testing English words with gradual grapheme injection.

	Graphemes			Predication accuracy of 10 runs					Average (s.e.)	Tree size
0	No graphemes			71.74 76.10 76.37 75.45			74.40		72.55 (1.12)	2555.1
				73.67 69.92 71.38 72.55			73.89			
1	tch	ear	ch	72.40 75.00 77.25 78.09			74.88		74.64 (0.58)	2554.8
	ea	th		74.33 72.60 73.33 74.71			73.89			
2	sh	our	eer	73.55 75.47 78.84 79.08			77.29		76.53 (0.55)	2475.0
	ee	are		76.17 74.80 76.10 77.54			76.45			
3	oor	oo	ough	74.21 75.79 79.19 79.57			77.78		76.92 (0.57)	2441.2
	ck	ar		76.67 74.33 77.40 76.87			77.47			
4	lle	ai	ore	73.72 76.57 78.66 78.25			77.46		76.75 (0.47)	2395.0
	ll	dge		77.00 74.80 76.75 77.20			77.13			
5	ow	or	oar	75.70 78.46 78.48 79.41			78.90		77.68 (0.56)	2401.8
	oa	ire		79.33 74.80 75.12 77.70			78.84			
6	ss	ier	ur	75.87 76.57 79.89 79.41			77.94		77.61 (0.53)	2361.0
	aw	wh		79.00 74.96 76.10 77.70			78.67			
7	ie	ir	ere	77.52 76.57 80.25 78.75			79.23		78.40 (0.41)	2310.6
	eigh	augh		78.17 77.01 77.40 78.70			80.38			
8	ew	er	au	79.17 78.93 81.66 81.05			79.71		79.84 (0.38)	2282.3
	oi	igh		79.83 77.80 79.02 80.03			81.23			
9*	wr	kn	oe	79.34 80.19 82.01 80.40			79.71		80.25 (0.40)	2235.8
	mb	ugh		80.17 77.64 80.16 81.03			81.91			

*The predictive accuracy at the phoneme level is 95.8% (standard error 0.68) after all of the 45 graphemes are injected.

comparable to the previous models. For example, Klatt (1987) cited Berstein and Pisoni (1980)'s result as the best human-engineered reading-aloud system — it reaches 97% correct at the phoneme level, and 85% correct for the whole word and the stress pattern. Although our learning algorithm is tested on a smaller set of short words and does not deal with stress, it seems to come close to the best performance.

Third, from the tree sizes listed in Table 1, we can see that the effective tree sizes[10] in the table are decreasing as graphemes are added. With graphemes, the regularities become simpler, so the tree size should decrease. On the other hand, however, more graphemes introduce more branches for each node in the tree. Without graphemes, each node in the tree has 28 branches (26 alphabet letters plus two marks, "<" and ">", for the word boundary). With 45 newly generated

---

[10] The effective tree size is the sum of the number of decision nodes and the number of non-empty leaves. A non-empty leaf is a leaf with at least one training example classified by it.

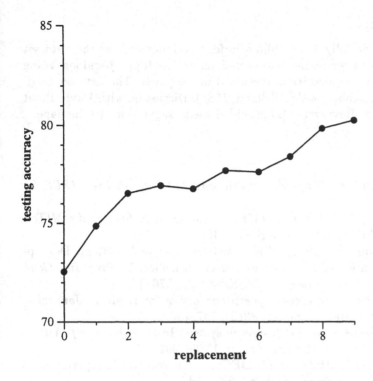

Fig. 1. Predictive accuracy on English words with gradual grapheme injections.

graphemes in the orthographic representation, there are 73 (28+45) branches in each decision node. Clearly, there is a trade-off in having more graphemes as a "macro" representation, similar to having more "macro" operators in the search space or chunking in problem space (Rosenbloom & Newell, 1986).

5   Conclusions

Graphemes are crucial in English reading since the spelling-sound regularities are primarily grapheme-phoneme correspondence (GPC) rules. A complete learning system of reading should be able to learn proper graphemes, a higher-level orthographic representation, rather than remaining at the level of 26 alphabet letters. In this paper, we described methods for generating useful graphemes in learning to read English words. We demonstrated that graphemes not only reduce the size of the decision tree learned, but also improve the generalization ability of the learning system in predicting unseen words.

Acknowledgements

We like to thank gratefully John Bullinaria for providing with us the data set used in his study, and for numerous discussions on the topic. Handong Wang implemented some of the algorithms discussed in the paper. The data set originally came from (Seidenberg & McClelland, 1989). Discussion with David Plaut has also been helpful. Reviewers also provided useful suggestions to the paper.

References

Allen, J. (1976). Synthesis of speech from unrestricted text. In *Proc. IEEE 64*, pp. 422–433.

Allen, J., Hunnicutt, S., & Klatt, D. (1987). *From Text to Speech: the MITalk System*. Cambridge U.P., Cambridge, UK.

Berstein, J., & Pisoni, D. (1980). Unlimited text-to-speech system: Description and evaluation of a microprocessor-based device. In *Proc. Int. Conf. Acoust. Speech Signal Process. ICASSP-80*, pp. 576–579.

Klatt, D. (1987). Review of text-to-speech conversion for English. *Journal of the Acoustic Society of America, 82*(3), 737–793.

Klatt, D. (1982). The Klattalk text-to-speech system. In *Proc. Int. Conf. Acoust. Speech Signal Process. ICASSP-82*, pp. 1589–1592.

Klatt, D. (1987). How Klattalk became DECtalk: An academic's experiences in the business world. *Speech Tech, 87*, 293–294.

Kurzweil, R. (1976). The Kurzweil reading machine: A technical overview. In Reden, M., & Schwandt, W. (Eds.), *Science, Technology and the Handicapped*, pp. 3–11.

Ling, C. X. (1994). Learning the past tense of English verbs: the Symbolic Pattern Associator vs. connectionist models. *Journal of Artificial Intelligence Research, 1*, 209 – 229.

Ling, C. X., & Marinov, M. (1993). Answering the connectionist challenge: a symbolic model of learning the past tense of English verbs. *Cognition, 49*(3), 235–290.

Ling, C. X., & Wang, H. (1997). Alignment algorithms for learning to read aloud. In *Proceedings of IJCAI-97 (Fifteenth International Joint Conference on Artificial Intelligence)*, pp. 874 – 879.

Ling, C. X., & Wang, H. (1998). A symbolic model for reading aloud: With automatic alignment and grapheme generation. Manuscript.

Plaut, D., McClelland, J., Seidenberg, M., & Patterson, K. (1996). Understanding normal and impaired word reading: Computational principles in quasi-regular domains. *Psychological Review, 103*, 56 – 115.

Quinlan, J. (1993). *C4.5: Programs for Machine Learning*. Morgan Kaufmann: San Mateo, CA.

Rosenbloom, P., & Newell, A. (1986). The chunking of goal hierarchies: A generalized model of practice. In Michalski, R., Carbonell, J., & Mitchell, T. (Eds.), *Machine Learning: An Artificial Intelligence Approach, vol. 2*. Morgan Kaufmann, Los Altos, CA.

Seidenberg, M., & McClelland, J. (1989). A distributed, developmental model of word recognition and naming. *Psychological Review, 96*, 523–568.

Sejnowski, T., & Rosenberg, C. (1987). Parallel networks that learn to pronounce English text. *Complex Systems, 1*, 145 – 168.

Venezky, R. (1970). *The structure of English Orthography*. Mouton, The Netherlands.

Wijk, A. (1969) In Haas, W. (Ed.), *Alphabets for English*. Manchester Univ. Press. Manchester, England.

A Trainable Bracketer for Noun Modifiers

Ken Barker

School of Information and Technology Engineering
University of Ottawa
Ottawa, Canada K1N 6N5
kbarker@site.uottawa.ca

Abstract. Noun phrases carry much of the information in a text. Systems that attempt to acquire knowledge from text must first decompose complex noun phrases to get access to that information. In the case of noun compounds, this decomposition usually means bracketing the modifiers into nested modifier-head pairs. It is then possible to determine the semantic relationships among individual components of the noun phrase.

This paper describes a semi-automatic system for bracketing an unlimited number of adjectival or nominal premodifiers. Since the system is intended to start processing with no prior knowledge, it gets trained as it brackets. That is, it starts from scratch and accumulates bracketing evidence while processing a text under user supervision.

Experiments show that generalizations of the structure of complex modifier sequences allow the system to bracket previously unseen compounds correctly. Furthermore, as more compounds are bracketed, the number of bracketing decisions required of the user decreases.

1 Introduction

The HAIKU system performs semi-automatic semantic analysis on three levels: between clauses, within clauses and within noun phrases. In the absence of precoded semantics HAIKU enlists the help of a cooperating user who oversees semantic decisions. To lessen the burden on the user, the system first attempts automatic analysis by comparing input structures to similar structures in the text that have already been semantically analyzed. Since it does not have access to a large body of pre-analyzed text, HAIKU starts processing from scratch for a text and acquires the needed data incrementally.

The clause level relationship (CLR) analyzer assigns semantic relationship labels to connected clauses based on their syntactic features. CLR analysis is described by Barker & Szpakowicz [2]. Within a clause, HAIKU assigns case relationships to arguments syntactically connected to the main verb. By comparing syntactic argument markers to syntactic patterns previously encountered, the case analyzer learns to make better analyses more autonomously. Delisle *et al.* [6] and Barker *et al.* [3] describe the case analyzer and HAIKU's case system. Within a noun phrase, HAIKU assigns noun modifier relationships (NMRs) to each of the head noun's premodifiers and postmodifiers. Similar previous instances of modifier-head pairs allow the NMR analyzer to improve the accuracy of its analyses while gradually decreasing its dependence on user input.

As a prologue to NMR analysis, the system must bracket lists of premodifiers into modifier-head pairs. Like the other components of HAIKU, the bracketer is semi-automatic. It uses previous modifier-head pairs to inform bracketing decisions, relying on the user to supply decisions when previous evidence is insufficient. As more noun phrases are bracketed, this reliance on the user decreases.

The subject of this paper is the subsystem of the NMR analyzer that brackets noun premodifiers. Section 2 looks at ideas and work related to noun phrase analysis and bracketing. Section 3 describes the syntactic input to the bracketer while section 4 places the bracketer in the larger context of noun phrase analysis in HAIKU. The algorithm for bracketing general sequences of premodifiers appears in section 5. Section 6 summarizes bracketer results that have been collected during the experimental evaluation of HAIKU.

2 Background and Related Work

2.1 Noun Compounds

A head noun along with one or more noun premodifiers is often called a noun compound. There are several different types of noun compounds: those whose meaning is derivable from the individual components and those whose meaning isn't; those that are a semantic subclass of the head noun and those that aren't; etc. HAIKU deals with the semantics of a particular kind of compound, namely compounds that are *transparent* and *endocentric*.

A transparent compound is one whose meaning can be derived from the meaning of its individual elements. For example, *laser printer* is transparent (a *printer* that uses a *laser*), whereas *guinea pig* is *opaque* since there is no obvious direct relationship to *guinea* or to *pig*.

An endocentric compound is a hyponym of its head. For example, *desktop computer* is endocentric because it is a kind of *computer*. A *bird brain* is *exocentric* because it does not refer to a kind of *brain*, but rather to a kind of person (whose brain resembles that of a bird).

Since HAIKU is intended to analyze technical text, the restriction to transparent endocentric compounds should not limit the utility of the system. The experiments described in section 6 found no opaque or exocentric compounds in the texts.[1] For these texts at least, little is lost by not dealing with such compounds.

2.2 Semantic Relationships in Noun Phrases

Most of the research on semantic relationships between nouns and their modifiers deals with noun-noun compounds. Usually researchers propose finite lists of semantic relationships that a compound may express.

---

[1] In fact, many exocentric compounds pose no particular problem for HAIKU's noun modifier relationship analyzer. The main difficulty is in recovering taxonomic information (section 4.3). Options for more flexible handling of exocentric compounds are under investigation.

Levi [15] argues that semantics and word formation cause noun-noun compounds to constitute a heterogeneous class. Instead, she looks at a class of opaque modifier-noun compounds, where the modifier may be a noun or a nominal, non-predicating adjective. For this more homogeneous class Levi offers nine semantic labels. According to her theory, these labels represent underlying predicates that were deleted during compound formation. George [9] disputes the claim that Levi's non-predicating adjectives never appear in predicative position.

Warren [21] describes a multi-level system of semantic labels for noun-noun relationships. The "Major Semantic Class" level consists of fourteen general relationships. Warren [22] extends the earlier work to cover adjective premodifiers as well as nouns. The similarity of the two lists suggests that many adjectives and premodifying nouns can be handled by the same set of semantic relations.

Computer systems for assigning semantic relationships to modifier-noun compounds usually depend on hand-coded semantic knowledge. Leonard [14] describes a system that assigns relationships to noun-noun compounds based on a dictionary that includes taxonomic and meronymic (part-whole) information, information about the syntactic behaviour of nouns and information about the relationships between nouns and verbs. Finin [8] produces multiple semantic interpretations of modifier-noun compounds (where a modifier is either a noun or a nominal, non-predicating adjective). The interpretations are based on precoded semantic class information and domain-dependent frames describing the roles that can be associated with certain nouns. Ter Stal [19] describes a system that identifies concepts in text and unifies them with structures extracted from a hand-coded lexicon containing syntactic information, logical form templates and taxonomic information for each word.

In an attempt to avoid the hand-coding required in other systems, Vanderwende [20] automatically extracts semantic features of nouns from online dictionaries. Combinations of these features imply particular semantic interpretations of the relationship between two nouns in a compound.

2.3 Bracketing Noun Compounds

When a head noun has more than one premodifying noun or adjective, the sequence has internal structure and requires bracketing. For example, phrase (1) is *left-branching* and has the bracketing shown in (2); phrase (3) is *right-branching* and has the bracketing shown in (4).

(1)   *laser printer manual*
(2)   *((laser printer) manual)*
(3)   *desktop laser printer*
(4)   *(desktop (laser printer))*

Several researchers have proposed empirical solutions to the bracketing problem. Liberman & Sproat [16], Pustejovsky *et al.* [17] and Resnik [18] follow a similar approach: for a given sequence X-Y-Z, compare the number of occurrences of X-Y in isolation in a corpus with the number of occurrences of Y-Z. Lauer [12] calls this the *adjacency model* and offers a different model, the *dependency model*. The dependency model compares the number of occurrences of X-Y to the number of occurrences of X-Z (instead of Y-Z). In Lauer's bracketer, the dependency model outperforms the adjacency model.

Ter Stal [19] confirms earlier results of Resnik [18] and Lauer & Dras [13] that between 60% and 70% of noun-noun-noun compounds in text are left-branching. He does not use bracketing in his compound analyzer, however, since his lexicon contains enough semantic information for direct identification of complex concepts.

HAIKU's bracketer differs from other approaches in three ways. First, it can be used to bracket phrases with an unlimited number of both adjective and noun premodifiers. Second, the evidence for bracketing can come from previous occurrences of a modifier-noun pair in isolation, previous occurrences of a pair *within* other compounds, as well as occurrences of a pair whose modifier and head are not adjacent in the text (see section 5). Finally, since it is interactive, the bracketer can bracket phrases even when there is no previous evidence.

3 Syntactic Input to the Bracketer

There are various ways to identify noun phrases in text. HAIKU performs semantic analysis on sentences parsed by the DIPETT parser [5]. For each noun phrase in a sentence DIPETT produces an *np* structure whose format appears in Figure 1.

The parts of the structure relevant to semantic analysis are *attributes*, *premodifiers*, the *head noun* and *np postmodifiers*. All adjectives that precede any premodifying nouns appear in the list of *attributes*. Premodifying nouns and adjectives that appear before the head but after the first premodifying noun appear in *premodifiers*. The *np postmodifiers* may include any number of postmodifying prepositional phrases as well as optional appositives or relative clauses.

The attributes and premodifiers must be bracketed before NMR assignment since some of the modifiers may modify other modifiers, not the head directly.

I said in section 2.3 that other systems that bracket premodifiers usually deal with the problem of bracketing three nouns: two premodifiers and a head (X-Y-Z). These systems compare occurrences of X-Y with occurrences of either Y-Z or X-Z (depending on the model). Since these pairs may occur infrequently in a text, it would be useful to generalize (X-Y-Z) and look for occurrences of the generalization. For example, Lauer [12] generalizes the nouns X, Y and Z to the Roget's Thesaurus categories that contain them: R_X, R_Y and R_Z. Instead of looking for other occurrences

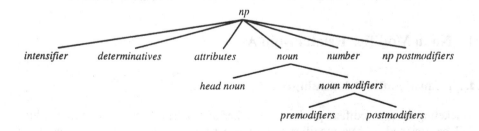

Figure 1. Syntactic structure of noun phrases

of X-Y and X-Z in the text, Lauer's bracketer looks for occurrences of U-V and U-W such that $R_U = R_X$, $R_V = R_Y$ and $R_W = R_Z$. The technique limits generalization to nouns that occur in Roget.

The problem of generalization is compounded in HAIKU since it deals with sequences of more than three words and allows adjectives as premodifiers. And since the fundamental tenet of HAIKU is to avoid precoding semantic information, a semantic generalization on the words is not readily available. What is needed is some way of increasing the number of hits when searching for previously analyzed noun phrases that can help analyze a new noun phrase.

Consider phrase (5) and a reasonable bracketing for it in (6).

(5)   *dynamic high impedance vocal microphone*
(6)   *(dynamic ((high impedance) (vocal microphone)))*

Each non-atomic element of each bracketed pair can be considered a *subphrase* of the original phrase. Given the bracketing in (6) the subphrases for phrase (5) are phrase (5) itself as well as the subphrases in (7). Assuming the compounds are endocentric, the subphrases will be well-formed.

(7)   *high impedance vocal microphone*
       high impedance
       vocal microphone

Each subphrase consists of one or more modifiers and a head local to the subphrase. Local heads in (6) are *microphone* (the head of three subphrases) and *impedance*. The subphrases are generalized by reducing modifiers and modificands to their local heads. If this concept of reduction is applied to a bracketed phrase, the result is a set of reduced subbracketings of the original phrase. The reduced subbracketings of (6) appear in (8).

(8)   *(dynamic microphone)*
       (impedance microphone)
       (high impedance)
       (vocal microphone)

The reduced subbracketings together are a structural generalization of the original noun phrase. Instead of simply memorizing complete noun phrases and their analyses, the system stores the subbracketings. This allows it to analyze different noun phrases that have only subbracketings in common with previous noun phrases. Section 5 will show how the reduced subbracketings help automate the bracketing procedure.

4 Noun Modifier Relationship Analysis

4.1 Noun Modifier Relationships

Bracketing the premodifiers produces a number of modifier-head pairs, each of which will be assigned a noun modifier relationship from the list in Table 1. The set of relationships is based primarily on research on the semantics of noun compounds,

Agent (AGT)	Instrument (INST)	Property (PROP)
Beneficiary (BENF)	Located (LED)	Purpose (PURP)
Cause (CAUS)	Location (LOC)	Result (RESU)
Container (CTN)	Material (MATR)	Source (SRC)
Content (CONT)	Object (OBJ)	State (STAT)
Destination (DEST)	Possessor (POSS)	Time (TIME)
Equative (EQUA)	Product (PROD)	Topic (TOP)

Table 1: The noun modifier relationships

such as the research described in section 2.2. Barker [1] offers definitions, paraphrases and examples for each NMR.

4.2 Naming NMR Arguments

The reduced subbracketings described in section 3 are used internally to help with the analysis of new noun phrases. The NMRs, however, apply to complete modifier-head sequences, not to reduced pairs. There are two NMRs for (9), since there are two modifier-head pairs:

(9)   small (gasoline engine)
(10)   gasoline-engine
(11)   small-(gasoline engine)

The NMR for (10) is Instrument, since *gasoline* is used by *gasoline engine*. Note that *gasoline* is an instrument of *gasoline engine*, not *engine* in general. The NMR for (11) is Property: *small* is a simple property of *small gasoline engine*, but not generally a property of *engine* or even of *gasoline engine*. The following structures are the semantic output for (9). When an argument name is built from more than one word, the individual words are concatenated with an underscore.

```
nmr_struct(inst,
           gasoline,
           gasoline_engine)
nmr_struct(prop,
           small,
           small_gasoline_engine)
```

The reduced pairs for (9) will be stored and used by the bracketing and NMR assignment algorithms to guide future processing:

(12)   (gasoline engine)
       (small engine)

4.3 Premodifiers as Classifiers

Warren [21] distinguishes two roles of modifiers orthogonal to the semantic relationship between premodifier and head: premodifiers as *classifiers* and premodifiers as *identifiers*. The identifying role is to point at some thing in the world referred to by the compound. As an identifier the modifier is relevant to such tasks as anaphora resolution and concept identification.

In NMRA the classifying role of modifiers in endocentric compounds allows us to glean taxonomic information directly from the semantic structures. Whenever an NMR is assigned between a modifier and modificand, there is an implicit hierarchical or *isa* structure as well. The reduced modifier subbracketings for (13) appear in (14); the corresponding *isa* structures appear in (15).

(13)   *((laser printer) stand)*
(14)   *(laser printer)*
         (printer stand)

(15)   `isa(laser_printer_stand, stand)`
         `isa(laser_printer, printer)`
         `isa(printer_stand, stand)`

5   Bracketing Noun Modifiers

5.1 The Algorithm

The algorithm for noun premodifier bracketing handles modifier sequences of any length by dealing with a window of three elements at a time, where an element is a word or a bracketed pair of elements.

1   Start with the rightmost three elements, X-Y-Z.

...	V	W	X	Y	Z

2a If X-Y-Z is confidently right-branching (see section 5.2), bracket it X-(YZ) and restart the algorithm with the rightmost three elements W-X-(YZ).

...	V	W	X	(YZ)

2b If X-Y-Z is confidently left-branching, move the window one element to the left and repeat the algorithm with W-X-Y. Note that X-Y-Z being confidently left-branching does not necessarily mean that it can be bracketed ...(XY)-Z, since left-branching may also be bracketed ...X)Y)-Z.

...	V	W	X	Y	Z

3   When the leftmost element in the whole sequence appears in the window, a left-branching triple U-V-W can be left-bracketed (UV)-W; restart with the three-element window expanded back to the right of the sequence.

(UV)	W	X	Y	...

5.2 Confidence in Branching Decisions

This section lists the conditions for deciding whether a given triple X-Y-Z is confidently right-branching or confidently left-branching.

The triple noun-adjective-noun is confidently right-branching since adjectives precede the nouns they modify. The exception is postpositive adjectives, which occur relatively infrequently within premodifier sequences.[2]

For any other sequence of three elements X-Y-Z, the bracketer reduces X, Y and Z to their local heads X_h, Y_h and Z_h. The sequence X-Y-Z is considered confidently right-branching if the frequency of previous occurrences of the reduced subbracketing $(X_h Z_h)$ is greater than the frequency of previous occurrences of the reduced subbracketing $(X_h Y_h)$ times a *threshold* value.[3] If $(X_h Y_h)$ has occurred more frequently than $(X_h Z_h)$, X-Y-Z is confidently left-branching.

In the absence of such evidence of confidence, the algorithm consults the user, in keeping with the semi-automatic approach of HAIKU. A fully automatic solution could just assume left-branching, based on results reported by Resnik [18] and Lauer & Dras [13] that left-branching is roughly twice as common as right-branching. However, these results were based on observations of noun-noun-noun triples only. For longer compounds and compounds with adjectives the ratio of left-branching to right-branching compounds might differ (see section 6.3).

5.3 What's Wrong with Adjacency?

Section 2.3 described two different models found in systems for bracketing compounds: the adjacency model and the dependency model. The algorithm presented above uses the dependency model, which compares frequencies of X-Y to X-Z when bracketing the triple X-Y-Z, ignoring previous occurrences of Y-Z.

For phrase (16) both left and right bracketings are possible. Previous occurrences of *small loan* would be evidence for right bracketing. Occurrences of *small business* would be evidence for left bracketing. Occurrences of *business loan* could be evidence for either bracketing. (17) restricts the loan; (18) restricts the business. But both refer to business loans. Therefore, occurrences of Y-Z do not count as evidence in favour of either bracketing.

(16)   small business loan
(17)   (small (business loan))
(18)   ((small business) loan)

---

[2] Examples such as *((machine readable) dictionary)* must be bracketed using HAIKU's manual bracketer. An NMR can then be assigned between *machine readable* and *dictionary*, though the semantic relationship between *machine* and *readable* cannot be handled by HAIKU. Ferris [7] gives a comprehensive account of adjective syntax and semantics (including a classification of several types of postpositive adjectives) that may suggest avenues for semantic analysis of composite adjectives in HAIKU.

[3] The threshold can be set to any value by the user. A higher value means that the frequency of $(X_h Z_h)$ must greatly exceed the frequency of $(X_h Y_h)$, or vice-versa. Section 6 examines the effect of different threshold values on the performance of the bracketer.

5.4 User Interaction

When the system cannot find sufficient evidence in favour of right-branching or left-branching, it turns to the user to supply the decision. Such decisions may be difficult and unintuitive. There are several ways to lessen the burden.

- ask only yes-no questions about right-branching — don't ask the user to supply bracketing information directly.

good: in the context of *tomato soup pot*,
does *tomato soup* make sense?

bad: does *tomato soup pot* bracket left or right?

- phrase questions in the context of three individual words by using subphrase reductions.

good: in the context of *steel soup pot*,
does *steel soup* make sense?

bad: in the context of *cotton soup pot cover holder*,
does *cotton soup pot cover* make sense?

- ask the user only about the acceptability of X-Y; do not ask the user to compare X-Y and X-Z — it is possible for *both* X-Y and X-Z to be unacceptable if X-Y-Z is in the middle of a modifier sequence, which would make the user's decision much more difficult.

good: in the context of *steel tomato soup*,
does *steel tomato* make sense?

bad: in the context of *steel tomato soup*,
which makes more sense: *steel tomato* or *steel soup*?

By using these techniques, a 'yes' answer to any question will provide confident left-branching; a 'no' answer will mean confident right-branching.

5.5 An Example

Assume that phrases (19) and (20) have already been bracketed. This section traces through the bracketing of (21).

(19)   (soup bowl)
(20)   (wooden (pot handle))
(21)   wooden French onion soup bowl handle

Start with the rightmost three elements, soup-bowl-handle.

wooden	French	onion	soup	bowl	handle

soup-bowl-handle is confidently left-branching, since *(soup bowl)* has occurred and *(soup handle)* has not. Move the window one element to the left and restart the algorithm.

wooden	French	onion	soup	bowl	handle

Neither *(onion soup)* nor *(onion bowl)* have occurred previously and *soup* is not an adjective, so there is no confidence in right-branching or left-branching. Ask the user if *onion soup* makes sense in the context of *onion soup bowl*. The user answers 'yes', providing confidence in left-branching. Move the window one element to the left and restart the algorithm.

wooden	French	onion	soup	bowl	handle

Neither *(French onion)* nor *(French soup)* have occurred previously. Ask the user if *French onion* makes sense in the context of *French onion soup*. The user answers 'no', so the sequence is confidently right-branching. Bracket *(onion soup)* and expand the window one element to the left.

wooden	French	(onion soup)	bowl	handle

French is an adjective, so *wooden-French-(onion soup)* is confidently right-branching. Bracket *(French (onion soup))*. Since there are no more elements to the left of *wooden*, expand the window back to the right.

wooden	(French (onion soup))	bowl	handle

Neither *(wooden bowl)* nor *(wooden soup)*, which is the reduction of *wooden-(French (onion soup))*, have occurred previously. *(French (onion soup))* is obviously not an adjective, so there is no confidence in either right-branching or left-branching. Ask the user if *wooden soup* makes sense in the context of *wooden soup bowl*, which is the reduction of *wooden-(French (onion soup))-bowl*. The user answers 'no', providing confidence in right-branching. Bracket *wooden-(French (onion soup))-bowl* as *wooden-((French (onion soup)) bowl)*. Since there are no more elements to the left of *wooden*, expand the window to the right.

wooden	((French (onion soup)) bowl)	handle

(wooden bowl), which is the reduction of *wooden-((French (onion soup)) bowl)* has not occurred previously; *(wooden handle)* has occurred previously as a reduction of *(wooden (pot handle))*. *wooden-((French (onion soup)) bowl)-handle* is therefore confidently right-branching. Bracket *(((French (onion soup)) bowl) handle)*.

wooden	(((French (onion soup)) bowl) handle)

Since there are only two remaining elements in the sequence, bracketing is trivial:

(wooden (((French (onion soup)) bowl) handle))

Finally, the system stores all of the reduced subbracketings (22) for future processing. It also stores the complete bracketing (23): if the phrase is ever encountered in its entirety, the bracketer can simply look up the complete bracketing instead of going through the steps of the algorithm.

(22)   (onion soup)
        (French soup)
        (soup bowl)
        (bowl handle)
        (wooden handle)
(23)   (wooden (((French (onion soup)) bowl) handle))

6   Evaluation

This section gives results of using the bracketer in the context of two experiments. The *sparc* experiment applied the NMR analyzer (including the bracketer) to the first 500 non-trivial noun phrases in a computer installation guide. In this context a non-trivial noun phrase has at least one premodifier (adjective or noun) or postmodifying prepositional phrase. Bracketing the 500 noun phrases in the test produced 645 bracketed pairs. Each of the bracketed pairs was assigned a single NMR from the list in Table 1.

The second experiment was a complete analysis of a book on the mechanics of small engines, including semantic analysis by HAIKU at the three levels described in section 1. Bracketing resulted in 733 premodifier-head pairs. Barker *et al.* [4] describe the *small engines* experiment and its results.

6.1 System Performance

In both experiments, most of the modifier-head pairs occurred in noun phrases with a single premodifier and head. These simple compounds required no bracketing decisions. In the *sparc* experiment, the 645 pairs required 188 bracketing decisions. The system made 122 (65%) of these decisions correctly, with the rest made by the user as described in section 5.3. Of the 66 user decisions, 47 (71%) were required during the first half of the experiment with only 19 in the second half. The running totals of user and system bracketing decisions appear in Figure 2.

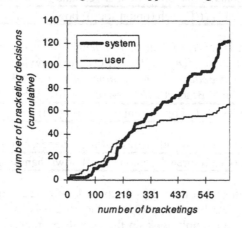

Figure 2. Bracketing decisions for *sparc*

The *small engines* experiment required 164 bracketing decisions. The system made 101 (62%) decisions correctly, with the rest made by the user. Due to the consistent terminology in the *small engines* text the cumulative number of decisions made automatically by the bracketer was always greater than the number required from the user.[4] The running totals for user and system bracketing decisions appear in Figure 3.

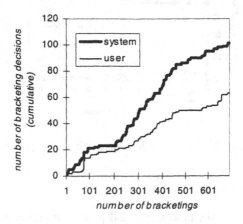

Figure 3. Bracketing decisions for *small engines*

6.2 The Effect of the Threshold

The bracketer determines whether a given triple X-Y-Z is confidently right-branching if the subbracketing (X_hZ_h) has previously occurred N times more frequently than the subbracketing (X_hY_h), where N is a threshold that can be set by the user. In the absence of sufficient evidence, the system asks the user to supply right-branching information.

If the value of the threshold is set high, the number of previous occurrences of (X_hZ_h) must greatly outweigh the number of occurrences of (X_hY_h) for the system to assume right-branching. High values of the threshold cause the system to be more conservative. Low values of the threshold (close to 1.0), make it more aggressive: the system requires less evidence to commit to a branching decision.

The *sparc* experiment was run twelve times with different threshold values. As expected, the number of system decisions, both correct and incorrect, was highest for low threshold values (see Figure 4). For higher threshold values, the number of incorrect system decisions decreased, but so did the number of correct decisions, and the user made more decisions.

For the *small engines* text, changing the threshold had no effect. This result suggests that for any triple X-Y-Z in that text, if (X_hZ_h) appears as a reduced pair, (X_hY_h) does not. In general, however, both may appear in any given text.

---

[4]   The user made the decision for the very first bracketing in the text. After the second bracketing, the cumulative number of system decisions overtook the number of user decisions.

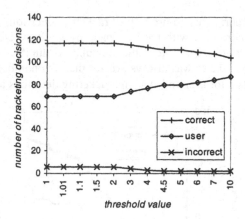

Figure 4. Effects of different threshold values on bracketing decisions for *sparc*

6.3 Branching Frequencies

Section 5.2 suggested that the bracketer could guess left-branching when there is no confidence in right-branching. Such a guess would be justified based on the predominance of left-branching compounds as reported by Resnik [18] and Lauer & Dras [13]. Results from the *small engines* experiment confirm the bias for left-branching. For the *sparc* experiment, however, the data in Table 2 show that guessing left-branching would have produced poor results.

		left-branching	*right-branching*
small engines	*noun-noun-noun*	47 (96%)	2 (4%)
	adjective-noun-noun	31 (84%)	6 (16%)
	total	78 (91%)	8 (9%)
sparc	*noun-noun-noun*	41 (55%)	33 (45%)
	adjective-noun-noun	11 (26%)	31 (74%)
	total	52 (45%)	64 (55%)

Table 2: Branching frequencies for *small engines* and *sparc*

The predominance of left-branching compounds is apparently not universal. If the system were modified to guess left in the absence of other evidence, there are texts (like the *sparc* text) for which the bracketer would perform poorly.

7 Future Work

Whenever the system brackets a list of premodifiers, it stores the reduced subbracketings to help bracket subsequent noun phrases. The system should be extended to store pairs resulting from postmodifying prepositional phrases as well.

For example, for the postmodifying prepositional phrase in (24) the system should store the pair (25).

(24)   *a bowl for soup*
(25)   *(soup bowl)*

Storing these extra pairs will increase the likelihood of the system finding evidence when bracketing new noun phrases.

Since HAIKU is an interactive semantic analyzer, it proceeds sentence by sentence through a text from the beginning. It cannot look ahead in the text at sentences that have not yet been analyzed. However, there may be unambiguous occurrences of modifier-head pairs in subsequent sentences that could help bracket phrases in the input sentence. The system could be modified to scan ahead in a text to look for such unambiguous pairs, although doing so may be costly.

Finally, there were two results in section 6 that need to be validated by further bracketing experiments. Left-branching triples do not always outnumber right-branching triples in a text. Counting the number of each in future experiments will determine whether the *sparc* text is unique in its predominance of right-branching triples. If left-branching predominance is confirmed, the system could be modified to guess left in the absence of other evidence.

The second result was the insensitivity of the bracketer to the value of the threshold. It is possible that a single technical text is unlikely to have both right-branching and left-branching evidence for a given triple. Future experiments may confirm this result or, if conflicting evidence is common, find a suitable threshold value for most texts.

Acknowledgments

This research is supported by the Natural Sciences and Engineering Research Council of Canada. I would like to thank Stan Szpakowicz for valuable input to the development of the ideas in this paper and to the paper itself. I am also grateful to Sylvain Delisle for comments on an earlier draft of the paper. The insightful comments of an anonymous reviewer helped shape the final version of this paper.

References

1. Barker, Ken (1997). "Noun Modifier Relationship Analysis in the TANKA System." TR-97-02, Department of Computer Science, University of Ottawa.
2. Barker, Ken & Stan Szpakowicz (1995). "Interactive Semantic analysis of Clause-Level Relationships." *Proceedings of the Second Conference of the Pacific Association for Computational Linguistics*, Brisbane, 22-30.
3. Barker, Ken, Terry Copeck, Sylvain Delisle & Stan Szpakowicz (1997). "Systematic Construction of a Versatile Case System." *Journal of Natural Language Engineering* 3(4), December, 1997.
4. Barker, Ken, Sylvain Delisle & Stan Szpakowicz (1998). "Test-driving TANKA: Evaluating a Semi-Automatic System of Text Analysis for Knowledge Acquisition." *Proceedings of the Twelfth Canadian Conference on Artificial Intelligence* (this volume), Vancouver.

5. Delisle, Sylvain (1994). "Text processing without A-Priori Domain Knowledge: Semi-Automatic Linguistic analysis for Incremental Knowledge Acquisition." Ph.D. thesis, TR-94-02, Department of Computer Science, University of Ottawa.
6. Delisle, Sylvain, Ken Barker, Terry Copeck & Stan Szpakowicz (1996). "Interactive Semantic analysis of Technical Texts." *Computational Intelligence* 12(2), May, 1996, 273-306.
7. Ferris, Connor (1993). *The Meaning of Syntax: A Study of Adjectives of English.* London: Longman.
8. Finin, Timothy W. (1986). "Constraining the Interpretation of Nominal Compounds in a Limited Context." in [10: 163-173].
9. George, Steffi (1987). *On "Nominal Non-Predicating" Adjectives in English.* Frankfurt am Main: Peter Lang.
10. Grishman, Ralph & Richard Kittredge, eds. (1986). *Analyzing Language in Restricted Domains: Sublanguage Description and Processing.* Hillsdale: Lawrence Erlbaum.
11. Jensen, Karen, George E. Heidorn & Stephen D Richardson, eds. (1993). *Natural Language Processing: The PLNLP Approach.* Boston: Kluwer Academic Publishers.
12. Lauer, Mark (1995). "Corpus Statistics Meet the Noun Compound: Some Empirical Results." *Proceedings of the 33rd Annual Meeting of the Association for Computational Linguistics.* Cambridge. 47-54.
13. Lauer, Mark & Mark Dras (1994). "A Probabilistic Model of Compound Nouns." *Proceedings of the 7th Australian Joint Conference on Artificial Intelligence.* Armidale. 474-481.
14. Leonard, Rosemary (1984). *The Interpretation of English Noun Sequences on the Computer.* Amsterdam: North-Holland.
15. Levi, Judith N. (1978). *The Syntax and Semantics of Complex Nominals.* New York: Academic Press.
16. Liberman, Mark & Richard Sproat (1992). "Stress and Structure of Modified Noun Phrases." *Lexical Matters (CSLI Lecture Notes,* 24). Stanford: Center for the Study of Language and Information.
17. Pustejovsky, James, S. Bergler & P. Anick (1993). "Lexical Semantic Techniques for Corpus Analysis." *Computational Linguistics* 19(2). 331-358.
18. Resnik, Philip Stuart (1993). "Selection and Information: A Class-Based Approach to Lexical Relationships." Ph.D. thesis, IRCS Report 93-42, University of Pennsylvania.
19. ter Stal, Wilco (1996). "Automated Interpretation of Nominal Compounds in a Technical Domain." Ph.D. thesis, University of Twente, The Netherlands.
20. Vanderwende, Lucy (1993). "SENS: The System for Evaluating Noun Sequences." in [11: 161-173].
21. Warren, Beatrice (1978). *Semantic Patterns of Noun-Noun Compounds.* Göteborg: Acta Universitatis Gothoburgensis.
22. Warren, Beatrice (1984). *Classifying Adjectives.* Göteborg: Acta Universitatis Gothoburgensis.

Lessons Learned in the Development and Implementation of a Bilingual Nationally Accessible Knowledge-Based System[1]

Brett Hodges* and Larry Hodgson**

* Interim Manager, Reporting and Research Section,
Revenue Collections Directorate, Revenue Canada
Room 7036, 400 Cumberland Street,
Ottawa, Ontario, K1A OL8
email: Bhodges@RC.GC.CA
**Consultant, DRT Systems International,
Deloitte & Touche Consulting Group,
Suite 200, 1101 Prince of Wales Drive
Ottawa, Ontario, K2C 3W7
email: Lhodgson@dttus.com

Abstract. The lessons learned in the development and implementation of a knowledge-based system at Revenue Canada are presented. Numerous development decisions were made including determining how to capture and represent a large set of complex rules and selecting the appropriate system development methodology. In addition, many technical challenges were overcome such as providing a fully bilingual system, and storing incomplete waiver determinations. This paper will discuss these issues and their resolution. The paper concludes with the characteristics of a successful knowledge-based project based on the experiences of Revenue Canada.

1 Introduction

The Waiver on Withholding System (WOW) assists officers in Revenue Canada's fifty-two Tax Service Offices (TSOs) in determining whether a waiver of withholding taxes should be granted. The Canadian Income Tax Act requires a withholding of tax from certain amounts paid to non-residents of Canada in respect of services rendered in Canada or to certain residents of Canada working abroad. If, however, a client can adequately demonstrate that the withholding taxes normally required are in excess of their ultimate Canadian tax liability, the Department may reduce the withholding tax accordingly [3].

---

[1] This work was carried out while the authors were with Revenue Canada's Information Technology Branch

WOW is the second component of the International Tax Advisory System (ITAS). The Residency Determination Advisor (RDA)[2] is the first component of ITAS and is also the first knowledge-based system developed by Revenue Canada for use nationally. RDA assists with the determination of residency for tax purposes. Prior to the implementation of RDA, residency determinations could take anywhere from forty-five minutes to three hours. Using RDA, employees were able to reduce the time required to make residency determinations to an average of seven minutes [6].

The WOW project began in the Fall of 1993. The Systems Development Methodology employed was DMR Productivity Plus (P+). The Opportunity Evaluation phase analyzed the suitability of using knowledge-based technology and outlined the scope of the project. This phase was completed in February 1994 and resulted in the recommendation that development using knowledge-based technology proceed.

The Preliminary Analysis phase was completed in May 1994. Version I of WOW was delivered nationally in March of 1996. Version I utilized Virtual Storage Access Method (VSAM) files for storage. Version II was implemented in May 1997 and utilizes a DB2 Version 4.0 Database for enhanced search and retrieval capabilities.

Both versions of WOW were developed using Platinum's Aion Development System (AionDS). AionDS is an object-oriented knowledge-based system development tool. Application development took place using AionDS version 6.40 on a PC running Windows 3.1. The application was then ported to the mainframe. Production access to WOW is through the Customer Information Control System (CICS) Version 4.1.0 to AionDS Version 6.50 on a Multiple Virtual System (MVS) IBM mainframe platform.

WOW was developed as a joint partnership between the system development team and the user development team. The system development team consisted of a project leader/knowledge engineer, a knowledge base programmer, and a database designer. The user development team consisted of a functional project manager/domain expert, a full-time domain expert, and additional domain experts from across the country.

The benefits of the WOW System are:
- provides accurate, consistent and timely waiver determinations;
- distributes specific knowledge to all Tax Service Offices;
- accurately tracks waiver determinations on a national basis;
- ensures compliance with the Canadian Income Tax Act; and
- assists in the training of new officers.

---

[2] Received the Federal Government Gold Medal Award in 1994 in the category of Renewing Services and Program Delivery as voted on by a panel of government and industry representatives [6].

2 Knowledge Engineering

Knowledge acquisition is the most critical element in the development of knowledge-based systems [2]. WOW is the largest rule-based system that Revenue Canada has undertaken to date incorporating approximately 600 rules. In selecting an appropriate methodology for acquiring and accurately representing domain knowledge, three main criteria were used:

- domain experts must be able to record the business rules with a minimum of assistance;
- procedural logic (control flow) and business logic (decision rules) must be represented together; and
- the line of reasoning must be easily understood from the representation by experts other than those who recorded the knowledge. This will assist in verification and validation activities in advance of prototype construction.

After reviewing a number of knowledge representations formats such as decision trees and narrative text, it was decided by the joint project team to employ a spread-sheet approach. An earlier version of this format was proposed by the user development team and utilized on prior projects. User prompts, business rules, outcomes based on those rules, and processing logic are represented in a Microsoft Excel spreadsheet. A modular approach was used with the knowledge to be captured divided into manageable segments. A set of spreadsheets was then developed for each segment. Together, the spreadsheets formed the knowledge dictionary for the project.

Figure 1 is an example of the knowledge and processing specifications for Article XV of the Canada-US Income Tax Treaty for Dependent employees with employment income. The entry condition refers to the state that must be true before this set of logic is executed. In this case, the user has selected "Other" from a list of possible entities.

Rules and their outcomes can be easily specified using this format. Rules can have either a yes or no value or a list of values as in Question #4. The outcome of a rule can be other rules (Go To Question X), instructional messages displayed to the user (Procedures to determine waiver), or processes (save completed waiver).

The WOW domain experts became comfortable enough with this approach that they could provide the spreadsheets with little or no assistance from a knowledge engineer. The spreadsheets served as an excellent way to capture, communicate, and document functional specifications. A process was implemented to ensure that the spreadsheets were linked to the source code.

Canada-U.S. Income Tax Treaty					
Dependents - Article XV					
Employment Income (Reg. 102)					
(entry condition is entity = other)					
3	Is waiver being requested by the non-resident employer of the applicant for the services being provided in Canada?	yes	no			
	Set waiver flag to true.	X				
	Go to question 4.	X	X			
	Message (1): Procedures to Determine Waiver - return to question 3			X		
4	Is the employee an:	Artiste	Athlete	Athlete	Athlete	Other
5	Did the athlete receive a signing bonus?		yes	yes	no	
	Message (2): 15% tax on signing bonus		X	X		
6	Does the athlete have employment income (not including signing bonus)?		yes	no		
7	Is the Artiste on tour in Canada?	yes				
	Message (3): "First TSO should process the entire tour."	X				
	Go to question 8.					X
	Go to question 10	X	X		X	
	Message (4): "Waiver Denied"			X		
	Go to Save Completed Waiver			X		

Figure 1. Example of WOW Knowledge Representation

3 Choice of System Development Methodology

As WOW employs a computer-initiated dialogue, it was important to provide an appropriate user-interface. A number of usability goals were set including; minimizing the time to learn, reducing the error rate and seeking high retention over time [1]. Development began by producing a mock-up prototype of the system to solicit user feedback and to emulate the processing logic used when a manual waiver determination was made. Many different offices were visited in order to receive feedback from the user population. The mock-up prototype was revised until the processing flow was being correctly emulated. The mock-up prototype also assisted in setting boundaries for the domain knowledge required.

For system development, it was decided to employ an evolutionary prototype methodology. Feedback from the users on the accuracy of the knowledge and the processing flow was solicited for each prototype and was incorporated into the subsequent prototype. Prototype agreements were drafted with the user development team which outlined the changes to be made based on feedback from the users, additional functionality, additional business rules, and the testing procedure.

4 Technical Challenges

4.1 Requirement to Provide a Bilingual System

WOW was required to provide both English and French user interfaces. The development team had two options for implementing this requirement, utilizing:
- two separate knowledge bases both containing the same business logic but different text; or
- one knowledge base with two separate texts attached to each object.

The features, advantages and disadvantages of each architecture were analyzed and are summarized in Figure 2.

It was decided to implement the twin knowledge-base design due to the potential performance degradation in utilizing one knowledge base with duplicate text.

As a result of using two knowledge bases, change control problems arose in keeping both knowledge-bases synchronized. This issue was resolved by implementing a rigorous change management system. Change control problems could have been averted by restructuring the internal design of the knowledge-base by separating the prompts and messages into their own classes. This would have permitted only one core knowledge base to be used which would import the language dependent areas as required. The text changes that would be made to those areas and the need to enter the code/rule changes into the two knowledge bases would be eliminated.

System Architecture	Features	Advantages	Disadvantages
Twin Knowledge Base Design	a) two copies of the * business rules * database access methods * functions b) different text messages and prompts c) user can select knowledge-base to execute depending upon language required	a) smaller knowledge-base to execute thus reducing execution time	a) higher maintenance cost as all changes have to be implemented twice
Knowledge Base with separate text for each object	a) one set of * business rules, * database access methods * functions b) user can select language to be displayed	a) lower maintenance costs as all changes except for text changes are implemented once	a) increased execution time due to text retrieval

Figure 2. Options for providing a Bilingual system

4.2 Storage of Incomplete Waiver Determinations

Users required the ability to save a waiver determination at any point during its processing, retrieve the determination and return to the same point. This can occur when a user does not have enough information to finish the waiver determination and must review pertinent documentation or consult with the client. This was complicated by the fact that users also required the option to backup and change the responses to previous questions during a waiver determination.

Version I of WOW, which employed VSAM files for storage, only allowed users to save completed waiver determinations. If a completed waiver determination could not be made, the user began the determination again and reentered all of the information. Version II of WOW employs a DB2 database for waiver determination storage. The relational structure allowed for greater search and retrieval functionality and increased performance.

Storage of partial waiver determinations was implemented by using the same techniques and built-in processes of AionDS that are employed in the backup function. AionDS allows the storage of user supplied answers. The waiver determination can be rerun at a later point using these answers. Some control information also had to be saved, such as identifier numbers and other system generated values. WOW stores the answers to incomplete waivers on the database so that reporting can be done against all determinations, even those in progress.

4.3 Database Access

There were two options available from AionDS to access the database, Automatic Data Interface or Application Programming Interface. Automatic Data Interface (ADI) is a feature that reduces the amount of work required to set up a data interface between a class and an external database file. A data interface consists of I/O statements, which select data from and update data in the database, and corresponding AionDS and database data structures. AionDS supports access to QSAM, dBASE, SQL, and VSAM databases [4].

The Application Programming Interface (API) is a knowledge-base to program interface. It provides AionDS with an open architecture that enables integrating knowledge bases with other applications in a variety of ways. The API architecture is based on the client/server model. Each participant (knowledge base or program) is considered a client. API acts as the server and is responsible for managing the clients and routing requests between them. Sessions, which are communications links between two clients, allow for the exchange of data and retrieval of object information [5].

The three main reasons that API was used over the ADI were:
- DB2 access through ADI only became available in AionDS release 6.5 which would not be installed in time for the implementation of WOW Version II;
- to allow the knowledge base to be as independent as possible from the database structure and platform; and
- to off-load as much processing from the knowledge base as possible.

4.4 Browsing Previous Waiver Determinations

Users were required the ability to browse prior waiver determinations on-line within WOW. This was implemented for Version I using two additional knowledge bases (English and French) that incorporated all the data retrieval and formatting processes. This implementation was chosen to try and keep the operational knowledge base as simple and efficient as possible by only including the required business rules and data access. In Version II API was used to off-load the data retrieval and formatting required for browsing to an external program, thus eliminating the need for the two "browse" knowledge bases.

218

5 Characteristics of a Successful Project

Based on the experience of Revenue Canada in developing knowledge-based systems, the following are the characteristics of a successful project:

- clearly defined business problem
    ⇒ describe the degree in which the business problem is to be solved
    ⇒ describe how the developed system will integrate into the organization;
- project champions in both the User and IT organizations;
- obtain user buy-in early in the development process;
- utilize more than one source of expertise;
- ensure scope of prototypes is well-defined and manageable;
- manage organization and user expectations;
- provide sound project management; and
- avoid handling every possible outcome
    ⇒ follow the 80/20 rule -- with 20% of the effort you can deal with 80% of the outcomes, the rest of the outcomes can be referred to human experts.

6 Future Direction

As knowledge-based system development is a relatively new area, it is important to apply past experience to ensure the success of future projects. Revenue Canada has realized the tremendous benefits of knowledge-based systems and is pursuing their development in other areas of the organization.

Acknowledgments

The authors would like to thank their colleagues at Revenue Canada, notably Martin Leigh (Revenue Collections) and Raymond Martinuk (Information Technology Branch) for their support and helpful suggestions. Richard Power and Glen Todd (International Tax Directorate) provided valuable comments from a user perspective.

References

1. Brown, M.R.: Usability and System Design. IBM (1992) 32-22.
2. McGraw, Karen L., Harbison-Briggs Karen: Knowledge Acquisition: Principles and Guide lines. Prentice Hall, 1989.
3. Platinum Technology: Source Book of Customer Successes and Technology Solutions - How Banks and Financial Service Companies are Automating Core Business Policies. Platinum Technology (October 1996) 15.
4. Platinum Technology: Aion Development System User's Guide (Character-Based), Release 7.0. Platinum Technology (1996).

5. Platinum Technology: Aion Development System Application Programming Interface for Windows Release 7.0. Platinum Technology (1996).
6. Shaw, Andy: Strategic Directions - Renewing Services and Program Delivery. In: Federal Awards Honouring the Winners. Supplement to January 1995 Technology in Government. Plessman Publications (1995) 14-15.

Selecting the Next Action with Constraints

Toby Donaldson and Robin Cohen

Dept. of Computer Science, University of Waterloo 200 University Ave. W.
Waterloo, Ontario, Canada, N2L 3G1
tjdonald@uwaterloo.ca, rcohen@uwaterloo.ca

Abstract. Traditional AI planning systems have focussed on *batch planning*, where an entire plan for achieving a goal is generated. An alternative approach is to select only the *next action*, a technique that has been used in situated planners, and, more recently, has been effectively applied to traditional AI planning domains. In this paper, we present an action selection framework sensitive to resource limits and based on constraint optimization. While the framework we present is very general, we are concerned with dynamic, time-pressured domains requiring reasoning under uncertainty. In such domains, batch planning is usually inappropriate or impossible to apply. We experimentally compare a number of local search algorithms, and give a detailed example of how action selection can be used to control the dialog of a course advising system, which allows for more flexible behaviour than in typical advice-giving systems.

1 Choosing What to Do Next

The *next action* (or *action selection*) problem is a planning problem where only the action to be executed next is found, as opposed to an entire plan for achieving a goal. This kind of planning can be useful in robotics, where a robot senses its local environment, and then makes a decision about what to do next; [5] shows that such planning need not be entirely reactive, but can involve deliberation about goals. A major advantage of such robots is that they operate much more quickly than general-purpose AI planners, and so robots can act reasonably (if simply) in an uncertain or changing environment.

The input to a next-action planner is $N = <A, I, G>$, where $A = \{a_1, \ldots, a_n\}$ is the set of all actions that can be executed, I is the initial state of the world, and G is the goal function to be optimized. The output is the best action to perform next. A next-action planner can be useful in domains with a highly dynamic or uncertain world, such as in multi-agent systems (where agents can never be completely certain what other agents are thinking), or when plan execution is interleaved with plan generation. For example, in a dynamic world, the goal function G might change over time, e.g. if you form a plan to go to your favorite Italian restaurant, but discover half-way there that it is closed, you can change your goal and go elsewhere. A next-action planner handles such situations in a natural way by allowing different next-action planning problems at each time-step of interest. If $N_t = <A_t, I_t, G_t>$ is the next-action planning problem to be solved at time t, an agent operates by solving a sequence of problems $N_1, \ldots, N_t, \ldots$. Strictly speaking, there need be no relation between N_t and N_{t+1}, but in practice one expects adjacent N_t's will usually be similar, and so a solution to N_t can be used to help solve N_{t+1}.

2 A Framework for Action Selection

We propose to solve the general action selection problem in two steps. The first is to reduce the number of actions by applying an application-specific heuristic filter to get rid of actions that are likely to be irrelevant. We will not address this point in this paper, except to say that we treat this as a quick and conservative technique for helping the planner to focus on the most relevant actions. The second step is to use local search to find a better ordering on the remaining actions, with the action appearing at the front of this list being the next action the agent will try to execute. Our goal is not just to solve the action selection problem, but to solve it using methods that are sensitive to time pressure and a dynamic/uncertain environment, so the solution strategies of interest to us must address these concerns.

2.1 Ordering Actions with Constraints

A *constraint satisfaction problem* (*CSP*) consists of a finite set of variables $V_1, \ldots, V_n$, where variable V_i has a corresponding (finite) domain of possible values, D_i. Constraints between sets of variables specify which values can be assinged to variables at the same time, and the problem is to find a complete assignment of values to variables that breaks no constraints. A *constraint optimization problem* (*COP*) is a CSP where not all constraints need be satisfied. Solving COPs requires different techniques than solving regular CSPs [6]. However, local search methods can be used to solve both CSPs and COPs, without any major change in the basic algorithm [8]. Local search is a general-purpose optimization strategy that repeatedly modifies a fully instantiated set of CSP variables in hopes of finding a better solution. Such methods often combine the characteristics of hill-climbing and greedy algorithms, although numerous variations are possible (e.g. simulated annealing).

We claim that local search is ideal for solving next-action planning problems in discourse, since conversants are typically working in a changing and time-pressured environment where goals can change due to information gathered during the dialog. Batch planning is inappropriate because, at any single time, too much information about the conversation is lacking to construct a useful complete plan. Recent planning systems relying on local search [1] and action selection [2] provide further evidence for the validity of using local search for planning.

Given: n actions, $A = \{a_1, \ldots, a_n\}$
k variables to fill, $1 < k \le n$
a penalty function $p(a_x, a_y) \ge 0$ that gives the penalty for
a_x coming before a_y
Find: a $1 - 1$ function $\sigma : \{1, \ldots, k\} \to \{1, \ldots, n\}$ that minimizes

$$G(A) = \sum_{i=1}^{k-1} \sum_{j=i+1}^{k} p(a_{\sigma(i)}, a_{\sigma(j)})$$

Fig. 1. The next-action problem.

3 The Next-Action Problem

Our main goal is to develop algorithms for enabling an agent to choose which action it should pursue next. Previously, we have studied this in the context of conversational turn-taking, where we referred to the items being ordered as *goals* instead of *actions* [3, 4]. We call them actions here since our perspective is more general, and actions and goals can be paired, i.e. the effect of executing action a_i is to satisfy goal g_i.

Figure 1 defines the next-action problem as a constraint optimization problem similar to the path asymmetric traveling salesman problem. This formalism allows us to partially order actions, where weights specify the strength of an ordering. If action a must be executed before b — represented by $a < b$ — then we assign a high penalty to $b > a$.

3.1 Algorithms and Empirical Results

We tested 28 basic local search algorithms for solving the $n = k$ case of the action selection problem of Figure 1. For each $n = 5, \ldots, 50$, 1000 random problems were generated and processed by each algorithm. For each problem, a random penalty function was created by assigning a random integer from 0 to n to each entry of an $n \times n$ matrix. The starting arrangement of each problem is a randomly chosen permutation of the n actions. Each algorithm was run on the same set of test problems and initial permutations for each n. Here, we will focus only on the algorithms that performed the best overall.

On average, the most successful algorithms were the greedy and choose-2 algorithms. The choose-2 procedure looks at all pairs of actions (a_i, a_j) in increasing numerical order, i.e. $(1, 2), \ldots, (1, n), (2, 3), \ldots, (2, n), (3, 4), \ldots, (n - 1, n)$, and swaps a_i with a_j if penalty/goal function G is decreased. The greedy algorithm works by looking at each position i in increasing order, and swaps the action at that position with the action that results in the greatest overall penalty decrease. The iterated version of an algorithm runs the basic algorithm repeatedly until the penalty score stops decreasing. As shown by the graph in Figure 2, the iterated greedy algorithm is the overall winner, followed by the greedy method, and then a simple variation on this called iterated left-right

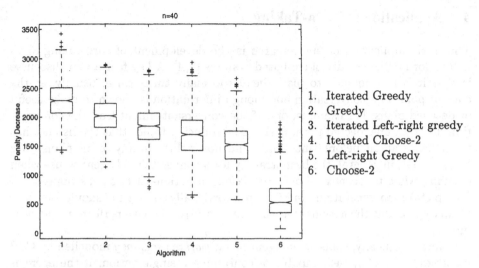

Fig. 2. Boxplots for the top three classes of algorithms. The notch in the box represents the mean penalty decrease for the 1000 runs with $n = 40$ actions, while the ends of a box denote the lower and upper quartiles of the data; a + represents an outlier.

greedy (explained below). The higher the "penalty decrease", the better the solution found for the problem.

While the iterated greedy method performed the best in terms of minimizing G, it is not necessarily the best choice for the action selection problem, at least for discourse. The problem is that at almost any time, the first action — the one that will be executed next if the agent is required to act — could be swapped with any of the later actions as the algorithm progresses. This can cause "unstable" behaviour, where the agent believes for a while that, say, action a_i is the best choice, but then, near the end of its processing, swaps a_i with another action. Instead, we would prefer an algorithm that allots its processing time in a more segmented manner, so all the processing choosing the next action is done near the beginning, not distributed over the entire processing time as in the greedy algorithm. The advantage is that we can then know when a reasonable next action has been selected without waiting for the entire algorithm to finish; any remaining time can be spent ordering the remaining actions for the future.

So instead of the basic greedy algorithm, we prefer either choose-2, or the greedy variation called left-right greedy which chooses the best value for variable i examining only the actions in variables to the right of i, i.e. $i+1, \ldots, n$ instead of $1, \ldots, i-1, i+1, \ldots n$. Both the choose-2 and left-right greedy algorithms can mark variables as having been filled, which can be used as a promise that the value of that variable will not change unless the action set or penalty function changes. Taking performance characteristics and the results of Figure 2 into account, we prefer the left-right greedy algorithm overall.

4 Application to Turn-Taking

The main application of our research is the development of turn-taking algorithms for intelligent, discourse-based systems [3, 4]. A key fact about discourse is that it is not possible to plan ahead too many turns since, usually, at the current point in a conversation not enough information is known to make useful or detailed plans. For example, one of the conversants might lead the conversation down an unexpected path, perhaps introducing topics that the listener has never heard about before (and thus could not include in any of his plans). We suggest that, in general, the best strategy for a conversational agent to use when deciding what to do next should be based on action-selection, as opposed to (complete) plan generation, and that proportionally more time should be spent "thinking" about the actions that the agent is most likely to perform in the near future.

More specifically, suppose an agent has a *working memory* modelled by CSP variables $V_1, \ldots, V_n$, each capable of containing a single action. If the agent is required to act, the action in V_1 will be executed, and then, if necessary, the action in V_2, V_3, etc. As the conversation progresses, the agent transforms relevant perceptions into actions to be executed and goals to be achieved. Simultaneously, the agent should also be thinking about what to do next, since conversation is generally intolerant of arbitrarily long pauses. Our proposal is for the agent to use a heuristic filter to first screen out irrelevant actions, and then work on ordering the actions in its working memory using a resource-sensitive local search algorithm such as choose-2 or left-right greedy.

4.1 Course Advising Example

Consider the domain of course advising, where an expert advisor helps a student construct a schedule of courses.[1] The schedule should not break any hard constraints (e.g. time conflicts, pre-requisites), and should try to satisfy as many of the student's preferences (soft constraints) as possible. For clarity, we use English examples, although our research does not assume the use of natural language. We contrast our work here with the CvBS system [7], where only single, as opposed to multiple, actions/goals are considered at a turn.

Suppose the student begins by asking:

(1) **S** Can I take cs246?

When the advisor sees input of the form "Can I take X?", we use a simple rule to automatically generate the following actions: ANSWER(X), CHECK-IF-COURSE(X), CHECK-PREREQS(X), CHECK-ANTIREQS(X), and CHECK-COREQS(X). Actions can be thought of as procedures for achieving their goals, and they can be simple or complex, even taking over control of the dialog for a period of time when fully general conversational behaviour is unnecessary. Actions can add new actions,

---

[1] We have implemented a Prolog/C++ system that handles most of the cases that follow, plus a number of other interesting examples.

	a	b	c	d	e	f	g
a	·	0	0	0	0	0	0
b	30	·	0	0	0	0	0
c	30	25	·	0	0	0	0
d	30	25	20	·	0	0	0
e	30	25	20	0	·	0	0
f	30	25	20	0	0	·	0
g	30	25	20	15	10	5	·

Goal ordering:

a = LINGUISTIC-REPAIR $< b$ = CHECK-COURSE
$< c$ = COURSE-REPAIR

$< \begin{cases} d = \text{CHECK-PREREQS} \\ e = \text{CHECK-ANTIREQS} \\ f = \text{CHECK-COREQS} \end{cases}$

$< g$ = ANSWER

Fig. 3. Penalty matrix for sample conversation, encoding goal orderings given on the right. For example, $p(f, c) = 20$ means putting f before c incurs a penalty of 20.

or can be removed from consideration when they have been achieved, or can never be achieved. Actions can be hierarchically related, and we require super-actions to be executed after their sub-actions. Action ANSWER is a super-action of CHECK-IF-COURSE, which is itself a super-action of the three "requisite" checking actions. Generally, if an action is removed from consideration, so are all of its sub-actions. As explained in [4], we assign types to each action, and constrain their order based on these types, and also domain-specific information. In this example, we use two repair actions, LINGUISTIC-REPAIR(X) and the domain specific action COURSE-REPAIR(X). A linguistic repair action is usually given first priority, as it is used in cases where some part of the utterance is garbled and not recognizable. A course repair is a higher-level action in the sense that it applies to utterances that are recognized as being linguistically acceptable, but are not part of the domain. Figure 3 shows the action ordering constraints, and the penalty matrix used to encode them for this example. Note that this particular example is a simple one, for illustration purposes, so that in fact algorithms other than local search could be used to solve it.

After utterance (1) is made by the student, the following actions are triggered and put into the system's working memory:

$A_1 =<$ ANSWER(cs246), CHECK-IF-COURSE(cs246),
    CHECK-PREREQS(cs246), CHECK-ANTIREQS(cs246), CHECK-COREQS(cs246) $>$

As soon as any of these actions appear in working memory, the advisor can begin to order them. Running the greedy left-right algorithm on A_1 moves ANSWER(cs246) to the end:

$A_2 =<$ CHECK-IF-COURSE(cs246), CHECK-PREREQS(cs246), CHECK-ANTIREQS(cs246),
    CHECK-COREQS(cs246), ANSWER(cs246) $>$

A_2 is a perfect solution, so the agent executes CHECK-PREREQS(cs246) and determines that cs246 is indeed a course, so the action is removed:

$A_3 =<$ CHECK-PREREQS(cs246), CHECK-ANTIREQS(cs246),
    CHECK-COREQS(cs246), ANSWER(cs246) $>$

Note that for a question of the form "Can I take X?", the advisor should always check that X is an actual course, but this should not be done automatically, because we want to allow for the possibility of handling a linguistic clarification action. For example, if the student instead asked "Can I take cd23L?", a low-level linguistic clarification action would be generated (by the agent's natural language processing module) to find out what "cd23L" means. In our example, the system would clarify this first before checking to see if it is a course.

What if CHECK-IF-COURSE could not find the supplied course? If the student had originally asked "What is cs239?", then CHECK-IF-COURSE(cs239) would add the action COURSE-REPAIR(cs239) to working memory, which should be the next action executed. A COURSE-REPAIR action could, for example, point out that cs239 is not a course name, and give the user a list of alternatives to select from. Then when the user picks the correct course, the course-repair goal is satisfied and removed, leaving us with A_3.

Continuing from A_3, the advisor next executes CHECK-PREREQS(cs246):

(2) **A** Have you taken the pre-requisite, cs134?

If the student answers "no", then the advisor can answer the student's question immediately. But instead the student answers:

(3) **S** Yes, last semester.

Now CHECK-PREREQS(cs246) is removed:

$A_4 =<$ CHECK-ANTIREQS(cs246), CHECK-COREQS(cs246), ANSWER(cs246) $>$

The system inquires about anti-requisites:

(4) **A** Have you taken cs241?
(5) **S** No.

Action CHECK-ANTIREQS(cs246) is removed, and CHECK-COREQS(cs246) generates no utterance because cs246 has no co-requisites. All that remains now is for the advisor to answer the user's original question:

$A_5 =<$ ANSWER(cs246) $>$

The systems says:

(6) **A** Okay, you are eligible to take cs246. (...)

5 Conclusions and Future Work

We have presented a general action selection paradigm applicable to highly uncertain or dynamic domains where forming a complete plan is not possible. Our experiments with local search algorithms and the desire to be sensitive to resource usage suggest that the greedy left-right algorithm is generally the best choice of the algorithms tested, even though others achieve lower average penalty scores.

A major concern of our research is to develop algorithms that work reasonably in time pressure. Hence, we have used local search algorithms in part because they are natural anytime procedures. This allows for an agent to be interrupted before it has completely finished thinking, although to deal with this explicitly requires being able to recognize *when* it is necessary to act. In particular, an agent should watch for turn-yielding/ending signals from other agents to know when they might be completing their turn. We are currently investigating how awareness of such signals can influence an agent's action selection process. Also, while we are mainly interested in multi-agent systems, it would be interesting to apply the action selection method to standard single-agent planning problems, wherein many of the resource-boundedness assumptions we have made could be relaxed.

References

1. José Ambite and Craig Knoblock. Planning by rewriting: Efficiently generating high-quality plans. In *Proceedings of AAAI-97*, pages 706–713, 1997.
2. Blai Bonet, Gábor Loerincs, and Héctor Geffner. A robust and fast action selection mechanism for planning. In *Proceedings of AAAI-97*, pages 714–719, 1997.
3. Toby Donaldson and Robin Cohen. Turn-taking in discourse and its application to intelligent agents. In *AAAI-96 Workshop on Agent Modeling*, pages 17–23, 1996. AAAI Technical Report WS-96-02.
4. Toby Donaldson and Robin Cohen. Constraint-based discourse agents. In *AAAI-97 Workshop on Constraints and Agents*, pages WS–97–05, 1997.
5. Pattie Maes. Situated agents can have goals. *Journal for Robotics and Autonomous Systems*, 6(1):49–70, 1990.
6. Edward Tsang. *Foundations of Constraint Satisfaction*. Academic Press, 1993.
7. Peter van Beek, Robin Cohen, and Ken Schmidt. From plan critiquing to clarification dialogue for cooperative response generation. *Computational Intelligence*, 9(2):132–154, 1993.
8. Richard Wallace and Eugene Freuder. Anytime algorithms for constraint satisfaction and sat problems. In *IJCAI-95 Workshop on Anytime Algorithms and Deliberation Scheduling*, 1995.

Poker as a Testbed for AI Research[1]

Darse Billings, Denis Papp, Jonathan Schaeffer, Duane Szafron

Department of Computing Science
University of Alberta
Edmonton, Alberta
Canada T6G 2H1
{darse, dpapp, jonathan, duane}@cs.ualberta.ca

Abstract. For years, games researchers have used chess, checkers and other board games as a testbed for artificial intelligence research. The success of world-championship-caliber programs for these games has resulted in a number of interesting games being overlooked. Specifically, we show that poker can serve as an interesting testbed for machine intelligence research related to decision making problems. Poker is a game of imperfect knowledge, where multiple competing agents must deal with risk management, agent modeling, unreliable information and deception, much like decision-making applications in the real world. The heuristic search and evaluation methods successfully employed in chess are not helpful here. This paper outlines the difficulty of playing strong poker, and describes our first steps towards building a world-class poker-playing program.

1. Introduction

Why study computer games? By writing programs that play games, some insights can be gained about machine intelligence. These lessons can then be used to develop useful non-game programs. Researchers have invested a lot of effort researching board games such as chess and checkers. These games all share the property that high performance can be achieved by brute-force search. This search emphasis was taken to the extreme by *Deep Blue*, which analyzed 200 million positions per second in its May 1997 match against World Chess Champion Garry Kasparov. This achievement only confirmed the effectiveness of brute-force search for some application domains. Can computer games give us any fresh insights into machine intelligence, beyond brute-force search?

We believe that the answer to this question is yes. However, real progress can only be made if we study games in which search is not the major criteria for success. Instead, we need to mimic real-world applications that are perceived to require intelligent behaviour. Activities such as financial trading, business negotiations, and

---

[1] This research is supported by the Natural Sciences and Engineering Research Council of Canada.

forecasting (from weather to politics) meet this criteria. The first column of Table 1 shows some of the characteristics of these applications from the AI point of view. We are not claiming that these are the only activities of interest, just that they are important considerations for a wide range of interesting problem domains. Unfortunately, games like chess and checkers do not have these characteristics, or involve them only in limited ways. Can these activities be studied in the context of computer games, and if so, what games?

Table 1. Characteristics of AI problems and how they are exhibited by poker.

General problem	Problem realization in poker
imperfect knowledge	opponents' hands are hidden
multiple competing agents	many competing players
risk management	betting strategies and their consequences
agent modeling	identifying opponent patterns and exploiting them
deception	bluffing and varying style of play
unreliable information	handling your opponents' deceptive plays

We are currently studying the game of poker and are attempting to build a high-performance poker program that is capable of beating the best human players. As shown in the second column of Table 1, poker exhibits all of the activities we are interested in studying.

Certain aspects of poker have been extensively studied by mathematicians and economists but, surprisingly, very little work has been done by computing scientists. There are two main approaches to poker research. One approach is to use simplified artificial variants [1] or simplified real variants [2] [3] that are easier to analyze. For example, one could use only two players or constrain the betting rules. The other approach is to pick a real variant, but to combine mathematical analysis, simulation and ad-hoc expert experience. Expert players with a penchant for mathematics are usually involved in this approach [4].

Simplification is a common technique for solving difficult problems. However, we must be careful that simplification does not remove the complex activities that we are interested in studying. For example, Findler worked on and off for 20 years on a poker-playing program for 5-card draw poker [5]. His approach was to model human cognitive processes and build a program that could learn. Unfortunately his simplified approach nullified many of the potential benefits of his research [6].

Recently, Koller and Pfeffer have been investigating poker from a theoretical point of view [7]. They implement the first practical algorithm for finding optimal randomized strategies in two-player imperfect information competitive games. This is done in their *Gala* system, a tool for specifying and solving problems of imperfect information. Their system builds trees to find the game-theoretic optimal (but not maximal) strategy, however only vastly simplified versions of poker can be solved due to the size of trees being built. The authors state that "...we are nowhere close to being able to solve huge games such as full-scale poker, and it is unlikely that we will ever be able to do so."

We have chosen to study the game of Texas Hold'em, the poker variation used in the annual World Series of Poker Championships. It is considered to be the most strategically difficult poker variant that is widely played, and requires all of the complex activities listed in Table 1. This paper describes our first steps towards building a strong poker program, called *Loki*. Section 2 gives the rules of Texas Hold'em. Section 3 discusses the requirements of a strong Hold'em program and provides evidence that all of the activities listed in Table 1 are necessary to play strong poker. Section 4 describes the *Loki* program and Section 5 gives some initial performance assessments. Section 6 discusses ongoing work on this project.

The research contributions of this paper include:

- showing that poker can be a testbed of real-world decision making,
- identifying the major requirements of high-performance poker,
- presenting new enumeration techniques for hand-strength and potential, and
- demonstrating a working program that successfully plays "real" poker.

2. Texas Hold'em

A hand of Texas Hold'em begins with the *pre-flop*, where each player is dealt two *hole* cards, face down, followed by the first round of betting. Then three community cards are dealt face up on the table, called the *flop*, and the second round of betting occurs. On the *turn*, a fourth community card is dealt face up and another round of betting ensues. Finally, on the *river*, a fifth community card is dealt face up and the fourth (final) round of betting occurs. All players still in the game turn over their two hidden cards for the *showdown*. The best five card poker hand formed from the two hole cards and the five community cards wins the pot. If a tie occurs, the pot is split. Typically Texas Hold'em is played with 8 to 10 players.

Limit Texas Hold'em uses a structured betting system, where the order and amount of betting is strictly controlled on each betting round[2]. There are two denominations of bets, called the small bet and the big bet. For simplicity, we will use a value of $10 for the small bet and $20 for the big bet. In the first and second betting rounds (pre-flop and flop), all bets and raises are $10, while in rounds three and four (turn and river), they are $20. In general, when it is a player's turn to bet, one of three options is available: *fold* (withdraw from the hand, leaving all previously wagered money in the *pot*), *call* (match the current outstanding bet; if there is no current bet, one is said to *check*), or *raise* one bet (put the current bet plus one into the pot; if there is no current bet, one is said to *bet*). There is usually a maximum of three raises allowed per betting round. The betting option rotates clockwise until each player that has not folded has put the same amount of money into the pot for the current round, or until there is only one player remaining. In the latter case, this player is the winner and is awarded the pot without having to reveal their cards.

There is a strategic advantage to being the last bettor in any given round, so to maintain fairness, the order of betting is rotated clockwise after each hand.

---

[2] In No-limit Texas Hold'em, there are no restrictions on the size of bets.

3. Requirements for a World-Class Poker Player

We have identified several key components (modules) that incorporate some of the required activities of a strong poker player and address most of the six characteristics listed in Table 1. However, these components are not independent. They must be continually refined as new activities are supported.

- **Hand strength:** assesses how strong your hand is in relation to what other players may hold. Hand strength is computed on the flop, turn and river. At a minimum, hand strength is a function of your cards and the community cards that have been dealt. A better hand strength computation takes into account the number of players still in the game, position at the table, and history of betting in the hand. An even better model considers different probabilities for each hidden hand, based on the relative chance of each hand being played to the current point in the game. This may be improved by varying the hidden hand probabilities for each player depending on a learned model of that opponent's play.

- **Hand potential:** assesses the probability of the hand improving (or being overtaken) as additional community cards appear. For example, having four cards in the same suit does not count toward hand strength, but has good potential to become a winning flush as more community cards are dealt. At a minimum, hand potential is a function of your cards and the community cards that have already been dealt. However, a better model can be evolved as capabilities are added to the program, similar to the hand strength computation described above.

- **Betting strategy:** determines whether to fold, call/check, or bet/raise in any given situation. A minimum model is based on hand strength. Refinements consider hand potential, pot odds (your winning chances compared to the expected return from the pot), bluffing, opponent modeling and unpredictability. Note that an accurate computation of your winning chances is necessary. This requires a sophisticated assessment of hand strength, as described above. Even with an accurate hand strength computation, the game-theoretic optimal folding/calling strategy may not be the best decision in practice, where bluffing, opponent modeling and unpredictability may be used to improve your betting strategy.

- **Bluffing[3]:** allows you to make a profit from weak hands. Even if you only break even on the bluffing plays, the false impression created about your play may improve the profitability of subsequent hands. Thus, bluffing is critical to successful play. Game theory can be used to compute a theoretical optimal bluffing frequency in certain situations. The minimal bluffing system merely bluffs this percentage of hands. In practice, you need to be able to predict the probability that your opponent will call in order to identify profitable bluffing opportunities. The better your opponent models are, the better your bluffing strategy will be.

- **Opponent modeling:** allows you to determine a likely probability distribution for your opponent's hidden cards or betting strategy. A minimal opponent model might use a single model for all opponents in a given hand. This can be improved

---

[3] Other forms of bluffing (semi-bluffing and betting a strong hand weakly) are not considered here.

by modifying the probabilities based on a classification of each opponent (e.g. weak/strong, passive/aggressive), betting history, and collected statistics. Opponent modeling has been attempted in two-player games but with limited success [8]. In poker, however, it is essential to success.

- **Unpredictability**: makes it difficult for opponents to form an accurate model of your strategy. By varying playing strategy over time (e.g. pre-flop hand selection, variable bluffing rate), opponents may be induced to make mistakes based on an incorrect model.

In addition, there are a number of less immediate concerns which may not be necessary to play reasonably strong poker, but may be required for world-class play.

This paper focuses on the issues of hand strength, hand potential and betting strategy. Other issues are the subject of on-going research.

4. Loki

Loki handles its play differently at the pre-flop, flop, turn and river. The play is controlled by two components: an evaluation of the hand and a betting strategy. The strategy is influenced both by the pot odds and our model of the opponent.

4.1. Pre-flop Evaluation

The hand strength for pre-flop play has been extensively studied in the poker literature [4]. These works attempt to explain the play in human understandable terms, by classifying all the initial two-card pre-flop combinations into nine betting categories. For each hand category, a suggested betting strategy is given, based on the strength of the hand, the number of players in the game, the position at the table, and the type of opponents (e.g. aggressive or conservative). For a poker program, these ideas could be implemented as an expert system, but a more general approach would be preferable.

For the initial two cards, there are {52 choose 2} = 1326 possible combinations, but only 169 distinct hand types. For each one of the 169 possible hand types, a simulation of 1,000,000 poker games was done against nine random opponents. This produced a statistical measure of the approximate *income rate* for each starting hand. A pair of aces had the highest income rate; a 2 and 7 (of different suits) had the lowest income rate for a 10-player simulation. There is a strong correlation between our simulation results and the pre-flop card ordering given in [4] (although there are a few interesting differences).

4.2. Hand Evaluation

Critical to the program's performance on the flop, turn and river is an assessment of the current strength of the program's hand. Enumeration techniques can provide an accurate estimate of the probability of currently holding the strongest hand.

For example, suppose our starting hand is A♦-Q♣ and the flop is 3♥-4♣-J♥. There are 47 remaining unknown cards and there are {47 choose 2} = 1,081 possible hands an opponent might hold. To estimate hand strength, the enumeration technique gives a percentile ranking of our hand. We simply count the number of possible hands that are better than ours (any pair, two pair, A-K, or three of a kind: 444 hands), how many hands are equal to ours (9 possible remaining A-Q combinations), and how many hands are worse than ours (628). Counting ties as half, this corresponds to a percentile ranking, or hand strength (HS), of 0.585. In other words there is a 58.5% chance that our hand is better than a random hand. This measure is with respect to one opponent but can be extrapolated to multiple opponents by raising it to the power of the number of active opponents. Against five opponents with random hands, the adjusted hand strength (HS$_5$) is $.585^5 = .069$. Hence, the presence of additional opponents has reduced the likelihood of our having the best hand to only 6.9%.

In practice, hand strength alone is insufficient to assess the quality of a hand. Consider the hand 8♦-7♦ with a flop of 9♦-6♣-2♦. The probability of having the strongest hand is very low, even against one random opponent. On the other hand, there is tremendous potential for improvement. With two cards yet to come, any ♦, 10, or 5 will give us a straight or a flush. Hence there is a high probability that this hand will improve substantially in strength, so the hand has a lot of value. We need to be aware of the potential changes of hand strength.

In addition to this positive potential (Ppot) of pulling ahead when we are behind, enumeration can also compute the negative potential (Npot) of falling behind if we are ahead. For each of the possible 1,081 opposing hands, we consider the {45 choose 2} = 990 combinations of the next two cards. For each subcase we count how many combinations of upcoming cards result in us being ahead, behind or tied.

The potential for A♦-Q♣ / 3♥-4♣-J♥ is shown in Table 2. The table shows, for cases where we were ahead, tied or behind after five cards, what the result would be after seven cards. For example, if we did not have the best hand after five cards, then there are 91,981 combinations of cards (pre-flop and two cards to come) for the opponents that will give us the best hand. Of the remaining hands, 1,036 will leave us tied with the best hand, and 346,543 will leave us behind. In other words, if we are behind we have roughly a 21% chance of winning against one opponent.

We use these values to generate Ppot and Npot. If $T_{(row,col)}$ refers to the values in the table (for brevity we use B, T, A, and S for Behind, Tied, Ahead, and Sum) then Ppot and Npot are calculated by:

Table 2. A♦-Q♣ / 3♥-4♣-J♥ potential.

5 Cards	7 Cards				
	Ahead	Tied	Behind	Sum	
Ahead	449,005	3,211	169,504	621,720 =	628x990
Tied	0	8,370	540	8,910 =	9x990
Behind	91,981	1,036	346,543	439,560 =	444x990
Sum	540,986	12,617	516,587	1,070,190 =	1,081x990

$$P_{pot} = (T_{\{B,A\}} + T_{\{B,T\}} / 2 + T_{\{T,A\}} / 2) / (T_{\{B,S\}} + T_{\{T,S\}} / 2) \qquad (1)$$

$$N_{pot} = (T_{\{A,B\}} + T_{\{A,T\}} / 2 + T_{\{T,B\}} / 2) / (T_{\{A,S\}} + T_{\{T,S\}} / 2) \qquad (2)$$

In the example Ppot is .208 and Npot is .274. The calculation for one card look-ahead is exactly the same as the above calculation, except there are only 45 possible upcoming cards instead of 990 (or 44 if we are on the turn). With only one card to come on the turn, Ppot is .108 and Npot is .145.

By enumerating all possible card combinations, the program uses a brute-force approach to calculating hand strength and potential. The calculations are easily done in real-time and provide accurate probabilities that take into account every possible scenario. Hence the calculation gives smooth and robust results.

4.3 Weighting the Enumeration

So far our calculations assume that all opponent hands are equally likely. In reality, this is not the case. Many weak hands like 4♥-J♣ would have been folded before the flop. However, with the example flop of 3♥-4♣-J♥, these hidden cards make a strong hand that skews the hand evaluations.

Accuracy of the estimates also depends strongly on models of our opponents. Ultimately, we want a different set of weights for each possible starting hand for *each* opponent. These weights could then be adjusted depending on the opponent's playing style. For example, raising on the flop probably indicates a strong hand that should be reflected in the weightings. We would then apply the appropriate weight for each of the 1,081 possible subcases when calculating hand strength and potential.

Although *Loki* treats all opponents the same, it was designed to support generalized opponent modeling. Currently the common weights are based on the simulations of the 169 different starting hand types, providing a reasonable starting template for unknown players.

4.4 Betting Strategy

Hand strength and potential are combined into *effective hand strength* (EHS):

$$EHS = HS_n + (1 - HS_n) \times P_{pot} \qquad (3)$$

where HS_n is the adjusted hand strength for n opponents and Ppot is the positive potential. This formula means that EHS is the probability that we are ahead, and in those cases where we are behind there is a Ppot chance that we will pull ahead. Currently, EHS is compared to some thresholds to determine when to bet. For example, with an EHS greater than 0.5 we can say there is a reasonable chance we are ahead of our opponents and will bet if no other opponent has bet. This is an optimistic estimate because we only consider positive potential. Npot is not considered for two reasons. First, we do not know if our opponent will play. Second, in many situations where we calculate a high Npot, it is often a better strategy to bet/raise to scare the opponent out of the hand.

Determining if the pot is large enough and whether we have enough equity to warrant calling a bet is different than deciding when to bet. This decision is made by comparing Ppot against the pot odds, where

$$pot\_odds = bets\_to\_us / (bets\_in\_pot + bets\_to\_us) . \qquad (4)$$

We call when Ppot $\geq$ *pot_odds*. Note that even on the flop we use only one card look ahead for Ppot. If we examine the situation two cards in the future we must consider whether we will face another bet (or more) after the first card. *Pot_odds* is based on the immediate situation. With the example hand of A♦-Q♣ / 3♥-4♣-J♥, if there are five opponents and we are first to act, EHS is 0.069 + (1 - 0.069) x 0.108 = 0.17 (assuming one-card Ppot) so we check. Assume the pot has $125 in it. If the first opponent behind us bets $10, two others call, and the fourth raises $10, then it is $20 to us and the pot is $175. Therefore *pot_odds* is 20 / (175 + 20) = 0.103, so we call (Ppot = 0.108 $\geq$ 0.103).

5. Experiments

A variety of different experimental methods have been used to evaluate *Loki* during its development. These include self-play simulations, play against human opposition, and play against other computer programs. Each type of evaluation has limitations, reinforcing the need for a wide range of experiments and testing methods.

Self-play simulations offer a convenient method for the comparison of two or more versions of the program. The simulations use a duplicate tournament system, based on the same principle as duplicate bridge. Since each hand can be played with no memory of preceding hands, it is possible to re-play the same deal, but with the participants holding a different set of hole cards. Our tournament system simulates a ten-player game, where each deal is replayed ten times, shuffling the seating arrangement each time so that every participant has the opportunity to play each set of hole cards once. This arrangement greatly reduces the "luck element" of the game, since each player will have the same number of good and bad hands. The differences in the performance of players will therefore be based more strongly on the quality of the decisions made in each situation. This large reduction in natural variance means that meaningful results can be obtained with a smaller number of trials than a typical game setting.

One simple application of a self-play simulation would be to play five copies of a new version against five copies of an older version, differing only in the addition of one new feature. If the new component improves the program, then that version will win against the older one. The margin of victory, in terms of expected number of bets per hand, can also give an indication of the relative value of the new enhancement.

However, there are limitations to how much can be concluded from a single experiment, since it is representative of only one particular type of game and style of opponent. It is quite possible that the same feature will perform much worse (or much better) in a game against human opposition, for example. A wider variety of testing is necessary to get an accurate assessment of the new feature. One approach is to change the context of the simulated game. The next self-play experiment might include a number of players who employ a different style of play, such as a more liberal selection of starting hands. If the new feature is successful over a wide variety of game types, we will have a more reliable indication of the value of that concept, with a metric to quantify its contribution.

As an example of a self-play experiment, Figure 1 shows the results of a tournament with five different versions of *Loki*. The average bankroll size (profit) is plotted against the number of hands played. Player A is the most advanced version of the program, including three major components that the most basic player does not have. Player E is a basic player, having no advanced features. The other three versions are the same as Player A, but with one of the major components removed. Player B lacks an appropriate weighting of subcases, using a uniform distribution for all possible opponent hands. Player C uses a simplistic pre-flop hand selection method, rather than the advanced system which accounts for player position and number of opponents. Player D lacks the computation of hand potential, which is used in modifying the effective hand strength and calling with proper pot odds.

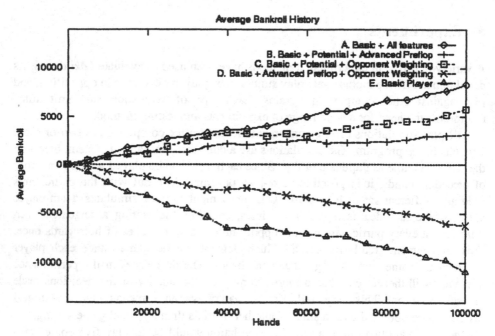

Fig. 1. A Tournament with different versions of *Loki*.

As expected, the complete system performs the best, while the basic system loses the most. The best program earned approximately +0.08 small bets per hand, while the worst lost at a rate of -0.11 small bets per hand.

Within the context of this particular experiment, the use of hand potential had the greatest impact on the strength of the program, since Player D, which lacked that component, performed poorly. Player B, missing the appropriate weighting of subcases, was still able to win against this field of opponents, but did not perform nearly as well as the version having this feature. Player C, differing only in the use of the advanced pre-flop hand selection method, did not lose much compared to the other weakened versions.

Loki must also be tested in more realistic games against human opposition. For this purpose, the program participates in an on-line poker game, running on IRC (Internet Relay Chat). Human players connect to the server and participate in games. No real money is at stake, but statistics on each player are maintained. Certain games are reserved for players who have earned enough virtual dollars to qualify, and those games are usually taken more seriously than the games open to all players. This provides an environment with several games, differing in styles of play and skill level.

Early versions of *Loki* had mixed results on the IRC server, but played at about the same level as the average human participant in the open games, roughly breaking even over the course of about 12,000 hands. When it qualified for the stronger game it lost slowly, averaging about -0.05 small bets per hand dealt (2,000 hands). This is not a large enough sample size for conclusive results, but strongly suggests it was a losing player overall in these games. Recent versions of *Loki* have performed much better, averaging about +0.20 small bets per hand (3,500 hands), which is comparable to a solid human player (probably in the top 10% of IRC players).

A third form of competition was introduced against other computer programs on the IRC server. Four programs participated, using three copies of each in a 12-player game. Two programs, *R00lbot* and *Loki*, were clearly dominant over the other two, *Xbot* and *Replicat*, with the more established *R00lbot* winning overall. Over 10,000 hands, *Loki* averaged about +0.03 small bets per hand. It should be noted, however, that this competition is representative of only one type of game, where all the players are quite conservative. *Replicat* in particular performs much better in the open games against human opposition than in this closed experiment.

6. Work in Progress

Loki still suffers from some obvious problems. Most importantly, it is a predictable player that reacts the same in a given situation irrespective of any historical information. This leaves it open to exploitation by an opponent who has deduced its simplistic playing style. The two major areas requiring improvement are opponent modeling and betting strategy. Both of these topics are open-ended, and will provide interesting challenges for future work.

When *Loki* is better able to infer likely holdings for the opponent, it will be capable of much better decisions. The hand strength and potential calculations will use a different table of weights for each particular opponent. Now the specific actions of that opponent can be taken into consideration, as well as historical and statistical information gathered on this opponent from previous games. A wide variety of properties can be measured and applied, such as betting frequencies, known bluffs, recent trends, etc. Additionally for each opponent we will also compute statistics to measure the betting strategy and thresholds for the various betting actions.

The current betting strategy is simplistic and predictable. A better betting system would bluff with high potential hands and occasionally bet a strong hand weakly. It would also predict opponent responses in order to choose the best practical action. Unpredictability and other advanced betting strategies can be incorporated.

The infrastructure is in place to incorporate these features. *Loki* is changing on a daily basis. It is only six months old and already at a level that exceeds our initial expectations. We understand many of the weaknesses in the program, but do not yet know if all of them can be addressed sufficiently to produce a world-class poker player.

References

1. J. von Neumann and O. Morgenstern, *Theory of Games and Economic Behavior*, Princeton University Press, 1944.
2. N. Ankeny, *Poker Strategy: Winning with Game Theory*, Basic Books, Inc., 1981.
3. M. Sakaguchi and S. Sakai, Solutions of Some Three-person Stud and Draw Poker, *Mathematics Japonica* 37, 6(1992), 1147-1160.
4. D. Sklansky and M. Malmuth, *Hold'em Poker for Advanced Players*, Two Plus Two Publishing, 1994.
5. N. Findler, Studies in Machine Cognition Using the Game of Poker, *Communications of the ACM* 20, 4 (1977), 230-245.
6. D. Billings, *Computer Poker*, M.Sc. thesis, Dept. of Computing Science, University of Alberta, 1995.
7. D. Koller and A. Pfeffer, Representations and Solutions for Game-Theoretic Problems, *Artificial Intelligence* 94, 1-2(1997), 167-215.
8. D. Carmel and S. Markovitch, Incorporating Opponent Models into Adversary Search, AAAI, 1996, 120-125.

Fault Prediction in the Telephone Access Loop Using a Neural Network

Bengt R. Knudsen

Department of Telematics,
Norwegian University of Science and Technology (NTNU),
7034 Trondheim, Norway.
Bengt.Knudsen@item.ntnu.no

Abstract. Fault prediction is a vital component of proactive maintenance in the telephone access loop. Indication of line problems are found by regularly measuring line parameters such as resistance and voltage. The suggested technique uses preprocessed line measurements as input to a neural network. Line repair records are used as fault indications when creating the training and test data set for the neural network. The collected data is found to be inconsistent and noisy. This limits the achievable correctness of the results. The method uses multiple measurements of the same line. Using hidden layers in the neural network was not found to improve the results significantly. The results show that around 25 - 50 % of the predicted faults are later reported by the customers. Unfortunately, few faults can be predicted with a high correctness.
Keywords: neural networks, telephone access loop, fault prediction, proactive maintenance.

1 Introduction

The access network consists mainly of separate twisted pairs connecting the telephones to the local exchange. On the average, a problem is reported by a customer every 9 years for each line. If the problem persists, a repairman is within a time limit sent out to investigate it. Travelling to the right location is an important cost factor. The total maintenance cost for millions of lines is very high, which means that even small improvements are significant.

Predicting a developing fault means that it may be rectified through proactive maintenance before it causes problems for the customer. Also, the potential revenue loss is avoided and the maintenance may be handled in a cost efficient manner.

Fault prediction in the access network has been addressed by Egan using Data Mining techniques [1]. The correctness reported is around 25 percent (3 of 4 predicted faults are false). A certain level of "randomness" was found in the data (messy or noisy data), thus lowering the achievable correctness. Thomas and Bell suggests that manual intervention and unusual weather conditions are the main fault drivers [2].

2 Approach

The overall processing of the presented method is shown in Figure 1. This figure shows that processing starts by combining measurement and repair logs. These are put through several stages of preprocessing to extract a compact and focused feature set for use by the neural network. The feature set is split into two disjoint sets, one for neural network training and one for result evaluation.

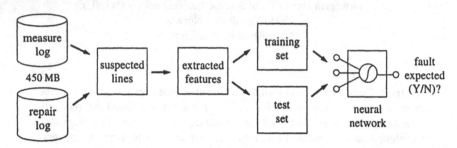

Fig. 1. Overall processing

2.1 Measurement and Repair Logs

The main data used is line measurements for 160000 lines collected once a week during a period of 8 months.

Table 1. Sample line measurement record. A twisted pair consists of two wires. One of the wires is labelled A and the other B. The ground potential is labelled J. Thus, A-J means a measurement between wire A and ground.

	A-J	B-J	A-B
Resistance (kOhm)	10000.0	8000.0	345.0
DC voltage (V)	0.1	0.0	0.0
AC voltage (V)	0.0	0.0	0.0
Capacitance (nF)	25	19	1230

Repair records are generated according to line problems and corresponding repair actions. The symptoms are mainly reported by the customers.

2.2 Abnormal Parameter Values

The probability of a future fault increases when a line parameter reading is abnormal. Critical threshold limits can be defined for each parameter which allows a simple classification into normal or abnormal line state. This allows the search for future potential failures to be limited to a subset of the lines. An example of current practise is to define abnormal parameter values to be resistance A-J or B-J lower than 1000 kOhm, or DC voltage above 7 Volts, or AC voltage above 2 Volts.

2.3 Temporal Processing

As a result of ageing and other causes, abnormal parameter values are found for some lines. This may start long before a problem is reported. By examining a series of samples, we find that the values for a parameter are equal or have variations. This information is be lost if only a single measurement is used. The "window" for generating a feature vector consists of the current measurement, and optionally a limited number of previous measurements (N-1). The window slides one step along the time axis when a new measurement becomes available by excluding the oldest one. A feature vector is generated at each step. The window is allowed to expand from 1 to N measurements, which means that a feature vector is also generated when only a single measurement is available. The window is reset to 0 when a problem report is detected.

2.4 Feature Extraction

All measured parameters are discretised into a set of binary fault indicators. The fault probability for each indicator can be calculated independently of the others. For instance, measuring resistance A-J between 10 - 30 kOhm means about 20 % probability of a near future problem report. These probability values was found to vary much from interval to interval, and was the main motivation for discretising the parameters. Several sets of discretisation intervals was constructed for comparison. The optimal number of intervals was found to be around 11. A near logarithmic scale for the interval boundaries was used because most samples are found in one end of the scale. The sample density decays fast when moving to the other end of the scale. This is typical for the resistance, DC and AC parameters.

The intervals for DC voltage are (in Volts): {0-0.1, 0.1-0.5, 0.5-1, 1-3, 3-7, 7-10, 10-15, 15-20, 20-30, 30-50, 50+}. For example, a DC voltage of 0.7 Volt is translated to {0,0,1,0,0,0,0,0,0,0,0} because 0.7 is in the middle of the third interval.

Also, features indicating simple parameter level changes from sample to sample was generated. Eight features for each parameter was selected after initial study of sample sequences. No optimisation of the initial setup have been tried. The features are: 30-500% level increase, >500% increase, increase in all the 3 latest samples (>100% accumulated), sudden high level (>500%) and return to first level in current sample (will detect a single abnormal value). Symmetric change features was used for negative changes.

The procedure is repeated for all measurements inside the current window. All extracted features (or a subset) are combined in a feature vector (a bit string).

2.5 The Applied Neural Network

The model applied is a basic neural network [3]. The neurons are divided into layers, and the output from one neuron is feed to the input of each neuron in the next layer. Training is done by the well known Backpropagation algorithm [4], p.142-157.

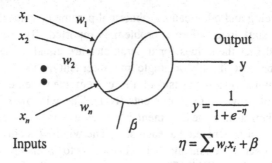

Fig. 2. A single neuron

The operation at each neuron is as follows. There are N input connections to the neuron. The input value at each connection is the output from a previous neuron multiplied by a constant weight. These values are added, together with an offset constant. The result is put through a sigmoid function. The output from the neuron is a real number ranging from 0 to 1.

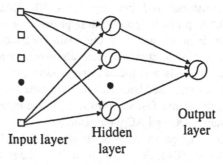

Fig. 3. A neural network with a hidden layer

Some modifications of the training algorithm was tried. The first is to reduce the influence of vectors which are almost correct. During training, a sequence of training vectors are applied one by one. The output from the neural network is compared to the desired value given by the vector, 1 (true) or 0 (false). However, for true vectors, only differences below a threshold of 0.82 result in an error different form 0. Similar, for false vectors, the output have to be above 0.18 to produce an error different from 0. When the error is 0, no training adjustments to the network is performed.

The second modification is to reduce the learning rate parameter ([4] p.147 and 149) gradually during training. This gradual reduction allows faster training and have a positive effect on the result. The reduction is done by multiplying the learning rate with a factor (0.998 - 0.9999) for every 100 applied training vector. Training stops by itself when this parameter gets close to zero. The reduction factor was changed during training, so that the reduction was smallest in the middle of the training. The initial learning rate was set to around 0.1 and the momentum to 0 ([4], p.149).

2.6 Result Evaluation Issues

The many vectors available for a single faulty or non-faulty line complicates the result evaluation. Multiple subsequent fault predictions for the same line are therefore counted as a single fault prediction. However, new fault predictions are accepted after a line repair or when a problem report has been cleared.

The aim is to predict problems before the customers reports them to enable rectifying actions in advance. This margin is set to 7 days unless otherwise stated.

Table 2. Applying a test set to the trained neural network using vectors where Res A-J below 1000 kOhm, or Res B-J below 1000 kOhm, or DC A-J above 3 Volt or AC A-B above 0.5 Volt.

	Predicted OK (negatives)	Predicted faulty (positives)
Observed OK (false)	8538	62
Observed faults (true)	782	27

$$correctness = (true\ positives) / (true\ positives + false\ positives) . \qquad (1)$$

An important factor is the correctness (1) of the predicted faults which in this case is 0.30 (27/(27+62)). The number of false positives should be as low as possible, because upgrading a line which is not going to fail should preferably be avoided.

Table 3 demonstrates the trade-off between the correctness of the prediction and the number of faults found. By adjusting the output detection level, it is possible to find the desired balance between the correctness and the number of faults found.

Table 3. Partitioning the neural network output into equal subintervals and counting the number of hits in each interval using a test set. The correctness is computed from accumulated values.

Detection level	0.0	0.1	0.2	0.3	0.4	0.5	0.6	0.7
True vectors (1)	0	28	120	59	16	5	2	0
False vectors (0)	8	729	1487	302	57	8	2	0
Correctness	0.08	0.08	0.09	0.18	0.25	0.41	0.50	-

Validation was done by repeating the training and testing of the neural network using the same vector set. The splitting was done randomly (10 % test vectors), but vectors generated from the same line stays grouped together. The arithmetic mean of the correctness and the number of faults found are the stated results. The arithmetic mean of the number of faults found is multiplied by 10 to compensate for the small test set size.

3 Results

Using a single neural network for all vectors was not found to deliver the expected results. Instead it was possible to obtain better results by using a subset of the vectors. A subset was obtained by defining a condition for the current measurement involving at least one parameter. Joining two subsets frequently made the result worse compared to using one of the subsets alone. This lead to the idea of finding an optimal combination of subsets. The main combination used (defined in Table 2) was found by trial and error.

Table 4. Selected subsets used for initial evaluation. Window = 3, margin = 7 days.

Vector subset	no of faults found	Correctness
Res A-J < 1000 kOhm	83	0.30
Res B-J < 1000 kOhm	106	0.31
1.0 V <= DC A-J < 2.0 V	117	0.30
0.5 V <= DC A-B < 1.0 V	38	0.29
Cap A-J >= 300 nF	66	0.27

The correctness was found to vary much for the different subsets tested. Resistance and DC voltage seems to be the best fault indicators.

Table 5. The main results.

Configuration	no of faults found	Correctness
3 hidden nodes, window = 3, margin = 7 days	29	0.49
	240	0.30
2 hidden nodes, window = 2, margin = 7 days	8	0.65
	734	0.25
no hidden layer, window = 3, margin = 7 days	12	0.73
	24	0.48
	356	0.29
no hidden layer, window = 3, margin = 1 day	588	0.30
	1139	0.26

The total number of faults for all lines in the period is close to 11000. Table 5 shows that few faults can be found with a high correctness. More faults can be found by accepting a lower correctness. Reducing the measurement margin before the fault report from 7 days to 1 day allows at least 50 % more faults to be detected. This indicates that a measurement interval of 7 days is probably too long for many faults. A relative small window (2-3 samples) gave the best results.

Using many vector features was found to increase the training quality, but the test set result improvement was generally small. Sometimes it was possible to obtain better results by removing features. The use of hidden nodes had similar effects.

4 Discussion and Conclusion

The data set used was found to be inconsistent and noisy. There are several causes of this. Measuring the telephone line once a week is probably too infrequent for some developing faults. Variations that happens faster may be detected improperly or not detected at all. Also, a huge amount of parameters is required to precisely describe the state of the individual lines. This should include a lot of ageing state parameters. Such parameters are not considered in this work. Besides, some customers are highly tolerant of background noise and other problems. This means that some problems are not reported.

False fault predictions is a problem, but may indicate an unacceptable line state which should be rectified. In many cases no faults are found, even if the customer have reported a problem. When performing a repair without a problem report, the probability of finding the fault is even lower. A positive fault prediction indicates a high failure probability for this line. If this situation can not be improved, the optimal strategy might be to replace this line by a new cable. This requires cost analysis.

Many different neural network models and configurations have been investigated. Surprisingly, the simplest neural network performed very good. The described method is able to predict only a few percent of the future faults. The correctness of the predicted faults is an important quality factor. Typical values range from 0.25 - 0.30 for a reasonable number of faults, and 0.73 is the best correctness found. The noisy and inconsistent data imposes an upper limitation on the achievable results for any method.

5 References

1. Egan, B.: Data Mining in the Telecommunications Industry, *subtopic* Network Fault Diagnosis. PKDD'97, Principles of Data Mining and Knowledge Discovery. Tutorial handout notes. First European Symposium, Trondheim, Norway (June 1997)
2. Thomas, M. R., Bell, P.: Fault rate analysis, modelling and estimation. BT Technical Journal, Vol . 14, No. 2 (April 1996) 133-139
3. Rumelhart, D., Widrow, B.: The Basic Ideas of Neural Network. Communications of the ACM, Vol.37, No.3 (March 1994) 87-92
4. Haykin, S.: Neural Networks, A Comprehensive Foundation. Macmillan College Publishing Company, Inc., 696 pages (1994)

Learning English Syllabification Rules

Jian Zhang and Howard J. Hamilton

Department of Computer Science, University of Regina

Regina, Saskatchewan, Canada, S4S 0A2

e-mail: {*jian, hamilton*}@cs.uregina.ca

Abstract. This paper describes LE-SR (Learning English Syllabification Rules), the first machine learning program that learns English *syllabification rules*, i.e., rules that tell how to divide English words into syllables for pronunciation. LE-SR uses a unique knowledge representation called C-S-CL-SS which effectively generalizes English graphemes. Given a 20,000 on-line pronouncing dictionary, LE-SR learned 423 syllabification rules from 90% of instances that have a predictive accuracy of 90.35% on the unseen 10% instances.

1 Introduction

LE-SR (Learning English Syllabification Rules) is the first machine learning program to learn English *syllabification rules*, i.e., rules that tell how to divide English words into syllables for pronunciation. The goal is produce a small number of syllabification rules that have high accuracy on *unseen words* (i.e., words that were not present in the training instances used to create the rules). Such rules are of interest to linguists, could be used in a speech synthesis system, and have been identified as essential to the LEP (Learning English Pronunciation) project.

LE-SR is one of four elements in the LEP project, which is a purely symbolic approach to learning English pronunciation based on separate steps for learning grapheme segmentation, syllabification, stress for syllables, and grapheme-to-phoneme translation [Zhang and Hamilton, 1996]. The overall approach is sketched in Figure 1. Four rule sets are learned separately and then applied in sequence. Currently, each component (LE-GS, LE-SR, LE-SS, or LE-PG) learns rules for one task directly from an on-line pronouncing dictionary. Future research will study interactive learning among the four learning components.

In a previous report, we described LE-SR 1.0, which learns syllabification rules based on counting the frequencies of inter-syllabic patterns [Zhang and Hamilton, 1997]. In this paper, we present LE-SR 2.2, which uses the Iterated Version Space Algorithm (IVSA) to generate, select, and order a set of syllabification rules; IVSA is described in [Hamilton and Zhang, 1996].

To explain the LE-SR approach, we give our definitions for graphemes and phonemes. A *phoneme* is the smallest unit of any spoken language that distinguishes sounds and meanings of words. For example, the phonemes /æ/ and /Λ/

distinguish the words *cat* and *cut*. A *grapheme* is a letter or a combination of letters that represents one sound unit (phoneme, cluster, or silent morphopheme). For example, the word "friend" has 6 letters but 5 graphemes: <f>, <r>, <ie>, <n>, and <d>.

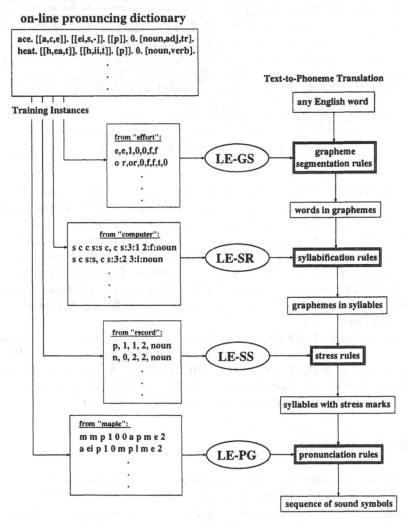

Fig. 1. The LEP Project

In the text-to-speech literature of the last 20 years, word syllabification has been ignored. Ling and Wang use a grapheme-to-phoneme method to translate all graphemes into phonemes [Ling and Wang, 1995]; PDtalk [Mudambi and Schimpf, 1994], DHtalk [Hochberg et al., 1991], NETtalk [Sejnowski and Rosenberg, 1987], DECtalk [Klatt, 1987], KLATtalk [Klatt, 1982], and NRLtalk [Elovitz et al., 1976] use letter-to-phoneme methods to translate each letter of a word into a phoneme; MITtalk [Allen et al., 1987] translates all morphs into

Symbol	Grapheme Type	Class	Graphemes / Cluster
C	consonant	−	b c d f g h j k l m n p q r s t v w c x z
			bb cc cch ch ck cq dd dg dj ff gg gh gm
			gn kk kn ll mb mm mn ng nn ph pn pp ps
			rr sc sh sl ss st tch th ts tt vv wh wr zz
S	syllabic	+	a i o u w c - aa ae ai ao ar au aw ay ea
			ear eau ee ei eo er err eu eur ew ey ia
			ie ier ieu iew io iou ir irr oa oar oe oi
			oir oo or orr ou our ow oy re ua ue uer
			ui uo uor ur ure urr uu uy yr
CL	cluster	−	bl br bbr bbl cl ckl cr dr fl fr gl gr
			kr pl pr tr
SS	special syllabic	+/−	e y

Table 1. The C-S-CL-SS Representation

phonemes. With these approaches, words in input text are not pronounced as syllables but as single sounds, and stresses are marked on individual vowels instead of syllables. This is one reason that the word utterance of commercial speech synthesizers does not sound as natural as human speech. Using the syllabification rules learned by LE-SR to divide any English word into syllables, a text-to-speech system could utter a word (regardless of whether it has been seen before) according to syllables instead of individual letters. Previous approaches to speech synthesis have either obtained syllabification from a dictionary or used a few hand-coded rules.

The remainder of this paper is organized as follows. In Section 2, syllabification is explained. Section 3 describes our approach by formulating the task of creating syllabification rules as a learning problem. A descriptive example is given in Section 4, and experimental results are presented in Section 5. Conclusions and suggestions for future research are given in Section 6.

2 Syllabification

For centuries, linguists of English have analyzed the syllables of English words. They discovered that an English syllable can have "zero, one, two or three consonants before the vowel and from zero to four consonants following the vowel" ([MacKay, 1987], pp. 41). This makes syllabification of English words very difficult. We have not found a piece of research that presents a complete set of English syllabification rules, although partial sets of rules are often given in linguistic books [Ladeforged, 1982], [MacKay, 1987], [Kreidler, 1989], [O'Grady and Dobrovolsky, 1992].

Informally, most English speakers know that a syllable must contain a vowel sound. Precisely, a written syllable must contain a *syllabic grapheme* that corresponds to a vowel sound. A syllabic grapheme is the "centre of a syllable" [Kreidler, 1989]. Vowel graphemes are usually syllabic (denoted "+syllabic"), but some can be non-syllabic ("–syllabic"), such as <e>, which can be silent. As well, the semi-vowel <y> is sometimes pronounced as a vowel and sometimes as a consonant. Some English speakers and dictionaries treat <m>, <n>, and <l> as syllabic consonants in some contexts, while others treat them as ordinary consonants in all contexts.

A syllable may include zero or more consonants. For example, the word *a* consists of one syllable, and this syllable contains the vowel sound /∂/. The word *syllabic* has three syllables, containing the /i/, /æ/, and /i/ sounds, which correspond to the syllabic graphemes <y>, <a>, and <i>, respectively. These examples suggest that identifying syllabic graphemes for English is essential for learning syllabification rules.

When formulating syllabification rules, we believe that is useful to extend the classification of +syllabic and −syllabic into a four-part classification, called the *C-S-CL-SS representation*. The symbols C, S, CL, and SS represent the class of phonemes that can be represented by the graphemes. In Table 1, we show the graphemes in each class, according to NETalk Corpus 2 (NTC2), which is an on-line pronouncing dictionary [Zhang et al., 1997]. Graphemes classified as C always correspond to consonant phonemes, and those classified as S always correspond to vowel phonemes in the dictionary. The symbol CL represents a *consonant cluster*, which here is treated as a sequence of consonant graphemes that frequently occur together. For convenience of expression, we refer to consonant clusters as if they were single graphemes, although they are not. SS represents a grapheme that corresponds to either a consonant or a vowel phoneme depending on context. The relationships are summarized in Figure 2.

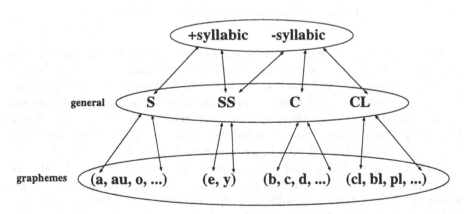

Fig. 2. Classification of Graphemes

Ordinary dictionaries divide syllables for hyphenation when printing rather than for pronunciation. When printing, if the last word in a line is too long, the word can be split across two lines according to dictionary hyphenation. According to the Gage Canadian Dictionary and the American Heritage Dictionary, the word *syllabic* is divided as *syl-lab-ic*. This division is not suited to pronunciation, because *syllabic* should be pronounced with the syllables *sy-lla-bic*.

We must make clear that syllabification done by LE-SR is for pronunciation rather than printing. In this description, *syllabification* means dividing words into segments according to the pronunciation of an on-line pronouncing dictionary, while *hyphenation* means dividing words into segments according to the lexical meaning of these segments. The problem of learning hyphenation rules has been specified, using rough data, in [Dietterich, 1997]. Table 2 shows a sample of words that are both hyphenated and syllabified. Differing cuts between syllables are indicated by ".".

Index	Word	Hyphenation	Syllabification
1	education	ed·u-ca-tion	e·du-ca-tion
2	dynamic	dy-nam·ic	dy-na·mic
3	folder	fold·er	fol·der
4	gravitation	grav·i-ta-tion	gra·vi-ta-tion
5	handy	hand·y	han·dy
6	infinitive	in-fin·i-tive	in-fi·ni-tive
7	jumpy	jump·y	jum·py
8	lemon	lem·on	le·mon
9	monotone	mon·o-tone	mo·no-tone
10	novel	nov·el	no·vel
11	recognize	rec·og-nize	re·cog-nize
12	shortcoming	short-com·ing	short-co·ming
13	talkative	talk·a-tive	tal·ka-tive

Table 2. Hyphenated and Syllabified Words

Words are usually hyphenated at affixes such as '-ic' in "dynamic", 'grav-' in "gravitation", '-on' in "lemon", 'mon-' in "monotone", 'nov-' in "novel", 'rec-' in "recognize", and 'ing' in "shortcoming". Most cuts for hyphenation happen to be identical with those for syllabification because the graphemes next to these affixes are consonant graphemes. Otherwise, cuts for hyphenation are frequently different from those for syllabification. The hyphenations and syllabification shown in Table 2 with index numbers 1, 2, 4, 6, 8, 9, 10, 11, and 12 are such examples. Other situations causing differences between syllabification and hyphenation are compound words such as 3, 5, 7, and 13 in Table 2. These words are formed by adding suffixes '-er', '-dy', '-py', and '-tive' to root words "fold", "hand", "jump", and "talk". It makes sense to separate the root words from their suffix when printing each word on two lines, but it would violate the usual pronunciation because English speakers say "fol-der" rather than "fold-er". We believe that syllabification poses a more difficult learning problem than hyphenation.

In our approach, before syllabifying a word for pronunciation, it is first divided into graphemes, such as <ll> and <gh>. The task of grapheme segmentation is discussed elsewhere [Zhang et al., 1997]. The goal of LE-SR is to produce

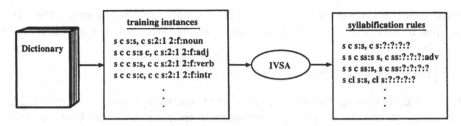

Fig. 3. Overview of LE-SR

a set of syllabification rules that can be applied to divide any English word, represented as a sequence of graphemes, into syllables. Identifying graphemes separately avoids a common difficulty with identical letter combinations that are cut in different places. For example, the word *uphill* is cut between *p* and *h* (*up·hill*), while the word *alphabet* is cut before *ph* (*al·pha·bet*). The letter combination "ph" sometimes forms one grapheme <ph> and sometimes forms two graphemes <p> and <h>. By resolving this difficulty beforehand, the problem of learning syllabification rules is simplified.

This paper does not discuss conflicting numbers of syllables for the same word due to individual usage of vocal organs (e.g., some people pronounce *sour* as one syllable and others pronounce it as two syllables). Instead, LE-SR learns a set of syllabification rules according to the NTC2 pronouncing dictionary.

3 The Learning Problem

Based on our previous work on learning English syllabification rules [Zhang and Hamilton, 1997], we hypothesize that this problem can be decomposed into two parts: (1) learning to identify which of the classes S, SS, C, and CL is most appropriate for each grapheme, and (2) using this information, learning to divide a sequence of graphemes into syllables. LE-SR 2.2 addresses the second problem, while assuming that the class of each grapheme has already been identified. After this information is added to input instances to create training instances, LE-SR uses the Iterated Version Space Algorithm [Hamilton and Zhang, 1996] to learn syllabification rules. As shown in Figure 3, LE-SR 2.2 first selects input instances from the on-line pronouncing dictionary and transforms them into training instances that use the C-S-CL-SS representation. These training instances are used by IVSA to generate a set of syllabification rules. The remainder of this section describes the learning problem faced by LE-SR.

Dictionary Description: The description of a word in the NTC2 pronouncing dictionary consists of six pieces of information: the word, the syllables of the word, the pronunciation symbols, the stress marks, a code (0 = regular, 1 = irregular, and 2 = foreign), and the parts of speech. Example:

  absent [[a,b],[s,e,n,t]] [[æ,b],[s,schwa,n,t]] [[p],[n]] 0 [adj,verb,tr]

Input: As retrieved from the NTC2 dictionary, the input instances are 3-tuples where the first element is a word, the second element contains the graphemes that comprise the word grouped into syllables, and the third identifies the parts of speech with this syllabification. The word "dictionary" is represented as a 3-tuple:

(dictionary, [[d,i,c],[t,io],[n,a],[r,y]], [noun]).

Creating Training Instances: As is common with applications of machine learning, we transform the input to produce training instances that explicitly represent features we believe are relevant; this transformation introduces an inductive bias since it influences the type of rules that can be produced. In an automatic preprocessing stage, the inter-syllabic patterns in the input words are identified. An *inter-syllabic pattern* (or simply *pattern*) includes all graphemes from the first possibly syllabic grapheme (S or SS) of the current syllable up to and including the last possibly syllabic grapheme of the next syllable. For example, the word 'biology' with syllabification [[bi][o][lo][gy]] is transformed into [[C S][S][C S][C S]], which has three patterns: 'S S' (i o), 'S C S' (o l o), and 'S C S' (o g y). All patterns from the input instances are collected together.

Then the input instances are examined again and transformed into training instances. The longest possible pattern in the pattern collection is matched to the input word starting with the first possibly syllabic grapheme in the input word. A training instance is created corresponding to this match. Then the process is repeated starting with the first unmatched portion of the input word, and so on.

A training instance is created by determining the cut into syllables in the pattern, the number of syllabic graphemes in the word, the positions of all possibly syllabic graphemes of the pattern among all possibly syllabic graphemes in the word, and the rough position (first, mid, last) of the current pattern in the word. Each training instance has 6 attributes, namely Pattern, Cut, S_SS, PS, PP, and POS.

- **Pattern**: all graphemes between the first S or SS of the current syllable and the last S or SS of the next syllable, inclusive.
- **Cut**: Pattern with '-' wherever the syllables are cut
- **S_SS**: number of S and SS graphemes in the word
- **PS**: positions of the S and SS graphemes in the word
- **PP**: rough position of the pattern in the word
- **POS**: part of speech
- Example: ⟨S C S, S - C S, 2, 1 2, last, adv⟩ (aback)

Output: The output is a set of syllabification rules that can be used by a text-to-speech system to syllabify words. The format of the rules is the same as that of the training instances except the rules can include '?', which matches anything, instead of a specific value for any field. An example rule is:

⟨S C SS CL S, S C SS - CL S, ?, 1 2 3, last, adj⟩

This rule can be interpreted as: if the pattern 'S C SS CL S' is found at the end of an adjective, and the S and SS graphemes are located in positions 1, 2, and 3, then the syllables are cut between 'S C SS' and 'CL S'.

4 A Descriptive Example

Consider the following input instances:

abacus [[a],[b,a],[c,u,s]] [noun]
biological [[b,i],[o],[l,o],[g,i],[c,a,l]] [adj,noun]
calculation [[c,a,l],[c,u],[l,a],[t,io,n]] [noun]
physically [[ph,y],[s,i],[c,a],[ll,y]] [adv]

The C-S-CL-SS representations are:

abacus $\langle$S C S C S C$\rangle$ $\langle$S - C S - C S C$\rangle$
biological $\langle$C S S SS S C S C S SS$\rangle$ $\langle$C S - S - SS S - C S - C S SS$\rangle$
calculation $\langle$C S SS C S SS S C S C$\rangle$ $\langle$C S SS - C S - SS S - C S C$\rangle$
physically $\langle$C S SS S C S C S$\rangle$ $\langle$C S - SS S - C S - C S$\rangle$

LE-SR begins by collecting all patterns. From 'abacus', LE-SR finds the same pattern $\langle$S C S$\rangle$ twice. From 'biological', LE-SR saves the patterns $\langle$S S$\rangle$, $\langle$S SS S$\rangle$, $\langle$SS S C S$\rangle$, and $\langle$S C S SS$\rangle$. The word 'calculation' has 3 patterns, $\langle$S SS C S$\rangle$, $\langle$S SS S$\rangle$, and $\langle$S C S$\rangle$. Since the patterns $\langle$S SS S$\rangle$ and $\langle$S C S$\rangle$ have already been saved from 'biological' and 'calculation', they are not saved again. The last word 'physically' includes 3 patterns that are already in the pattern collection. So, they are not saved.

From the above four words, the following 12 training instances are produced:

1. $\langle$S C S, S - C S, 3, 1 2, first, noun$\rangle$ (abacus)
2. $\langle$S C S, S - C S, 3, 2 3, last, noun$\rangle$ (abacus)
3. $\langle$S S, S - S, 7, 1 2, first, adj$\rangle$ (biological)
4. $\langle$S SS S, S - SS S, 7, 2 3 4, middle, adj$\rangle$ (biological)
5. $\langle$SS S C S, SS S - C S, 7, 3 4 5, middle, adj$\rangle$ (biological)
6. $\langle$S C S SS, S - C S SS, 7, 5 6 7, last, adj$\rangle$ (biological)
7. $\langle$S SS C S, S SS - C S, 6, 1 2 3, first, noun$\rangle$ (calculation)
8. $\langle$S SS S, S - SS S, 6, 3 4 5, middle, noun$\rangle$ (calculation)
9. $\langle$SS S C S, SS S - C S, 6, 4 5 6, last, noun$\rangle$ (calculation)
10. $\langle$S SS S, S - SS S, 5, 1 2 3, first, adv$\rangle$ (physically)
11. $\langle$SS S C S, SS S - C S, 5, 2 3 4, middle, adv$\rangle$ (physically)
12. $\langle$S C S, S - C S, 5, 4 5, last, adv$\rangle$ (physically)

From these training instances, IVSA generates candidate rules. From instances 1, 2 and 12, the candidate set includes only one rule: $\langle$S C S, S - C S, ?, ?, ?, ?$\rangle$ where '?' means no restriction. From number 4, 8, and 10, we have: $\langle$S SS S, S - SS S, ?, ?, ?, ?$\rangle$. Suppose we have example number 13 which is $\langle$S SS S, S SS - S, 8, 3 4 5, middle, noun$\rangle$. Then IVSA will produce another rule $\langle$S SS S, S SS - S, 8, ?, ?, ?$\rangle$ and place it before $\langle$S SS S, S - SS S, ?, ?, ?, ?$\rangle$. IVSA arranges the rules for each pattern from more specific to more general. The order of the rules is important for LE-SR because the learned rules are applied in sequence by the syllabifier.

5 Experimental Results

5.1 Ten-Fold Test Results

LE-SR was tested on NTC2 [Zhang et al., 1997], a 20,000 word pronouncing dictionary for English derived from the NETalk Corpus [Sejnowski and Rosenberg, 1988]. LE-SR was applied to 90% of the input words and tested on the unseen 10% of words. Accuracy is based on the fraction of patterns that are correctly divided into syllables.

In the experiments described in Table 3, LE-SR used two sets of SS graphemes, shown as $SS_1 = \{e, y\}$ and $SS_2 = \{e, y, l, -\}$. The average ten-fold testing accuracy on 10% unseen instances with SS_1 is 90.35% using 423 rules, while with SS_2 it is 89.02% using 810 rules.

Run	$SS_1 = \{e, y\}$					$SS_2 = \{e, y, l, -\}$				
	# of Instances		Accuracy			# of Instances		Accuracy		
#	90%	10%	Learning	Testing	Rules	90%	10%	Learning	Testing	Rules
1	37,349	4,089	92.15%	91.27%	426	37,331	4,045	92.58%	89.67%	801
2	37,465	4,141	92.15%	90.87%	426	37,183	4,170	92.54%	90.38%	829
3	37,465	4,141	92.06%	90.39%	417	37,286	4,101	92.24%	88.56%	774
4	37,465	4,135	92.06%	92.41%	417	37,245	4,096	92.32%	90.53%	806
5	37,417	4,150	92.06%	90.55%	420	37,291	4,103	92.45%	89.47%	800
6	37,521	4,048	92.04%	90.66%	427	37,325	4,015	92.54%	90.09%	821
7	37,504	4,038	92.06%	90.34%	429	37,296	3,988	90.33%	86.33%	836
8	37,740	4,134	92.16%	86.31%	404	37,513	4,087	92.47%	86.74%	823
9	37,416	4,132	91.95%	90.63%	434	37,275	4,083	92.53%	89.59%	818
10	37,430	4,121	92.14%	90.10%	428	37,307	4,089	92.54%	88.85%	800
Ave.	37,466	4,113	92.08%	90.35%	423	37,305	4,077	92.25%	89.02%	810
S.D.	106.36	38.36	0.06	1.48	8.11	80.23	48.30	0.65	1.37	17.26

Table 3. Ten-Fold Test on 20,000 Words

5.2 Rule Usage

The frequency of rule usage (for cases where patterns were correctly classified in testing) in a single run (Run 1 with {e,y} of Table 3) is shown in Table 4. The results indicate that about 85% of the testing instances are covered by only 29 (7%) of the syllabification rules, while 157 (38%) rules are used to cover the rest of the instances. Although 231 (55%) of the rules are not used for the 10% unseen instances, they are useful for the 90% instances (see statistics in Table

4). The natural logarithms of the frequencies are also graphed in Figures 4 and 5. The rules in Figure 5 are shown in the order they will be applied. Heavy rule usage is well distributed among these rules.

Frequency (F)	10% Unseen Instances		90% Training Instances	
	# of Rules (%)	Usage (%)	# of Rules (%)	Usage (%)
$F = 0$	231 (55.40)	0 (00.00)	0 (00.00)	0 (00.00)
$F = 1$	56 (13.43)	56 (01.40)	116 (27.82)	115 (00.30)
$F = 2$	32 (07.67)	64 (01.50)	49 (11.75)	98 (00.26)
$F = 3$	15 (03.60)	45 (01.45)	42 (10.07)	126 (00.33)
$F = 4$	14 (03.36)	56 (00.86)	22 (05.28)	88 (00.23)
$F = 5$	9 (02.16)	45 (01.07)	16 (03.84)	80 (00.21)
$5 < F \leq 15$	31 (07.43)	281 (05.40)	61 (14.63)	582 (01.51)
$15 < F \leq 35$	11 (02.64)	277 (07.15)	35 (08.39)	912 (02.37)
$35 < F \leq 100$	12 (02.88)	515 (12.68)	39 (09.35)	2,451 (06.38)
$100 < F \leq 1,000$	5 (01.20)	1,169 (32.91)	30 (07.19)	9,525 (24.79)
$1,000 < F \leq 1,500$	1 (00.24)	1,128 (35.57)	2 (00.48)	2,712 (07.07)
$1,500 < F \leq 5,000$	0 (00.00)	0	4 (00.96)	10,775 (28.04)
$5,000 < F \leq 11,000$	0 (00.00)	0	1 (00.24)	10,959 (28.52)
Total	417 (100.00)	3,636 (100.00)	417 (100.00)	38,430 (100.00)

Table 4. Rule Usage Summary

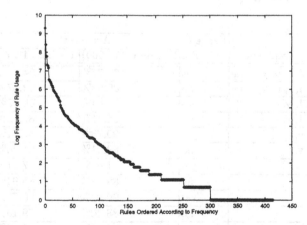

Fig. 4. Frequency of Rule Usage, in Descending Order

5.3 Experiments with Grapheme Classifications

In this section, we examine the appropriateness of the C-S-CL-SS representation introduced in Section 3. Our experiments relate to two questions: (1) should a CL

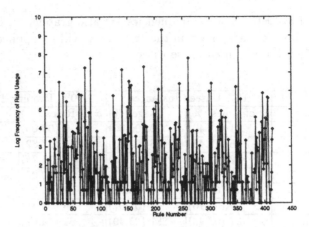

Fig. 5. Frequency of Rule Usage, in Rule Order

set be used, i.e., should separate CL and C sets be used or should all consonant graphemes always be treated as members of the C set? (2) which graphemes should be classified as $+/-$ syllabic, i.e., included in the SS set?

Table 5 presents the results of preliminary experiments using different sets of graphemes in the SS set with or without using the CL set. We tested a sample of 6,000 words using six possible sets of SS graphemes. In each of the six sets of tests, the test using the CL set gave higher testing accuracy than the one with no CL set. Nonetheless, further investigation of the C-S-SS representation is warranted given the relatively high predictive accuracy in Run 4 and the small number of rules in Run 8.

Test Number	SS Graphemes	Usage of CL Set	Accuracy		Number of Rules
			Learning (15,000)	Testing (4,200)	
1	e, i, l, u, y, -, ue	yes	91.77%	84.19%	534
2	e, i, l, u, y, -, ue	no	89.98%	82.37%	545
3	e, l, y, -	yes	93.44%	89.29%	467
4	e, l, y, -	no	91.71%	87.55%	505
5	l, y, -	yes	90.78%	86.71%	308
6	l, y, -	no	89.01%	84.26%	326
7	e, y	yes	91.61%	87.91%	443
8	e, y	no	89.91%	85.94%	261
9	l, -	yes	90.07%	80.73%	280
10	l, -	no	88.40%	79.15%	286
11	l, ue	yes	90.15%	86.12%	283
12	l, ue	no	88.32%	83.93%	292
13	none	no	85.61%	81.31%	211

Table 5. Tests on LE-SR with Different Amounts of Basic Knowledge

The experiments also showed that choosing different SS sets affects both the accuracy and number of rules. However, the results do not simply improve as more graphemes are added to SS. Run 3 gives the highest learning and testing accuracy, but it does not use the most SS graphemes. Run 13 produces the fewest rules, but it also gives the lowest accuracy for both learning and testing. Our experiments suggest that whenever <e> and <y> are classified as SS, LE-SR obtains better results (Runs 1, 3, and 7).

Although the preliminary experiments on SS graphemes shown in Table 5 predicted that using set {e, y, l, -} produces highest accuracy, the ten-fold tests presented in Table 3 show that using {e, y} gives better results. Examination of the rules shows that keeping <l> as a SS grapheme all the time is not suitable. Therefore, further research on learning to classify particular occurrences of SS graphemes (such as <l>) as either syllabic or non-syllabic may yield improvements.

6 Conclusions

This paper has described LE-SR, the first machine learning application for learning English syllabification rules. In our ten-fold testing, LE-SR learned 423 syllabification rules from 90% of instances (average of 37,466 patterns) that gave predictive accuracy of 90.35% on the unseen 10% instances (4,120). Further experimentation with various classifications of graphemes within the C-S-CL-SS framework is warranted. Future research could also try to automate the process of identifying syllabic graphemes.

References

[Allen et al., 1987] Allen, J., Hunnicutt, S., and Klatt, D., editors (1987). *From Text to Speech: The MITalk System*. Cambridge University Press, London.

[Dietterich, 1997] Dietterich, T. (1997). CS534 programming assignment 5. http://www.cs.orst.edu:80/ tgd/classes/534/programs/prog5/prog5.html.

[Elovitz et al., 1976] Elovitz, H., Johnson, R., Mchugh, A., and Shore, J. (1976). Automatic translation of English text to phonetics by means of letter-to-sound rules. Technical Report NRL 7948, Naval Research Laboratory, Washington, D.C.

[Hamilton and Zhang, 1996] Hamilton, H. J. and Zhang, J. (1996). The iterated version space algorithm. In *Proc. of Ninth Florida Artificial Intelligence Research Symposium (FLAIRS-96)*, pages 209–213, Daytona Beach, Florida.

[Hochberg et al., 1991] Hochberg, J., Mniszewski, S., Calleja, T., and Papcun, G. (1991). A default hierarchy for pronouncing English. *IEEE Transactions on Pattern Analysis and Machine Intellegence*, 13(9):957–964.

[Klatt, 1982] Klatt, D. (1982). The Klattalk text-to-speech system. In *Proc. Int. Conf. Acoustics Speech Signal Processing*, pages 1589–1592.

[Klatt, 1987] Klatt, D. (1987). How KLATTalk became DECtalk: An academic's experience in the business world. In *Official Proceedings Speech Tech'87: Voice Input/Output Applications Show and Conference*, pages 293–294.

[Kreidler, 1989] Kreidler, C. W. (1989). *Pronunciation of English*. Basil Blackwell, Oxford, UK.

[Ladeforged, 1982] Ladeforged, P. (1982). *A Course in Phonetics*. Harcourt Brace Jovanovich, New York.

[Ling and Wang, 1995] Ling, C. and Wang, H. (1995). A decision-tree model for reading aloud. http://www.csd.uwo.ca/faculty/ling/sub-pub.html.

[MacKay, 1987] MacKay, I. R., editor (1987). *Phonetics: the Science of Speech Production*. Pro-Ed, Austin, Texas.

[Mudambi and Schimpf, 1994] Mudambi, S. and Schimpf, J. (1994). Parallel CLP on heterogeneous networks. Technical Report ECRC-94-17, European Computer-Industry Research Centre GmbH, Munich, Germany.

[O'Grady and Dobrovolsky, 1992] O'Grady, W. and Dobrovolsky, M. (1992). *Contemporary Linguistic Analysis*. Copp Clark Pitman, Toronto.

[Sejnowski and Rosenberg, 1987] Sejnowski, T. and Rosenberg, C. (1987). Parallel networks that learn to pronounce English text. *Complex Systems*, 1:145–168.

[Sejnowski and Rosenberg, 1988] Sejnowski, T. and Rosenberg, C. (1988). NETtalk corpus, (am6.tar.z). ftp.cognet.ucla.edu in pub/alexis.

[Zhang and Hamilton, 1996] Zhang, J. and Hamilton, H. (1996). The LEP learning system. In *International Conference on Natural Language Processing and Industrial Applications*, pages 293–297, Moncton, New Brunswick, Canada.

[Zhang and Hamilton, 1997] Zhang, J. and Hamilton, H. (1997). Learning English syllabification for words. In *Proc. of Tenth International Symposium on Methodologies for Intelligent Systems*, pages 177–186, Charlotte, North Carolina.

[Zhang et al., 1997] Zhang, J., Hamilton, H., and Galloway, B. (September, 1997). English graphemes and their pronunciations. In *Proceedings of Pacific Association for Computational Linguistics*, pages 351–362, Ohme, Japan.

Characterizing Tractable CSPs

Wanlin Pang[1] and Scott D. Goodwin[2]

[1] Institute for Information Technology, National Research Council of Canada,
Ottawa, Ontario, Canada K1A 0R6   Email: wpang@ai.iit.nrc.ca
[2] Department of Computer Science, University of Regina,
Regina, Saskatchewan, Canada S4P 0A2   Email: goodwin@cs.uregina.ca

Abstract. In this paper, we introduce the notion of ω-graph as a representative graph for the hypergraph associated with general constraint satisfaction problems (CSPs) and define a new form of consistency called ω-consistency. We identify relationships between the structural property of the ω-graph and the level of ω-consistency that are sufficient to ensure tractability of general CSPs and we prove that the class of tractable CSPs identified here contains the class of tractable CSPs identified with some related conditions reported previously.

1 Introduction

Constraint satisfaction problems (CSPs) are NP-complete problems in general [21]. However, many practical problems have special properties that allow them to be solved in polynomial time. It is known that one of the most important criteria for identifying tractable CSPs is the structure of the constraints; that is, which variable is constrained by which other variables and which constraint is connected to which other constraints. The structure of binary constraints is represented by the underlying constraint graph and research has been conducted on identifying relationships between the topological property of the constraint graph and the level of local consistency needed to ensure that a binary CSP is tractable [9]. A general CSP is associated with a constraint hypergraph, where nodes are variables and the hyperedges are constraints. The underlying constraint hypergraph represents the constraint structure, but the topological property of hypergraph has not been well studied in the area of constraint satisfaction problems. Instead, representative graphs such as *line graphs*[1] and *join graphs* are graphical tools used to capture the structure of general constraints [14, 11].

In this paper, we address the issue of characterizing tractable general CSPs. We introduce a new representative graph called ω-graph for the underlying constraint hypergraph. The ω-graph captures the structure of general constraints more concisely than other related representative graphs and therefore allows a more precise characterization of tractable CSPs. We define a new form of consistency called ω-consistency in general CSPs, which includes some existing forms of consistency in general CSPs [14, 10]. We then identify relationships between

---

[1] The line graph is also called inter graph [14] and dual-graph [6].

the structural property of the ω-graph and the level of ω-consistency that are sufficient to ensure the tractability of a CSP, and we show that the class of tractable CSPs identified here contains the class of tractable CSPs identified with some related conditions reported previously in [1, 10, 14].

The ω-graph can be constructed and ω consistency can be achieved in a polynomial time. The algorithms for constructing the ω-graph and for enforcing ω-consistency will not be presented in this paper but can be found in [18].

2 Preliminaries

2.1 Constraint Satisfaction Problems

A *constraint satisfaction problem (CSP)* is a structure (X, D, V, S). Here, $X = \{X_1, X_2, \ldots, X_n\}$ is a set of variables that may take on values from a set of domains $D = \{D_1, D_2, \ldots, D_n\}$, and $V = \{V_1, V_2, \ldots, V_m\}^2$ is a family of ordered subsets of X called *constraint* or *relation schemes*. Each $V_i = \{X_{i_1}, X_{i_2}, \ldots, X_{i_{r_i}}\}$ is associated with a set of tuples $S_i \subseteq D_{i_1} \times D_{i_2} \times \ldots \times D_{i_{r_i}}$ called *constraint* or *relation instance*, and $S = \{S_1, S_2, \ldots, S_m\}$ is a family of such constraint instances. Together, an ordered pair (V_i, S_i) is a *constraint* or *relation* which permits the variables in V_i to take only value combinations in S_i. A *solution* is an n-tuple from $D_1 \times D_2 \times \ldots \times D_n$ such that all the constraints are satisfied. The task of solving a CSP is to find one or all solutions.

A *binary CSP* is a CSP with unary and binary constraints only, that is, every constraint scheme contains at most two variables. A CSP with constraints not limited to unary and binary is referred to as a *general CSP*.

Since constraints are defined as relations, we use some relational operators, specifically, *join* and *projection*. Let $C_i = (V_i, S_i)$ and $C_j = (V_j, S_j)$ be two constraints, $t_i \in S_i$ and $t_j \in S_j$ two tuples, and V_h a subset of V_i. The *join* of C_i and C_j is a constraint denoted by $C_i \bowtie C_j$. The *projection* of $C_i = (V_i, S_i)$ on $V_h \subseteq V_i$ is a constraint denoted by $\Pi_{V_h}(C_i)$. The *projection* of t_i on V_h, denoted by $t_i[V_h]$, is a tuple consisting of only the components of t_i that correspond to variables in V_h. t_i and t_j are *compatible* if $t_i[V_i \cap V_j] = t_j[V_i \cap V_j]$. If t_i and t_j are compatible, the *join of t_i and t_j*, denoted by $t_i \bowtie t_j$, is a tuple such that $(t_i \bowtie t_j)[V_i] = t_i$ and $(t_i \bowtie t_j)[V_j] = t_j$.

A constraint (V_h, S_h) in a CSP (X, D, V, S) is redundant if its removal does not change the relation represented by the CSP; that is, there is a set of constraints $\{(V_{p_1}, S_{p_1}), \ldots, (V_{p_k}, S_{p_k})\}$ such that $V_h \subset \cup_{i=1}^{k} V_{p_i}$ and $\Pi_{V_h}(\bowtie_{i=1}^{k} S_{p_i}) \subseteq S_h$.

A CSP is *globally consistent* if any consistent instantiation of variables in any variable set can be extended to a consistent instantiation of all the variables. A CSP is said to *have backtrack-free solutions* if there is a variable ordering such that the backtrack search along this ordering is backtrack-free. If a CSP is globally consistent then it has backtrack-free solutions, but the converse may not be true.

---

[2] Throughout this paper, we assume that $\forall i, j (V_i \in V \wedge V_j \in V \wedge i \neq j \Rightarrow V_i \not\subseteq V_j \wedge V_j \not\subseteq V_i)$.

2.2 Related Work

Much work has been done on consistency ([17, 15, 8, 12, 4, 3, 23, 16]) and tractability of CSPs ([9, 1, 10, 14, 7, 22, 13]). In this section, we briefly review some related work.

In binary CSPs, Mackworth [15] introduced three local consistencies called *node*, *arc*, and *path consistency*, and Freuder [8] generalized them into *k-consistency*. In general CSPs, one of the well-known consistencies is originally introduced in databases [1] which is called *pairwise-consistency*. In terms of CSPs, pairwise-consistency can be stated as follows:

Definition 1. (Beeri et al. [1]) *A CSP* (X, D, V, S) *is* pairwise consistent *if for any* $V_i, V_j \in V$, $\Pi_{V_i}(S_i \bowtie S_j) = S_i$ *and* $\Pi_{V_j}(S_i \bowtie S_j) = S_j$.

The pairwise consistency is generalized into *k-wise consistency* in [10] and *hyper-k-consistent* in [14], respectively:

Definition 2. (Gyssens [10]) *A CSP* (X, D, V, S) *is* k-wise consistent *if for any* $V_{p_1}, V_{p_2}, \ldots, V_{p_{k-1}}, V_{p_k} \in V$, $\Pi_{V_{p_k}}(\bowtie_{i=1}^{k} S_{p_i}) = S_{p_k}$.

Definition 3. (Jegou [14]) *A CSP* (X, D, V, S) *is* hyper-k-consistent *if for any* $V_{p_1}, V_{p_2}, \ldots, V_{p_{k-1}}, V_{p_k} \in V$, $\Pi_{(\cup_{i=1}^{k-1} V_{p_i}) \cap V_{p_k}}(\bowtie_{i=1}^{k-1} S_{p_i}) \subseteq \Pi_{(\cup_{i=1}^{k-1} V_{p_i}) \cap V_{p_k}}(S_{p_k})$. *A CSP is* strongly hyper-k-consistent *if it is hyper-l-consistent for all* $1 \leq l \leq k$.

Even though hyper-2-consistency is equivalent to 2-wise consistency (since both equal pairwise consistency), hyper-k-consistency and k-wise consistency are different when $k > 2$, which is discussed in [18].

Dechter and van Beek [7] extended arc, path, and k-consistency of binary CSPs to general CSPs, which are called *relational arc, path,* and *k-consistency*. As shown in [18], their work is not related to ours.

The problem of identifying restrictions to CSPs which are sufficient to ensure global consistency or to ensure that a CSP has backtrack-free solutions has been investigated by several researchers. These restrictions may either involve the structure of constraints, or they may require some particular properties of constraint instances. In the following, we review some of the work related to the structural properties of the constraint graph.

Freuder [9] identifies sufficient conditions which involve a property called the *width* of the constraint graph and the level of local consistency for a binary CSP to yield backtrack-free solutions. As a special case:

Theorem 1. (Freuder [9]) *If a binary CSP has a tree-structured constraint graph, then enforcing arc consistency ensures that it has backtrack-free solutions.*

For CSPs with cyclic constraint graphs, Freuder introduces the *width* of a graph and gives a general form of the backtrack-free condition.

Theorem 2. (Freuder [9]) *If a binary CSP is strongly k-consistent and if it has a constraint graph of width less than k, then it has backtrack-free solutions.*

If a CSP has a tree structured constraint graph, enforcing arc consistency guarantees backtrack-free solutions. However, for CSPs with a cyclic constraint graph, Theorem 2 can only be used to check if the given CSP satisfies the required condition, since enforcing k-consistency ($k > 3$) may add non-binary constraints and the theorem is no longer applicable.

A general CSP is associated with a hypergraph. The original result concerning acyclicity of the hypergraph and global consistency comes from databases. In terms of CSPs, it can be stated as follows:

Theorem 3. (Beeri et al. [1]) *If a CSP has an acyclic constraint hypergraph, then enforcing pairwise consistency ensures global consistency.*

This theorem is generalized by Gyssens and Jegou in two different ways (the cyclicity and the width of hypergraphs are defined in [10] and [14]).

Theorem 4. (Gyssens [10]) *If a CSP is k-wise-consistent and if its constraint hypergraph is k-cyclic, then it is globally consistent.*

Theorem 5. (Jegou [14]) *If a CSP is strongly hyper-k-consistent and if its constraint hypergraph has a width less than k, then it has backtrack-free solutions.*

Theorem 5 can also be considered as a generalization of Theorem 2, so it has a same problem that Theorem 2 does. Also it is not clear to us how to achieve hyper-k-consistency for $k > 2$. On the other hand, Theorem 4 is seldom considered as a sufficient condition for backtrack-free search, but it provides a theoretical basis for the *hinge decomposition method* for solving CSPs [11].

3 ω-Graph

We assume that readers are familiar with notations in graph theory such as *partial graph, subgraph, path* or *chain, articulation node, block,* and so on ([2]).

A general CSP (X, D, V, S) has an associated constraint hypergraph $H = (X, V)$ whose nodes are variables and whose hyperedges are constraint schemes. A hypergraph $H = (X, V)$ has a *linegraph* $l(H) = (V, L)$ whose nodes are hyperedges of H and with two nodes V_i and V_j joined with an edge $(V_i, V_j) \in L$ if $V_i \cap V_j \neq \emptyset$. A *join graph of H* is a partial linegraph, $j(H) = (V, J)$, where $J \subseteq L$ and for every pair V_i, V_j in V, if $V_i \cap V_j \neq \emptyset$, then there exists in $j(H)$ a chain $V_i = V_{p_1}, V_{p_2}, \ldots, V_{p_q} = V_j$ such that $V_i \cap V_j \subseteq V_{p_k} \cap V_{p_{k+1}}$ for all $1 \leq k < q$. A join graph $j(H) = (V, J)$ is *minimal* if there is no partial graph $j(H) = (V, J')$ such that $J' \subset J$ and (V, J') is a join graph.

Examples of a hypergraph, its linegraph and its join graphs are shown in Figure 1 (A), (B), (C), and (D).

It is known that a general CSP can be converted into a binary one according to an associated join graph. As a graph representation of CSPs, we observed that a join graph can be further simplified by deleting some nodes resulting in an ω-graph. However, there are special kinds of nodes, called ω-covers that cannot be removed. An ω-cover is a subset of constraint schemes with the property that any constraint scheme not in the ω-cover can be covered by two constraint schemes in the ω-cover. More formally,

Definition 4. *Given a hypergraph $H = (X,V)$. A subset $W \subseteq V$ is called an ω-cover of X if $\cup W = X$ and if for any $V_k \in V - W$, there exist $V_i, V_j \in W$ such that $V_k \subseteq V_i \cup V_j$. An ω-cover W is minimal if there is no $V_i, V_j, V_k \in W$ such that $V_k \subseteq V_i \cup V_j$. If a linear order is specified on the elements of W, then W is called an* ordered ω-cover.

For example, given a hypergraph $H = (X,V)$ as in Figure 1 (A), where $X = \{1,2,3,4,5,6,7\}$ and $V = \{\{1,2\}, \{1,4,7\}, \{2,3\}, \{2,4,7\}, \{3,5,7\}, \{3,6\}\}$, a subset of V, $W_1 = \{\{1,4,7\}, \{2,3\}, \{2,4,7\}, \{3,5,7\}, \{3,6\}\}$ is an ω-cover, since for $\{1,2\} \in V - W$, there are $\{1,4,7\}, \{2,4,7\} \in W_1$ such that $\{1,2\} \subset \{1,4,7\} \cup \{2,4,7\}$. The subset $W_2 = \{\{1,4,7\}, \{2,4,7\}, \{3,5,7\}, \{3,6\}\}$ is a minimal ω-cover. Notice that V itself is a ω-cover but not necessarily a minimal ω-cover.

In general, we can also define the notion of high order ω-covers as follows:

Definition 5. *Given a hypergraph $H = (X,V)$. A subset $W^k \subseteq V$ is called a k-th order ω-cover of X if $\cup W^k = X$ and if for any $V_k \in V - W^k$, there exist in W^k a set of $k - 1$ edges $V_{p_1}, V_{p_2}, \dots, V_{p_{k-1}}$ such that $V_k \subseteq \cup_{i=1}^{k-1} V_{p_i}$. An k-th order ω-cover W^k is minimal if there is no $V_{p_1}, V_{p_2}, \dots, V_{p_{k-1}}, V_{p_k}$ in W such that $V_{p_k} \subseteq \cup_{i=1}^{k-1} V_{p_i}$.*

¿From an ω-cover and a hypergraph, we can construct an ω-graph whose node set is an ω-cover.

Definition 6. *Let $H = (X,V)$ be a hypergraph and W an ω-cover. An ω-linegraph of $H = (X,V)$ is a graph $\omega_l(H) = (W,E)$, where the node set W is an ω-cover and there is an edge joining two nodes V_i and V_j if either $V_i \cap V_j \neq \emptyset$ or there is $V_k \in V - W$ such that $V_k \subset V_i \cup V_j$.*

Let (X,D,V,S) be a CSP, $H = (V,X)$ the hypergraph, W an ω-cover, and $\omega_l(H) = (W,E)$ an ω-linegraph. For each arc $(V_i, V_j) \in E$, we define the *variable arc-check-set of V_i and V_j with respect to W* as $vks_a(V_i, V_j) = \{V_k | V_k \in V - W, V_k \subset V_i \cup V_j\}$. Accordingly, the *constraint arc-check-set of V_i and V_j with respect to W* is defined as $cks_a(V_i, V_j) = \{C_k = (V_k, S_k) | V_k \in vks_a(V_i, V_j)\}$. The *variable check-set of V_i and V_j* is the variable check-set of V_i and V_j with respect to V, that is, $vks(V_i, V_j) = \{V_h \in V | V_h \subseteq V_i \cup V_j\}$, and the *constraint check-set of V_i and V_j* is $cks(V_i, V_j) = \{C_h = (V_h, S_h) \in C | V_h \in vks(V_i, V_j)\}$. Notice that $vks_a(V_i, V_j) \subseteq vks(V_i, V_j)$ and $cks_a(V_i, V_j) \subseteq cks(V_i, V_j)$. We define the *variable path-check-set of V_i and V_j with respect to W* as $vks_p(V_i, V_j) = \{V_k | V_k \in vks_a(V_p, V_q)\}$ where (V_p, V_q) is any edge on any path connecting V_i and V_j.

Definition 7. *Let $\omega_l(H) = (W,E)$ be an ω-linegraph of a hypergraph $H = (X,V)$. An ω-graph of H is a partial ω-linegraph $\omega(H) = (W,F)$, where $F \subseteq E$*

such that for any $(V_i, V_j) \in E$, (i). if $V_i \cap V_j \neq \emptyset$, then there exists in $\omega(H)$ a chain $V_i = V_{p_1}, V_{p_2}, \ldots, V_{p_q} = V_j$ such that $V_i \cap V_j \subseteq V_{p_k}$ for all $1 \leq k \leq q$; and (ii). if $vks_a(V_i, V_j) \neq \emptyset$, then $vks_a(V_i, V_j) \subseteq vks_p(V_i, V_j)$.

A minimal ω-graph is an ω-graph $\omega_m(H) = (W, F_m)$ where there is no $F' \subset F_m$ such that (W, F') is an ω-graph.

For example, given a hypergraph $H = (X, V)$ as in Figure 1 (A) and an ω-cover $W = \{(147), (247), (357), (36)\}$. An ω-linegraph and an ω-graph are shown in Figure 1 (E) and (F). Notice that an ω-linegraph is an ω-graph but not necessarily a minimal ω-graph.

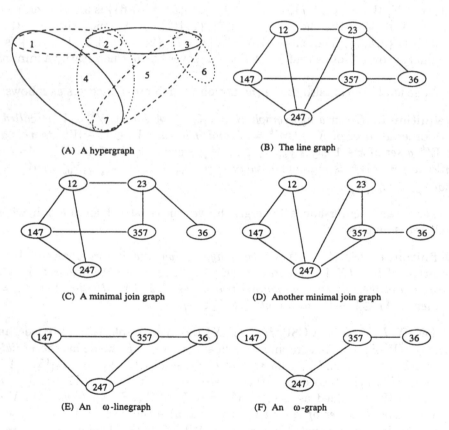

(A) A hypergraph

(B) The line graph

(C) A minimal join graph

(D) Another minimal join graph

(E) An ω-linegraph

(F) An ω-graph

Fig. 1. A hypergraph and its representative graphs

If V is chosen as an ω-cover, then the ω-linegraph $\omega_l(H) = (V, L)$ is the ordinary linegraph of the hypergraph, an ω-graph is a join graph, and a minimal ω-graph is a minimal join graph. Therefore, a join graph is only a special ω-graph. Accordingly, we have the following results:

Theorem 6. *If a hypergraph $H = (X, V)$ has a tree-structured join graph, then H also has a tree-structured ω-graph. Whereas the converse does not necessarily hold.*

The proof is trivial, since V itself is an ω-cover, and the join tree is a tree-structured ω-graph. Figure 1 shows an example of a cyclic hypergraph (A) which only has cyclic minimal join graphs (C) and (D) but an acyclic ω-graph (F).

Since a simple graph can also be considered as a hypergraph, it has an ω-graph. There is a similar relationship between a simple graph and its ω-graph:

Corollary 1. *If a simple graph $G = (X, V)$ is a tree, then it has a tree structured ω-graph. Whereas the converse does not necessarily hold.*

Proof. If the simple constraint graph $G = (X, V)$ is a tree, then the corresponding hypergraph $H = (X, V)$ has no cycle in it; that is, it is acyclic, thus H has a tree-structured ω-graph. $\Box$

We say that an ω-graph is *k-cyclic* if the number of nodes in its largest block is at most k.

For a given hypergraph and an ω-cover, there exists exactly one ω-linegraph but more than one ω-graphs. An algorithm is given in [18] for constructing an ω-graph from the linegraph such that the cyclicity of constructed ω-graph is at most the cyclicity of the hypergraph.

An ω-graph is a simple graph so its width can be normally defined as the minimum width of all the node orderings. However, we are only interested in the properties which are useful for analyzing and solving CSPs, and we noticed that some node orderings in an ω-graph, which we call *illegal*, may not be possible orderings for instantiating variables. In general, we give a definition as follows:

Definition 8. *A node ordering is legal in a join graph (V, J) if for any ordered pair of nodes V_i and V_j such that $V_i \cap V_j \neq \emptyset$ and $(V_i, V_j) \notin J$, there exists in (V, J) a chain $V_i = V_{p_1}, V_{p_2}, \ldots, V_{p_q} = V_j$ such that $V_i \cap V_j \subseteq V_{p_k}$ and $p_k < j$ for all $1 < k < q$. The legal width of a join graph is the minimum width of all its legal node orderings.*

According to an ω-graph $\omega(H) = (W, F)$, a general CSP (X, D, V, S) can be converted into a binary CSP (W, S^w, F, R), where each $V_i \in W$ is considered a singleton variable that takes on values from a set of domains $S^w = \{S_i | V_i \in W\} \subseteq S$. F is a set of constraint schemes and R is a set of constraint instances. Each edge $F_{ij} = \{V_i, V_j\}$ in F is associated with a subset $R_{ij} \subseteq S_i \bowtie S_j$ in R such that $\Pi_{V_h}(R_{ij}) \subseteq S_h$ for all $C_h \in cks_a(V_i \cup V_j)$. In other words, the binary constraint posed on V_i and V_j requests that the instantiation of variables in V_i and V_j has to satisfy the compatible constraint as well as the original constraints in the constraint arc-check-set $cks_a(V_i \cup V_j)$. We prove that such a binary CSP is equivalent to the original general CSP; that is, they represent the same relation over X.

Theorem 7. *If (W, S^w, F, R) is a binary CSP converted from a general CSP (X, D, V, S) and an ω-graph $\omega(H) = (W, F)$ as described above, then they represent the same relation on X.*

Proof. Assume $W = \{V_1, V_2, \ldots, V_w\}$. Let an n-tuple $t_g = (x_1, x_2, \ldots, x_n)$ be a solution to (X, D, V, S), we show the instantiation of $V_1, V_2, \ldots, V_w$, $t_b = (t_g[V_1], t_g[V_2], \ldots, t_g[V_w])$, is a solution to (W, S^w, F, R), i.e., for any $(V_i, V_j) \in F$, $(t_g[V_i], t_g[V_j]) \in R_{ij}$. If $V_i \cap V_j \neq \emptyset$, $t_g[V_i][V_i \cap V_j] = t_g[V_i \cap V_j] = t_g[V_j][V_i \cap V_j]$. If $vks_a(V_i, V_j) \neq \emptyset$, for any $V_h \in vks_a(V_i, V_j)$, $(t_g[V_i] \bowtie t_g[V_j])[V_h] = t_g[V_i \cup V_j][V_h] = t_g[V_h] \in S_h$. In both cases, $(t_g[V_i], t_g[V_j]) \in R_{ij}$.

Let $t_b = (t_1, t_2, \ldots, t_w)$ be a solution to (W, S^w, F, R), we show that $t_g = (t_1 \bowtie t_2 \bowtie \ldots \bowtie t_w)$ is a solution to (X, D, V, S), i.e., for any $V_k \in V$, $t_g[V_k] \in S_k$. Trivially, if $V_k \in W$, $t_g[V_k] = t_k \in S_k$. If $V_k \notin W$, then there are $V_i, V_j \in W$ such that $V_k \in V_i \cup V_j$. So, $t_g[V_k] = t_g[V_i \cup V_j][V_k] = (t_g[V_i] \bowtie t_g[V_j])[V_k] = (t_i \bowtie t_j)[V_k] \in S_k$. $\square$

It should be advised that the ω-graph based binary representation of a general CSP is much simpler than other binary representations such as the one based on the join graph, it is still not practical to solve a general CSP by converting it and then solving the converted binary CSP.

4 ω-Consistency

Arc-consistency in binary CSPs is related to the binary constraint graph and pair-wise consistency is related to the join graph. In this section, we give a definition of ω-consistency for general CSPs related to the ω-graph and we discuss the relationship between ω-consistency and other forms of consistency.

Definition 9. *Given a CSP (X, D, V, S) and an ω-cover W. An ordered pair of V_i and V_j in W is ω-consistent with respect to W if for any tuple $t_i \in S_i$ there exists a tuple $t_j \in S_j$ such that t_i and t_j are compatible and the joined tuple $t_i \bowtie t_j$ satisfies every constraint in $cks_a(V_i \cup V_j)$. A pair V_i and V_i in W is ω-consistent with respect to W if both ordered pairs (V_i, V_j) and (V_j, V_i) are ω-consistent with respect to W. The CSP is ω-consistent with respect to W if every pair V_i and V_j in W is ω-consistent with respect to W.*

Definition 10. *A CSP is ω-consistent if it is ω-consistent with respect to every ω-cover.*

For a pair V_i and V_j, if for any $t_i \in S_i$ ($t_j \in S_j$) there is $t_j \in S_j$ ($t_i \in S_i$) such that t_i and t_j are compatible and $t_i \bowtie t_j$ satisfies every constraint in $cks(V_i, V_j)$, then the pair is said to be ω-consistent.

Lemma 1. *emmaA CSP (X, D, V, S) is ω-consistent iff every pair V_i and V_j in V is ω-consistent.*

Proof: Sufficiency is obvious, we prove necessity; that is, if a CSP is ω-consistent, then every pair V_i and V_j in V is ω-consistent.

For any V_i and V_j, $W = V - cks(V_i, V_j)$ is an ω-cover. Thus V_i and V_j is ω-consistent with respect to W. Since the constraint arc-check-set of V_i and V_j with respect to W $cks_a((V_i, V_j)$ is $cks(V_i, V_j)$, the pair V_i and V_j is ω-consistent. $\square$

Equally, we can define that a CSP is ω-consistent if every pair in V is ω-consistent.

It is less expensive to achieve ω-consistency with respect to an ω-cover than to achieve general ω-consistency as defined above. Further, to achieve ω-consistency with respect to an ω-cover can be done by achieving ω-consistency with respect to an ω-graph.

Definition 11. *Given a CSP (X, D, V, S) and an ω-graph $\omega(H) = (W, F)$. The CSP is ω-consistent with respect to $\omega(H)$ if every adjacent pair V_i and V_j in $\omega(H)$ is ω-consistent with respect to W.*

Lemma 2. *A CSP is ω-consistent with respect to an ω-cover W iff it is ω-consistent with respect to an ω-graph $\omega(H) = (W, F)$.*

Proof. We only need to prove sufficiency; that is, if a CSP is ω-consistent with respect to an ω-graph $\omega(H) = (W, F)$, then it is ω-consistent with respect to W. For any pair V_i and V_j in W, if $(V_i, V_j) \in F$, then the pair is ω-consistent. Now, assume that $(V_i, V_j) \notin F$.

If $V_i \cap V_j \neq \emptyset$, from the definition of ω-graph, there exists in $\omega(H)$ a chain $V_i = V_{p_1}, V_{p_2}, \ldots, V_{p_q} = V_j$ such that $V_i \cap V_j \subseteq V_{p_l}$ for all $1 \leq l \leq q$. Since every adjacent pair V_{p_l} and $V_{p_{l+1}}$ is ω-consistent, for any tuple $t_i \in S_i$ ($t_j \in S_j$), there exists a tuple $t_j \in S_j$ ($t_i \in S_i$) such that $t_i[V_i \cap V_j] = t_j[V_i \cap V_j]$.

If $vks_a(V_i, V_j) \neq \emptyset$, then for any $V_k \in vks_a(V_i, V_j)$ there is (V_p, V_q) on a path connecting V_i and V_j such that $V_k \in vks_a(V_p, V_q)$. Since (V_p, V_q) is on a path connecting V_i and V_j, we have $(V_i \cap V_p) \cup (V_i \cap V_q) = V_i \cap V_k$ and $(V_j \cap V_p) \cup (V_j \cap V_q) = V_j \cap V_k$. Then for any $t_i \in S_i$ and $t_j \in S_j$ we have $t_i[(V_i \cap V_p) \cup (V_i \cap V_q)] = t_i[V_i \cap V_k]$ and $t_j[(V_j \cap V_p) \cup (V_j \cap V_q)] = t_j[V_j \cap V_k]$, that is, $t_i[V_i \cap V_p] \bowtie t_i[V_i \cap V_q] = t_i[V_i \cap V_k]$ and $t_j[V_j \cap V_p] \bowtie t_j[V_j \cap V_q] = t_j[V_j \cap V_k]$. Based on that $V_i \cap V_p \neq \emptyset$ implies $t_i[V_i \cap V_p] = t_p[V_i \cap V_p]$, there are $t_p \in S_p, t_q \in S_q$ such that $t_p[V_i \cap V_p] \bowtie t_q[V_i \cap V_q] = t_i[V_i \cap V_k]$ and $t_p[V_j \cap V_p] \bowtie t_q[V_j \cap V_q] = t_j[V_j \cap V_k]$. Therefore, $(t_i \bowtie t_j)[V_k] = t_i[V_i \cap V_k] \bowtie t_j[V_j \cap V_k] = t_i[V_i \cap V_p] \bowtie t_i[V_i \cap V_q] \bowtie t_j[V_j \cap V_p] \bowtie t_j[V_j \cap V_q] = t_p[(V_i \cap V_p) \cup (V_j \cap V_p)] \bowtie t_q[(V_i \cap V_q) \cup (V_j \cap V_q)] = (t_p \bowtie t_p)[(V_i \cap V_p) \cup (V_j \cap V_p) \cup (V_i \cap V_q) \cup (V_j \cap V_q)] = (t_p \bowtie t_p)[V_k]$. Since $V_k \in vks_a(V_p, V_q)$ and $(V_p, V_q) \in F$, there is a $t_k \in S_k$ such that $(t_p \bowtie t_q)[V_k] = t_k$. So we have $(t_i \bowtie t_j)[V_k] = t_k$, that is $(t_i \bowtie t_j)[V_k] \in S_k$. This proves that V_i and V_j are ω-consistent. $\square$

Following Dechter and Pearl [5] we can also define *directional ω-consistency*.

Definition 12. *Let W be an ordered ω-cover and $\omega(H) = (W, F)$ an ordered ω-graph. A CSP is directional ω-consistent with respect to $\omega(H)$ if every adjacent pair V_i and V_j in $\omega(H)$, where $i < j$, is ω-consistent with respect to W.*

ω-consistency can be achieved in polynomial time. Algorithms for achieving (directional) ω-consistency are given in [18].

In what follows, we generalize ω-consistency into two different high-level ω-consistencies which are called ω-k-wise-consistency and ω-k-consistency. First, we given some notations to simplify the description.

Let (X, D, V, S) be a CSP, W an ω-cover, and $\{V_{p_1}, V_{p_2}, \dots, V_{p_k}\} \subseteq W$ a subset of constraint schemes. We denote the union set of variable arc-check-set involved in the subset as $vks_a(V_{p_1}, V_{p_2}, \dots, V_{p_k}) = \bigcup_{1 \le i,j \le k} vks_a(V_{p_i}, V_{p_j})$. Similarly, $vks(V_{p_1}, V_{p_2}, \dots, V_{p_k}) = \bigcup_{1 \le i,j \le k} vks(V_{p_i}, V_{p_j})$.

Definition 13. *A CSP is ω-k-wise-consistent with respect to W if for any $V_{p_1}, V_{p_2}, \dots, V_{p_{k-1}}, V_{p_k} \in W$, $\Pi_{V_{p_k}}((\Join_{i=1}^{k} S_{p_i}) \Join S_h) = S_{p_k}$ for all $V_h \in vks_a(V_{p_1}, \dots, V_{p_k})$.*

A CSP is ω-k-wise-consistent if for any $V_{p_1}, V_{p_2}, \dots, V_{p_{k-1}}, V_{p_k} \in V$, $\Pi_{V_{p_k}}((\Join_{i=1}^{k} S_{p_i}) \Join S_h) = S_{p_k}$ for all $V_h \in vks(V_{p_1}, V_{p_2}, \dots, V_{p_k})$.

Definition 14. *A CSP is ω-k-consistent with respect to W if for any $V_{p_1}, V_{p_2}, \dots, V_{p_{k-1}}, V_{p_k} \in W$, $\Pi_A((\Join_{i=1}^{k-1} S_{p_i}) \Join S_l) \subseteq \Pi_A(S_{p_k} \Join S_h)$, where $A = (\bigcup_{i=1}^{k-1} V_{p_i}) \cap (V_{p_k} \cup V_h)$, for all $V_l \in vks_a(V_{p_1}, V_{p_2}, \dots, V_{p_{k-1}})$ and for all $V_h \in vks_a(V_{p_i}, V_{p_k})$ such that $i \ne k$. A CSP is strongly ω-k-consistent with respect to W if it is ω-l-consistent with respect to W for all $1 \le l \le k$.*

A CSP is ω-k-consistent if for any $V_{p_1}, V_{p_2}, \dots, V_{p_{k-1}}, V_{p_k} \in V$, $\Pi_A((\Join_{i=1}^{k-1} S_{p_i}) \Join S_l) \subseteq \Pi_A(S_{p_k} \Join S_h)$, where $A = (\bigcup_{i=1}^{k-1} V_{p_i}) \cap (V_{p_k} \cup V_h)$ for all $V_l \in vks(V_{p_1}, V_{p_2}, \dots, V_{p_{k-1}})$ and for all $V_h \in vks(V_{p_i}, V_{p_k})$ such that $i \ne k$. A CSP is strongly ω-k-consistent if it is ω-l-consistent for all $1 \le l \le k$.

A CSP (X, D, V, S) is pairwise consistent if and only if it is ω-consistent with respect to a special ω-cover V. So the pairwise consistency is a special case of ω-consistency. Similarly, a CSP (X, D, V, S) is k-wise-consistent if and only if it is ω-k-wise-consistent with respect to V, and a CSP is hyper-k-consistent if and only if it is ω-k-consistent with respect to V. Notice that ω-2-wise-consistency equals to ω-2-consistency since they both equal to ω-consistency. In [18] we show that ω-k-wise-consistency does not equal to ω-k-consistency when $k > 2$, and we have algorithms for achieving ω-k-wise-consistency and ω-k-consistency.

5 Characterizing Tractable CSPs

The main result of this section is that if a CSP has a tree-structured ω-graph and it is ω-consistency, then it has backtrack-free solutions. To prove it, we need a technical lemma.

Lemma 3. *Let (W, S^w, F, R) be a binary CSP converted from a general CSP (X, D, V, S) and an ω-graph $\omega(H) = (W, F)$ as described above. The general CSP is ω-consistency with respect to $\omega(H)$ iff the binary CSP is arc-consistency.*

Proof. If (X, D, V, S) is ω-consistent with respect to $\omega(H) = (W, F)$, then any pair V_i and V_j such that $(V_i, V_j) \in F$ is ω-consistent with respect to W; that is, for any $t_i \in S_i(t_j \in S_j)$ there is $t_j \in S_j(t_i \in S_i)$ such that $t_i[V_i \cap V_j] = t_j[V_i \cap V_j]$ and $(t_i \bowtie t_j)[V_h] \in S_h$ for all $C_h \in cks_a(V_i \cup V_j)$; thus, $(t_i, t_j) \in R_{ij}$. Therefore, any pair V_i and V_j in the binary CSP is arc-consistent; so the binary CSP is arc-consistent.

If (W, S^w, F, R) is arc-consistent, then any pair V_i and V_j in W is arc-consistent; that is, for any $(V_i, V_j) \in F$ and for any $t_i \in S_i(t_j \in S_j)$, there is $t_j \in S_j(t_i \in S_i)$ such that $(t_i, t_j) \in R_{ij}$; thus, $t_i[V_i \cap V_j] = t_j[V_i \cap V_j]$ and $(t_i \bowtie t_j)[V_k] \in S_k$ for all $C_h \in cks_a(V_i \cup V_j)$. So the general CSP is ω-consistent with respect to $\omega(H)$. $\square$

Theorem 8. *If a CSP has a tree-structured ω-graph, then enforcing ω-consistency with respect to that ω-graph ensures that it has backtrack-free solutions.*

Proof. We convert the given CSP into an equivalent binary CSP as described previously. The ω-graph of original CSP is the constraint graph of the converted binary CSP. If the original CSP has a tree-structured ω-graph, then the constraint graph of the converted binary CSP is a tree. Based on Lemma 3, the original CSP is ω-consistent with respect to the ω-graph iff the converted binary CSP is arc-consistent. And based on Theorem 2, enforcing arc consistency ensures the tractability of the converted binary CSP. So enforcing ω-consistency with respect to the ω-graph ensures that the original CSP has backtrack-free solutions. $\square$

Based on Theorem 6 and Corollary 1, we can see that the class of tractable CSPs identified with Theorem 8 contains that identified with Theorem 2 or 3. In other words, for those CSPs in which enforcing arc consistency (or pairwise consistency) ensures tractability, enforcing ω-consistency also ensures that these CSPs has backtrack-free solutions; and there is a class of CSPs in which enforcing arc consistency (or pairwise consistency) is not enough to ensure tractability, enforcing ω-consistency still guarantees that those CSPs can be solved by search without backtracking. As an example, suppose that we have a CSP which is associated with the hypergraph in Figure 1 (A). Since the constraint hypergraph has only cyclic join graphs such as those in (C) or (D), the CSP will not be identified as tractable by using Theorem 3 or Theorem 1. It will be identified as a tractable CSP by using our theorem because it has a tree-structured ω-graph (F).

For the sake of computational effort, if a CSP has a tree-structured ω-graph, enforcing directional ω-consistency is enough to ensure its tractability.

Theorem 9. *If a CSP has a tree-structured ω-graph, then enforcing directional ω-consistency respect to that ω-graph ensures that it has backtrack-free solutions.*

In the following, we give general forms of Theorem 8, which include Theorem 10 and 11 as special cases:

Theorem 10. *If a CSP is ω-k-wise-consistent with respect to an ω-graph and if this ω-graph is k-cyclic, then the CSP is globally consistent.*

Proof. If the ω-graph is k-cyclic, then the number of nodes in every block is at most k. Enforcing ω-k-wise-consistent with respect to the ω-graph ensures: (i) for each block, every instantiation of variables in any variable subset within this block has consistent extension to all the variables involved in this block; and (ii). every instantiation of variables in any block can be extended to a whole solution. Therefore, every consistent instantiation of variables in any variable set can be extended into a solution; that is, the CSP is globally consistent. $\square$

Theorem 11. *If a CSP is strongly ω-k-consistent with respect to an ω-graph and if the legal width of this ω-graph is less than k, then the CSP has backtrack-free solutions.*

Proof. If the legal width of the ω-graph is less than k, then there is a legal node ordering whose width is less than k. We can choose this node ordering as an ordering of instantiating variables in each variable set. At any stage of instantiation, the current variable set are connected directly with at most $(k-1)$ preceding variable sets, and since it is ω-k-consistent, the instantiation of instantiated variables has a consistent extension to variables in current variable set. $\square$

Further, with the notion of high order ω-covers, we derive another sufficient condition of backtrack-free search. Let W^k be a kth order ω-cover.

Lemma 4. *If a CSP is strongly ω-k-consistent where $k \geq 3$, then any constraint (V_h, S_h) such that $V_h \in V - W^k$ is redundant.*

Proof. Let (V_h, S_h) be a constraint such that $V_h \in V - W^k$. From the definition of kth order ω-cover, we have a set of $(k-1)$ variable sets $V_{p_1}, V_{p_2}, \ldots, V_{p_{k-1}}$ such that $V_h \subset \cup_{i=1}^{k-1} V_{p_i}$. Since the CSP is strongly ω-k-consistent, it is also strongly ω-k-consistent with respect to V, so we have $\Pi_{V_h}(\bowtie_{i=1}^{k-1} S_{p_i}) \subseteq S_h$. This proves that (V_h, S_h) is redundant. $\square$

Lemma 5. *Let (X, D, V, S) be a CSP, let $V^c \subseteq V$ be a cover of X such that any constraint (V_h, S_h) is redundant if $V_h \in V - V^c$, and let S^c be a subset of S corresponding to V^c. If (X, D, V, S) is strongly ω-k-consistent then the CSP (X, D, V^c, S^c) is also strongly ω-k-consistent.*

Proof. Suppose the opposite, that is, (X, D, V^c, S^c) is not strongly ω-k-consistent, then there is an ω-cover W such that (X, D, V^c, S^c) is not strongly ω-k-consistent with respect to W; that is, there is a set of k variable sets $V_{p_1}, V_{p_2}, \ldots, V_{p_{k-1}}, V_{p_k} \in W$, such that the following property does not hold in (X, D, V^c, S^c): $\Pi_A((\bowtie_{i=1}^{k-1} S_{p_i}) \bowtie S_l) = \Pi_A(S_{p_k} \bowtie S_h)$, where $A = (\cup_{i=1}^{k-1} V_{p_i}) \cap (V_{p_k} \cup V_h)$, for all $V_l \in vks_a(V_{p_1}, V_{p_2}, \ldots, V_{p_{k-1}})$ and for all $V_h \in vks_a(V_{p_i}, V_{p_k})$ such that $i \neq k$. Let $W^o = W \cup (V - V^c)$, then W^o is an ω-cover for (X, D, V, S). For the same set of k variable sets which are also in W^o, the same property does not hold in (X, D, V, S). That is, (X, D, V, S) is not strongly ω-k-consistent with respect to W^o, then it is not strongly ω-k-consistent. This is a contradiction. $\square$

Theorem 12. *If a CSP is strongly ω-k-consistent and if the width of partial hypergraph (X, W^k) is less than k, then the CSP has backtrack-free solutions.*

Proof. Based on Lemma 4, we have that all the constraints (V_h, S_h) such that $V_h \in V - W^k$ is redundant. Base on Lemma 5, we have that the CSP (X, D, W^k, S^w) is also strongly ω-k-consistent. Based on Theorem 5, (X, D, W^k, S^w) has backtrack-free solutions. Since both CSPs are equivalent, (X, D, V, S) has backtrack-free solutions. $\square$

¿From the proof of Lemma 4, we noticed that only strong ω-k-consistency with respect to V is needed as a part of the condition, and strong ω-k-consistency with respect to V is the same as strong hyper-k-consistency. Since the width of a partial hypergraph is at most the width of the hypergraph, we have the following corollary identifying a sufficient condition that is much weaker than the condition in Theorem 5.

Corollary 2. *If a CSP is strongly hyper-k-consistent and if the width of partial hypergraph (X, W^k) is less than k, then the CSP has backtrack-free solutions.*

6 Conclusion

We introduced the ω-graph which captures the constraint graph more precisely than other representative graphs. We defined ω-consistency for general CSPs which generalizes some notions of consistency. We identified relationships between the property of ω-graphs and the level of ω-consistency that are sufficient to ensure tractability of a CSP, and we proved that the class of tractable CSPs identified here contains the class of tractable CSPs identified with some related conditions reported previously. The ω-graph is also a useful tool for developing efficient algorithms for solving general CSPs. Achieving ω-consistency also simplifies a general CSP for subsequent programs to solve it. The detailed discussion of these issues can be found in [18–20].

References

1. C. Beeri, R. Fagin, D. Maier, and M. Yannakakis. On the desirability of acyclic database schemes. *J. ACM*, 30(3):497–513, 1983.
2. C. Berge. *Graphs and Hypergraphs*. North-Holland, New York, 1973.
3. C. Bessiere and M. Cordier. Arc-consistency and arc-consistency again. In *Proceedings of AAAI-93*, pages 108–113, 1993.
4. M. Cooper. An optimal k-consistency algorithm. *Artificial Intelligence*, 41:89–95, 1989.
5. R. Dechter and J. Pearl. Network-based heuristics for constraint-satisfaction problems. *Artificial Intelligence*, 34:1–38, 1988.
6. R. Dechter and J. Pearl. Tree clustering for constraint networks. *Artificial Intelligence*, 38:353–366, 1989.

7. R. Dechter and P. van Beek. Local and global relational consistency. In *Proceedings of the 1st International Conference on Principles and Practices of Constraint Programming*, pages 240–257, Cassis, France, September 1995.

8. E. Freuder. Synthesizing constraint expressions. *Communications of the ACM*, 21(11):958–966, 1978.

9. E. Freuder. A sufficient condition for backtrack-free search. *J. of the ACM*, 29(1):25–32, 1982.

10. M. Gyssens. On the complexity of join dependencies. *ACM Transactions on Database Systems*, 11(1):81–108, 1986.

11. M. Gyssens, P. G. Jeavons, and D. A. Cohen. Decomposing constraint satisfaction problems using database techniques. *Artificial Intelligence*, 66:57–89, 1994.

12. C. Han and C. Lee. Comments on Mohr and Henderson's path consistency algorithm. *Artificial Intelligence*, 36:125–130, 1988.

13. P. Jeavons, D. Cohen, and M. Gyssens. A test for tractability. In *Proceedings of the 2nd International Conference on Principles and Practice of Constraint Programming (CP96)*, pages 267–281, Cambridge, MA, 1996.

14. P. Jegou. On the consistency of general constraint satisfaction problems. In *Proceedings of AAAI-93*, pages 114–119, 1993.

15. A. Mackworth. Consistency in networks of relations. *Artificial Intelligence*, 8(1):99–118, 1977.

16. R. Mohr and T. Henderson. Arc and path consistency revisited. *Artificial Intelligence*, 28:225–233, 1986.

17. U. Montanari. Networks of constraints: Fundamental properties and applications to picture processing. *Information Science*, 2:95–123, 1974.

18. W. Pang. *A Constraint-Directed Approach for Analyzing and Solving General Constraint Satisfaction Problems*. PhD thesis, University of Regina, Canada, 1997.

19. W. Pang and S. D. Goodwin. A new synthesis algorithm for solving CSPs. In *Proceedings of the 2nd International Workshop on Constraint-Based Reasoning*, pages 1–10, Key West, FL, May 1996.

20. W. Pang and S. D. Goodwin. Constraint-directed backtracking. In *The 10th Australian Joint Conference on AI*, pages 47–56, Perth, Western Australia, December 1997.

21. E. Tsang. *Foundations of Constraint Satisfaction*. Academic Press, San Diego, CA, 1993.

22. P. van Beek. On the minimality and decomposability of constraint networks. In *Proceedings of AAAI-92*, pages 447–452, 1992.

23. P. Van Hentenryck, Y. Deville, and C. Teng. A generic arc-consistency algorithm and its specialization. *Artificial Intelligence*, 57:291–321, 1992.

An Attribute Redundancy Measure for Clustering

Teresa Gonçalves and Fernando Moura-Pires

Departamento de Informática, Faculdade de Ciências e Tecnologia,
Universidade Nova de Lisboa, Quinta de Torre
2825 Monte da Caparica, Portugal
{tcg,fmp}@di.fct.unl.pt

Abstract. Several information theory based measures have been used in machine learning. Using the definition of the Kullback-Leibler entropy, this paper presents a new measure for clustering objects - the attribute redundancy measure. First, an introduction to clustering is made, with its interpretation from the machine learning point of view and a classification of clustering techniques pointed out. Then, a description of the use of information theory based measures in machine learning, both in supervised and in unsupervised learning is made, including the application of the mutual information. Next, the new measure is presented, highlighting its ability to capture relations between attributes and outlining its closeness to other concepts of information theory. Finally, and a genetic algorithm as the search procedure to find the best clustering, a comparison between the attribute redundancy measure and the mutual information is made.

1 Introduction

The first clustering techniques appeared in the Botanical and Zoological areas as an auxiliary instrument to construct taxonomies [17]. Soon they extended to other scientific areas such as medicine, economy and linguistics [9] and began to be generically called as Cluster Analysis.

More recently, Michalski [13] introduced the concept of Conceptual Clustering as an extension to Cluster Analysis. These methods should propose not only a cluster (object's aggregation) representation through object enumeration but also, a characterization of each cluster [6].

In a conventional view, a clustering system consists in a process that

Given: a set of examples, E

Tries to find: a clustering of elements of E, $\{c_1, \ldots, c_K\}$, where the similarity between instances of the same cluster is maximum and between instances of different clusters is minimum. A set of clusters of E is named *clustering*.

From the machine learning point of view, clustering is a form of unsupervised learning or learning by observation in contrast to supervised or learning by examples, where examples are already classified.

Clustering techniques differ in the clustering structure, the method used to search the space of solutions and function used to measure similarities between examples.

The clustering organization varies from a hierarchy to a list of clusters. Moreover, there are algorithms where each instance resides only in one cluster and others where an example can belong to several clusters. In this last kind of technique, known as a clumping, cluster membership can be presented through probabilities or membership grades.

In some algorithms, the number of clusters formed is settled automatically from the data and in others that number is given a priori. In this last case, the number of different partitions visited by an algorithm that performs a complete search in the space of partitions is approximately K^N (being K the number of clusters and N the number of examples in the data set).

Since this number becomes huge even for small data sets, it is necessary to use other approaches to obtain the "best" clustering. Most of them rely on local search algorithms but, nowadays there are heuristic search techniques like simulated annealing, tabu search and genetic algorithms that can be applied to this field (see, for instance, [16]).

This paper presents an evaluation function for clustering using the Kullback-Leibler entropy and uses a genetic algorithm as the search method chosen to explore the space of solutions and devise the "best" clustering of objects.

The presented function is compared to other one that has already been used in several machine learning algorithms - the Mutual Information sum for all attributes. Both functions are based on Information Theory.

The comparison between functions is made both in terms of accuracy rate (examples correctly placed, given the original partition) and specialization performance (examples correctly placed by clusters' aggregation, given two partitions of different sizes, obtained by varying the number of formed clusters).

2 Information Theory and Machine Learning

Several functions, used in Machine Learning to evaluate solutions, are based on Information Theory measures. The concepts of Entropy, Mutual Information and Kullback-Leibler entropy (see, for instance, [4]) have been used both in supervised and unsupervised learning; specifically, they have been applied in decision tree and rules induction and in conceptual clustering, respectively.

The relevant information theory concepts for this work are presented in the appendix.

CART [10], a decision tree algorithm, uses the maximization of the Gini index (equation A8) as the criterion to obtain the "best" tree.

CN2 [1][2], an algorithm that induces rules to classify unseen instances, uses the entropy to evaluate complexes' quality and the Kullback-Leibler entropy (equation A7) as the stop criterion to test partition's significance. The entropy is minimized, since the lower the entropy, the better the complex, and the Kullback-

Leibler entropy is measured between the probabilities distribution before and after the partition of the training set.

The evaluation function used in the decision tree algorithms ID3 [14] and C4.5 [15], is the mutual information between the classes and the attribute. In each tree node, the chosen attribute is the one that maximizes the mutual information. This value is divided by the attribute's entropy to cut the bias towards attributes with many possible values.

Another criterion for partitioning data sets, also based on Information Theory, was proposed by Mántaras [11] and is based on the concept of distance normalization between two partitions. This criterion is similar to the one proposed by Quinlan when the mutual information normalization is done by the joint entropy between the class and the attribute.

Gluck and Corter [8][3], working in psychology, proposed two measures of category usefulness to predict instances' features. These measures, generically designated by *category utility* (CU), are based on the Information Theory, CU_{IT}, and on the Guessing-Game Measure, CU_{GG}, being, respectively, the Mutual Information and the Gini Index measures:

$$CU_{IT}(C, A) = I(C; A) = H(A) - H(A|C) \tag{1}$$
$$= \sum_c p(c) \cdot \sum_a p(a|c) \cdot \log\ p(a|c) - \sum_a p(a) \cdot \log\ p(a)\ ,$$

$$CU_{GG}(C, A) = \sum_c p(c) \cdot \sum_a p(a|c)^2 - \sum_a p(a)^2\ . \tag{2}$$

As Gluck and Corter say, these two measures are closely related and produce the same results since $\log(p)$ approximates to p for small numbers.

Fisher [7] used the Gini index measure to implement COBWEB, a hierarchical incremental conceptual clustering algorithm that uses a local search procedure to find the "best" tree of concepts. Categories' quality is measured using the Gini index for all features and, to cut the bias towards clusterings with many classes, the number of classes, K, divides this value, resulting in the following measure

$$\frac{1}{K} \cdot \sum_{i=1}^{J} CU_{GG}(C, A_i) \approx \frac{1}{K} \cdot \sum_{i=1}^{J} CU_{IT}(C, A_i) = \frac{1}{K} \cdot \sum_{i=1}^{J} I(C; A_i)\ . \tag{3}$$

3 The Evaluation Function

There are clustering techniques that base themselves on the reduction of the redundancy between variables. For example, and for continuous domains, there is a well-known tool in statistics, the so-called Principal Component Analysis.

For discrete domains, exists, also, an Information Theory function that measures the redundancy between variables. That function, described in [5], is the generalized multidimensional mutual information. It is defined as

$$I(X_1; \ldots; X_K) = D\left(p(X_1, \ldots, X_k) \parallel \prod_{i=1}^{K} p(X_i)\right), \qquad (4)$$

where $D(.\|.)$ is the Kullback-Leibler entropy (equation A7). Notice that, larger values correspond to greater redundancy between variables and when this function equals zero, the variables are statistically independent (no redundancy between them).

Our purpose, as a clustering function, is then to find the examples' distribution in clusters (the clustering) that minimizes the redundancy between attributes. For that, we will use the conditional multidimensional mutual information, naming it the *attribute redundancy quantity*, ARQ. This function can be formalized as

$$ARQ(A_1, \ldots, A_J, C) = D\left(p(A_1, \ldots, A_J|C) \parallel \prod_{i=1}^{J} p(A_i|C)\right). \qquad (5)$$

Using the Kullback-Leibler entropy definition, we can rewrite ARQ as

$$ARQ(A_1, \ldots, A_J, C) = \sum_{c} \sum_{a_1} \cdots \sum_{a_J} p(a_1, \ldots a_J, c) \ \log \frac{p(a_1, \ldots a_J|c)}{\prod_{i=1}^{J} p(a_i|c)}, \qquad (6)$$

and, using the conditional entropy definition (equation A3), it can be described in terms of entropies by the following equation

$$ARQ(A_1, \ldots, A_J, C) = \sum_{i=1}^{J} H(A_i|C) - H(A_1, \ldots A_J|C). \qquad (7)$$

Making use of the chain rule for the joint entropy, given by equations A2 and A3, on equation 7, we obtain

$$ARQ(\ldots) = \sum_{i=1}^{J} H(A_i|C) - \left(H(A_1|C) + \sum_{i=2}^{J} H(A_i|A_{i-1}, \ldots, A_1, C)\right) \qquad (8)$$

$$= \sum_{i=2}^{J} H(A_i|C) - H(A_i|A_{i-1}, \ldots, A_1, C),$$

and using the mutual information definition (equation A5), we achieve

$$ARQ(A_1, \ldots, A_J, C) = \sum_{i=2}^{J} I(A_i; A_{i-1}, \ldots A_1|C). \qquad (9)$$

Notice that there is no ordering between different A_i attributes and that the sum starts with $i = 2$. This expression can be interpreted as mutual information sums, adding one attribute at a time.

As expected, the ARQ function equals zero if, given the class, all attributes are independent among each other.

4 The Search Procedure

Instead of using a local search procedure, we decided to make use of the genetic algorithm paradigm to search for the "best" clustering.

To encode the partitions in a way that allows genetic operators manipulation, we matched each example's class to a gene in the chromosome. For partitioning a data set with N examples into K classes, chromosomes have length N, with each gene representing an example; each gene has a value between one and K, corresponding to the class assigned to the example. Setting each chromosome's gene to a random integer between one and K, randomly generates the initial population.

A very simple mutation operator was implemented: genes are randomly selected and their values are modified. This means that the examples they represent change to another class.

As said before, a comparison between two different functions will be made: the mutual information sum and the ARQ function. The search for the "best" clustering, implies the maximization of the first and the minimization of the second.

Both functions were simplified assuming that examples were equiprobable. The simplification was made taking into account that the expected probability values were given by frequencies, $i.e.$

$$p(c_k) = \frac{n(c_k)}{n} \tag{10}$$

$$p(a_{ij}, c_k) = \frac{n(a_{ij}, c_k)}{n}$$

where, n is the number of examples in the data set, $n(c_k)$ is the number of examples that belong to class k and $n(a_{ij}, c_k)$ is the number of examples that have value j in attribute i and belong to class k.

The simplified expression for the mutual information sum is

$$\sum_i I(C; A_i) = I \cdot \log n - \sum_i \sum_j \frac{n(a_{ij})}{n} \cdot \log n(a_{ij}) - \tag{11}$$

$$-I \cdot \sum_k \frac{n(c_k)}{n} \cdot \log n(c_k) + \sum_i \sum_j \sum_k \frac{n(a_{ij}, c_k)}{n} \cdot \log n(a_{ij}, c_k)$$

and, for the ARQ function is

$$ARQ(A_1, \ldots, A_J, C) = (I - 1) \cdot \sum_k \frac{n(c_k)}{n} \cdot \log n(c_k) - \qquad (12)$$

$$- \sum_i \sum_j \sum_k \frac{n(a_{ij}, c_k)}{n} \cdot \log n(a_{ij}, c_k) ,$$

where I is the number of attributes, K is the number of classes and J_i is the number of attribute values for attribute i.

5 Experimental Results

Several data sets were chosen to compare the ARQ measure to the Mutual Information sum. As said before, two different studies were made: one to test functions' accuracy, other to verify their specialization behavior. For the first, an experiment was done, asking for a number of clusters equal to the number of original classes. For the other, several experiments were conducted by varying the number of classes to be created.

A comparison between the ARQ results and the ones obtained by COBWEB will not be made since COBWEB is an incremental algorithm. Instead, we will compare the evalaution function used by COBWEB (the Mutual Information sum) to the one proposed here.

The options, choices and results obtained are presented in the next subsections.

5.1 Data Sets

The data sets were selected from the ML Repository [12]. They differ in the number of instances, attributes and number of classes but, they all have nominal attributes only, since the measures, as defined, only apply to this kind of values.

The data sets used were the Breast cancer, the Lymphography Domain, and the Zoo. The Breast cancer and the Lymphography are databases dated by 1988, obtained from the Institute of Oncology, University Medical Centre, Ljubljana, Yugoslav and donated by Matjaz Zwitter and Milan Soklic. The Zoo database was conceived by Richard Forsyth in 1990.

Table 1 summarizes the characteristics of the original databases.

Table 1. Original database characteristics

data sets	classes	attributes	values/att	instances	instances/class
Breast	2	9+class	2..13	286	201, 85
Lympho	4	18+class	2..8	148	2, 81, 61, 4
Zoo	7	16+class	2..6	101	41, 20, 5, 13, 4, 8, 10

The class attribute was taken out from the data sets in order to verify the functions' ability to obtain the original partition. Repeated instances and instances with missing values were after taken out. The resulting data sets have the characteristics shown in Table 2.

Table 2. Used database characteristics

data sets	values/att	instances	instances/class
Breast	2..11	260	183, 77
Lympho	2..8	148	2, 81, 61, 4
Zoo	2..6	59	8, 19, 12, 5, 5, 4, 6

5.2 Genetic algorithm

Several experiments were conducted by varying the number of clusters to be created from 2 to 5 (for the Zoo database the range was from 2 to 8 classes).

After testing several sets of genetic algorithms' parameters, the following ones were selected for all experiments:

- number of generations: 500
- normalisation: reverse-mean-scale, bias=2
- selection: roulette
- crossover: two-point, rate=0.8
- mutation: change, rate=3 (per chromosome)
- replacement: tournament, rate=0.8 (unconditional, without elitism)

The population size was modified according to the number of generated classes and the size of the data sets. For two clusters, a population of 5000, 2500 and 1250 was used for the Breast, Lympho and the Zoo data sets, respectively. In order to maintain diversity of chromosomes, an increment of 1000, 500 and 250 chromosomes was made for each data set, when increasing by one the number of generated clusters.

5.3 Outcome Analysis

Since genetic algorithms are a heuristic method, 30 different runs were made for each experiment and the results were averaged. As said before, two different studies were made to assess functions ability: the accuracy rate and the specialization performance. They are described in the next points jointly with the results obtained.

In the tables, *MI* represents the simplified mutual information sum (equation 11) and *ARQ* represents the simplified *ARQ* function (equation 12). The figures represent the percentage of correct placed examples.

Accuracy rate. To examine the skill exhibited by each function, the best partition returned by the algorithm (the best chromosome achieved through all generations) was compared to the one given by the original classification. The function's accuracy rate is the percentage of correct placed examples. This number is obtained by finding the correspondence between the original classes and retrieved clusters that minimizes the number of misplaced examples.

Table 3 shows, for each function, the best, worst, mean and standard deviation for the 30 runs.

Table 3. Accuracy Rate

data set	classes	function	best	worst	mean	std. dev.
Breast	2	MI	71.2	70.8	70.8	0.07
		ARQ	73.1	71.5	72.5	0.23
Lympho	4	MI	61.5	48.6	54.6	3.01
		ARQ	71.6	60.8	64.7	2.13
Zoo	7	MI	93.2	86.4	89.9	1.24
		ARQ	93.2	84.7	90.0	1.60

Looking at the results, we can see that the ARQ function performs better than the mutual information. For the Lympho database, the difference is of about 10%.

Table 4 shows the results obtained by some supervised learning algorithms[1] (CN2, ASSISTANT-86 and AQ15). The figures from Table 3 are not comparable to the ones of Table 4, since the first one are obtained by an unsupervised algorithm where the class is unknown. Table 4 is presented here, just to see the differences between reached accuracy.

Table 4. Results obtained by other algorithms

data set	CN2	ASSISTANT-86	AQ15
Breast	65-72	78	66-72
Lympho	82	76	80-82

Specialization performance. Another test was made in order to access what happened to the partition when a classification specialization was made (achieved by increasing the number of retrieved clusters). For that, the best partition of K clusters was compared to the best partition of $L \neq K$ clusters retrieving the percentage of correct placed examples.

When comparing a partition of K clusters to a partition of $L > K$ clusters, one can consider that a classification specialization was made. Therefore, to

---

[1] Information obtained in [12].

compare the partitions, clusters of the second clustering were grouped in a way to obtain the same number of clusters as first one (K). The grouping chosen is the one that minimizes the number of misplaced examples and the percentage of correct placed examples is returned.

Table 5 shows, for each function and for the Breast and Lympho data sets, the mean percentage of correct placed examples, when comparing each partition of K clusters to each partition of $L > K$ clusters. The upper figures stand for the mutual information function, and the bottom ones to ARQ. For example, we obtained, for the Breast data set, an average precision of 96.9% for the ARQ function and 88.4% for the mutual information, with a partition's specialization from 2 to 3 clusters.

For all experiments, the standard deviation had a magnitude order of 0.001.

We do not present the results for the Zoo data set because they were very similar for both functions, with the majority having values above 96%.

Table 5. Data sets' specialization

Breast	2	3	4	5	
2	–	88.4	91.6	91.4	
3	96.9	–	77.1	77.6	MI
4	96.0	95.6	–	77.0	
5	95.0	95.0	94.0	–	
		ARQ			

Lympho	2	3	4	5	
2	–	93.7	94.6	91.1	
3	94.2	–	86.8	83.4	MI
4	94.2	90.3	–	81.0	
5	93.3	90.5	86.0	–	
		ARQ			

Observing Table 5 we can conclude that both functions specialize well (around 90% of the examples are well placed and, many times, even more), but the ARQ function outperforms the mutual information, especially for the Breast data set.

6 Conclusions and Future Work

As expected, the results obtained by the ARQ function are better than the ones obtained by the mutual information, suggesting that ARQ is better in catching the existing relations between the data. This arises from the fact that ARQ searches for the best examples' aggregation that reduces attributes redundancy.

We think that, if not assuming the equiprobability of examples, the differences would be more significant, since the ARQ function takes into account the relations between all attributes and the mutual information only handles one attribute at a time.

Concerning the specialization, we, also, obtained better results for the ARQ function. We consider partition's specialization an important point, since with it, is possible to create hierarchical clustering structures.

As future work we intend to further study ARQ function's potential, by applying it to other data sets and comparing the results with other clustering algorithms, like CLUSTER/2 and COBWEB.

On the other hand, and with the same goal, we wish to apply this function to supervised learning, in particular to decision tree induction, for choosing the best partition of data in each tree node. For that, we are planning to substitute C4.5's evaluation function (the Mutual Information) by this one and compare the results.

We further intend to compare both functions using data sets where examples are not equiprobable in order to confirm our expectations.

We also want to try a cross-validation approach to verify the results by using a training set to create the partition (using or not the class as a regular attribute) and then apply it to a test set.

Acknowledgements

This research was carried out in the Computer Science Department of Faculdade de Ciências e Tecnologia - Universidade Nova de Lisboa and was supported by JNICT, the Portuguese Council for Science and Technology.

The work was conducted using the SUGAL (SUnderland Genetic ALgorithm) package, developed by Dr. Andrew Hunter at the University of Sunderland, England.

The authors would also like to thank M. Zwitter and M Soklic for providing the Lymphography and the Breast cancer databases.

References

1. P. Clark. Functional specification of CN and AQ. Technical Report IT/P21154/PC/1.2, The Turing Institute, 1989.
2. P. Clark and T. Niblett. The CN2 induction algorithm. *Machine Learning Journal*, 3:261–283, 1989.
3. James E. Corter and Mark A. Gluck. Explaining basic categories: Features predictability and information. *Psychology Bulletin*, 111(2):291–303, 1992.
4. Thomas M. Cover and Joy A. Thomas. *Elements of Information Theory*. Wiley Series in Telecomunication. John Wiley and Sons, Inc, New York, 1991.
5. Gustavo Deco and Dragan Obradovic. *An Information-Theoretic Approach to Neural Computing*. Springer-Verlag, New York, 1996.
6. Douglas Fisher and Pat Langley. *Conceptual Clustering and its Relation to Numerical Taxonomy*, pages 77–116. Addison-Wesley Publishing Company, 1986.
7. Douglas H. Fisher. *Knowledge Acquisition Via Incremental Conceptual Clustering*. PhD thesis, 1987.
8. Mark A. Gluck and James E. Corter. Information, uncertainty, and the utility of categories. In *The Seventh Annual Conference of Cognitive Science Society*, pages 283–288, Hillsdade, NJ, 1985.
9. J. A. Hartigan. *Clustering Algorithms*. John Wiley and Sons, 1975.
10. Richard A. Olshen Leo Breiman, Jerome H. Friedman and Charles J. Stone. *Classification and Regression Trees*. Wadsworth and Brooks/Cole Advanced Books and Software, Pacific Grove, 1984.
11. Ramon L. Mántaras. A distance-based attribute selection measure for decision tree induction. *Machine Learning Journal*, 6:81–92, 1991.

12. C. J. Merz and P. M. Murphy. Uci repository of machine learning databases, 1996.
13. R. S. Michalski. Knowledge acquisition through conceptual clustering: A theoretical framework and an algorithm for partitioning data into conjunctive concepts. *International Journal of Policy and Information Systems*, 4(3):219–244, 1980.
14. J. R. Quinlan. Induction of decision trees. *Machine Learning*, 1:81–106, 1986.
15. J. R. Quinlan. *C4.5: Programs for Machine Learning*. Morgan Kaufmann Publishers, San Mateo, California, 1993.
16. Colin R. Reeves. *Modern Heuristic Techniques for Combinatorial Problems*. MacGraw-Hill, London, UK, 1995.
17. P. H. Sneath and R. R. Sokal. *Numerical Taxonomy: The Principles and Practice of Numerical Classification*. W. H. Freeman and Company, San Francisco, 1973.

Appendix: Some Concepts of Information Theory

The main information theory concepts can be found, for instance, in [4]. Some of them are presented below.

1. *Joint entropy.* The joint entropy $H(A_1, \ldots, A_J)$ of J discrete random variables $A_1, \ldots, A_J$ with a joint distribution $p(a_1, \ldots, a_J)$ is defined as

$$H(A_1, \ldots, A_J) = \sum_{a_1} \cdots \sum_{a_J} p(a_1, \ldots, a_J) \cdot \log p(a_1, \ldots, a_J) . \tag{A1}$$

The chain rule for entropy allows the following development for the joint entropy

$$H(A_1, \ldots, A_J) = \sum_{i=1}^{J} H(A_i | A_{i-1}, \ldots, A_1) . \tag{A2}$$

2. *Conditional entropy.* The conditional entropy, $H(A|C)$, of a random variable A, given C, is defined as

$$H(A|C) = \sum_{c} p(c) \cdot H(A|c) = - \sum_{c} \sum_{a} p(a, c) \cdot \log p(a|c) . \tag{A3}$$

3. *Mutual information.* The mutual information, $I(C; A)$, between two variables A and C is given by

$$\begin{aligned} I(C; A) &= H(C) - H(C|A) \\ &= H(A) - H(A|C) \\ &= H(C) + H(A) - H(C, A) \end{aligned} \tag{A4}$$

The conditional mutual information, $I(C; A|B)$, is defined by

$$I(C; A|B) = H(C|B) - H(C|A, B) \tag{A5}$$

The mutual information for several variables, $I(C; A_1, \ldots, A_J)$, is defined by

$$I(C; A_1, \ldots, A_J) = H(C) - H(C|A_1, \ldots, A_J) \tag{A6}$$

4. *Kullback-Leibler entropy.* The Kullback-Leibler entropy, also called relative entropy or cross-entropy, is defined between two probability distributions $p(x)$ and $q(x)$ over the same set of values and measures the distance between them. It is given by

$$D(p\|q) = \sum_x p(x) \cdot \log \frac{p(x)}{q(x)} \tag{A7}$$

This quantity is not a true distance, but a quasi-distance since $D(p\|q) \neq D(q\|p)$. However, $D(p\|q)$ is always positive and $D(p\|p)$ is always zero.

5. *GiniIndex.* The Gini index measures the predictability of an attribute A given a set of classes C and is defined by

$$GiniIndex(C, A) = \sum_c p(c) \sum_a p(a|c)^2 - \sum_a p(a)^2 \tag{A8}$$

It was proven that this measure is similar to the mutual information since $p \cdot \log(p)$ approximates to p^2 for small numbers [8][3][10].

On the Complexity of VLSI-Friendly Neural Networks for Classification Problems

Sorin Draghici

Vision and Neural Networks Laboratory
Department of Computer Science, Wayne State University,
431 State Hall, Detroit, 48202 MI, USA
Fax: (313) 577-6868, Email: sod@cs.wayne.edu

Abstract. This paper presents some complexity results for the specific case of a VLSI friendly neural network used in classification problems. A VLSI-friendly neural network is a neural network using exclusively integer weights in a narrow interval. The results presented here give updated worst-case lower bounds for the number of weights used by the network. It is shown that the number of weights can be lower bounded by an expression calculated using parameters depending exclusively on the problem (the minimum distance between patterns of opposite classes, the maximum distance between any patterns, the number of patterns and the number of dimensions). The theoretical approach is used to calculate the necessary weight range, a lower bound for the number of bits necessary to solve the problem in the worst case and the necessary number of weights for several problems. Then, a constructive algorithm using limited precision integer weights is used to construct and train neural networks for the same problems. The experimental values obtained are then compared with the theoretical values calculated. The comparison shows that the necessary weight precision can be estimated accurately using the given approach. However, the estimated numbers of weights are in general larger than the values obtained experimentally.

Introduction

One particular approach for creating adaptive systems able to learn from examples is the neural network paradigm. In the last decade, the efforts of the neural network research community have been concentrated on investigating the abilities and limits of the neural networks in general. This focus was both necessary and timely. Before trying to use a tool, we must understand its possibilities and limits. However, now we *know* that neural networks are able both to learn from examples and to adapt to changes in their inputs. We also know they are *not* a universal panacea but we do know a lot about how and when we *can* deploy this technology very successfully.

A necessary and essential step in continuing the diffusion of this paradigm in our day by day use is their hardware implementation. The ability of the neural systems to be implemented in hardware is crucial because the normal requirements for many applications include: i) a small volume, ii) a reduced weight and iii) a high resistance to shocks, vibrations and adverse environmental conditions and iv) a high execution speed. Furthermore, the hardware implementation is by far the most cost-effective solution for large scale use.

A VLSI friendly neural network is defined as a neural network which can be conveniently implemented in VLSI hardware. Although some of the considerations made in this paper hold for other types of implementations as well, our focus is on requirements specific to VLSI implementations.

Most neural network models have been studied using software simulations. In such set-up, features like the fan-in of the neurons or the precision used for the weights are simply irrelevant. At the same time, other features like floating point processing at the unit level are taken as granted. Further characteristics like the number of units or the number of weights used are sometime discussed (perhaps as part of a more general point of view dealing with complexity) but they still bear little impact as criteria for assessing different algorithms and/or architectures. However, all these issues have a crucial importance when the VLSI implementation is considered. Storing weights in double precision, performing floating point processing at neuron level and having network architectures with non-homogeneous fan-in units can raise dramatically the price of the VLSI chip implementing a given architecture.

On the other hand, a network using integer weights within a limited interval and a constant fan-in [2] are much better suited to hardware implementation in VLSI. For instance, if the weight values are restricted to integer values in the interval [-3, 3], a weight can be stored on 3 bits only. For a chip containing potentially hundreds or thousands of weights, the reduction from 32 or 64 to 3 bits per weight would translate in an important reduction of the size of the VLSI chip and thus of its price

These considerations have determined a recent surge of interest in neural networks using limited precision integer weights. Several recent results in this area which are also relevant to the present paper will be reviewed very briefly in the following section.

Previous results

Training algorithms using limited precision integer weights

One approach is to find algorithms able to train neural networks which use limited precision weights while still being able to solve difficult problems. There are various approaches to this problem. [11], [27], [3] and [22] re-scale the weights dynamically whilst adapting the gain of the activation function. [12], [26] use probabilistic rounding whereas [8], [15], [18], [19], [20], [21] and [22] restrict the weight values to powers of two. The latter approach is of particular interest because powers of two values and multiplications of such are particularly easy to handle in binary circuitry.

The question is: how far can this approach be used? Given a problem, what sort of precision should we use so that a solution will still exist? In general, it is acknowledged that integer weight neural networks with weight values limited at powers of two lack in capabilities in comparison to the real-valued networks [16]. At the same time, empirical experiments suggest that the weaker learning capabilities of such networks can be compensated by an increase in the number of layers. In this case, how many layers should we expect to need for a given problem? In general, what is a reasonable *complexity* of the network we should use?

Theoretical results

There are various general results establishing relationships between the complexity of a neural network and its capabilities. The initial justification for the possibilities of multilayer networks comes from Kolmogorov's superposition theorem and its refinements. These results assume different unknown activation functions for each function to be approximated. They also specify an exact upper limit for the number of intermediate elements (implemented by hidden units in the case of a neural network). However, in the neural network framework, the usual situation is that there is a single fixed activation function and the number of hidden units is not limited a priori.

Hornik in [13] and [14] demonstrates a result which is more appropriate in this framework: a standard multilayer feedforward network with a single hidden layer using arbitrary squashing functions is capable of approximating any Borel measurable function from one finite-dimensional space to another to any desired degree of accuracy, provided sufficiently many hidden units are available.

This result must be seen as an answer to the question regarding the existence of the solution. Provided that enough hidden units are available, in general, a solution weight state will exists. However, the theorem does not give a method to estimate the necessary number of hidden units given a function to be approximated nor does it give a training algorithm able to find the solution starting from arbitrary weights. Although reassuring, such result cannot be used directly when a practical application is contemplated.

Following the original idea suggested by Kolmogorov's theorem, Hecht-Nielsen [10] and Kurkova [17] have proved results related to the capabilities of the multilayer feedforward neural network. Sprecher in [23], [24] and [25] has given a method for constructing the activation functions of a two layer network able to approximate any given I/O mapping.

However, all these results apply to neural networks using arbitrary precision weights. For instance, the algorithm presented in [24] requires a precision of at least 50 bits for some numerical values. Such precisions are very expensive when the VLSI implementation is considered because using so many bits per weight and floating point arithmetic-logic units (ALU's) take up a lot of space on the chip.

Recent results have shown that the limited precision integer weights neural networks are still able to solve classification problems if the precision used for the weights is adapted to the difficulty of the problem as characterized by the minimum distance between two patterns from opposite classes. More precisely, it has been shown that one can establish a relationship between the minimum distance between two patterns from opposite classes and the range necessary for the weights. This relationship is stated in the following proposition (from [5]):

Proposition 1 *Using integer weights in the range [-p, p], one can correctly classify any set of patterns for which the minimum distance between two patterns of opposite classes is* $d_{min} \geq 1 / p$.

The proof is based on induction on p and on the number of dimensions n and will not be presented here. Also, one should note that this result is existential. In other words, for a given minimum distance d_{min}, there exists a neural network using weights in the given range (calculated according to **Proposition 1**) that solves the problem. However, this result does not say anything about the complexity or architecture of the solution network and nor does it say anything about *finding* such network i.e. about the training process itself.

The complexity issue is addressed by a second range of results presented in [5] and [6]. These results give bounds on the complexity of the network as characterized by the number of bits in the information entropy sense. **Proposition 2** gives a simple lower bound for the chosen conditions.

Proposition 2 *Let us consider a set of m patterns (in general positions) from two classes in the hypersphere of radius $D \le 1$ centered in origin of R^n. Let us consider $d_{min} = 1/p$ the minimum distance between two patterns belonging to different classes. Then, the number of bits necessary for the separation of the patterns (in general positions) using weights in the set {-p, -p+1, ...,0, 1, ..., p} is lower bounded by:*

$$N_H = \lceil m \cdot n \cdot \log(2 \cdot p \cdot D) \rceil \tag{1}$$

In this expression, m is the number of patterns, n is the number of dimensions, p is the half-range of the weights (i.e. the weights are restricted to integer values in the range $[-p, p]$), and D is the radius of the smallest sphere including all patterns. In this expression and throughout the rest of this paper, all logarithms are in base 2. Furthermore, we will drop the ceiling function keeping in mind that whenever discrete quantities are involved, the values should be rounded up to the nearest integer.

Theoretical considerations regarding the possibilities of limited precision neural networks

Proposition 1 and **Proposition 2** offer the theoretical base for designing the network in accordance with the necessities of a given problem. The weight range can be calculated easily after finding the minimum distance between patterns of opposite classes d_{min}. Subsequently, one can calculate lower bounds for the number of bits that the network will need in order to solve the problem. The radius D of the smallest sphere containing all patterns can be approximated by the maximum distance between any two patterns (as shown in [4]). This approximation will yield a lower bound larger than the actual value and therefore, it will not compromise the ability of the network to solve the problem.

Using the lower bound on the number of bits calculated as above and the number of bits used to store one weight (which is $\lceil \log(2p + 1) \rceil$ for integer weights in the range $[-p,p]$), one can calculate a lower bound on the necessary number of weights:

$$w \ge \frac{N_H}{\log(2 / d_{min} + 1)} \tag{2}$$

A network thus designed will offer the guarantees that i) there exists a weight state with weights in the given range that solves the problem and ii) the architecture is not undersized for the given problem.

Two important observations are needed here. Firstly, the number of bits which is calculated by the formula given in **Proposition 2**, refers to bits in the informational entropy sense and these bits do not correspond directly to the bits used to store the weights because the neural codification is less than optimal. One should consider an implementation factor k, which would characterize the efficiency of the implementation. In other words, k would be the number of storage bits corresponding to one bit in the informational entropy sense. In principle, this implementation efficiency would be the number of storage bits needed to implement a network able to make a binary decision in the context of the given problem. Thus,

$$k = \frac{N_S}{N_H} \tag{3}$$

where N_s is the number of storage bits and N_H is the number of bits in the information entropy sense. The number of weights of the network could then be chosen according to:

$$w \geq \left\lceil \frac{k \cdot N_H}{\log(2p+1)} \right\rceil \tag{4}$$

$$w \geq \left\lceil \frac{k \cdot N_H}{\log(2/d_{\min}+1)} \right\rceil \tag{5}$$

For input patterns in arbitrary positions, a neural network cannot implement a binary decision using less than one hyperplane. A neuron implementing a hyperplane in an n-dimensional space needs n+1 weights. If the weights are integers in the given range, a weight will need $\log(2p+1)$ storage bits. Therefore, the minimum number of storage bits necessary to implement a binary decision in the general case will be $k = (n+1)\log(2p+1)$. This value can be interpreted as the worst-case implementation efficiency. As the network scales up, this interpretation can become less accurate because most networks will need a second and perhaps a third hidden layer in order to combine the outputs of the units in the first hidden layer. These units will tend to decrease the overall efficiency.

Taking into consideration this worst-case implementation efficiency, the lower bound on the number of weights becomes:

$$w \geq \frac{(n+1) \cdot \log(2p+1) \cdot N_H}{\log(2p+1)} = (n+1) \cdot N_H \tag{6}$$

It has been recently shown that using neurons with small, constant fan-in is VLSI optimal in the AT^2 sense (see [2] and references therein). If we now consider this particular case in which all neurons have the same fan-in, we can extract the number of neurons as:

$$neurons \geq \frac{w}{fan\_in} \tag{7}$$

The second observation is that the above lower bound was calculated in the worst-case scenario which assumes that the network will need to isolate each pattern in their own classification region. In practice, this happens only very seldom. In most cases, a classification region will contain several patterns belonging to the same class. In consequence, the number of bits in the information entropy sense must be corrected by a factor nl which will take into consideration the average number of patterns of the same class grouped together in the same classification region.

$$N_{Hnl} = N_H / nl \tag{8}$$

This factor is highly dependent on the problem and, intuitively, it is inversely proportional with the degree of non-linearity of the problem. At one extreme, there is the class of linearly separable problems. If the weights are real valued i.e. the dividing hyperplanes can take any position, a linearly separable problem can be solved by grouping all patterns of the same class in just one classification region and the factor nl will be maximum for the given problem and equal to the number of patterns in the least numerous class (in a two class problem, we only need to separate one class from the other). At the other extreme, one can imagine an infinite n-dimensional hyper-grid in which adjacent patterns always belong to opposite classes. Such problem is representative for the worst-case situation considered in **Proposition 2** in which each pattern will be classified in its own classification region. In this worst-case scenario, nl will be at its minimum value of 1. In general one could consider an average value of nl which will represent the average number of patterns classified in the same region. One can imagine various ways of extracting approximate values of nl from the pattern set but this computation is outside the scope of the present paper.

A last observation is due on the number of patterns m considered in calculating the number of entropy bits in **Proposition 2**. In theory, one should consider the minimum number of pattern in the two classes. This is because in a two class problem as considered here, it is sufficient to separate just the class with fewer patterns. However, since one cannot know in advance which class is going to be used by the training algorithm (or because the training algorithm uses both), it is more appropriate to take the number of patterns equal to the average of the number of patterns in the two classes $m/2$.

A statistical view

One can trade-in the absolute guarantee regarding the existence of the solution in exchange for a better approximation for practical use. The worst-case considered calculated the necessary weight range based on the minimum distance between patterns of opposite classes. The approximation proposed here is based on the assumption that the data set is such that the distance between patterns of opposite classes follows a Gaussian distribution. If this assumption holds, most pairs of points will be separated by a distance situated in an interval centered in the average distance and with a width equal to 3σ (standard deviations). Therefore, most patterns from opposite classes will be separated by at least $\tilde{d} = \bar{d} - 1.5 \cdot \sigma$.

This approximation is made even more plausible by the observation that a pair of very close patterns of opposite classes will cause a training failure only if they are situated in particular positions which cannot be separated by the hyperplanes available. Two patterns can be even infinitely closed to each other if they are positioned on different sides of at least one available hyperplane. It is reasonable to assume that there are relatively few such particularly unfavorable positions. Therefore, the new limit can be taken as:

$$w \geq \left\lceil (n+1) \cdot m \cdot n \left[1 + \log d_{\max} - \log\left(\overline{d} - 1.5 \cdot \sigma\right) \right] \right\rceil \tag{9}$$

Keeping in mind these observations, let us see how such results could be used. If one could indeed customize the size of the network to the given problem, one could apply the training algorithm of one's choice being confident that i) the given network has the possibility of solving the problem (i.e. there exists a solution weight state for the given configuration) and ii) the chosen configuration is not wasteful and it can be translated into a VLSI chip with a cost close to the minimum possible (for the given problem).

The present paper aims at investigating how well the results given by these theoretical instruments fit with practical experiments. This can be done by comparing the theoretical bounds obtained using the formulae above with the number of weights effectively used by trained networks.

Experiments

Experimental setup and results

Experiments were run using both classical benchmark problems (the exclusive-or XOR and the 2-spirals problem) and a real world problem. The XOR was chosen because is the simplest non-linear problem one can imagine. Such a problem allows us to test the validity of our approach at the lower end of the complexity scale when parameters like the non-linearity factor and the number of units on the second and third hidden layer are kept to a minimum. The 2 spiral problem can be seen as "pathologically difficult" [1] and allows us to test the validity of the approach as the difficulty of the problem increases. Since numerous experiments have been performed on these problems in the past, the results presented here can be easily put into perspective. One real world problem has been chosen to investigate the validity of the approach in those cases in which there is no a priori information available regarding the degree of non-linearity of the problem. The USER data set represents two classes of computer usage at the University of London Computer Centre [9].

Although the theoretical method presented and the bounds calculated using it do not depend on any particular training algorithm, all experimental results will unavoidably depend on such algorithm. Different algorithms might yield solutions using different number of neurons and weights.

	XOR	User data	2 Spirals
Minimum distance between patterns of opposite classes	1	0.026877	0.143527
Maximum distance between any two patterns	1.414213	1.659804	2
Average distance between patterns	1.138071	0.627921	0.764195
Standard deviation	0.203945	0.345186	0.38158
Weight range p (theoretical)	1	37.20585	6.967348
Weight range p (statistical)	1.2017	9.07920	5.2131
Weight range p (experimental)	1	5	5
Lower bound for entropy bits (theoretical)	6	294	970
Lower bound for entropy bits (statistical)	8	245	873
Min # of weights necessary (with theory p)	18	1021.4	2793.9
Min # of weights necessary (with statistical p)	21.1	722.2	2550.4
Number of patterns classified in the same region (experimental average)	1.333	4.067	2.419
Min # of weights necessary (with theory p)	13.5	251.1	1154.9
Min # of weights necessary (with statistical p)	15.8	177.5	1054.2
Number of weights (experimental average)	12.4	73.2	551.4

Table 1 Summary of experimental results

The particular algorithm used here was the VLSI-friendly Constraint Based Decomposition (VCBD) presented in [7]. This algorithm is a constructive algorithm which builds the network starting from scratch and adds neurons as they are needed. Although the algorithm is able to produce networks with a limited, user chosen fan-in, this feature was disabled for these experiments because the mechanism which ensures the limited fan-in tends to increase the number of weights used.

Sample solutions for the XOR, USER and 2-spiral problems are given in Fig. 1, Fig. 2 and Fig. 3, respectively. In the particular case of the XOR problem, the patterns have been shifted with -0.5 along both axes to avoid having some patterns on the very boundary of the region in which the results where demonstrated. Both the 2 spiral and the USER patterns have been scaled to fit in the [-1,1] square. All I/O images are drawn in the same square.

Since for the chosen algorithm the shape of the solution can depend on the order of the patterns in the training set, a set of 30 trials were performed for each problem. The patterns were randomly shuffled before each trial. The number of hyperplanes and weights used in each trial are presented in Fig. 4, Fig. 5 and Fig. 6 for the XOR, USER and 2-spiral problems, respectively.

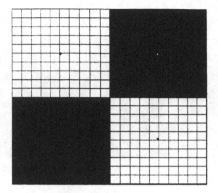

Fig. 1 The XOR problem solved with integer weights in the range [-1, 1]. The solution used 2 hyperplanes with a total number of 14 weights * 1 bit/weight = 14 bits of storage.

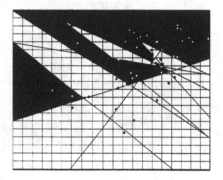

Fig. 2 The USER data set. This solution used 11 hyperplanes with a total number of 78 weights in the range [-5, 5]. The total number of storage bits used was 78 * 4 = 312.

Fig. 3. The 2 spiral problem. This solution used 31 hyperplanes with a total number of 272 weights in the range [-5, 5]. The total number of storage bits used was 272 * 4 = 1088

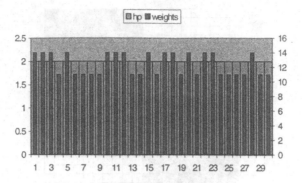

Fig. 4 The number of hyperplanes and weights used for the XOR problem (30 trials).

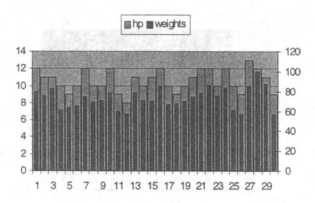

Fig. 5 The number of hyperplanes and the number of weights used for the USER data set (30 trials).

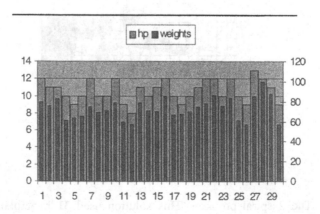

Fig. 6 The number of hyperplanes and weights for the 2 spiral problem (30 trials).

Discussion

For each problem, the minimum distance between two patterns of opposite classes (d_{min}) and the maximum distance between any two patterns (d_{max}) were calculated.

The minimum distance between patterns of opposite classes was used to calculate the minimum theoretical weight range p. The values obtained were 1, 37.20, and 6.96 for the XOR, USER and 2 spirals respectively (see row 5 in Table 1). Then, experiments were performed trying to obtain a solution using a range p as low as possible. The lowest values obtained were 1, 5 and 5 for the XOR, USER and 2 spirals respectively (row 7 in Table 1).

One can note that in practice, for two out of the three problems tested, it was possible to use weight ranges much below the theoretical values. This is because, the theoretical value offers the guarantee that the solution exists for *any* pattern set respecting the minimum distance condition. The discrepancy between the theoretical value and the practical range used can be also seen as a measure of the difficulty of the problem. Note that for the 2 spiral problem the theoretical value is very close to the value actually needed. This might be taken as a confirmation that the 2 spiral problem is indeed "pathologically difficult" as characterized in [1].

However, the USER data set shows that the theoretical bounds can be quite far from the values that can be used experimentally

Using the statistical assumptions detailed above, we have used the average distance between patterns and the standard deviation to calculate a statistical estimation for the necessary weight range p. These values are presented in row 6 in Table 1. A comparison between these values and the values actually needed (row 7 in the same table) shows that the estimated yielded by the statistical approach was much more accurate than the worst-case estimate given by the theoretical approach.

The theoretical and statistical estimates of p were used to calculate a theoretical and statistical estimate for the lower bounds on the number of entropy bits (calculated according to equation (1)). These values are given in row 8 and 9. Equation (6) was then used to calculate theoretical and statistical estimates for the number of weights necessary. These values are presented in rows 10 and 11. As explained in the previous section, these values were calculated in the assumption that each pattern will be classified in its own region. In order to be able to assess the results, we have calculated the average number of patterns classified in the same region for each of the problems analyzed. These values correspond to the non-linearity factor discussed in the previous section and were used to correct the values calculated. The rows 13 and 14 present the theoretical and statistical estimated which take into consideration the average number of patterns per region. These values are to be compared with the average number of weights used for each problem.

The experiments presented have shown that the experimental values obtained for the number of weights are consistently smaller than the values calculated in the worst-case scenario considered by the approach presented. In practical terms this means that if a network is designed according to the method given, the size of the network will be sufficient even for the worst-case scenario but rather wasteful in most practical cases. It is believed that this is mainly due to the approximation introduced by approximating the radius D of the smallest hypersphere containing all patterns with the largest distance between any two patterns d_{max}. In all problems considered here, the radius D can be calculated and leads to much more accurate bounds for the number of weights. However, in the general case, d_{max} is much more convenient.

In practice, the number of weights calculated as above (with $D \cong d_{max}$) can be used as an upper limit for the network design. The network will never need more weights than the number of weights resulted from the given method. If a more precise estimation is needed, one can calculate the centroid c of the patterns and approximate:

$$D \cong \max\left\{|p_i - c|, p_i \in C_1 \cup C_2\right\} \tag{10}$$

Conclusions and future work

The paper presented a method for calculating a worst-case estimate for the size of a VLSI-friendly network for a given classification problem. The method is based on previous theoretical results and was further detailed and completed.

Several experiments involving two benchmarks and a real-world problem have been presented. The experiments showed that the theoretical results based on a worst-case scenario yielded unnecessary large lower bounds for the necessary weight range. Modifications based on statistical considerations have been suggested and tested. The experiments performed showed that these modifications yield good approximations for the weight range. However, the estimations obtained for the number of necessary weights are still rather pessimistic and may lead to an oversized network.

The worst-case values calculated are valuable as an upper limit for the number of weights to be used. Thus, the approach guarantees that a network having the appropriate number of weights will be able to solve any classification problem and there is no need for designing architecture with a larger number of weights. It is believed that this can be corrected with a better approximation or an exact calculation of the radius D of the smallest hypersphere containing all patterns.

Future work will investigate the case in which this radius D is approximated using the centroid (as in equation (10)). It is expected that this combine a feasible computation with a better accuracy for the necessary number of weights.

References

[1] Baffes, P.T., J.M. Zelle - Growing layers of perceptrons: introducing the extentron algorithm, Proc. of 1992 Intl. Joint Conf. on Neural Networks, II, pp. 392-397, IEEE Press, 1992.

[2] Beiu V., Draghici S., Makaruk H.E. - On Limited Fan-in Optimal Neural Networks, Proc. of the IV Brazilian Symposium on Neural Networks, SBRN (Goiana, Brazil, 3-5 December, 1997). Also published as Technical Report LA-UR-97-1567, Los Alamos National Laboratories, 1997.

[3] Coggins R., M. Jabri, Wattle: A Trainable Gain Analogue VLSI Neural Network, Advances in NIPS 6 (NIPS*93, Denver, CO), Morgan Kaufman, San Mateo, CA, 874-881, 1994.

[4] Draghici S., Beiu, V. - Entropy based comparison of neural networks for classification, in Proc. of The 9-th Italian Workshop on Neural Nets, WIRN Vietri-sul-mare, 22-24 May, Springer-Verlag, 1997. Also published as Technical Report LA-UR-97-483, Los Alamos National Laboratory, 1997.

[5] Draghici S., Sethi, I.K: On the possibilities of the limited precision weights neural networks in classification problems, *Proc. of International Work-Conference on Artificial and Natural Neural Networks IWANN'97*, Lanzarote, Canary Islands, June 4-6, 1997.

[6] Draghici S., Beiu V., Entropy based comparison of neural networks for classification, *Proc. of The 9-th Italian Workshop on Neural Nets*, WIRN Vietri-sul-mare, 22-24 May, 1997.

[7] Draghici S., Sethi I.K. - Adapting theoretical constructive algorithms to hardware implementations for classification problems, *Proc. of the International Conference on Engineering Applications of Neural Networks*, Stockholm, Sweden, 16-18 June, 1997.

[8] Dundar G., K. Rose, The Effect of Quantization on Multilayer Neural Networks, *IEEE Transactions on Neural Networks* 6 (6), pp. 1446-1451, 1995.

[9] Hand D.J., Discrimination and Classification, John Wiley, 1981.

[10] Hecht-Nielsen, R., Kolmogorov's mapping neural network existence theorem. Proc. of the IEEE Conference on Neural Networks III, pp. 11-13, New York, IEEE Press. 1987.

[11] Hohfeld M., S.E. Fahlman, Learning with limited numerical precision using the Cascade-Correlation Algorithm, *Tech.Rep. CMU-CS-91-130*, School of Comp. Sci. Carnegie Mellon, May 1991. Also *in IEEE Transactions on Neural Networks*, NN-3(4), 602-611, 1992.

[12] Hohfeld M., S.E. Fahlman, Probabilistic rounding in neural networks with limited precision. In U. Ruckert and J.A. Nossek (eds.): *Microelectronics for Neural Networks* (Proc. MicroNeuro'91 - Munich, Germany), Kyrill & Method Verlag, 1-8, October 1991. Also in *Neurocomputing*, 4, 291-299, 1992.

[13] Hornik K.,, M. Stinchcombe, H. White, Multilayer feedforward networks are universal approximators, Neural Networks, vol. 2, pp. 359-366, 1989.

[14] Hornik K., Some new results on neural network approximation, Neural Networks, vol. 6, pp. 1069-1072, 1993.

[15] Khan A.H., E.L. Hines, Integer weight neural networks, *Electronics Letters*, 30 (15), pp. 1237-1238, 1994.

[16] Khan A.H., R.G. Wilson, Integer weight approximation of continuous-weight multilayer feedforward nets, Proc. *IEEE Int. Conf. on Neura. Networks*, vol. 1, pp. 392-397, Washington DC, June 1996, IEEE Press, New York, NY, 1996.

[17] Kurkova, V. - Kolmogorov's theorem and multilayer neural networks. Neural Networks 5, 501-506, 1992.

[18] Kwan H.K., Tang C.Z., Designing Multilayer Feedforward Neural Networks Using Simplified Activation Functions and One-Power-of-Two Weights. *Electronic Letters*, 28 (25), pp. 2343-2344, 1992.

[19] Kwan H.K., Tang C.Z., Multiplierless Multilayer Feedforward Neural Networks Design Suitable for Continuous Input-Output Mapping, *Electronic Letters*, 29 (14), pp. 1259-1260, 1993.

[20] Marchesi M., G. Orlandi, F. Piazza, L. Pollonara, A. Uncini, Multilayer Perceptrons with Discrete Weights, *Proc. Int. Joint Conf. on Neural Networks IJCNN'90*, San Diego, Vol. II, pp. 623-630, June, 1990.

[21] Marchesi M., G. Orlandi, F. Piazza, A. Uncini, Fast Neural Networks without Multipliers, *IEEE Transactions on Neural Networks*, NN-4 (1), pp. 53-62, 1993.

[22] Tang C.Z., H.K. Kwan, Multilayer Feedforward Neural Networks with Single Power-of-Two Weights. *IEEE Trans. On Signal Processing*, SP-41(8), 2724-2727, 1993.

String Clustering and
Statistical Validation of Clusters

M. Sebban & A.M. Landraud-Lamole
Equipe RAPID
Reconnaissance, Apprentissage et Perception Intelligente à partir de Données
UFR Sciences, Université des Antilles et de la Guyane
Jeune Equipe de Mathématiques et d'Informatique
Campus de Fouillole, 97159 Pointe à Pitre (France)
{Marc.Sebban,Anne.Lamole}@univ-ag.fr

Abstract. In this article we present a new string clustering algorithm and a statistical validation of discovered clusters. They are obtained by searching for common structures of strings and by grouping those sharing wide words. The application of a statistical test, estimating cluster homogeneity, allows to find automatically the number of classes. We apply our method to extract key-structures in 40 biological sequences of about 100 characters each in order to build clusters, and to find three original families again.

1 Introduction

Trying to find repeated structures in character strings presents numerous interests and can be encountered in areas such as *speech recognition, odors detection, images comparison, etc.* In the case of searching for exactly repetitions, efficient algorithms have been proposed, such as the Karp-Miller-Rosenberg's algorithm [2] and the Knuth-Morris-Pratt's algorithm (KMR) [3]. In the case of approximately repeated structures, an algorithm has been developed and proposed by Landraud-Avril-Chretienne (LAC) in [4], derived from the KMR one, and working with time complexity $O(N^2L^2\log_2 L)$, where N is the number of strings and L the maximum length. Nevertheless, this previous approach does not tackle the clustering problem. The goal being to search for common structures of a string family, it deals with strings already belonging to the same class. This way to proceed is comparable to a supervised learning process. Actually, once structures are discovered, a pattern recognition process is then possible in order to affect a new string to a class. Unfortunately, the problem is sometimes more difficult to treat, and no knowledge is *a priori* available about the belonging class of the considered objects.

In this article, we decide to do without this knowledge *a priori*, while using discovered common structures to cluster the set of strings. Thus, the interest of our approach is double: (i) *to search for the best string clustering*; (ii) *to explain (thanks to discovered common structures) the grouping of two strings*. To tackle this problem, we use a modified version of the efficient algorithm of Landraud-Avril-Chretienne [4] to find automatically, step by step, string clusters from common structures. In order to validate the current clusters and their number, we apply a statistical test (the *test of edges*) which estimates their homogeneity degree. The test is based on the construction of the *Minimum Spanning Tree* [7] from the set of distances between strings. From the information contained in this connected graph, the test verifies if the repartition functions of strings in clusters can be statistically considered as being different.

The organization of this paper is the following: in Section 2, we review the useful aspects of the KMR and LAC algorithms. Section 3 describes our algorithm derived from the previous ones. We formulate our statistical test which requires some knowledge in computational geometry. Finally, we apply our method on the problem of 40 biological molecules, trying to find three original classes again.

2 Methodological Review

Published in 1972, the KMR algorithm proposes a solution to search for exactly repeated runs in a S string, and notably the longest word that occurs the more often. This algorithm is based on the search for a set of equivalence relations E_k. E_k is defined at each location of the string S as: the iE_kj relation means that both words, with k characters, beginning at locations i and j are identical and belong to the same class.

Example: in the string $S = $ 'AABCAA', the relation $1E_25$ means that the same word 'AA' begins at locations 1 and 5 of the S string.

The algorithm starts with $k = 1$ and finds recurrently E_k relations. At the beginning ($k = 1$), each character taken in a lexicographical order is considered as a class, if this one is not already a class (cf figure 1.a). The E_1 relation is represented by a vector $v^{(1)} = [v_1^{(1)}, ..., v_i^{(1)}, ..., v_n^{(1)}]$, where $v_i^{(1)}$ corresponds to the label of the class of E_1 at the position i (cf figure 1.b), and n the length of S.

To obtain the next equivalence relation E_k from two stacks P and Q, we use the following procedure :

1. For each C_m class, we create a $P(C_m)$ stack, which stores positions i of S where the word of C_m occurs (cf figure 1.c).
2. Each $P(C_m)$ is sequentially cleared. All numbers i such that a k-length word (of a given class $C_{m'}$) begins at the position $i+1$ are put in the same $Q(C_{m'})$ (cf figure 1.d).
3. Each $Q(C_m)$ is sequentially cleared. Each considered number i is compared to the latter extracted number. If both of them do not belong to the same P stack (that is also the case for the top of each stack that we do not compare to anything) a class counter (initialized to 0) is incremented before being stored at the ith position of the vector $v^{(k)}$ (cf figure 1.e). Otherwise, *i.e.* both of them belong to the same P stack, the current class counter is kept

unchanged and stored at the ith position of the vector $v^{(k)}$. New classes are inferred from $v^{(k)}$ (cf figure 1.f).

4. While $\exists i, j \quad i \neq j \, / \, v_i^{(k)} = v_j^{(k)}$ return to step 1, *i.e.* while it exists at least a word which occurs twice in the string, the algorithm continues working (cf figure 1.g).

In [4], Landraud-Avril-Chretienne propose an extension of the KMR algorithm to find common structures (which can be approximately identical) in a set of N strings belonging to a same family. The principle is based on the concatenation of the N strings into a single S vector and the application of a modified KMR algorithm. Each string in S is characterized by the position of its first and last characters. These boundaries are important because each repeated word found in S must fully belong to only one interval. In this algorithm, words can occur in the N strings with some allowed distortions: *substitution of one character for another one, deletion or insertion of one character.* To estimate the degree of distortions, authors propose three distances: distance between two words, distance between the neighborhood of two words, and a star-distance which is the sum of the N-1 neighborhood distances between a word and its N-1 nearest neighbors.

These distances are taken into account to find *anchoring patterns* in S, corresponding to a configuration in which the same word occurs with some allowed distortions (figure 2).

When the first anchoring pattern is found, the same process is applied to the remaining substrings. In this algorithm, different parameters must be fixed in advance :

1. The number q of strings among the N ones which must occur without any distortion.
2. The length l of the considered neighborhood (l characters on the left and on the right of the word)
3. The degree d of tolerance between the main word of the anchoring pattern and a word with distortions.

The establishment of these parameters is not always easy, because they often depend on the complexity of the problem to treat. Thus, a lot of experiments are often necessary to converge to the best configuration. Moreover, this algorithm is applicable only for a family of strings, where all the N strings share a common structure. The problem becomes more difficult to treat when the N strings belong to different classes of patterns, and where no information *a priori* about classes is known.

3 Algorithm for String Clustering

3.1 Presentation

The problem we propose to deal with belongs to the unsupervised learning frame. Actually, the goal is to use common structures found in N strings to identify

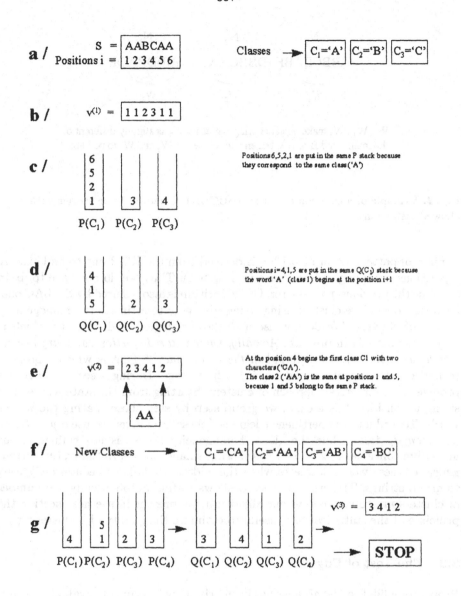

Fig. 1. Application of the KMR algorithm. The longest word 'AA' is found at locations 1 and 5.

$$N_1 \qquad N_2 \qquad N_3$$

$$\underbrace{ABBCBABH}_{W_1}\Big|\underbrace{DBBCBAYL}_{W_2}\Big|\underbrace{GBBDBAOP}_{W_3}$$

W_1, W_2, W_3 make an «anchoring pattern». W_3 is slightly different of the main word BBCBA, but enough close to W_1 and W_2 to be kept.

Fig. 2. Example of a common structure (BBCBA) shared by three strings with some allowed distortions.

families of patterns. Our algorithm is derived from the KMR one to find exactly repetitions occurring at least *twice* in S ($q > 1$). Thus, we do not have to fix in advance the previous q parameter. Our algorithm is also inspired by the LAC one, because we validate clusters using string distances to estimate the homogeneity degree of clusters. We do not use a d allowed degree of distortions which is very difficult to fix in practice. *Actually, what is the distortion boundary beyond which two words are wrongly put in the same class ?* That is why we propose to find exactly repeated words during a first stage. During a second stage, we propose a constructive approach of clusters. Starting from the state where each string is considered as a class, we group step by step those sharing the widest words. To evaluate the pertinence degree of these groupings, we use a *population homogeneity test*. While the global homogeneity degree is not sufficient, our algorithm continues to group strings sharing smaller words. Actually, the current length of these words decreases when the widest words have been already used to group strings. This way to proceed allows to find automatically the number of clusters m. To understand our algorithm, we present in the next section the principle of the statistical test, useful to estimate the quality of a clustering.

3.2 The Test of Edges

Proposed in [9], the *test of edges* has been originally imagined to evaluate *a priori* the quality of a given representation space for a pattern recognition problem. Usually, the expert of a given field (*doctor* for example) establishes an a priori list of features (*number of red and white corpuscles in blood, the blood pressure, etc.*) to allow the construction of a φ classification function by a learning algorithm. φ automatically determines the state of a Y variable (*operation or not ?*). The goal of *the test of edges* consists in estimating the quality of this feature set, before the construction of φ. It allows to estimate statistically difficulties *a priori* to build a model in this space. The general principle of this test is the following:

Different classes (for example *healthy and ill patients*) are well represented by p features, if the representation space (characterized by p dimensions) shows

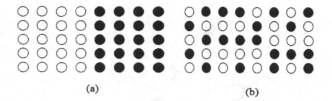

(a)   (b)

Fig. 3. Two classes in the space of features ; for example, black points could represent "healthy patients" and white points the "ill patients" class.

wide geometrical structures (or clusters) of points belonging to these classes (figure 3.a). In fact, when we build a model, we always search for the farthest representation space from the situation where each point of each class constitutes one structure. Thus, the quality of a representation space can be estimated by the distance to the worst situation which is: *equality of the probability functions of classes* (figure 3.b).

To solve this problem, we can use one of the numerous statistical tests of population homogeneity. Unfortunately, none of these tests is both nonparametric and applicable in R^p. The *test of edges* cancels these constraints. We consider the null hypothesis H_0:

$$H_0 : F_1(x) = F_2(x) = ... = F_m(x) = F(x)$$

where $F_i(x)$ corresponds to the repartition function of the class i

Intuitively, figure 3.b accepts the null hypothesis according to the mixing of classes. On the contrary, on figure 3.a $F_1(x)$ seems to be different to $F_2(x)$. In this case, the null hypothesis must be rejected.

In order to construct this test in practice, we use information contained in the well known *Minimum Spanning Tree* (figure 4). This graph consists in connecting by an edge nearest neighbors and building a path with a *minimal edge length* on the set. Afterwards, our approach is based on the research of structures of points belonging to the same class, called *homogeneous subsets*. To obtain these *homogeneous subsets* and evaluate the quality of the representation space, we propose the following procedure :

1. Construction of the *Minimum Spanning Tree*.
2. Construction of *homogeneous subsets*, deleting edges connecting points which belong to different classes.
3. Comparison of the *proportion of deleted edges* (S/N_c) with the probability obtained under the null hypothesis. We proved in [9],

$$S \equiv H(\frac{N(N-1)}{2}, n_c, p)$$

and then the asymptotic normality of the number of deleted edges S,

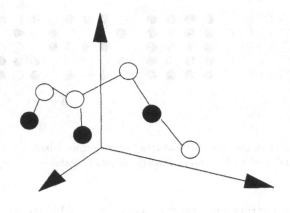

Fig. 4. Example of the Minimum Spanning Tree

where N is the number of objects, n_c is the number of created edges, S is the number of deleted edges, and p is the probability under the H_0 hypothesis to delete an edge. We proved in [9] that

$$p = \frac{\sum\limits_{i=1}^{m-1} n_i \sum\limits_{j=j+1}^{m} n_j}{\frac{N(N-1)}{2}} * \frac{n_c}{\frac{N(N-1)}{2}}$$

where n_i is the number of points of the class i

The decision rule is the following: if the proportion of deleted edges $\frac{S}{n_c}$ is smaller than the probability p, then the H_0 hypothesis is not accepted and the "quality" of the space is verified.

This test, originally created to estimate the quality of a representation space, can also be apply to evaluate the quality of a given clustering of strings. Actually, once a clustering is obtained, i.e. once a label is awarded to each string, we can estimate the quality of this configuration, testing if clusters are wide enough to reject the H_0 hypothesis.

Nevertheless, the problem of this type of population is the following: each string is not a point in $\mathbb{R}^p$ (as a patient characterized for example in $\mathbb{R}^3$, by the *number of red corpuscles in blood, the number of white corpuscles, and the blood pressure*) in which distances between two points are easy to compute. In order to apply the test of edges, we must establish a array of $\frac{N(N-1)}{2}$ distances between the N strings, from which we can build the *Minimum Spanning Tree*.

Between two strings, the distance concept is based on the minimum number of changes, *i.e.* the minimum cost to go from one string to another. First works on string distances come from Levenshtein [5] (the Levenshtein's distance), and Wagner & Fisher [10] (string edit distance), about spelling corrections. Elementary operations are :

○ S_1 = «THE-CAT- IS-GREY»
● S_2 = «THE-DOG-IS-BLACK»
○ S_3 = «THE-CAT-IS-SMALL»
● S_4 = «THE-DOG-IS-BIG»

$D(S_i,S_j)$	S_1	S_2	S_3	S_4
S_1		8	5	7
S_2			8	4
S_3				8
S_4				

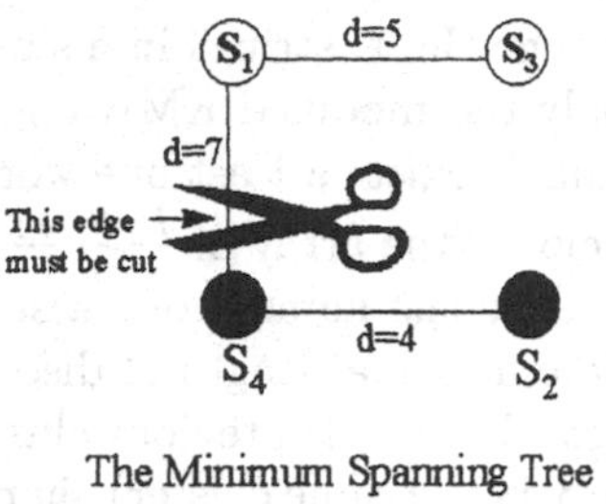

The Minimum Spanning Tree

○ Class 1
● Class 2

Corresponding to an a priori knowledge

Fig. 5. Illustration of the construction of the Minimum Spanning Tree on a set of strings. Classes have been allocated by a given clustering procedure.

1. *substitution of one character by another one*
2. *deletion of one character*
3. *insertion of one character*

To each change, we attribute a cost which can be constant, or dependent on considered strings. For example, distances between proteins can be computed using a substitution matrix, such as the Dayhoff's matrix [1]. This matrix uses probabilities to weight the transformations.

Among recent works dealing with string distances, we can cite Ristad & Yianilos [8], which propose a stochastic model for string edit distance, and Marzal & Vidal [6].

In this article, we decided to assign the same cost to the different distortions which change a word into another one: *substitution of one character, deletion of one character, and insertion of one character*. Thus, we can apply the test of edges if we know the belonging class of each string (figure 5).

To establish automatically this belonging class, without *a priori* knowledge, we propose in the next section a clustering heuristic. It consists in grouping step by step strings sharing wide words, and testing the validity of clusters with the test of edges.

3.3 Clustering Algorithm and Cluster Validation

Starting from the following adage "*Birds of a feather flock together*", we propose to apply the following clustering criterion: *two strings sharing a wide word have a biggest probability to belong to the same class than two words sharing a small word*. Starting from this criterion, we can apply the following stages of our algorithm to create a string clustering :

1. Arrange the N strings in a single vector S.
2. Apply the modified KMR algorithm to extract exactly repeated structures (while it exists a least one word occurring twice in S).
3. Compute the array of $\frac{N(N-1)}{2}$ distances between the N strings.
4. Initialize the number of classes m as the number of strings ($m = N$), and l as the maximal length of discovered structures.
5. According to the previous clustering heuristic, group the two strings (not already in the same cluster) sharing a l-length word; $m \longleftarrow m-1$. If numerous couples of strings share a word of same length, we give greater importance to the closest ones. If no l-length word is found then $l \longleftarrow l-1$.
6. Apply the test of edges with a α critical risk (5% for example). If the α_c critical threshold calculated during the test is bigger than α then Return to step 5 (*i.e.* the H_0 hypothesis is still accepted) else Stop (*i.e.* the H_0 hypothesis has been rejected and the clustering is validated).

4 Experimental Results

In this section, we apply our algorithm to a Ω set of 40 biological macromolecules of maximum length 100, belonging *a priori* to three families (figure 6):

- twenty-three ferredoxins (proteins): N_1 to N_{23}
- seven mammalian RN-ases (proteins): N_{24} to N_{30}
- ten tRNA from Escherichia Coli (nucleic acids): N_{31} to N_{40}

This data base has already been used in [4] to test the LAC algorithm. Nevertheless, it treated families independently to search for common structures shared by all the strings. Here, we deal with the three classes without using the belonging label of strings. Grouping together strings sharing discovered structures, and testing clusters, our algorithm allows to find the three original families again.

In order to understand our algorithm on this real example, let us explain in detail the example of figure 7. It considers a subset of 12 strings, and explains the different steps of the algorithm.

We know *a priori* that these 12 strings belong to 3 classes, but we do not use this knowledge during the procedure. Thus, the goal is the following: (i) find the common structures linking two strings; (ii) finding the 3 original classes again. Above all, our algorithm searches for common structures that occur at least twice in S, which represents the concatenation of the 12 strings. The widest word is shared by N_3 and N_5 (ITDCRETGSSKYPNCAYK). Thus, N_3 and N_5

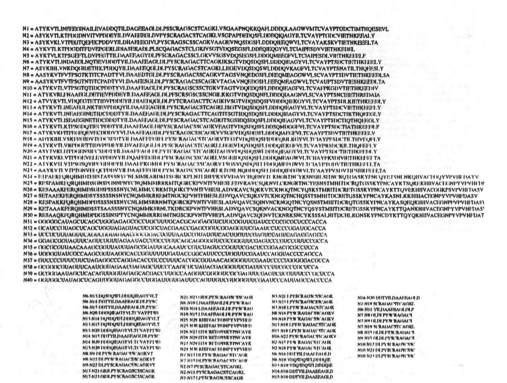

Fig. 6. Set of 40 sequences of biological macromolecules.

are grouped together in the same cluster (see the first graph). At this step, there are only 11 classes left. Applying the test of edges (see the *Minimum Spanning Tree* built from the array of distances), we accept the H_O hypothesis because the proportion of deleted edges (10/11) is too high comparing to the theoretical p. During the second step, N_3 and N_{10} are grouped together (TGSSKYP-NCAYKT), and so on. The last iteration appears when the H_0 hypothesis is refused, *or when the current number of classes is too small* (usually $m = 2$). For this example, the H_0 hypothesis is refused after the grouping of N_6 and N_8. We obtain at the end three classes, finding the three original classes again. The same procedure has been applied on the whole set of macro-molecules; the three classes has been found again.

5 Conclusion

Efficient algorithms have been proposed in literature to find common structures (exactly or approximately repeated) in a set of strings. These approaches are very interesting to explain the link between objects belonging to the same family. The

N01 = AYKTVLKTPSQEFTLDVPEGTTILDAAEEAGYDL/FSCRAGACSSCLGKVVSGSVIXQSEGSFLDDGQMEEGFVLTCIAIPESDLVIETHKEEELF

N02 = ETPAEKFQRQHMDTEHSTASSSNYCNLMMKARDMTSGRCKPLNTFIHEPKSVVDAVCHQENVTCKNGRTNCYKSNSRLSITNCRQTGASKY
PNCQYETSNLNKQIIVACEGQYVPVHFDAYV

N03 = KESAAAKFERQHMDSGDSPSSSSNYCNLMMCCRKMTQGKCPVNTFVHESLADVKAVCSQKKVTCKNGQTNCYQSKSTMRITDCRETGSSKY
PNCAYKTTQVEKHIIVACGGKPSVPVHFDASV

N04 = AYKVTLKTPDGDITFDVEPGERLIDIASEKADLPLSCQAGACSTCLGKIVSGTVDXQSEGSFLDDEQIEQGYVLTCIAIPESDVVIETHKEDEL

N05 = SETAAFKFERQHMDSYSSSSNSNYCNQMMKRREMTNOCKPVNTFIHESLEDVQAVCSQKSVTCKNGQTNCHQSSTSMHITDCRETGSSKYPNCA
YKASNLKKHIIACEGNPYVPVHFDASV

N06 = GGAGCGGUAGUUCAGUCGGUUAGAAUACCUGCCUGUCAGCAGGGGGUCGCGGGUUCGAGUCCCGUCCGUUCCGCCA

N07 = ASYKVKLVTPEGTQEFECPDDVYILDHAEEEGIVLPYSCRAGSCSSCAGKVAAGEVNQSDGSFLDDDQIEEQWVLTCVAYAKSKVTIETHKEEELTA

N08 = GGCGCGUUAACAAAGCGGUUAUGUAGCGGAUUGCAAAUCCGUCUAGUCCGGUUCGACUCCGGAACGCGCCUCCA

N09 = UGGGGUAUCGCCAAGCGGUAAGGCACCGGUUUUUGAUACCGGCAUUCCCUGGGUUCGAAUCCAGGUACCCCAGCCA

N10 = RESPAMKFQRQHMDSGNSPGNNPNYCNQMIMMRRKMTQGRCKPVNTFVHESLEDVKAVCSQKNVLCKNGRTNCYESNSTMHITDCRQTGSSKY
PNCAYKTSQKEKHIIVACEGNPYVPVHFINSV

N11 = GUCCCCUUUCGUCUAGAGGCCCAGGACACCGCCUCUUUCACCGCGGUAACAGCGGGUUCGAAUCCCCUGGGGGACCCCA

N12 = ASYKVTLKTPDGDNVITVPDDEYILDVAEEBGLDVPYSCRAGACSTCAGKLVSGPAPDEIXQSFLDDDQIQAGYILTCVAYPTGDCVIETHKEEALY

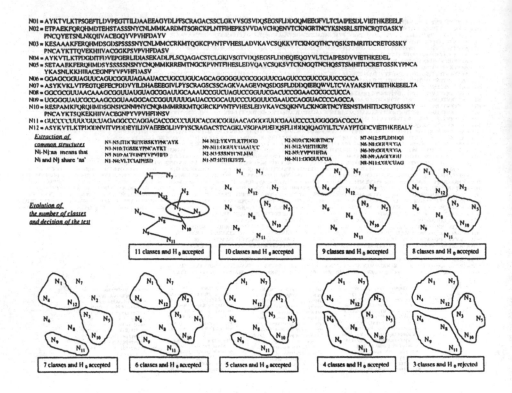

Extraction of common structures
Ni-Nj:aa means that Ni and Nj share 'aa'

Evolution of the number of classes and decision of the test

11 classes and H_0 accepted
10 classes and H_0 accepted
9 classes and H_0 accepted
8 classes and H_0 accepted
7 classes and H_0 accepted
6 classes and H_0 accepted
5 classes and H_0 accepted
4 classes and H_0 accepted
3 classes and H_0 rejected

Fig. 7. Illustration of our algorithm : 12 strings are tested belonging to 3 a priori known classes, but this knowledge is not used during the procedure.

algorithm proposed in this paper goes further, because it tries on the one hand to discover common structures, and on the other hand to cluster strings sharing these structures. The test of edges, which has already proved its performances in the pattern recognition frame, is used in a new context to validate the discovered clusters. Applied to the particular problem of biological molecules, our approach shows interesting results. Even if other heuristics could be applied to create clusters, we wanted to use extracted information (common structures) to solve the problem. Nevertheless, this clustering heuristic which consists in grouping strings sharing wide local words can be discussed, and is worth being compared.

References

1. M. DAYOFF. *Atlas of protein sequences and structure*. Nat. Biomed. Res. Found, 1978.
2. R. KARP, R. MILLER, and L. ROSENBERG. Rapid identification of repeated patterns in strings, trees and arrays. In *Proceedings 4th Annu. ACM Symp. Theory of Computer*, pages 125–136, 1972.

3. D. KNUTH. *The Art of Computer Programming.* vols 1,2,3, Reading, MA: Addison-Wesley, 1973.

4. A. LANDRAUD-LAMOLE, J. AVRIL, and P. CHRETIENNE. An algorithm for finding a common structure shared by a family of strings. *IEEE Transactions on Pattern Analysis and Machine Intelligence*, 11:890–895, 1989.

5. V. LEVENSHTEIN. Binary code capable of correcting deletions, insertions and reversals. *Soviet Physics-Doklady 10*, 10:707–710, 1966.

6. A. MARZAL and E. VIDAL. Computation of normalized edit distance and applications. *IEEE Trans. PAMI 15*, 9:926–932, 1993.

7. F. PREPARATA and M. SHAMOS. *Computational Geometry.* Springer-Verlag, 1985.

8. E. RISTAD and P. YIANILOS. Learning string edit distance. *Research Report CS-TR-532-96*, 1997.

9. M. SEBBAN. *Modèles Théoriques en Reconnaissance de Formes et Architecture Hybride pour Machine Perceptive.* PhD thesis, Université Lyon 1, 1996.

10. C. WAGNER and M. FISCHER. The string to string correction problem. *J.A.C.M.*, 21:168–173, 1974.

Finding Partitions for Learning Control of Dynamic Systems

Michael McGarity

University of New South Wales, 2052, Australia.

Abstract. When a dynamic systems is controlled by a learning controller, the state space is required to be coarsely partitioned to make the learning task computationally feasible. This partition forms the representation of the dynamic system to the learning algorithm. However, such representations normally make the system non-Markovian and thus hard to control, do not naturally allow for asymptotic approach of the setpoint, and often necessitate large control actions.

By analysing the partitioning function as an information channel providing partial observation of the underlying Markovian process, it can be shown that the problems of hidden state, selective perception and partially observable systems are not brought about by having the wrong number of cells, which could be improved by pruning or splitting nodes, nor can it be improved by augmenting observations with a history of observations, but is rather due to a poor choice of base representation.

Using an information loss metric and sliding mode design heuristics, it is possible to find more appropriate partitions of the state space which remove or reduce the learning and controlling problems associated with partitioned representations of dynamic systems. The practical benefits of these partitions are demonstrated controlling a benchmark process.

1 Introduction

Intelligent control algorithms aims to develop controllers capable of dealing with a wide variety of conditions and operating points without re-tuning or other human intervention. Although intelligent controllers contain some adaptive element designed to find such a controller, the dynamic system representation is usually specified before learning begins. This paper demonstrates one way of finding this representation.

Reinforcement Learning Controllers (RLCs) usually represent the space in which the system moves as a set of disjoint regions. A different control law may operate when the state of the system is in each box. Learning and controlling a dynamic system are made vastly more difficult in the context of partitioning the state space, because that partitioning the system makes it non-Markovian. Treating the system as Markovian, as RLC algorithms inevitably do, then creates the appearance of a non-deterministic system.

We retain the notion of disjoint regions in state-space defined by a grid in $\mathbb{R}^n$, but claim that rotating the grid which defines the regions can make the system seem more deterministic, thus improving learning and control.

2 Intelligent Controllers

Control literature has suggested that we need a new definition of what makes a good controller [1, 6]. The most important points of this new definition are *robustness* in the face of parameter uncertainty and disturbance, being *goal-driven*, and being *intuitively understandable by humans*.

Most reinforcement learning controllers attempt to satisfy these goals by assuming that there are a finite number of separate regions, or partitions of the state space, and a choice between a finite number of responses to make in each of these regions. The framework is simple, the produced rule base being of a form easily broken down into human understandable blocks. Producing goal-optimal (within the restrictions of this finite set of responses) behaviour given these constraints is thus reduced to a finite decision process. The complication is that, without significant domain knowledge, the imposed constraint of a finite (and usually small) number of distinct regions and responses can easily restrict the set of possible control laws that may be produced by the decision tree to quite poor ones. The optimal set of decisions can thus still produce a infeasible or unrobust control law.

As I see it, the two main problems facing designers of RLCs for achieving the intelligent control criteria above are these:

To design a decision making algorithm which copes with the fact that most or all choices of finite representation preclude the possibility of a deterministic model, and To find a good representation of the dynamic system. The representation should be designed to give some behaviour guarantees given the small amount of a priori knowledge available, and to minimise the effect of the necessarily non-deterministic model of the dynamic system given a heterogeneous representation.

Although the first problem has received considerable attention [3, 5], the second has not. In this paper, I propose in this paper to lay the framework for addressing the problem of representation.

3 Definition of the Quantised System

Say we have a deterministic, discrete time system with n-vector describing the state. The state space in which the system moves is partitioned into regions. The functiomn $z = \mathcal{Q}(x)$ returns the region z within which the state x in currently contained. The region z is often called an observation. We could write such a system as:

$$x_{n+1} = F(x_n, u_n) \qquad (1)$$
$$z_n = \mathcal{Q}(x_n)$$
$$\text{where}$$
$$x \in \mathbb{R}^n$$

$$u \in \mathbb{R}^m$$

$$z \in \Omega, |\Omega| \text{ finite.}$$

Note that the future states are defined to be functions of the current state and the control applied, so that with respect to the state x, the system is a Markov chain. However it has been shown [2] that, with respect to the observations z, the system may not exhibit the Markov property. If the Markov property does not hold when we are only supplied with the observations z, the task of modeling or controlling the system is more difficult, since we cannot always be sure of the effect of a control.

The qualitative observer Q is an indicator function $\mathbb{R}^n \to \mathbb{Z}^n$ for a partition P of the continuous state space. Usually, the sides of each partition are parallel to the dimension boundaries, so that the z^i, the n components of z are functions of x^i, the n components of x

$$z^i = [x^i]_{P^i} \tag{2}$$

where

$$[a]_{P^i} = \max\{p \in P^i : p < a\}$$

The model given by (1) and (3) is one we will use in the following analysis. We might also propose a model based entirely on the observations,

$$z_{n+1} = \hat{F}(z_n, u_n) \tag{3}$$

where

$$z(t) \in \Omega, |\Omega| \text{ finite.}$$

$$u(t) \in \mathbb{R}^m.$$

but we find that $\hat{F}$ is not in general a function, not usually being singularly-valued. This model, and $\hat{F}$, is well defined only if the system is deterministic with respect to the observations.

4 Properties of the Non-deterministic Model

If we accept that the quantised system is non-deterministic [2], the definition of the transition probabilities should be stated. The transition probabilities follow directly from the definition of the system $x_{n+1} = F(x_n)$ and $z_n = Q(x_n)$ and depend on the distribution μ of $x \in \mathbb{R}^n$, which in turn depends on the control policy (or control strategy, or control law).

$$\hat{p}_{ij} = \int_{\tau \in P_i} I_{F(\tau) \in P_j} \partial\mu(\tau) \tag{4}$$

where

I_S is the indicator function for set S

$\mu(\tau)$ is the distribution of x under closed loop

This makes clear upon what the transition probabilities depend, but does not give a true picture of what is meant by them. A transition of a quantised system is generally taken to be between *different* observations, which the above definition does not guarantee. This might be viewed in terms of qualitative dynamics as a feedback of landmark values, where the only noteworthy events are when the system crosses a boundary. Movement within the partition is not seen to be of importance. With this in mind, let us try again.

$$p_{ij} = \int_{\tau \in P_i} I_{\tau \in P_i^j} \partial \mu(\tau) \tag{5}$$

where

$$P_i^j = \{\tau \in P_i : \exists n > 0 F^n(\tau) \in P_j, \forall 0 < m < n F^m(\tau) \in P_i\}$$

I_S is the indicator function for set S

$\mu(\tau)$ is the distribution of x_n under closed loop

Obviously, $\hat{p} \neq p$. Less obviously, p cannot be defined in terms of $\hat{p}$ in the usual way, thus,

$$p_{ij} \neq \frac{\hat{p}_{ij}}{1 - \hat{p}_{ii}}$$

This is because the transitions between finite states are not really Markovian probabilities, but represent a lack of information. As such, they are useful only in predicting the next observation that will be made, and matrix algebra cannot be used to predict observations multiple time steps into the future. Care is needed to not use the identified p beyond that for which they are defined.

Furthermore, we restrict our discussion to ergodic systems. The essential feature of ergodic systems that we require is that the experimental distribution converges to the true distribution of any random variables. This property holds even if the transitions are not independent, as the Markov property requires. This means that we can estimate the transition probabilities by recording how often they occur, but we cannot use a combination of transition probabilities to predict a sequence of observations.

5   A More Predictable Transformation

It is clear that system which partitions the state space will not be Markovian in the quantized state z, given that it does not fit the restrictive conditions given in Lunze [2], and the last two sections have shown that this makes the system non-deterministic. These are the conditions uder which the majority of learning algorithms work. An important question is, how may we find partitions that minimise this effect?

We approach this problem by assigning *a priori* a partition, but transform the state space by $\tilde{x} = Tx$ before the quantisation occurs. We then attempt to find a transformation matrix T such that the new quantised state $\tilde{z}$ is more predictable along trajectories of the system.

If we now assume that the system is a Markovian, non-deterministic finite state machine, each transition will introduce entropy, since the observation will not be known given only past data. Let us consider how the transition entropy may be minimised, and the system made to appear more predictable. Define a metric of information loss h_c in transitions from each observation cell c as,

$$h_c = \sum_{z \in \Omega} p_{cz} \log_2 \left(\frac{1}{p_{cz}} \right) \tag{6}$$

This metric gives the number of bits lost by making a transformation according to the non-deterministic transition matrix. Note that $h_c = 0$ if observation c' always follows observation c. It would be nice if we could re-arrange the partitions, which would also change the values of the p_{cz}, reducing the value of h_c. If we could alter p_{cz}, the following result might be useful,

$$\frac{\partial J_c}{\partial p_{cz}} = \log \left(\frac{G}{p_{cz}} \right) \tag{7}$$

where $\tag{8}$

$$G = {}_{|\bar{C}|}\sqrt{\prod_{i \in \bar{C}} p_{ci}}$$

$$\bar{C} = \{i \in \Omega : i \neq c \text{ and } 0 < p_{ci} < 1\}$$

The heuristic interpretation of this result is that if it is possible to change the values of the p_{ij}, it is best to increase the value of those probabilities that are larger than the geometric mean of the rest of the probabilities, and decrease the rest. To go further, if we notice that transitions after an observation c leave the observation cell in one of a small set of directions, the orientation of the partitions around c should move so as to minimise J_c. The orientation does this by reducing the number of observations that likely follow observation c given the known system behaviour after making observation c.

This is a difficult task, and the technique described in the next section does not guarantee to solve it. To make it slightly easier, in the following we assume in the following that $F(x)$ is convex for all x. This means that there is only one connected image of each partition, and we need only attempt to maximise the p_{cz} with the largest magnitude and reduce the rest of the transition probabilities.

6 Experimental Framework

Before learning begin, we specify a uniform directionwise quantiser by which we produce a series of quantised states. A uniform directionwise quantiser is defined as in (3) as $[\cdot]_{Z\!\!\!Z}$. A naive search is then performed for a transformation matrix T so that the the transformed $\tilde{z}$ are more predictable along trajectories.

If we linearly transform the state before it is quantised, we have a lot of freedom in dictating how the system is viewed. If we have a system:

$$x_{n+1} = \Phi x_n + \Gamma u_n$$

of which we have quantised observations through a quantiser $\mathcal{Q}$, can we linearly transform the states before quantisation to produce more useful discrete observations.

$$z_n = \mathcal{Q}(T x_n T^{-1})$$

We would like to find the transform T that produces the best predictive information in the observations z_n

It is appreciated that, in combining the system variables in this way, one loses some ability to describe both the behaviour of the system, and the action of the controller, in simple, human understandable ways.It is hoped that the advantages in control and learning speed offset this slight loss of descriptive ability.

7   A Naive Search

We examine the behaviour of our benchmark process under the influence of a random controller. Of course, it may be beneficial to to control the system in the way it was designed or intended to move. In these experiments, however, we do not attempt to find such an initial controller. This allows for future work to move to an adaptive algorithm which attempts to generate controller and representation simultaneously.

The behaviour upon which we need to focus is the transition behaviour of the boxes, and more specifically, the expected transition entropy (TE) of the system. If the system is currently in one box, we would like to determine which partition the system will move to (if and when it moves to another box). Section 4 suggests that we assume that the quantised system is not deterministic, so that the mapping of current observation to next observation will show several possible next quantised states.

Calculation of the TE associated with a given transformation matrix T proceeds by dividing each region into small sub-regions. In our experiemnts, we divided each region into 10^n sub-regions, where n is the number of dimensions. Then, by projecting each subregion forward until it hits a partition, or a certain number of time steps is reached, an estimation of the transition probability from that region to adjoining regions is found. This is done for each of the control actions available in that region, and for each region in the partition. The approximate transition probability into a partition is calculated as the number of small regions that hit the boundary entering that partition divided by the total number of subregions which leave the region. Those regions which stay within the partition until the time limit are deemed to be stable, and are not include in the transition probabilities.

A simple genetic algorithm was then established, using the TE for each transformation matrix as the fitness funtion, and the $n \times n$ elements of the transition matrix as the basis vector. Random additive variations to the matrix T were included as the mutation phase, periodically elements of T were swapped with elements from the same position in other population matrices to simulate crossover.

It was noticed that the transformation matrix produced by the genetic algorithm grew unbounded. This has the effect of forming very small regions, as small changes in x result in large changes in $\tilde{x}$. However, the improvements due to an increase in the size of the regions were insignificant compared to those due to the orientation of the transformation. This was a surprising result, and to explore the effect of orientation independantly from region size, we altered the algorithm so that before determining the transition probabilities between transformed cells, each genetically created transition matrix was normalised to a determinant of one, to retain constant cell volume. Badly conditioned matrices were discarded as unfit to be tested.

Obviously, the above technique is not designed for computational efficiency, and it is not surprising that the genetic algorithm needed a very long time to converge. It was run from scratch five times, producing matricies which were very similar, aside from inconsequential permutations. These permutations were of a form so that transformation T_i found on the ith run of the algorithm would satisfy $T_i \approx ST$ where S is a permutation matrix (ie, exactly one 1 in each column and row) and and T is the transformation found by the minimum TE algorithm. Also, even though the transformations found were not always the same, the minimum average information loss per transition was always found to be close to to 1.5 bits, assuming uniform occupancy probabilities throughout the allowed space. Applying the permutation S to each T_i (by finding the column vector in T most closely resembling a column vector in T_i), we can find the renormalised element-wise mean for our estimation of T, shown in Tab. 1. The transition entropy for this renormalised mean matrix was found to be similar (within 0.08 bits/transition) to those found by genetic algorithm.

$$
T = \begin{bmatrix}
0.58 & 0.64 & 0.51 & 0.02 \\
0.07 & 0.01 & -0.07 & -0.99 \\
0.51 & 0.20 & -0.83 & 0.09 \\
0.63 & -0.74 & 0.21 & 0.02
\end{bmatrix}
$$

Table 1. Renormalised element-wise mean of maximally predictable transforms found by the GA. Transition entropy of 1.47 bits/transition

7.1 Testing the transformation

To test the effectiveness of the partitions formed by our simple partition in conjunction with the newly found genetic algorithm, we ran several experiments using known learning algorithms, a well known plant in the pole and cart, and our representation. The simple partition used is very similar (although with fewer partitions) to that which have previously (e.g. [7]) been used to learn to control the pole and cart. The partition is shown in Tab. 2. The transformation shown

If $\hat{x} = Tx$,

$$\hat{x}_1 \in (-\infty, 0) \text{ or } [0, \infty)$$

$$\hat{x}_2 \in (-\infty, 0) \text{ or } [0, \infty)$$

$$\hat{x}_3 \in (-\infty, -0.1) \text{ or } [-0.1, 0.1) \text{ or } [0.1, \infty)$$

$$\hat{x}_4 \in (-\infty, -0.1) \text{ or } [-0.1, 0.1) \text{ or } [0.1, \infty)$$

Table 2. Simple partition for these experiments

in Tab. 1 was then applied to our example plant, and we attempt to learn to control it by reinforcement learning techniques. In the discussion above, it was hoped that the minimum TE transform would result in faster learning (from the Markovian argument) and better control(due to the sliding surface argument). Let us examine the results of the experiment for evidence of these advantages.

Using Boxes [4], 1-step Q-learning [8], P-trace [5], $Q(\lambda)$, and Mahadavan's R-learning [3], we now look at how the transformation improves the ability of a reinforcement learning controller to learn a physical system that has been made more predictable.

Tables 3 and 4 show a comparison between the learning algorithms that are provided the transformation found by the GA described above, and the same learning algorithm given the same basic partition, but without any transformation. We required that each algorithm produce a controller that kept the pole and cart within the specified bounds for 50 seconds. Each combination was tested 10 times, and the results averaged. The tables show the mean number of trials $\bar{N}_T$ resulting in failure that were required before a successful trial. The length of a successful trial is 50 seconds. Also shown is the standard deviation of $\bar{N}_T$, as well as the minimum and maximum number of trials required.

It is clear from Tab. 3 and 4 that the transformation makes it substantially easier for an RLC algorithm to learn to control the example system using the simple partition that we are using. In addition to this, we would like to see whether it improves the quality of control. Section 2 lists the qualities we would like from control and singles out frugal control effort and reaching the setpoint asymptotically as those qualities that are often lacking from RLC controllers. Let us compare two illustrative examples. Figures 2 and 1 shows the behaviour of

Algorithm	$\bar{N}_T$	σ	Min	Max
Boxes	127.5	99.7	41	343
PTrace	†472.5	†30.4	451	DNF
Q learning	‡	‡	‡	‡
Q($\lambda = 0.9$)	†99.0	†41.7	72	DNF
Q trace	‡	‡	‡	‡
Mahadavan	†401.3	†145.6	233	DNF

† Not all of the trials succeeded, so the average is incomplete.

‡ None of the trials succeeded. No information about the usefulness of this algorithm with no transformation.

DNF The maximum number of trials required is unknown, as not all of the experiments completed learning successfully.

Table 3. Performance of the test algorithms on the pole and cart using a *very* simple representation, but no transformation.

Algorithm	$\bar{N}_T$	σ	Min	Max
Boxes	17.5	9.7	11	34
Boxes	35.6	17.1	13	58
PTrace	24.5	10.6	15	41
Q learning	164.2	84.2	59	291
Q($\lambda = 0.9$)	49.0	24.7	9	71
Q trace	51.4	23.3	29	87
Mahadavan	159.4	161.0	29	401

Table 4. Results for each algorithm using the minimum transition entropy transformation provided by the offline GA algorithm. The time taken to learn to control the pole and cart is noticeably better than those shown in Tab. 3

the pole and cart under the control of two RLCs. The first shows the behaviour, starting from initial conditions $[\theta, \dot{\theta}, x, \dot{x}] \approx [0.1, 0, 1, 0]$, using a RLC with a standard axis parallel partition (i.e. no transformation). The second shows the behaviour when the transformation given in Tab. 1 is used.

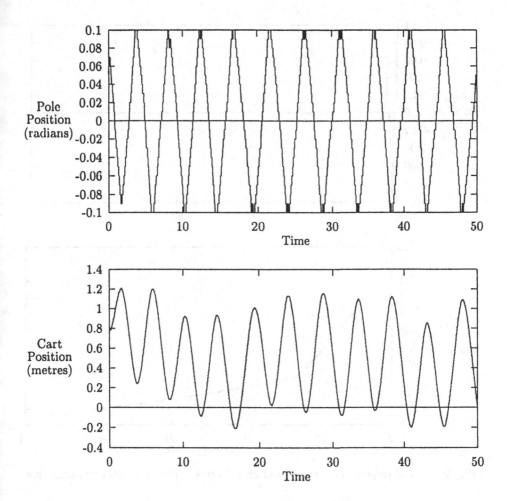

Fig. 1. Typical response of the pole and cart (respectively) *without* the transformation

The improved quality of control should be obvious from these plots. The "robustness" of the resulting controllers is tested in the literature by trying them a number of times and recording in how many of these trials the controller keeps the plant inside the required limits. Table 5 show these results. Clearly, the transformed controllers are far more robust as well.

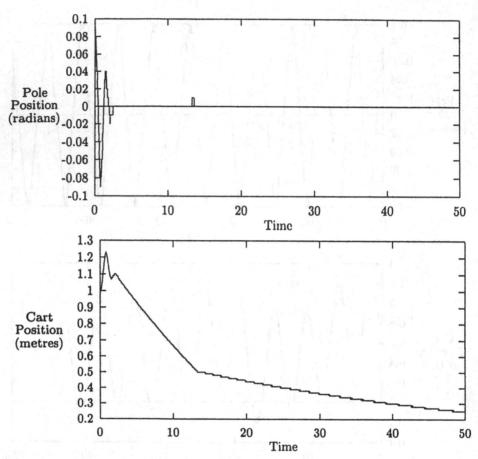

Fig. 2. Typical response of the pole and cart (respectively) *with* the transformation

Algorithm	% of Robustness Trial Successful		
	No Transform	Published	Offline Transform
Boxes	10	35	76
PTrace	5	60	97
Q learning	0	20	52
$Q(\lambda = 0.9)$	10	35	50
Q trace	0	55	66
Mahadavan	0	25	50

Table 5. Robustness of the test algorithms on the pole and cart using each of the representations used above.

8 Conclusion

The methodology developed in this paper has two potential problems. First, we assumed that the occupancy probability of the state within a region in constant, to allow us to produce an offline function which estimated the transition entropy of the quantised system state $\tilde{z}$. Second, the genetic algorithm used was very basic and used no heuristics to improve convergence time.

Note that the occupancy probability is affected by the control actions of the learner, and will therefore change as the learner learns. Further work will examine an adaptive algorithm based on these ideas which will be able to address this problem by making an estimate of them directly instead of estimating the transition probabilities by means of average flows of small subregions at a given boundary. An adaptive algorithm will also be able to deal with plants for which no good model exists, another restriction of this offline algorithm.

These two points notwithstanding, the controllers produced by this offline algorithm described in this paper exhibit improved learning times and qualitatively improved quality of control. Despite the problems with this algorithm, and despite the loss in descriptive power that transformation matrices bring about, improvements in learning and control suggest that finding transformation to improve predictability is a good framework for finding partitions for reinforcement learner controllers.

References

[1] B. Hayes-Roth. Intelligent control. *Artificial Intelligence*, 59:213–220, 1993.
[2] Jan Lunze. Qualitative modelling of linear dynamical systems with quantized state measurements. *Automatica*, 30(3):417–431, 1994.
[3] Sridhar Mahadevan. Average reward reinforcement learning: Foundations, algorithms, and empirical results. *Machine Learning*, 22:159–195, 1996.
[4] Donald Michie and R.A. Chambers. Boxes: An experiment in adaptive control. In E. Dale and D. Michie, editors, *Machine Intelligence 2*. Oliver and Boyd, 1968.
[5] Mark Pendrith and Malcolm Ryan. Reinforcement learning for real-world control applications. In *Proc. of the 11th Canadian Artificial Intelligence Conf.* Springer-Verlag, 1996.
[6] Herbert E. Rauch. Autonomous control reconfiguration. *IEEE Control Systems Magazine*, 15(6):37–48, 1995.
[7] Claude Sammut and James Cribb. Is learning rate a good performance criterion for learning. In B.W. Porter and R.J. Mooney, editors, *Proceedings of the Seventh International Machine Learning Conference*. Morgan Kaufman, 1990.
[8] Christopher J.C.H. Watkins. *Learning from delayed rewards*. PhD thesis, King's College, Cambridge, 1989.

A Relational Modeling of Cognitive Maps

B. Chaib-draa

Département d'Informatique
Université Laval
Ste-Foy, PQ, Canada G1K 7P4
chaib@ift.ulaval.ca

Abstract. Causal reasoning involves many interacting concepts that make them difficult to deal with, and for which analytical techniques are inadequate. A cognitive map can be employed, as a tool for qualitative reasoning, to cope with this type of knowledge. Cognitive maps have been used for decision analysis, administrative sciences, management sciences, distributed AI and distributed group decision support. In this paper, we present a formal model for cognitive maps with a precise semantics based on relation algebra. In this way, we justify the classical intuitive inference mechanisms, based on reasoning from causes to effects.

1 Introduction

Generally, causal knowledge involves many interacting concepts that make them difficult to deal with, and for which analytical techniques are inadequate [10]. A cognitive map (*CM*) can be used, as a tool for qualitative reasoning, to cope with this kind of knowledge.

Generally, the basic elements of a *CM* are simple. The concepts an individual uses are represented as *points*, and the causal links between these concepts are represented as *arrows*. This representation gives a graph of points and arrows, called a *cognitive map*. The strategic alternatives, all of the various causes and effects, goals, and the ultimate utility of the decision-making agent can all be considered as concept variables, and represented as points.

Causal relationships can take on different values based on the most basic values + (positive), − (negative), and 0 (neutral). Logical combinations of these three basic values give the following: "neutral or negative" (⊖), "neutral or positive" (⊕), "non-neutral" (±), "ambivalent" (*a*) and, finally, "positive, neutral or negative" (i.e.,"universal") (?) [1],[2],[9].

The real power of this approach appears when a *CM* is pictured in graph form. It is then relatively easy to see how concepts and causal relationships are related to each other and to see the overall causal relationships of one concept with another, particularly if these concepts are the concepts of several agents.

For instance, the *CM* of Figure 1, taken from [8], explains how the Japanese made the decision to attack Peal Harbor. Indeed, this *CM* states that "remaining idle *promotes* the attrition of Japanese strength while *enhancing* the defensive preparedness of the US, both of which *decrease* Japanese prospects for success in war". Thus, a *CM* is a set of concepts as "Japan remains idle", "Japanese attrition", etc. and a set of signed edges representing causal relations like "promote(s)", "decrease(s)", etc.

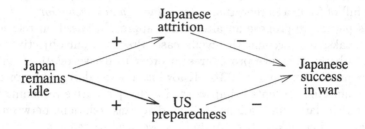

Fig. 1. A *CM* (from [Levi and Tetlock, 1980]).

Note that the concepts' domains are not necessarily defined precisely since there are no obvious scales for measuring "US preparedness", "success in war", etc. Nevertheless, it seems easy to catch the intended meaning of the signed relationships in this model [14]. As any cognitive map, the *CM* of Figure 1 can be transformed in a matrix called an adjacency or valency matrix which is a square matrix with one row and one column for each concept.

Inferences that we can draw from a *CM* are based on a qualitative reasoning similar to "friend's enemy is enemy, enemy's enemy is friend, etc.". Thus, in the case of Figure 1, "remaining idle" decreases the prospects for Japanese success in a war along two causal paths. Notice that the relationship between idleness and war prospects is negative since both paths agree. In these conditions, Japan has interest to start war as soon as possible if he believes that war is inevitable.

Notice that *CMs* may be more complex than that given in this paper (see for example [2] for larger examples). In fact, *CMs* follow *personal construct theory*, first put forward by Kelly [5]. This theory provides a basis for representing an individual's multiple perspectives. Kelly suggests that understanding how individuals organize their environments requires that subjects themselves define the relevant dimensions of that environment. He proposed a set of techniques, known collectively as *repertory grid*, in order to facilitate empirical research guided by the theory. Personal construct theory has spawned many fields and has been used as a first step in generating *CMs* for decision support. *CMs* have been used for decision analysis in the fields of international relations [1],[2], administrative sciences [11], management sciences [4],[13], and distributed group decision support [15]. In the latter context, the authors provided the notions of NPN (Negative-Positive-Neutral) logic, NPN relations, and neural networks. In this model, quantities are combined along the paths but there is no other connection to the original spirit of *CMs*, that is, the causal reasoning.

Except for Zhang's work, all other approaches to *CMs* were based on simple inference mechanisms in order to give rise to a qualitative calculus about the consequences of a *CM*. Thus, the definition of a precise semantic interpretation of qualitative causality has received very little attention. The only work that we are aware of in this context is Wellman's approach [14]. This author used an approach based on graphical dependency models, for probabilistic reasoning, and sign algebras, for qualitative reasoning. However, his techniques are only applicable in the acyclic case (i.e., a graph with no cycles) although *CMs* are generally full of feedbacks reflecting *interesting dynamic behavior*.

In this paper, we propose an alternative approach, based on relation algebra, which takes into account the cyclic case. Precisely, our objective is to use propagation-based inference procedures in order to derive relations among arbitrary connected concepts in *CMs*. Knowing how to derive relations among arbitrary connected concepts is important for the qualitative reasoning in some domains, particularly applications such as diagnosis, relations between agents, qualitative decision making, etc. To do this, we need to define a precise semantics interpretation of qualitative causality. In this paper, we give a semantic interpretation based on relation algebra.

2 Classical Theory of Causal Maps

Usually, causal links between two concepts v_i and v_j can have one of the eight values indicated in Table 1. The eight types of causal relations are represented by sets of the three causal relations, $+$, $-$ and 0 [1],[9]. Specifically, $\oplus = 0 \cup +$ (i.e., $\{0, +\}$); $\ominus = 0 \cup -$ (i.e., $\{0, -\}$); $\pm = + \cup -$ (i.e., $\{+, -\}$); $? = 0 \cup + \cup -$ (i.e., $\{-, 0, +\}$); $a = x \cap y$ with $x, y \in \{+, 0, -\} \wedge x \neq y$. As we see, a denotes the conflicting assertions about the same link and its set value is $\{\}$.

Table1: Causal Links in a Causal Map

Relations	Descriptions
$v_i \xrightarrow{+} v_j$	v_i facilitates, helps, promotes, $\ldots v_j$
$v_i \xrightarrow{-} v_j$	v_i hinders, hurts, prevents, $\ldots v_j$
$v_i \xrightarrow{0} v_j$	v_i has no effect on, is neutral to, $\ldots v_j$
$v_i \xrightarrow{\oplus} v_j$	v_i does not retard, does not hurt, $\ldots v_j$
$v_i \xrightarrow{\ominus} v_j$	v_i does not promote, does not help, $\ldots v_j$
$v_i \xrightarrow{\pm} v_j$	v_i affects in some non-zero way v_j
$v_i \xrightarrow{?} v_j$	$+$, $-$, and 0 can exist between v_i and v_j.
$v_i \xrightarrow{a} v_j$	Conflicting assertions about the same relation have been made, this relation is called *ambivalent*.

Researchers have given some informal rules to determine effect of one concept on another in a serie-parallel combination. In a serie combination, on establish the *indirect effect*, that is, the result of combining direct effects of relationships that are in sequence. For instance, from $v_i \xrightarrow{+} v_j \xrightarrow{+} v_k$, there is an indirect effect $v_i \xrightarrow{+} v_k$. Usually, this operation is called "multiplication" ($*$) and its rules are as follows [9]:

$$+ * y = y \text{ if } y \in R, \qquad (1)$$
$$0 * y = 0 \text{ if } y \in R, \qquad (2)$$
$$a * y = a \text{ if } y \in R - \{0\}, (3)$$
$$- * - = +, \qquad (4)$$
$$* \text{ distributes over } \cup \qquad (5)$$
$$x * y = y * x, \text{ if } x, y \in R. \quad (6)$$

These six rules seem to be reasonable. In the case of parallel combination on determine the *total effect* of v_i on variable v_j which is the sum of the indirect effects of all the paths and cycles from v_i to v_j. Usually, the rules governing the sum ($|$) are the following [9]:

$$0|y = y \text{ if } y \in R, \qquad (7)$$
$$a|y = a \text{ if } y \in R - \{0\}, (8)$$
$$x|x = x \text{ if } x \in \{+, -\}, (9)$$
$$+|- = ?, \qquad (10)$$
$$| \text{ distributes over } \cup \qquad (11)$$
$$x|y = y|x \quad x, y \in R. \qquad (12)$$

These rules also seem to be reasonable except rules (8) and (10). We will explain why latter.

The operators $*$ and $|$ can be lifted to matrices. Assume that V and W are square matrices of size n. Addition and multiplication of matrices are defined as follows:

$$(V|W)_{ij} = (V)_{ij}|(W)_{ij}, \qquad (13)$$
$$(V * W)_{ij} = (V_{i1} * W_{1j})| \cdots |(V_{in} * W_{nj}) (14)$$

The nth *power* of a square matrix V, for $n > 0$, is then naturally defined by $V^1 := V$ and $V^n := V * V^{n-1}$.

In these conditions, the *total effect matrix* V_t is the matrix that has as its ij^{th} entry the total effect of v_i on v_j. That is, $V_t = V|V^2|V^3|\ldots$. It is easy to check that the sum operator is $\subseteq$-monotonic. This implies that there is a k such that

$$V_t = V|V^2|\cdots|V^k \qquad (15)$$

In summary, we note that the classical view of causal maps, is an intuitive view with ad-hoc rules to calculate direct and indirect effects. Furthermore, there is no a precise meaning of the primitive concepts, neither a sound formal treatment of relations between concepts. These considerations brought us to develop the formal model presented in the next section.

3 A Relational Model of Causal Maps

3.1 Relations in General

Intuitively, a relation indicates a connection between two or more things. Formally, a relation R on a set F is a subset of the cartesian product $F \times F$. Elements $x, y \in F$ are said to be in relation R if $(x, y) \in R$.

We are using the usual symbols $(\vee, \wedge), (\cup, \cap)$, and $(\sqcup, \sqcap)$ for the two binary Boolean operations on truth values, subsets and relations, respectively. $\vee$ and $\wedge$ are the *conjunction* and *disjunction* for truth values. $\cup$ and $\cap$ are *union* and *intersection* of two sets. Finally, $\sqcup$ and $\sqcap$ are *union* and *intersection* of relations. Other symbols used in this text are: $\Longrightarrow$ consequence; $\Longleftrightarrow$ metalanguage equivalence; $:\Longleftrightarrow$ metalanguage definition, $:=$ definitional equality; $\rightarrow$ "if–then" in propositional logic.

Notice that relations are sets, and consequently we can consider their intersection, union, complement, and inclusion. What follows is a definition of some of the usual operations on relations.

Definition 1 Let $R, S \subseteq F \times F$ and let S be a set of relations on F. The usual operations on relations are:

1. union $R \sqcup S := \{(x,y) \mid (x,y) \in R \vee (x,y) \in S\}$,
2. intersection
   $R \sqcap S := \{(x,y) \mid (x,y) \in R \wedge (x,y) \in S\}$,
3. complement $\overline{R} := \{(x,y) \mid (x,y) \notin R\}$,
4. product $R \circ S := \{(x,z) \mid \exists y \in F : (x,y) \in R \wedge (y,z) \in S\}$,
5. transposition $R^\top := \{(x,y) \mid (y,x) \in R\}$,
6. inclusion
   $R \subseteq S :\Longleftrightarrow \forall x, y : [(x,y) \in R \rightarrow (x,y) \in S]$,
7. identity $I := \{(x,y \mid x = y\} \subseteq F \times F$. •

Priority of operations: The unary operations $(^\top, ^-)$ are performed first, followed by the binary relation operation $(\circ)$, and finally by the binary operations $(\sqcup, \sqcap)$.

Sometimes and for convenience, we will simply write RS for the product $R \circ S$, and $R^2 (= RR)$, $R^3 (= RRR)$, ... for the powers of R.

A finite relation R can be represented by a Boolean matrix, using the convention $R_{xy} = 1 \Longleftrightarrow (x,y) \in R$ and $R_{xy} = 0 \Longleftrightarrow (x,y) \notin R$. The definition of the relational operators for Boolean matrices follows: we use $\wedge$ and $\vee$ as operators on the set $\{0,1\}$, considered as a set of truth values in the usual way.

$$(V \sqcup V')_{ik} := V_{ik} \vee V'_{ik}, \qquad (\overline{V})_{ik} := \neg V_{ik} \text{ (negation)},$$
$$(V \circ V')_{ik} := \bigvee_{j=1}^{n} V_{ij} \wedge V'_{jk}, \ (V \sqcap V')_{ik} := V_{ik} \wedge V'_{ik},$$
$$(V^\top)_{ik} := V_{ki}, \qquad\qquad (16)$$

Thus, for example, if $F = \{a, b\}$, we have

$$O = \begin{array}{c} \\ a \\ b \end{array}\!\!\begin{array}{cc} a & b \\ \begin{pmatrix} 0 & 0 \\ 0 & 0 \end{pmatrix} \end{array}, \quad L = \begin{array}{c} \\ a \\ b \end{array}\!\!\begin{array}{cc} a & b \\ \begin{pmatrix} 1 & 1 \\ 1 & 1 \end{pmatrix} \end{array},$$

$$\begin{pmatrix} 0 & 1 \\ 1 & 1 \end{pmatrix}^\top = \begin{pmatrix} 1 & 1 \\ 1 & 0 \end{pmatrix}, \quad \begin{pmatrix} 0 & 1 \\ 1 & 1 \end{pmatrix} \circ \begin{pmatrix} 0 & 0 \\ 0 & 1 \end{pmatrix} = \begin{pmatrix} 0 & 1 \\ 0 & 1 \end{pmatrix}$$

(this example also shows that the labels of rows and colums may be explicit or implicit).

3.2 Relation Algebras

We now state concepts and results concerning relation algebras that are needed for our model.

Definition 2 A *Boolean algebra* is an algebra of the form $(B, \sqcup, \sqcap, ^-, O, L)$, with B a set of relations, which satisfies the identities [7]:

1. $(Q \sqcup R) \sqcup S = Q \sqcup (R \sqcup S)$,
2. $(Q \sqcap R) \sqcap S = Q \sqcap (R \sqcap S)$,
3. $(Q \sqcap R) \sqcup S = (Q \sqcup S) \sqcap (R \sqcup S)$,
4. $(Q \sqcup R) \sqcap S = (Q \sqcap S) \sqcup (R \sqcap S)$,
5. $R \sqcup S = S \sqcup R$,   6. $R \sqcap S = S \sqcap R$,
7. $(Q \sqcap R) \sqcup Q = Q$, 8. $(Q \sqcup R) \sqcap Q = Q$,
9. $R \sqcup \overline{R} = L$,   10. $R \sqcap \overline{R} = O$,
11. $R \sqcup R = R$,   12. $R \sqcap R = R$,
13. $R \sqcup O = R$,   14. $R \sqcap O = O$,
15. $R \sqcup L = L$,   16. $R \sqcap L = R$,
17. $\overline{\overline{R}} = R$,   18. $\overline{R \sqcap S} = \overline{R} \sqcup \overline{S}$,
19. $\overline{R \sqcup S} = \overline{R} \sqcap \overline{S}$.

The partial ordering of a Boolean algebra is defined thus: $R \subseteq S \iff R \sqcap S = R$.

Definition 3 $\mathcal{R}$ is a *relation algebra* iff

$$\mathcal{R} := (U, \sqcup, \sqcap, ^-, O, L, \circ, ^\top, I),$$

where $(U, \sqcup, \sqcap, ^-, O, L)$ is a Boolean algebra (called the *reduct* of $\mathcal{R}$), $\circ$ is a binary operation, $^\top$ is a unary operation, $I \in U$, and the following identities hold:

1) $(Q \circ R) \circ S = Q \circ (R \circ S)$,
2) $(Q \sqcup R) \circ S = Q \circ S \sqcup R \circ S$,
3) $R \circ I = R = I \circ R$,   4) $R^{\top^\top} = R$,
5) $(R \sqcup S)^\top = R^\top \sqcup S^\top$,   6) $(R \circ S)^\top = S^\top \circ R^\top$,
7) $R^\top \circ \overline{R \circ S} \sqcap S = O$.

We refer to L as the *Boolean unit* of $\mathcal{R}$, and to I as the *identity element* of $\mathcal{R}$.

Schmidt and Ströhlein (1993) mention that the set of all $n \times n$ matrices with coefficients from a homogeneous relation algebra again form a relation algebra, with the relational operators on these matrices defined as follows:

$$(V \sqcup V')_{ik} := V_{ik} \sqcup V'_{ik}, \quad (\overline{V})_{ik} := \overline{V_{ik}},$$
$$(V \circ V')_{ik} := \bigsqcup_{j=1}^{n} V_{ij} \circ V'_{jk}. \; (V \sqcap V')_{ik} := V_{ik} \sqcap V'_{ik},$$
$$(V^\top)_{ik} := (V_{ki})^\top, \tag{17}$$

Thus, in the same manner than a valency matrix can be associated to a causal map, one can associate to a relational matrix a graph with arrows labeled by relations. Thus, if we had relations modeling the classical causal relations

$(+, -, \ominus,$ etc.), and relational operations modeling the operations on classical causal relations $(\sqcup, \sqcap, |, *)$, we would have a *relational model* of *CMs*. This model is now presented.

3.3 The Relation Algebra of Causal Maps

Let $\Delta := \{-1, 0, 1\}$. Numbers in Δ are intended to represent changes (variations) in a concept variable, with $-1, 0, 1$ denoting decrease, stability and increase, respectively. How these variations are measured and what exactly is varying does not concern us here; it could be, e.g., the utility of a variable, an amount of something, etc. Next, we define the relations $+, 0, -$ on the set Δ. These are under matrix representation:

$$+ := \begin{array}{c} \\ 1 \\ 0 \\ -1 \end{array} \begin{array}{ccc} 1 & 0 & -1 \\ \begin{pmatrix} 1 & 0 & 0 \\ 0 & 1 & 0 \\ 0 & 0 & 1 \end{pmatrix} \end{array} \quad 0 := \begin{array}{c} \\ 1 \\ 0 \\ -1 \end{array} \begin{array}{ccc} 1 & 0 & -1 \\ \begin{pmatrix} 0 & 1 & 0 \\ 0 & 1 & 0 \\ 0 & 1 & 0 \end{pmatrix} \end{array} \quad - := \begin{array}{c} \\ 1 \\ 0 \\ -1 \end{array} \begin{array}{ccc} 1 & 0 & -1 \\ \begin{pmatrix} 0 & 0 & 1 \\ 0 & 1 & 0 \\ 1 & 0 & 0 \end{pmatrix} \end{array}$$

Recall that these relations are used to label arrows of a relational causal map, thus linking cause variables to effect variables. Consider relation $+$. It is interpreted as follows: an increase in the cause variable causes an increase in the effect variable, a decrease in the cause variable causes a decrease in the effect variable, and stability of the cause variable promotes stability of the effect variable (note that $+$ is just the identity relation and could be written I). Relation 0 says that the cause variable promotes stability of the effect variable, no matter how it changes. Relation $-$ is interpreted similarly.

We use the primary relations $+, -$ and 0 to define $\oplus, \ominus, \pm, ?$ and $!$.

$\oplus := 0 \sqcup +, \quad \ominus := 0 \sqcup -, \quad \pm := + \sqcup -,$

$! := + \sqcap -, ? := + \sqcup - \sqcup 0.$ •

Before discussing further the interpretation of the various relations (in particular $O, 0$ and $!$), we present the tables showing the result of the application of the relational operators $\sqcup, \sqcap, \circ$ to the above relations. These tables are constructed by using Equation (??). Thus, for instance, it is easy to verify that $- \circ - = +$ by multiplying the matrix representing $-$ by itself.

So far, we have defined and interpreted all our relations $R \in S$. Now, we can give rules for $\sqcup, \circ,$ and $\sqcap$. These rules are given by Tables 2, 3 and 4. These tables are constructed by using equation (17). Thus for instance, it easy to verify that $- \circ - = +$ by multiplying the matrices representing $-$.

The relational composition operation $(\circ)$ corresponds to the multiplication operation $(|)$ of classical causal maps. Comparing Table 3 and rules $(7) - (12)$, we see that, with the exception of the classical a and the relational $!$, there is an exact correspondence. Also, the classical 0 corresponds to both the relational O and the relational 0. Although the status of the classical a is not clear, the fact that it is interpreted by the empty set leads us to compare it to the relation O; the match is not too bad.

Table 2: Table for ⊔

⊔	O	0	+	−	⊕	⊖	±	!	?
O	O	0	+	−	⊕	⊖	±	!	?
0	0	0	⊕	⊖	⊕	⊖	?	0	?
+	+	⊕	+	±	⊕	?	±	+	?
−	−	⊖	±	−	?	⊖	±	−	?
⊕	⊕	⊕	⊕	?	⊕	?	?	⊕	?
⊖	⊖	⊖	?	⊖	?	⊖	?	⊖	?
±	±	?	±	±	?	?	±	±	?
!	!	0	+	−	⊕	⊖	±	!	?
?	?	?	?	?	?	?	?	?	?

Table 3: Table for ∘

∘	O	0	+	−	⊕	⊖	±	!	?
O	O	O	O	O	O	O	O	O	O
0	O	0	0	0	0	0	0	0	0
+	O	0	+	−	⊕	⊖	±	!	?
−	O	0	−	+	⊖	⊕	±	!	?
⊕	O	0	⊕	⊖	⊕	⊖	?	0	?
⊖	O	0	⊖	⊕	⊖	⊕	?	0	?
±	O	0	±	±	?	?	±	!	?
!	O	!	!	!	!	!	!	!	!
?	O	0	?	?	?	?	?	0	?

Table 4: Table for ⊓

⊓	O	0	+	−	⊕	⊖	±	!	?
O	O	O	O	O	O	O	O	O	O
0	O	0	!	!	0	0	!	!	0
+	O	!	+	!	+	!	+	!	+
−	O	!	!	−	!	−	−	!	−
⊕	O	0	+	!	⊕	0	+	!	⊕
⊖	O	0	!	−	0	⊖	−	!	⊖
±	O	!	+	−	+	−	±	!	±
a	O	!	!	!	!	!	!	!	!
?	O	0	+	−	⊕	⊖	±	!	?

The relational union operation (⊔) has similarities with both classical union (∪) and classical sum (|). For example, assuming that the classical 0 corresponds to the relational 0, we have the classical law $0 \cup + = \oplus$ and the relational law $0 \sqcup + = \oplus$. Assuming that the classical 0 corresponds to the relational O, we have the classical law $+|0 = +$ and the relational law $+ \sqcup O = +$. The most conspicuous divergence concerns the classical a. The law $a|y = a$ means that it is not possible to weaken any contradiction; contradictions propagate in the calculation of the total effect, because of law (8). In fact, Nakamura *et al.* [9] find it difficult to accept $a|y = a$. In our case, no relation plays the role of a.

In our approach, the empty relation O is used to denote "unrelatedness" or "ambivalence". Asserting that there is no relationship between a cause variable and an effect variable is just the same as making a contradictory assertion about this relationship.

Note that we distinguish between the two relationships O and 0 since, in our model, 0 indicates that the relationship between two concepts *exists* and is "neutral" Also, the relation $! = + \sqcap - = + \sqcap 0 = - \sqcap 0$ is partially ambivalent (somewhat less than O); it is a weak ambivalent relation.

There are at least two ways to obtain a relation algebra $\mathcal{A} = (A, \sqcup, \sqcap, \bar{\ }, O, L, p\circ, {}^{\top}, +)$ from the set of relations $\{+, 0, -\}$. One way is to take for A the full set of relations over the set $\Delta = \{n, z, p\}$ (the full set of 3×3 matrices). This gives $2^9 = 512$ relations. The other way is to take for A the closure of $\{+, 0, -\}$ under the five relational operations; the result is a set of 32 relations, whose atoms (minimal non-O relations) are

$$\begin{pmatrix} 1 & 0 & 0 \\ 0 & 0 & 0 \\ 0 & 0 & 1 \end{pmatrix} \quad \begin{pmatrix} 0 & 1 & 0 \\ 0 & 0 & 0 \\ 0 & 1 & 0 \end{pmatrix} \quad \begin{pmatrix} 0 & 0 & 1 \\ 0 & 0 & 0 \\ 1 & 0 & 0 \end{pmatrix}$$

$$\begin{pmatrix} 0 & 0 & 0 \\ 1 & 0 & 1 \\ 0 & 0 & 0 \end{pmatrix} \quad \begin{pmatrix} 0 & 0 & 0 \\ 0 & 1 & 0 \\ 0 & 0 & 0 \end{pmatrix}$$

(these could be taken as primitive relations instead of $+, 0, -$).

A *CM* can then be built using relations in A to label the arrows. Alternatively, one can construct the associated (relational) valency matrix V. Indirect effects of length k are given by the k-th power of V, V^k. Indirect effects are added by means of $\sqcup$. The total effect matrix is the transitive closure of V, which is $V^+ := \bigsqcup_{k>0} V^k$; this matrix corresponds to the matrix V_t of previous expression (15) (we use V^+ rather than V_t because it is the standard notation for transitive closure). A $n \times n$ matrix whose entries are 3×3 matrices is a $3n \times 3n$ matrix. This implies that $V^+ = \bigcup_{k=0}^{3n-1} V^k$ (see [12]). It also means that V^+ can be computed in $O((3n)^3) = O(n^3)$ steps using the Roy-Warshall algorithm; better algorithms also exist [12]. Furthermore, large systems with few interconnections may use space-efficient representations (the implementation need not use the matrix view). Hence the approach developed here can be used beyond a few agents and a few concepts.

4 Discussion

CMs were originally proposed to capture the qualitative causal relationships that exist between concepts in a structure of decision. Some *intuitive* inference mechanisms, based on reasoning from cause to effect, were proposed [1],[9],[2]. In this paper, we have defined a precise semantics interpretation of qualitative causality in terms of relation algebra, to justify these intuitive inference mechanisms. Indeed, as discussed in the previous subsection, our model justifies most of the rules proposed by Nakumara *et al.* As we have pointed out, the main difference concerns ambivalence. Another difference is our law $+ \sqcup - = \pm$ versus $+|- = ?$. According to [9], $+|- = ?$ says that the sum of $+$ and $-$ depends on which of the indirect effects $+$ or $-$ is stronger; the rule expresses that the total effect is plus $(+)$ if the indirect effect $+$ is stronger than the indirect effect $-$, is minus $(-)$ if $+$ is weaker than $-$, and is zero (0) if $+$ is as strong as $-$. It may be argued, however, that in a qualitative approach it is difficult to know how a relation can be as strong or stronger than another. It seems more reasonable to retain $+$ and $-$ for further reasoning. Our model takes this point of view into account by having $+ \sqcup - = \pm$.

Our model also takes into account nonreversible causation, contrary to classical models of causal maps. An example of nonreversible causation is "an increase in v_i causes an increase in v_j, but a decrease in v_i does not cause a decrease in v_j". For instance, the normal interpretation of "smoking causes illnesses" involves nonreversible causation, because stopping smoking does not put out illnesses. In classical *CM* theory, only reversible causation is allowed, because, e.g., $v_i \xrightarrow{+} v_j$ is taken to mean *both* that "an increase in v_i causes an increase in v_j" *and* "a decrease in v_i causes a decrease in v_j". In our model, reversible causation can be expressed by choosing the appropriate relation among the set of 512 possible relations; for example, $\{(+1,+1),(0,0),(-1,0),(-1,+1)\}$ expresses that an increase in the cause variable causes an increase in the effect variable; it also says that a decrease in the cause variable causes anything but a decrease in the effect variable.

The $\sqcap$ operation is used to combine relations when they are asserted together. Suppose, for instance, that an agent A wants to produce a matrix V by combining the matrices V_1 and V_2 transmitted by two other agents A_1 and A_2. If A considers the information sent by A_1 and A_2 to be reliable, then she should define $V := V_1 \sqcap V_2$; the result might be that some concepts become related by ambivalent relations $(O, !)$. On the other hand, if A considers both V_1 and V_2 to be possible (e.g., they represent a range of opinions), then she should define $V := V_1 \sqcup V_2$; the result is fuzzier information than that of either V_1 or V_2.

We have just mentioned that many more relations can be asserted than the few causal relations of the classical theory. There are also two new operations, complementation and converse, which still have to be exploited. Complementation allows to say that the relationship between two concepts is, e.g., anything but 0 (expressed by $\overline{0}$). Converse allows talking about "backward causality" (consequence).

An important advantage of the model is that it can be easily contracted or extended, by starting with a different set Δ. Choosing $\Delta := \{-1, +1\}$ results in a smaller model. Choosing $\Delta := \{-2, -1, 0, +1, +2\}$ gives a larger model, in which finer distinctions can be made; for example, it becomes possible to say that a large increase $(+2)$ in the cause variable causes a large decrease (-2) in the effect variable.

5 Implementation and Application to Multiagent Environments

The crisp causal reasoning model presented in this paper has been implemented in a system used as a computational tool supporting the relational manipulations. This tool is called $\mathcal{SR} \circ \Psi lab$ and is built over the Ψlab software[1], a freeware package developed by INRIA, France. This tool enables users 1) to edit matrices about relations, 2) store matrices in the working memory, 3) execute algebraic operations on matrices and 4) calculate the total effect matrix $V^+ := \bigsqcup_{k>0} V^k$ as precised in Section 3. Any session begins by presenting a matrix called "working copy" which is displayed on the screen for editing. Using this matrix allows users to represent relations like $+$, $-$, etc. A whole set of matrices can be kept in the working session to allow any combination of relations.

With this tool, we are investigating the causal reasoning in multiagent environments [3]. Causal reasoning is important in multiagent environments because it allows to model interrelationships or causalities among a set of individual and social concepts. This provides a foundation to 1) test a model about the prediction of how agents will respond to expected (or not) events; 2) explain how agents have done specific actions; 3) make a decision in a distributed environment; 4) analyze and compare the agents' causal representations. All these aspects are important for coordination, conflict solving and the emergence of cooperation between agents.

6 Conclusion and Future Work

We have proposed a *CM* formulation for relationships between agents' beliefs. With this formulation, based on relation algebra, we have particularly: (1) defined a precise semantics interpretation of qualitative causalities; (2) justified the classical intuitive inference mechanisms based on reasoning from cause to effect; (3) provided users with formulas to determine certain quantitative and qualitative features of *CMs*.

Here are many directions in which the proposal made here can be extended.

- The full possibilities of relation algebra have yet to be exploited. In particular, it allows equation solving, which would certainly be useful.
- Another option is to study "fuzzy relations" between agents' concepts [6, 15]. Our approach might be extended in this direction to take into account many degrees and vague degrees of influence between agents such as: none, very little, sometimes, a lot, usually, more or less, etc.
- Tools, must be built to support the relational manipulations and the reasoning process. In fact, the first version of this type of tools is available yet. It has built over the Ψlab software, a freeware package developed by INRIA, France.

---

[1] This software can be obtained by anonymous ftp from "ftp.inria.fr:/INRIA/Scilab".

References

1. Axelrod, A. editor: Structure of Decision: The Cognitive Maps of Political Elites. Princeton University Press (1976)
2. Buede, D. M. and Ferrell, D. Convergence in problem solving: A prelude to quantitative analysis. IEEE Trans. Syst., Man, Cybern. **23** (1993) 746-765
3. Chaib-draa, B. Causal Reasoning in Multiagent Systems. MAAMAW'97–Agents and Multiagent Systems. M. Boman (ed.), LNAI, Springer–Verlag (1997)
4. Eden, C. J. and Sims, D. Thinking in organizations. Macmillan, London (1979)
5. Kelly, G. A. The Psychology of Personal Constructs. New:Norton (1955)
6. Kosko, B. Neural Networks and Fuzzy Systems. Prentice Hall (1992)
7. Ladkin, L. B. and Maddux, R. D. On binary constraint problems. Jour. of ACM. **41(3)** (1994) 435–469
8. Levi, A. and Tetlock, P. E. A cognitive analysis of Japan's 1941 decision for war. Journ. of Conflict Resolution. **24** (1980) 195-211
9. Nakumara, K., Iwai, S. and Sawaragi. T. Decision support using causation knowledge base. IEEE Trans. Syst., Man, Cybern. **12** (1982) 765-777.
10. Park, K. S. and Kim, S. H. Fuzzy cognitive maps considering time relationships. Int. J. Human-Computer Studies. **42** (1995) 157-168
11. Ross, L. L. and Hall, R. I. Influence diagrams and organizational power. Admin. Sci. Q. **25** (1980) 57-71
12. Schmidt, G. and Ströhlein, T. Relations and Graphs. Monog. on Theor. Comput. Science, Springer-Verlag, Berlin (1993)
13. Smithin, T. and Sims, D. Ubi Caritas?—Modeling beliefs about charities. Eur. J. Opl Res. **10** (1982) 273-243
14. Wellman, M. P. Inference in cognitive maps. Math. and Comp. in Simul. **36** (1994) 1-12
15. Zhang, W. R., Chen, S. S. and King, R. S. A cognitive map based approach to the coordination of distributed cooperative agents. IEEE Trans. Syst., Man, Cybern. **22(1)** (1992) 103-114

Distance Constraint Arrays:
A Model for Reasoning on Intervals with
Qualitative and Quantitative Distances

Steffen Staab and Udo Hahn

Computational Linguistics Lab, Freiburg University
Werthmannplatz 1, D-79085 Freiburg, Germany
http://www.coling.uni-freiburg.de

Abstract. We outline a model of one-dimensional reasoning on interval relations with quantitative and qualitative distances. At the core of this model lie constraints on interval boundaries, partial ordering and subsumption relations on interval relations and interval boundary constraints, and the transformation of interval relations to interval boundary constraints and vice versa. By way of subsumption and approximation criteria on distance constraint arrays, a significant level of conceptual abstraction from the underlying interval boundary constraints is realized when new relations are inferred.

1 Introduction

When humans reason about temporal or spatial relations or even degree expressions in evaluative discourse (*"tall"*, *"fast"*, etc.), they are highly proficient at seamlessly integrating different types of scalar information. We here distinguish three types, *viz.* ordinal relations, e.g., the relations in the point algebra [14] or in Allen's calculus [1], quantitative relations, such as in the framework given by Dechter, Meiri & Pearl [5], and relations with qualitative distances, e.g., the mechanism provided by Clementini, Di Felice & Hernández [3,8]. Unfortunately, formal models for temporal reasoning — or one-dimensional reasoning, in general — have so far not integrated all three types of knowledge. In this paper, we develop a formal framework which tries to fill this gap.

In order to illustrate the need for such an integration consider example (1):

(1)   a. Hein's flight from Frankfurt to New York takes 8 hours.

   b. John's plane from Chicago to New York will start one hour after Hein's.

   c. John's flight will be rather short.

If you planned to meet John and Hein at their arrivals, you would have to integrate quantitative (1a,b) and qualitative information (1c) in order to draw a conclusion such as (2).

(2) John will reach New York before Hein.

This paper describes how previous research on ordinal relations [1, 14], quantitative temporal distances [2, 5] and work on qualitative spatial distances [3, 8] can be integrated in a single, homogeneous framework to allow for a tight coupling between ordinal, quantitative and qualitative knowledge. Moreover, previous proposals support only reasoning mechanisms on fairly low-level relations. What is missing then are adequate means to adjust the level of inferences to be made according to the needs of various levels of abstraction. For instance, given information like "*the end of X is clearly after the start of Y and the start of X is clearly before the end of Y*", we aim at interval relations that convey high level abstractions, such as "*X is clearly contemporary with Y*". This distinction between fine-grained and coarser types of knowledge is often discussed in terms of different *granularities* of knowledge [9].

In Section 2 we introduce *distance constraint arrays* as representation structures for interval relations with distances. A crucial point of this approach is the easy conversion between the distance constraints of these arrays and higher-level interval relations. Reasoning by composition on distance constraints is then described in Section 3. Whereas in Section 2 we are able to abstract from the kinds of distances involved, these will become very important for the definition of the composition rules. Finally, in Section 4, we turn to the overall reasoning scheme and elaborate example (1) in detail in order to illustrate our approach.

2 Representation by Interval Boundary Constraints

In order to represent and reason with ordinal knowledge [1, 14], quantitative distances [2, 5] and qualitative distances [3, 8], we aim at the combination of two sorts of requirements. On the one hand, we use relations on intervals that allow for a high degree of abstraction in order to express the adequate representation level for temporal and spatial relations. On the other hand, we integrate knowledge about distances into constraints between the boundaries of intervals in order to provide a homogeneous representation format for a large variety of expressions.

2.1 Distance Constraints

It has often been noted (e.g., [14, 2]) that Allen's primitive relations on intervals [1] can also be represented by conjunctions of constraints expressed by the operators ">" and "$\geq$" on the boundaries of the intervals. We here follow this line of research, but elaborate on the type of constraints that may hold between two interval boundaries. Instead of the sort of common constraints just mentioned we will here incorporate formal constructs for boundaries the semantics of which read as "*a boundary is at least/more than a distance x after another boundary*" or "*a boundary is at most/less than a distance x before another boundary*".

We here assume a set of time points which are totally ordered. An interval consists of an upper and a lower bound. The distances x are members of a set D from the distance structure $\mathcal{D}^*$. We here commit ourselves to only few restrictions, because we want to consider abstractions in this section which are independent from the particular type of distances involved. In Section 3, we spell out some possibilities for concrete distance structures in detail.

Definition 1 (Distance Structure). A distance structure $\mathcal{D}^*$ is a triple $(D, >_{|D}, 0)$. It consists of a set D of elements, which are strictly partially ordered by $>_{|D}$, and a least element $0 \in D$. The elements of D are called distances.

Given such a structure $\mathcal{D}^*$ we may define distance constraints as follows:

Definition 2 (Distance Constraints). For all $x \in D$: "$\succ_x$", "$\succeq_x$", "$\succ_{-x}$", "$\succeq_{-x}$" and "$\top$" are distance constraints.

These constraints can be characterized as follows: $\top$ denotes a non-restricting constraint which is weaker than all the others. $a \succeq_x b$ means that a is later[1] than b and the interval in between has at least the length x (cf. Fig. 1). $a \succ_x b$ is similar but requires for the temporal distance between a and b to be strictly larger than x.

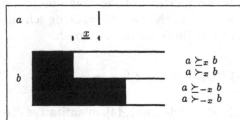

$a \succeq_x b$	
$a \succ_x b$	
$a \succeq_{-x} b$	
$a \succ_{-x} b$	

Assuming $x \in D$, the set of distances in the distance structure $\mathcal{D}^*$, the grey color indicates the regions to which b is restricted with respect to a by the constraints $\succeq_x$ and $\succ_x$ ($\succeq_{-x}$ and $\succ_{-x}$, respectively). In contrast to $\succ$, $\succeq$ allows b to lie on the borderline, too.

Fig. 1. Distance Constraints

The occurrence of "$-$" in the index of such a constraint, e.g., $a \succeq_{-x} b$, indicates a slightly different semantics, namely that a is either before b with at most the distance x between a and b or a is after b. A corresponding proposition holds for $a \succ_{-x} b$. Since "$-$" results in weaker constraints and since we want to compare the strengths of constraints on the basis of their indices, "$-$" is introduced as an operator that is used to extend $\mathcal{D}^*$ to $\bar{\mathcal{D}}^*$:

Definition 3 (Operator "$-$"). $-$ is a bijective function that maps $\bar{D} := D \cup \{-x | x \in D\}$ onto itself such that $-0 = 0$ and $x \in D \setminus \{0\} \Leftrightarrow -x \in \bar{D} \setminus D$.

Definition 4 (Extended Distance Structure). The extended distance structure $\bar{\mathcal{D}}^*$ is the quadruple $(\bar{D}, >, 0, -)$ derived from $\mathcal{D}^*$ (as defined in Def. 1) by extending D to $\bar{D} := D \cup \{-x | x \in D\}$ and $>_{|D}$ to $>$ and using 0 and "$-$" (as defined in Def. 3). Thereby, the strict partial ordering $>$ on $\bar{D}$ is defined as follows: $(1), \forall x \in D, y \in \bar{D} \setminus D : x > y, (2), \forall x, y \in D : x >_{|D} y \Leftrightarrow x > y$, and, $(3), \forall x, y \in \bar{D} : x > y \Leftrightarrow -y > -x$.

---

[1] Whenever we use a temporal expression, it is also valid for corresponding spatial and degree expressions and the reasoning on these expressions.

Given this basic definition of $\bar{\mathcal{D}}^*$, axioms can be stated (cf. Table 1) that describe how boundaries are related to itself (reflexivity), what constraints are contradictory (contradiction), and how constraints can be compared (subsumption). In this list of axioms those for composition are still missing. They will be considered in Section 3, since they require further assumptions concerning the respective distance structure from which we abstract in this section. Irrespective of the distance structure, $\succ_0$ and $\succeq_0$ will be required to define a partial ordering. To facilitate further descriptions, we also use several notational shortcuts (cf. Table 2).

$\forall a, b \in B$, the set of time points, $\forall x, y \in \bar{D}$:	
1. $x \leq 0 \Rightarrow (a \succeq_x a)$	(reflexivity 1)
2. $x < 0 \Rightarrow (a \succ_x a)$	(reflexivity 2)
3. $x > 0 \Rightarrow (a \succeq_x a \Rightarrow \bot)$	(contradiction 1)
4. $x \geq 0 \Rightarrow (a \succ_x a \Rightarrow \bot)$	(contradiction 2)
5. $(a \succ_x b \wedge a \succeq_x b) \Leftrightarrow a \succ_x b$	(subsumption 1)
6. $(a \succeq_x b \wedge a \succeq_y b) \Leftrightarrow a \succeq_{\max(x,y)} b$	(subsumption 2)
7. $(a \succ_x b \wedge a \succ_y b) \Leftrightarrow a \succ_{\max(x,y)} b$	(subsumption 3)

$\forall a, b \in B, \forall x \in \bar{D}$:
A. $a \prec_x b :\Leftrightarrow b \succ_x a$
B. $a \preceq_x b :\Leftrightarrow b \succeq_x a$
C. $a \doteq_x b :\Leftrightarrow a \succeq_{-x} b \wedge b \succeq_{-x} a$
D. $a \doteq_x b :\Leftrightarrow a \succ_{-x} b \wedge b \succ_{-x} a$

Table 1. Axioms for Constraints on Time Points Involving Distances

Table 2. Logical Equivalences for Notational Shortcuts

All conjunctions of constraints that may hold between two intervals can now be uniquely described in terms of "distance constraint arrays".[2]

Definition 5 (Distance Constraint Array). A distance constraint array for two intervals, X and Y, is an array $[c_1, \ldots, c_{12}]$ of 12 distance constraints (cf. Def. 2). These constraints describe all possible restrictions between the beginnings (X_b, Y_b) and endings (X_e, Y_e) of these intervals in the following ordering:
$X_b c_1 Y_b \wedge Y_b c_2 X_b \wedge X_b c_3 Y_e \wedge Y_e c_4 X_b \wedge X_e c_5 Y_b \wedge Y_b c_6 X_e \wedge X_e c_7 Y_e \wedge Y_e c_8 X_e \wedge X_e c_9 X_b \wedge Y_e c_{10} Y_b \wedge X_b c_{11} X_e \wedge Y_b c_{12} Y_e$.

Furthermore, we also allow for disjunctions of distance constraint arrays to represent non-neighboring ambiguities. For instance, "X is disjoint of Y" is represented by a disjunction of constraint vectors,

$$X\{[\top, \top, \succ_0, \top, \ldots], [\top, \top, \top, \top, \top, \succ_0, \top, \ldots]\}Y,$$

while neighboring alternatives like "X precedes or meets or overlaps Y" require only a single distance constraint array, e.g.,

$$X\{[\top, \succ_0, \top, \top, \top, \top, \top, \succ_0, \top \ldots]\}Y.$$

---

[2] Some distance constraint arrays require special consideration, since they are always true (e.g., when they only require that $X_e \succ_0 X_b$), or since they are always invalid (e.g., when they require that $X_b \succ_0 X_e$). However, for the structural arguments made here, they do not pose any problems.

2.2 Converting between Interval Boundary Constraints and Interval Relations

Constraints on interval boundaries are on a rather low level of abstraction and, therefore, Allen's approach is usually preferred over boundary constraint representations. This is true, even though the conversion between common qualitative boundary constraints $(>, \geq)$ and common qualitative interval relations is so trivial (cf., e.g., [7]) that choosing any of the two approaches hardly makes a difference. In contradistinction, as far as reasoning with distances is concerned, it is almost precluded to encode all the possibly ensueing interval relations, as it has been done for interval relations without distances. This motivates our efforts in representing interval relations by boundary constraints with distances. Nevertheless, abstractions are entirely necessary to deal with interval relations in settings such as natural language understanding, planning systems, or geographic information systems.

From Interval Relations to Boundary Constraints. While for qualitative interval relations a widely spread set of standard relations already exist (e.g., those given by Allen), this is not the case for interval relations with distances. We have the impression that the appropriateness of such interval relations is strongly influenced by the underlying domain and, thus, cannot be fully determined in advance. However, some exemplary, general-purpose interval relations with distances are given together with their abbreviating labels in Tables 3 and 4 in term of interval boundary constraints. The binary relations allow to state propositions about interval lengths (cf. Table 3), while the ternary relations describe distance constraints between two intervals (cf. Table 4). Thus, conversion from interval relations to boundary constraints boils down to a simple table lookup.

$\forall X \in I$, the set of intervals, X_b being the lower and X_e being the upper boundary of X, and $\forall n \in D$:		
Relation	Label	Constraints
is at most n long[3]	$maxlo_n$	$X_b \succeq_{-n} X_e$
is at least n long	$minlo_n$	$X_e \succeq_n X_b$
is n long	$length_n$	$X_e \succeq_n X_b \wedge X_b \succeq_{-n} X_e$

Table 3. Binary Interval Relations Including Length Constraints

From Boundary Constraints to Interval Relations. Converting conjoined constraints into interval relations cannot be done so straightforwardly. The goal of this conversion is to find a conjunction of interval relations that subsumes

---

[3] $X_b \prec_0 X_e$ need not be added, because it is entailed by the general knowledge that the beginning of an interval is before its ending. This knowledge must generally be made available.

$\forall X, Y \in I$, the set of intervals, X_b and Y_b being the lower and X_e and Y_e being the upper boundaries of X and Y, respectively, and $\forall n \in D$:		
Relation	Label	Constraints
n older	$older_n$	$X_b \preceq_n Y_b \wedge Y_b \preceq_{-n} X_b$
survives at least with n	$svmin_n$	$X_e \succeq_n Y_e$
survives, but less than n	$svless_n$	$X_e \succ_0 Y_e \wedge X_e \prec_{-n} Y_e$
precedes with more than n	$minpr_n$	$X_e \prec_n Y_b$
precedes, but less than n	$maxpr_n$	$X_e \prec_0 Y_b \wedge X_e \succ_{-n} Y_b$
head to head with a tolerance of n	hh_n	$X_b \hat{=}_n Y_b$
contemporary for more than n	$minct_n$	$X_b \prec_n Y_e \wedge X_e \succ_n Y_b$

Table 4. Ternary Interval Relations with one Parameter for Distances

all the given boundary constraints. Furthermore, these interval relations, when remapped to boundary constraints, should equal the originally given ones. In general, this is neither easily realized nor need it be useful at all. It is hard to realize, since the number of possible constraint combinations increase drastically by the additional distance parameters and, thus, require plenty of new interval relations to account for additional combinations. It may even not be useful, since such a bounty of interval relations would possibly obscure the essential distinctions to be made.

Consider, e.g., a simple domain where the only interval relation which incorporates a distance and which is available is a binary relation that describes an interval length. This allows one to infer, in principle, that one interval X is a distance d before another interval Y. If, however, no interval relation incorporating such a distance constraint is specified, an ordinal relation, e.g., *"precedes"*, would be an adequate means to approximate the boundary constraints. This need not be considered a disadvantage at all, since approximations that are valid but not necessarily complete descriptions often constitute the right level of abstraction (e.g., "Schiller died before Goethe" seems to be a reasonable abstraction for "Schiller died at least 27 years before Goethe").

Therefore, given a set of interval relations (e.g., Tables 3 and 4) and a set of boundary constraints on two intervals, we do not require the "reconverted" interval relations to equal the given boundary constraints. Instead, we just set up the requirement that they should *approximate* them as narrowly as possible. In order to define "approximation", we here introduce the concept of *"subsumption of constraint arrays"* as a core notion of our approach.[4]

Definition 6 (Subsumption of Constraint Arrays). A constraint array $[c_{1,1}, \ldots, c_{1,12}]$ subsumes another constraint array $[c_{2,1}, \ldots, c_{2,12}]$, iff for all $i \in [1, 12]$ $c_{1,i}$ subsumes $c_{2,i}$ (cf. Table 1 for subsumption axioms).

---

[4] We here handle boundary constraints on two intervals with at most one parameter and the constraints $\succ_0$ and $\succeq_0$. Interval relations with more than one parameter (and/or more constant constraints) can be defined at the cost of slightly more complicated definitions of approximation.

Subsumption of constraint arrays defines a partial ordering of a (semi-)lattice with $[\top, \ldots, \top]$ as its largest element (cf. Fig. 2).[5]

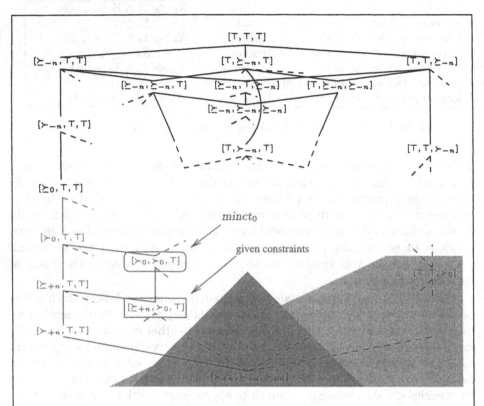

Let us assume the following order for the constraint array with at most one parameter n: $[X_e?Y_b, Y_e?X_b, X_b?X_e]$. The graph depicts three important aspects of this lattice:

1. The transitive subsumption relations between arrays (esp. in the upper part of the graph).
2. Arrays that are subsumed by contradictory constraints ($X_b \succ_0 X_e$), and which are, as a consequence, contradictory, too. They are indicated by grey regions.
3. A given constraint array is abstracted by subsuming, best-approximating interval relations. For instance, $[\succeq_{+n}, \succ_0, \top]$ is abstracted by the interval relation $minct_0$.

Fig. 2. The lattice structure of constraint combinations — a simplified version with 3 constraints.

---

[5] If we postulate an infinite distance "∞" then $[\succeq_\infty, \ldots, \succeq_\infty] = [\bot, \ldots, \bot]$ can be considered the complement to $[\succ_{-\infty}, \ldots, \succ_{-\infty}] = [\top, \ldots, \top]$ and, thus, the least element of the lattice.

Definition 7 (Best Approximation for One Parameter). Let a set of
boundary constraints on two intervals with at most one parameter n be represented by a constraint array C_1. An interval relation represented by a constraint
array C_2 with its possibly single parameter n fixed is called the best approximation for C_1, iff C_2 subsumes C_1 and there is no other interval relation with
one parameter (represented by a constraint array C_3) such that C_2 subsumes C_3
and C_3 subsumes C_1 and $C_2 \neq C_3$.[6]

This definition may yield several best-approximating interval relations, since
it is based on a partial ordering. A unique best approximation is given by the
conjunction of these interval relations.

3 Treatment of Different Types of Distances

So far, we have left out of consideration the types of distances that are allowed
in our approach. An almost trivial one is the restriction to the zero distance.
This one exactly allows to represent Allen's relations, since "$\succ_0$" and "$\succeq_0$" are
equivalent to the common relations "$>$" and "$\geq$", respectively. Much more interesting are non-trivial quantitative or qualitative distances and their combination.
Several strategies to handle them are discussed in this section.

3.1 Quantitative Distances

Quantitative distances shall here be treated equivalently to non-negative real
numbers. All the axioms and equivalence rules from Tables 1 and 2 still apply.
Furthermore, composition axioms for quantitative distances can be formulated
(cf. Table 5). These are very simple, and even though distances marked with "$-$"
embody a slightly different meaning, their composition with unmarked distances
simply boils down to addition with negative reals. For the number zero the
composition is simply equivalent to the transitivity property of "$>$" and "$\geq$".

$\forall a, b, c \in B, \forall x, y \in \bar{D}$
8. $(a \succeq_x b \ \wedge \ b \succeq_y c) \Rightarrow a \succeq_{x+y} c$ (composition 1)
9. $(a \succeq_x b \ \wedge \ b \succ_y c) \Rightarrow a \succ_{x+y} c$ (composition 2)
10. $(a \succ_x b \ \wedge \ b \succeq_y c) \Rightarrow a \succ_{x+y} c$ (composition 3)
11. $(a \succ_x b \ \wedge \ b \succ_y c) \Rightarrow a \succ_{x+y} c$ (composition 4)

Table 5. Composition Axioms for Quantitative Distances

---

[6] When the constraints in C_1 come with parameters n_i then these parameters are
appropriate candidates for the single parameter n.

3.2 Qualitative Distances

Let us now consider qualitative distances (cf. example (1c)). Basically, we adapt the composition rules stated by Clementini, Di Felice & Hernández [3, 8]. They assume a totally ordered set of qualitative distances (cf. Definition 1), *viz.* $\{\Delta_i | i \in [0, n] \wedge \forall j \in [1, n-1] : \Delta_{j+1} > \Delta_j > \Delta_0 = 0\}$ (with $\Delta_n \hat{=} \infty$). Depending on the availability of further restrictions, different composition rules are given. What is especially remarkable in this context here is that Clementini *et al.* always compute *upper* and *lower bounds*. Nevertheless, they do not directly represent these bounds. Instead they choose a disjunction of distance regions as a representation format. For some small n (i.e., few different distance regions), their representation schema is as convenient as ours. For larger numbers, however, the computational costs become unnecessarily large in their approach.

In order to demonstrate how the composition rules for qualitative distances described in [3] can be applied to our approach, we describe some of them in our notation in Table 6.[7] While the rule for the lower bound condition is straightforward, the other ones for the upper bound condition require further considerations such as made in [3]. Note that the more complicated composition rules for heterogeneous structures or the absorption rule Clementini *et al.* define can be directly translated into our approach, if the proper conditions are fulfilled. Composition for a "positive" with a "negative distance" can be derived from the rules given by Clementini *et al.* for opposite directions.

$\forall a, b, c \in B, \forall \Delta_i, \Delta_j \in D :$		
Application Conditions		**Composition Rule**
"Lower Bound" $x = \Delta_i, y = \Delta_j$		$a \succ_x b \wedge b \succ_y c$ $\Rightarrow a \succ_{\Delta_{\max(i,j)}} c$
"Upper Bound" $x = -\Delta_i, y = -\Delta_j$	"monotonicity": $\forall i \in [1, n] : \delta_{i+1} > \delta_i$	$a \succ_x b \wedge b \succ_y c$ $\Rightarrow a \succ_{-\Delta_{\min(i+j,n)}} c$
	"range restriction": $\forall i \in [1, n] : \delta_{i+1} > \Delta_i$	$a \succ_x b \wedge b \succ_y c$ $\Rightarrow a \succ_{-\Delta_{\min(\max(i,j)+1,n)}} c$

Table 6. Exemplary Composition Rules for Constraints with Qualitative Distances

Moreover, our approach allows for a partial ordering of qualitative distances. This reflects a requirement that can be traced to the use of qualitative distances in natural language expressions. These expressions often do not constitute a total ordering, but only a partial one. Consider, e.g., the expressions *"somewhat later"*, *"a little later"* and *"much later"*. The precedence between *"somewhat"* and *"little"* is not clearly drawn, while both expressions are certainly ordered with respect to *"much"*.

---

[7] We assume that $\delta_i = \Delta_i - \Delta_{i-1}$. The composition rules are applicable if the respective triggering conditions on the boundaries ("lower bound" and "upper bound"), as well as the respective structural restrictions on the distance system $\mathcal{D}^*$ ("monotonicity", "range restriction") are fulfilled. The condition names in "..." are taken from [3].

With the composition rules described so far, the derivation of conclusions relating to two distances which are not ordered with respect to each other is not supported. However, a simple scheme which is easily illustrated by the following small example allows to do exactly this. Let us assume four distances, $\Delta_1, \Delta_{2a}, \Delta_{2b}, \Delta_3$, with $\Delta_1 < \Delta_{2a} < \Delta_3$ and $\Delta_1 < \Delta_{2b} < \Delta_3$, and the knowledge $a \succ_{-\Delta_{2a}} b \wedge b \succ_{-\Delta_{2b}} c$. The subsumption axioms from Table 1 require — and therefore allow to infer — that $a \succ_{-\Delta_3} b \wedge b \succ_{-\Delta_{2b}} c$ and $a \succ_{-\Delta_{2a}} b \wedge b \succ_{-\Delta_3} c$ to which the total ordering composition rules can be applied. Depending on the circumstances, the result may be a conjunction of two non-comparable constraints on an interval boundary pair, which requires a revision of the definitions 5 and 6, respectively.

Definition 8 (Multiple Distance Constraint Array). A multiple distance constraint array for two intervals, X and Y, is an array $[s_1, \ldots, s_{12}]$ of 12 distance constraint sets s_i, where all $c_j \in s_i$ are distance constraints, such that for all $i \in [1, 12]$ no constraint $c_j \in s_i$ subsumes another one $c_k \in s_i, k \neq j$ (i.e., s_i is a minimal representation).

Definition 9 (Subsumption of Multiple Distance Constraint Arrays). A multiple distance constraint array $C_1 = [s_{1,1}, \ldots, s_{1,12}]$ subsumes another one $C_2 = [s_{2,1}, \ldots, s_{2,12}]$, iff for all $i \in [1, 12]$: $(\forall c_k \in s_{2,i} : \exists c_j \in s_{1,i} : c_j$ subsumes c_k).

Consider an array like $[\{\succ_{-\Delta_{2a}}, \succ_{-\Delta_{2b}}\}, \{\top\}, \ldots]$, which describes a conjunction of constraints $X_b \succ_{-\Delta_{2a}} Y_b \wedge X_b \succ_{-\Delta_{2b}} Y_b$. Composition rules must be applied to both constraints and the usual subsumption rules must enforce the minimality of entries in the arrays. Despite this proposed extension, the main idea of computing compositions for quantitative and qualitative distances (cf. Tables 5 and 6) and computing a best approximation (cf. Def. 7) remains unchanged.

3.3 Combining Quantitative and Qualitative Distances

The major advantage of our reformulation is that it allows for inferencing with either Allen's relations, or interval relations with quantitative distances, or interval relations with qualitative distances in an integrated framework.

The latter two modes both provide zero distances and, hence, both subsume Allen's calculus. Though, they really are complementary, they interact nevertheless. This interaction can be described on the basis of a partial ordering between quantitative and qualitative distances. For instance, world knowledge may specify that "rather short" describes a temporal length which is less than three hours.[8] Composition rules for mixed quantitative/qualitative measures can then be handled analogously to partially ordered qualitative distances, namely

---

[8] In general, this might also be a two-sided restriction like *"between one and three hours"*, but for the sake of simplicity we here avoid the second parameter that merely complicates the approximation.

by referring to common subsuming constraints (cf. Section 3.2). Of course, a fundamental aspect of mapping "rather short" onto "less than three hours" is the context in which the qualitative description is made. Staab & Hahn [13] give an algorithm to deduce "comparison classes"[9] which is sensitive towards contextual criteria, and Hernández *et al.* sketch an articulation rule mechanism that is designed to find the correct mapping. However, the general problem concerning context influence still needs further research [8].

What is even more interesting is that such a reformulation allows for the expression of new interval relations with qualities or quantities, ones that are cognitively plausible in that they involve a single act of perception. For instance, we can now introduce the relation *"roughly meets"* or the relation *"meets with a measuring tolerance of 100ms"*, which can be defined by the boundary constraints[10] (cf. also Table 2):

$$\{[X_e \doteq_{\Delta(\text{roughly})} Y_b, X_b \prec_0 Y_b, X_e \prec_0 Y_e]\} = X \ \{[\{\top\}, \{\succ_0\}, \{\top\},$$
$$\{\top\}, \{\succ_{-\Delta(\text{roughly})}\}, \{\succ_{-\Delta(\text{roughly})}\}, \{\top\}, \{\succ_0\}, \{\top\}, \{\top\}, \{\top\}, \{\top\}]\} \ Y$$

or

$$\{[X_e \doteq_{\Delta(100\text{ms})} Y_b, X_b \prec_0 Y_b, X_e \prec_0 Y_e]\} = X \ \{[\{\top\}, \{\succ_0\}, \{\top\},$$
$$\{\top\}, \{\succ_{-\Delta(100\text{ms})}\}, \ \{\succ_{-\Delta(100\text{ms})}\}, \{\top\}, \{\succ_0\}, \{\top\}, \{\top\}, \{\top\}, \{\top\}]\} \ Y.$$

Naturally, "roughly meets" subsumes "meets", but it also subsumes some parts of neighboring relations. Thus, its scope is a new kind of "conceptual neighborhood" [7] that arises when only one parameter at a time is varied — in this case, the distance parameter.

4 Reasoning Scheme on Interval Relations with Distances

In this section, we will join the data structures and inference steps defined so far in a reasoning algorithm. The capabilities of this algorithm are then demonstrated by referring to example (1) and solving the underlying scheduling problem in formal terms.

4.1 Reasoning Algorithm

The reasoning algorithm on interval relations with distances is composed of the following steps:

1. Use a lookup table to convert interval relations into disjunctions of constraint arrays.
   For instance, X $\{minpr_n, \text{"overlaps"}\}$ Y $\mapsto X\{C_1, C_2\}Y$; cf. Tables 3 and 4.
2. The composition axioms (cf. Section 3) are applied to pairs of constraint arrays until no new inferences can be drawn.
   For instance, $X\{C_1, C_2\}Y \wedge Y\{C_3, C_4\}Z \Rightarrow X\{C_{1,3}, C_{1,4}, C_{2,3}, C_{2,4}\}Z.$

---

[9] The notion of "comparison class" in the natural language understanding community is roughly equivalent to "frame of reference" in the spatial reasoning community.

[10] We here assume that the function Δ maps expressions like "100ms" or "roughly" onto elements of the distance structure $\mathcal{D}^*$ using the proper frame of reference.

3. Subsumption tests (cf. Def. 6) eliminate redundant disjunctions.
   For instance, $X\{C_{1,3}, C_{1,4}, C_{2,3}, C_{2,4}\}Z \Leftrightarrow X\{C_{1,3}, C_{1,4}\}Z$, where $C_{1,3}$ and $C_{1,4}$ subsume $C_{2,3}$ and $C_{2,4}$, respectively.
4. Compute the best approximation (cf. Def. 7) from the boundary constraints.[11]
   Determine the best approximation for each array of the array set.
   For instance, $X\{C_{1,3}, C_{1,4}\}Z \mapsto X \{minct_n, \text{"precedes"}\} Z$.

Thus, the subsumption criterion does not only yield the best approximating interval relation, but it also reduces unnecessary ambiguities.[12]

4.2 A Sample Reasoning Process

To illustrate this reasoning process, let us return to example (1) in more technical detail. We assume, that H and J denote the time intervals that are needed for Hein's and John's flights, respectively. Then, the sentences can be captured as follows:[13]

(3) a. $length_{\Delta(8h)}(H) = \{[H_e \succeq_{\Delta(8h)} H_b, H_b \succeq_{-\Delta(8h)} H_e]\} =$
   $H\{[[\{\top\}, \{\top\}, \{\top\}, \{\top\}, \{\top\}, \{\top\}, \{\top\}, \{\top\}, \{\succeq_{\Delta(8h)}\},$
   $\{\succeq_{\Delta(8h)}\}, \{\succeq_{-\Delta(8h)}\}, \{\succeq_{-\Delta(8h)}\}]]\}H$

   b. $older_{\Delta(1h)}(H, J) = \{[J_b \succeq_{\Delta(1h)} H_b, H_b \succeq_{-\Delta(1h)} J_b]\} = H\{[[\{\succeq_{-\Delta(1h)}\},$
   $\{\succeq_{\Delta(1h)}\}, \{\top\}, \{\top\}, \{\top\}, \{\top\}, \{\top\}, \{\top\}, \{\succ_0\}, \{\succ_0\}, \{\top\}, \{\top\}]]\}J$

   c. $maxlo_{\Delta(\text{rather short})}(J) = \{[J_b \succeq_{-\Delta(\text{rather short})} J_e]\} =$
   $J\{[[\{\top\}, \{\top\}, \{\top\}, \{\top\}, \{\top\}, \{\top\}, \{\top\}, \{\top\}, \{\succ_0\}, \{\succ_0\},$
   $\{\succeq_{-\Delta(\text{rather short})}\}, \{\succeq_{-\Delta(\text{rather short})}\}]]\}J$

For the reasoning process, these constraints together with the assumption that *"rather short"* in the intended frame of reference (cf. Section 3.3) means a distance which is not exactly specified but which is certainly less than three hours are taken for granted. We may then conclude the following additional constraints by propagation and application of composition rules: $H_b \succ_{-\Delta(4h)} J_e$, $J_e \succ_{\Delta(1h)} H_b, H_e \succeq_{\Delta(7h)} J_b, J_b \succeq_{-\Delta(7h)} H_e, H_e \succ_{\Delta(4h)} J_e, J_e \succ_{-\Delta(7h)} H_e$.
Combining the entire knowledge available from the initial data and the results of reasoning, we get:
$H\{[[\{\succeq_{-\Delta(1h)}\}, \{\succeq_{\Delta(1h)}\}, \{\succ_{-\Delta(4h)}\}, \{\succ_{\Delta(1h)}\}, \{\succeq_{\Delta(7h)}\}, \{\succeq_{-\Delta(7h)}\}, \{\succ_{\Delta(4h)}\},$
$\{\succ_{-\Delta(7h)}\}, \{\succeq_{\Delta(8h)}\}, \{\succ_0\}, \{\succeq_{-\Delta(8h)}\}, \{\succeq_{-\Delta(\text{rather short})}\}]]\}J$.
Since we employ only a trivial qualitative distance system with one distance,

---

[11] If there are interval relations that are defined by disjunctions of constraint arrays, one can adjust definitions to allow disjunctions to be elements of the lattice, too.

[12] A more elaborate redundancy avoidance mechanism might be based on the least common subsumer *lcs* of two constraint arrays, C_1 and C_2, respectively. If all constraint arrays subsumed by *lcs* do either subsume C_1 or C_2 or are subsumed by C_1 or C_2 then *lcs* is equivalent to the disjunction of C_1 and C_2.

[13] We here formally capture binary interval relations $R_n(X)$ by ternary relations $\bar{R}_n(X, X)$, such that composition rules can be applied on the left and on the right side of other relations $R'_m(X, Y)$ and $R''_k(Z, X)$.

Δ(rather short), no composition rules can be applied to yield qualitative distance constraints (and, thus, non-singleton constraint sets), too.

Step 3 need not apply, since no ambiguities exist. Given exactly the interval relations from Tables 3 and 4 in step 4 the subsumption test would recognize that the relations *maxlo*, *minlo*, and *length* could be applied to H and *maxlo* to J, respectively. However, for H *length*$_{\Delta(8h)}$ approximates better than either "*maxlo*" or "*minlo*" — this is just the information given in (3a). Furthermore "*older*", "*svmin*", "*svless*", "*hh*" and "*minct*" also subsume the constraints, but "*older*" is subsumed by "*hh*" and, therefore, the conjunction

$$\text{"svmin}_{\Delta(4h)}(H, J) \wedge \text{svless}_{\Delta(7h)}(H, J) \wedge \text{minct}_0(H, J)\text{"}$$

is returned as result conjoined with the three input relations. The direct interpretation is that Hein's flight ends ("survives") at least 4 ($\text{svmin}_{\Delta(4h)}(H, J)$), but less than 7 hours ($\text{svless}_{\Delta(7h)}(H, J)$) after John's, and their flights happen contemporarily at some time point ($\text{minct}_0(H, J)$). Hence, if you plan to meet John and Hein at the airports in New York, after, first, meeting John you will, second, have between 4 and 7 hours to meet Hein, finally.

5 Related Work

Since the goal of this paper is to integrate rather than to substitute existing quantitative and qualitative approaches, it is similar to them with respect to several aspects. Still, our proposal achieves considerable extensions and an advanced level of conceptual abstraction in comparison to all other approaches.

Early studies on duration reasoning, such as work by Allen [1] and Kautz & Ladkin [10] do not tightly integrate quantitative reasoning and reasoning on Allen's relation, but rather combine two different, interacting networks. Meiri [11] more tightly integrated Allen's calculus with the model for temporal constraint satisfaction problems (TCSP; cf. [5]). But still Meiri's model keeps quantitative constraints on time points and Allen's relations on intervals rather separate. Constraints for relations like *"meets with a tolerance of n units"* could be formulated, but would be spread across the network without any connection and without the capability for abstraction, while relations like *"is clearly disjoint"* could principally not be formulated at all. Meiri's model could perhaps be extended to include qualitative scales, but one of the main benefits of our approach is our mechanism for computing high-level abstractions, which is not provided in Meiri's account. The same problems occur in Zimmermann's model [15] which is based on a similar primitive as ours, namely on $a(>, d)b \Leftrightarrow a = b + d$, but which does not allow for an abstraction into those constraints that belong together. Moreover, we extend the partial ordering he uses to allow for the easy embedding of different types of distances. Badaloni & Berati [2] recognized the need to capture all constraints between the boundaries of two intervals in one place. However, their only primitive is a rather unwieldy quadrupel of numerical intervals. No abstraction mechanisms are provided.

As for qualitative distances, Clementini, Di Felice, & Hernández [8, 3] present the most elaborate work and thus serve as a blueprint for our qualitative distances reasoning part. Again, they only consider one constraint at a time. Furthermore, we extend their mechanism to account for partially ordered distance systems, too (cf. Section 3.2).

Common interval label propagation networks that represent interval boundaries by *restrictions on time points* (cf. [4]) do not offer the same level of expressiveness as our proposal, since simple transitive conclusions, e.g., "*a* later *c*" cannot be inferred from "*a* later *b* and *b* later *c*". However, our approach can be reduced to such a network with *constraints on distances*. But then the implications are not structured in a way that is easily accessible from outside the reasoning system.

We build on Freksa's consideration [7] who favors conjoined partial specifications (similar to the notion of "convex relation" by Vilain, Kautz & van Beek [14]) to allow for lucid reasoning about knowledge at a coarser level of specification. We do, however, not subscribe to his point of view when he introduces new labels for semi-interval relationships instead of simply using the constraints between the interval boundaries. The reason for this is that by adding the distance parameter to the boundary constraints we are able to consider a new type of important conceptual neighborhoods. The relation *"roughly meets"* was given as an example for that claim.

6 Conclusion

In this paper, we presented a mechanism for an integrated reasoning on interval relations with qualitative and quantitative distances that combines proposals by Allen [1], Clementini, Di Felice & Hernández [3, 8] and Badaloni & Berati [2]. We claim, however, that our proposal considerably increases the reasoning power of the underlying calculus compared with either of these.

Our approach builds on *distance constraint arrays* as a new way of uniquely representing interval relations with different types of distances. Central to the reasoning scheme are the notions of *subsumption* and *approximation* which allow to infer interval relations that are much more lucid from the human designer's point of view, since they achieve a considerable degree of conceptual abstraction from the underlying interval boundary constraints.

Four major points could not be considered in detail in this paper. First, for knowledge like "A's flight is much shorter than B's" metareasoning on the different lengths of flights is required. This can be achieved by considering the distances, D, as being bounded by metaintervals to which our mechanism can be applied, too. Second, though our approach requires exponential time at worst, it remains efficient when the input is restricted to input conditions that describe convex relations. Similarly to the way Schwalb & Dechter [12] proceeded for TCSP relations, one may also employ approximating defragmentation procedures. But in addition to their approach, we may exploit the interdependencies between distance constraints from the set of arrays between two intervals in order to derive plausible, approximating distance constraint arrays instead of single constraints — and thereby achieve a tighter approximation. Third, we did not consider subsumption and approximation for disjunctions. However, they can be neatly defined as a clipping procedure in 6-dimensional space (cf. [6] on clipping). Fourth, we abstracted from how to actually assign numerical bounds to qualitative distances. This is a highly context-dependent problem for which preliminary solutions exist (cf. Section 3.3), but which still needs further investigation. However, to the best of our knowledge, no other proposal neither offers a similarly tight integration of constraints with qualitative and quantitative distances for reasoning nor a similarly high level of knowledge abstraction about interval relations with distances as the proposal we have outlined in this paper.

References

1. James F. Allen. Maintaining knowledge about temporal intervals. *Communications of the ACM*, 26(11):832–843, 1983.
2. Silvana Badaloni and Marina Berati. Hybrid temporal reasoning for planning and scheduling. In *TIME-96: Proc. of the 3rd Int. Workshop on Temporal Representation and Reasoning*, Los Alamitos, CA, 1996. IEEE Computer Society Press.
3. Eliseo Clementini, Paolino Di Felice, and Daniel Hernández. Qualitative representation of positional information. *Artificial Intelligence*, 95:317–356, 1997.
4. Ernest Davis. Constraint propagation with interval labels. *Artificial Intelligence*, 32:281–332, 1987.
5. Rina Dechter, Itay Meiri, and Judea Pearl. Temporal constraint networks. *Artificial Intelligence*, 49(1-3):61–95, 1991.
6. James Foley, Andrew van Dam, Steven Feiner, and John Hughes. *Computer Graphics: Principles and Practice*. Addison-Wesley, Reading, MA, 1996.
7. Christian Freksa. Temporal reasoning based on semi-intervals. *Artificial Intelligence*, 54(1-2):199–227, 1992.
8. Daniel Hernández, Eliseo Clementini, and Paolino Di Felice. Qualitative distances. In A. U. Frank, editor, *Spatial Information Theory: A Theoretical Basis for GIS*, number 988 in LNCS, pages 45–56, Berlin, 1995. Springer.
9. Jerry R. Hobbs. Granularity. In *IJCAI-85: Proc. of the 9th Int. Joint Conference on Artificial Intelligence*, pages 432–435, Los Altos, CA, 1985. Morgan Kaufmann.
10. Henry A. Kautz and Peter B. Ladkin. Integrating metric and qualitative temporal reasoning. In *AAAI-91: Proc. of the 9th National Conf. on Artificial Intelligence*, pages 241–246, Menlo Park, CA; Cambridge, MA, 1991. AAAI Press; MIT Press.
11. Itay Meiri. Combining qualitative and quantitative constraints in temporal reasoning. *Artificial Intelligence*, 87:343–385, 1996.
12. Eddie Schwalb and Rina Dechter. Processing disjunctions in temporal constraint networks. *Artificial Intelligence*, 93:29–61, 1997.
13. Steffen Staab and Udo Hahn. "Tall", "good", "high" — Compared to what? In *IJCAI-97:Proc. of the 15th International Joint Conference on Artificial Intelligence*, pages 996–1001, San Francisco, CA, 1997. Morgan Kaufmann.
14. Marc Vilain, Henry Kautz, and Peter van Beek. Constraint propagation algorithms for temporal reasoning: A revised report. In Daniel S. Weld and Johan de Kleer, editors, *Readings in Qualitative Reasoning about Physics*, pages 373–381. Morgan Kaufmann, San Mateo, CA, 1989.
15. Kai Zimmermann. Measuring without measures. The Δ-calculus. In A. U. Frank, editor, *Spatial Information Theory: A Theoretical Basis for GIS*, number 988 in LNCS, pages 59–67, Berlin, 1995. Springer.

Revising TimeGraph-II

James P. Delgrande and Arvind Gupta

School of Computing Science,
Simon Fraser University,
Burnaby, BC, V5A 1S6 Canada
jim,arvind@cs.sfu.ca

Abstract. TimeGraph-II is a system for efficient point-based temporal reasoning, developed by Schubert, Gerevini, and collaborators. For our purposes, temporal relations are represented in a directed acyclic graph, where vertices represent time points and directed edges are labelled $\leq$ or $<$, with no redundant edges. The graph is partitioned into a set of *chains*, supported by a *metagraph* data structure. Temporal reasoning can be carried out efficiently: reasoning within a chain takes constant time; reasoning between chains is less efficient, but is determined by a graph (the metagraph) significantly smaller than the original. We suggest two enhancements to TimeGraph-II, both of which lead to improvements in the original approach. First, the original approach does not consider updates to the structure. We show that additions to chains can be accomplished very efficiently, with manageable degradation in reasoning ($O(\log n)$ in both cases). Second, we argue that basing the representation on trees rather than chains leads to a strictly more powerful reasoner. More queries can be answered in constant time, and at the same time, for general queries, the size of the metagraph is decreased.

1 Introduction

Temporal reasoning is essential in many areas of Artificial Intelligence, including planning, reasoning about action and causality, and natural language understanding. Unfortunately, the temporal reasoning component in a knowledge-based system is frequently a severe bottleneck. One problem is that of *scalability*: even if an algorithm has good complexity bounds requiring, say, $O(n)$ or $O(n^2)$ time, such a bound is unacceptable for a large database, particularly if frequent use is to be made of such an algorithm. On the other hand, some temporal reasoning tasks may simply require a large amount of time; for example computing the closure of a set of assertions in the point algebra has an $O(n^4)$ worst case time complexity.

Consequently, there has been interest in investigating the tradeoff between expressive power and complexity, and in particular in investigating tractable subcases (see for example [VKvB90,GS93,NB94]). However, such work does not address the problem of scalability since, as indicated, even a low-order polynomial algorithm may be too slow for large problems. In response, there has been work in investigating restrictions of problems for which very efficient algorithms exist. These fast, restricted reasoners may then be embedded in a more general reasoner, with the expectation that overall performance would be improved. In point-based reasoners, several approaches have been proposed. The best-know and best-developed of these is the *TimeGraph* approach of Schubert, Gerevini and collaborators [MS90,GS95]; the most recent incarnation is called *TimeGraph-II* [GS95]. In this approach, one begins (for our purposes) with an arbitrary set of assertions concerning points in time. These assertions are processed so that one obtains a directed acyclic graph (DAG) with edges labelled from $\{\leq, <\}$, representing assertions between time points represented by the vertices. *Chains* of point assertions are extracted from this graph, and it is shown that reasoning within a chain takes constant time. Reasoning between chains is less efficient, but is determined by a *metagraph* that (ideally) is significantly smaller than the original. If the original structure is dominated by chains of points, this results in a very efficient reasoner.

The original approach however did not consider updates to the structure. We begin by describing a modification to the base approach designed to address this shortcoming. We show that additions to chains can be accomplished very efficiently. It would appear that this requires $O(n)$ time. However, we present an approach based on 2-3 trees that allows us to accomplish event additions in $O(\log n)$ time. The tradeoff is that determining implicit $<$ relations in a time chain now also requires $O(\log n)$ time.

Second we provide a strict enhancement to the base TimeGraph-II reasoner. Rather than basing the reasoner on a collection of chains in a (general) DAG, we show that the same performance can be obtained in a spanning tree of the graph. That is, we show that determining implicit $<$ and $\leq$ relations can be determined in constant time (after a suitable compilation) for points lying on a directed path in this tree. Since many more relations can be determined in a tree than in a set of chains over the same set of vertices, the result is a strictly more powerful reasoner. In the worse case, $O(n)$ chains are required to cover all vertices in a graph, while obviously only a single spanning tree is required.

It is clear that both modifications outlined above lead to improvements in the original structure. It remains an interesting open problem whether both improvements can be realized simultaneously with no degradation in time complexity for either.

In related work, [GM89] also employs a spanning tree in place of chains, but in a somewhat different fashion. Reasoning within the tree is argued to require $O(\log n)$ time (compared to our $O(1)$); as well only $<$ relations can be handled. In [DG96] we showed how to reason efficiently in the class of *series-parallel graphs*, in that, after $O(n)$ preprocessing, arbitrary $\leq$ and $<$ queries can be answered in constant time. Series-parallel graphs are used to model, for example, the temporal progress of process execution, where a process can overlay itself with another, or spawn subprocesses but must wait for all spawned processes to terminate before it can terminate. In particular, series-parallel graphs subsume trees. The approach taken in [DG96] has also been extended to series-parallel graphs embedded in a general DAG. The speedup for general graphs is similar in manner to that in TimeGraph-II; an implementation is currently being tested and will be described elsewhere.

The next section reviews related work and describes TimeGraph-II in more detail. Section 3 describes our modifications to allow efficient updating of chains, while Section 4 describes replacing chains with a spanning tree. In Section 5 we briefly summarise our work and compare it with other approaches.

2 Related Work

In temporal reasoning there is a fundamental choice between whether time points or time intervals are the primitive objects. [All83] proposed the *interval algebra* (IA) of temporal relations wherein time intervals are primitive. Reasoning within this algebra (that is, reasoning about implied interval relations or determining the consistency of a set of assertions) is NP-complete [VK86]. The *point algebra* (PA) was introduced in [VK86,VKvB90], based on the notion of (primitive) time points in place of intervals. In PA, the basic relations between two points are $<$, $=$, and $>$. Allowing disjunctions of the basic relations yields the relations $\{<, \leq, >, \geq, =, \neq, \emptyset, ?\}$. The subset of the IA that can be translated into the PA is called the *pointisable interval algebra* (SIA) [vB90]. Finding a consistent scenario (i.e. interpretation) for a set of assertions in the PA and SIA takes $O(n^2)$ time for n points while computing the closure takes $O(n^4)$ time [vB92]. Again, these bounds are too big to permit large scale applications. [GS93] consider complexity characteristics of various restrictions of the IA, while [NB94,DJ96] and others consider maximum tractable subclasses of IA relations.

Other approaches attempt to provide good expected performance, rather than guaranteed bounds. [Dor92] develops the notion of a *sequence graph*, based on the observation that frequently in applications, processes, for example, will execute or recur sequentially. In sequence graphs, only "immediate" relations are stored. No information is lost, and the reduction in complexity is claimed to be significant. [DG96] address reasoning in series-parallel graphs; these graphs are appropriate for modelling process execution, for example, where a process can spawn any number of children, or overlay itself, but must wait for all children to terminate before it terminates. Informally a series-parallel graph (SP-graph) is a DAG that is inductively constructed by a set of *series* steps (the source of one SP-subgraph is identified with the sink of another), and *parallel* steps (a set of SP-subgraphs share a common source and sink). Notably, [DG96] show that if edges are labelled over $\{\leq, <\}$, then determining implicit $\leq$ and $<$ relations between arbitrary vertices can be accomplished in $O(1)$ time.

An emerging general approach is to begin with assertions in the point algebra, and process these assertions as follows (see [vB92] and [GS95]). Given an arbitrary graph, first eliminate "=" relations; this can be performed efficiently by identifying the strongly-connected components. As well we can efficiently determine (so called) *implicit* $<$ relations and make these relations *explicit*. Lastly we can isolate $\neq$ relations, by using table lookup to determine these. The resulting

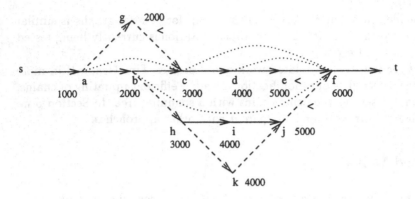

Fig. 1. An example of a timegraph.

graph has $<$ and $\leq$ edge relations only; moreover we can ensure that there are no redundant edges, in that no explicit $<$ or $\leq$ relation is implied by a transitive path. Call the resultant graph the *($<, \leq$)-graph* of the original. This graph can then be further compiled into structures for (presumably) efficient reasoning. In [GM89] a spanning tree underlying a DAG of time points is used for achieving efficient indexing. Performance for retrieving and updating temporal relations is argued experimentally to be linear. In TimeGraph-II (see the next subsection), chains are extracted from the DAG, while in forthcoming work from the authors, series-parallel graphs are extracted from the graph. In all these cases, a special-purpose reasoner derived from the ($<, \leq$)-graph is used for efficient reasoning by, first, providing very efficient reasoning within this special-purpose reasoner, and, second, by allowing general reasoning to be carried out on a graph substantially smaller than the original ($<, \leq$)-graph.

2.1 TimeGraph-II

In TimeGraph-II [MS90,GS95] temporal reasoning is centred on *chains* of events. Assertions in the point algebra are compiled into a ($<, \leq$)-graph. From this, a *timegraph* is formed,[1] where a timegraph consists of the ($<, \leq$)-graph partitioned into a set of *time chains* such that every vertex is on exactly one chain. A timegraph has a unique source, or start time, and a unique sink, or end time. Every vertex v of a timegraph is assigned a *pseudotime* consisting of the $\leq$-rank of the vertex multiplied by an increment, where the $\leq$-rank is the longest path from the source to that vertex. A vertex in a chain may have a *nextgreater* link, an edge connecting it to the nearest vertex on the chain that is strictly greater than that vertex (according to the edge labels). Distinct chains of a timegraph can be connected by *cross-edges*. Endpoints of cross-edges are called *metavertices*. Each metavertex also has two additional edges associated with it, the *nextout* edge that points to the closest vertex on the same chain with an outgoing cross-edge

---

[1] *TimeGraph-II* is the name of the system described here; a *timegraph* is the data structure on which reasoning is based.

and the *nextin* edge pointing to the closest vertex on the same chain with an incoming cross-edge. Finally, the *metagraph* of a timegraph is the graph with vertices consisting of the metavertices, and with edges consisting of the cross-edges as well as the nextgreater, nextout, and nextin edges. Although seemingly complex, the underlying structure is actually quite simple: a $(<, \leq)$-graph is partitioned into a set of chains, together with the metagraph representing the information of the original graph not given in the chains.

Figure 1 gives an example of a timegraph. Unlabelled directed edges are assumed to be $\leq$ edges. There are four chains, consisting of the solid directed paths from s to t and from h to j, as well as degenerate chains consisting of the single vertices g and k. Meta-edges are given by dashed directed edges, while dotted edges give the nextgreater edges. Nextout and nextin edges are not given.

Assuming that temporal event histories are dominated by chains of events, one would expect that the metagraph would be substantially smaller than the original graph. This in turn leads to efficient algorithms for reasoning. Reasoning within a chain takes constant time: for two points within the same chain, examining pseudotimes will determine a $\leq$ relation, and a $<$ relation is determined by examining the nextgreater link. In Figure 1, for example, $a < d$ since $a < c$ (by a's nextgreater link) and $c \leq d$. (Note that the nextgreater link for a was determined not from a's chain but from crossedges $a \leq g < c$). For points on different chains, reasoning about relations relies on standard graph-search techniques; however the graph searched is (effectively) the metagraph which, as indicated, is presumably significantly smaller than the original. Finding a path has time complexity $O(\hat{v})$ where $\hat{v}$ is the number of metavertices.[2]

This concludes our discussion of the most recent implementation of timegraphs, TimeGraph-II. There are a number of aspects of the system that we have not discussed. In particular [GS95] go on to consider the incorporation of some disjunctions of point assertions; this work builds on top of, and is independent of, the timegraph structure and does not concern us here.

3   Updating Time Chains

In this section we consider the formal problem of updating a time chain. Our main result is that an update can be carried out in $O(\log n)$ time, where queries now are answered also in $O(\log n)$ time. This result is somewhat surprising. If one considers the example given in Figure 2, the addition of the $<$ relation given by the dashed arc makes $O(n)$ edges redundant. A naive implementation of this update operation would clearly require $O(n)$ time.

Consider a set of time events $\mathcal{V} = \{v_1, v_2, \ldots, v_n\}$ occurring along a time line. Let $t(v_i)$ be the time at which v_i occurred. Then we will assume that there is a permutation π of these events so that $t(v_{\pi(1)}) \leq t(v_{\pi(2)}) \leq \cdots \leq t(v_{\pi(n)})$. We will refer to this as the *linearity condition* and it will correspond to a chain in a

---

[2] [GS95] give the time complexity as $O(k + \hat{e} + \hat{v})$ where k is a constant and $\hat{e}$ is the number of meta-edges. Since [GS95] assume that the number of edges is proportional to the number of vertices, this is equivalent to $O(\hat{v})$.

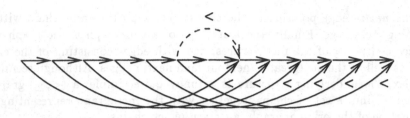

Fig. 2. When the dashed arrow is added, all other < edges become redundant.

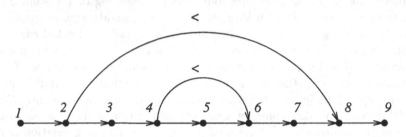

Fig. 3. Edge $(2, 8)$ is redundant as it is implied by the edge $(4, 6)$.

timegraph. We can assume without loss of generality that there are two identified events v_0 and v_∞ such that $t(v_0) \leq t(v_i) \leq t(v_\infty)$ for all i, corresponding to the source and sink of the timegraph.

Suppose we also know some relative temporal information about the events in $\mathcal{V}$; this takes a set of the form $\mathcal{E} = \{(x, y)\}$ for some $x, y \in \mathcal{V}$ with an edge (x, y) interpreted as "event x occurs strictly before event y" or $t(x) < t(y)$. The temporal reasoning question is that of determining, given two events v_i and v_j, the strongest known relationship about these events, that is, for $\pi(i) < \pi(j)$, whether or not $t(v_{\pi(i)}) < t(v_{\pi(j)})$. Then $(\mathcal{V}, \mathcal{E})$ is a directed acyclic graph $\mathcal{G}$ where those edges defining the linearity condition are labelled by "$\leq$" and those in $\mathcal{E}$ by "$<$"; we call these the $\leq$-edges and $<$-edges respectively. Notice that all vertices in $\mathcal{G}$ except the source and sink have exactly one incoming and one outgoing $\leq$-edge. As well, some "$<$" edges can be redundant. Figure 3 illustrates a redundant edge.

In their paper, Gerivini and Schubert showed that it is possible to answer temporal reasoning questions in constant time after a $O(n)$ time preprocessing step (Section 2.1). We extend that work by considering the case in which temporal information is not static but rather new temporal information is learned over time. This new information can be viewed as adding vertices and edges to the graph $\mathcal{G}$. Our problem is to add this information to $\mathcal{G}$ so that temporal reasoning questions can still be answered quickly.

We will assume that contradictory information is never placed into $\mathcal{G}$ (that is, if $(x, y) \in \mathcal{E}$ then $(y, x) \notin \mathcal{E}$) and that information is monotonically increasing (so that neither $\mathcal{V}$ or $\mathcal{E}$ ever get smaller). We therefore restrict ourselves to the following two updates:

New Vertex Add a new time event v to $\mathcal{V}$ such that the linearity condition is maintained.

New Edge Add a new time relation (x, y) to $\mathcal{E}$. This signifies that $t(x) < t(y)$.

Viewed as operations on a graph, the **New Vertex** relation adds a new vertex to $\mathcal{G}$ and **New Edge** adds a new directed edge. Furthermore, because of the linearity condition, we assume that **New Vertex** actually specifies a pair (v, v_i) where v is the new event, $v_i \in \mathcal{V}$ and $t(v_{\pi(i)}) \leq t(v) \leq t_{\pi(i)+1}$.

We present an algorithm that performs the updates outlined above as well as answers temporal reasoning questions in $O(\log n)$ time where $n = |\mathcal{V}|$. Therefore, given a sequence of m requests, each either an update or a temporal question, all m requests can be processed in $O(m \log m)$ time.

Throughout we will make the assumption that events are given labels over a dictionary (that is, the labels for events are unique, totally ordered and can be compared in constant time). Furthermore, to simplify notation, for $t(v) \leq t(v')$, we write $v \leq v'$; similarly for $(v, v') \in \mathcal{E}$, we write $v < v'$.

3.1 Data Structures

Our algorithms use 2-3 trees (see [LD91] for an example) as their data structure; we will call the 2-3 tree associated with $\mathcal{G}$, $T_{\mathcal{G}}$. To avoid confusion, we refer to elements of $\mathcal{V}$ as vertices or time events and to elements of $V(T_{\mathcal{G}})$ as nodes. In our 2-3 data structure, nodes will store names of events; if a node is empty we say it stores a *null* event. We will also store information on edges which are implemented as pointers; we call an empty pointer a *nil* pointer.

Each node of the 2-3 tree will store the following information:

- up to two events (of which at most one can be null);
- pointers to 3 children with the number of nil pointers for non-leaves equal to the number of null events;
- with each non-nil child pointer p, an event $NextGreater(p)$ (which is possibly null);
- with each non-nil pointer p, a pair of events,
    $NextRange(p) = [NextLower(p), NextUpper(p)]$.

All events will appear inside exactly one leaf of $T_{\mathcal{G}}$ (our tree is a like a B^* tree in this regard). An event v appears to the left of an event v' in the leaves of $T_{\mathcal{G}}$ if and only if $v \leq v'$; therefore the linearity condition is implicit in the leaves. The internal nodes of $T_{\mathcal{G}}$ store event names and are used for performing searchs. With each node p of $T_{\mathcal{G}}$, we associate a range of consecutive events $R(p)$; these are the events appearing at the leaves of the subtree of $T_{\mathcal{G}}$ rooted at p. In particular, the range of the root is the set of all events.

If the root contains a single event v then it has two children q_1 and q_2 with $R(q_1)$ the set of all events w for which $w \leq v$ and $R(q_2)$ the set of all events w other than v for which $v \leq w$. Similarly, if the root contains two events v_1 and v_2 then it has three children q_1, q_2 and q_3 with $R(q_1) = \{w | w \leq v_1\}$,

$R(q_2) = \{w|v_1 \leq w \leq v_2\}\backslash\{v_1\}$ and $R(q_3) = \{w|v_2 \leq w\}\backslash\{v_2\}$. This notion of range extends in a natural way to other nodes of $T_{\mathcal{G}}$.

The events appearing in internal nodes are used for searching within the tree. The events associated with non-null pointers are used to store nextgreater information. Our nextgreater's are inherited. That is, the nextgreater value for an event w is defined as follows: Let ℓ_w be the leaf of $T_{\mathcal{G}}$ containing w. Following a path from the root to ℓ_w, consider the first pointer p in an ancestor of ℓ_w such that $NextGreater(p)$ is non-null. This ancestor might be w itself. Then nextgreater of w will be $NextGreater(p)$. Note that if all $NextGreater(p)$ are null for ancestors of ℓ_w then $NextGreater(\ell_w)$ must be non-null. Furthermore, it will always be the case that $NextGreater$ values are stored at the highest possible pointers in the tree. We call this the **inheritance property**.

Finally, the values for $NextRange$'s are also inherited in the same sense as those for $NextGreater$. For a pointer p, $NextRange(p)$ is the range of $NextGreater$ values for elements of $R(p)$. A graph $\mathcal{G}$ with its associated 2-3 tree is given in Figure 4.

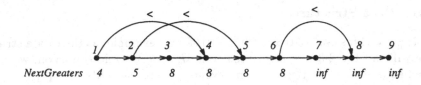

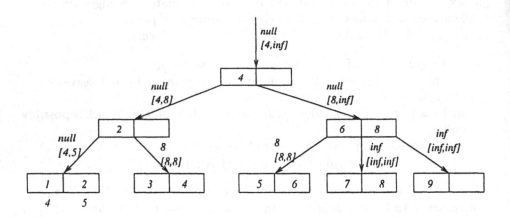

Fig. 4. A graph $\mathcal{G}$ with its associated 2-3 tree. NextGreater values are given in the graph below the vertex.

3.2 Algorithms

We present $O(\log n)$ time algorithms for handling both updates and for answering temporal reasoning questions.

Temporal Query Handling Suppose we are given two events v_1 and v_2 where $v_1 \leq v_2$ and we want to determine if $v_1 < v_2$. As outlined in Section 2.1, $v_1 < v_2$ if and only if $NextGreater(v_1) \leq v_2$. Therefore, we need only determine $NextGreater(v_1)$; this is easily done by searching for v_1 in $T_{\mathcal{G}}$. Since $T_{\mathcal{G}}$ has height $O(\log n)$ and is a search tree the total time is $O(\log n)$.

New Vertex Suppose we are given a new v that must be added to V with $v_1 \leq v \leq v_2$. Clearly $NextGreater(v) = NextGreater(v_2)$. We begin by searching for v in $T_{\mathcal{G}}$; this is equivalent to searching for v_2 in $T_{\mathcal{G}}$. The search results in a leaf ℓ. The following lemma is straightforward.

Lemma 1. *For v and ℓ as above, v_2 is contained in ℓ.*

If ℓ contains exactly one event then we add v to ℓ, set $NextGreater(v_2) = NextGreater(v)$ and we are finished. By the inheritance property the updated tree satisfies the necessary conditions.

Finally, suppose ℓ contains two events $w_1 \leq w_2$. Then it is either the case that $w_1 = v_2$ (in which case $v \leq w_1 \leq w_2$) or $w_2 = v_2$ (in which case $v_1 = w_1 \leq v \leq w_2$). We detail the former case here, the latter case is similar.

Using the insertion algorithm for 2-3 trees, we can divide ℓ into two new nodes ℓ_1 and ℓ_2 with ℓ_1 containing v and w_1 and ℓ_2 containing w_2. Now w_1 is recursively added to the parent of ℓ using the standard insertion procedure in 2-3 trees: If the parent contains one event then w_1 is added and we are done. Otherwise it is recursively divided into two nodes with the middle key pushed up.

We next update the $NextGreater$ and $NextRange$ values. By the inheritance property $nextgreater(w_1) = nextgreater(v) = NextGreater(p)$ for some pointer p on the root to ℓ path in $T_{\mathcal{G}}$; this is the highest pointer in the tree along this path such that all events in its subtree have the same nextgreater value. If p is above ℓ then it remains unchanged. Otherwise p is inside ℓ and it may be necessary to propagate $NextGreater$ information to the parent of ℓ. Notice that the $NextRange$ values remain unchanged. To see that this operation works in $O(\log n)$ time note that the total complexity of this operation is no worse than the complexity of insertion in a 2-3 tree.

New Edge The most difficult update to handle is **NewEdge**. In this section we assume that the time relation (v, v') (corresponding to adding the information $v < v'$) must be added to $\mathcal{G}$. Notice that adding such information can render other edges redundant and significantly change nextgreater values. Recall that in the worst case, $O(n)$ edges can be rendered redundant in this way (see Figure 2 for an example).

To add a new edge, we begin by determining the nextgreater of v by following the path from the root of $T_{\mathcal{G}}$ to the leaf ℓ containing v, picking up along the way $nextgreater(v)$. If $nextgreater(v) \leq v'$ in $\mathcal{G}$ then (v, v') does not yield new information and we are finished.

Now suppose that $v' < nextgreater(v)$ in $\mathcal{G}$. This will necessitate updating both $NextGreater$ and $NextRange$ values in $T_\mathcal{G}$. We make use of the inheritance property to accomplish this in $O(\log n)$ time. Notice that in $\mathcal{G}$ there is an interval of events $[x, y]$ such that $v \in [x, y]$ and $nextgreater(x) = nextgreater(y)$. Then, it is the case that in the updated graph, $[x, y]$ is broken into two subintervals $[x, v]$ and $[v_1, y]$ such that $nextgreater(x) = nextgreater(v) = v'$, v_1 is the event immediately following v in the linear ordering and $nextgreater(v') = nextgreater(y)$. Furthermore, because of redundancy, there may even be events $z \leq x$ such that in $\mathcal{G}$, $nextgreater(z) < nextgreater(x)$ but in the updated graph $nextgreater(z) = nextgreater(x)$. We must handle all these cases in our updates. The procedure for updating $NextGreater$'s is as follows:

Procedure $Edge\text{-}Updates$ (v, v') {Add a new edge (v, v') where $v < v'$}

If $v' \geq nextgreater(v)$ halt.
Let ℓ be the leaf of $T_\mathcal{G}$ containing v.
Find vertex $z \leq v$ such that in $\mathcal{G}$, $nextgreater(z) > v'$,
    but for all $z' \leq z$ in the linear ordering, $nextgreater(z') < v'$.

Let ℓ' be the leaf of $T_\mathcal{G}$ containing z. Notice that we must assign
    $nextgreater(w) = v'$ for $z \leq w \leq v$.
Let $\mathcal{P}'$ be the path from the root to ℓ' in $T_\mathcal{G}$.
Following $\mathcal{P}'$ back from ℓ', let a be the last node on $\mathcal{P}'$ such that the
    outgoing pointer p from a on $\mathcal{P}'$ is the left-most pointer.
Set $NextGreater(p) = v'$.
Let $\mathcal{P}$ be the path from the root to ℓ in $T_\mathcal{G}$.
Following $\mathcal{P}$ back from ℓ, let a be the last node on $\mathcal{P}$ such that the
    outgoing pointer p from a on $\mathcal{P}'$ is the right-most non-null pointer.
Set $NextGreater(p) = v'$.

A similar procedure is used for updating $NextRange$ values. Notice that the procedure involves traversing the 2-3 tree at most 4 times and therefore the entire operation takes $O(\log n)$ time.

4 Basing TimeGraph-II on Trees

In this section we argue that strictly improved performance can be obtained in TimeGraph-II by basing the reasoner on a spanning tree of the $(<, \leq)$-graph. The argument in favour of this proposition is straightforward. Within a chain, one just looks "forward" in the chain in reasoning (using pseudotime values for $\leq$ relations and in addition the nextgreater link for $<$ relations). In our extension, the final vertex in a chain will be connected to either another chain or to the sink of the graph. A spanning tree rooted at the sink of the graph can be constructed consisting of the chains and some outgoing edge from each final vertex in a chain. In the tree, every vertex "sees" a chain of vertices terminated by the sink.

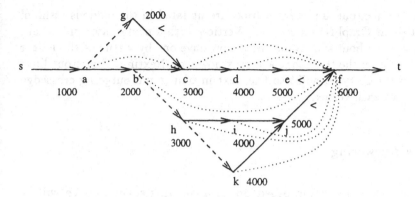

Fig. 5. An example of a timegraph based on a spanning tree.

So beginning with a timegraph, we construct the spanning tree based on the chains of the timegraph.[3] This involves adding a meta-edge from the sink of every chain to form the spanning tree. (Since strongly-connected components have been collapsed in the formation of the $(<, \leq)$-graph, it is impossible to form a cycle in this fashion.) Vertices that do not have a nextgreater link in their original chain may have a nextgreater link in the spanning tree. Figure 5 illustrates the timegraph example from Figure 1, with the spanning tree given by solid edges. Several new nextgreater links have been added to the structure.

The procedure for constructing a tree from the underlying graph is straight-forward. In the following E is the set of edges in the $(<, \leq)$-graph (i.e. the set of chain edges and crossedges). Each vertex has a flag, accessed via $Searched(\cdot)$, initialized to **false**. The procedure is initially called on the sink of the timegraph.

Procedure $Process(v)$
{spanning tree construction procedure.}
{Inputs: v where v is a vertex in the $(<, \leq)$-graph.}

> $Searched(v) \leftarrow$ **true**
>   for every $(u, v) \in E$ do
>   if $CrossEdge((u, v))$ do
>   If $IsChainSink(u) \wedge Searched(u) =$ **false**
> $AddToTree((u, v))$
>   end
>   else { edge in chain }
> $AddToTree((u, v))$
> $Process(u)$
>   end
> end {$Process$}

---

[3] We have a two-step process since it appears advantageous to favour longer chains over shorter ones.

The nextgreater, nextout, and nextin links are updated in the obvious fashion, using extant (TimeGraphII) procedures. Vertices with a nextgreater link retain the link; vertices without such a link may now have one by virtue of the longer "chains" (i.e. path in the tree) that a vertex now sees. Nextin and nextout links are updated if necessary to point to the next incoming and outgoing crossedge (respectively) for each vertex.

4.1 Query Answering

It is clear that query answering based on an underlying spanning tree will be faster than that based on a set of chains. The spanning tree strictly subsumes the original set of chains, and so more queries (those involving a path in the tree) can be answered in constant time. For arbitrary queries, the metagraph must still be searched, resulting in an $O(\hat{v})$ algorithm. However the metagraph associated with the spanning tree will be smaller than that associated with a set of chains; this will yield superior performance.

We can use the algorithms of Gerevini and Schubert for reasoning about temporal relations, with one elaboration: we need to determine whether two points lie on a common directed path in the tree. For an arbitrary tree this can be accomplished in constant time, given an initial $O(n)$ preprocessing step. For example [SPT83] provides an algorithm based on a numbering of nodes determined by a preorder traversal of the spanning tree. Each vertex is assigned a *number bracket* consisting of the vertex's number in a preorder traversal and the highest preorder number of its descendants. Vertex v is a descendant of w (i.e. $v \leq w$ is implied in the spanning tree) exactly when the number bracket of v (regarded as an interval) is contained in that of w. [DG96] give an algorithm where a *series-parallel* graph (a class of graphs including trees among its instances) is embedded in the Cartesian plane. In this approach $v \leq w$ just if for coordinates (x_v, y_v) and (x_w, y_w) associated with v and w respectively, we have $x_v < x_w$ and $y_v < y_w$.

Clearly our extension represents a strict enhancement of the TimeGraph-II approach. To determine whether vRw for vertices v and w, and $R \in \{<, \leq\}$:

1. If v is a descendant of w in the spanning tree, then if $nextgreater(v) \leq w$ in the spanning tree then $v < w$; otherwise $v \leq w$.
2. If v is not a descendant of w then search the metagraph as in the original approach.

This is the query algorithm for TimeGraph-II, generalized to allow for a spanning tree rather than a set of chains. Queries answered using 1. can be determined in time $O(1)$ with constant space overhead, while those answered using 2. require a search of the metagraph, as in TimeGraph-II, but on a smaller metagraph than in TimeGraph-II.

5 Discussion

We have presented two modifications to the base structure of TimeGraph-II. In the first case we considered the problem of adding additional information to chains of events; this information could consist either of the addition of new edges (new < relations) or the addition of new vertices (new events). We showed that for a chain of n events, such updates as well as queries can be carried out in time $O(\log n)$. Our approach was based on storing nextgreater information for a vertex in a novel construction in a 2-3 tree. Since 2-3 trees are balanced (that is, have height $O(\log n)$ for n nodes), modifying or searching such a tree takes $O(\log n)$. As well there is only a constant factor increase in storage.

Second, we showed that basing the representation on a spanning tree rather than chains leads to a strictly more powerful reasoner. Queries can be answered in constant time for two vertices on the same path in the tree, rather than just two nodes on a common path in a chain.

For both modifications we have nothing to say about the metagraph (although in the second modification one generally obtains a strictly smaller metagraph). Therefore, in both cases the metagraph is dealt with as in the original approach. Lastly, although these two enhancements can be combined, doing this in a straightforward manner does not yield better time complexity. Rather, a question for further research concerns the efficient updating of the spanning tree.

References

[All83]   James Allen. Maintaining knowledge about temporal intervals. *Communications of the ACM*, 26(1):832–843, 1983.

[DG96]   J.P. Delgrande and A. Gupta. A representation for efficient temporal reasoning. In *Proceedings of the AAAI National Conference on Artificial Intelligence*, pages 381–388, Portland, Oregon, August 1996.

[DJ96]   T. Drakengran and P. Jonsson. Maximal tractable subclasses of allen's interval algebra: Preliminary report. In *Proceedings of the AAAI National Conference on Artificial Intelligence*, pages 389–394, Portland, OR, 1996.

[Dor92]   Jurgen Dorn. Temporal reasoning in sequence graphs. In *Proceedings of the AAAI National Conference on Artificial Intelligence*, pages 735–740, 1992.

[GM89]   Malik Ghallab and Amine Mounir Alaoui. Managing efficiently temporal relations through indexed spanning trees. In *Proceedings of the International Joint Conference on Artificial Intelligence*, pages 1297–1303, Detroit, 1989.

[GS93]   M. Golumbic and R. Shamir. Complexity and algorithms for reasoning about time: A graph-theoretic approach. *JACM*, 40(5):1108–1133, 1993.

[GS95]   Alfonso Gerevini and Lenhart Schubert. Efficient algorithms for qualitative reasoning about time. *Artificial Intelligence*, 74(2):207–248, April 1995.

[LD91]   H.R. Lewis and L. Denenberg. *Data Structures and their Algorithms*. Harper-Collins, New York, NY, 1991.

[MS90]   S.A. Miller and L.K. Schubert. Time revisited. *Computational Intelligence*, 6:108–118, 1990.

362

[NB94]   B. Nebel and H.-J. Bürckert. Reasoning about temporal relations: A maximal tractable subclass of allen's interval algebra. In *Proceedings of the AAAI National Conference on Artificial Intelligence*, pages 356–361, Seattle, WA, 1994.

[SPT83]   L.K. Schubert, M.A. Papalaskaris, and J. Taugher. Determining type, part, colour, and time relationships. *IEEE Computer*, 16(10):53–60, 1983.

[vB90]   Peter van Beek. Reasoning about qualitative temporal information. In *Proceedings of the AAAI National Conference on Artificial Intelligence*, pages 728–734, 1990.

[vB92]   Peter van Beek. Reasoning about qualitative temporal information. *Artificial Intelligence*, 58(1-3):297–326, 1992.

[VK86]   Marc Vilain and Henry Kautz. Constraint propagation algorithms for temporal reasoning. In *Proceedings of the AAAI National Conference on Artificial Intelligence*, pages 377–382, Philadelphia, PA, 1986. temporal reasoning.

[VKvB90]   Marc Vilain, Henry Kautz, and Peter van Beek. Constraint propagation algorithms for temporal reasoning: A revised report. In *Readings in Qualitative Reasoning about Physical Systems*, pages 373–381. Morgan Kaufmann Publishers, Inc., Los Altos, CA, 1990.

Temporally Invariant Junction Tree for Inference in Dynamic Bayesian Network

Y. Xiang

Department of Computer Science
University of Regina
Regina, Saskatchewan, Canada S4S 0A2
Phone: (306) 585-4088, E-mail: yxiang@cs.uregina.ca

Abstract. Dynamic Bayesian networks (DBNs) extend Bayesian networks from static domains to dynamic domains. The only known generic method for *exact* inference in DBNs is based on dynamic expansion and reduction of active slices. It is effective when the domain evolves relatively slowly, but is reported to be "too expensive" for fast evolving domain where inference is under time pressure.

This study explores the *stationary* feature of problem domains to improve the efficiency of exact inference in DBNs. We propose the construction of a temporally invariant template of a DBN directly supporting exact inference and discuss issues in the construction. This method eliminates the need for the computation associated with dynamic expansion and reduction of the existing method. The method is demonstrated by experimental result.

Keywords: probabilistic reasoning, temporal reasoning, knowledge representation, dynamic Bayesian networks.

1 Introduction

Dynamic Bayesian networks (DBNs) [5,9] extend Bayesian networks (BNs) [10] from static domains to dynamic domains, i.e., domains that change their states with time. A DBN consists of a finite number of "slices" each of which is a domain dependence model at a particular time interval. Slices corresponding to successive intervals are connected through arcs that represent how the state of the domain evolves with time. Collectively, the slices represent the dynamic domain over a period of time.

When inference must be performed over an extended period of time, it is not feasible to maintain all slices accumulated in the past. Kjaerulff [9] proposed a method, which we shall refer to as the *dynamic expansion and reduction* (DER) method, to perform *exact* inference by dynamically adding new slices and cutting off old slices. To the best of our knowledge, it is the only method explicitly designed for exact inference in DBNs. However, as networks become more complex, the method does not provide satisfactory performance in time-critical domains [7].

In this paper, we investigate ways to improve the efficiency of exact run time inference computation when the domain is either *stationary* or close to be stationary. In Section 2, we define the terminology. Graph-theoretic terms that may not be familiar to some readers are included in Appendix. In Section 3, we propose the construction of a temporally invariant representation to support exact run time inference computation. We discuss technical issued involved in the subsequent two sections and demonstrate our method with an experiment in Section 6.

2 Dynamic Bayesian Networks

A DBN [5, 9] is a quadruplet

$$\mathcal{G}^K = (\bigcup_{i=0}^{K} N_i, \bigcup_{i=0}^{K} E_i, \bigcup_{i=1}^{K} F_i, \bigcup_{i=0}^{K} P_i).$$

Each N_i is a set of nodes labeled by variables. N_i represents the state of a dynamic domain at time interval $t = i$ ($i = 0, \ldots, K$). Collectively, $N = \bigcup_{i=0}^{K} N_i$ represents the states of the dynamic domain over $K + 1$ intervals. Each E_i is a set of arcs between nodes in N_i, which represent conditional independencies between domain variables at a given interval. Each F_i is a set of *temporal* arcs each of which is directed from a node in N_{i-1} to a node in N_i ($i = 1, \ldots, K$). These arcs represent the Markov assumption: the future states of the domain is conditionally independent of the past states given the present state. The subset of N_i ($0 \le i < K$)

$$FI_i = \{x \in N_i | (x, y) \in F_{i+1}\}$$

is called the *forward interface* of N_i, where (x, y) is a temporal arc from x to y. The subset of N_i ($0 < i \le K$)

$$BI_i = \{y \in N_i | (x, y) \in F_i\} \cup \{z \in N_i | z \in \pi(y) \ \& \ (x, y) \in F_i\}$$

is called the *backward interface* of N_i, where $\pi(y)$ is the set of parent nodes of y. Arcs of E_i and F_i are so directed that $D_i = (N_i \cup FI_{i-1}, E_i \cup F_i)$ is a directed acyclic graph (DAG). Each P_i is a conditional probability distribution

$$P_i = \begin{cases} P(N_0) & i = 0 \\ P(N_i | FI_{i-1}) & i > 0 \end{cases}$$

specified by a set of probability tables one for each variable x in N_i conditioned on $\pi(x)$. The pair $S_i = (D_i, P_i)$ is called a *slice* of the DBN and D_i is called the structure of S_i. Collectively, the slices of a DBN define a Bayesian network, whose structure is the union of slice structures and whose joint probability distribution (jpd) is the product of probability tables in all slices.

Figure 1 shows the structure of a DBN where $N_1 = \{a_1, b_1, c_1, d_1, e_1, f_1\}$, $E_1 = \{(a_1, b_1), (b_1, c_1), (b_1, d_1), (c_1, e_1), (d_1, e_1), (e_1, f_1)\}$, $F_1 = \{(a_0, b_1), (f_0, f_1)\}$, $FI_1 = \{a_1, f_1\}$ and $BI_1 = \{a_1, b_1, e_1, f_1\}$.

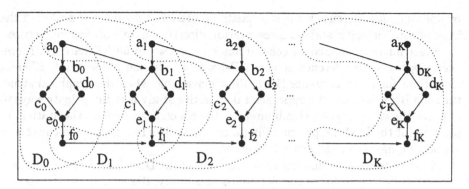

Fig. 1. A dynamic Bayesian network.

At any time $t = j \leq K$, the slices $S_0, \ldots, S_{j-1}$ represent the domain history and $S_{j+1}, \ldots, S_K$ predict the future. Evidence (observations obtained in the past and present) may be entered into $S_0, \ldots, S_j$. Limited by computational resource, normally only $S_i, \ldots, S_K$ ($i \leq j \leq K$) are explicitly maintained, called *active slices* of the DBN.

We assume that the DBN is *connected*. Otherwise the domain can be partitioned into independent subdomains each of which can be represented by a separate DBN.

3 Temporally Invariant Template

Kjaerulff [9] proposed the DER method to perform *exact* inference in DBNs. The method dynamically adds new slices to the front of active slices, converts the expanded slices into a junction tree (JT) [8] representation, reduces the JT by removing the parts corresponding to slices in the most remote history, and uses the reduced JT to process new evidence.

The DER method is effective for domains that evolve relatively slowly, e.g., monitoring the effect of medical therapy [1] or commercial forecasting [3]. However, for fast evolving domains where inference computation is under time pressure, e.g., mobile robot navigation [6] or automated vehicles [7], the computation is "too expensive" as reported in [7].

We attribute the unsatisfactory performance of the DER method partially to the expensive computation during dynamic expansion and reduction. We argue that in many practical applications, the domain is *stationary* or at least is stationary for an extensive period of time before changing to a different (stationary) state. When the domain is stationary, the slices of the DBN are invariant with time. If the number of active slices is also a constant, then dynamic expansion/reduction by the DER method is unnecessarily repeated over and over again.

Forbes et al. [7] recognized this opportunity for improvement. They proposed to precompile the slice of a stationary DBN into a "temporally invariant network". However, since the approach that they took was to replace exact inference by approximate inference using stochastic simulation, they did not deal with the issue of establishing a stable representation directly capable of *exact* inference.

Exact inference in BNs in general has been shown to be NP-hard [2]. Moreover, approximate inference is also NP-hard [4]. On the other hand, efficient algorithms for exact inference [10, 8, 13] are available when the graphical structure of a BN is sparse. The approach taken in this study is to investigate ways to improve the efficiency of exact inference. To this end, we explore the stationary property of the DBN by precompiling a run-time slice representation capable of supporting more efficient exact inference.

We assume that the number of active slices of the DBN is a constant (relaxed in Section 7) $m \geq 1$. Since the domain is stationary, the m active slices at any two time intervals are identical. For the study of inference efficiency, it makes no difference to treat the m slices as one big slice. Therefore, without loss of generality, we can consider only the case $m = 1$.

As stated, we want to precompile some slice representation of a stationary DBN that supports more efficient exact inference. The representation consists of a graphical structure and the associated conditional probabilities. Once such a representation is constructed, a copy of it can be stored as a *template* which we shall denote by T. Inference using the template works as follows:

At any time interval $t = i$, place an active copy T_i of T in the memory. T_i is identical to T except that it has absorbed all evidence acquired when $t < i$. To proceed in time, we evolve T_i into T_{i+1}. First, we cache the belief on some interface (defined below) between T_i and T_{i+1}. Then belief of T is copied into T_i. This effectively makes T_i identical to T without changing the overall data structure of T_i (e.g., the internal representation of the graphical structure). The belief of T_i is then updated using cached belief, which turns (physical) T_i into (logical) T_{i+1}. Now T_{i+1} has emerged and is ready to process new evidence while T_i has vanished.

We emphasize that the above inference uses only two *physical* copies of the template, T and T', and only the belief of T' is modified from interval to interval. Much computation required by DER method is no longer needed.

4 Defining Subnet

In order to construct the template, a portion of the DBN must be selected, which we refer to as a *subnet*. It may or may not be identical to a slice. The subnet may be multiply connected in general. To allow efficient exact inference, we convert it into a JT representation [8] as the run-time template.

Instead of defining the subnet first and then converting to template, we may *conceptually* first convert the DBN into a JT, then select a subtree T of it as the template, and finally determine the corresponding subnet. The subnet/template pair must be such that the template contains exactly the set of variables of the subnet, namely, no clique in T contains variables outside the subnet. When this is the case, we say that the subnet and the subtree template *covers* each other. We will define the subnet in this way.

As in the standard method [8], the process of converting the DBN into a JT consists of moralization, triangulation, organizing cliques into a JT, and assigning belief to each clique. As we shall see, to ensure that the subnet is covered by a subtree, triangulation is the key step in this process.

We define some minimum separator of the moral graph of DBN as the interface between T_i and T_{i+1}, denoted by I_i. This is semantically correct since variables in a separator renders the two groups of variables it separates conditionally independent.

We use node elimination to triangulate (Appendix) the moral graph. The elimination order will be consistent with the order that each T_i emerges and vanishes. That is, for each T_i ($0 < i \le K$), nodes contained in T_j ($0 \le j < i$), except I_i, are eliminated before any node of T_i. We shall call any such order a *temporal elimination order*. We show that in the resultant triangulation, the interface I_i is complete.

Proposition 1 *Let $G = \{N, E\}$ be the moral graph of a stationary DBN. Let $I_i \subset N_{i-1} \cup N_i$ ($1 < i \le K$) be a minimum graph separator of G. Let $\{N_a, I_i, N_b\}$ be a partition of N such that N_a and N_b are separated by I_i. Let G be triangulated into G' by eliminating all nodes in N_a before any node in $I_i \cup N_b$ is eliminated.*
  Then I_i is complete in G'.

Proof:
  We show that an arbitrary pair of nodes in I_i is connected in G'. Since the DBN is stationary, there exists $I_{i-1} \subset N_{i-2} \cup N_{i-1}$ for $i \ge 2$. Consider a pair of nodes x_i and y_i in I_i and the corresponding node x_{i-1} in I_{i-1}.

Since the DBN is connected and I_i is minimum, there exists a path from x_i to x_{i-1} such that all nodes on the path are contained in N_a, except x_i. Otherwise, for every path from x_i to x_{i-1}, there exists a node $z_i \in I_i$. In that case, x_i may be removed from I_i such that I_i is still a separator, which contradicts the assumption that I_i is minimum.

For the similar argument, there exists a path from y_i to x_{i-1} such that all nodes on the path are contained in N_a. Hence, there exists a path from x_i to y_i such that all nodes on the path are contained in N_a. Due to Lemma 4 in Rose et al. [11], the link $\{x_i, y_i\}$ is in G'. $\square$

Proposition 1 implies that I_i is contained in a clique of G' and so is I_{i-1}. If we organize cliques of G' into a JT, then all nodes of the DBN between I_i and I_{i-1} can be covered by a subtree that connects to the rest of the JT through these two cliques. This subtree (a JT) can then be used as the run-time template. This is justified in Theorem 3. Proposition 2 prepares for its proof.

Proposition 2 *Let I be a complete separator between nodes x and y in a triangulated graph G. Let C_x and C_y be two cliques of G such that $x \in C_x$ and $y \in C_y$. Then there exists a JT T of G such that I is either a sepset on the simple path from C_x to C_y in T or is contained in a clique on that path.*

Proof:

The set N of nodes of G can be partitioned into $\{N_x, I, N_y\}$ such that $x \in N_x$, $y \in N_y$, and N_x and N_y are separated by I. Since I is a complete separator, the subgraph G_x spanned by $N_x \cup I$ is triangulated and so is the subgraph G_y spanned by $N_y \cup I$. Hence, a JT T_x of G_x exists and so does a JT T_y of G_y.

The two JTs can be combined into a single JT as follows: Identify a clique Q_x in T_x containing I and a clique Q_y in T_y containing I. If one of the cliques equals I, then join the two JTs by unioning Q_x and Q_y. If none of the cliques equals I, then join the two JTs by a sepset I. The resultant is a JT that satisfies the requirement. $\square$

The following theorem shows that a JT of a DBN can be found that consists of a sequence of (sub)JTs chained together. The subJT will be our template.

Theorem 3 *Let $G = \{N, E\}$ be the moral graph of a stationary DBN. Let $I_i \subset N_{i-1} \cup N_i$ $(1 < i \leq K)$ be a minimum graph separator of G. Let $\{N_a, I_{i-1}, N_b, I_i, N_c\}$ be a partition of N, where N_a and N_b are separated by I_{i-1}, and N_b and N_c are separated by I_i.*

Then there exists a temporal elimination order triangulating G into G', and there exists a JT T of G' that satisfies the following conditions:

1. *There exists a subtree T_i connected to the rest of T through two cliques $C_{i-1} \supseteq I_{i-1}$ and $C_i \supseteq I_i$ such that every clique in T_i is a subset of $I_{i-1} \cup N_b \cup I_i$ except that C_{i-1} may contain nodes in N_a and C_i may contain nodes in N_c.*
2. *For each $y \in N_b$, y is contained in nowhere in T except in T_i.*

Proof:

It suffices to show that for any $x \in N_a$ and $y \in N_b$ where x is contained in a clique C_x and y is contained in a clique C_y, it must be the case that $C_x \neq C_y$ and C_{i-1} is on the path between C_x and C_y in some T obtained by some temporal elimination order.

According to a temporal elimination order, x is eliminated before y. They are in a same clique of G' iff they are connected when x is eliminated. Since I_{i-1} is the separator between x and y, y is not in the adjacency of x, and hence they are not connected at the time x is eliminated. Hence $C_x \neq C_y$.

By Proposition 1, since I_{i-1} is a minimum separator, I_{i-1} is complete in G' using any temporal elimination order. Hence C_{i-1} exists in G'. By Proposition 2, it follows that C_{i-1} is on the path between C_x and C_y. $\square$

We can now define the subnet based on such a template.

Definition 4 *Let I_i be a minimum separator in the moral graph of a DBN. Let $\{N_a, I_{i-1}, N_b, I_i, N_c\}$ be a partition of N such that N_a and N_b are separated by I_{i-1}, and N_b and N_c are separated by I_i. The subgraph spanned by $I_{i-1} \cup N_b \cup I_i$ defines the structure of a subnet relative to separator I_i.*

Through previous *conceptual* analysis, we have understood what the structure of a subnet should be. In *practice*, the subnet obtained by Definition 4 will be the starting point in the construction of a template.

5 Choosing Separator

Given the moral graph of a DBN, there are many minimum separators. We first consider two immediate choices: the forward and backward interface. The following propositions show that both can be used as the basis in choosing the separator.

Proposition 5 *Backward interface BI_i is a separator in the moral graph of DBN.*

Proof:

BI_i contains the head of each temporal arc and the parents of the head. In the moral graph, every simple path from a node in N_{i-1} to a node in N_i must contain either a temporal link or a moral link. Hence, deletion of BI_i renders them separated. □

Proposition 6 *Forward interface FI_i is a separator in the moral graph of DBN.*

Proof:

FI_i contains the tail of each temporal arc. In the moral graph, every simple path from a node in N_{i-1} to a node in N_i must pass the tail of a temporal arc, and then either the corresponding temporal link or a moral link. Hence, deletion of BI_i renders them separated. □

It should be noted that both forward and backward interface may not be minimum separators. For example, let $x \in N_i$ be the head of a temporal arc, and $y \in N_i$ be a parent of x. If y has no parent nor other child, then the minimum separator based on BI_i includes x but not y.

Similarly, if the tail of a temporal arc has no parent nor other child, then the minimum separator based on the forward interface does not include this node.

Construction of the template requires assignment of belief to cliques of the template JT. This is performed by assigning each node in the subnet to a unique clique in the JT that contains the family of the node. The belief of a clique C is initialized to the product of $P(x|\pi(x))$ for each x assigned to C. The family of a node in the subnet may not be identical to its family in the DBN. This may or may not cause problem in the belief assignment as discussed below:

First, consider a subnet defined based on forward interface FI_{i-1} and FI_i. The family of each node in this subnet is identical to that in the DBN except for nodes in FI_{i-1}. Since during inference, the belief on FI_{i-1} will be *replaced* by the belief on FI_{i-1} from the previously active template, the belief on these nodes can be left unassigned (equivalent to a constant belief). Hence, difference of family size for nodes in separator FI_{i-1} causes no problem to belief assignment.

On the other hand, if the subnet is defined based on backward interface BI_{i-1} and BI_i, the situation is different. For example, let $x \in N_i$ be the head of a temporal arc, and $y \in N_i$ be a parent of x. The parents of y in the DBN may not be contained in the subnet. Therefore, $P(y|\pi(y))$ as specified in the DBN cannot be included in the belief assignment. Without this piece of knowledge, a correct belief assignment of the template cannot be accomplished. Therefore, the belief assignment of a template cannot be performed *locally* using only the subnet defined by backward interface.

Since forward interface separator allows local belief assignment and thus simplifies the implementation of the template constructor, it is generally preferred over backward interface separator. We shall call forward interface a *self sufficient* separator. In fact, it is not the only self sufficient separator. We characterize such separators as follows:

Definition 7 *Let I_i be a minimum separator in a DBN and S be a subnet defined by separators I_{i-1} and I_i. I_i is* self sufficient *if for each node in S, its family is identical to that in the DBN except nodes in I_{i-1}.*

Since self sufficient separators simplify template constructor, they are generally preferred over separators that are not self sufficient.

Among self sufficient separators, different separators may produce templates of different run-time computational complexity. It is known that the amount of inference computation in a JT of a BN increases as the size of the total state space (STSS) of the JT [12]. Hence a template of smaller STSS is preferred. As finding a JT with the minimum STSS is NP-hard [12], we have to settle for heuristic methods.

According to Proposition 1, the separator will be completed during triangulation. Therefore, a larger separator creates a larger clique and tends to increase the STSS of the resultant template. Furthermore, a larger separator needs more fill-ins to complete. These fill-ins may cause additional cycles which in turn require more fill-ins to triangulate the graph. The result is the additional increase of the STSS. Therefore, one useful heuristics is to choose the separator of the smallest state space, which we shall term as a *minimal* separator.

6 Experimental Demonstration

The method proposed has been implemented and tested in WEBWEAVR-III environment, a research testbed that supports many aspects of representation and inference with uncertain knowledge. The modules involved in this work include a Bayesian network editor for specifying a slice or subnet, a template constructor, and a dynamic inference engine. In the following, we demonstrate the method proposed using our implementation.

We shall demonstrate using the monitoring of a digital counter since understanding the problem requires very little domain knowledge. The counter consists of three D flip-flops (DFFs). The first DFF is driven by an external clock signal. Its output is used to drive the second DFF, whose output is in turn used to drive the third DFF. The circuit, a clock input and its normal output are shown in Figure 2.

The counter cannot be modeled using standard Bayesian networks. This is because the input and output of each DFF are changing with time. The state of each DFF can also change with time. A DFF may be initially normal but becomes abnormal. However, the topology of the circuit is fixed. The state of each DFF

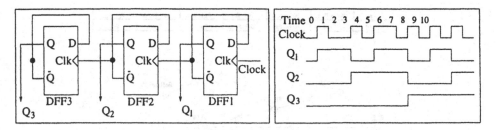

Fig. 2. Left: a digital counter made of three D flip-flops. Right: the input and output of the counter.

can be modeled as temporally changing between two types of behavior: normal and abnormal. Each type can be described without reference to time. Hence the domain is *stationary* and our proposed method is applicable.

The first DFF toggles at the positive edge (not positive level) of the clock. The edge monitoring can be modeled by a variable GotLow. At each time interval, GotLow = true if the input clock level is negative. The value implies that the next positive level will be a positive edge. When the input clock level is positive, two possible previous clock levels should be considered. If the previous clock level has been positive, then GotLow should be false since the negative level has not been seen yet. If the previous clock level has been negative, then the current positive level represents a positive edge. The value of GotLow should be reset to start the next cycle of monitoring. Hence, GotLow = false whenever the input clock level is positive. We have $P(GotLow = true|Clock = 0) = 1$ and $P(GotLow = true|Clock = 1) = 0$.

The toggling decision is made based on both GotLow value and the current clock level. This decision can be modeled by a variable Flip. Flip = yes if and only if GotLow = true and Clock = 1.

The output Q_1 is determined by the previous value of Q_1 and the Flip decision. Q_1 toggles if and only if Flip = yes.

To model the abnormal behavior of a DFF, we assume that if the DFF is abnormal, it will not toggle when it should 80% of the time. It may toggle when it shouldn't 10% of the time.

The other two DFFs can be similarly modeled. Since each of them is driven by $\overline{Q}$ of another DFF, it toggles at the negative edge of Q of the other DFF. Hence the variable GotHigh is used to model the edge monitoring.

We model the persistence of the state of a DFF as follows: If a DFF is normal at $t = i$, it may become abnormal at $t = i + 1$ with 1% probability. If it is abnormal at $t = i$, it will stay abnormal. A subnet of the DBN specified using the Bayesian network editor is shown in Figure 3, where each node is labeled by the variable name followed by the index of the node. The subnet is defined based on the forward interface. FI_{i-1} contains nodes 0, 2, 3, 4, 6, 7, 8, 10 and 11. FI_i contains nodes 13 through 21.

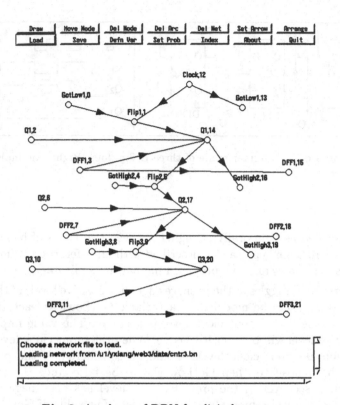

Fig. 3. A subnet of DBN for digital counter.

Once the subnet is specified, we use the template constructor to generate the template. The constructor module converts subnet into a template JT with belief assigned and initialized. The template JT generated based on the subnet is shown in Figure 4, where each clique is labeled by the indexes of member variables. The clique C_8 contains FI_{i-1} and is used to propagate evidence from the previous active template into the current template during inference. The clique C_0 contains FI_i and is used to propagate evidence from the current template into the next active template.

After the template is generated, inference can be performed using the dynamic inference engine. In our experiment, we assume that all DFFs are normal at $t = 0$. At $t = 4$, DFF2 breaks down and did not toggle. Since DFF3 is driven by the output of DFF2, the output of DFF3 is also affected. The corresponding output of DFF2 and DFF3 are shown in Figure 5. Note the difference from Figure 2.

We assume that the initial values of all variables at $t < 0$ are known, e.g., $Q_i = 0$, $GotLow1 = false$, $DFF1 = good$, etc. We assume that clock can be cheaply observed and is observed at every time interval. The observation of output of each DFF incurs a cost, and hence only one DFF is observed at a time interval. The first observation is made on Q_1 at $t = 4$. At $t = 5, 6$ and 7, Q_2, Q_3

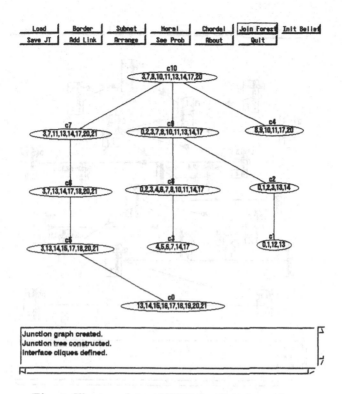

Fig. 4. The template of DBN for digital counter.

and Q_1 are observed respectively, and so on. No other variables are observable after $t = 0$.

Figure 6 shows the belief at $t = 3$. Since no observation has been made except on clock, the inference engine has simulated the expected output of each DFF from $t = 0$ to $t = 3$ essentially based on their normal behavior. The first observation on Q_1 is made at $t = 4$ (not shown in figures due to space limit). Although Q_2 becomes abnormal and does not toggle at this interval, the observation on Q_1 does not reflect the problem yet.

Figure 7 shows the belief at $t = 5$. Since the observed value of Q_2 is inconsistent with the expected value 1, its abnormality is being suspected. Due to

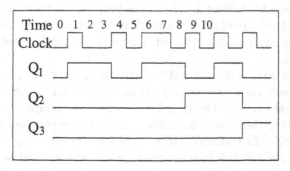

Fig. 5. Incorrect output due to breading down of DFF2 at $t = 4$.

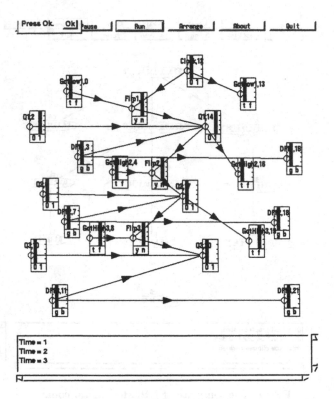

Fig. 6. The belief at $t = 3$.

limited observation, DFF1 is also suspected. The suspicion on the abnormality of DFF1 is denied by subsequent observations. Hence at $t = 10$, the belief becomes $P(DFF1 = bad) = 0.05$, $P(DFF2 = bad) = 0.98$, and $P(DFF2 = bad) = 0.08$ (not shown in figures due to space). At this time, the monitor is fairly certain about the problem of the counter through tying together observations made across different time intervals.

7 Conclusions

In this work, we explore the stationary feature of problem domains to improve the efficiency of exact inference in DBNs. We propose the construction of a temporally invariant template of a DBN which can be reused at run time. This saves the run time computation associated with dynamic expansion and reduction by the DER method.

We show that once a slice of DBN is specified, the forward and backward interface form direct basis to select a minimum separator in the moral graph of the DBN. A subnet can then be defined from which the template is constructed. Unlike backward interface and other non-self sufficient separators, forward interface and other self sufficient separators allow local belief assignment using the subnet only. Thus self sufficient separators should be preferred as they simplify template construction.

Besides the property of self sufficiency, using a minimal separator appears to be a useful heuristics in order to reduce the size of total state space of the

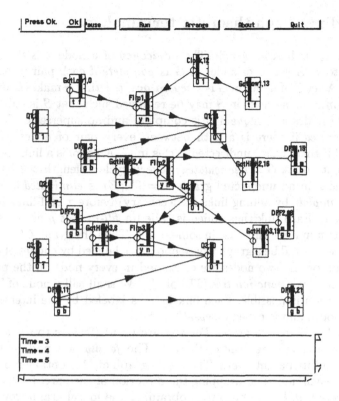

Fig. 7. The belief at $t = 5$.

resultant template. Further experimental study is being conducted to test this heuristics.

Our approach can be extended to close-to-stationary domains. If the DBN can be expressed by a small number of distinct slices, several templates may be created for each distinct slice, one for each distinct preceding slice. The assumption of a constant number of active slices (Section 3) can also be lifted in the same way.

Our presentation has focused on inference that supports *estimation* (estimating the current state of some unobserved variables) and *forecast* (predicting the future state of the domain). The template constructed can also support *backward smoothing* (re-estimating the past state of some unobserved variables). The extension is straightforward.

Acknowledgement

This work is supported by the Research Grant OGP0155425 from NSERC.

Appendix: Graph-theoretic terminology

Let G be an undirected graph. The *adjacency* of a node x is the set of nodes adjacent to x. A set X of nodes in G is *complete* if each pair of nodes in X is adjacent. A set S of nodes in G is a *separator* if deleting S makes G disconnected. S is *minimum* if no node in S may be removed such that S is still a separator. A set C of nodes is a *clique* if C is complete and no superset of C is complete. G is *connected* if there is a path between every pair of nodes. G is *multiply* connected if there exists undirected cycles in G. A *chord* is a link connecting two nonadjacent nodes. G is *triangulated* if every cycle of length > 3 has a chord.

A node x in an undirected graph $G = (N, E)$ is *eliminated* if its adjacency is made *complete* by adding links (if necessary) before x and links incident to x are removed. Each link thus added is called a *fill-in*. Let ρ be the set of fill-ins added in eliminating all nodes in some order. Then the graph $G' = (N, E \cup \rho)$ is triangulated. Let T be a graph whose nodes are labeled by cliques of G' such that intersection of any two nodes are contained in every node on the path between them. Then T is a *junction tree* (JT) of G'. We shall call a node of T as a clique if no confusion is possible. Each link in T is labeled by the intersection of the two end nodes and is called a *sepset*.

Let D be a directed graph. For any arc (x, y) (from x to y), x is called the *tail* and y is called the *head* of the arc. The *family* of a node is the union of the node and its parent nodes. The *moral* graph of D is obtained by completing parents of each node and dropping the direction of each arc. Each link added is called a *moral link*. The process of obtaining the moral graph from D is called *moralization*.

References

1. S. Andreassen, R. Hovorka, J. Benn, K.G. Olesen, and E.R. Carson. A model-based approach to insulin adjustment. In *Proc. 3rd Conf. on Artificial Intelligence in Medicine*, pages 239–248. Springer-Verlag, 1991.

2. G.F. Cooper. The computational complexity of probabilistic inference using Bayesian belief networks. *Artificial Intelligence*, 42(2-3):393–405, 1990.

3. P. Dagum, A. Galper, and E. Horvitz. Dynamic network models for forecasting. In D. Dubois, M.P. Wellman, B. D'Ambrosio, and P. Smets, editors, *Proc. 8th Conf. on Uncertainty in Artificial Intelligence*, pages 41–48, Stanford, CA, 1992.

4. P. Dagum and M. Luby. Approximating probabilistic inference in Bayesian belief networks is NP-hard. *Artificial Intelligence*, 60(1):141–153, 1993.

5. T.L. Dean and K. Kanazawa. A model for reasoning about persistence and causation. *Computational Intelligence*, (5):142–150, 1989.

6. T.L. Dean and M.P. Wellman. *Planning and Control*. Morgan Kaufmann, 1991.

7. J. Forbes, T. Huang, K. Kanazawa, and S. Russell. The batmobile: towards a bayesian automated taxi. In *Proc. Fourteenth International Joint Conf. on Artificial Intelligence*, pages 1878–1885, Montreal, Canada, 1995.

8. F.V. Jensen, S.L. Lauritzen, and K.G. Olesen. Bayesian updating in causal probabilistic networks by local computations. *Computational Statistics Quarterly*, (4):269–282, 1990.

9. U. Kjaerulff. A computational scheme for reasoning in dynamic probabilistic networks. In D. Dubois, M.P. Wellman, B. D'Ambrosio, and P. Smets, editors, *Proc. 8th Conf. on Uncertainty in Artificial Intelligence*, pages 121–129, Stanford, CA, 1992.

10. J. Pearl. *Probabilistic Reasoning in Intelligent Systems: Networks of Plausible Inference*. Morgan Kaufmann, 1988.

11. D.J. Rose, R.E. Tarjan, and G.S. Lueker. Algorithmic aspects of vertex elimination on graphs. *SIAM J. Computing*, 5:266–283, 1976.

12. W.X. Wen. Optimal decomposition of belief networks. In *Proc. 6th Conf. on Uncertainty in Artificial Intelligence*, pages 245–256, 1990.

13. Y. Xiang, D. Poole, and M. P. Beddoes. Multiply sectioned Bayesian networks and junction forests for large knowledge based systems. *Computational Intelligence*, 9(2):171–220, 1993.

Utility Theory-Based User Models for Intelligent Interface Agents

Scott M. Brown[1], Eugene Santos Jr.[2], and Sheila B. Banks[1]

[1] Department of Electrical and Computer Engineering
Air Force Institute of Technology
Wright-Patterson AFB, OH 45433-7765 USA
{sbrown,sbanks}@afit.af.mil
[2] Computer Science and Engineering
University of Connecticut
Storrs, CT 06269-3155 USA
eugene@eng2.uconn.edu

Abstract. An underlying problem of current interface agent research is the failure to adequately address effective and efficient knowledge representations and associated methodologies suitable for modeling the users' interactions with the system. These *user models* lack the representational complexity to manage the uncertainty and dynamics involved in predicting user intent and modeling user behavior. A utility theory-based approach is presented for effective user intent prediction by incorporating the ability to explicitly model users' goals, the uncertainty in the users' intent in pursuing these goals, and the dynamics of users' behavior. We present an interface agent architecture, CIaA, that incorporates our approach and discuss the integration of CIaA with three disparate domains — a probabilistic expert system shell, a natural language input database query system, and a virtual space plane —that are being used as test beds for our interface agent research.

Keywords: cognitive modeling, uncertainty, knowledge representation

1 Introduction

As computers have become common place in the business work force and at home, researchers and the software industry have become painfully aware of the need to help users perform their every day tasks. To that end, research continues into *interface* or "personal assistant" agents. The purpose of these agents is to reduce information overload by collaborating with the user, performing tasks on the users behalf [28]. Examples of interface agents include office assistance agents, such as e-mail, scheduling, and financial portfolio management agents [28, 38], tutor and coach agents [11, 12], and character-based assistants for word processors, spreadsheets, and presentation software, such as the Office Assistants found in the Microsoft's Office 97 software [20].

The remainder of this paper is organized as follows: The motivation and background information for our current research efforts is provided in Section 2. Section 2.1 briefly outlines requirements we believe interface agents must meet, metrics to measure those requirements, and a methodology for determining if an agent is meeting those requirements. In Section 3, we discuss our utility theory-based approach to offering assistance to a user in an environment. Section 4 describes three of the environments we are using as test beds for our research. In Section 5, we discuss research related to our work. Finally, we discuss some pertainent issues, and drawing conclusions from our research and showing promising areas for future research.

2 Background

Shifting responsibility for final design decisions from the initial software developers to the users or to people who are closer to the users has long been realized as a desirable goal for software systems. This approach has been central to the research performed by the human-computer interaction (HCI) community. *Customizable* systems allow end users to adjust a system to their specific needs and tasks. These adjustments can be as simple as allowing a user to choose from predetermined alternatives to providing users a way to alter the system itself. Adaptive interfaces are one customization technique, but one where the user is not in complete control. Adaptations are typically done either via statistical averages of users' actions or dynamic user models (see Baeker, et. al [2] for examples of systems utilizing both approaches). We feel statistical approaches fail to adequately model a user's intent. In particular, situation-action pairs [27] ignore the correlation between actions (i.e., behaviors) and the goals being pursued. Situations are matched with a single action to perform given the situation. However, in many situations, a user may perform a series of actions to accompilsh some higher level goal. Simple situation-action pairs can not model situation-goal-actions.

Maes [27] discusses the basic problems Artificial Intelligence researchers have with adaptive autonomous agents, of which interface agents are a subset. The two basic problems are the following:

- **Action selection** — what to do next given time-varying goals?
- **Learning from experience** — how to improve performance over time?

To address the problem of action selection, interface agents must be capable of determining which goal the user is pursuing so the interface agent can determine what to do next. Since the purpose of interface agents is to offer beneficial assistance to the user, it is important to have a keen understanding of the goals the user is pursuing over time. We use the term *user intent* to denote the actions a user intends to perform in pursuit of his/her goal. Therefore, for an interface agent to be able to assist the user in pursuing those goals, the agent must be capable of ascribing user intent.

With respects to the action selection problem stated by Maes, we present a utility theory-based approach for user modeling. Our approach determines *what is important* to model in the domain. Our knowledge representation captures an explicit representation of users' goals within the domain, with associated metrics to determine *when* a user is pursuing those goals and *how* to offer assistance, and allows an agent to predict the user's intent. By infusing utility theory into our approach, we can not only determine the probability that assistance should be offered on the user's behalf, but also the utility of offering this assistance. Determining *when* and *how* to offer assistance is paramount to providing timely, beneficial assistance to the user.

To address the problem of learning from experience, we must determine *what* to improve over time. What should we learn from past experiences? Ascription of user intent is inherently uncertain. Due to the simple fact most environments where interface agents are utilized are very dynamic and not static, user models must be capable of adapting over time to better model the user with the domain. Due to space constraints, we can not fully address this problem here; the problem of learning from experience is addressed elsewhere [5, 10].

2.1 Interface Agent Development

We believe it is a necessity to first develop concrete, measurable requirements and then use these metrics to determine the effectiveness of an interface agent within an environment. We levy the following requirements on our agent: **adaptivity** — "the ability to modify an internal representation of the environment through sensing of the environment in order to change future sensing, acting, and reacting for the purpose of determining user intent and improving assistance", **autonomy** — "the ability to sense, act, and react over time within an environment without direct intervention", **collaboration** — "the ability to communicate with other agents, including the user, to pursue the goal of offering assistance to the user", and **robustness** — "the ability to degrade assistance gracefully." We have developed an associated set of requirement metrics to measure the effectiveness of the interface agent in meeting these requirements. For example, the *precision metric* measures the interface agent's ability to accurately suggest assistance to the user. We define our precision metric as

$$M_{precision} \triangleq \frac{number\ of\ correct\ suggestions}{number\ of\ suggestions}. \tag{1}$$

Details on the requirement metrics set may be found elsewhere [10].

3 Utility Theory-Based User Models

The elicitation, specification, design, and maintenance of an accurate cognitive user model of the user is necessary for effective ascription of user intent. The driving goal of our research is to develop a comprehensive software engineering, knowledge engineering, and knowledge acquisition methodology for Symbiotic

Information Reasoning and Decision Support (SIRDS) [5]. SIRDS requires the development of an adaptive, intelligent, learning human computer interface. Intelligent agents are a key aspect of SIRDS; they perform information fusion, analysis, and abstraction, as well as deriving information requirements and controlling information display.

User modeling is concerned with how to represent the user's knowledge and interaction within a system to adapt those systems to the needs of users. Researchers from the fields of artificial intelligence, human-computer interaction, psychology, and education have all investigated ways to construct, maintain, and exploit user models. The benefit of utilizing a dynamic user model within a system is to allow that system to adapt over time to a specific user's preferences, workflow, goals, disabilities, etc. To realize this benefit, the user model must effectively represent the user's knowledge and intent within the domain to accurately predict how to adapt the system.

Unfortunately, ascribing user intent is made difficult because many times users do not follow pre-planned goals. They perform actions that can be ascribed to one plan, and other actions that can be ascribed to another plan. As a result, observing a user's actions in an attempt to predict intention to those actions can be next to impossible. One way of avoiding this is to observe only the most recent actions [16]. A *fading function* is used to "forget" past actions. Not only does the fading function have the advantage focusing attention on the most recent actions making prediction of user intent in certain domains (e.g., web browsing) easier, but it has the side effect of reducing the complexity of reasoning over all the past actions to determine a user's intent. Another way to handle this problem is to introduce uncertainty into the model. Jameson describes how a causal planning model can be used to construct Bayesian networks [24]. The networks are constructed based on the observable events within each phase of the model.

One failing of purely statistical approaches is their inability to determine the utility of offering assistance for an action. We are interested in not only offering assistance based on what is *probable*, but assistance that is beneficial for the user. Utility theory is concerned with the problem of making informed decisions, taking into account all preferences and factors affecting the decisions, and assessing the *utility* of all the outcomes of our decisions. Utility theory has been used in such diverse domains as graphics rendering [22], display of information for time-critical decision making [21], prioritization of repairs [8], and categorization [23].

3.1 Approach

Brown, et al. state that to ascribe user intent, we must identify the salient characteristics of our domain environment and specifically determine goals a user is trying to achieve and the actions to achieve those goals [10]. Social scientists use intentions (as determined by surveying subjects) to measure possible future behaviors (i.e., actions) [31]. That is, what a user says they intend to do is indicative of what they really might do. They note intentions do not necessarily translate into action. Brown, et al., on the other hand, observe behavior (and other environmental events), in an attempt to predict a user's intent so as to predict future behavior.

This approach is based on the belief that what a user intends to do in an environment is the result of environmental stimuli (i.e., events) occurring in the environment, and by the goals they are trying to obtain as a reaction to stimuli. These goals can be explicit (e.g., landing an aircraft) or implicit (e.g., reduce work load). To achieve a goal, a user must perform certain actions to achieve the goal. Goals can be composed of multiple actions, with many pre- and post-conditions. Pre-conditions include directly observable events in the environment (e.g., the plane is going to crash) as well as indirectly observable events (e.g., an increase in the user's cognitive load). These pre-conditions cause a user to pursue a goal. We can use a directed acyclic graph to show causality between the stimuli, goals, and actions. For example, Figure 1 shows three goals — auto pilot landing, manual pilot landing, and reduce cognitive load. Pre-conditions in this figure are the roots of the tree and the actions (e.g., activate ILS) are the leaves of the tree.

There are several advantages to representing users' intentions in a directed acyclic graph, such as the following:

- Goal abstraction allows us to design and detect higher level goals, in pursuit of lower level goals.
- Evidence can be easily and intuitively added and removed (in the form of pre- and post-conditions) as a user interacts with system.
- Pre- and post-conditions for goals and actions are explicitly stated.
- Keyhole plan recognition[1] is made easier by explicitly enumerating atomic actions composing goals [1, 39].
- Natural language explanations of actions based on prediction of goals can be easily generated.

Benyon and Murray use the term *task* or *intentional level* to describe the component of a user model containing knowledge about the user's goals [7]. The task level knowledge is used to infer what goals the user is pursuing. Benyon and Murray state "failure to recognise the intentions underlying some user action will result in less satisfactory interaction" as a result of failing to recognize the pursuit of one goal versus another.

3.2 Architecture

Prediction of user intent is inherently uncertain. Knowledge representations that can dynamically capture and model uncertainty in human-computer interaction as well as the causal relationships between goals, environmental stimuli, and actions as described above are needed to effectively model users.

---

[1] Plan recognition is the task of ascribing intentions about plans to an agent (human or software), based on observation of the agent's actions. With keyhole plan recognition, the agent is unaware of or indifferent to the plan recognition process.

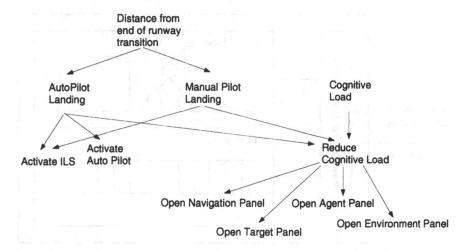

Fig. 1. A directed acyclic graph representation of a user model.

One knowledge representation well suited to representing uncertainty is a Bayesian Network [30]. Bayesian Networks are a probabilistic knowledge representation used to represent uncertain information. The directed acyclic graph structure of the network contains representations of both the conditional dependencies and independencies between elements of the problem domain. The knowledge is represented by nodes called random variables (RVs) and arcs representing the (causal) relationships between variables. The strengths of the relationships are described using parameters encoded in conditional probability tables. A Bayesian network is a mathematically correct and semantically sound model for representing uncertainty, providing a means to show probabilistic relationships between the RVs — in this case goals, actions, and stimuli.

Our Core Interface Agent Architecture (CIaA) is shown in Figure 2. The main component of the architecture is our Bayesian network-based user model. The network consists of three different RV types — goal, action, and pre-condition. Each action RV has an associated utility function used to determine the expected utility of offering assistance to achieve the parent goal. The utility functions and their relationship to ascribing user intent are discussed in the next section. Pre-condition RVs are used to capture environmental events (e.g., psychological factors).

For each observable event in the environment (e.g., button press, altitude change, user is confused, etc.), the host application sends a message, via the message passing interface[2], to the interface agent. This observable is modeled in the user model as either an action or pre-condition. The evaluator stores the observed event in a observation history stack (i.e., most recent event is on top of the history stack).

---

[2] We use the knowledge query and manipulation language (KQML) [29] due to its general acceptance in the agent community.

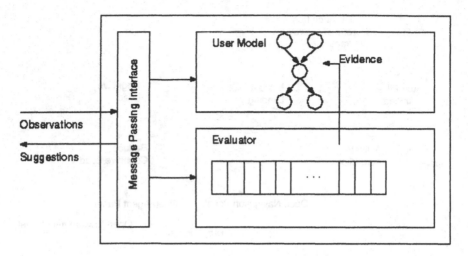

Fig. 2. The Core Interface Agent Architecture.

Periodically (currently once a second) or when new observations arrive from the host application, the interface agent determines if the user needs assistance. The determiniation is based on two factors: the expected utility of offering assistance to acheive a goal and user defined assistance thresholds. The interface agent performs Bayesian network belief updating on all of the goal random variables. All of the relevant observations in the history stack are used as evidence in the Bayesian network. The interface agent then uses the updated probabilities and the utility functions associated at the action RVs to calculate the expected utility of each goal.

The two user defined thresholds, one for offering assistance and one to autonomously perform actions on the user's behalf to obtain a user's goal, determine how/if the interface agent will offer assistance. This approach is the same as Maes [28], except she bases her thresholds on statistical probabilities and we base ours on the expected utility function. The interface agent autonomously performs the actions associated with the highest ranked goal (based on its expected utility) if the goal's expected utility is greater than the autonomy threshold. Else, if the goal's expected utility is above the suggestion threshold, the interface agent sends a request to the user to perform the goal's actions on the user's behalf. Otherwise, the interface agent offers no assistance. Additionally, the interface agent calculates the values of the requirement metrics to determine if the interface agent needs to correct the user model to more accurately reflect the user's intent.

3.3 User Model Design

Our utility theory-based approach addresses the aforementioned deficiencies of statistical-based agents. As mentioned briefly above, we determine the expected utility of offering assistance for a goal, based not only on the probability of an action as determined by performing belief updating of the Bayesian Network, but on the utility of performing the action given the user is pursuing the goal. Let $\mathcal{G}$ be a finite collection of goals. For each goal $G \in \mathcal{G}$ there will be a finite collection of actions A_G for achieving that goal. Let Δ denote the set of applicable discriminators that may also impact the utility (e.g., cognitive load, skill, user preferences). Let $\mathbf{E}$ denote any observed evidence and ξ any background information on the user. Given an action $a \in A_G$, let $U(G, a, \Delta)$ be a positive real-valued utility function, denoting the utility of action a with respect to goal G. Let $Pr(a|\mathbf{E}, \xi)$ denote the probability of action a given evidence E and ξ. Let our expected utility function, $EU(G, \Delta)$, be defined as

$$EU(G, \Delta) = \sum_{a \in A_G} \Pr(a|\mathbf{E}, \xi) U(G, a, \Delta). \tag{2}$$

The interface agent suggests the goal with the greatest expected utility taking into account the user chosen assistance thresholds. Utility theory, using Bayesian techniques for assessing the probabilities, is a non-ad hoc approach for predicting user intent. The utility function $U(G, a, \Delta)$ can take into account *relevancy* of the goal with respect to any number of metrics and/or discriminators in the environment. These metrics tell us what is important, explicitly enumerating those factors that impact the utility of choosing the goal. Δ may take into account the psychological factors, such as the user's cognitive load or preferences; system factors, such as processor load, explicit requirements placed on the system by the designer (e.g., reaction time); or simply the goal at hand[3].

We can use our utility function to determine what actions to take — the ones with the highest expected utility, when to take them — when the expected utility is above some chosen threshold, why to take an action — the action helps the user achieve the goal they are pursuing, and how to take it — the action itself. Key to this determination is realizing metrics that capture relevancy to an action, given the current state of the world.

Constructing the Bayesian network user model and associated utility functions is a difficult research question. For environments where the user's goals and actions are relatively static, we can use any number of well known knowledge elicitation techniques [13]. An approach for determining the goals, actions, and pre- and post-conditions within an environment for adaptive systems is one offered by Benyon and Murray [7]. They point out five analysis phases that must be considered when designing adaptive systems. The first two, functional and data analysis, are analogous to the software engineering techniques of function-oriented and state-oriented problem analysis [14]. Task knowledge analysis focuses on cognitive characteristics required of users by the system (e.g., cognitive loading). User analysis determines the scope of the user population where the system is able to respond. This analysis is concerned with obtaining attributes of users of the application. Environmental analysis is, obviously, concerned with

---

[3] The current implementation uses a user profile consisting of psychological factors that include spatial and temporal memory, domain expertise, and perceptual acuity.

the environment within which the system is to be situated in, including physical aspects of the system.

However, certain environments do not allow us to fully specify the user model a priori. In these cases, we must realize that our user model must be dynamic. We therefore look to research on dynamic Bayesian networks.

Some researchers take an expert systems approach, where the utility functions are elicited from knowledge experts [21]; some preliminary results for determining utility functions from users exist [15, 17, 35]. However, typically, and certainly in our case, the utility functions are very much determined by individual users. We therefore desire to capture the user-specific utility functions. However, because our user model is dynamic and therefore changes over time (with the possibility of adding and removing goals, actions, pre-conditions), we must be able to specify utility functions dynamically also. It should be obvious we would prefer not to query the user for his/her utility of a particular action.

Therefore, we must determine heuristics for determining the utility functions dynamically. Currently, we feel the user performs the most utilitarian actions first to achieve a goal. Using this simplistic approach, for a given action $a \in A_G$, we can proportionally rank $U(G, a, \Delta)$ based on the order in which the user performs the various actions, normalizing the utility functions.

4 User Models in Practice

Many researchers have used restricted domains (e.g., interface agents for e-mail and news readers) [27] as application domains for their interface agents. While the interface agents used in these domains may be adequate, scalability of the methodologies and techniques used to more complex domains is a problem. We are concerned with integrating intelligent interface agents into complex and dynamic environments, thereby possibly revealing insights into interface agent research not previously recognized with restricted domains.

Our own research in the field of intelligent interface agents is demonstrated by our integration into an expert system shell called PESKI [18, 19, 9], a virtual spaceplane environment [37], and a natural language interface database query system.

PESKI (Probabilities, Expert Systems, Knowledge, and Inference) is an integrated probabilistic knowledge-based expert system shell. PESKI provides users with knowledge acquisition [32], verification and validation [33, 6], data mining [36], and inference engine tools [34], each capable of operating in various communication modes. For more information on PESKI, see the United States Air Force Institute of Technology's Artificial Intelligence Laboratory web site[4]. PESKI was used for our initial tests concerning implementation and usability of our intelligent interface agent [3].

The Virtual SpacePlane (VSP) is a prototype of the Manned SpacePlane (MSP), a spacecraft capable of supporting the United States Air Force's mission

---

[4] http://www.afit.af.mil/Schools/EN/ENG/LABS/AI/

of providing worldwide deployment of space assets, with minimal preflight and in-orbit support from a mission control center. The goals of the VSP project are to uncover, develop and validate the MSP's user interface requirements, develop a prototype virtual spaceplane to demonstrate MSP missions, and to conduct preliminary training experiments. The VSP environment is an accurate, high fidelity presentation of the ground, the Earth's surface as seen from orbit, and the contents of the space environment. The architectural design of the VSP allows for rapid prototyping of the cockpit's user interface and flight dynamics.

Our interface agent is currently being integrated into the VSP to support VSP assistance such as real-time information visualization of real-time data and automation of the landing sequence. Figure 3 shows the preliminary integration of the interface agent within the VSP environment. Here, the interface agent has suggested the user land at Edwards Air Force Base. The suggestion is based on a number of observable environmental stimuli. If the user chooses to allow the agent to achieve this goal (by clicking on the "ok" button in the agent panel), the agent performs the necessary actions to land the spaceplane.

The Clavin System[5] project is a natural language interface database query system. Our CIaA is responsible for adding context to the spoken queries. For example, if the user asks "Which missile hit the plane" the system returns information about F-16s and F-22s and Stinger missiles; then the user's next query asks "What is the cost of these planes", the interface agent determines the user is requesting information specifically about F-16s and F-22s. The use of the interface agent in this system is different from the other two systems in that the user does not perform explicit actions per se in the environment that are observable. However, the robustness of our architecture and knowledge representation allow us to model the spoken queries from the user as well as the return answers to the database queries to effectively help the user.

5   Related Work

Several authors have investigated the use of probabilistic approaches, including Bayesian networks, for plan recognition and generation.

Kirman, et al. investigate the use of a Bayesian network of the world — in the authors' case, a simple room with a mobile robot and a target to be found — and a utility measure on world states to generate plans (sequences of actions) with high expected utility [26]. The number of plans investigated are restricted to those with high utility with respects to attaining a goal. In the authors' work, the goals are known with certainty and the plans to achieve the goals must be found. They show that by using decision-theoretic methods, they can drastically reduce the number of plans that must be investigated.

Waern uses keyhole plan recognition to determine what a user is doing within a route guidance domain and Internet news reader [39]. She uses pre-compiled

---

[5] The system is named after Cliff Clavin from the T.V. show *Cheers*. Cliff Clavin was known for being a know-it-all.

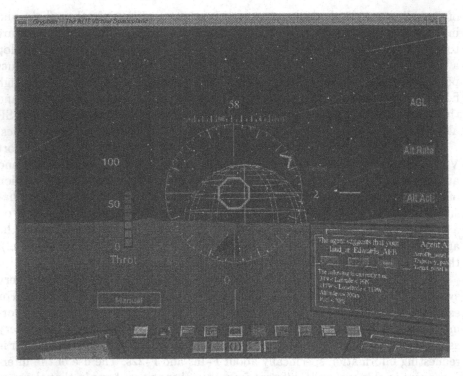

Fig. 3. The Virtual SpacePlane with an Interface Agent.

plans, called *recipes*. Assistance is offered for attaining a goal based on the probability the user is pursuing the goal. Her approach does *not* address the utility of offering assistance. She only considers the probability that offering to perform an action will help the user obtain a goal. Furthermore, her approach is not dynamic; that is, there is no adaptation of the pre-compiled plans. Lastly, there is no way to *trace* the user's execution of a plan nor offer explanations of assistance.

Conati, et al. present a system, ANDES, for long-term knowledge-assessment, plan recognition, and prediction of students' action during physics problem solving [12]. ANDES uses Bayesian networks constructed dynamically from static knowledge bases of specific physics problems as well as physics concepts, laws, formulas, etc. The plan recognition component is used to tailor support for the students when they reach impasses in their problem solving process. Their approach uses explicitly stated goal and problem solving strategy nodes to model the user's problem solving, but does *not* use a utility-based approach. The authors note they are researching methods to expand the fixed knowledge based used to construct the Bayesian networks; in particular, they are adding knowledge to determine common "misconceptions" within the domain and changing the static parameters.

The Pilot's Associate Program was a research effort using plan recognition within a real-time domain to determine goals from actions [4]. The Pilot's Associate was a software agent providing assistance — in the form of wanted and needed information at the correct time — to a combat pilot. They used AND/OR plan-and-goal trees with an associated "dictionary form" for explanations of plans a user was pursuing, and offered assistance to help the pilot. The graph's hierarchical structure produces a common planning language for use among heterogeneous modules. One of the main problems with their approach was due to the technology available at the time for representing and reasoning about uncertainty. Their approach did not account for the uncertainty nor utility in obtaining goals by performing actions. As stated in the authors' conclusions, Pilot's Associate pushed the envelope in uncertainty knowledge representation and reasoning techniques.

The intelligent multimedia presentation systems (IMMPS) project [25] presents an approach to determine, within its domain, the what, when, why, and how, to adapt the system's presentation. Central to their approach is an explicit decomposition of the adaptation process into adaptivity constituents (the "what"), determinants (the "when"), goals (the "why"), and rules (the "how"). They use a decision-theoretic approach to determine what adaptation is best for the current user context (e.g., the user is confused). Their approach does not address agent-based environments since the project is mainly concerned with information presentation and not with processing information from the user. However, their approach appears to be extensible to an agent-based paradigm. There is no way of determining whether a particular method of adaptation, the "how", is feasible within their approach, nor its impact. We believe this places an unnecessary burden on the application designer to account for this and/or limits the allowable adaptations.

6   Issues, Future Research, and Conclusions

In this paper, we described our utility theory-based user model for interface agents. Our approach explicitly models user intent by identifying the goals a user is trying to achieve, with the associated actions to achieve those goals, as well as the pre-conditions that cause a user to pursue the goals. The use of utility theory allows our interface agent to not only reason about the statistical probability that a user is pursuing a goal, but the utility of offering assistance to achieve that goal. Our utility function can use any relevant factor to calculate the utility of offering assistance for a user's goal and we can use our utility function to determine what actions to take, when to take them, why to take an action, and how to take it. The underlying knowledge representation, a Bayesian Network, is capable of representing uncertainty and is dynamic. That is, we can correct the user model over time.

Future efforts propose to provide tools to developers for constructing interface agent user models. Current agent development environments focus on the collaboration and autonomy requirements of an agent (more the former than the latter), while ignoring the adaptivity and robustness requirements. We propose to address these issues explicitly within our development environment, while additionally concentrating on environment specification and agent knowledge base and reasoning mechanisms.

References

1. David W. Albrecht, Ingrid Zukerman, Ann E. Nicholson, and Ariel Bud. Towards a bayesian model for keyhole plan recognition in large domains. In Anthony Jameson, Cécil Paris, and Carlo Tasso, editors, *Proceedings of the Sixth International Conference on User Modeling (UM '97)*, pages 365–376. SpringerWien New York, 1997.

2. Ronald M. Baecker, Jonathan Grudin, William A. S. Buxton, and Saul Greenberg. From customizable systems to intelligent agents. In *Readings in Human-Computer Interaction: Toward the Year 2000*, chapter 12, pages 783–792. Morgan Kaufmann, second edition, 1995.

3. Sheila B. Banks, Robert A. Harrington, Eugene Santos Jr., and Scott M. Brown. Usability testing of an intelligent interface agent. In *Proceedings of the Sixth International Interfaces Conference (Interfaces 97)*, pages 121–123, May 1997.

4. Sheila B. Banks and Carl S. Lizza. Pilot's associate: A cooperative, knowledge-based system application. *IEEE Expert*, pages 18–29, June 1991.

5. Sheila B. Banks, Martin R. Stytz, Eugene Santos Jr., and Scott M. Brown. User modeling for military training: Intelligent interface agents. In *Proceedings of the 19th Interservice/Industry Training Systems and Education Conference*, pages 645–653, December 1997.

6. David Bawcom. An incompleteness handling methodology for validation of bayesian knowledge bases. Master's thesis, Air Force Institute of Technology, 1997.

7. D. Benyon and D. Murray. Adaptive systems: from intelligent tutoring to autonomous agents. *Knowledge-Based Systems*, 6(4):197–219, December 1993.

8. Jack Breese and David Heckerman. Decision-theoretic troubleshooting: A framework for repair and experiment. In *Proceedings of the Twelfth Conference on Uncertainty in Artificial Intelligence*, pages 124–132, 1996.

9. Scott M. Brown, Eugene Santos Jr., and Sheila B. Banks. A dynamic bayesian intelligent interface agent. In *Proceedings of the Sixth International Interfaces Conference (Interfaces 97)*, pages 118–120, May 1997.

10. Scott M. Brown, Eugene Santos Jr., Sheila B. Banks, and Mark E. Oxley. Using explicit requirements and metrics for interface agent user model correction. In *Proceedings of the Second International Conference on Autonomous Agents (Agents '98)*, May 1998. to appear.

11. D. N. Chin. Intelligent interfaces as agents. In J. W. Sullivan and S. W. Tyler, editors, *Intelligent User Interfaces*. ACM, New York, 1991.

12. Cristina Conati, Abigail S. Gertner, Kurt VanLehn, and Marek J. Druzdzel. Online student modeling for coached problem solving using Bayesian networks. In Anthony Jameson, Cécile Paris, and Carlo Tasso, editors, *User Modeling: Proceedings of the Sixth International Conference, UM97*, pages 231–242. Springer Wien New York, Vienna, New York, 1997. Available from http://um.org.

13. Nancy J. Cooke. Varieties of knowledge elicitation techniques. *International Journal of Human-Computer Studies*, 41(6):801–849, 1994.

14. Alan M. Davis. *Software Requirements: Objects, Functions & States.* P T R Prentice Hall, 1993.

15. Marek J. Druzdzel and L. van der Gaag. Elicitation of probabilities for belief networks: Combining qualitative and quantitative information. In *Proceedings of the Eleventh Conference on Uncertainty in Artificial Intelligence*, pages 141–148, 1995.

16. Leonard Newton Foner. Paying attention to what's important: Using focus of attention to imporve unsupervised learning. Master's thesis, Massachusetts Institute of Technology, June 1994.

17. Vu Ha and Peter Haddawy. Problem-focused incremental elicitation of multi-attribute utility models. In *Proceedings of the Thirteenth Conference on Uncertainty in Artificial Intelligence*, pages 215–222, 1997.

18. Robert A. Harrington, Sheila Banks, and Eugene Santos Jr. Development of an intelligent user interface for a generic expert system. In Michael Gasser, editor, *Online Proceedings of the Seventh Midwest Artificial Intelligence and Cognitive Science Conference*, 1996. Available at http://www.cs.indiana.edu/event/maics96/.

19. Robert A. Harrington, Sheila Banks, and Eugene Santos Jr. GESIA: Uncertainty-based reasoning for a generic expert system intelligent user interface. In *Proceedings of the 8th IEEE International Conference on Tools with Artificial Intelligence*, pages 52–55, 1996.

20. Eric Horvitz. Agents with beliefs: Reflections on Bayesian methods for user modeling. In Anthony Jameson, Cécile Paris, and Carlo Tasso, editors, *User Modeling: Proceedings of the Sixth International Conference, UM97*, pages 441–442. Springer Wien New York, Vienna, New York, 1997. Available from http://um.org.

21. Eric Horvitz and Matthew Barry. Display of information for time-critical decision making. In *Proceedings of the Eleventh Uncertainty in Artificial Intelligence*, pages 296–305, 1995.

22. Eric Horvitz and J. Lengyel. Perception, attention, and resources: A decision-theoretic approach to graphics rendering. In *Proceedings of the Thirteenth Conference on Uncertainty in Artificial Intelligence*, August 1997.

23. Eric J. Horvitz and Adrian C. Klein. Utility-based abstraction and categorization. In David Heckerman and Abe Mamdani, editors, *Proceedings of the Ninth Conference on Uncertainty in Artificial Intelligence*. Morgan Kaufmann, 1993.

24. Anthony Jameson. Numeric uncertainty management in user and student modeling: An overview of systems and issues. *User Modeling and User-Adapted Interactions*, 5:193–251, 1995.

25. Charalampos Karagiannidis, Adamatios Koumpis, and Constantine Stephanidis. Deciding 'what', 'when', 'why', and 'how' to adapt in intelligent multimedia presentation systems. In G.P. Faconti and T. Rist, editors, *Proceedings of the Twelvth European Conference on Artificial Intelligence Workshop "Towards a Standard Reference Model for Intelligent Multimedia Presentation Systems"*. John Wiley & Sons, Ltd., August 1996.

26. Jak Kirman, Ann Nicholson, Moises Lejter, Thomas Dean, and Eugene Santos Jr. Using goals to find plans with high expected utility. In *Proceedings of the Second European Workshop on Planning*, pages 158–170, Linkoping, Sweden, 1993.

27. Patti Maes. Modeling adaptive autonomous agents. *Artificial Life Journal*, 1(1 & 2), 1994. MIT Press (C. Langton, Ed.).

28. Pattie Maes. Agents that reduce work and information overload. *Communications of the ACM*, 37(7):811–821, July 1994.

29. James Mayfield, Yannis Labrou, and Tim Finin. Evaluation of kqml as an agent communication language. In Michael J. Woolridge, Jörg P. Müller, and Milind Tambe, editors, *Intelligent Agents II: Agent Theories, Architectures, and Languages*, pages 347–360. Berlin: Springer, 1996.

30. Judea Pearl. *Probabilistic Reasoning in Intelligent Systems: Networks of Plausible Inference*. Morgan Kaufmann, San Mateo, CA, 1988.

31. H. Frances G. Pestello and Fred P. Pestello. Ignored, neglected, and abused: The behavior variable in attitude-behavior research. *Symbolic Interaction*, 14(3):341–351, 1991.

32. Eugene Santos Jr., Darwyn O. Banks, and Sheila B. Banks. MACK: A tool for acquiring consistent knowledge under uncertainty. In *Proceedings of the AAAI Workshop on Verification and Validation of Knowledge-Based Systems*, pages 23–32, 1997.

33. Eugene Santos Jr., Howard T. Gleason, and Sheila B. Banks. BVAL: Probabilistic knowledge-base validation. In *Proceedings of the AAAI Workshop on Verification and Validation of Knowledge-Based Systems*, pages 13–22, 1997.

34. Solomon Eyal Shimony, Carmel Domshlak, and Eugene Santos Jr. Cost-sharing heuristic for bayesian knowledge-bases. In *Proceedings of the Thirteenth Conference on Uncertainty in Artificial Intelligence*, pages 421–428, 1997.

35. Yoav Shoham. Conditional utility, utiltiy independence, and utility networks. In *Proceedings of the Thirteenth Conference on Uncertainty in Artificial Intelligence*, pages 429–436, 1997.

36. Daniel J. Stein III, Sheila B. Banks, Eugene Santos Jr., and Michael L. Talbert. Utilizing goal-directed data mining for incompleteness repair in knowledge bases. In Eugene Santos Jr., editor, *Proceedings of the Eighth Midwest Artificial Intelligence and Cognitive Science Conference*, pages 82–85. AAAI Press, 1997.

37. Martin R. Stytz and Sheila B. Banks. The virtual spaceplane: A modeling and simulation tool for advanced prototyping, requirements development, and training for the manned spaceplane project. In *Proceedings of the 19th Interservice/Industry Training Systems and Education Conference*, December 1997.

38. Katia Sycara, Keith Decker, Anandeep Pannu, Mike Williamson, and Dajun Zeng. Distributed intelligent agents. *IEEE Expert*, 11(6):36–46, December 1996.

39. Annika Waern. *Recognising Human Plans: Issues for Plan Recognition in Human-Computer Interaction*. PhD thesis, Royal Institute of Technology, 1996.

A Hybrid Convergent Method
for Learning Probabilistic Networks

Jun Liu, Kuo-Chu Chang, and Jing Zhou

Center of Excellence in Command, Control, Communications, and Intelligence (C³I)
School of Information Technology and Engineering
Fairfax, VA 22030, U.S.A.
kchang@gmu.edu

Abstract. During past few years, a variety of methods have been developed for learning probabilistic networks from data, among which the heuristic single link forward or backward searches are widely adopted to reduce the search space. A major drawback of these search heuristics is that they can not guarantee to converge to the right networks even if a sufficiently large data set is available. This motivates us to explore a new algorithm that will not suffer from this problem. In this paper, we first identify an asymptotic property of different score metrics, based on which we then present a hybrid learning method that can be proved to be asymptotically convergent. We show that the algorithm, when employing the information criterion and the Bayesian metric, guarantee to converge in a very general way and is computationally feasible. Evaluation of the algorithm with simulated data is given to demonstrate the capability of the algorithm.

1 Introduction

Probabilistic network, or Bayesian network as one of the major techniques in modeling a probabilistic space has been gradually recognized in an increasing number of application areas. Much research has been done in the literature. One of the important area is the automatic construction of network structure with database and domain knowledge. The resulting network is expected to be a graphical representation that explicitly demonstrates the probabilistic relationships among the variables presented in the database.

Many learning algorithms for Bayesian networks have been proposed in recent years. An important class of such algorithms is the score metric based method. Similar to solving a mathematical optimization problem, these methods first define a quantity metric that measures the quality of the network structures or the conditional dependence among variables given the database, then apply a search procedure to identify the structure that maximizes the metric over the structure space. One of the first work of such kind is Cooper and Herskovits's K2 algorithm [1]. The others include the Kutato algorithm [2], the Lam-Bacchus algorithm [3], the PC algorithm, Buntine's B-search algorithm [4], the method by Heckerman, et al. [5], and various combinations of these algorithms. Most of these algorithms employed a greedy search procedure (single step look ahead or backward). The goal is to reduce the search complexity so that the maximization over the structure space that contains more than an exponential number of structures becomes computationally feasible. As a widely adopted learning procedure, the greedy search works reasonably well for some probabilistic models. However it suffers from the problem of non-convergence for the other models. The critical remarks by Xiang, et al. [6] indicated that there exists a class of probabilistic domain models such as pseudo-independent (PI) model, on which the greedy search will theoretically lead to an incorrect result. Therefore, better techniques are needed in general.

This paper summarizes our recent research results in developing new learning algorithms that tackle the problem of learning convergency. The problem is divided into two subjects--the asymptotic properties of the score metric and the asymptotic convergence of the search procedure. Roughly speaking, given a sufficiently large database, a consistent score metric should favor the correct models of the underlying distribution of the database, and an asymptotically convergent search procedure when employing such a score metric, should return one of these correct models. In this paper, we first review our previous research on the consistence of the score metrics. We then introduce a hybrid learning method that can be proved to be asymptotically convergent.

This paper is organized as follows. In Section 2, we introduce notations and a set of score metrics used in the paper. The hybrid learning algorithm is given in Section 3, which is based on a previously developed method--the Simple Search algorithm [7]. In Section 4, we evaluate the new approach with a popular test example. A comparison between the new approach and the B-search is also presented. We give the concluding remarks in Section 5.

2 Preliminaries

Throughout the discussion, we consider a domain $U=\{X_1, ..., X_n\}$ of $n>1$ discrete variables defined on a probability space. Each variable may take on a finite number of values. We use capital letters, such as X, Y, and Z to denote variables, and lowercase letters, such as x, y, and z to represent the specific values the corresponding variables take. A set of variables are denoted by boldface capital letters, V, W and Z, and the corresponding assignments of values (instantiations), by v, w, and z. For the sets of variables, we use $U, \cap$, and $-$ denote the set union, intersection, and difference, respectively. A sample over U is a value assignment to every variable in U. A database D_N over U is a list of samples. In this paper, we assume that the samples in a database are independent and identical distributed (i.i.d.) with an underlying distribution. Furthermore, we assume that there is no sample with missing values in the database.

A *probability distribution* p_V over $V \subseteq U$ is defined as $p_V(v)=P(V=v)$, $\forall v$, or simply denoted as $p(v)$ whenever the context is clear. Let V and W be subsets of U. The *conditional probability distribution* of V given W is defined as $p(v|w)=p(v,w)/p(w)$, $\forall v$ and w, where $p(w)>0$. Consider V, W, and Z be three disjoint subsets of U. V and W

are *conditionally independent* given **Z**, denoted as $I_P(\mathbf{V}, \mathbf{Z}, \mathbf{W})$, or simply $I(\mathbf{V}, \mathbf{Z}, \mathbf{W})$, if $p(v|w,z)=p(v|z)$, $\forall v$ and w.

2.1 Bayesian networks

Since we use graphs to represent independence relations among variables where each node in the graph represent each variable in **U**, we shall interchangeably use nodes and variables. Let three disjoint subsets **V**, **W**, and **Z** of nodes in a graph. If **V** *separates* **W** from **Z**, it is denoted as <**V**, **Z**, **W**> [8]. In a directed graph, the link between nodes is called *arc*. A graph G is an *independence map* (*I-map*) of p if each node in the graph corresponds to a variable in **U** and for all disjoint subsets **V**, **W**, and **Z** such that <**V**, **Z**, **W**>, $I(\mathbf{V}, \mathbf{Z}, \mathbf{W})$ must hold in p. That is, in an I-map, variables that are graphically separated are conditionally independent. A *minimal I-map* of p is an I-map in which no link can be deleted such that the resulting graph is still an I-map of p. Since there are only a finite number of network structures for a given problem domain, there is a finite number of I-maps for a given p. Among these I-maps there must exist at least one network structure that needs the least number parameters to define a Bayesian network representing p. This structure (could be more than one) is called the simplest I-map of p. For more details on graphical representation of dependency models, see [8].

Definition 1 Let $G = \{\Pi_1, \Pi_2, ..., \Pi_n\}$ be a directed acyclic graph over **U** where Π_i is the parent set of the ith node corresponds to the random variable X_i in **U**, and Θ be a set of specified conditional probability distributions $p(x_i|\pi_i)$, $\forall x_i$ and $\forall \pi_i$, $i = 1, ..., n$. Then a *Bayesian network B* is defined to be a pair $B=(G, \Theta)$. G is the topological structure, and Θ the parameter set of B.

By this definition, the network structures are not restricted to the minimal I-map of the joint probability distribution which is the product of the n conditional probabilities with respect to n variables, that is, redundant arcs are allowed. Since the redundant arcs introduce redundant parameters and increase the complexity of the network, an alternative definition of Bayesian network is to remove this allowance by adding the minimality. However, the latter definition is very hard to verify in practice even if a network has only a moderate number of variables. For this reason, we prefer the above definition.

An important property of a network structure is the node order, in which the preceding nodes are not allowed to be descendants of the successor nodes. For example, the structure $\{X \leftarrow Y \rightarrow Z\}^1$ has the node order (YXZ) or (YZX), and $\{X \rightarrow Y \rightarrow Z, X \rightarrow Z\}$ has an order (XYZ). A well-known fact is that if p is positive, then there is a unique minimal I-map corresponding to every node order.

---

[1] $A \leftarrow B$ means there is a directed arc from node B to node A.

2.2 Convergency of learning procedures

Given a joint probability distribution p, there are many Bayesian network presentations, of which the network structures are necessarily to be I-maps of p. Not all I-maps are "good" presentations of a given p. For example, a complete network that is a trivial I-map of every p reveals no conditional independency among variables and hence is almost useless. Since a minimal I-map has no redundant arcs, and needs less parameters than all network structures that are its super-maps, it is a preferable presentation. Similarly, in learning Bayesian networks from data, we expect to find one of the minimal I-map of p that generates the data. However, due to the randomness of the data generating process this expectation is too unrealistic for a finite database. A reasonable consideration is to design a learning procedure that is *asymptotically convergent* to one of the minimal I-maps of p that generates the database, as the sample size in the database increases. This introduces the formal definition of the convergency of learning procedures.

Definition 2 Let p be a joint distribution over U. Let **D** be a database containing infinite i.i.d. random samples with respect to p, and $\mathbf{D}_N$ contain the first N samples in **D**, $N=1, 2, ...$ Let $\mathcal{L}$ be a learning procedure that returns a network structure G given a $\mathbf{D}_N$, that is $G=\mathcal{L}(\mathbf{D}_N)$. Let $\mathcal{M}$ be the set of all minimal I-maps of p. Then $\mathcal{L}$ is said to be (asymptotically) convergent, if $\lim_{N\to\infty}P(\mathcal{L}(\mathbf{D}_N) \in \mathcal{M}) = 1$.

The asymptotic convergency states that a learning procedure will return a minimal I-map with probability approaching to 1 as the sample size of database goes to infinity, or alternatively, the probability that it will return a non minimal I-map approaches zero as the sample size of database goes to infinity.

As mentioned before, a score metric based method employs a metric that measures the quality of network structures given the data. It can be imagined that a necessary condition for a learning procedure to be convergent is that the employed score should favor minimal I-maps among all I-maps, and favor the simplest I-maps among all minimal I-maps, especially when the sample size of the database is sufficiently large. This introduces the formal definition of the *consistency* of score metrics.

Definition 3 Let p be a probability distribution on U. Let $\mathbf{D} = \{U_1, U_2, ...\}$ be a database with infinite sequence of i.i.d. samples over U. Let $S(G, \mathbf{D}_N)$ be a score metric where G is a Bayesian network structure defined on U, and $\mathbf{D}_N=\{U_1, U_2, ..., U_N\}$ is a database containing the first N samples in **D**. Let G_{sim} be a simplest I-map of p. The score metric S is called (*asymptotically*) *consistent*, if for any network structure G, where G is not a simplest I-map of p, we always have

$$\lim_{N\to\infty} P(S(G_{sim}, \mathbf{D}_N) > S(G, \mathbf{D}_N)) = 1.$$

In addition to the asymptotic convergency, we would mention another expected property of a learning procedure: capability to find simpler minimal I-map. An I-map with properly defined parameters can be a valid presentation for a given p. A minimal I-map is more preferable than a non minimal I-map. However, not every minimal I-map is desirable. To see this, consider two network structures $\{X \leftarrow Y \rightarrow Z\}$ and $\{X \rightarrow Y \rightarrow Z, X \rightarrow Z\}$. It is easily to define parameter sets for both structures such that both networks represent the same joint probability distribution p and they both are minimal I-map of p. But the latter is a complete structure that reveals no conditional independence $I(X, Y, Z)$. We therefore expect a good learning algorithm would converge to the first structure. In general, the sparser the network structure is, the more conditional independencies it would reveals. Therefore, we expect a learning procedure that would not only be convergent, but also converge to a simpler or sparser structure among all minimal I-map.

3 Learning Bayesian Networks

The focus of this section is to develop a learning algorithm that is theoretically convergent. The algorithm employs the information criterion as the score metric, and a hybrid search procedure that originates and is modified from a so-called *simple search* approach [7]. We first investigate asymptotic properties of the information criterion that form the theoretical basis of the learning algorithm. Secondly, we introduce the simple search procedure and prove its convergency. We then present the main algorithm, which is designed to converge to a minimum I-map of the underlying distribution when a sufficiently large data set is available. Not to clutter the main context, detailed proofs of the theorems are omitted. For details, see [9].

3.1 Asymptotic properties of the score metric

A popular score metric in the Bayesian learning field is the information criterion. Let Let $U = \{X_1, X_2, ..., X_n\}$, where each X_i can take a value from $\{x_{i1}, x_{i2}, \cdots, x_{ir_i}\}$, $r_i \geq 2$, $i=1,..., n$. Let G denote a network structure over U, and let Π_i be the parent set of X_i defined by G. Furthermore, for each Π_i, let w_{ij} denote the jth instantiation of Π_i, $j = 1, ..., q_i$, $q_i \geq 1$. Let $\Theta = \{\theta_{ijk}\}$ be a parameter set where $\theta_{ijk} = P(X_i = x_{ik} | \Pi_i = w_{ij})$, $i=1,..., n$, $j=1,..., q_i$, $k=1,...,r_i$. On Θ, the only constraint is $\sum_{k=1}^{r_i} \theta_{ijk} = 1$ for $\forall i$ and j.

Therefore the total number of free parameters in Θ is equal to $K = \sum_{i=1}^{n} q_i(r_i - 1)$.

Now, let $d_N = \{u_1, u_2, ..., u_N\}$ be an observed database with respect to D_N. let N_{ijk} be the number of observations in d_N where the variable X_i has the value x_{ik} and Π_i is instantiated as w_{ij}. Finally, let $N_{ij} = \sum_{k=1}^{r_i} N_{ijk}$. Then the information criterion with a penalty function f of N is defined by

$$I_f(G, d_N) = -N \times H(G, d_N) - K \times f(N). \tag{1}$$

where

$$H(G, \mathbf{d}_N) = -\sum_{i=1}^{n} \sum_{j=1}^{q_i} \sum_{k=1}^{r_i} \frac{N_{ijk}}{N} \log \frac{N_{ijk}}{N_{ij}} \qquad (2)$$

is a non-negative quantity that represents the conditional entropy of the database $\mathbf{d}_N$ given the network structure G. H is also the posterior log likelihood of $\mathbf{d}_N$ given G with the conditional probabilities estimated by the relative frequencies on the samples.

Given a probability distribution p, the preferable structure is the minimal I-maps among which the simplest I-map is the best. A good score metric that measures the quality of network structures given the data therefore should favor I-map against non-I-map, favor minimal I-map among all I-maps, and favor the simplest I-maps among all minimal I-maps, especially when the sample size of the database is sufficiently large. The following theorem states that for a class of penalty functions the information criterion has such properties.

Theorem 1 (*Asymptotic properties of the Information Criterion*) Let p be a strictly positive probability distribution defined over $\mathbf{U}$. Let $\mathbf{D}_N = \{\mathbf{U}_1, ..., \mathbf{U}_N\}$ be N i.i.d. samples of $\mathbf{U}$. Let I_f be the information criterion with a penalty function f: $f(N) \to \infty$, and $f(N)/N \to 0$ ($N \to \infty$). Let G and G' be two network structures over $\mathbf{U}$. Then for any $M \geq 0$,

$$\lim_{N \to \infty} P(\log I_f(G, \mathbf{D}_N) - \log I_f(G', \mathbf{D}_N) > M) = 1$$

if one of the following conditions holds:
  (a) G and G' are I-maps of p with K and K' ($K < K'$) parameters, respectively, or
  (b) G is a complete network structure, G' is not an I-map of p, and they obey the same node order.
  (c) G is an I-map of p, but G' is not.
  (d) G is a simplest I-map, but G' is not (consistency).

From Theorem 1, we could conclude that a "high quality structures" is more likely to have a higher scores, and conversely, a structure that has a higher score is more likely to be a "high quality structure". The larger the database is, the more likely this is true. Based on this theorem, it can be concluded that if there exists an algorithm that can find a structure with maximum score for any given finite database, this algorithm is a convergent algorithm. Unfortunately, the structure space is so large that such an algorithm is very difficult, if not impossible, to be developed, except an exhaustive search that is computationally prohibited.

Our new algorithm is an alternative approach. Before going on, we need to introduce another asymptotic property associated with the information criterion, the *consistency of the local scores*. Let $G = \{\Pi_1, ..., \Pi_n\}$ be a structure defined by n parent sets corresponding to n variables. By (1), the information criterion can be rewritten as a summation of local scores: $I_f(G, \mathbf{d}_N) = \sum_{i=1}^{n} I_{f,i}(\Pi_i, \mathbf{d}_N)$, where

$$I_{f,i}(\Pi_i, \mathbf{d}_N) = \sum_{j=1}^{q_i} \sum_{k=1}^{r_i} N_{ijk} \log \frac{N_{ijk}}{N_{ij}} - q_i(r_i - 1)f(N), \quad i = 1, ..., n. \tag{3}$$

Then we have the following theorem.

Theorem 2 (*asymptotic property of the local score*) Let p, $\mathbf{D}_N$, and I_f be as in Theorem 1. Let $G_m = \{\Pi_1^m, ..., \Pi_n^m\}$, $G = \{\Pi_1, ..., \Pi_n\}$, and $G_c = \{\Pi_1^c, ..., \Pi_n^c\}$ be three network structures obeying the same node order O, where G_m is a minimal I-map of p, G_c is a complete structure, and G is a subgraph of G_c, i.e., $\exists i$ such that $\Pi_i \subset \Pi_i^c$. Then we have the following:

(a) if $\Pi_i^m \subseteq \Pi_i$, then $\lim_{N \to \infty} P(I_{f,i}(\Pi_i, \mathbf{D}_N) > I_{f,i}(\Pi_i^c, \mathbf{D}_N)) = 1$;

(b) if $\Pi_i^m \not\subset \Pi_i$, then $\lim_{N \to \infty} P(I_{f,i}(\Pi_i^c, \mathbf{D}_N) > I_{f,i}(\Pi_i, \mathbf{D}_N)) = 1$.

Theorem 2 is very important and is the theoretical basis of the new learning algorithms to be developed. To explain the basic idea clearly, we first introduce two algorithms that are convergent, but require a node order as input. Based on analysis of these algorithms, we then develop the hybrid learning algorithm that does not require a node order.

3.2 The Simple Search Algorithm and the Modified Simple Search Algorithm

Given a database $\mathbf{d}_N$ with an underlying distribution p, and a node order, we are to construct a minimal I-map $G_m = \{\Pi_1^m, ..., \Pi_n^m\}$ of p. This is equivalent to find each Π_i^m, $i = 1, ..., n$. To do this, we begin from a complete network $G_c = \{\Pi_1^c, ..., \Pi_n^c\}$ that obeys the input node order. Secondly, we examine all arcs in G_c to determine which arc is in G_m and which is not. We delete one arc at a time in G_c to form a new network structure $G = \{\Pi_1, ..., \Pi_n\}$. Assuming the deleted arc is in the ith parent set Π_i^c, i.e., $\Pi_i \subset \Pi_i^c$, then if the local score difference between Π_i and Π_i^c is greater than zero, that is $I_{f,i}(\Pi_i, \mathbf{d}_N) > I_{f,i}(\Pi_i^c, \mathbf{d}_N)$, by Theorem 2 (b), the arc just deleted is more likely not in Π_i^m, otherwise, it is more likely in Π_i^m by Theorem 2 (a). Note that there are only $n(n-1)/2$ arcs to be examined. Finally, only those arcs whose deletion causes the score to decrease are identified and used to comprise a network structure.

Figure 1 presents this algorithm. The algorithm, called the *simple search* (SS), is composed of a subroutine and a main routine. The subroutine, called "SS", is to reduce a Π_i^c by checking every arc in it using the procedure described above. The main routine is to globally construct a network structure.

===

Main routine: the Simple Search (SS)

    Input: a list of nodes $\{X_1, ..., X_n\}$, a observed database $\mathbf{d}_N$, and
                         a node order O: $i_1, i_2, ..., i_n$;

    $\Pi_{i_1} = \varnothing$;

    for $k = 2, ..., n$

        $\Pi_{i_k}^c = \{X_{i_1}, X_{i_2}, ..., X_{i_{k-1}}\}$;

        $\Pi_i = SS(X_i, \Pi_i^c, \mathbf{d}_N)$;

    end;

    Output: $G = \{\Pi_1, ..., \Pi_n\}$;

Subroutine: $SS(X_i, \Pi_i^c, \mathbf{d}_N)$

    Input: X_i, a complete parent set Π_i^c, and a database $\mathbf{d}_N$

    $\Pi_i = \varnothing$;

    for each $X \in \Pi_i^c$

        if $I_{f,i}(\Pi_i^c - \{X\}, \mathbf{d}_N) < I_{f,i}(\Pi_i^c, \mathbf{d}_N)$

        then $\Pi_i = \Pi_i \bigcup \{X\}$;

    end

    Return: Π_i

===

Figure 1. The Simple Search (SS) algorithm

The Simple Search algorithm can be proved to be convergent. This is shown in the following theorem.

Theorem 3. The Simple Search (SS) algorithm is asymptotically convergent, and it converges to the minimal I-map of p that obeys the input node order, if (1) the underlying distribution p that generates the database is positive, and (2) the information criterion has a penalty function f: $f(N) \to \infty$, and $f(N)/N \to 0$ $(N \to \infty)$.

The SS algorithm is simple and convergent, but the convergent speed may be slow. This is because it does not include a maximization procedure. For example, the parent set Π_i returned by the subroutine SS in the ith step, may not have the highest local score. A consideration is to take this Π_i as the initial parent set, then use the greedy search, forward or backward, one node at a time, to maximally increase the local score of Π_i. This procedure is stopped until no further improvement on the local score is found. This modified algorithm, called the *Modified Simple Search* (MSS) is illustrated in Figure 2. In Figure 2, the main routine is the same as in the SS search.

===

Main routine: the Modified Simple Search (MSS)

> **Input:** a list of nodes $\{X_1, ..., X_n\}$, a observed database $\mathbf{d}_N$, and
> a node order O: $i_1, i_2, ..., i_n$;

$$\Pi_{i_1} = \varnothing;$$

> **for** $k = 2, ..., n$
>
> $$\Pi_{i_k}^c = \{X_{i_1}, X_{i_2}, ..., X_{i_{k-1}}\};$$
>
> $$\Pi_i = MSS(X_i, \Pi_i^c, \mathbf{d}_N);$$

end;

Output: $G = \{\Pi_1, ..., \Pi_n\}$;

Subroutine: $MSS(X_i, \Pi_i^c, \mathbf{d}_N)$

> **Input:** X_i, a complete parent set Π_i^c, and a database $\mathbf{d}_N$
>
> $$\Pi_i = \varnothing;$$
>
> **for each** $X \in \Pi_i^c$
>
> > **if** $I_{f,i}(\Pi_i^c - \{X\}, \mathbf{d}_N) < I_{f,i}(\Pi_i^c, \mathbf{d}_N)$
> >
> > **then** $\Pi_i = \Pi_i \cup \{X\}$;
>
> **end**
>
> **Repeat**
>
> > **Repeat**
> >
> > $$X = \arg \max_{X \in \Pi_i^c - \Pi_i} I_{f,i}(\Pi_i \cup \{X\}, \mathbf{d}_N)$$
> >
> > **if** $I_{f,i}(\Pi_i \cup \{X\}, \mathbf{d}_N) > I_{f,i}(\Pi_i, \mathbf{d}_N)$
> >
> > **then** $\Pi_i = \Pi_i \cup \{X\}$;
> >
> > **until** no further improvement in $I_{f,i}$ by adding any node to Π_i
> >
> > **Repeat**
> >
> > $$X = \arg \max_{X \in \Pi_i} I_{f,i}(\Pi_i - \{X\}, \mathbf{d}_N)$$
> >
> > **if** $I_{f,i}(\Pi_i - \{X\}, \mathbf{d}_N) > I_{f,i}(\Pi_i, \mathbf{d}_N)$
> >
> > **then** $\Pi_i = \Pi_i - \{X\}$;
> >
> > **until** no further improvement in $I_{f,i}$ by removing any node from Π_i
>
> **until** no further improvement in $I_{f,i}$

Return: Π_i

===

Figure 2. The Modified Simple Search (MSS) algorithm

Using the MSS algorithm, in each step, the subroutine MSS would return a parent set with a local score greater than or equal to the one returned by the subroutine SS. Hence, a structure constructed by the MSS algorithm would have a global score greater than or equal to that of the one constructed by the SS algorithm. It can be imagined that the MSS algorithm is also convergent, and the convergent speed should be faster than that of the SS algorithm. In deed, this is verified by the following theorem.

Theorem 4   The Modified Simple Search (MSS) algorithm is asymptotically convergent, and it converges to the minimal I-map of p that obeys the input node order, if (1) the underlying distribution p that generates the database is positive, and (2) the information criterion used in the algorithm has a penalty function f: $f(N) \rightarrow \infty$, and $f(N)/N \rightarrow 0$ ($N \rightarrow \infty$).

3.3   A hybrid learning algorithm for Bayesian networks

Two algorithms introduced in the previous section are relatively simple and theoretically convergent. However, they both need a node order as input. In this section, we develop an algorithm that employs the MSS subroutine as the local search method and a greedy global search method as described below.

At beginning, a node is chosen as the initial point, and it will become a root node of the resulting network. The root node can be chosen arbitrarily, randomly, or based on the domain knowledge. If such a node is difficult to choose, we can run the algorithm several times, each starts with a different node, and choose the best result, e.g., the network structure that has the highest score. The worst case is to run the algorithm n times.

Whenever a root node is determined, the network structure is recursively constructed in the way that each time only one node is added into the current network until all nodes are included in the network. To add a node to the current network, first, all parent sets of the remaining nodes are identified using MSS algorithm. This is done by starting from a complete parent set that contains all nodes in the current network. Then a node is chosen by applying one of the following decision rules:

(1)   it has the least number of parents, or
(2)   it has the least number of local parameters, $q_i(r_i-1)$, or
(3)   it has the highest local score.

Since at each step we optimize the selected decision rule, it is expected that the resulting network structure would either be sparse, or have fewer number of parameters, or have a higher score. Figure 3 presents the above procedure with the decision rule (3). It should be mentioned that if we denote O as the resulting sequential order in which the nodes were actually added, the network structure obtained using this algorithm will be identical to that obtained using the SS search with the order O as input.

===

Main routine: the Hybrid Learning Algorithm (HLA)

    Input: a list of nodes $\{X_1, ..., X_n\}$, a observed database $\mathbf{d}_N$, and

               an index k_1 such that X_{k_1} is the root node;

    $\Pi_{k_1} = \varnothing$;

    $G = \{ \Pi_{k_1} \}$;   (the current network)

    $\mathbf{V} = \{ X_{k_1} \}$;   (the set of nodes within the current network)

    $\mathbf{W} = \{X_1, ..., X_n\} - \{ X_{k_1} \}$;   (the set of nodes not in the current network)

    for $i = 2, ..., n$

        for every $X_j \in \mathbf{W}$

            $\Pi_j = MSS(X_j, \mathbf{V}, \mathbf{d}_N)$;

        end

        $k_i = index(\arg \max_{\forall X_j \in \mathbf{W}} I_{f,j}(\Pi_j, \mathbf{d}_N))$;**   (*index* returns the index of a node)

        $\mathbf{V} = \mathbf{V} \cup \{ X_{k_i} \}$;

        $\mathbf{W} = \mathbf{W} - \{ X_{k_i} \}$;

        $G = G \cup \{ \Pi_{k_i} \}$;

    end;

    Output: $G = \{\Pi_1, ..., \Pi_n\}$;

Subroutine: $MSS(X_i, \mathbf{V}, \mathbf{d}_N)$

    (The same as in the Modified Simple Search algorithm)

===

Figure 3. The Hybrid Learning Algorithm (HLA)

The decision rule (1) or (2) can also be applied to this algorithm. One simply substitutes the decision line (marked **) with the alternative decision rule. As mentioned before, since we optimize the selected decision rule, it is expected that the resulting network structure would either be sparse, or have the fewer parameters, or have a higher global score. By the asymptotic properties of the information criterion explained in Theorem 1 and 2, we can see that these three decision rules are more or less consistent since an I-map with a higher score is also more likely to be simpler and have fewer parameters, and *vice versa*. Therefore, regardless of which decision rule is used, the resulting network tends to be sparser or simpler. This algorithm can also be proved to be convergent. This is verified by the following theorem.

Theorem 5   The Hybrid Learning Algorithm (HLA) is asymptotically convergent, and it converges to a minimal I-map of p that obeys the resulting node order, if (1) the underlying distribution p that generates the database is positive, and (2) the information criterion has a penalty function f: $f(N) \to \infty$, and $f(N)/N \to 0$ ($N \to \infty$).

It should be mentioned that for the local search method, the subroutine SS can be used in the HLA instead of the subroutine MSS, and the convergency property of the algorithm will remain unchanged. In addition, it is worth to point out that the information criterion is not the only score metric that has asymptotic properties. Another popular score metric, the Bayesian score, developed by Cooper and Herskovits [1], has similar asymptotic properties as described in Theorem 1 and 2. Hence, if it is used in the SS, MSS, and HLA algorithms, the convergency property of the algorithms remains unchanged as well. For detailed discussion and theoretical proof, readers are referred to [9].

4 Performance Analysis

The main purpose of this paper is to develop learning algorithms that are theoretical convergent. As mentioned in Introduction, those algorithms which employ the greedy search can not guarantee to obtain a correct solution (I-map of the underlying distribution). Particularly, if the underlying distribution is a PI model, theoretical analysis shows that these algorithm would result in an empty graph (the graph without arcs) [6]. An implementation example that shows the non-convergency of the greedy search, and the convergency of the SS search and the Descent Greedy search (the other convergent method), can be found in [9]. This section presents the evaluation of the developed algorithms on learning a popular network, "Alarm System" by Beinlich et al. [10].

Figure 4 illustrates the structure of the "Alarm System" which contains 37 nodes, and 47 arcs. The network parameters are not listed. All nodes have less than three parents, so this network is relatively sparse. In the figure, the numbers represent the indexes of variables.

We will compare the learning results obtained by the HLA algorithm to those obtained by a comparable algorithm, the B-search algorithm [4], because both algorithms do not require a node order. In both algorithms, we use the information criterion with a penalty function $f(N) = 1/2\log N$, which is also called the Minimum Description Length (MDL) score [5].

In order to compare the performance of the two learning methods (HLA and B), we use these methods separately to construct Bayesian networks from a databases. This database contains 10,000 samples generated by simulation based on the network structure and parameters. The learning algorithms are then applied using these data with a sample size from 100 to 10,000. After the resulting network structures are obtained, we then use the same learning samples to estimate the network parameters (conditional probabilities). To avoid a zero probability estimate, the Bayesian estimator is used,

$$\hat{\theta}_{ijk} = \hat{P}(X_i = x_{ik} \mid \Pi_i = wij) = \frac{N_{ijk} + 1}{N_{ij} + r_i},$$

where the notations are defined as in Section 3.1. For each learning algorithm, top 10 network structures were obtained. Three criteria were used to evaluate the 20 resulting networks.

They are:

    (i)   The MDL score of the resulting network structure. Based on Theorem 1, the higher the score is, the better the quality of network structure would be.

    (ii)   The number of extra and missing arcs. Intuitively, the less the number, the closer the resulting network structure would be to the original. Note that if an arc in the resulting network is in a reversal direction with respect to the original network, it would be counted as one extra arc and one missing arc.

    (iii)   The cross entropy $II_p(p,q) = E_p \log(p/q) \geq 0$, a non-negative quantity, where p and q are the joint probability distributions represented by the original network and the resulting network, respectively. The lower the entropy, the closer the q would be to p, and $II = 0$ if and only if $p=q$.

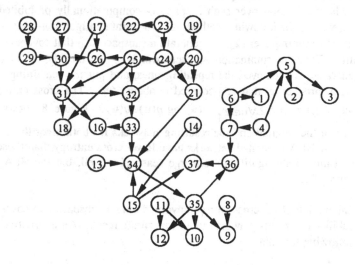

Figure 4. Alarm System

Figure 5 shows the score difference between the HLA and the B-search vs. the sample size. As expected, the HLA tends to return the network structures that have the higher scores. This tendency is more and more significant as the sample size increases, especially, when it exceeds 1,000. This tendency indicates that the HLA would return network structure with higher quality given a finite database, if its sample size attains to certain level. This can be seen in Figure 6 and Figure 7.

Figure 6 and Figure 7 show the number of extra arcs and missing arcs, respectively. We can see that the HLA has a smoother performance than the B-search does. The number of extra arcs fluctuates in a range from 6 to 9, and the missing arcs tend to decrease. When the sample size is bigger than 1,000, the most of "mistakes" are direction reversals, and this happens in most cases for those nodes that have only one parent. In other word, the resulting network is more likely to be an equivalent I-map of the original network. We also can see that the B-search has an oscillatory performance, where the absolute number of mistake arcs are much more than in that of the HLA. This is due to the deficiency of the B-search that it is hard to provide a decision rule in determining the direction when adding an arc during the learning process. In a network, not every arc can be reversed such that the resulting network is still an I-map. Therefore the more the arcs are reversed, the more likely the resulting network would not be an I-map.

Next, we shall show the cross entropy between the original and the resulting networks for both learning algorithms. To do this, we have to address a computational problem. For a discrete variable domain U, we are to compute

$$H_p(p, q) = \sum_{\forall \mathbf{u}} p(\mathbf{u}) \log p(\mathbf{u}) / q(\mathbf{u}). \tag{4}$$

For the alarm system, thirty seven discrete variables with each one having about three values would have a joint configuration space with an order approximately equal to 4.5×10^{17}. The summation over such a space is computationally prohibited. In our performance, we use the following method. Let the joint configuration space denoted as Ω_U. Instead of summing over Ω_U, we generate a subspace Ω'_U that covers certain mass of probability. Then the summation is taken over Ω'_U. To do this, out of the 10,000 samples generated, we removed the repeating ones, and put the remaining samples in Ω'_U. The total probability that Ω'_U covered is about 60%. The cross entropy is then estimated as $\hat{H}_p(p, q) = \sum_{\forall \mathbf{u} \in \Omega'_U} p(\mathbf{u}) \log p(\mathbf{u}) / q(\mathbf{u})$. Figure 8 shows the cross entropy between the original and the resulting networks for both algorithms. For most sample sizes, the HLA generated networks have lower cross entropy than those of the B-search algorithm. Both algorithms converge reasonably well, but the HLA converges faster and smoother.

Since our calculation of the cross entropy involved only a subspace that cover only 60% of the probability mass, this may lead to an inaccurate result. An alternative method is to use the following formula:

$$H_p(p, q) = \sum_{\forall \mathbf{u}} p(\mathbf{u}) \log p(\mathbf{u}) / q(\mathbf{u})$$

$$= \sum_{\forall \mathbf{u}} p(\mathbf{u}) \log p(\mathbf{u}) - \sum_{\forall \mathbf{u}} p(\mathbf{u}) \log q(\mathbf{u})$$

$$= \sum_{\forall \mathbf{u}} p(\mathbf{u}) \log p(\mathbf{u}) - \sum_{\forall \mathbf{u}} p(\mathbf{u}) \log \prod_{i=1}^{n} q(x_i \mid \pi_i^q)$$

$$= \sum_{\forall \mathbf{u}} p(\mathbf{u}) \log p(\mathbf{u}) - \sum_{i=1}^{n} \sum_{\forall \mathbf{u}} p(\mathbf{u}) \log q(x_i \mid \pi_i^q)$$

$$= \sum_{\forall \mathbf{u}} p(\mathbf{u}) \log p(\mathbf{u}) - \sum_{i=1}^{n} \sum_{\forall x_i, \pi_i^q} p(x_i, \pi_i^q) \log q(x_i \mid \pi_i^q), \tag{5}$$

where the first term is a constant that is irrelevant to the resulting distribution q, and Π_i^q, $i=1,...,n$, are the parent sets defined by the resulting network. The double summation in the second term of (5) is much simpler than that in (4). However, this involves the computations of the marginal distributions, $p(x_i, \pi_i^q)$, which can be obtained using any query algorithm such as the SPI algorithm [12].

5 Conclusions

In this paper, we developed a hybrid learning algorithm that is theoretically convergent in a very general way. The algorithm is designed such that no prior information about the network structure is needed. However, if such information is available, it can be easily incorporated into the learning procedure. The detailed discussion can be found in [9]. The algorithm requires selecting a node as the starting point. We pointed out in Section 3.3 that this initial node can be chosen arbitrarily, randomly, or based on domain knowledge. In the worst case if such a node is difficult to choose, we can run the algorithm n times, and choose the best result. In Section 3.3, we proposed three decision rules to determine the priority of the nodes to be added to the existing network. We stress that regardless which initial node or which decision rule is used, the convergency property of the learning algorithm will not be affected.

The performance of the algorithm on the Alarm System showed that it is superior to the B-search in terms of the network score, the incorrect arcs, and the cross-entropy. In our performance analysis, we used the MDL score which is a special case of the information criterion. It would be worthwhile to evaluate the algorithm using different penalty functions in the information criterion. The other interesting work is to analyze the sample complexity of the algorithm. That is, given a finite database, how much confidence can we have that the algorithm will return a minimal I-map, or in turn, given a confidence level, how many samples do we need such that the algorithm will return a minimal I-map. This research is very important since it will provide a quantifiable measure on the usefulness of the algorithm in real world applications.

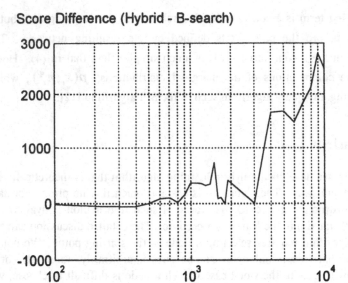

Figure 5. The score difference vs. sample size

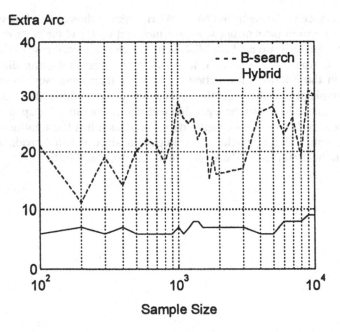

Figure 6. The extra arc vs. sample size

Missing Arc

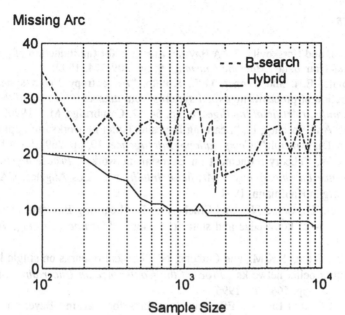

Figure 7. The missing arc vs. sample size

Cross Entropy x 10^{-5}

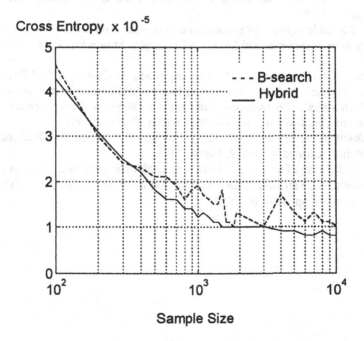

Figure 8. The cross entropy vs. sample size

References

[1] Cooper, G. and Herskovits, E, "A Bayesian method for the induction of probabilistic networks from data", *Machine Learning*, 9, pp. 309-374, 1992.

[2] Herskovits, E.H. and Cooper, G.F., Kutato, "An entropy-driven system for the construction of probabilistic expert systems from databases", *Proc. of the Conf. on Uncertainty in Artificial Intelligence*, pp. 54-62, Cambridge, MA, 1990.

[3] Lam, W. And Bacchus, F., "Learning Bayesian belief networks, an approach based on the MDL principle", *Computational Intelligence*, 10, pp. 269-293, 1994.

[4] Buntine, W, "Theory refinement on Bayesian networks", *Proceedings of Seventh Conference on Uncertainty in Artificial Intelligence*, Los Angeles, CA, pp. 652-660, Morgan Kaufmann, 1991.

[5] Heckerman, D., Geiger, D., and Chickering, D. "Learning Bayesian networks: The combination of knowledge and statistical data". *Machine Learning*, 20, pp.197-234, 1995.

[6] Xiang, Y., Wong, S.K.M., and Cercone, N., "Critical remarks on single link search in learning belief networks", *Proc. of the Conference on Uncertainty in Artificial Intelligence*, pp. 564-571, 1996.

[7] Chang, K.C. and Liu, J., "Efficient algorithms for learning Bayesian networks", *1996 IEEE International Conference on Systems, Man, and Cybernetics*, Vol. 2, pp. 1274-1279, 1996..

[8] Pearl, J, *Probabilistic reasoning in intelligent systems*. San Mateo, CA, Morgan Kaufmann, 1988.

[9] Liu, J., Model learning with probabilistic networks, a Ph.D. dissertation, School of Information Technology and Engineering, George Mason University, Fairfax, VA, 1997.

[10] Beinlich, I.A., Suermondt, H.J., Chavez, R.M., & Cooper, G.F, "The ALARM monitoring system: A case study with two probabilistic inference techniques for belief networks", *Proceedings of the Second European Conference on Artificial Intelligence in Medicine*, pp. 247-256, London, England, 1989.

[11] Bouckaert, R. R, Bayesian belief networks: from construction to inference, Ph.D. dissertation, University Utrecht, Dutch, 1995.

[12] Chang, K.C. and Fung, R., "Symbolic probabilistic inference with both discrete and continuous variables", *IEEE Transaction on Systems, Man, and Cybernetics*, Vol. 25, No. 6, pp. 910-916, 1995.

Relational Concepts and the Fourier Transform: An Empirical Study

Eduardo Pérez[1] and Larry Rendell[2]

[1] Universidad Autónoma de Madrid, E.T.S. Informática,
Madrid E-28049, Spain
e-mail: eduardo.perez@ii.uam.es
[2] University of Illinois, Dept. of Computer Science and Beckman Institute
Urbana, IL 61801, USA
e-mail: rendell@cs.uiuc.edu

Abstract. Lack of domain knowledge may impose primitive data representations. Then, complex (non-linear) relationships among attributes complicate learning, especially for typical learning methods. These methods fail because their bias does not match the complex relational structures relevant to the domain. However, more recent approaches to learning have implemented biases that allow learning of structured, albeit complex, concepts. One of such approaches, based on the Fourier transform of Boolean functions, is studied and compared empirically to others, based on constructing new features or extracting relations from propositional training data. Controlled experiments help to characterized the kinds of concept that allow each approach to outperform the others. This characterization, which implicates parameters of Fourier complexity, other measures of concept difficulty, and the relational structure of the target concepts, is also discussed with respect to difficult real-world domains.

1 Introduction: Motivation and Background

When lack of domain knowledge forces the use of primitive data representations, complex relations among attributes prevail and complicate learning significantly. Then, typical learning methods fail because their similarity-based bias does not match the complex relational structures relevant to the domain. It is true that any learner must be biased in some way [18,8]. Thus, no learning system can be the best uniformly over all concepts [16], mainly because of the extremely large number of random (unstructured) concepts [1]. However, more recent approaches to learning have implemented biases that allow learning of structured, albeit complex, concepts. One of such approaches is to change the representation of the examples, introducing new terms (features or relations among attributes) to narrow the gap between primitive input representation and target concept [4]. Some machine learning methods, such as Fringe [9] and MRP [10], automate this representation change. Another approach, studied in computational learning theory [2,6], explicitly introduces a representation based on the Fourier transform of Boolean functions in order to capture complex relations underlying the target concept. This paper empirically compares both approaches and characterizes the kinds of concept that allow each approach to outperform the other. This characterization, which implicates parameters of Fourier complexity, other measures of concept difficulty, and the relational structure of the target concepts, is also discussed with respect to difficult real-world domains.

The rest of this section reviews basic definitions and terminology relevant to the Fourier transform, and illustrates this representation in the context of learning. In Section 2, the learning accuracy of four learning systems is described empirically as a function of Fourier complexity. The results from these experiments are discussed and compared with previous ones regarding Concept Variation, another measure of learning difficulty. Then, Section 3 extends the empirical comparison by considering one algorithm from the computational learning theory literature, which is explicitly designed to learn in terms of the Fourier transform. This algorithm is compared again, in Section 4, to the other learners, but this time using target concepts that cover a wider range of the Fourier complexity spectrum and include combinations of complex relations among attributes. Section 5 discusses algorithm limitations and extensions suggested by the empirical comparisons, and analyzes related work.

To consider the Fourier transform in the context of learning Boolean functions, it is convenient to view every Boolean function f as

$$f : \{0,1\}^n \to \{+1, -1\} . \tag{1}$$

Any such function, or concept, can be expressed as the sign of a linear combination of Fourier terms $\chi_z(x)$, that is,

$$f(x) = sign\left(\sum_{z \in \{0,1\}^n} \hat{f}(z)\chi_z(x)\right), \tag{2}$$

where $sign(x) = +1$ if $x \geq 0$, and $sign(x) = -1$ otherwise. To simplify the notation, the $sign$ function is often left out but implicitly understood when converting real numbers to Boolean values. Each $\hat{f}(z)$ is the coefficient of a Fourier term, and each Fourier term $\chi_z(x)$ is a parity function defined by

$$\chi_z(x) = (-1)^{z_1 x_1 + z_2 x_2 + \ldots + z_n x_n} . \tag{3}$$

That is, the characteristic vector z of the Fourier term $\chi_z(x)$ is a binary vector whose $active$ bits (i.e., bits set to 1) serve to select the corresponding bits (or attribute values) from an example input vector x, and then the parity of the selected input bits is the value of $\chi_z(x)$. The number of active bits in z defines the $degree$ of a Fourier term $\chi_z(x)$ or a coefficient $\hat{f}(z)$. The coefficient of the Fourier series of f are real numbers that can be computed by

$$\hat{f}(z) = \frac{1}{2^n} \sum_{x \in \{0,1\}^n} f(x)\chi_z(x) . \tag{4}$$

Although each real function has a unique Fourier series, different real functions can be interpreted as the same Boolean function (since only the sign is retained). Hence, learning systems approximating Boolean functions by real functions may choose among several Fourier decompositions for the same Boolean function.

The *spectral norm* of f, denoted by $L(f)$, is defined as the sum of absolute values of all Fourier coefficients of f:

$$L(f) = \sum_{z \in \{0,1\}^n} |\hat{f}(z)| \, . \tag{5}$$

It can be shown that $L(f) \geq 1$, for all f. However, $L(f)$ is the sum of 2^n absolute values of Fourier coefficients, possibly resulting in a large sum unless there are only a few non-zero coefficients, or unless the number of coefficients that are "large" is "small". Some classes of Boolean functions have only a few non-zero Fourier coefficients, and consequently have small spectral norm. It is common terminology to refer to polynomially bounded spectral norms as "small". Having small spectral norm implies learnability (with membership queries and under uniform distribution assumptions) [5].

The spectral norm depends on the absolute value, not the degree, of the non-zero coefficients. Consider, for instance, the following functions, each with a single non-zero coefficient of degree 1, 2, 3 and 4 respectively:

$$
\begin{aligned}
p_1(x) &= -1 \cdot \chi_{1000...0}(x) & [&\equiv x_1] \, , \\
p_2(x) &= -1 \cdot \chi_{1100...0}(x) & [&\equiv x_1 \oplus x_2] \, , \\
p_3(x) &= -1 \cdot \chi_{1110...0}(x) & [&\equiv x_1 \oplus x_2 \oplus x_3] \, , \\
p_4(x) &= -1 \cdot \chi_{1111...0}(x) & [&\equiv x_1 \oplus x_2 \oplus x_3 \oplus x_4] \, .
\end{aligned}
\tag{6}
$$

They all have spectral norm equal to 1, but may not be equally difficult to learn. In particular, for learning methods based on the similarity-based bias [14], the first function is a trivial target concept; the others are typically considered of highest difficulty. Nevertheless, the small spectral norm of these and other *hard* concepts suggests that an algorithm based on the Fourier transform can learn them under certain circumstances (e.g., with the help of membership queries).

The set of Fourier terms constitutes a basis that allows any function to be expressed as a linear combination of the basis (parity) functions. Thus, non-linear relationships among variables are captured *within* the Fourier terms, not by the Fourier series itself. That is, complex attribute interaction can be expressed as simple (linear) combinations of complex basis functions. This is also a goal of some machine learning methods considered in the next section.

2 Fourier Complexity and Learning Performance

This section empiricallly studies learning performance as a function of Fourier complexity. The complexity of a Fourier series can be characterized by two parameters: the number and the degree of Fourier terms with non-zero coefficients. The following experiments show the effect of these parameters on the learning accuracy of several learning systems. The systems considered here are C4.5

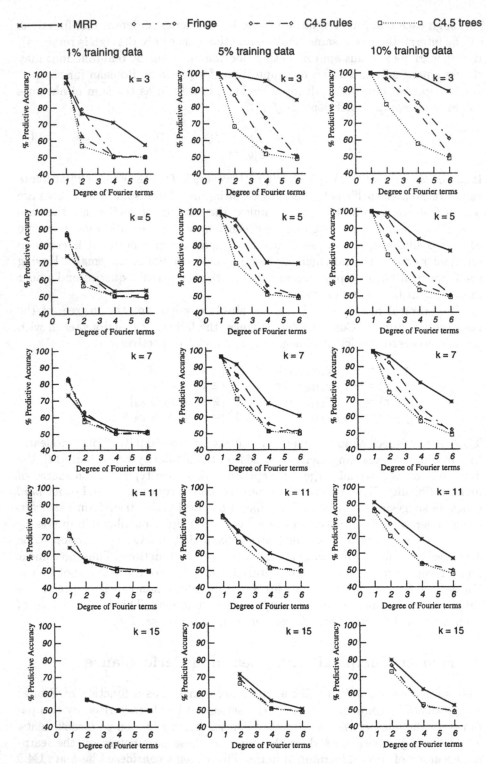

Fig. 1. Predictive accuracy as a function of Fourier complexity

trees, C4.5 rules, Fringe, and MRP. C4.5 provides the baseline performance of a similarity-based learner that does not change the representation of the examples during learning [13]. Fringe, however, changes the representation by introducing new features that result from combining attribute pairs at the end of each path from the root of a decision tree constructed using a previous representation [9]. MRP, which finds relations among primitive attributes by means of multidimensional projection, extracts their extensional representation from the training data, and uses them as new predicates for the test nodes of a decision tree [10].

The Boolean functions used here as target concepts are characterized by two parameters: they have at most k non-zero Fourier terms, and each term has degree d. For each pair of values (k, d), 8 functions of 12 variables were generated by randomly choosing their Fourier coefficients from $\{0.0, 0.1, 0.2, \ldots, 0.9, 1.0\}$. The performance measure used was predictive accuracy (i.e., percentage of correct classification measured over all data points not used for training). Each algorithm was run 5 times for each function and size of training data, except that Fringe was too slow to be run for $k > 7$. For each algorithm, its average accuracy for different values of k, d, and training size are shown in Figure 1. Each of these averages summarizes 40 accuracy values (5 values for each of 8 target concepts). The number of terms k was set to values 3, 5, 7, 11, and 15 to observe its effect in learning difficulty. The three graphs in each row of Figure 1 correspond to a particular value of k. Each column corresponds to a different size of training data. Each graph plots an algorithm's accuracy as a function of d, the degree of the Fourier terms (or number of parity bits). Note that $d = 1$ is the extreme case of no parity involved, and so the functions generated with $d = 1$ are weighted linear thresholds of at most k input variables.

Figure 1 shows an expected degradation of performance for the four learning systems as either parameter, k or d, of the Fourier series increases. However, d seems to have a stronger effect than k. Consider the leftmost column of graphs. Even for a very small number of terms (e.g., 3), $d = 6$ is sufficient to bring all learning curves to the level of guessing, and thus increasing k cannot make things worse once d is high (≥ 6). When d is low (e.g., 2), then increasing the number of terms reduces accuracy notably. However, this effect is more gradual (for the k values used here). Note that d is bounded by n, but k can be as large as $n(n-1)\ldots(n-d+1)$. Since the spectral norm (i.e., the sum of absolute values of the Fourier coefficients) does not depend on d, it seems to capture only a certain aspect of learning difficulty: *one which is independent of the degree of parity involved*. However, most current learning systems are extremely sensitive to (even small) increases in the degree of the Fourier terms.

The performance of MRP (relative to that of the other learners) in this context is similar to what was observed in the context of increasing concept variation [11]. Here, MRP's degradation with increasing d (degree of parity) is not worse and sometimes considerably better than the degradation experienced by the other learners. Also, as training data increases (from left to right column in Figure 1), MRP is the only one of the four systems studied that can take advantage of increasing data regardless of function complexity. Nevertheless, when the number of Fourier terms becomes large (e.g., 15), a training sample of 1% is not sufficient to allow learning by any of the systems used here.

The leftmost column of graphs in Figure 1 also shows that MRP's advantage has a counterpart. When $d = 1$, no complex interactions are involved; the target functions are linear thresholds. The other learners can find a more accurate hypothesis because their SBL bias is appropriate for these concepts. MRP's less restrictive bias is more likely to overfit spurious regularities appearing in small data samples. On the other hand, larger data samples remove this disadvantage (e.g., consider the accuracies for $d = 1$ in graphs $k = 7$ and 11 as data increases).

The above analysis, in particular with respect to the effect of the degree of Fourier terms in performance, suggests a link between Fourier complexity and Variation (used in [11] as a measure of concept difficulty). The (average) variation of a Boolean concept is defined in [15] as

$$V_n = \frac{1}{n2^n} \sum_{i=1}^{n} \sum_{neigh(x,y,i)} \delta(x,y) \,, \tag{7}$$

where the inner summation is taken over all 2^n pairs of neighboring points that differ only in their i-th attribute, and $\delta(x,y)$ equals 0 if two neighboring examples x and y belong to the same class, or equals 1 otherwise. Intuitively, V_n measures the roughness of a Boolean concept as a surface in instance space. If many pairs of neighboring examples (i.e., having Hamming distance 1 in Boolean domains) do not belong to the same class, then variation is high. Then, the connection

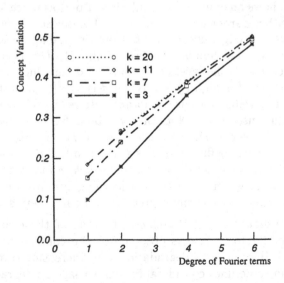

Fig. 2. Concept variation increases with Fourier complexity

between Variation and Fourier Complexity can be partly anticipated by noting that the two parity functions of n inputs have the highest variation, and the variation captured individually by each Fourier term of degree d is at most d/n (being exactly that fraction when no overlap with other Fourier terms occurs). That is, variation tends to diminish proportionally with d. Thus, functions with only a few non-zero Fourier coefficients of moderate to high degree can still be difficult to learn by most current systems due to the high variation involved in the Fourier series of such functions. Similarly, increasing the number of non-zero Fourier terms also brings up variation, but at a significantly lower rate. This is confirmed empirically as Figure 2 illustrates. All curves show a rapid increase of variation with d. Although increasing k raises each curve as a whole, this effect becomes almost imperceptible for $k > 11$.

Because the spectral norm $L(f)$ depends on the absolute value of the non-zero coefficients but not on their degrees, it is not correlated to variation. For instance, parity functions with the highest variation still have the lowest spectral norm. Thus, the spectral norm might also seem unrelated to the notion of learning difficulty as witnessed by the performance of many typical learning systems. However, results in computational learning theory strongly tie the spectral norm to learnability. In particular, any class of functions with polynomially bounded spectral norm is learnable through membership queries (under uniform distribution over the input space) [5]. Thus, it is important to find good upper bounds of spectral norm for interesting classes of functions. The difficulty of such task is acknowledged by Bellare [2], and he only gives upper bounds for simple classes (e.g., conjunctions, disjunctions, and parity trees) and classes of functions whose inductive structure simplifies the direct computation of the spectral norm (e.g. comparison functions, and each output bit in addition) . Some functions in the latter group, such as majority functions and linear thresholds on the number of bits, will be part of those used in the remaining experiments.

3   Algorithms Based on the Fourier Transform

A survey of learning methods based on the Fourier transform highlights two algorithms, one for each of two different kinds of function described next [6]. These algorithms do not rely directly on the spectral norm but on the distribution of the non-zero Fourier coefficients with respect to the degree of the terms. Thus, some Boolean functions have good approximations in terms of a few low-degree terms, and others can be accurately approximated using only a few high-degree terms. That is, the factor discriminating two relevant kinds of function is not the spectral norm itself (i.e., the sum of absolute values of Fourier coefficients) but its growth rate with respect to the coefficients' degree. For one kind of function, most of the spectral norm accumulates rapidly (on low-degree terms); for the other, the spectral norm concentrates on high-degree terms. Both cases are illustrated with the thin-line curves in Figure 3; the straight line represents a borderline between the two kinds of function and, hence, an unfavorable case for algorithms specifically targeting either kind of function. Because the spec-

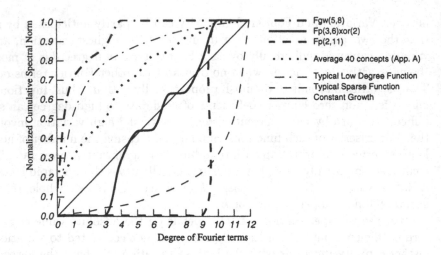

Fig. 3. Spectral norm growth for benchmark concepts from Appendix A

tral norm of different functions can vary greatly in absolute terms, we focus on the *normalized cumulative* spectral norm, using this as vertical axis in Figure 3. This axis measures the sum of *squared* Fourier coefficients (instead of their absolute values), up to a certain degree indicated by the horizontal axis. Thus, since $\sum_{z\in\{0,1\}^n}(\hat{f}(z))^2 = 1$ (as shown in [6]), the normalized cumulative norm of any function is 0 for $d = 0$, and 1 for $d = n$, regardless of how large the actual spectral norm of that function is.

For each of the two kinds of functions characterized above as extreme cases, Mansour [6] describes one learning algorithm: the Low Degree algorithm (LD), and the Sparse Function algorithm. The latter relies on membership queries, and is consequently excluded from our experiments since none of the other learners considered here uses such queries. The Low Degree algorithm uses $\mathcal{O}(n^d)$ randomly selected examples to estimate the Fourier coefficients of degree d or smaller. Recall that the Fourier coefficients can be computed by

$$\hat{f}(z) = \frac{1}{2^n} \sum_{x\in\{0,1\}^n} f(x)\chi_z(x) \,. \tag{8}$$

However, since f is not known at learning time, the coefficients are estimated by

$$\hat{f}_{est}(z) = \frac{1}{2^n} \sum_{i=1}^{m} f(X_i)\chi_z(X_i) \,, \tag{9}$$

from a set of classified examples $\{X_1, X_2, \ldots, X_m\}$ randomly chosen for training. Thus, the Low Degree algorithm, LD(d), outputs the Boolean function

$$h(x) \stackrel{\text{def}}{=} sign \left(\frac{1}{2^n} \sum_{z\in\{0,1\}^n,\ \text{degree}(z)\leq d} \hat{f}_{est}(z)\chi_z(x) \,. \right) \tag{10}$$

As d increases, the number of terms to consider grows quickly, and so does the number of coefficients that need to be estimated. Consequently, increasing d means that more examples are required for accurate estimation.

Table 1. Algorithm comparison based on Fourier series controlled by k and d

Parameters of the target function's Fourier series		Predictive Accuracy					
		1% Training data			10% Training data		
		MRP	LD(d)	Difference	MRP	LD(d)	Difference
$k = 3$	$d = 2$	76.3	73.0	**3.3**	100.0	94.4	**5.6**
	$d = 4$	70.9	56.4	**14.5**	98.5	71.0	**27.5**
	$d = 6$	57.5	52.8	**4.7**	89.0	59.5	**29.5**
$k = 7$	$d = 2$	61.3	69.3	-8.0	96.1	87.9	8.2
	$d = 4$	52.5	55.5	-3.0	80.3	68.1	**12.2**
	$d = 6$	51.2	53.3	-2.1	68.8	58.1	**10.7**
$k = 15$	$d = 2$	56.6	67.0	-10.4	79.9	85.4	-5.5
	$d = 4$	50.2	55.2	-5.0	62.3	67.2	-4.9
	$d = 6$	49.9	52.7	-2.8	52.6	57.9	-5.3

To observe the influence of d in LD's performance, we ran LD under the same experimental design discussed in Section 2 except that now, due to LD's longer running times, only a subset of the original values of k, d, and training size are used. Here, LD is compared only to MRP, the system that was more resistant to Fourier complexity in the previous experiments. In each run, LD is provided with the actual value of d used to generate the target concept. The results are shown in Table 1, together with the corresponding results for the best performer from Section 2. It was observed in Figure 1 that the accuracy of four learners degrades quickly as d grows. Like the others, LD experiences a performance degradation for any given k. However, the accuracy degradation observed in Figure 1 for increasing k seems to affect LD to a lesser extent than the other four learning systems. As shown in Table 1, LD's resistance to increasing k is superior to MRP's, and is due to its ability to retain a large number (n^d) of Fourier terms in its hypothesis, but this also slows down its learning and classification. This feature, initially presented as beneficial, can also reduce LD's predictive accuracy when learning other concepts, such as those considered next.

4 Relational Concepts and the Fourier Transform

The above comparison of systems' performance is based on randomly generated concepts with controlled Fourier complexity. We now extend the comparison to consider the benchmark concepts used in [10] to evaluate MRP (see Appendix A). These concepts were designed to have small representation in terms of relations (some of which could be complex relations). Despite their complexity, these concepts have a clearer structure than those generated randomly for the previous experiments. Now, we characterize also these benchmark concepts in terms of their Fourier complexity. First, they all have small spectral norm, ranging from 1.0 to 17.4 and averaging 5.3 (over all 40 concepts). Thus, they should be efficiently learnable by membership queries, as suggested in [5]. However, the learning model and systems studied here do not consider exploiting the benefit of membership queries. Despite their small spectral norm, some of these concepts still have a relatively large number of Fourier terms, ranging from 1 to 512, with an overall average of 103 terms per concept.

These concepts can also be characterized with respect to how fast their spectral norm grows with respect to the degree of Fourier terms. This allows positioning each benchmark concept within the range between the two kinds of function described in Section 3 (thin lines in Figure 3). The result of such process is that these concepts are scattered throughout the entire range between the two extreme cases. To illustrate this, four curves corresponding to spectral norm growth measured on benchmark concepts are shown as thick lines in Figure 3. Three of the thick-line curves correspond to individual concepts, each one selected as a close match to one the previous curves. The fourth one corresponds to the average over all 40 benchmark concepts. This average is slightly skewed toward the case of quickly growing spectral norm (i.e., the case of functions mostly defined on low-degree terms). This suggests that on average these concepts are closer to the extreme favorable to LD than to the opposite end. However, because these concepts are scattered between both ends, LD's performance varies considerably from concept to concept.

Figure 4 summarizes how LD's accuracy varies with respect to d, for the benchmark concepts of Appendix A. All curves are based on five learning trials per concept, each one using a randomly generated training sample covering 10% of the 12-dimensional instance space. The top three graphs correspond to the same three concepts selected for Figure 3 as representatives of two extreme cases and one intermediate case of spectral norm growth. For each extreme case, LD achieves its highest accuracy at a different end of the d axis. The leftmost graph, corresponding to a concept with mostly low-degree terms, indicates a clear loss in accuracy as the complexity of the model being fit (that is, d) increases. The rightmost graph corresponds to a parity concept, that is, a concept with just one Fourier term, but a term of a high-degree. Although LD is not designed for this kind of concept, this rightmost graph serves to illustrate some problems that may affect LD in other situations as well. Note that LD's accuracy increases sharply at $d = 10$, and that the target concept is a parity function of 10 inputs. Thus, for concepts involving parity of p bits, LD(d)'s accuracy misleadingly decreases as d grows from 0 to $p - 1$. This is the same behavior observed in the leftmost graph. However, in the parity case, d must be allowed to grow more if the highest accuracy is to be reached, whereas in the leftmost graph, any increase in d was to produce only less accurate hypotheses (due to overfitting). Thus, hill-climbing approaches to grow d gradually can be misled easily.

The top middle graph in Figure 4 corresponds to a concept whose Fourier coefficients are more or less evenly distributed over mid-degree terms (from $d = 4$

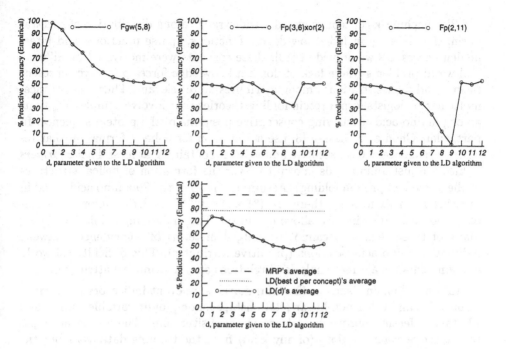

Fig. 4. LD(d)'s accuracy on benchmark concepts from Appendix A

to $d = 9$). Again, this is not the case most favorable to LD, as witnessed by its highest accuracy of about 50%. The structure of this concept is such that can be expressed concisely in terms of two relations: a parity of 4 bits and a combination of two linear threshold functions over the same set of 6 bits. Note again some sharp increases in accuracy at $d = 4$ and $d = 10(= 4 + 6)$. Thus, the previous observation about the misleading decay in accuracy as d grows also affects this concept (although to a lesser degree).

On average over these 40 concepts, LD(d)'s accuracy (bottom of Figure 4) has a smooth peak toward the low degree end, which is consistent with the observation that the average spectral norm growth is skewed toward quickly growing for small d (recall the dotted line in Figure 3). LD's average performance over these concepts is lower than MRP's, shown as dashes in the bottom graph of Figure 4. Even after selecting d^* as the best d for each benchmark concept individually, LD(d^*) still has an average accuracy (dotted line) about 10 percentage points below MRP's.

5   Discussion: Results, Extensions and Related Work

Our experiments show that LD(d) is better than other algorithms when learning low-degree functions (Figure 1 and Table 1), but worse when learning other benchmark concepts (Figure 4). In both test environments, all concepts have low spectral norm (possibly a general necessary condition for learning). However,

MRP's benchmark concepts covered a wider range along distribution of spectral norm; that is, they included low-degree functions, sparse functions, and intermediate cases. As we argued in [10], these concepts were motivated by difficult real-world problems where lack of domain knowledge forces primitive representations and makes relations among attributes more relevant. Thus, for instance, molecular biologists form protein folding theories that involve complex relations among amino acids occupying consecutive positions in the protein sequence. In particular, Chou and Fasman [3] use a condition for α-helix formation that requires a sequence of 6 consecutive amino acids containing at least 4 *helix formers* (which are just amino acids known to favor the formation of helical structures in the process of protein folding). Assuming that 5 of the 20 amino acids used in proteins are helix formers, there are $\binom{6}{4} \times 5^4 \times 20^{(6-4)} = 3.75$ million sequences of amino acid satisfying the above condition. The underlying similarity among many of those sequences cannot be judged in terms of coincidences between individual amino acid positions (primitive attributes). This difficult real-world domain demands a direct analysis of relations among primitive attributes.

In other domains, such as financial markets, relevant indicators are derived from ratios and other non-linear relationships among input variables. MRP and LD take different approaches to learn in these situations. The former attempts to extract relevant relations (of any kind) from the training data available; the latter tries to construct such relations in terms of a low-degree Fourier transform. There are ways for each algorithm to mutually benefit from the other, as we will discuss next.

We have used the most straightforward implementation of the Low Degree algorithm [6]. This could be extended with parameters to control the maximum number of terms in the hypotheses, or the minimum absolute value acceptable for a Fourier coefficient to keep the corresponding term. Also, knowledge about which inputs (not just how many inputs) need to be considered in the Fourier terms can reduce running times considerably. Instead of considering all n^d terms, it would then be enough to consider the 2^d terms involving the selected attributes as suggested by [6]. Similarly, additional knowledge can constrain LD's search even further. The learner can be given knowledge of related sets of input attributes, or it can obtain such knowledge by techniques similar to those used in MRP. This type of knowledge can speedup new versions of the $LD(d)$. On the other hand, the explicit incorporation of the Fourier basis into the search for new representations performed by algorithms like MRP can also be beneficial.

An alternative approach related to the Fourier transform and similar to the Low Degree algorithm was developed by Seshu [17]. He proposed a decision-tree learner, *R-splitter*, that could split the data using any of the 2^R parity functions (or parity features) over a subset of R variables, previously selected by the system from the original set of n input variables. Here, R is a system parameter similar to LD's d. Unlike LD, R-splitter does not express hypotheses as sums of possibly exponentially many parity features (or Fourier terms). Instead, at each decision node, R-splitter first estimates the information provided by each split based on any individual input variable, and then if such splits are not useful, it considers splitting on parity features. Although the system considers all 2^R parity features like LD does, R-splitter chooses only one parity feature to split the data at the current node, and then proceeds to recursively refine each child of the current node. Thus, R-splitter decides dynamically how many parity functions (of degree at most R) to keep in its final hypothesis. This is similar to the way MRP dynamically finds relations in the training data, but MRP is not limited to using parity relations. It extracts the extensional representation of the relevant relations from the data.

The second basic algorithm reviewed in [6] is the Sparse Function algorithm [5]. It learns functions that can be accurately approximated by a small number of Fourier coefficients corresponding to high-degree terms. Both algorithms, Low Degree and Sparse Function, learn classes of Boolean functions *in terms of* a different class [12], namely, the class of real functions. The algorithms are not restricted to output a Boolean function, that is, one whose only possible values are -1 and $+1$. Instead, they output a real function to be interpreted as Boolean (see Section 1). This suggests that separating the two Boolean values at zero may not always be the best choice [7]. A new question related to this issue is whether the method used to estimate the Fourier coefficient is always the best. Both algorithms base their coefficient estimation in the (canonical) definition of the coefficients given by

$$\hat{f}(z) = \frac{1}{2^n} \sum_{x \in \{0,1\}^n} f(x)\chi_z(x) . \tag{11}$$

This definition forces the Fourier transform to be a strictly Boolean function. Thus, for instance, the function *majority of four inputs* (which returns true if and only at least two of its inputs are 1) has the following Fourier series:

$$
\begin{aligned}
maj_4(x_1, x_2, x_3, x_4) = \\
+0.375\chi_{0000}(x) - 0.375\chi_{0001}(x) - 0.375\chi_{0010}(x) - 0.125\chi_{0011}(x) \\
-0.375\chi_{0100}(x) - 0.125\chi_{0101}(x) - 0.125\chi_{0110}(x) + 0.125\chi_{0111}(x) \\
-0.375\chi_{1000}(x) - 0.125\chi_{1001}(x) - 0.125\chi_{1010}(x) + 0.125\chi_{1011}(x) \\
-0.125\chi_{1100}(x) + 0.125\chi_{1101}(x) + 0.125\chi_{1110}(x) + 0.375\chi_{1111}(x) .
\end{aligned}
$$

However, being a linear threshold, this function can be expressed more concisely in terms of low-degree coefficients only, as follows:

$$maj_4(x_1, x_2, x_3, x_4) = -0.5\chi_{0001}(x) - 0.5\chi_{0010}(x) - 0.5\chi_{0100}(x) - 0.5\chi_{1000}(x) .$$

These series are two different real functions, but the same Boolean function (when considering only their sign). Learners based on estimation of Fourier coefficients should be prepared to choose among competing sets of coefficients.

6 Conclusion

This paper has brought together approaches from the machine learning community and the computational learning theory community. The unifying context was to explore the use of new representations that facilitate learning from primitive attributes, when complex relationships are involved. The Fourier transform suggests new measures of learning difficult, and provides a way to express structured, albeit complex, concepts as simple combinations of the parity basis functions. However, without the help of membership queries, current algorithms for learning in terms of the Fourier transform perform better than other learning algorithms only for Low Degree functions. Despite the small spectral norm of the benchmark concepts from [10], $LD(d)$ did not learn then more accurately than MRP, on average. $LD(d)$ was not able to extract the relevant relation because it insisted on expressing them in terms of low-degree Fourier terms. The simple structure of these concepts, when expressed in terms of the appropiate relations, make them realistic in the context of difficult real-world domains where only primitive input representations are available. Our discussion of empirical results relates concept characteristics and learning algorithm design, suggesting directions to improve current learning systems.

Acknowledgments

This research was supported in part by grant IRI 92-04473 from the US National Science Foundation. We thank Lenny Pitt for bringing to our attention the literature on learning through the Fourier transform, and for his suggestions.

References

1. Yaser S. Abu-Mostafa. Complexity of random problems. In Yaser S. Abu-Mostafa, editor, *Complexity in Information Theory*, chapter VI, pages 115–131. Springer-Verlag, NY, 1988.
2. Mihir Bellare. A technique for upper bounding the spectral norm with applications to learning. In *Proc. of the Fifth Annual Conf. on Computational Learning Theory*, pages 62–70, 1992.
3. Peter Y. Chou and Gerald D. Fasman. Prediction of protein conformation. *Biochemistry*, 13(2):222–245, 1974.
4. Li-Min Fu and Bruce G. Buchanan. Learning intermediate concepts in constructing a hierarchical knowledge base. In *Proc. of the Ninth Int. Joint Conf. on Artificial Intelligence*, pages 659–666, 1985.
5. Eyal Kushilevitz and Yishay Mansour. Learning decision trees using the fourier transform. In *Proc. of the 23rd Annual ACM Symp. on Theory of Computing*, pages 455–464. ACM Press, 1991.
6. Yishay Mansour. Learning boolean functions *via* the fourier transform. In V. P. Roychodhury, K-Y. Siu, and A. Orlitsky, editors, *Advances in Neural Computation*, pages 151–155. Kluwer Academic Publishers, 1994.
7. Yishay Mansour and Sahar Sigal. Implementation isssues in the fourier transform algorithm. In *Proc. of the Neural Information Processing Systems, Natural and Synthetic*, 1995.
8. Tom M. Mitchell. The need for biases in learning generalizations. Technical Report CBM-TR-117, Computer Science Department, Rutgers University, New Brunswick, NJ 08903, May 1980.

9. Giulia Pagallo and David Haussler. Boolean feature discovery in empirical learning. *Machine Learning*, 5:71–99, 1990.

10. Eduardo Pérez and Larry A. Rendell. Using multidimensional projection to find relations. In *Proc. of the 12th Int. Conf. on Machine Learning*, pages 447–455. Morgan Kaufmann Publishers, Inc., 1995.

11. Eduardo Pérez and Larry A. Rendell. Learning despite concept variation by finding structure in attribute-based data. In *Proc. of the 13th Int. Conf. on Machine Learning*, pages 391–399. Morgan Kaufmann Publishers, Inc., 1996.

12. Leonard Pitt and Leslie G. Valiant. Computational limitations of learning from examples. *Journal of the Association for Computing Machinery*, 35(4):965–984, October 1988.

13. J. Ross Quinlan. *C4.5: Programs for Machine Learning*. Morgan Kaufmann Publishers, Inc., Palo Alto, CA, 1993.

14. Larry Rendell. A general framework for induction and a study of selective induction. *Machine Learning*, 1(2):177–226, 1986.

15. Larry A. Rendell and Raj Seshu. Learning hard concepts through constructive induction: Framework and rationale. *Computational Intelligence*, 6:247–270, 1990.

16. Cullen Schaffer. A conservation law for generalization performance. In *Proc. of the Eleventh Int. Conf. on Machine Learning*, pages 259–265, 1994.

17. Raj Seshu. Solving the parity problem. In *Proc. of the 4th European Working Session on Learning*, pages 263–271, Montpellier, France, December 1989.

18. Satosi Watanabe. *Knowing and Guessing*. John Wiley & Sons, New York, 1969.

Appendix A. Benchmark Concepts

The following concepts, used as benchmark in [10], are members of the groups described below, where the notation $x_{i..j}$ is shorthand for $x_i, x_{i+1}, x_{i+2}, ..., x_j$:

$F_{p(2,11)}$	$F_{p(3,10)}$	$F_{p(4,9)}$	$F_{p(5,8)}$	$F_{cp(2,11)}$	$F_{cp(3,10)}$
$F_{cp(4,9)}$	$F_{cp(5,8)}$	$F_{cdp(1,9)}$	$F_{cdp(2,10)}$	$F_{cdp(3,11)}$	$F_{p(3,6)\wedge(2)}$
$F_{p(3,6)\vee(2)}$	$F_{p(3,6)\oplus(2)}$	$F_{p(3,6)\wedge(3)}$	$F_{p(3,6)\vee(3)}$	$F_{p(3,6)\oplus(3)}$	$F_{p(3,6)\wedge(2\text{-or-}3)}$
$F_{p(3,6)\vee(2\text{-or-}3)}$	$F_{p(3,6)\oplus(2\text{-or-}3)}$	$F_{mj(4,8)}$	$F_{mj(3,9)}$	$F_{mj(2,10)}$	F_{mx6}
$F_{mx6c(6,7)}$	$F_{mx6c(5,8)}$	$F_{mx6c(4,9)}$	$F_{mx6c(3,10)}$	$F_{rk(5,7)}$	$F_{rk(6,7)}$
$F_{rk(6,9)}$	$F_{rk(7,9)}$	$F_{nm(4,5,7)}$	$F_{nm(5,6,9)}$	$F_{gw(3,10)}$	$F_{gw(4,9)}$
$F_{gw(5,8)}$	$F_{sw(3,10)}$	$F_{sw(4,9)}$	$F_{sw(5,8)}$		

Parity. Let odd(s)=true *iff* an odd number of bits in s are 1. Then,
$F_{p(i,j)} \stackrel{\text{def}}{=} \text{odd}(x_{i..j})$, $F_{cp(i,j)} \stackrel{\text{def}}{=} \text{odd}(x_{i..6}) \wedge \text{odd}(x_{7..j})$, and
$F_{cdp(i,j)} \stackrel{\text{def}}{=} \text{odd}(x_{i..4}) \wedge [\text{odd}(x_{i+j/2..8}) \vee \text{odd}(x_{j..12})]$

Majority. $F_{mj(i,j)} \stackrel{\text{def}}{=} \text{maj}(x_{i..j})$, maj($s$)=true *iff* at least half of the bits in s are 1.

Parity and counters. Let l-in(s)=true *iff* exactly l bits in s are 1. Then, for $l \in \{2, 3, 2\text{-or-}3\}$ and $\nabla \in \{\wedge, \vee, \oplus\}$, $F_{p(i,j)\nabla(l)} \stackrel{\text{def}}{=} \text{odd}(x_{i..j}) \nabla\ l\text{-in}(x_{7..12})$.

Multiplexors. Let $\text{mx}(i, j, d_0, d_1, d_2, d_3) = d_{2i+j}$, $\text{mx}_c(0, 0, d_{0..i}) = \bigwedge(d_{0..i})$, $\text{mx}_c(0, 1, d_{0..i}) = \bigvee(d_{0..i})$, $\text{mx}_c(1, 0, d_{0..i}) = \bigoplus(d_{0..i})$, and $\text{mx}_c(1, 1, d_{0..i}) = \neg \bigoplus(d_{0..i})$. Then, $F_{mx6} \stackrel{\text{def}}{=} \text{mx}(x_1, x_2, x_3, x_6, x_9, x_{12})$, and $F_{mx6c(i,j)} \stackrel{\text{def}}{=} \text{mx}_c(x_1, x_2, x_{i..j})$

Linear thresholds. Let w(s) be the number of ones in s. Then, we define $F_{rk(i,k)} \stackrel{\text{def}}{=} \text{w}(x_{6-\lfloor k/2\rfloor..7+\lfloor k/2\rfloor}) = i$, $F_{nm(i,j,k)} \stackrel{\text{def}}{=} \text{w}(x_{6-\lfloor k/2\rfloor..7+\lfloor k/2\rfloor}) \in \{i, j\}$, $F_{gw(i,j)} \stackrel{\text{def}}{=} \text{w}(x_{i..6}) > \text{w}(x_{7..j})$, and $F_{sw(i,j)} \stackrel{\text{def}}{=} \text{w}(x_{i..6}) = \text{w}(x_{7..j})$.

ELEM2: A Learning System for More Accurate Classifications

Aijun An and Nick Cercone

Department of Computer Science, University of Waterloo
Waterloo, Ontario N2L 3G1, Canada

Abstract. We present ELEM2, a new method for inducing classification rules from a set of examples. The method employs several new strategies in the induction and classification processes to improve the predictive performance of induced rules. In particular, a new heuristic function for evaluating attribute-value pairs is proposed. The function is defined to reflect the degree of relevance of an attribute-value pair to a target concept and leads to selection of the most relevant pairs for formulating rules. Another feature of ELEM2 is that it handles inconsistent training data by defining an unlearnable region of a concept based on the probability distribution of that concept in the training data. To further deal with imperfect data, ELEM2 makes use of the post-pruning technique to remove unreliable portions of a generated rule. A new rule quality measure is proposed for the purpose of post-pruning. The measure is defined according to the relative distribution of a rule with respect to positive and negative examples. To show whether ELEM2 achieves its objective, we report experimental results which compare ELEM2 with C4.5 and CN2 on a number of datasets.

1 Introduction

Induction is a process that reasons from specific cases to general principles. Rule induction covers a special, and prevalent, case of induction, in which the results of induction are expressible as condition-action rules. A number of rule induction systems, such as C4.5 [15], AQ15 [12] and CN2 [4], have been constructed and applied to discover knowledge from collected data in different applications, yet many suffer from poor performance in prediction accuracy in many practical domains. It has been shown repeatedly that each method works best in some, but not all [2, 7]. While it seems unlikely to have an algorithm to perform best in all the domains of interest, it may well be possible to produce learners that perform better on a wide variety of real-world domains.

Our objective is to work towards this direction by proposing ELEM2, a new rule induction method that employs new strategies to enhance the induction and classification processes. Similar to some other learning algorithms (such as CN2 [4] and PRISM [3]), ELEM2 generates rules from a set of training examples by searching for a hypothesis in a general-to-specific manner in which an attribute-value pair is selected at each specification step. However, ELEM2 differs from other algorithms in several aspects. First, to select an attribute-value pair, ELEM2 employs a new heuristic function for evaluating attribute-value pairs. Various evaluation criteria have been used in different learning algorithms. For example, ID3 [14] employs an entropy-based information gain to find the most relevant attribute to grow decision trees. PRISM [3] uses another form of information gain which can be characterized in terms of apparent classificatory accuracies on the training set to measure the relevance of attribute-value pairs with respect to a target concept. LEM2 [8] basically considers as the most relevant selector the attribute-value pair that has the largest coverage over the positive examples. We argue that both coverage and information gain should be considered when measuring the relevance of selectors. Selectors that cover a large number of positive examples may also cover negative examples well. On the other hand, when only considering information gain, no matter whether the consideration is in terms of entropy or apparent classificatory accuracies, such consideration can lead to generation of rules covering few examples [15]. Such rules tend to have higher predictive error rates [10]. We propose an alternative evaluation function. The new function is defined in terms of both an classification gain and the coverage of an attribute-value pair over a set of the training data and also reflects the degree of relevance of the attribute-value pair to a target concept with regard to the training data.

Secondly, ELEM2 addresses the issue of handling inconsistent examples. Inconsistent examples in the training set usually confuse a learning system when the system tries to identify common properties of a set of objects. One way to handle this problem is to remove all or part of the inconsistent examples to reduce confusion. This may not be a good idea, especially in very noisy environments in which most of the examples may need to be eliminated. Also, inconsistent examples may provide useful information for probability analysis during induction. To handle this problem, ELEM2 defines an unlearnable region for each concept based on the probability distribution of the concept over the training data. The unlearnable region of a concept is used as a stopping criterion for the concept learning process: if the positive examples that are not yet covered by the already generated concept descriptions fall into the unlearnable region of the concept, the process for learning that concept stops.

Thirdly, ELEM2 employs a new rule quality measure for the purpose of handling imperfect data by post-pruning generated rules. Post-pruning is a technique that prevents a generated rule from *overfitting* the data.[1] There have been several post-pruning methods in the literature. For example, C4.5 [15] uses an error-based technique called *pessimistic* pruning for pruning decision trees, which estimates the predictive error rate of concept descriptions by adjusting the apparent error rate on the training set. Another example is AQ15 [12], which associates conjunctions in a generated rule with weights and the ones with the least weights were removed to avoid overfitting the data. The weight is defined as the number of training examples explained *uniquely* by the conjunction. A

---

[1] We say that a rule *overfits* the training examples if it performs well over the training examples but less well over the entire distribution of instances (i.e., including instances beyond the training set).

problem with AQ15 is that it is hard to specify when to stop the pruning. ELEM2 takes another route in doing post-pruning. It defines a rule quality measure based on the relative distribution of a rule with respect to the positive and negative examples the rule covers. The rule quality formula is chosen from four alternatives that represent different kinds of distributions. We choose from these four alternatives the one with the most information and the best experimental results.

The rest of the paper is organized as follows. In Section 2, we present the strategies that ELEM2 uses for selecting attribute-value pairs. In particular, we describe how ELEM2 groups attribute-value pairs to formulate a search space and how the evaluation function is defined. In Section 3, an unlearnable region of a concept is defined which is used by ELEM2 for handling inconsistency in the training data. In Section 4, we discuss the rule quality measure used by ELEM2 for post-pruning generated rules. The ELEM2 induction algorithm and its classification strategy are presented in Sections 5 and 6. Section 7 reports some experimental results for evaluating ELEM2. We conclude the paper with a summary of ELEM2 and some suggestions for future work.

2 Selection of Attribute-Value Pairs

An *attribute-value pair* is a relation between the attribute and its values, which is represented in the form $\langle a \ rel \ v \rangle$, where a is an attribute, rel denotes a relational operator (e.g. $=, \neq, \leq, >, \cdots$, or $\in$) and v is a specific value or a set of values of the attribute. Let t denote an attribute-value pair. We use a_t, rel_t and v_t to denote the attribute, the relational operator and the value in t, respectively. We define that the *complement* of an attribute-value pair t is the attribute-value pair $\langle a_t, \neg rel, v_t \rangle$, where $\neg$ is the negation of rel. For example, the complement of $\langle a = v \rangle$ is $\langle a \neq v \rangle$.

ELEM2 induces rules for a target concept by selecting relevant attribute-value pairs from a space of attribute-value pairs. This section addresses two issues related to the attribute-value pair selection in ELEM2. First, we discuss how ELEM2 formulates the attribute-value pair space. Then we introduce the evaluation function that ELEM2 uses to select an attribute-value pair from the formulated space.

2.1 Grouping Attribute-Value Pairs

In formulating the space of attribute-value pairs, many induction algorithms consider only single-valued attribute-value pairs. This consideration may cause the learning algorithm to generate more rules that cover small portions of examples. To overcome this problem, ELEM2 works with attribute-value pairs whose value may be a disjunction or a range of values. We refer to the combination of values as grouping attribute values. Since there are a large number of possible combinations, ELEM2 considers only reasonable groupings that can be easily made use of or refined by the learning algorithm. This strategy avoids producing an exponentially large search space. In grouping values, we use different strategies for different kinds of attributes.

Grouping discrete attribute values There are two kinds of discrete attributes: *nominal attributes* and *ordered discrete attributes*. The values of a nominal attribute do not show any inherent order among themselves, while an ordered discrete attribute has an ordered set of values. For example, an attribute *colour* with a set of values being $\{red, blue, yellow, orange\}$ is a normal discrete attribute, while an attribute *temperature* with a value set being $\{low, medium, high\}$ is an ordered discrete attribute.

For a nominal attribute, ELEM2 uses a dynamic grouping strategy, i.e., the value groups are determined after an attribute-value pair of this attribute is chosen as a candidate selector during the induction process. The initial search space of attribute-value pairs before induction is made of attribute-value pairs with single values. Details about how to dynamically group these single-valued attribute-value pairs will be described in the ELEM2 rule induction algorithm in Section 5.

For an ordered discrete attribute, grouping of its values is carried out before the induction process commences. The grouping method is based on $n - 1$ binary splits, where n is the number of all possible values of the attribute. Let $\{s_1, s_2, ..., s_n\}$ be the set of values of an ordered discrete attribute a, where $s_i < s_{i+1}$ for $i = 1, ..., n-1$. For each value $s_i (i = 1, ..., n-1)$, two groups: $\{s_1, ..., s_i\}$ and $\{s_{i+1}, ..., s_n\}$, are generated, i.e., two attribute-value pairs: $\langle a \in \{s_1, ..., s_i\}\rangle$ and $\langle a \in \{s_{i+1}, ..., s_n\}\rangle$, are obtained. In this way, a total of $2(n - 1)$ pairs can be obtained for an attribute with n possible values. We put half of these pairs into the search space for the selection process. For each value $s_i (i = 1, ..., n-1)$, only the first pair, $\langle a \in \{s_1, ..., s_i\}\rangle$, is included in the search space. We drop off the second pair because it is the complement of the first pair and its degree of relevance to a target concept, measured by our evaluation function described in the next section, is the additive inverse of the degree of relevance for the first pair. We can use the evaluation information about one pair to judge the other one. Therefore, in our method, only $n - 1$ attribute-value pairs need to be examined during induction instead of $2^n - 2$ possibilities.

Grouping continuous attribute values In ELEM2, continuous attributes are discretized by using user-supplied discretization formulas or by applying one of the automatic discretization methods[6]. Suppose $\{x_1, x_2, ..., x_n\}$ is the set of cut-points for a discretized continuous attribute a. Our grouping method for this kind of attributes is similar to the one for an ordered discrete attribute. For each cut-point x_i, $(i = 1, ..., n)$, two attribute-value pairs: $\langle a \le x_i\rangle$ and $\langle a > x_i\rangle$, are generated. The search space consists of only the first pairs in these binary splits. Therefore, the search space has a total of n attribute-value pairs for a continuous attribute with n cut-points.

2.2 Evaluating Attribute-Value Pairs

ELEM2 generates decision rules for a target concept by performing a general-to-specific search in a hypothesis space. At each step of specialization, a heuristic function is used to evaluate attribute-value pairs. The function assigns a significance value to each considered pair in order for the most significant attribute-value pair to be selected. The significance function is defined according to the relevance of an attribute-value pair to the target concept. An attribute-value pair av is *relevant* to a concept c with respect to a set, S, of examples if

$$P(av) > 0 \text{ and } P(c|av) \neq P(c),$$

where $P(av)$ denotes the probability that an example in S satisfies the relation expressed by av, $P(c)$ denotes the probability of the examples occurring in S that belong to concept c, and $P(c|av)$ is the probability that an example in S belongs to c given that the example satisfies av.[2] Under this definition, av is relevant to the concept c if it can change the probability of c, or in other words, if c is conditionally dependent on av.

In a set of training samples, there may exist more than one attribute-value pair that are relevant to a concept. Some pairs may be strongly relevant, while others may not be relevant. To measure the degree of relevance, we use an evaluation function to assign a significance value to each attribute-value pair. The function is defined as

$$SIG_c(av) = P(av)(P(c|av) - P(c)). \tag{1}$$

According to this definition, if $P(c|av) = P(c)$, i.e., av is not relevant to the concept c, then the degree of relevance of av to c is equal to 0; if $P(c|av) \neq P(c)$, i.e., av is relevant to c, then the degree of relevance is proportional to both the difference between $P(c|av)$ and $P(c)$ and the coverage of av over the training set currently being considered. The range of this function is $(-1, 1)$. If the value stays positive, then the higher the value, the more relevant the attribute-value pair av with respect to the target concept c; if the value is negative, the lower the value, the more relevant the attribute-value pair $\neg av$ (i.e., the complement of pair av) with respect to c. We use $P(av)$ as a coefficient of the function since we believe that, say, a 95% accurate rule which covers 1000 training cases is better than a 100% accurate rule that covers only one case. This helps avoid the overfitting problem.

The significance function has a nice property, expressed as follows. Given a concept c, it can be proved that [1]

$$SIG_c(av_i) = -SIG_c(\neg av_i). \tag{2}$$

This means that the SIG values for a selector and its complement are additively inverse. This observation allows us to narrow the search space of selectors by

---

[2] The probabilities here are determined by analysing a set S of training examples. Therefore, they can be considered as posterior probabilities.

half since the value for one of them can be obtained from the value for the other. Therefore, using this evaluation function is more efficient in practice than using other functions that do not have this feature.

3 Handling Inconsistency

In real-world applications, the set of training data may be inconsistent due to incomplete or noisy information. Two examples are inconsistent if they have identical attribute values for the condition attributes, but are labelled as belonging to different concepts. Inconsistent data in the training set may confuse a learning algorithm and result in a failure in deriving decision rules. ELEM2 handles the problem of inconsistency by computing an unlearnable region for each concept, inspired by [9]. Let $R = \{X_1, X_2, \cdots, X_n\}$, where X_i $(1 \leq i \leq n)$ is a set of examples that are identical in terms of condition attribute values and there are a total of n sets of this kind in the training set. We can predict that any example that matches the condition part of the examples in X_i belongs to the concept c with the probability $P(c|X_i)$, which is the probability that an example belongs to c given that the example is in X_i. The *classification gain* of X_i with respect to a concept c is defined as [9]:

$$CG_c(X_i) = P(c|X_i) - P(c),$$

which measures how much is gained by classifying a new example into c based on the information of the probabilities of the set X_i and the concept c. The *negative region* of a concept c is defined as

$$NEG(c) = \bigcup_{P(c|X_i) < P(c)} X_i,$$

which means, if $CG_c(X_i) < 0$, then X_i belongs to the negative region of c. The *unlearnable region* of a concept c, denoted as $ULR(c)$, is defined as the set of positive examples of c that exist in $NEG(c)$.

During ELEM2's rule induction, if the positive members of the currently considered set of training examples belong to the unlearnable region of the target concept, the induction process for this concept is stopped. This prevents ELEM2 from learning from the inconsistent examples that do not provide positive classification gain.

4 Post-Pruning Induced Rules

Systems interacting with real-world data must address the issues raised by imperfect training data. The training data are imperfect when there is noise in the data or when the number of training examples is too small to produce a representative sample of the true target function. The noise or coincidental regularities within the training data can lead to serious problems for the learning task. One problem is that learning algorithms can be misled by the imperfect data to produce long and distorted concept descriptions. By trying to fit every example into the concept descriptions, faulty and noisy examples are included, leading to cluttered and complex concept descriptions which cover a small number of anomalous examples in the training set. These descriptions are commonly known as *small disjuncts* [10]. Generating these small disjuncts not only increases the induction time and the complexity of the concept description but also decreases predictive performance of the learned knowledge on unknown objects since the rules applied to the noisy examples may misclassify correct examples. Post-pruning is a technique that rule induction algorithms use to handle the small disjunct problem. *Post-pruning* allows the induction process to run to completion (i.e., form a concept description completely consistent with the training data or as nearly consistent as possible if the complete consistency is impossible.) and then 'post-prunes' the over-fitted concept description by removing the components deemed unreliable. A criterion is needed in post-pruning to check whether a component in a concept description should be removed.

	Positive	Negative	Total
Covered by r	m	$n - m$	n
Not covered by r	$M - m$	$N - M - n + m$	$N - n$
Total	M	$N - M$	N

Table 1. Example Distribution for Rule r

In ELEM2, a rule quality measure is used as a criterion for post-pruning. The measure is defined according to the relative distribution of a rule with respect to the positive and negative examples it covers. We consider several alternatives when defining the rule quality measure. Given a set S of training data and a rule r learned from S, let N denote the number of examples in S, M be the number of positive examples in S, n denote the number of examples covered by r, and m be the number of positive examples covered by r. Consider the contingency table of example distribution for r (See Table 1). We assume that rule quality formulae have to in some way reflect the relative distribution of rules with respect to positive and negative examples. Specifically, four formulae can be derived from the table as follows:

$$Q_1 = \frac{\left(\frac{m}{M}\right)}{\left(\frac{n}{N}\right)} \tag{3}$$

$$Q_2 = \frac{\left(\frac{m}{M}\right)}{\left(\frac{n-m}{N-M}\right)} \tag{4}$$

$$Q_3 = \frac{\left(\frac{m}{M-m}\right)}{\left(\frac{n}{N-n}\right)} \tag{5}$$

$$Q_4 = \frac{\left(\frac{m}{M-m}\right)}{\left(\frac{n-m}{N-M-n+m}\right)} \tag{6}$$

Informally, for the given rule r, Q_1 represents the ratio of the proportion of positive examples which r covers to the proportion of the entire training set S which r covers, while Q_2 represents the ratio of the proportion of positive examples to that of negative examples. Q_3 represents the ratio between the "positive odds" for the rule (*i.e.* the ratio between the number of positive examples which r covers and the number which it does not cover) and the "total odds" for r, while Q_4 represents the ratio between the rule's positive odds and its "negative odds". Thus, Formulae Q_1 and Q_2 are related by using proportions, while Q_3 and Q_4 use odds; but Q_1 and Q_3 respectively are related by comparing the positive example distribution of a rule to its entire collection distribution, while Q_2 and Q_4 are related by comparing positive and negative distributions.

Analyze the formulae in another way. Given a training set and a concept in it, N and M are independent with the rule generated from the set. Thus, Q_1 is actually determined by the apparent accuracy of the rule, which is usually estimated as $\frac{m}{n}$. Since the apparent accuracy does not usually reflect the predictive accuracy, Q_1 is not a good choice for measuring rules' quality because our objective is to learn rules that classify *new* examples well. Q_2 has the flavour of measuring both coverage and accuracy. It can be specified in terms of probabilities as follows:

$$Q_2 = \frac{P(satisfy(r,e)|positive(e))}{P(satisfy(r,e)|negative(e))}$$

where P denotes probability, $satisfy(r,e)$ means r is satisfied by example e, $positive(e)$ means that e is a positive example, and $negative(e)$ means e is negative. Similarly, Q_4 can be represented as:

$$Q_4 = \frac{P(satisfy(r,e)|positive(e))P(\neg satisfy(r,e)|negative(e))}{P(satisfy(r,e)|negative(e))P(\neg satisfy(r,e)|positive(e))}$$

Although $P(\neg satisfy(r,e)|negative(e))$ and $P(\neg satisfy(r,e)|positive(e))$ depend on $P(satisfy(r,e)|negative(e))$ and $P(satisfy(r,e)|positive(e))$ respectively, the distinction between the two formulae concerns *explicit* recognition of rule unsatisfaction in calculation of probabilities. We argue that Q_4 is better than Q_2 in the sense that Q_4 explicitly contains more information than Q_2. A similar conclusion can be drawn between Q_1 and Q_3 that Q_3 explicitly contains more information than Q_1.

The difference between Q_3 and Q_4 is that Q_3 compares the positive distribution of a rule to its entire set distribution, while Q_4 compares positive and negative distributions. To see which one is a better measure for rule quality, we conducted experiments. In the experiments, we run ELEM2 with measure Q_3 and ELEM2 with Q_4 for ten-fold evaluation on 14 randomly selected datasets. The results (presented in [1]) show that the program with Q_4 gives better predictive accuracy means and accuracy deviations than the one with Q_3 on most of the tested datasets Therefore, we choose Q_4, which represents the ratio between the rule's positive odds and its negative odds (see Formula 6 and Table 1), as a criterion for measuring rule qualities and this criterion is used by ELEM2 to decide when to stop post-pruning. The post-pruning process is as follows:

1. Sort the selected pairs in a rule in the reverse order to that in which they were selected;
2. Check the pairs in this order to see if they can be removed without causing the rule quality to decrease. If yes, remove them.

5 The ELEM2 Induction Algorithm

ELEM2 induces rules using the *separate and conquer* strategy, i.e., it induces one rule at a time, removes the data covered by the rule and then iterates the process. The learning algorithm is briefly described as follows. If the training set contains examples of more than one concept, then for each concept c:

1. Compute the unlearnable region of the concept: $ULR(c)$;
2. Let CS be the current training set;
3. Calculate the significance value, $SIG(av_i)$, of each attribute-value pair av_i in the attribute-value pair space with respect to CS;
4. Select the pair av for which $|SIG(av)|$ is a maximum;
5. If the attribute a in the selected pair av is a nominal attribute and av's SIG value is positive, dynamic grouping is performed as follows:
   (a) Let TCS be the set of examples in CS that are not covered by av;
   (b) Compute the SIG values of all other pairs of attribute a with respect to TCS;
   (c) Group with the selected pair av the pairs with SIG value greater than or equal to $|SIG(av)|$;
6. Remove from CS the examples that are not covered by av;
7. Repeat Steps 3-6 until CS contains only examples of the concept c or the positive examples it contains belong to $ULR(c)$. The induced rule r is a conjunction of all the attribute-value pairs selected;
8. Post-prune the induced rule r using the rule quality measure $Q_4(r)$;
9. Remove all the examples covered by this rule from the current training set;
10. Repeat Steps 2-9 until all the examples of c have been removed or the remaining examples of c belong to $ULR(c)$.

When the rules for one concept have been induced, the training set is restored to its initial state and the algorithm is applied again to induce a set of rules describing the next concept.

6 Classification Using Induced Rules

In general, rules induced from a set of data are used to classify new objects into an appropriate concept. The central task of a classification algorithm is to determine if an example satisfies a rule. This is also referred to as the example matching a rule. Three cases are possible for matching an example with a set of rules: there may be only one match (i.e., the example matches only one rule), more than one match (i.e., the example matches more than one rules), or no match (i.e., the example does not match any rules). We refer to these three cases as single-match, multiple-match and no-match. The single-match is not a problem since the example can be classified into the concept indicated by the matched rule. In the multiple-match case, if the matched rules indicate the same concept, then the example is classified into this concept. If the matched rules do not agree on the concepts, then the system activates a conflict resolution scheme for the best decision. The conflict resolution scheme computes a decision score for each concept that the matched rules indicate. The decision score of a concept c is defined as:

$$DS(c) = \sum_{i=1}^{n} RB(r_i),$$

where r_i is a matched rule that indicates c, n is the number of this kind of rules, and $RB(r_i)$ is the reliability of rule r_i, which is defined as

$$RB(r_i) = log(Q_4(r_i))$$

After computing the decision scores for all the concepts indicated by the matched rules, ELEM2 classifies the example into the concept with the highest decision score.

In the case of no-match, partial matching is considered where some attribute-value pairs of a rule may match the values of corresponding attributes in the new example. A partial matching score between an example e and a rule r with n attribute-value pairs, m of which match the corresponding attributes of e, is defined as follows:

$$PMS(r) = \frac{\sum_{k=1}^{m} RB(mav_k)}{\sum_{j=1}^{n} RB(av_j)} \times RB(r),$$

where av_j $(j = 1, \cdots, n)$ denotes a pair in r, mav_k $(k = 1, \cdots, m)$ denotes a matched pair in r, $RB(r)$ is the reliability of rule r, $RB(mav_k)$ and $RB(av_j)$ stand for the reliabilities of pairs mav_k and av_j respectively. The reliability of an attribute-value pair av is defined similar to the definition of the reliability of a rule as:

$$RB(av) = log \frac{P(av|pos)P(\neg av|neg)}{P(av|neg)P(\neg av|pos)},$$

where $P(av|pos)$ denotes the probability that an example satisfies av conditioned on the example is positive, $P(av|neg)$ denotes the corresponding probability for negative examples, $P(\neg av|pos)$ is the probability that an example does not satisfy av conditioned on the example is positive, and $P(\neg av|neg)$ is the corresponding probability given that the example is negative. Based on the partial matching scores of the partially-matched rules, ELEM2 assigns a decision score to each concept indicated by these rules. The decision score of a concept c is defined as follows:

$$DS(c) = \sum_i PMS(r_i),$$

where $i = 0$ to the number of partially matched rules indicating concept c. In decision making, the new example is classified into the concept with the highest value of the decision score.

7 Empirical Evaluation

ELEM2 has been implemented in C under Unix environments. To evaluate the system, we have conducted experiments with ELEM2 on a number of actual data sets taken from the UCI repository [13]. Our objective is to check the usefulness of the rule sets generated by ELEM2 in terms of their predictive accuracy. We report the experimental results and compare them with the results from C4.5 and CN2.

7.1 Evaluation Methods

One method for evaluating a learning system is to artificially construct a training and a test dataset so that the characteristics of the training data, such as the complexity of concepts and the noise level of the training data, are available for analyzing the learner's capability. Three artificially designed domains, the MONK's problems, were obtained from the UCI repository to evaluate ELEM2 for this purpose. Each MONK's problem contains a training and a test dataset. The classification accuracy over the testing set is measured to show the learner's predictive performance.

Another evaluation method is x-fold cross validation. At the expense of computational resources, this method gives a more reliable estimate of the accuracy of a learning algorithm than a single run on a held-out test set. x-fold cross validation involves randomly partitioning the database into x disjoint data sets, then providing the learning algorithm with $x - 1$ of them as training data and using the remaining one as test cases. This process is repeated x times using different possible test sets. Each time a classification accuracy is obtained. The mean of the accuracies from the x runs and the standard deviation of the accuracy can then be calculated to measure testing performance. Ten-fold cross validation is used in our experiments to compare ELEM2 with two other algorithms on actual data sets.

7.2 Evaluation of ELEM2 on MONK's Domain

MONK's Problems The MONK's problems are three artificially constructed problems. They are derived from an artificial robot domain, in which robots (examples) are described by six nominal attributes [16]. The sizes of the value sets of the six attributes are 3, 3, 2, 3, 4 and 2, respectively as shown below:

$$head\_shape \in \{round, square, octagon\}$$
$$body\_shape \in \{round, square, octagon\}$$
$$is\_smiling \in \{yes, no\}$$
$$holding \in \{sword, balloon, flag\}$$
$$jacket\_color \in \{red, yellow, green, blue\}$$
$$has\_tie \in \{yes, no\}$$

Consequently, the example space contains 432 ($3 \times 3 \times 2 \times 3 \times 4 \times 2$) possible examples. The three MONK's problems, referred to as $M1$, $M2$, and $M3$, are all binary classification tasks defined over the same space. They differ in the type of concept to be learned and in the amount of noise in the training examples. Each problem is given by a logical description of a concept. Robots belong either to this concept or not, but instead of providing a complete concept description to the learning problem, only a subset of all 432 possible robots with its classification is given. The learning task involves generalizing over these examples and, if the particular learning technique at hand allows this, to derive a simple class description. The three MONK's problems are specially designed as follows:

- Problem M_1: ($head\_shape = body\_shape$) OR ($jacket\_color = red$)
  From 432 possible examples (referred to as MonkTest 1, 216 positive and 216 negative), 124 (62 positive and 62 negative) were randomly selected for the training set (referred to as MonkTrain 1). There were no misclassifications in the training set.
- Problem M_2: *exactly two of the six attributes have their first value*
  From 432 possible examples (referred to as MonkTest 2, 142 positive and 290 negative), 169 (64 positive and 105 negative) were randomly selected as training examples (referred to as MonkTrain 2). Again, there was no noise in Training Set 2.
- Problem M_3: ($jacket\_color = green$) AND ($holding = sword$) OR ($jacket\_color$ is NOT blue) AND ($body\_shape$ is NOT octagon) From 432 possible examples (referred to as MonkTest 3, 228 positive and 204 negative), 122 (60 positive and 62 negative) were selected randomly, and among them there were 5% misclassifications, i.e. noise in the training set (referred to as MonkTrain 3).

Problem 1 is in standard disjunctive normal form and is supposed to be easily learnable by a symbolic learning algorithm such as C4.5, CN2 and ELEM2. Conversely, problem 2 is similar to parity problems. It combines different attributes in a way which makes it complicated to describe in DNF or CNF using the given attributes only. Problem 3 is again in DNF and serves to evaluate the algorithms under the presence of noise.

Performance Comparison with C4.5 and CN2 A performance comparison of ELEM2 with C4.5 and CN2 has been conducted on the MONK's problems.

All three systems provide the facilities for inducing rules from a training set and evaluating the induced rules on a test set.[3] In the experiment on each problem M_i, we presented each learning system with the training set MonkTrain i, recorded the number of rules generated from each algorithm, and examined the performance of the induced rules on the test set MonkTest i.

Algorithms	MonkTest 1	MonkTest 2	MonkTest 3
C4.5	100%	64.8%	94.4%
CN2	98.6%	75.7%	90.7%
ELEM2	100%	78.7%	96.3%

Table 2. Comparison in Predictive Accuracy

A comparison in terms of the percentage of the test examples correctly classified is illustrated in Table 2. In all cases, ELEM2 produces more accurate rules than CN2. For the simple problem M_1, both C4.5 and ELEM2 gives 100% accurate predictions. For the problem M_2, which is difficult to describe in CNF or DNF using the given attributes only, all three algorithms do not produce accurate classification rules since the concept description languages used by the three algorithms do not fit the problem well. Nevertheless, ELEM2 has the best classification accuracy among the three algorithms. Problem M_3 is not difficult for the three learners, but it involves noisy data. From the table, we can see that ELEM2 better handles the noise in this problem than C4.5 and CN2.

7.3 Comparison of ELEM2 with C4.5 and CN2 on Actual Data Sets

To further compare ELEM2 with C4.5 and CN2, we have conducted experiments with these algorithms on 14 real-world data sets from the UCI repository [13]. Description of these datasets in terms of their number of concepts, number of condition attributes, number of examples and application domain is given in Table 3. Table 4 shows the results of ten-fold evaluation of C4.5, CN2 and ELEM2 on the 14 data sets. For each data set and each algorithm, we report the average of accuracies from the ten runs and their standard deviation.[4] When running C4.5, we used the option '-s' to allow grouping of attribute values. Other

---

[3] C4.5 can generate both decision trees and decision rules. We chose to use generation of decision rules. The decision rules are generated from unpruned decision tree(s) and are then generalized using pessimistic pruning technique. CN2 can generate both ordered and unordered sets of rules. We used the default settings which generate unordered sets of rules and use Laplacian error estimate as the search heuristic.

[4] The standard deviation is calculated using the following formula:

$$stdev = \sqrt{\frac{n \sum x_i^2 - (\sum x_i)^2}{n(n-1)}}$$

Datasets	No. of Concepts	No. of Cond. Attr.	No. of Examples	Domain
australia	2	14	690	Credit card application approval
balance-scale	3	4	625	Balance scale classification
breast-cancer	2	9	683	Medical diagnosis
bupa	2	6	345	Liver disorder database
diabetes	2	8	768	Medical diagnosis
german	2	20	1000	Credit database to classify people as good or bad credit risks
glass	6	9	214	Glass identification for criminological investigation
heart	2	13	270	Heart disease diagnosis
iris	3	4	150	Iris plant classification
lenses	3	4	24	Database for fitting contact lenses
segment	7	18	2310	image segmentation database
tic-tac-toe	2	9	958	Tic-Tac-Toe Endgame database
wine	3	13	178	Wine recognition data
zoo	7	16	101	Animal classification

Table 3. Description of Datasets.

options in C4.5 were kept as default settings. For CN2, all runs used default parameters so that Laplacian estimate was employed as the search heuristic and unordered rules were generated, which means that the improved version of CN2 was used.

The best result for each problem is highlighted in boldface in the table. Among the 14 problems, ELEM2 gives the best results in terms of predictive accuracy for 10, C4.5 for 3 and CN2 for 1. In terms of standard deviation, on 7 out of 12 data sets, ELEM2 gives the smallest number; C4.5 does it on 5 data sets; and CN2 on 2. At the bottom of the table, the average of the accuracy means or deviations of each algorithm over the 14 datasets indicate that ELEM2 is generally able to learn more accurate and more stable representations of the hidden patterns in the data than C4.5 and CN2.

8 Conclusions

We have presented ELEM2, a new method for inducing classification rules from a set of examples. The method employs a number of new strategies to improve the predictive performance of generated rules. We proposed a significance function for evaluating attribute-value pairs based on the degree of their relevance to a target concept. A new method for handling inconsistent training examples by

---

where x_i ($i = 1, 2, \cdots, n$) is the accuracy from the ith run on a data set. Here, for ten-fold cross validation, $n = 10$.

Datasets	Accuracy Mean			Accuracy Standard Deviation		
	C4.5	CN2	ELEM2	C4.5	CN2	ELEM2
australian	82.9%	84.92%	**86.52%**	5.45%	6.19%	**3.55%**
balance-scale	78.10%	79.05%	**81.14%**	5.63%	**3.23%**	5.29%
breast-cancer	95.6%	95.17%	**96.19%**	**1.56%**	2.77%	2.51%
bupa	68.4%	62.00%	**69.24%**	**4.00%**	9.53%	7.88%
diabetes	70.8%	71.21%	**74.10%**	5.53%	6.12%	**4.82%**
german	69.3%	**74.30%**	74.00%	**3.40%**	4.90%	4.62%
glass	68.7%	55.17%	**72.88%**	13.96%	12.11%	**10.11%**
heart	**80.8%**	77.85%	79.63%	**6.93%**	10.51%	7.46%
iris	**95.3%**	88.68%	94.67%	6.31%	8.34%	**5.26%**
lenses	73.3%	75.01%	**76.67%**	34.43%	**22.56%**	26.29%
segment	**96.6%**	86.24%	95.93%	**0.84%**	2.99%	2.14%
tic-tac-toe	96.8%	98.44%	**99.17%**	1.79%	1.51%	**1.28%**
wine	92.8%	86.00%	**97.78%**	7.44%	5.91%	**3.88%**
zoo	92.1%	92.09%	**98.00%**	6.30%	7.87%	**4.22%**
AVERAGE	82.96%	80.43%	**85.42%**	7.39%	7.04%	**6.38%**

Table 4. Performance Comparison of ELEM2 with C4.5 and CN2.

determining the unlearnable region of each concept is also presented. To further handle imperfect training data, post-pruning generated rules is used to prevent rules from overfitting the training data. A new rule quality measure based on example distribution is proposed as a criterion for stopping the post-pruning process. We have conducted empirical evaluation of ELEM2 on a number of designed and real-world databases. The results show that ELEM2 outperforms C4.5 and CN2 in terms of predictive accuracies on most of the tested problems. In future work, we will investigate how much each of the new ideas employed in ELEM2 contributes to the performance improvement. We also plan to clarify the bias of ELEM2. ELEM2 reduces the error rates on many data sets, but not all. More studies need to be done to find out the relations between the algorithm and the nature of problems.

9 Acknowledgements

This research was conducted when the first author was a PhD student at the University of Regina under the supervision of Professors Nick Cercone and Christine Chan. We would like to acknowledge the financial support received from Natural Science and Engineering Research Council of Canada (NSERC) and Telecommunications Research Laboratories (TRLabs). We would also like to thank Mr. Ning Shan for his suggestions on early versions of this work.

References

1. An, A. 1997. *Analysis Methodologies for Integrated and Enhanced Problem Solving.* Ph.D. Thesis, Dept. of Computer Science, University of Regina, Regina, Canada.
2. Brodley, C.E. 1993. "Addressing the Selective Superiority Problem: Automatic Algorithm/model Class Selection." *Proceedings of the 10th Machine Learning Conference.* pp.17-24.
3. Cendrowska, J. 1988. "PRISM: An Algorithm for Inducing Modular Rules". In Gaines, B. and Boose, J. (eds.): *Knowledge Acquisition for Knowledge-Based Systems.* Academic Press.
4. Clark, P. and Niblett, T. 1989. "The CN2 Induction Algorithm". *Machine Learning,* 3, pp.261-283.
5. Cooper, W.S. 1973. "On Selecting a Measure of Retrieval Effectiveness." *Journal of the American Society for Information Science.* Vol.24.
6. Creecy, R.H., Masand, B.M., Smith, S.J. and Waltz, D.L. 1992. "Trading MIPS and Memory for Knowledge Engineering". *Communications of the ACM,* 35, pp.48-64.
7. Domingos, P. 1995. "Rule Induction and Instance-Based Learning: A Unified Approach." *IJCAI-95.* Montreal, Canada. pp.1226-1232.
8. Grzymala-Busse, J.W. 1992. "LERS-A System for Learning From Examples Based on Rough Sets", in Slowinski, R.(ed.): *Intelligent Decision Support: Handbook of Applications and Advances of Rough Sets Theory,* Kluwer Academic Publishers, pp.3-18.
9. Hamilton, H.J., Shan, N. and Cercone, N. 1996. "RIAC: A Rule Induction Algorithm Based on Approximate Classification". *Technical Report CS-96-06,* University of Regina.
10. Holte, R., Acker, L. and Porter, B. 1989. "Concept Learning and the Problem of Small Disjuncts". *Proceedings of the Eleventh International Joint Conference on Artificial Intelligence,* Detroit, Michigan.
11. Kerber, R. 1992. "ChiMerge: Discretization of Numeric Attributes", *Proceedings of the 10th National Conference on Artificial Intelligence AAAI-92,* San Jose, CA.
12. Michalski, R.S., Mozetic, I., Hong, J. and Lavrac, N. 1986. "The Multi-Purpose Incremental Learning System AQ15 and Its Testing Application to Three Medical Domains". *Proceedings of AAAI 1986.* pp.1041-1045.
13. Murphy, P.M. and Aha, D.W. 1994. *UCI Repository of Machine Learning Databases.* URL: http://www.ics.uci.edu/ mlearn/MLRepository.html. For information contact ml-repository@ics.uci.edu.
14. Quinlan, J.R. 1983. "Learning efficient classification procedures and their application to chess end games". In Michalski, R.S., Carbonell, J.G. and Mitchell, T.M. (eds.): *Machine Learning: An Artificial Intelligence Approach.* Vol.1.
15. Quinlan, J.R. 1993. *C4.5: Programs for Machine Learning.* Morgan Kaufmann Publishers. San Mateo, CA.
16. Wnek, J., Sarma, J., Wahab, A. and Michalski, R. 1990. "Comparison Learning Paradigms via Diagrammatic Visualization: A Case Study in Single Concept Learning Using Symbolic, Neural Net and Genetic Algorithm Methods". *Technical Report,* Computer Science Department, George Mason University.

Sequential Instance-Based Learning

Susan L. Epstein[1] and Jenngang Shih[2]

[1]Department of Computer Science
Hunter College and The Graduate School of The City University of New York
695 Park Avenue, New York, NY 10021
epstein@roz.hunter.cuny.edu
[2]Department of Computer Science
The Graduate School of The City University of New York
33 West 42nd Street, New York, NY 10036
jshih@broadway.gc.cuny.edu

Abstract. This paper presents and evaluates sequential instance-based learning (*SIBL*), an approach to action selection based upon data gleaned from prior problem solving experiences. SIBL learns to select actions based upon sequences of consecutive states. The algorithms rely primarily on sequential observations rather than a complete domain theory. We report the results of experiments on fixed-length and varying-length sequences. Four sequential similarity metrics are defined and tested: distance, convergence, consistency and recency. Model averaging and model combination methods are also tested. In the domain of three no-trump bridge play, results readily outperform IB3 on expert card selection with minimal domain knowledge.

1. Introduction

In domains where a solution is a sequence of decisions, experts often address problems with *action patterns*, contiguous subsequences of those decisions that establish subgoals (e.g.,(Korf 1990)). These macros are purposeful and often named. For example, a finesse in bridge is an action pattern, part of a plan intended to win. Our thesis is that reusable action patterns can be inductively learned from sequences of expert decisions. Specifically, in game playing, a set of sequences from previously played contests can yield action patterns that accurately select expert choices in a new contest. The principal contributions of this paper are a general method to learn action patterns called *SIBL* (Sequential Instance-Based Learning), and a demonstration of its efficacy for three no-trump card play in the game of bridge.

Game playing may be viewed as a planning problem, with an initial state, one or more goal states and a set of operators that transforms one state into another. A plan consists of an ordered set of operators that transforms the initial state into a goal state. Some planning approaches, such as non-linear and hierarchical planners, rely on complete domain knowledge to derive plans (Hendler, Tate, & Drummond 1990). Some learning methods that readily enhance planning, such as explanation-based learning (*EBL*), also assume complete domain knowledge (Minton 1985). Others, such as case-based planners, reuse past planning experience through matching and adaptation but require large quantities of knowledge (Alterman 1988; Hammond 1989; Kambhampati 1990). SIBL, the inductive learning approach described here, addresses planning tasks but does not require extensive domain knowledge. Instead, it reuses information about past solutions to identify likely sequences of actions.

Because SIBL is intended to rely on relatively little domain knowledge, it could require substantial quantities of data. Rather than collect thousands of expertly-played bridge deals, we perturbed 72 input deals into about 90,000 training instances. We then used SIBL (and a modicum of domain knowledge, described in Section 7), to mine the resultant database for action patterns to direct expert play.

The next section provides a foundation for work with action patterns. Section 3 explains variants of SIBL and the need for good matching heuristics. Section 4 details four metrics developed for SIBL on matches between sequences of states. Section 5 describes an application of SIBL to the game of bridge, and provides results. The final sections survey related and future work.

2. Sequential Dependency

This section defines relevant terms and considers the extraction from problem solving experiences of sequences that could be used to support expert decisions. Consider, then, a problem solving experience

$$s_1 \xrightarrow{a_1} s_2 \xrightarrow{a_2} \cdots \xrightarrow{a_{i-1}} s_i \xrightarrow{a_i} s_{i+1} \xrightarrow{a_{i+1}} \cdots \xrightarrow{a_{n-1}} s_n \tag{1}$$

represented as a sequence of n states and $n-1$ actions, where the expert's action a_i moves the problem state from s_i to s_{i+1} for $i = 1, 2, ..., n-1$. Each such experience contains many *transition sequences*, contiguous subsequences of states and actions within the experience that end in a particular state from which an action will be taken. In the notation of (1), a transition sequence is of the form:

$$s_j \xrightarrow{a_j} s_{j+1} \xrightarrow{a_{j+1}} \cdots \xrightarrow{a_{i-1}} s_i \tag{2}$$

Traditional learning methods assume that a_i, the action to be selected from state s_i, is dependent upon the nature of s_i, and therefore those methods seek features within s_i that mandate the selection of a_i. *Sequential dependency*, however, postulates that the reasons for the selection of a_i actually reside within a broader context, the particular sequence of states $s_j, s_{j+1}, ..., s_i$ that precede a_i. SIBL seeks to learn that broader context.

Let a *sequential instance*, or *s-instance*, be a sequence of states followed by an action a, denoted:

$$s_j, s_{j+1}, ..., s_i \Rightarrow a \qquad (3)$$

Observe that an s-instance describes both the current state s_i and some number of consecutive, immediately prior states s_j, s_{j+1}, ..., s_i, but that the s-instance omits the intermediate actions of the transition sequence (2). (Assuming an adequate state description, an intermediate action could be deduced from the differences between two consecutive states.) The *length* of an s-instance is the number of states it includes. Thus the length of (3) is $i-j+1$.

Given a transition sequence like (2), the *chronological expansion* of it is the set of s-instances terminating in the action that leads to s. For example, in the experience

$$
\begin{array}{ccccccccc}
& a_1 & & a_2 & & a_3 & & a_4 & \\
s_1 & \to & s_2 & \to & s_3 & \to & s_4 & \to & s_5
\end{array}
\qquad (4)
$$

the chronological expansion of s_4 is three s-instances:

$$s_3 \Rightarrow a_3$$
$$s_2 s_3 \Rightarrow a_3 \qquad (5)$$
$$s_1 s_2 s_3 \Rightarrow a_3$$

We call each of the s-instances in the chronological expansion of a transition sequence a *partial s-instance*. Clearly, if the transition sequence is at the kth state in a problem solving experience, then there are k-1 partial s-instances in its chronological expansion.

Each partial s-instance offers a different context that may have determined the selection of action a. In (5), for example, all of s_1 s_2 s_3 may have determined the choice of a_3, or perhaps only s_2 s_3, or simply the nature of s_3 alone. It may also be necessary, for computational efficiency, to limit consideration to the l most recent partial s-instances. SIBL learns and makes decisions based on sequential dependency.

3. SIBL

SIBL is an extension to instance-based learning (*IBL*). IB3, the version of IBL we use here, represents input examples and output concept descriptions as feature-value pairs, and ordinarily retains the prototypical examples for reuse (Aha 1992; Aha, Kibler, & Albert 1991) . When IB3 is used for planning from state s, it retrieves the best-matching *simple instance* of the form $s_i \Rightarrow a_i$ from its database, and applies the action of the recommended instance, a_i. SIBL is an IB3 approach that applies sequential dependency to decision making, using a database of s-instances like (3) instead of simple instances.

Figure 1 is an overview of learning with SIBL. It shows how a training instance is expanded into a set of one or more partial s-instances that are then matched against a database. Unless the database's best match predicts the training action, the database is updated with the partial s-instances derived from the training instance.

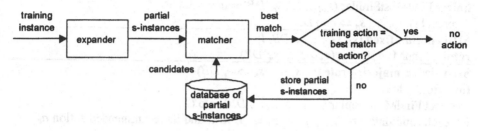

Figure 1. An overview of learning in SIBL

Table 1 gives high-level pseudocode for the SIBL algorithms. The length of the s-instances to be learned is an important issue. Is there a "best" length partial s-instance or does the length of the best partial s-instance vary from one decision to another? Although some actions may depend upon the entire sequence of states that preceded them, others may not require a complete chronological sequence to interpret the current situation. The relevant sequence of events may be shorter, even of length one. Table 1 therefore contains three approaches, one that assumes a parameterized best length l, and two that accommodate varying lengths.

Each approach incrementally constructs a database DB from a set of problem solving experiences, and uses it to make decisions. All three approaches begin the same way: each problem solving experience like (1) is expanded into training instances, s-instances like (3) where the expert made a decision. Here, the three methods deviate.

3.1 Fixed-length SIBL

For fixed-length partial s-instances, SIBL-learn-fixed in Table 1 retrieves from the database DB the most similar s-instance of length l. For example, given training data

$$s_1, s_2, s_3, s_4 \Rightarrow a \qquad (6)$$

and $l = 2$, SIBL-learn-fixed would select from DB the s-instance most similar to $s_3 s_4$, using the distance metric described in Section 4.1 below. Unless the action the re-trieved s-instance recommends is identical to the action in the training instance, the database is updated with the training instance. For $l = 1$, SIBL-learn-fixed is IB3.

Once DB has been constructed, SIBL makes decisions based upon it. In Table 1, SIBL-decide-fixed merely retrieves the most similar s-instance of length l and mandates that action. For example, given the training data in (6) and $l = 3$, SIBL-decide-fixed recommends the action taken by the s-instance in DB most similar to $s_2 s_3 s_4$. Similarity here is measured by distance, defined in Section 4.1 below.

Table 1. The SIBL algorithms.

SIBL-learn-fixed $(s_1, s_2, ..., s_n \Rightarrow a, DB, l)$
unless FindMostSimilar $(s_{n-l+1}, ..., s_n, DB) = a$
  append $s_1, s_2, ..., s_n \Rightarrow a$ to DB

SIBL-decide-fixed $(s_1, s_2, ..., s_n, DB, l)$
return FindMostSimilar $(s_{n-l+1}, ..., s_n, DB)$

SIBL-learn-majority-vote $(s_1, s_2, ..., s_n \Rightarrow a, DB)$
for i from 1 to n
  collect FindMostSimilar $(s_i, s_{i+1}, ..., s_n, DB)$ into C
for each candidate $c = s'_c, s'_{c+1}, ..., s'_n \Rightarrow a_c$ in C and its recommended action a_c
  vote$(a_c) \leftarrow$ vote$(a_c) + 1$
unless $a = a_c$ where vote(a_c) is a maximum
  for i from 1 to n
    append $s_i, s_{i+1}, ..., s_n \Rightarrow a$ to DB

SIBL-decide-majority-vote $(s_1, s_2, ..., s_n, DB)$
for i from 1 to n
  collect FindMostSimilar $(s_i, s_{i+1}, ..., s_n, DB)$ into C
for each candidate $c = s'_c, s'_{c+1}, ..., s'_n \Rightarrow a_c$ in C and its recommended action a_c
  vote$(a_c) \leftarrow$ vote$(a_c) + 1$
return a_c where vote(a_c) is a maximum

SIBL-learn-SSM $(s_1, s_2, ..., s_n \Rightarrow a, DB)$
for i from 1 to n
  collect FindMostSimilar $(s_i, s_{i+1}, ..., s_n, DB)$ into C
unless FindMostSimilarCandidate $(s_1, s_2, ..., s_n, C) = a$
  for i from 1 to n
    append $s_i, s_{i+1}, ..., s_n \Rightarrow a$ to DB

SIBL-decide-SSM $(s_1, s_2, ..., s_n, DB)$
for i from 1 to n
  collect FindMostSimilar $(s_i, s_{i+1}, ..., s_n, DB)$ into C
return FindMostSimilarCandidate $(s_1, s_2, ..., s_n, C)$

FindMostSimilar $(s_i, s_{i+1}, ..., s_n, DB)$
$\sigma \leftarrow s_i, s_{i+1}, ..., s_n$
for each partial s-instance s in DB of length $n - i + 1$
  minimize distance(σ, s) as smallest
return action of smallest

FindMostSimilarCandidate $(s_1, s_2, ..., s_n, C)$
if candidate c in C has significant minimum distance$(s_1, s_2, ..., s_n, c)$,
  then return its recommended action a_c
else if candidate c in C has significant maximum convergence$(s_1, s_2, ..., s_n, c)$,
  then return its recommended action a_c
else if candidate c in C has significant maximum consistency$(s_1, s_2, ..., s_n, c)$,
  then return its recommended action a_c
else if candidate c in C has significant maximum recency$(s_1, s_2, ..., s_n, c)$,
  then return its recommended action a_c
else select a random candidate c in C, **return** its recommended action a_c

3.2 Varying-length SIBL

For decisions rely on varying-length s-instances, there are two methods in Table 1: one relies on a voting process and the second on similarity metrics. Both methods chronologically expand each s-instance into a set of partial s-instances. Then, for each partial s-instance in each chronological expansion, both methods retrieve a *candidate* (the most similar partial s-instance of the same length as the newly expanded partial s-instance) from the partial s-instances already recorded in *DB*. Since a current experience with k states gives rise to $k-1$ partial s-instances, there will be $k-1$ candidates, each a partial s-instance of a different length. For example, if (6) is a training instance and we restrict partial instances to at most length $l = 3$, SIBL identifies a candidate of length one to match s_4, a second of length two to match s_3, s_4, and a third of length three to match s_2, s_3, s_4. Both varying-length SIBL methods collect these candidates along with the actions they recommend. They differ, however, in how they learn and decide with these candidates.

3.2.1 Majority vote

As described above, for a given s-instance SIBL-learn-majority-vote retrieves the best matching candidates of varying lengths from *DB*. Then each partial s-instance retrieved by FindMostSimilar casts one vote for the action it recommends. If the action that receives the *majority vote* (the most support) among the different length candidates matches the action to be learned, no change is made to *DB*. Otherwise, each of the partial s-instances in the expansion is appended to *DB*. Given the training data in (6) and $l = 3$, for example, SIBL-learn-majority-vote would retrieve three candidates and vote for the actions they indicate. Unless the best supported action were a, all three partial s-instances would be added to *DB*.

Once the database *DB* has been constructed by SIBL-learn-majority-vote, to make a decision SIBL-decide-majority-vote retrieves the candidates from *DB*. Each candidate casts one vote for the action it recommends, and the action that receives the majority vote is selected. Given the training data in (6) and $l = 3$, for example, SIBL-learn-majority-vote would retrieve three candidates, vote for the actions they indicate, and select the best supported action. In the event of a tie, both the training and testing majority vote algorithms choose at random from among the top-ranked actions.

3.2.2 Sequential similarity metrics

As described above, for a given s-instance SIBL-learn-SSM retrieves the best matching candidates of varying lengths from *DB*. Next, SIBL-learn-SSM uses FindMostSimilarCandidate in Table 1 to identify the *best-matching* candidate, the one whose state sequence is most similar to the training instance. The metrics that measure the quality of a match between two partial s-instances are called *sequential similarity metrics* and defined in the next section. In the example of (6) with $l = 3$, some candidate of length $1 \leq l \leq 3$ is identified. If the best-matching candidate's recommended action already corresponds to the action taken in the training instance, no change is made to the database. When the database's best match, however, recommends an action different from that taken by the expert in the training in-stance, each of the partial s-instances in the expansion is appended to *DB*.

Once the database *DB* has been constructed by SIBL-learn-SSM, to make a decision SIBL-decide-SSM retrieves the candidates from its database. Then the algorithm selects the most similar candidate and returns its recommended action. The next section describes the sequential similarity metrics that underlie this method.

4. Metrics for Sequential Similarity

FindMostSimilarCandidate in Table 1 applies up to four metrics to select the best matching partial s-instance of length n in *DB* to the training s-instance of length n. Each metric is defined for two same length, partial s-instances whose states are represented by a finite set of v features. To avoid bias toward shorter s-instances, every metric is normalized to return values in [0,1]. For clarity, normalization is omitted from the examples shown here.

A metric m is said to *distinguish* between two s-instances s and s' if and only if $m(s) \neq m(s')$ to some precision, say, the nearest tenth. In the order of presentation below, each metric is a refinement of the one that precedes it. For example, convergence is a way to distinguish between two partial s-instances with equal distance. FindMostSimilarCandidate applies these metrics one at a time to a set of same-length candidates. The first metric to distinguish among the different-length candidates returns its choice. We report the frequency to which they were resorted in Section 5.

Throughout, we let one partial s-instance be

$$s = s_p \rightarrow s_{p+1} \rightarrow ... \rightarrow s_k \quad (7)$$

and the second be

$$s' = s'_p \rightarrow s'_{p+1} \rightarrow ... \rightarrow s'_k \quad (8)$$

4.1 Distance

The *distance metric* quantifies the feature-based differences between the individual states in s and s' as:

$$distance(s,s') = \sqrt{\sum_{i=1}^{v} difference_i^2(s,s')} \quad (9)$$

The *difference* between the values of feature f_i in s and s' is defined as:

$$difference_i(s,s') = \begin{cases} |f_i(s) - f_i(s')| & \text{if } f_i \text{ is numeric} \\ 0 & \text{if } f_i \text{ is discrete and } f_i(s) = f_i(s') \\ 1 & \text{otherwise} \end{cases} \quad (10)$$

In FindMostSimilarCandidate, the candidate s' with minimal distance to the same length, partial s-instance s of the current experience is selected.

Table 2 is a hypothetical example where $E = s_1s_2s_3$ is the current experience, and Y_i is the stored s-instance of length $i = 1, 2, 3$, the best candidate of length i for the partial s-instance $s_{3-i+1}...s_3$ of E. If the distances between the partial s-instances of E and the stored s-instances were given as 0.67, 0.69 and 0.68, FindMostSimilarCandidate could select action A_1 for E, because Y_1 is the most similar (least distant) stored partial s-instance to E.

Table 2. Applying sequential similarity metrics.

	$Y_1 \Rightarrow A_1$	$Y_2 \Rightarrow A_2$	$Y_3 \Rightarrow A_3$
Distance to E	0.67	0.69	0.68
Convergence to E	0.55	0.58	0.56
Consistency with E	1	1	2
Recency to E	1	1	2

4.2 Convergence

Although the distance metric in Table 2 shows Y_1 as most similar to E, all three values round to 0.7, so FindMostSimilarCandidate would not distinguish among the candidates to the nearest tenth with the distance metric. The algorithm therefore resorts to a second metric. The *convergence metric* quantifies the change in the distance between partial s-instances, measured from their first states to their last states. Convergence is the change in distance between s and s' from one end to the other:

$$convergence(s, s') = distane(s_p, s'_p) - distance(s_k, s'_k) \qquad (11)$$

In SIBL, the candidate s' with maximal convergence to the same length, partial s-instance s of the current experience is selected. Continuing the example in Table 2, since the convergence values between E and the candidates are 0.55, 0.58 and 0.56, FindMostSimilarCandidate could select action A_2 for E, because Y_2 is the most similar (most convergent) stored partial s-instance to E.

4.3 Consistency

Convergence, like distance, may not adequately discriminate among the candidates, as shown in Table 2 to the nearest tenth. Therefore, in the ongoing example Find-MostSimilarCandidate would now resort to a third metric. For each partial s-instance of the current experience and the candidate retrieved for it, the *consistency metric* tallies the maximum number of consecutive non-increases in distance between the states in the current experience and the states in each candidate. Consistency between s and s' is measured by:

$$consistency(s, s') = t \text{ such that}$$

$$distance(s_j, s'_j) \geq distance(s_{j+1}, s'_{j+1}) \text{ for } j = m \text{ to } m + t \text{ in } [p, k] \text{ where} \qquad (12)$$

$$p \leq j \leq k \text{ and } t \text{ is the largest such value}$$

In FindMostSimilarCandidate, the candidate s' with maximal consistency to the same length, partial s-instance s of the current experience is selected. In Table 2, continuing the example, since the consistency values between E and the candidates are 1, 1, and 2, FindMostSimilarCandidate could select action A_3 for E, because Y_3 is the most similar (most consistent) stored partial s-instance to E.

4.4 Recency

When consistency fails to discriminate adequately among candidates, FindMostSimilarCandidate resorts to the *recency metric* that identifies the latest point where distance did not increase between consecutive states. Recency between s and s' is measured by:

$$recency(s, s') = \text{the largest } j \text{ in } [p, k] \text{ such that}$$

$$distance(s_j, s'_j) \geq distance(s_{j+1}, s'_{j+1}) \qquad (13)$$

If, for example, all the consistency values in Table 2 had been 1 but the recency values between E and the candidates 1, 1, and 2, FindMostSimilarCandidate would select action A_3 for E, because Y_3 is the most similar (most recent) stored partial s-instance to E.

5. Experimental Design and Results

The domain of investigation for this work is card play in the game of bridge, a four-player planning domain. A bridge *deal* distributes 52 distinct cards equally among the players into four *hands*. There are 13 cards in each of four suits; in increasing order of strength: 2, 3, 4, 5, 6, 7, 8, 9, 10, jack, queen, king, ace. The game has two phases: bidding and play. During *bidding*, the *contract* (a specific number of tricks for winning and a trump suit) is determined. During *play*, one contestant, identified by the bidding, is the *declarer* and another contestant, sitting opposite the declarer, is the *dummy*. The declarer tries to achieve the contract, controlling both declarer's and dummy's cards, while the other two contestants try to defeat it. (After the first card is played, the dummy's cards are exposed on the table for all to see.) Play consists of 13 tricks; a *trick* is constructed when each contestant in turn plays a single card. The first card's suit in the trick is the suit *led*. This work is restricted thus far to declarer play for three no-trump contracts, where the highest card in the suit led takes the trick, and the declarer is expected to take at least nine tricks. The problem addressed here is to select a sequence of actions (card plays) that enables the declarer to reach the contract.

A bridge state is a situation in which someone is expected to select a card, the *target feature*. We represent such a state as a set of 23 feature-value pairs. The features describe the suit strengths held by declarer and dummy, the suit strengths played by each of the opponents in all previous tricks, the cards played thus far in the current trick, who must play the next card, the target feature, and whether or not the declarer wins the trick. Since high cards are most likely to win tricks, cards below 9 are considered indistinguishable and are represented by the symbol X.

A bridge deal is a problem-solving experience, a sequence of 53 states and 52 actions, 26 of which are situations where the declarer had to play a card from its own or the dummy's hand. Our program calculates the chronological expansion of each training instance as a set of partial s-instances of various lengths in the context of the deal where the training instance appears. Every s-instance of length five or less is then represented as a sequence of one or more states plus a selected card. (Five was chosen as an upper bound based on preliminary experiments.) Thus an s-instance represents the current state and zero or more (up to four) states immediately prior to the current state.

Our data began as 108 three no-trump bridge deals, each fully played by human experts who successfully made the contract. We first separated the deals into training (72 deals) and test (36 deals) sets. In any given deal, however, there are 26 decision situations, and 325 partial s-instances of lengths from 1 to 25. Furthermore, each partial s-instance can be permuted (by varying its suits, declarer and dummy) into 48 partial s-instances. At this point, when every deal yields 1248 $(26 \cdot 48)$ training instances and 15,600 partial s-instances, computing resources become a consideration. We therefore divided the training set into three smaller ones.

Each smaller training set of 24 deals was used to produce a database, which we call here a *model*. Thus each model was based on almost 30,000 $(24 \cdot 26 \cdot 48)$ training instances, and could be tested on the $26 \cdot 36 = 936$ withheld instances in the testing set. A *run* randomized the order of the training instances, and then a decision maker learned on them. To gauge the learner's development and the value of continued training, after each tenth of the training set was presented, the program was tested on the 936 testing instances with learning turned off. An *experiment* averaged the results over 10 runs for a decision maker.

We ran experiments for decision makers based upon each of the following models:
- Length-one instances (IB3).
- Fixed-length instances for $l = 2, 3, 4$ and 5
- Majority vote among s-instances of lengths $l \leq 5$ learned with SIBL-learn-majority-vote for $l \leq 5$.
- *Model averaging*, where a single model built with SIBL-learn-SSM was used for decision making, but performance reported as the average of the performance of the three individual models.
- *Model combination*, where the three models built with SIBL-learn-SSM voted equally to make a decision whose performance was monitored.

All fixed-length models were built with SIBL-learn-fixed. As a benchmark, we also tested random legal (suit-following) play.

We tested each SIBL decision maker on the 936 withheld instances, noting how often it selected the correct (expert's move) card. If the program selected a card in a different suit, the result was scored as 0 (error). If the program selected the identical card, the result was scored as 1 (correct). If the program selected a card in the same suit as the correct card and consecutively adjacent to the target feature, the result was also considered correct and scored as 1. (For example, 10, jack, and queen in the same suit are consecutively adjacent and have the same effect on a trick.) Because the database is constructed from different deals, the recommended action may not always be legal in the current state, that is, SIBL may recommend a card not held but in the correct suit. Therefore, if the card SIBL selected was in the same suit as the correct card but neither identical nor consecutively adjacent, the result was assigned a numeric value between 0 and 1 based on the distance between the correct card and the card recommended by SIBL. In this case, the program plays the closest holding to the card SIBL recommends, and if two cards are equally close, the higher. With six possible actions in a suit (ace, king, queen, jack, 10, 9 and X), the difference to the adjacent card was scored as 5/6, to two adjacent cards as 4/6, and so on.

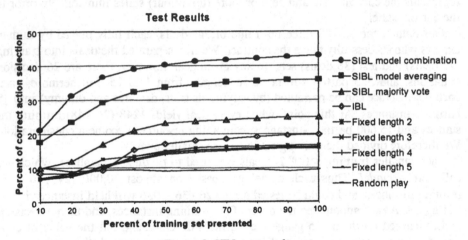

Figure 2. SIBL test results

Figure 2 shows how often each decision maker selected the correct action. The horizontal axis indicates the percentage of the training set seen before testing; the vertical axis shows the percentage of correct decisions. All the instance-based learners were substantially better than random play. Among the fixed-length SIBL experiments, after learning on all the training instances, $l = 1$ (IB3) outperformed all longer fixed-length sequences at the 99% confidence level. All three versions of SIBL outperformed IB3 at the 99% confidence level. Both model averaging and model combination with sequential similarity metrics were consistently better than majority vote. In addition, model combination outperformed (43% correct) model averaging (36% correct).

The sequential similarity metrics did indeed refine action selection. 80% of the decisions were made on distance alone. 17% of the time, distance did not distinguish among the candidates but convergence did. 2% of the decisions were made on consistency, and the final 1% relegated to recency or random selection among the most recent. Would more training (i.e., additional hands) have provided even better performance? The curves in Figure 2 (except the random play benchmark) appear to flatten in the last 10-20% of training. This suggests that 72 hands, as permuted, may be enough.

6. Related Work

Projective Visualization (*PV*) projected future states from the current one by following a set of state links (Goodman 1994) . The link between two states was defined by a set of state features that associated the two states. Initially, the state features were built one at a time with decision tree algorithms. At runtime these decision trees were used to find matching states with the same features. Like SIBL, PV tried to learn the state transition patterns. PV, however, used only lookahead information, with the risk of compounding projection errors. PV did not take advantage of historical state transition information, nor did it exploit the relative strengths of transition sequences of various lengths. The primary domain of investigation was Bilestoad, a computer game between two gladiators.

CAP learned action patterns with constructive induction. CAP's representation was a subset of Horn clause logic (Hume 1990) . It defined primitive properties of objects, relations, and actions for the target action pattern. A logical expression described a sequence of actions. Like EBL, given the basic definitions of a domain, CAP could learn domain concepts from a few descriptive examples. Unlike SIBL, CAP relied on a well-defined logical representation to assist learning domain concepts. The primary domain of investigation was mountaineering.

Moore's system used a form of reinforcement learning on a sequence of situation-action pairs to learn the effect of an action for robot arm control (Moore 1990) . It divided the search space into hierarchical segments to limit the search. It matched only the current state description to select an action, whereas SIBL matches a sequence of state descriptions to select an action. In a domain such as bridge, that is sensitive to sequential relationships, a sequence of states is more advantageous.

GINA was a program that learned to play Othello from experience, with a sequential list of situations encountered, actions taken, and final outcome (DeJong & Schultz 1988) The representation of its experience base was a subtree of the min-max game tree. Bridge, however, has concealed information (the opponents' hands), that makes its branching factor much higher than Othello's, and GINA's approach less practical.

SIBL is a general method to learn action patterns, that is, to reuse stored expert knowledge to make decisions in similar subsequent situations. An expert bridge program should also rely on substantial domain knowledge and a model of its opponents. SIBL could ultimately be one component in such a program. For these reasons, we do not compare our program's decision making skill to other expert bridge programs' here.

7. Conclusion

Although there are about $5 \cdot 10^{28}$ possible decision states in bridge, the strongest version of SIBL described here achieves more than twice the accuracy of IB3 on card play after training on only 72 deals. The only domain knowledge provided to the program was the need to follow suit, the ranking of the cards in a suit, and a preference for a higher card in the same suit when SIBL's recommendation was not present in the hand.

Bridge play includes units of four decisions (tricks), yet no fixed-length SIBL method performed as well as IB3 (length-1 sequences) did. This is probably due to the nature of the domain, that is, bridge play is dependent on recent experience, but the extent of the relevant recent experience varies. This theory is supported by the fact that the varying-length SIBL methods substantially outperformed IB3. Majority vote from a database of varying-length, rather than fixed-length, sequences is correct 27% more often than IB3. With the similarity metrics defined here and model combination, SIBL makes correct decisions 118% more often than IB3.

These experiments demonstrate that SIBL is an effective way to detect action patterns in bridge play, and represents a substantial improvement over IB3. As described here, SIBL seeks a match in its database for past states. In that sense, it only completes plans that are already underway. Current research enhances SIBL with planning-oriented lookahead.

References

Aha, D. W. 1992. Tolerating Noisy, Irrelevant and Novel Attributes in Instance-Based Learning Algorithms. *International Journal of Man-Machine Studies*, 36 : 267-287.

Aha, D. W., Kibler, D. and Albert, M. K. 1991. Instance-based Learning Algorithms. *Machine Learning*, 6 : 37-66.

Alterman, R. 1988. Adaptive Planning. *Cognitive Science*, 12 : 393-421.

DeJong, K. A. and Schultz, A. C. 1988. Using Experience-Based Learning in Game Playing. In *Proceedings of the Fifth International Machine Learning Conference*, 284-290. Ann Arbor, Michigan: Morgan Kaufmann, San Mateo.

Goodman, M. 1994. Results on Controlling Action with Projective Visualization. In *Proceedings of the Twelfth National Conference on Artificial Intelligence*, 1245-1250.

Hammond, K. J. 1989. *Case-based Planning: Viewing Planning as a Memory Task* . Boston: Academic Press.

Hendler, J., Tate, A. and Drummond, M. 1990. AI Planning: Systems and Techniques. *AI Magazine*, 11 (2): 61-77.

Hume, D. V. 1990. Learning Procedures by Environment-Driven Constructive Induction. In *Proceedings of the Seventh International Conference on Machine Learning*, 113-121. Austin: Morgan Kaufmann.

Kambhampati, S. 1990. Mapping and Retrieval during Plan Reuse: A Validation Structure Based Approach. In *Proceedings of the Eighth National Conference on Artificial Intelligence*, 170-175. Boston: AAAI Press.

Korf, R. 1990. Real-Time Heuristic Search. *Artificial Intelligence*, 42 (2-3): 189-211.

Minton, S. 1985. Selectively Generalizing Plans for Problem-Solving. In *Proceedings of the Ninth International Joint Conference on Artificial Intelligence*, 596-599. Los Angeles.

Moore, A. W. 1990. Acquisition of Dynamic Control Knowledge for a Robotic Manipulator. In *Proceedings of the Seventh International Conference on Machine Learning*, 244-252. Austin.

Predicate Invention from a Few Examples

Riverson Rios[1]   Stan Matwin

School of Information Technology and Engineering
University of Ottawa
K1N6N5 Canada
+1(613)562-5800 ext. 6667   +1(613)562-5800 ext. 6679
{riverson, stan}@csi.uottawa.ca

Abstract. One main difficulty of Inductive Logic Programming lies in learning recursively defined predicates. Today's systems strongly rely on a set of supporting predicates known as the background knowledge, which assumes that the user knows in advance what sort of predicates are required by the target definition. Predicate invention can remedy the situation by extending the specification language with new concepts that appear neither in the examples nor in the background knowledge, and finding a definition for them. A serious concern is that no examples of the invented predicate are explicitly given but rather of the target predicate, so learning has to be done in the absence or scarcity of examples. This work shows an autonomous learning method based on inverting clausal implication that can invent the recursive predicates it needs. The learner is endowed with means to work from a small data set.

Keywords: learning, inductive logic programming

1. Introduction

Inductive Logic Programming (ILP) is one of the new and fast growing sub-fields in artificial intelligence. ILP lies somewhere between machine learning, from which it inherits an empirical approach, and logic programming, from which its theoretic foundation and representation are derived. Given a specification language, the goal is to induce a logic program from examples of how the program should work (and also of how it should *not* work). The potential of this emerging field of study has already been proven, considering the number of successful uses of ILP in domains ranging from satellite fault diagnosis ([2]) to drug design ([16]) and others ([15]). An introduction to ILP is provided in [3] and [10].

One main difficulty lies in learning recursively defined predicates. Recursion happens to be the principal control structure in logic programming languages such as Prolog. Since terms, the most important data structure in those languages, are also

---

[1] On leave from Universidade Federal do Ceará, Brazil. Partially supported by CAPES, Brazil.

recursively defined, it is natural that the predicates that transform them be recursive as well. The important issues in learning such predicates concern the number of clauses, the number of recursive calls, their placement in the clause, and the choice of predicates and arguments to include in the recursive clauses. Today's systems strongly rely on a set of supporting predicates K, known as the *background knowledge*, that help define the recursive clause.

The dependence on background knowledge has drawbacks. It assumes that the user knows in advance what sorts of predicates are to be required by the target definition. While a lack of the essential predicates results in an ineffective learning, an excess of (useless or irrelevant) predicates inevitably leads to a combinatorial explosion of the hypothesis space, thereby degrading the performance of the system. Moreover, care must be taken with respect to the correctness and structure of the information in the background knowledge. For some systems, even the order of the predicates can make a difference.

Another problem regards the *implication* operation. The ILP task of finding a program that behaves like the given positive examples (and *not* like the negative examples) can be seen as a *generalization task*. Since the induction of a program is defined in terms of a logical consequence, it is natural to use implication as the sole basis for generalization. The ILP task can, therefore, be "simplified" to finding a program that implies the set of given examples. Unfortunately, though, it is not a straightforward task to invert implication. Not only is implication undecidable between clauses ([20]) but also between Horn clauses ([12]). Stronger forms of relations have been proposed such as *T-implication* ([5]) and *θ-subsumption* ([17]). Unfortunately, they are incomplete or do not guarantee that the result of a generalization is a Horn clause.

From a practical point of view, the current learners that are based on inverting clausal implication have serious limitations. The system Lopster ([9]), for instance, requires that either the base clause or examples in the same resolution chain be given. Crustacean ([1]) relaxes this requirement but limits itself to pure recursion. Clam ([18]) extends Crustacean by allowing left recursion but is still dependent on the background knowledge. Finally, Smart ([14]) and TIM ([6]) are restricted to n-bound and right-recursive clauses, respectively. None of them are capable of inventing the predicates they need.

A serious concern is that no examples are explicitly given of the invented predicate but rather of the target predicate. This means that a recursive definition of the new predicate will have to be induced from such a sparse set of positive examples only. Much often, non-dense example sets are not sufficient for a logic program to be learned when inverse resolution is used. They generally lack what is called a basic representative set (BRS), that is, a set of examples one single resolution step apart that provide a minimum amount of information about the program to be identified ([11]). Hence, it is essential that techniques be developed to endow systems with means to learn recursive definitions (RDs) from small data sets.

This work focuses on the problem of learning RDs based on inverting implication, especially when a small, sparse data set is given. We describe a learning method that does not rely on background knowledge (and thus invents the recursive predicates it needs). Two principles have guided the development of the system Shrinp ([19]):

1) Autonomy - Shrinp was conceived to be an *autonomous* learner. That is, no input is necessary other than the examples and the modes of the target relation, i.e. the input/output nature of each argument. If negative examples are missing or are incomplete, it is up to Shrinp to create them. If a supporting predicate is needed, it is up to Shrinp to invent it and if no examples exist for it, it is up to Shrinp to find them. No background knowledge, no domain descriptions, no external help from the user, no oracle, no type system are allowed.

2) Scarcity of examples - Real-world examples may be scarce or hard to dig up. If Shrinp is to be used by, say, first-year students, one would not expect them to provide all possible examples of a predicate like *length* even from a small model. Or if Shrinp is to be used on the fly, the system has to be able to deal with the unavailability or even the absence of examples. A system like Champ ([7]) requires that a BRS be present in the set of training examples. But when only a few examples are available, it is very unlikely that two examples will be only one single resolution step apart not to mention in the same resolution chain.

This work is organized as follows. Section 2 presents predicate invention. Section 3 introduces Shrinp. Section 4 has some results on using the system and the last section concludes this paper with suggestions for future work.

2. Predicate Invention

There are situations when a fixed initial specification language is not enough for the learning task at hand to be successfully completed. *Constructive Learning* is the capacity to automatically extend the specification language by adding new non-observational representation primitives ([8]). This idea is today an active research topic in ILP where it involves the invention of new predicates, i.e. the process of:

1. extending the specification language with concepts (denoted by predicates) that appear neither in the examples nor in the background knowledge and

2. finding a definition for these new concepts.

Predicate invention (PI) assumes that the choice of vocabulary for the given task has not yet been completely solved and, thus, represents a crucial theoretical topic in learning. [13] sees two main advantages in PI:

- **Simplicity:** In the best case, the new predicates correspond to the relations that were missing in the specification language and which have a particular meaning in the domain;

- **Completeness:** Some learning problems can be solved only if the language is widened through the invention of new predicates. In this sense, PI allows the expressiveness of the language to be augmented without seriously sacrificing its efficiency, thereby increasing the completeness of the learning process.

As the new relations don't appear in K, a burden is taken from the user's shoulders, who won't have to provide them. For a new predicate to be *necessary*, it must be recursively defined. If not, it will, at most, compact the learned program and K will still be needed.

The *predicate invention task* is similar to the ILP problem. Given an incomplete clause $C \in L$, $C = (C_0 :- C_1, C_2, ...,C_n)$ and a set of positive and negative examples of C_0, C_0^+ and C_0^-, the idea is to find a new literal Q and provide its definition D so that:

- $C' = C \cup Q$
- $C', D, K \vdash c^+$ for all $c^+ \in C_0^+$
- $C', D, K \not\vdash c^-$ for all $c^- \in C_0^-$

In Shrinp's case, K is not necessary. Four main steps are involved in PI, namely:

1. Choosing the incomplete, over-general clause C to be specialized through the addition of the new literal Q-. Decision criteria for introducing new predicates are discussed in [21].

2. Determining an argument structure for the call to Q in the new clause C'. A decision has to be made regarding:

   - The *arity n* of the new predicate
   - An adequate argument structure for the call to Q in C.

   The number of combinations is infinite for any small n as several terms can take part. Any number of the following potential terms is acceptable:

   - A variable or constant that already appears in C
   - A new variable or constant
   - A function applied to any of the above
   - Repeated terms

3. Finding the sets of examples for the new predicate, Q^+ and Q^-. Here, information about covered examples can be used. By instantiating the clause C' with the values provided by the examples of C the two sets can be found by calculating:

   - $Q^+ = \{Q\theta \mid C_0\theta \in C^+\}$
   - $Q^- = \{Q\theta \mid C_0\theta \in C^-\}$

4. Building its definition D. This step can be carried out by merely calling the learner itself recursively.

A few restrictions help reduce the size of the tuples to be considered. Whatever the choice, it must be enough for the completed clause $C' = C \cup Q$ to *completely discriminate* the examples of C_0. That is, there should be no $e^+ \in Q^+$ such that $C' \vdash \not\vdash e^+$ and at the same time no $e^- \in Q^-$ such that $C' \vdash e^-$. The arguments must be structured so as to comply with the principle that the sets of positive and negative examples should not overlap. It has been proven that it suffices to consider simple terms ([22]), that is, terms composed of constants and variables. Even so, while these restrictions eliminate potential argument tuples, a large number of tuples are still left over for consideration.

3. Shrinp

Unrestricted inverse implication has the problems mentioned earlier. Therefore, restrictions have to be imposed on the hypothesis language in order to make it efficient and useful. Shrinp's language bias allows for several important predicates to be learned, which includes those that have purely recursive definitions (PRDs), left-recursive definitions (LRDs) or right-recursive definitions (RRDs) with at most two literals in the body.

Shrinp can be roughly divided into three main modules: the *inducer*, the *filter* and the *predicate inventor* (Fig. 1).

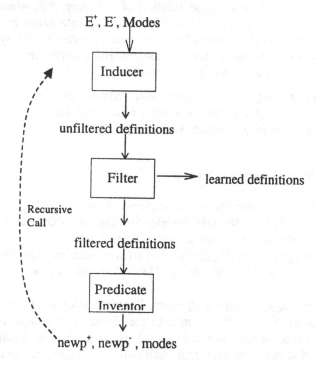

Fig. 1. Shrinp's modules.

The inducer accepts the examples and the modes from the user, induces potential PRDs and passes them onto the Filter Module, which tests them for endless loops, coverage, etc. The program stops when a definition passes the screening, yielding the learned clauses. If none does, the filtered definitions are regarded as potential RRDs or LRDs that need to be completed through the addition of a new literal. It is the Predicate Inventor Module (PIM) that is in charge of providing the missing literal and a definition of this new relation by recursively calling the inducer after computing examples for the new relation.

As can be seen, the process can be repeated indefinitely. An incomplete definition gives rise to a recursive call to Shrinp, which produces another incomplete definition that forces a new call to Shrinp, and so on recursively. The sequence of calls stops when the last definition in the chain of recursive calls is a correct PRD. In the best scenario, once such a definition is found in the bottom of the calls, all the previous incomplete definitions will get completed one by one, until the target predicate is learned, covering all given positive and no given negative examples. At this point, Shrinp outputs all the definitions found and stops. Note that in practice the learned definitions are relatively shallow in that they require the invention of only one or two new predicates. The main features of the system are:

- **The automatic generation of negative examples**. Negative examples work as a means to fine tune the final solution of a learner. But when Shrinp is called recursively to learn a definition of a new predicate *newp*, not enough negative instances of *newp* are given. To circumvent the problem, the system corrupts the positive examples of the new relation according to certain rules, thereby coming up with adequate negative examples.

- **The relearning of the base clause**. Shrinp extends Clam's capability of correcting the base clause by using a similar algorithm to the one presented in [18] that is adapted to include RRDs.

3.1 Predicate Invention in Shrinp

The Predicate Inventor Module specializes an incomplete clause by adding a new literal to its left or to its right, thereby forming an RRD or an LRD, respectively. The steps addressed in Section 2 are treated as follows:

Choosing an incomplete clause. PIM tries all clauses in the order that they are received from the Filter Module (see [18] for details on how incomplete clauses are induced).

Determining an argument structure. Discrimination is not possible because the number of examples is not enough for the clause, once completed, to discriminate between them. Shrinp uses a series of *argument-binding chains* (ABCs), short programs that bind arguments in the call to the new predicate, for selecting variables and creating new ones.

Finding examples. The guidelines discussed Section 2 are followed. Special algorithms remove non-ground positive instances and complete non-ground negative instances that result from running the extended clause C' on the examples of the target predicate. System-generated negative examples are also used.

Finding a definition. Shrinp is called recursively with Q^+ and Q^- as examples. A sequence of recursive calls may occur when the definition of a new predicate requires the invention of another new predicate and so on. The algorithm stops as soon as a PRD is found or a fixed number of recursive calls is reached.

3.1.1 Argument structure

Special care has to be taken while finding an adequate argument structure for the new literal Q. Given the small number of examples, not only is it impossible to find a minimal set of variables, the computation of negative examples for Q becomes seriously compromised.

The choice of arguments for Q has to be based solely on the terms that already appear in C. The approach followed by Shrinp mixes these terms with new variables depending on the type of recursive definition being induced. The creation of new terms, complex or not, from those that are already in the clause would result in a combinatorial explosion. Our approach avoids this problem and is even more general than Champ's. The choice of arguments is simplified by the fact that some terms are disallowed. If a *constant*, for instance, is placed as the argument in position i of Q, it will appear in the same position in all elements of Q^+. That means that any definition induced for the new predicate will also have the same constant in the ith position both in the base clause and in the head and body of the recursive clause. The use of constants, thus, has no effect and is not allowed in Shrinp. The *repetition* of arguments is also useless. They will simply duplicate the value of an argument, thereby yielding the same terms on the base and recursive clauses of the induced definition. Finally *new variables* are useful only in RRDs. In an LRD, a new variable V can only be included if it is repeated as an argument of Q as there is no other literal to the right of the Q where V can be referenced. New variables on LRDs are not allowed. Therefore, the complexity of choosing an argument structure for Q is simplified to considering the variables and simple terms that already appear in C and a new variable.

Five argument-binding chains for creating RRDs are defined:

1. no common variables (**NCV**). This is the simplest ABC and is also a starting point for all the others. All NCV does is to come up with a new literal whose arguments do not intersect with those of the recursive call. All variables must be used at least twice in the clause.

2. repeat body input variable (**RBV**). This ABC allows one input variable of the recursive call at a time to be repeated as an input argument of the new literal. For each variable that is repeated, a new clause is produced. Only body variables that are not yet present in the new literal yet are considered. The variables that appear only once in the clause are first added to the new literal.

3. repeat head input argument (**RHA**). Here head input arguments whose terms do not appear in the new literal are added as input arguments to the latter. As before, each inclusion gives rise to a different clause and the variables that appear only once in the clause are first added to the new literal.

4. New input variable (**NVI**). A variable that has not been used in the clause is successively substituted for each body input argument in this argument chain.

The new variable is then added to the output arguments of the new literal. Arguments in the head are also included into the new literal as long as the terms that appear in the head do not intersect with any current variable of the new literal, in which case they replace the variable. All variables have to be used twice.

5. New output variable (**NVO**). The arguments of the recursive call are successively substituted by a new variable that is included as an output argument of the call to the new predicate. All input arguments of the head are also inserted into the new literal.

A slight adjustment is necessary before LRDs can be learned. The incomplete clause received by PIM usually contains complex terms as output arguments of both the head and body literals. First, Shrinp replaces each of these arguments with a different new variable. Once the modification is performed, the problem is then reduced to inventing a predicate that takes as input the body output variables and produces as output the output variables in the head. The idea is to let the new literal provide the connection between the recursive call's and the clause's output. Two ABCs are defined:

1. classic (**CLA**). In this ABC, the new predicate will contain only the variables that are used exactly once in the incomplete clause. Of course it will contain the new variables introduced to the head and body literals in the first step. This is the simplest and most common case of LRD.

2. repeat head input argument (**LHA**). A little like RHA, LHA extends the literal produced by the classic ABC with one or more of the input arguments in the head. Arguments that share variables with the new literal are ignored.

4. Experimental Results

As a test of Shrinp's main feature, the ability to learn from a small number of examples, we chose eight relations that are usually found in Prolog textbooks. We also want to see if Shrinp can correctly invent the predicates it needs and find a definition for them. The hypothesis is that Shrinp can learn various relations if given the appropriate examples and modes. So no extra help from the user and no background knowledge are allowed. The number of examples was kept to a minimum, averaging four.

The effect of the ABCs for learning RRDs can be observed in Table 1. The predicate *isSorted*, for instance, is learned through the use of RBV by repeating as an input argument of the new predicate the variable B, which appears in the input argument of the recursive call to *isSorted*. The induced definition found for the new predicate equals that of the *lessEq* predicate.

Table 1. Predicates invented through the use of the RRD chains.

C	Incomplete clause	Induced Clauses	Invented predicate

N
C
V
	doubles([],[]).
	doubles([A|B],[C|D]) :-
	   doubles(B,D).
		doubles([],[]).
		doubles([A|B],[C|D]) :-
		   twice(A,C),
		   doubles(B,D).
			twice(0,0).
			twice(s(A),s(s(B))) :-
			   twice(A,B).

R
B
V
	isSorted([A]).
	isSorted([A,s(B)|C]) :-
	   isSorted([s(B)|C]).
		isSorted([A]).
		isSorted([A,s(B)|C]) :-
		   lessEq(A,B),
		   isSorted([s(B)|C]).
			lessEq(0,A).
			lessEq(s(A),s(B)) :-
			   lessEq(A,B).

R
H
A
	subset([],[A|B]).
	subset([A|B],[C|D]) :-
	   subset(B, [C|D]).
		subset([],[A|B]).
		subset([A|B],[C|D]) :-
		   member(A,[C|D]),
		   subset(B,[C|D])
			member(A,[A|B]).
			member(A,[B,C|D]) :-
			   member(A,[C|D]).

N
V
I
	eqList([],[]).
	eqList([A|B],[C|D]) :-
	   eqlist(B,D).
		eqList([],[]).
		eqList([A|B],[C|D]) :-
		   myDelete(A,[C|D],E),
		   eqList(B,E).
			myDelete(A,[A|B],B).
			myDelete(A,[B,C|D],[B|E]) :-
			   myDelete(A,[C|D],E).

N
V
O
	repeat([A|B],[A|B]).
	repeat([A|B],[C,D|E]) :-
	   repeat([A|B],[D|E]).
		repeat([A|B],[A|B]).
		repeat([A|B],[C,D|E]) :-
		   remFront([A|B]
		   ,[C,D|E],F),
		   repeat([A|B],F).
			remFront([],[A|B],[A|B]).
			remFront([A|B],[A,C|D],
			   [E|F]) :-
			   remFront(B,[C|D],[E|F]).

The ABCs for learning LRDs are enough to make Shrinp learn the predicates shown in Table 2. The predicate *select*, for instance, is learned when Shrinp tries to induce an LRD for the predicate *permut*. Note how the output argument of the head, *[C\|D]*, was changed to a new variable, *E*, that is later used in the call to *select*. The predicate *plus* was learned both for *sum* and for *sumToN*.

5. Conclusion

We showed a new method based on inverse implication that is capable of inventing recursive predicates. The method was implemented in the system Shrinp with successful results. Shrinp was designed to learn RDs of a single predicate and to operate with few examples. These characteristics make it the first inverse implication-based constructive learner. The ability to deal with few examples and to require no external aid contributes to the system's principal applications:

- **as a specialized learner.** In this case, a general-purpose learner calls Shrinp as a specialized learner of simple RDs, as it is more efficient in such circumstances. Shrinp can take advantage of the knowledge that the program to be learned must be recursive. The recursive nature of necessary invented predicates fits perfectly in this conjecture. Indeed, when a general-purpose technique detects the necessity of inventing a new predicate, it is preferable to invoke the specialized learner for such auxiliary purposes, rather than to have the general-purpose learner do the task. Chances are the general-purpose learner will most likely do a poor job in inventing the new relation.

Table 2. Predicates invented through the use of the LRD chains.

C	Incomplete Definition	Induced Definition	Invented predicate
	permut([],[]).	*permut([],[]).*	*select(A,B,[A|B]).*
	permut([A|B],[C|D]) :-	*permut([A|B],E) :-*	*select(A,[B|C],[B,D|E]) :-*
	permut(B,D).	*permut(B,D),*	*select(A,C,[D|E]).*
C		*select(A,D,E).*	
L	*sum([],0).*	*sum([],0).*	*plus(0,A,A).*
A	*sum([A|B],s(s(C))) :-*	*sum([A|B],E) :-*	*plus(s(A),B,s(C)) :-*
	sum(B,C).	*sum(B,D),*	*plus(A,B,C).*
		plus(A,D,E).	
L	*sumToN(0,0).*	*sumToN(0,0).*	*plus(0,A,A).*
H	*sumToN(s(A),s(s(s(C)))):-*	*sumToN(s(A),E) :-*	*plus(s(A),B,s(C)) :-*
A	-	*sumToN(A,D),*	*plus(A,B,C).*
	sumTo(A,C).	*plus(s(A),D,E).*	

- **as a tool for teaching logic programming languages.** Shrinp can work as a tool for *algorithm discovery* in that beginner Prolog students would devise experiments by supplying the system with different sets of positive and negative examples of a target predicate. The advantage is that the students would not have to provide a valid set of background predicates and could limit themselves to a small number of examples on each run. It would be tedious to enter, for instance, tens of examples for a single predicate. Algorithm discovery means playing with predicates, adding and removing examples, changing modes, experimenting, creating, learning. Shrinp's efficiency in such a task makes it ideal to an application like this.

A study on the learnability of recursive logic programs ([4]) suggests that to learn complex recursive hypotheses, some extra information must be given in addition to the training set. This may be achieved either through the knowledge of some special properties of the target concepts or with the availability of the complete sets of examples. The ABCs represent a step in this direction especially when only a few instances are available. Further work on Shrinp could focus on developing new bindings that may account for the definition of relations not yet learnable.

Perhaps the main limitation is Shrinp's strong bias. Given the unavailability of the background knowledge, it is hard to overcome the small size of the recursive clauses. However, although it would require a great computational effort for Shrinp to add two or more new predicates to an incomplete clause, there still is room for introducing other recursive calls, which would at least make divide-and-conquer-based relations such as *quickSort* learnable.

What would be the effect of using background knowledge together with the predicate invention facility? A hybrid system would be produced that could use the supporting relations and generate its own predicates whenever the background knowledge proved to be insufficient to learn a definition. Consequently, the user would not have to worry about providing *the* necessary set of definitions for a given relation to be learned. A relatively small, structured general-purpose set would probably do. The number of programs that can be induced would be much larger in the sense that a call to non-recursive predicates could be inserted into the recursive clause. An alternative consists of letting the system cumulatively keep the predicates it invents. This way, the restriction to obtain no further help from the user would still prevail through the use of such system-generated background knowledge. In any case, it would be a challenge to automatically simulate the human ability of dynamically organizing such knowledge according to the relevance to a problem. The presence of background knowledge, on the other ledger, brings up what is called the *background knowledge usage bottleneck*. Questions regarding the choice and placement of the new predicates would result in a combinatorial explosion, not to mention the choice of arguments for the added literals from the background knowledge. Anyway, the system would also have to deal with incorrect or incomplete background information.

Shrinp was designed to learn from a small number of examples. However, if too many examples are given to the system, the performance will certainly degrade considerably as more tentative definitions will be produced, thereby, requiring more memory. We are currently working on an experiment with random examples that can empirically show this fact.

Acknowledgements

Thanks go to NSERC and Capes for supporting this research.

References

[1] Aha, D.W., Lapointe, S., Ling, C. & Matwin, S. (1994). Inverting implication with small training sets. In *Proc. ECML* (31-48). Catania, Italy

[2] Feng, C. (1992). Inducing temporal fault diagnostic rules from a qualitative model. In *Inductive Logic Programming* (473-493). San Diego, CA

[3] Bergadano, F. & Gunetti, D. (1993). An interactive system to learn functional logic programs. In *Proc. 13th IJCAI* (1044-49). Chambéry, France

[4] Cohen, W. (1995). Pac-learning recursive logic programs: negative results. *Journal of Artificial Intelligence Research* 2:541-573

[5] Idestam-Almquist, P. (1993). *Generalization of Clauses*. Ph.D. Thesis. Dept. of Computer and System Sciences. Stockholm University. Stockholm, Sweden

[6] Idestam-Almquist, P. (1996). Efficient induction of recursive definitions by structural analysis of saturation. In (L. De Raedt, ed.) *Advances in ILP* (192-205). Amsterdam, The Netherlands

[7] Kijsirikul, B., Numao, M. & Shimura, M. (1992). Discrimination-based constructive induction of logic programs. In *Proc. 10th National Conference on Artificial Intelligence* (44-49). San José, CA

[8] Lapointe, S., Ling, C. & Matwin, S. (1993). Constructive inductive logic programming. In *Proc. of the 13th IJCAI* (273-281). Chambéry, France

[9] Lapointe, S. & Matwin, S. (1992). Sub-unification: A tool for efficient induction of recursive programs. In *Proc. 9th ICML* (273-281). Aberdeen, Scotland

[10] Lavrac, N & Dzeroski, S. (1994). *Inductive Logic Programming: Techniques and Applications*. Ellis Horwood

[11] Ling, C. (1991). Inductive learning from good examples. In (J. Mylopoulos, R. Reiter, eds.) *Proc. 12th IJCAI* (751-756). Sydney, Australia

[12] Marcinkowski, J. & Pacholski, L. (1992). Undecidability of the Horn clause implication problem. In *Proc. 33rd IEEE Symposium on the Foundations of Computer Science* (354-362). Pittsburgh, PA

[13] Martin. L. & Vrain, C. (1997). Systematic predicate invention in inductive logic programming. In *Proc. Seventh International Workshop on ILP*. Prague, Czech Republic

[14] Mofizur, C. & Numao, C. (1996). Top-down induction of recursive programs from small number of sparse examples. In (L. De Raedt, ed.) *Advances in ILP* (236-253). Amsterdam, The Netherlands

[15] Muggleton, S. (1994). Inductive logic programming: derivations, successes and short-comings. *SIGART Bulletin* 5(1):5-11

[16] Muggleton, S., King, R. & Sternberg, M. (1992). Protein secondary structure prediction using logic. In *Proc. 2nd Int'l Workshop on ILP*. Tokyo, Japan

[17] Plotkin, G.D. (1971). *Automatic Methods of Inductive Inference*. Ph.D. Thesis. Edinburgh University, Edinburgh, Scotland

[18] Rios, R. & Matwin, S. (1996). Efficient induction of recursive Prolog definitions. In *Proc. 11th Canadian Artificial Intelligence Conference* (240-248). Toronto, Canada

[19] Rios, R. (1998). *Learning Recursive Definitions in Prolog*. Ph.D. Thesis. School of Information Technology and Engineering, University of Ottawa. Ottawa, Canada

[20] Schmidt-Schauß, M. (1988). Implication of clauses is undecidable. *Theoretical Computer Science* 59:287-296

[21] Stahl, I. (1996). Predicate invention in inductive logic programming. In (L. De Raedt, ed.) *Advances in ILP* (34-47). Amsterdam, The Netherlands

[22] Stahl, I., Weber, I. (1994). The arguments of newly invented predicates in ILP. In *Proc. 4th Int'l Workshop on ILP*. Bad Honnef/Bonn, Germany

Author Index

Lecture Notes in Artificial Intelligence (LNAI)

Lecture Notes in Computer Science

Springer
and the
environment

At Springer we firmly believe that an international science publisher has a special obligation to the environment, and our corporate policies consistently reflect this conviction.

We also expect our business partners – paper mills, printers, packaging manufacturers, etc. – to commit themselves to using materials and production processes that do not harm the environment. The paper in this book is made from low- or no-chlorine pulp and is acid free, in conformance with international standards for paper permanency.